VIRGINIA WOOLF
AND THE BLOOMSBURY AVANT-GARDE

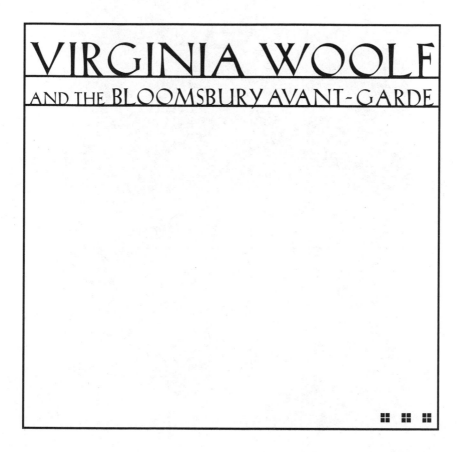

GENDER AND CULTURE

VIRGINIA WOOLF

AND THE BLOOMSBURY AVANT-GARDE

WAR ▪ CIVILIZATION ▪ MODERNITY

CHRISTINE FROULA

COLUMBIA UNIVERSITY PRESS ▪ NEW YORK

Columbia University Press
Publishers Since 1893
New York   Chichester, West Sussex
Copyright © 2005 Columbia University Press

Library of Congress Cataloging-in-Publication Data

Froula, Christine, 1950–
    Virginia Woolf and the Bloomsbury avant-garde :
war, civilization, modernity / Christine Froula.
        p. cm. — (Gender and culture)
    Includes bibliographical references and index.
    ISBN 0–231–13444–4 (cloth : alk. paper)
        1. Woolf, Virginia, 1882–1941—Criticism and interpretation.
    2. Bloomsbury (London, England)—Intellectual life—20th century.
    3. World War, 1914–1918—England—London—Literature and the war.
    4. Women and literature—England—London—History—20th century.
    5. Experimental fiction, English—History and criticism.   6. Avant-garde
    (Aesthetics)—England—London.   7. Modernism (Literature)—England—
    London.   8. Civilization, Modern, in literature.   9. Bloomsbury group.
    I. Title. II. Series.

    PR6045.072Z6435   2004
    823'.912—dc22   2004052774

Columbia University Press books are printed on permanent
and durable acid-free paper.

Printed in the United States of America

c 10 9 8 7 6 5 4 3 2 1

Frontispiece: Courtesy of the Harvard Theatre Collection, the Houghton Library,
Harvard University

for Sasha, voyaging out

■ ■ ■ CONTENTS

∷ ∷ ∷ ABBREVIATIONS

Epigraph citations to "Woolf" always refer to Virginia Woolf. "Leonard Woolf" is cited in full. Unless otherwise stated, citations are to the Harcourt, Brace, Jovanovich current editions. The date of first publication is given here.

Works by Virginia Woolf

BA	*Between the Acts.* 1941.
CDB	*The Captain's Death Bed and Other Essays.* 1950.
CR	*The Common Reader.* 1925.
CR2	*The Second Common Reader.* 1932.
CS	*Congenial Spirits: The Selected Letters of Virginia Woolf.* Edited by Joanne Trautmann Banks. 1989.
CSF	*The Complete Shorter Fiction of Virginia Woolf.* 2nd ed. Edited by Susan Dick. 1989.
D	*The Diary of Virginia Woolf.* 5 vols. Edited by Anne Olivier Bell. 1977–84.
DM	*The Death of the Moth and Other Essays.* 1942.
E	*The Essays of Virginia Woolf.* Vols. 1–4. Edited by Andrew McNeillie. 1986–94.
GR	*Granite and Rainbow: Essays.* 1958.
H	*The Hours: The British Museum Manuscript of* Mrs. Dalloway. Transcribed and edited by Helen Wussow. New York: Pace University Press. 1997.
JR	*Jacob's Room.* 1922.
L	*The Letters of Virginia Woolf.* Edited by Nigel Nicolson and Joanne Trautmann. 1975–80.
M	*Melymbrosia: An Early Version of* The Voyage Out. Edited by Louise A. DeSalvo. New York: New York Public Library. 1982.
MB	*Moments of Being: Unpublished Autobiographical Writings.* 2d ed. Edited by Jeanne Schulkind. 1985.
MD	*Mrs. Dalloway.* 1925.
MDP	*Mrs. Dalloway's Party: A Short Story Sequence by Virginia Woolf.* Edited by Stella McNichol. 1973.

ND   *Night and Day.* 1919.

O   *Orlando.* 1928.

Oh   *Orlando: The Original Holograph Draft.* Transcribed and edited
        by Stuart Nelson Clarke. London: S. N. Clarke. 1993.

P   *The Pargiters: The Novel-Essay Portion of* The Years. Edited by
        Mitchell A. Leaska. 1977.

PA   *A Passionate Apprentice: The Early Journals 1897–1909.* Edited
        by Mitchell A. Leaska. 1990.

PH   *Pointz Hall: The Earlier and Later Typescripts of* Between the
        Acts. Edited by Mitchell A. Leaska. New York: University Pub-
        lications. 1983.

RF   *Roger Fry: A Biography.* 1940.

RO   *A Room of One's Own.* 1929.

TG   *Three Guineas.* 1938. First American edition, with illustrations.

TL   *To the Lighthouse.* 1927.

TLhd   To the Lighthouse: *The Original Holograph Drafts.* Transcribed
        by Susan Dick. Toronto: University of Toronto Press. 1982.

VO   *The Voyage Out.* 1915.

W   *The Waves.* 1931.

Wh   The Waves: *The Two Holograph Drafts.* Transcribed and edited
        by J. W. Graham. Toronto: University of Toronto Press. 1976.

WF   *Women & Fiction: The Manuscript Versions of* A Room of One's
        Own. Edited by S. P. Rosenbaum. Oxford and Cambridge,
        Mass.: Blackwell's. 1992.

Y   *The Years.* 1937.

Supplementary Works

BGMC   *The Bloomsbury Group: A Collection of Memoirs and
        Commentary.* Edited by S. P. Rosenbaum. Rev. ed. Toronto:
        University of Toronto Press. 1995.

BGR   *A Bloomsbury Group Reader.* Edited by S. P. Rosenbaum. Oxford:
        Blackwell's. 1993.

HL   Lee, Hermione. *Virginia Woolf.* New York: Alfred A. Knopf.
        1997.

QB   Bell, Quentin. *Virginia Woolf: A Biography.* 1971.

VW:CH   *Virginia Woolf: The Critical Heritage.* Edited by Robin Majumdar
        and Allen McLaurin. London: Routledge and Kegan Paul.
        1975.

VWM   *Virginia Woolf Miscellany.* Nos. 1–63. Fall 1973–Summer 2003.

Bertie [Bertrand Russell] . . . thinks he's going to found new civilisations.

—Woolf, *Letters*, 23 January 1916

[You women] who are trying to earn your livings in the professions . . . call out . . . all those sympathies which, in literature, are stimulated by the explorers who set out in crazy cockle shells to discover new lands, and found new civilisations.

—Woolf, *The Pargiters*, 1932

 his book situates Virginia Woolf and Bloomsbury within a modernity understood as a "permanent revolution" in the sense Thomas Jefferson evoked when he wrote that he could die content if he knew that the revolution he had helped to make would never be written in stone but would remain always alive— not laying down the law for generations to come but always debated and contested, actively reaffirmed or creatively transformed by the living.[1] Twenty years ago the intellectual historian Perry Anderson could write, "My own country England, the pioneer of capitalist industrialization and master of the world market for a century, . . . beachhead for Eliot or Pound, offshore to Joyce, . . . produced virtually no significant native movement of a modernist type in the first decades of this century—unlike Germany or Italy, France or Russia, Holland or America."[2] Today Virginia Woolf has emerged on the world stage, read around the world in English and translation amid an array of Bloomsburies: Leon Edel's house of lions, Raymond Williams's oppositional fraction of England's ruling class, S. P. Rosenbaum's interconnected writers, as well as wide-ranging discussions of Bloomsbury biographies, personalities, sexualities, friendships, lifestyle, decor, and affinities with material culture, consumer culture, and the popular imagination. Still, it is easy to overlook Bloomsbury's import and specificity as a *modernist movement*, in part because its enormous multidisciplinary archive tends to obscure the strong lines of force in its associates' work and thought beneath the glitter and glamour of their everyday lives.

But if we understand modernity's permanent revolution as a perpetual effort to reclaim the purpose and vitality of the Enlightenment project— as an unfinished and unfinishable struggle for human (including economic) rights, democratic self-governance, world community, and peace—then Bloomsbury puts England on the map of modernist movements as decisively as more commonly recognized movements do Germany, Italy, France, Russia, Holland, and America. In a half-century blighted by two European "civil wars," Bloomsbury carried forward and made new the Enlightenment project's self-critical and emancipatory force and meaning. As the 1914 war plunged Europe into crisis, as belligerent nationalisms (even in England) and rising totalitarianisms threatened to eclipse Europe's Enlightenment ideal, Bloomsbury artists and intellectuals entered a struggle not to "save" their civilization but to help advance Europe toward its own unrealized ideal, a civilization that had never existed. Bloomsbury carries the Enlightenment struggle for civilization dialectically into the twentieth century in its pacifism and internationalism, its sense of history not as inevitable progress but as an unending fight for a future that is always open and free, and—most tellingly—its address to barbarity *within* Europe and the West.

Along with Freud and Keynes, Virginia Woolf is as powerfully analytic, critical, and imaginative a proponent as the Enlightenment project has had in the last century. In alliance with Bloomsbury and in some measure against it, Woolf linked the breakdown of England's sex/gender economy and women's emergence into public voice with Bloomsbury's critique of the class system, imperial domination, racialized economic exploitation, and militant nationalisms. Like her contemporary James Joyce, who, inspired by Ibsen, saw women's struggle for economic, political, and social emancipation as the greatest revolution of their time, Virginia Woolf framed the women's movement as an avant-garde in the struggle for freedom, peace, and the rights of all within modernity's unfinished project.

Vanessa Bell recalled that her sister's first short story was "a wildly romantic account of a young woman on a ship," rejected by *Titbits* (the same that Leopold Bloom peruses in *Ulysses*) (*BGR* 335). From this first, lost story to her last novel in which the playwright La Trobe voyages away from the shore toward her next play, Woolf made the voyage of exploration her central metaphor for modernity's great adventure toward "new lands, . . . new civilisations." Her first novel departs from Joseph Conrad's inaugural modernist voyage to the heart of European barbarism, which brings Marlow to tell an evil-tasting lie to help women "stay in a beautiful world of their own, lest ours gets worse." As Marlow confronts the lies that found racialized imperialism, Woolf parlays the European rhetoric of imperialist exploration and conquest into a metaphysical voyage toward a civilization that has never existed. A woman "writing against the current" yet (as Clive Bell thought) too much of a genius to believe in either sex, Woolf ventured upon seas of thought that her male contemporaries left unexplored (D 5:189). With her family birthright of radical skepticism and a fortuitous education in her father's library and Cambridge-educated Bloomsbury, she embarked on a writing career that now seems scarcely less a miracle than she considered Jane Austen's to be, her pen flying after the elusive "wild goose" of modern experience to net its traces in the "silver-grey flickering moth-wing quiver of words" (O 313, W 215). If, as Philippe Sollers put it, "they who know not language serve idols; they who could see their language could see their gods," Woolf's novels, diaries, letters, and essays embody this unending quest for and responsiveness to the world as a luminous alternative to the twentieth century's totalitarian longings for "a new god."[3] Entering into modernity as a permanent revolution, Woolf forges a dialogic art that shatters outworn conventions not "for art's sake"—in isolation from everyday life and the social world—but to call her public to active debate of an ever changing *sensus communis* or common understanding. Bringing readers in sight of new lands, new civilizations, her writings inspire "modern men and women" to "yearn for change: not merely to be open to changes in their personal and social lives but positively to demand them, actively to seek them out and carry them through."[4]

In framing Woolf and Bloomsbury in this way, this book joins the contemporary effort across several disciplines to rethink European modernity's Enlightenment project in face of modern and antimodern forms of violence and exploitation.[5] We are not accustomed to seeing Woolf and Bloomsbury in this light, and I have accordingly emphasized their contributions more than their lapses and failures, their critical and creative opposition to the wartime nationalism that shadowed British foreign policy and public culture from 1914 to the Second World War more than their implication in class privilege and racialized imperialism—in the unenlightened barbarism that post-World War II and postmodern critiques rightly address. Yet my purpose is not to present Kant and Freud, Woolf and Bloomsbury, as incontestable heroes, paragons of Enlightenment modernity. Rather, believing that in speaking only of their failures we risk forfeiting what is potentially most vital and most fruitful in their historical legacy, I pose the question of that legacy for a world still struggling with the economic, political, social, and ethical challenges that confront women and men, races, religions, and cultures, classes and nations, as they seek to negotiate differences not by violence but through the power of speech, the effort and "the art of understanding other people's lives and minds" (*TG* 50).

⁘ ⁘ ⁘

This project evolved over many years, and I am deeply grateful for the help and support of innumerable benefactors—colleagues, students, friends, libraries, institutions—along the way. Nancy K. Miller, the late Carolyn Heilbrun, and Jennifer Crewe, the humanities editor at Columbia University Press, encouraged this project from its beginnings. Carolyn's pioneering work on Woolf and Bloomsbury was an early inspiration and her generosity to me, as to so many other scholars, was a tremendous force in my life. I cherished the gift of her friendship, and I cherish her memory. Maud Ellmann, Susan Stanford Friedman, Karen R. Lawrence, and Brenda R. Silver gave invaluable support; and Marianne DeKoven and Karen Lawrence offered excellent advice on the entire manuscript. I thank Gayle Rogers and Emily Sheffield for help in preparing the manuscript and Susan Heath, Anne McCoy, Michael Haskell, and Liz Cosgrove at Columbia University Press for their meticulous and imaginative care.

For inviting me to present aspects of this work in a variety of venues, I warmly thank Rebecca Beasley, Catherine Bernard, Deborah Clarke, Pamela Caughie, Antoine Compagnon, Beth Rigel Daugherty, Maud Ellmann, Susan Manning, Natalya Reinhold, Christine Reynier, Natania Rosenfeld, Pierre-Eric Villeneuve, and Nicola J. Watson. For thoughtful and challenging responses and conversation that strengthened this book in countless ways, I thank Brian Artese, Nina Auerbach, Miriam Bailin, Gillian Beer, Kevin Bell, Shari Benstock, Paul Berliner, Diana Black, Françoise Bort, Rachel Bowlby, Paul Breslin, Marilyn Brownstein, Dorit Cypis, Patricia Dailey, Scott Durham, Rosa Eberly, Betsy Erkkila, Penelope Farfan, Daniel Ferrer, Elzbieta Foeller-Pituch, Nancy Fraser, Reginald Gibbons, Michal Ginsburg, Susannah Young-Ah Gottlieb, Christopher Herbert, T. William Heyck, Margaret Homans, Myra Jehlen, Christopher Johnson, Patricia Klindienst, Cassandra Laity, Christopher Lane, Jules Law, Karen Leick, Joanna Lipking, Larry Lipking, Michael Maness, Celia Marshik, Stephanie McCurry, Leslie Melchert, Adrienne Munich, Barbara Newman, Richard Pearce, Christina Pugh, Alessia Ricciardi, Carol Rifelj, Julie Rivkin, Gayle Rogers, Mary Beth Rose, Mireille Rosello, Carol Shloss, Carl Smith, Lynne Sowder, Glenn Sucich, Patricia

Swindle, Marian Tolpin, Joseph Urbinato, Robert von Hallberg, Paul Wallich, Sarah Winter, Anne Winters, Randall Woods, John Young, and Linda Zerilli. I have also benefited enormously from the work, friendship, and conversation of many people in the ever widening community of Woolf scholars, including Elizabeth Abel, Murray Beja, Melba Cuddy-Keane, Laura Davis, Louise DeSalvo, Maria diBattista, Rachel Blau duPlessis, Jane Garrity, Sally Greene, Molly Hite, Mark Hussey, Ellen Carol Jones, Jane Lilienfeld, Jane Marcus, Vara Neverow, Merry Pawlowski, Lisa Ruddick, Susan Squier, and Diana Swanson. My students at Yale, Northwestern, and Washington University—far too many to name here, some now colleagues and friends—have made teaching Woolf a perennial adventure and a seemingly inexhaustible source of joy and surprise.

Several grants for the academic year 2002–2003 enabled me to consolidate the work of many years into this book. I am deeply indebted to Northwestern's Alice Berline Kaplan Humanities Center for a Senior Faculty Fellowship that freed me for a year of research, thinking, and writing. I am also grateful to Clare Hall, Cambridge, for a Visiting Fellowship in spring 2003; and, for support for research travel abroad, to Northwestern's University Research Grants Committee, Dan Linzer (dean) and Adair Waldenberg (associate dean) of the Weinberg College of Arts and Sciences, and Reginald Gibbons (chair) and Kathy Daniels (administrative goddess) of the English department. I thank President Ekhard Salje, Lisa Salje, Elizabeth Ramsden, Ann Little, Andrew Goadby, and all the staff and friends at Clare Hall who made my family's stay there so happy and productive, and, again, Maud Ellmann, whose hospitality, sense of fun, and delightful friends made our sojourn as much a social and gastronomic adventure as an intellectual one. I am fortunate to have held a Guggenheim Fellowship, a National Endowment for the Humanities Summer Stipend, a Northwestern University President's Fund Fellowship, a Yale Senior Faculty Fellowship, and research grants from Northwestern's Office of Research and Sponsored Projects during earlier periods of work on this project, and I thank Lawrence B. Dumas, former dean of the college, for the Herman and Beulah Pearce Miller Research Professorship in Literature, which supported my work from 1992–1994.

My work on this book has been greatly assisted by the librarians and archivists of the Northwestern University Library, Yale University Library, Houghton Library of Harvard, Harvard Theatre Collection, British Library, Cambridge University Library, Berg Collection of the New York Public Library, Virginia Woolf Archive at the University of Sussex, the Fitzwilliam Museum (who kindly made room for me to study the manuscript of *A Room of One's Own* in their temporary quarters during renovations), the Wren Library at Trinity College (who enabled me to see the word Milton changed in the manuscript of "Lycidas"), Clare College Library, and the Freud Museum in London. I owe very special thanks to Elisabeth Inglis, curator of the Virginia Woolf Archive at Sussex, who not only made my visits fruitful beyond all expectation but each time extended a splendid welcome with unforgettable excursions to Firle, Lewes, Monk's House, Charleston, Asheham House (now razed), the river Ouse, Newhaven, Glyndebourne, some memorable pubs, and her own home; and to Rachel Bowlby, who joined us in some of these pilgrimages, conversed about the genius loci, shared the pleasures of her life in Brighton, and bestowed warm hospitality. I also thank Jeffrey Garrett, until recently our library's humanities bibliographer, who in the course of keeping up the Woolf holdings acquired the Primary Source Media CD-ROM Virginia Woolf Archive, edited by Mark Hussey, which makes nearly all of Woolf's writings available on one's computer. And I thank Russell Maylone, curator of our Charles Deering McCormick Library of Special Collections, who not only showed my students and me the library's extensive early Hogarth Press holdings but—in what can only be called a labor of love—guided us expertly and patiently through a Woolfian printing project on the library's 1837 Washington and Hoe hand press.

I acknowledge with thanks the following editors and publishers. *Modernism/Modernity* published chapter 4, "*Mrs. Dalloway*'s Postwar Elegy" (special issue on gender and war, winter 2002); *Tulsa Studies in Women's Literature* published a version of chapter 8, "St. Virginia's Epistle to an English Gentleman: Sex, Violence and the Public Sphere in Woolf's *Three Guineas*" (spring 1994). An early version of chapter 2 appeared as "War, Civilization, and the Conscience of Modernity: Views from *Jacob's Room*," in *Selected Papers from the Fifth Annual Virginia Woolf Conference*, ed. Beth Rigel Daugherty and Mark Hussey (1996). Part of chapter 6 appeared as "'A Fin in a Waste of Waters': L'Esthétique Moderne et la [Femme] dans *The Waves*," trans. Pierre-Eric Villeneuve, in *Virginia Woolf: Le Pur et l'Impur, Colloque de Cerisy-2001*, ed. Catherine Bernard and Christine Reynier (Rennes: Presses Universitaires de Rennes, 2002). I also draw briefly on my "Out of the Chrysalis: Female Authority and Female Initiation in Virginia Woolf's *The Voyage Out*" (*Tulsa Studies in Women's Literature* [spring 1986]); "Virginia Woolf as Shakespeare's Sister," in *Women's Re-Visions of Shakespeare*, ed. Marianne Novy (Urbana: University of Illinois Press, 1990), and "Modernism, Genetic Texts, and Literary Authority in Woolf's Portraits of the Artist as the Audience," *Romantic Review* (special issue on *critique génétique*, ed. A. Compagnon and A. Grésillon [spring 1996]).

My deepest thanks go to John Austin, who inspired, discussed, read, pruned, queried, and otherwise improved this book in ways no words can touch while buoying me along on that great voyage life's adventure. Finally, I thank Sasha Austin Schmidt for illuminating Lily Briscoe's struggle to picture the world, for the everyday joys of her young family, and for her own adventurous spirit. I dedicate this book to her.

VIRGINIA WOOLF
AND THE BLOOMSBURY AVANT-GARDE

■■ ■■

We were in the van of the builders of a new society.
—Leonard Woolf, *Sowing: An Autobiography of the Years 1880 to 1904*

Let us never cease from thinking—what is this "civilization" in which we find ourselves?
—Woolf, *Three Guineas*, 1938

The barbarian . . . is not only at our gates; he is also within the walls of our civilization, within our minds and hearts.
—Leonard Woolf, *Barbarians Within and Without*, 1939

■■ ■■

ONE

Civilization and "my civilisation"
Virginia Woolf and the Bloomsbury Avant-Garde

orn in London in 1882 and educated in her father's library, Virginia Woolf came of age at a moment when, as Leonard Woolf put it, political and social movements gave hope that Europe "might really be on the brink of becoming civilized."[1] Leonard's prospective formulation reanimates Kant's dynamic understanding of Enlightenment as no completed, secure achievement but an unfinished and unfinishable struggle against barbarism *within* Europe.[2] In the early twentieth century, Bloomsbury modernism addressed barbarities "within the walls" of European civilization, "within our minds and our hearts": belligerent nationalisms, racialized imperialisms, the class system, the sex/gender system, genocidal persecution, and war.[3] For the artists and thinkers of Bloomsbury—among them the Woolfs, Clive Bell, Vanessa Bell, John Maynard Keynes, Roger Fry, Duncan Grant, and Sigmund Freud, published in English by the Woolfs' Hogarth Press—as for many others, the 1914 war was a "Civil War" that rent what had been an increasingly international civilization.[4] This eruption of collective violence not only destroyed the illusion that Europe was "on the brink" of an international, economically egalitarian civilization committed to human rights, political autonomy, and world peace but threatened to eclipse even its idea. Before, during, and after the First World War, when democracy's triumph over fascism and communism was by no means assured, Bloomsbury's thinkers and artists contributed richly to the struggle for "civilization" in debates on Europe's future: among other works, Keynes's *Economic Consequences of the Peace* (1919); Leonard Woolf's *Empire and Commerce in Africa* (1920) and *Imperialism and Civilization* (1928); Woolf's great postwar elegy, *Mrs. Dalloway* (1925), as well as *A Room of One's Own* (1929) and *Three Guineas* (1938); Freud's *Future of an Illusion* (1927) and *Civilization and Its Discontents* (1929/30).[5]

When Woolf wonders, "But what about my civilisation," urges readers never to cease asking "what is this 'civilization' in which we find ourselves," or pictures women entering the professions as "explorers who set
out in crazy cockle shells to discover new lands, and found new civilisations," the word registers the critical and visionary usages of her moment
and milieu.[6] As Clarissa Dalloway "owed" Peter Walsh "words: 'sentimental,' 'civilised,' " Woolf owes *civilization* to a discourse formed by
Europe's imperial history, her public-school professional class and its culture, the Stephen family heritage of radical skepticism, and the crisis of
liberal democracy after 1914.[7] As an unschooled daughter of an educated
man and an "Outsider," Woolf entered public discourse by the side door
of Bloomsbury—at once heir to the Enlightenment concept of a public
sphere independent of state and market, in which private individuals
debate the community's interests, values, and future, and a local, liminal
version of England's masculinized public sphere. Within that extraordinary intellectual and artistic milieu, evolved from her brother Thoby's
Cambridge friendships, Woolf honed her public voice. Through Leslie
Stephen and Bloomsbury she inherited the Kantian idea of Enlightenment
as unending struggle for human rights, self-governance, and peace in the
name of a "sociability" conceived as humanity's highest end. At the same
time, she extended Bloomsbury's critique of the barbarity within Europe
to the women's movement, not simply as the voice of a "subaltern coun-
terpublic" but on the principles articulated by its leaders: " 'Our claim
was no claim of women's rights only' " but " 'a claim for the rights of all—
all men and women—to the respect in their persons of the great principles
of Justice and Equality and Liberty' " (*TG* 155, citing Josephine Butler).
With this gesture, Woolf not only writes the women's movement into
Europe's Enlightenment project but asserts its continuity with England's
interwar struggles against rising anti-Semitism and totalitarianism: "The
words are the same as yours; the claim is the same as yours," she tells the
male correspondent who has asked her to join a society to prevent war.
"The daughters of educated men who were called, to their resentment,
'feminists' were in fact the advance guard of your own movement. They
were fighting the tyranny of the patriarchal state as you are fighting the
tyranny of the Fascist state" (*TG* 156).

To frame Bloomsbury in this way is to recover something of its specificity as, in E. M. Forster's words, the "only genuine *movement* in English
civilisation."[8] More often considered a rearguard action in defense of a
liberal modernity's pre-1914 gains, Bloomsbury's claims as a modernist
avant-garde rest on the extent to which it managed to translate the energies of the "hopeful and exciting" prewar European political and social

movement into the postwar battle for Europe's future. If, as Lucy McDiarmid writes, Britain's major poets contemplated "saving civilization" with fatalistic despair, nostalgia, and "embarrassment," Bloomsbury's internationalist thinkers and artists fought in public debate across the disciplines—economics, politics, psychoanalysis, social criticism, arts and letters—for a civilization that had never existed (hence could not be "saved").[9] Like Peter Bürger's historical avant-gardes, Bloomsbury rejects bourgeois culture's "means-end rationality" and engages art-for-art's-sake in the cause of "forg[ing] a new life praxis from a basis in art."[10] But whereas Bürger misconstrues Kantian aesthetic autonomy as "the pathos of universality," Bloomsbury integrates political and suprapolitical thinking with aesthetics and everyday praxis in addressing a public sphere conceived, in Hannah Arendt's words, as "a form of being together where no one rules and no one obeys"; where the community's interest in disinterestedness is continually proposed, if never perfectly enacted; and where the work of art calls people not to see as one but to see differently and then seek to "persuade each other" in arduous negotiation of an always changing *sensus communis*, or common understanding.[11]

This view of Bloomsbury diverges at critical points from Raymond Williams's influential 1980 summation of its "theory and practice":

> from Keynesian economics to its work for the League of Nations, it made powerful interventions towards the creation of economic, political and social conditions within which, freed from war and depression and prejudice, individuals could be free to be and to become civilized. Thus in its personal instances and in its public interventions Bloomsbury was as serious, as dedicated and as inventive as this position has ever, in the twentieth century, been.[12]

This "oppositional fraction" of England's ruling class, Williams observes, deployed "bourgeois enlightenment" values against "cant, superstition, hypocrisy, pretension, . . . public show, . . . ignorance, poverty, sexual and racial discrimination, militarism, and imperialism." Yet he concludes that, because Bloomsbury's "supreme value" was not an "alternative idea of a whole society" but the "free . . . civilized individual," its "embarrassing" if unwitting legacy is the "conspicuous and privileged consumption" to which bourgeois individualism is now largely reduced.[13]

But Williams's tracing of post-1945 consumer culture's "fashionably distorted tree" (which even he finds strange "fruit") to Bloomsbury's "hopefully planted seed" risks losing sight of the woods. First, his construction of Bloomsbury as an "evidently incoherent" array of positions falsely naturalized by the notion of "the 'civilized individual' " both neglects strong, significant affinities among their works and silently discounts the qualifier *civilized*.[14] Second, his opposition of Bloomsbury's free civilized individual to "the idea of a whole society" obscures the more relevant oppositions between the civilized individual and the unfree, uncivilized individual—whether a barbaric and tyrannical leader (Hitler, Mussolini, Franco, Stalin) or a person of any class whose freedom of mind is sacrificed, in Roger Fry's words, to "the herd with 'its immense suggestibility more than ever at the mercy of unscrupulous politicians' "; and, further, between democratic and totalitarian social systems—ideas of a whole society that foster or repress freedom to think for oneself, the sine qua non of democratic governance.[15] Third, Williams's insistence that Bloomsbury was not a "cause" but a liberal modern "style" of "personal relations, aesthetic enjoyment, and intellectual openness" both trivializes the integration of the economic, political, and aesthetic dimensions of public life in its art and thought and turns a blind eye to its "idea of a whole society": a democratic, economically egalitarian, international civilization, far from realized before the First World War, in crisis and under threat from 1914 until Hitler's defeat (and beyond) (154, 163). In Bloomsbury's modernist transformation of and contributions to this "cause" lies a different legacy for a new century still struggling toward global economic equity, human rights, community, and peace.[16]

Bloomsbury and the Barbarism Within

It would require a book in itself to survey Bloomsbury's contributions to modernist discourse on civilization. Here I just sketch some deep lines of force across authors and disciplines: its internationalist stance at a moment when virulent nationalism prevailed even in England; its analysis of the violence within that "dark continent" Europe and within the self; and its Darwinian sense of history as (in Freud's figure) a struggle between the "immortal" adversaries "Eros and Death, between the instinct of life and the instinct of destruction, as it works itself out in the human species."[17] While Bloomsbury surely epitomizes what Lyotard sums up as the "Enlightenment narrative in which the hero of knowledge works toward a good ethico-political end—universal peace," its historical moment resists both any reified, positivist notion of "knowledge" and any postmodern reduction to a totalizing belief in "Progress—Science—Reason—Truth."[18] Thus Leonard Woolf saw his life after 1918 "ruthlessly" shaped by the fight against totalitarianism and war: "(1) 1919 to 1933, the . . . struggle for civilization that ended with Hitler's rise to power; (2) 1933 to 1939, . . . in which civilization was finally destroyed and which ended with war; (3) 1939 to 1945, the six years of war; (4) the post-war world."[19] Of course, neither Freud, driven from Vienna in 1938, nor Virginia Woolf, who wrote in 1940 "Thinking is my fighting," nor Keynes, a historic presence at Bretton Woods, nor indeed Leonard, who published *Barbarians Within and Without* in 1939, abandoned the struggle for civilization on Hitler's becoming German chancellor (*D* 5:285, 15 May 1940). If, as Woolf wrote, "It was no longer possible to believe that the world generally was becoming more civilised" after 1918, they continued to fight against barbarism within (*RF* 213).

As the 1914 war sucked even "liberal and pacifist" contemporaries such as H. G. Wells and G. M. Trevelyan into its "religion of Nationalism," Bloomsbury seemed by contrast, Clive Bell wrote, almost a "shrine of civilization," of belief in reason's power to emancipate human beings from prejudice and violence.[20] Crucial to its "experiment in civilization" was its radical practice of the free speech England's liberal democracy protected and fostered, at least in principle. As Arendt observes, in a historical crisis "thinking ceases to be a marginal affair": when everyone else is "swept away," critical questioning of unexamined opinions, values, doctrines, theories, and convictions "is political by implication," and the public and principled "refusal to join," "a kind of action."[21] Bertrand Russell's dismissal from his Cambridge lectureship and imprisonment for protesting the war; Clive Bell's pamphlet *Peace at Once* (1915), "publicly burned by the Common Hangman" by order of London's Lord Mayor; Keynes's resignation in protest from the Versailles Peace talks; Leonard's critique of European imperialism in Africa; Virginia's of the "egg" of fascism in England's sex/gender system: all exemplify thinking as fighting in the "war for peace" (one of Leonard's titles).[22]

Bloomsbury argued eloquently against a European civil war in the conflict's early days. Bell's *Peace at Once*, for example, deplored the diversion of vast resources that might have gone to combat class oppression to nationalist military violence and asked whether "crushing Germany" "is worth killing and maiming half the serviceable male population of Europe, starving to death a quarter of the world, and ruining the hopes of the next three generations."[23] Confident that the British Navy would in any case keep England from becoming "a German province," Bell doubted, in light of Europe's "morally and materially" international civilization, whether an ordinary Englishman would rather kill and die "than have his children taught German." The true enemy, he argued, is not Germany but the class system: "everywhere the people are under the thumb of the ruling class," and ruling classes "are pretty much alike everywhere" (21–22). Pre-1914 Germany, he contended, had been "moving towards a more democratic theory and a more generous view of life"; had English diplomats worked for peace instead of buying into "the game of German militarists," it would soon have purged the "relics of barbarism" from its political system and joined the "humane, intellectual movement that was gaining ground so rapidly in France and England." Foreshadowing Keynes, Bell warned that "every month of war" strengthened "the German jingo Party, which will become . . . the Party of revenge," and urged his government to propose peace terms acceptable to "the more reasonable part of the German nation," since "the surest means to another European war would be a peace that humiliated someone" (31–33, 42, 45).

Keynes famously propounded such an internationalist vision at the Versailles Peace talks in 1919, where he served as the British delegation's chief Treasury representative.[24] Condemning the Allied reparations against Germany as a barbaric relic of the militant nationalisms that had led to the war, Keynes sought to persuade the Allied leaders—Wilson, Lloyd George, Clemenceau—to rise above nationalist psychology and lead Europe toward a truly international civilization. As the war was a "civil war," the Peace was civil war by other means: an instrument of nationalist aggression calculated to enrich the Allied victors at the expense of the vanquished Germans. As such, it could only create the conditions for another war. In *The Economic Consequences of the Peace*, written after he resigned from the Peace talks, Keynes pointed out that what was at stake was Europe's future not Germany's: the burden of reparations would drive the Germans to "submerge civilization itself" in the attempt to meet their "overwhelming needs" (228) and thereby "destroy, whoever is victor, the civilization and the progress of our generation" (268). Written against an economic policy bound to foment nationalist aggression, *The Economic Consequences of the Peace* not only prophesies Hitler but frames him as a barbarian *within* European civilization, partly spawned by the Allies' regressive postwar nationalism (a point to which chapter 4 returns).

Leonard Woolf pursued his vision of an internationalist Europe through work on the League of Nations, anti-imperialism, and democratic socialism.[25] Recounting the events that led to the 1914 war, military historian John Keegan stresses the Russian czar's failed initiative of an international court for the peaceful arbitration of disputes between nations, which ran aground on the principle of national sovereignty.[26] The League's failure to avert a second war contributed to Leonard's view that totalitarian aggression had "finally destroyed" European civilization by 1939. Leonard's 1905–1911 experience as a British colonial official in Ceylon left him appalled at how long it took his "imperialist soul" to "doubt" his right to be "a ruler of subject peoples."[27] Having witnessed "the white man's burden of lucrative imperialism"—the agent of "more bloodshed than ever religion or dynasties" and the "chief cause" of the 1914 war—he envisioned the League of Nations as an agency not just to arbiter international disputes but to dismantle Europe's rival imperialisms and redress some of the damage wrought by "barbarian" Europe upon Africa.[28]

Following Conrad's 1899 *Heart of Darkness* and Edward Morel's 1913 declaration of partial victory in his long campaign to stop King Leopold's criminal exploitation of Congo, Leonard's 1920 *Empire and Commerce in Africa: A Study in Economic Imperialism* (1920) analyzed the "almost wholly evil" effects of "Christian European civilization" on African peoples and the "deadly" "material results" of British, French, and German perversions of "such elusive 'imponderables' as civilization and barbarism" to serve "racial passion and national ambitions."[29] Reluctantly, skeptically, only on stringent conditions of oversight, and (to judge from his rhetoric) with less faith than profound doubt of reason's sway over capitalist interest, he proposed making the League a paternalistic "trustee for the native population"—its "only duty" to promote Africans' political, social, and economic interests by systematic education in self-governance and by overseeing the return of all land and all profits from their land and labor in a "gradual expropriation" of European "capitalist enterprises" in Africa (*ECA* 362). Like Conrad, Leonard describes the heart of darkness within Europe—the "primitive" barbarity of that "alien civilization" whose "social policy is mainly directed towards safeguarding its most cherished principles, the sacred rights of property" and profit; and whose "right . . . to civilize" has meant in practice "the right . . . to rob," "exploit," and "enslave" (352–53). Proposing a "science of civilisation" as his "visionary and nonexistent" subject, and anticipating being dismissed as "a doctrinaire, a visionary, and a crank," he frames "semi-civilized" Europe's imperialist enterprises as a violent "conflict of civilizations" and (not unlike Keynes) attacks its capitalist "economic ideals" with its human-rights ideal (360).[30]

From the other side of the Peace, Freud enters the debate on Europe's future with a searching analysis of civilization's material and psychosocial economies and (with Bell and Keynes) a critique of class oppression as a cause of war. In *The Future of an Illusion* and *Civilization and Its Discontents*, he points to the war as incontrovertible evidence that human aggression is no aberration but an instinct, innate and ineradicable. In exchange for material, social, and psychic rewards, civilization induces its subjects to renounce aggression; but, since instincts can only be suppressed, not eradicated, everyone remains "virtually an enemy of civilization," and civilization's economy of renunciation and reward is inherently fragile, easily unbalanced by social and economic inequities that intensify its enemy-subjects' grievances.[31] The "decisive question" for war-ravaged Europe, Freud argues, is whether the burden of "instinctual sacrifices" can be lessened and civilization's enemies reduced to "a minority" (*FI* 5, 8). As Keynes saw the Peace as an economic war, Freud judges class oppression a formidable threat to civilization, which can pacify its citizen-enemies only by a reasonably equitable distribution of rewards.[32] Watching a defeated, oppressed Germany move toward the vengeance Keynes predicted and Russia struggling to consolidate its revolution into an alternative political economy, Freud distinguished privations that affect everyone from those affecting "only groups, classes or even single individuals": a society that exists by the labor of people allotted too meager a share of its wealth, he predicted, would inevitably incur their "intense hostility" and "neither has nor deserves the prospect of a lasting existence" (*FI* 12, 15–16).

Freud's critique of class oppression is inseparable from his attack on "religious illusion," which he, like Marx, sees as a powerful means of controlling aggression (*FI* 81). Against its irrational picture of a cosmos populated by anthropomorphic gods that exorcise nature's terrors, reconcile believers to fate, and promise future compensation for earthly discontents, Freud advocates an *"education to reality"* (*Ananke*: necessity); in place of the quiescent Christian fantasy of heaven, an activist vision of improving collective life in the here and now.[33] If European civilization is to survive, he concludes, it must relegate religion's "practical fictions" to its childhood and turn instead to science, which subjects its representations of reality to empirical verification, and art, which makes no truth claims and, in its symbolic gratification of instincts, reconciles people to the sacrifices civilization demands as nothing else can.[34]

In *Three Guineas*, her 1938 public epistle to an English gentleman who asks her to join a society dedicated to preventing war and to sign "a manifesto in favour of disinterested culture and intellectual liberty," Virginia Woolf pictures the barbarian within—"called in German and Italian Führer or Duce; in our own language Tyrant or Dictator"—as "ourselves" (*TG* 148, 217). As we shall see in chapter 8, her argument that "we cannot dissociate ourselves from that figure" does not consign humanity to the fatality of its own aggression but (like Freud) calls readers to fight on the side of Eros: "we are not passive spectators doomed to unresisting obedience but by our thoughts and actions can ourselves change that figure" (*TG* 217).

Leonard's 1939 *Barbarians Within and Without* also addresses the barbarism within. Citing Freud on civilization's economy of aggression renounced in exchange for benefits (65 and n. 11), Leonard tracks the flawed historical incarnations of Europe's democratic ideal from Periclean Athens, with its economic basis of slavery, to Marx, Lenin, and the Russian Revolution on one hand and to its "semi-civilized" "travesty" in modern Britain and France on the other (*BWW* 45). The Soviets have "fatally compromised" *The Communist Manifesto*'s radical democratic spirit by corrupting the economic foundation for "what might have been the greatest civilization in human history."[35] Meanwhile, despite essentially similar ideals, social democrats, communists, and socialists fight each other instead of uniting against their common enemy the Nazi "barbarians," whom they would otherwise have vanquished (*BWW* 162). As for Keynes, Freud, and Virginia Woolf, Hitler is a barbarian within as well as without: a monster (from Latin *monstrum*: a portent; *monere*: to warn) created by the Allied victors, a pariah who both mocks and mirrors Europe's semibarbaric "civilization" in scapegoating the Jewish people for Germany's economic desperation while promising to throw off the Allies' economic domination and reclaim the German people's "right to live" (*BWW* 97, 108). Still, Leonard discounts Hitler's and Mussolini's "importance" to Europe's future, since "even a semi-civilized state like Britain or France" would triumph over fascism if it held to "the principles and traditions of its semi-civilization" (*BWW* 176–77).

Bloomsbury's "cause," in short, was not the grand one of "saving" civilization but the more modest one of fighting for its possibility, in the spirit of Kant as indeed of Gandhi, who remarked that Western civilization would be a good idea. In 1916 Freud had predicted that "our high opinion" of civilization's riches would lose "nothing from our discovery of their fragility"; "We shall build up again all that the war has destroyed, and perhaps on firmer ground and more lastingly than before."[36] Against Williams's identification of Bloomsbury's "supreme value" as no "alternative idea of a whole society" but the free civilized individual, their internationalism, critique of the violence within, and assertion of human agency toward a future understood not as certain progress but as open and free pursue the possibility of rebuilding European civilization on firmer ground and more lastingly. Although Keynes's intimate 1938 Memoir Club essay, "My Early Beliefs," has been taken for a sweeping repudiation of Bloomsbury's utopian faith in "rational individualism," Keynes no less than the Woolfs and Freud proposed and advocated legal, social, political, and economic institutions to counteract (in Freud's words) the "truth . . . which people are so ready to disavow . . . that men are not gentle creatures who want to be loved" but instinctively aggressive against their "neighbour," who "tempts them to . . . exploit his capacity for work without compensation, to use him sexually without his consent, to seize his possessions, to humiliate him, to cause him pain, to torture and to kill him. *Homo homini lupus.* Who, in the face of all his experience of life and of history, will have the courage to dispute this assertion?"[37] For Bloomsbury it was a question not of any simple belief that "civilized" or "rational" individuals will spontaneously produce a just social order but (as Kant wrote) of creating political and social institutions such as to enable even a "race of devils" to have "a good state" so long as they are rational (that is, unable to will as a general law what would be destructive to themselves), without sacrificing more of freedom and possibility than necessary for one's "neighbor's" protection; in short, without resort to totalitarianism.[38]

Thus Virginia Woolf, attending the 1928 *Well of Loneliness* trial as a potential witness on the book's behalf, found herself

> impressed by the reason of the law, its astuteness, its formality. Here have we evolved a very remarkable fence between us & barbarity; something commonly recognised; half humbug & ceremony therefore—when they pulled out calf bound books & read old phrases I thought this; & the bowing & scraping made me think it; but in these banks runs a live stream. What is obscenity? What is literature? What is the difference between the subject & the treatment? In what cases is evidence allowable? . . . After lunch we heard an hour more, & then the magistrate, increasingly deliberate & courteous, said he would read the book again & give judgment next Friday at two [on] the pale tepid vapid book which lay damp & slab all about the court.[39]

It is "the reason of the law"—as institution, abstract rule, deliberative procedure—and not the "rational individual" that she finds "a remarkable fence" against barbarity; "the reason of the law" that, however imperfectly, civilizes aggression, transforms it into a luxury one can survive by creating an alternative to human sacrifice. To see Bloomsbury's idea of civilization as more individual than collective, "more a state of mind than a nation-state," overlooks the interdependence of individual freedom and rational political and social institutions in their thought and art.[40] To see the "cesspool" discussed in *Between the Acts* as "a rude metaphor for everything the characters call civilization" flattens the novel into one-note critique, shorn of the depth and complexity of Woolf's critical and creative vision.[41]

One way that Leonard and Virginia Woolf publicly deployed their freedom of speech in the struggle for civilization was by creating the Hogarth Press. Founded as a hobby and run on a shoestring ("L. never makes a penny; I mean—tries to, & I could almost wish we were more lavish in our ways," wrote Virginia), the Press reflects its owners' internationalist vision (*D* 3:176, 18 February 1928). Eventually its list had six Nobel Prize authors—Ivan Bunin, T. S. Eliot, and Bertrand Russell in literature, Viscount Cecil, Fridtjof Nansen, and Philip Noel-Baker in Peace—as well as the three world figures Keynes (the Prize in Economics was not yet established in his lifetime), Freud, and Virginia Woolf.[42]

With volumes on economic, political, and social questions standing cheek by jowl with art and literature, the Hogarth Press shelves present a cross-section of multidisciplinary thought toward "a new life praxis," as for example in the convergence of modernist aesthetics and feminism. In "What Is Enlightenment?" Kant had criticized those self-appointed cultural "guardians" who would deny freedom of thought to "the largest part of mankind (including the entire fair sex)."[43] By the early twentieth century, Woolf's exact contemporary James Joyce considered women's emancipation "the greatest revolution of our time, . . . the revolt of women against the idea that they are the mere instruments of men"; and Ibsen, whose "ideas have become part of our lives," "the greatest influence on the present generation."[44] When Woolf began writing her first novel, *The Voyage Out* (1915), the suffrage battle was raging; in her second, *Night and Day* (1919), one character envisions each suffrage meeting as "a step onwards in the great march—humanity, you know," and the campaign's success as "A great day not only for us but for civilization" (*ND* 170). Interrupting that struggle, the 1914 war—which, Woolf intimated in a public letter of 1920, might seem almost to have demonstrated men's unfitness to govern—brought to a crisis a civilization appropriated to masculine interests and existing to a very great extent by women's uncompensated labor. As *Three Guineas* argues, Europe's "civil war" had a parallel in the war at home as women challenged men's monopoly on public resources, policy, and cultural institutions from education and the professions to the church and political economy.

Virginia Woolf's work extends Bloomsbury's dialectical modernization of the Enlightenment "cause" to rights and freedoms long denied "the entire fair sex."[45] *Three Guineas* analyzes the "half-civilized barbarism" of the sex/gender system and challenges both her Bloomsbury friends' and her public's uncritical acquiescence in that barbarism (*CS* 127). Her novels weave the "greatest revolution of our time" into the fabric of everyday life: thus Charles Tansley complains that "Women made civilisation impossible" while Mrs. Ramsay, cringing under a verbal "pelt of jagged hail," marvels that her husband rends "the thin veils of civilisation so wantonly, so brutally," pursuing truth "with such an astonishing lack of consideration for other people's feelings" (*TL* 85, 32). From the novel's stereophonic standpoint, what makes civilization impossible is the barbarous system of masculine domination and feminine sacrifice, even as *To the Lighthouse* is read today in dozens of languages for the freedom and power of its vision and art—an implicit critique of a civilization based "more on the light of instinct than of reason" (*WF* 6).

The convergence of women, freedom, and aesthetics brings us to a crux of Bloomsbury's claim as a modernist avant-garde, for here as in Enlightenment thought sociopolitical critique is integrated with aesthetics. To do justice to the ways (both obvious and subtle) that the influence of Kant, that towering intellectual ancestor of modernity, stamps the work of Leslie Stephen, Freud, George Moore, Roger Fry, and Clive Bell, is beyond this chapter's scope.[46] I shall instead attempt to draw out some salient implications of the words *sentimental* and *civilized* that Clarissa owes Peter, himself once one of those "young men"—lovers of abstract principles, readers of science and philosophy—on whom "the future of civilisation" depends (*MD* 50). These words, I suggest, are opposed terms of judgment, to which a third word, *disinterested*—missing here, but elsewhere in Bloomsbury aesthetics allied with *civilized*, opposed to *sentimental*—offers a key. As S. P. Rosenbaum observes, "The essential disinterestedness of art was . . . a fundamental conviction of Bloomsbury's aesthetics, which suggests that . . . Bloomsbury's . . . aesthetic attitudes descend mainly from Kant"—that is, from the Third Critique, the *Critique of Judgment*.[47]

In Kant's aesthetics, we judge an artwork beautiful when our disinterested contemplation of it gives rise to aesthetic pleasure, which arises from the free play of imagination and understanding. In making aesthetic judgments, we try to set aside "interest," personal prejudice, and preference—in a word, *sentiment* (does it go with my couch? does it remind me of my honeymoon? will it appreciate in value? does owning it enhance my social status?). In this sense, aesthetic judgments are—or at least we try to make them—"pure." By virtue of this disinterestedness, we posit "*subjective universal validity*" for them: that is, when we judge a work of art beautiful, we *posit* that anyone who contemplates it apart from personal prejudice and preference will experience aesthetic pleasure—quite apart from whether or not this proves to be the case in practice.[48] One's aesthetic judgment, in other words, is binding not on other people but on oneself, in that it requires one to put aside personal interest—*sentiment*—in making it. By the same token, in putting personal interest aside, one seeks common ground with others, whether or not experience confirms it. In offering disinterested aesthetic pleasure—free from personal interest, use, or purpose; relatively free, too, of particular local, national, and cultural contexts—art indirectly mediates the sociability that Kant considers humanity's "highest end," in line with the Enlightenment sociopolitical ideal, the "right to go visiting" (*LK* 8, 16).

Bloomsbury's modernist aesthetics resonates with Kant's emphasis on the artwork's purely formal beauty, apart from content, truth claims, and external rule.[49] The artist, Kant writes, does not copy nature but creates "another nature"—a form complete in itself, apart from any worldly design or use, given by no concept and to which no concept is adequate, which arises from the free play of imagination and understanding in the artist and gives rise to the same in the beholder (*CJ* §49 157, *CPJ* 192). A work of art that is "beautiful" in Kant's sense manifests "purposiveness without purpose" in its form (*CJ* §10 55, *CPJ* 105). Yet something more than the usual understanding of "art for art's sake" is at stake in art's freedom from imitation and use, from the everyday life of purpose and gain. In Kant's aesthetics it is genius, "nature in the subject," that gives the rule to art—unlike science, which must subject its claims to empirical validation, and moral reason, which must submit its judgments to moral law (*CJ* §46 150, *CPJ* 186). In this originality, the artwork actualizes a freedom that belongs to the noumenal (supersensible) realm, beyond reach of nature's sensible, phenomenal realm and beyond human will. By creating "another nature . . . out of the material that actual nature gives it," endowed with a "completeness" nowhere found in nature, the artist throws a bridge from nature's realm to the realm of freedom. "We feel our freedom," writes Kant, in the artist's transformation of nature's "material" "into something different which surpasses nature" and occasions thought to which "no concept can be fully adequate" (*CJ* §49 157–58, Introduction IX 32; *CPJ* 192, 81). As a form subject to no rule but that given by the artist's genius—nature in the subject, since genius is inborn—the artwork manifests a freedom beyond human will.[50] And for Kant, of the "three pure rational ideas" God, immortality, and freedom, freedom alone "proves its objective reality" by its effects in nature (*CJ* §91 327, *CPJ* 338).

In this light, "art for art's sake" might accurately be said to exist for the sake of a freedom that mediates sociability. For the freedom we sense in the disinterested contemplation of art entails an escape from personality, or (in Clive Bell's memorable phrase) one's "thick little ego."[51] To exercise reflective judgment in making or contemplating art is to try to see "things in themselves," beyond one's thick little ego (that is, apart from interest, possession, utilitarian purpose); to posit "subjective universal validity" for one's judgments; to think as oneself in the place of the other.[52] In respect to Clarissa's two words, art cultivates a *civilized* (and civilizing) disinterestedness that tends to enhance the common life and the *sensus communis*, not by eradicating always interested *sentiment* but by making us conscious of it as such and so keeping it in its "proper" (from Latin *proprius*: one's own) place.

For Woolf, a "feminist" aesthetics is subsumed within such a Kantian aesthetics of freedom from personality and sentiment, of detachment from everyday means-ends concerns, with Shakespeare its example par excellence:

> it is impossible to conceive the speed & the control, the violence & the calm, that were needed to write a scene say in Antony & Cleopatra; always to be flying before the break of that gale . . . now to be [?Pompey[53]] now to be Caesar, to be some old soldier next & then a girl singer: . . Is it not the freedom of it that most amazes us? . . . it is the freedom of it that remains overwhelming. One has been liberated; set free—one finishes Antony & Cleopatra feeling that . . . If Shakespeare had said "I am this sort of man" . . . had kept popping his head in, . . . "Daffodils that come before the swallow dares" wd not have been. (WF 163–64)

Far from setting art off from the world, Bloomsbury, like Kant, finds in its beauty a manifestation of freedom that mediates sociability and community—not by imposing canons of taste but by transporting its beholders beyond egotism into (possible) disinterested pleasure, and thence into noncoercive dialogue about the *sensus communis*, or common values—a function of spectatorship we shall explore in chapter 9. As one spectator of La Trobe's pageant says, "I thought it brilliantly clever"; as another replies, "O my dear, I thought it utter bosh" (BA 197).

Bell thought Roger Fry's 1909 "Essay on Aesthetics" the most valuable "contribution to the science" since Kant.[54] Whatever the merits of that claim, Kant's influence on Fry, Woolf, and Bloomsbury aesthetics can hardly be overestimated. For Fry, the key to art's mediation of what he calls "decency and good" is not content or usefulness but purely formal beauty, apprehended in "a disinterested intensity of contemplation" that is not remote from but actually belongs to the sphere of everyday social practices.[55] Woolf notes that Fry honored the painter Watts because "'he looked upon art as a necessary and culminating function of civilised life— as indeed the great refining and disinterested activity, without which modern civilisation would become a luxurious barbarity'" (RF 115). Fry's lectures "encourage[d] the individual to enjoy the rarest of his gifts, the disinterested life, the life of the spirit, over and above our mere existence as living organisms" (RF 236). In the same terms he presented to an appalled British public the landmark "Manet and the Post-Impressionists" exhibition at London's Grafton Gallery from November 1910 to January 1911: these artists have abandoned "the merely representative element" for "expressive form in its barest, most abstract elements"; and the spectator who can "look without preconception" and "allow his senses to speak" will discover "a discretion and a harmony of color, a force and completeness of pattern" that "suggest visions to the imagination, rather than impose them upon the senses."[56] Introducing the second Post-Impressionist Exhibition in October 1912, Fry continued,

> these artists . . . do not seek to give what can, after all, be but a pale reflex of actual appearance, but to arouse the conviction of a new and definite reality. They do not seek to imitate form, but to create form, not to imitate life, but to find an equivalent for life[;] . . . to make images which . . . shall appeal to our disinterested and contemplative imagination with something of the same vividness as the things of actual life appeal to our practical activities. In fact they aim not at illusion but at reality. (*RF* 177–78)

Disinterested and contemplative imagination; not a *reflection of actual appearance* but *conviction of a new and definite reality*; not an imitation of nature but *an equivalent for life*: these phrases flag Fry as a modernist heir of the Third Critique. Remote from mimetic representation, from nature's "actual appearance," modern art's abstract forms incarnate his understanding of art as an "equivalent for life" that inspires "conviction of a new and definite reality," to be valued not for the sake of knowledge or truth but in itself, for no other purpose than beauty and "the disinterested life, the life of the spirit" that aesthetic pleasure mediates.

The First Post-Impressionist exhibition—Fry's single-handed intervention in British taste—illustrates the way art offered for no purpose but the disinterested contemplation of beauty can mediate transformations of the *sensus communis*.[57] Woolf describes in some detail the "paroxysms of rage and laughter" into which the show threw the public of 1910.[58] Nonetheless, life was soon imitating art. Two years later, at the Second Post-Impressionist Exhibition Ball, Virginia and Vanessa "dressed . . . as Gauguin pictures and careered around Crosby Hall," scandalizing respectable ladies (*MB* 200). In 1923 the National Gallery acquired a Gauguin; in 1939 a Cézanne centenary exhibit was mounted to benefit a London hospital. "The pictures are the same," Woolf observes. "It is the public that has changed" (*RF* 153). For Woolf herself, as we shall shortly see, 1910 was an *annus mirabilis*: the English debut of "the Post Is. & ourselves" marked a momentous change in "human character" and a crucial advance in her modernist "re-form" of the novel (*L* 1:356, 19 August 1908). Integrating aesthetics with internationalist perspectives on economic, political, and social institutions at a moment when the *sensus communis* was under urgent debate, Bloomsbury challenges myths of modernism as an antirealism "remote from the sphere of everyday practices." Neither Williams's "evidently incoherent" group of "civilized individuals" nor advocates of "mere aesthetic[ism]," Bloomsbury contested contemporary *reality* against conventions masquerading as "realism."[59]

Voyages in a Library: From Leslie Stephen's Daughter to Shakespeare's Sister

Leonard Woolf would have been Leonard Woolf, Keynes Keynes, and Freud Freud without Bloomsbury, but what would Virginia Woolf have been? And what would Bloomsbury have been without her? To pose this question is to recall the rare patrimony to which Virginia Stephen was born. Her father, Leslie Stephen, philosopher, author, and editor of the *Dictionary of National Biography*, delighted in her brilliance, tutored her in history, arranged her Greek lessons, and predicted that she would become a writer. His tyrannical temper outraged her, but his powerful, uncompromising, truth-seeking intellect helped to form hers. On the whole he disliked educated women, and he did not send his daughters to Cambridge.[60] Woolf always insisted that she was "uneducated," yet her home schooling as this particular educated man's daughter founded her art and thought on a deeper, more radical skepticism than perhaps even Cambridge, with its centuries of church affiliation, could have done.[61]

In fact Leslie Stephen had left Cambridge for just this reason. At twenty-two he was elected a fellow of Trinity Hall; the next year he was ordained, as his fellowship required; in 1859, at twenty-six, he took priest's orders. By 1860 he had read Mill, Comte, Kant, Kant's Scottish interpreter (or misinterpreter) William Hamilton, Hobbes, Locke, Berkeley, and Hume. His philosophical bent, his biographer Noel Annan notes, "cut short his career at Cambridge": by 1862 he had lost his faith and resigned as tutor.[62] Stephen often remarked "the astonishing insularity of the English in the early nineteenth century, their sublime ignorance of the German language and their indifference to German thought and literature" (173–74). I Iis *An Agnostic's Apology* (Stephen coined the word and made "agnosticism a party name") translates Kant's demonstration that pure reason cannot prove or disprove religious ideas into the language of British empiricism: "There was a simple answer to the theologians. You denied that their subject had any right to exist. The agnostic declared that there were limits to human knowledge and that beyond those limits" lay dogmatism (234, 233).

Woolf's portrait of the Ramsays in *To the Lighthouse* honors the legacy of her parents' radical skepticism. As the Ramsays' boat flies before the wind in "The Lighthouse," sixteen-year-old Cam remembers how she often slipped into her father's study to overhear him talk with his visitors:

> Just to please herself she would take a book from the shelf and stand there, watching her father write, . . . with . . . something said briefly to the other old gentleman opposite. . . . [O]ne could let whatever one thought expand here like a leaf in water; and if it did well here, among the old gentlemen smoking and *The Times* crackling then it was right. . . .
>
> "Come now," said Mr. Ramsay, suddenly shutting his book.
>
> Come where? To what extraordinary adventure? . . . Where was he leading them? . . . This is right, this is it, Cam kept feeling, . . . as she did in the study. . . . Now I can go on thinking whatever I like, and I shan't fall over a precipice or be drowned, for there he is, keeping his eye on me. (*TL* 189, 204–5)

Cam's "Come where? To what extraordinary adventure?" evokes Virginia's adventures in her father's library and company. Born English, "restless, . . . with the waves at their very door," the Stephen children were tossed naked into the sea by their father at St. Ives and set sail in their London nursery by hoisting a bedsheet over an upended table (*DM* 31). At fifteen Virginia was "enraptured" by Hakluyt's *Voyages*, lugged home for her from the London Library by her father. Later, she described it as less a book than "a great bundle of commodities," an Elizabethan "lumber room"; these were the prose writers she loved "first and most wildly," and she found "on mature inspection" that Hakluyt justified "over & over again my youthful discrimination."[63] In the Elizabethans' "hopes for the future and their sensitiveness to the opinion of older civilisations," she felt "much the same susceptibility that sometimes puzzles us among the younger countries today, the sense that broods over them of what is about to happen, of an undiscovered land on which they are about to set foot," and much the same "excitement that science stirs in the minds of imaginative English writers of our own time" (*CR2* 15–16). These voyages of discovery endow her own metaphysical voyages toward new "lands" and "civilizations" from *The Voyage Out* on.

While Virginia was "devouring" her father's library, Thoby Stephen, two years older, was at Trinity College, Cambridge, cultivating the friendships that would evolve into Bloomsbury.[64] In a letter to her brother, nineteen-year-old Virginia confesses a change of heart as to the merits of "a certain great English writer":

I read Cymbeline just to see if there mightnt be more in the great William than I supposed. And I was quite upset! Really and truly, I am now let in to [the] company of worshippers—though I still feel a little oppressed by his—greatness I suppose. I shall want a lecture when I see you; to clear up some points about the Plays. I mean about the characters. Why aren't they more human? Imogen and Posthumous and Cymbeline—I find them beyond me—Is this my feminine weakness in the upper region? But really they might have been cut out with a pair of scissors—as far as mere humanity goes—Of course they talk divinely. I have spotted the best lines in the play—almost in any play I should think—

Imogen says—Think that you are upon a rock, and now throw me again! and Posthumous answers—Hang there like fruit, my Soul, till the tree die. [Cymbeline 5:5.262–65] Now if that doesn't send a shiver down your spine, even if you are in the middle of cold grouse and coffee—you are no true Shakespearian! Oh dear oh dear—just as I feel in the mood to talk about these things, you go and plant yourself in Cambridge. (L 1:45–46, 5 November 1901)

Shut out from the education that passed the mantle of cultural authority to young men like Thoby, Virginia portrays herself belatedly "let in," in spirit if not body, to the elite "company" who worship this sacred text in Trinity's hallowed halls. While Thoby duly inherits Shakespeare, Virginia seeks secondhand wisdom from him and veers between doubt of Shakespeare's greatness and anxiety about her possible "feminine weakness." Yet far from acquiescing in her own sidelining, she parlays her "oppressed" admiration into an audacious sibling rivalry—with Shakespeare no less than Thoby. This aspiring Shakespeare's sister is not too much abashed to criticize Shakespeare's characters or to pit her judgment against Thoby's, whose ear for poetry she hints Cambridge luxury might dull. In this epistolary debate on "the great William," Virginia adroitly moves from uninitiated scoffer to chagrined worshipper to exacting critic to "true Shakespearian": thrilling to Shakespeare's "best lines," she paints herself his true inheritor. And the Shakespeare she fashions foreshadows that of Room: a genius whose characters leave vast regions of "humanity" yet untouched; a national trophy enshrined in bastions of masculine privilege but open to claim by sisters outside the line of succession.[65]

In a 1903 diary-essay, "The Country in London," Virginia continues to amass intellectual capital from her outsider's position. "I read—then I lay down the book & say—what right have I, a woman, to read all these things men have done?" she begins, adding cheerily, "But I am going to forget all that in the country. . . . All the big books I have read I have read in the country" (PA 178). In one breath she doubts her "right" to partake of a man-made world culture and eagerly anticipates a country sojourn that allows her free if covert trespass into the quasi-public arena of "big books" as she practices in private the world spectatorship that is preparing her to enter a masculinized public sphere.

In 1904 the Stephen children nursed their father through his final illness, sold 22 Hyde Park Gate, and together created a new household in Bloomsbury. Virginia had lost her mother at thirteen, her beloved half sister Stella two years later, and now, at twenty-two, her father. In her late memoir she recalls feeling too young at her mother's death to "master it, envisage it, deal with it"; after Stella's, "But this is impossible; things aren't, can't be, like this," and then "that if life were thus made to rear and kick, it was a thing to be ridden; nobody could say 'they' had fobbed me off with a weak little slip of the precious matter" (*MB* 124, 137). To be forced to grapple with loss was to appreciate life's "extreme reality" (*MB* 137). Educated thus in her father's library and the University of Life, Virginia Stephen entered a Bloomsbury soon to become a London extension of Cambridge.

Bloomsbury's Aeolian Island

> "Aeolian women were not confined to the harem like Ionians, or subjected to the rigorous discipline of the Spartans. While mixing freely with male society, they were highly educated and accustomed to express their sentiments to an extent unknown elsewhere in history—until, indeed, the present time."
>
> —Woolf, letter to the *New Statesman* (October 1920), citing Symonds on Sappho
>
> Well, I was educated in the old Cambridge school.
>
> —Woolf to Vita Sackville-West, *Letters*, 23 January 1924

Woolf would have had to invent Bloomsbury—for her, not just Cambridge in London but a liminal public where she honed her writer's voice—had fate not landed her there.[66] Indeed, she did invent it to a considerable extent, inseparably with herself. Bloomsbury rose from the Stephen family's ashes as the beautiful, genial, charismatic Thoby invited his brilliant friends to their declassé household near the British Museum for "Thursday evenings." Vanessa doubted that he meant to include his sisters; "still there they were" (*BGMC* 105). Many of these young men belonged to the Apostles, the elite Cambridge Conversazione Society devoted to "Athenian liberty of speech and speculation."[67] When Vanessa ("strong of brain," "quick to detect . . . fallacy") and Virginia were mixed into this elixir of talk, "These Apostolic young men found to their amazement that they could be shocked by the boldness and skepticism of two young women."[68] In Desmond MacCarthy's account, the openly homosexual Lytton Strachey had enlarged G. E. Moore's "realistic commonsense" philosophy into a "school" of "personal emotions and personal relations," of "literature, art and themselves." Transplanted to Bloomsbury, this free speech flourished in the unprecedented company of women—"a most important change" in social history, MacCarthy notes (*BGMC* 71).

Virginia, once accustomed to the long silences of "these inanimate creatures," found she had never "listened so intently to each step and half-step in an argument. Never have I been at such pains to sharpen and launch my own little dart. And then what joy it was when one's contribution was accepted" (*L* 1:208, 1 October 1905; *MB* 190). (Note the shift from *I* to *one*: as Virginia begins to speak on equal terms with educated men, including some of her generation's most distinguished minds, she subsumes the personal pronoun within the impersonal "one"—a point to which we shall shortly return.) However fortuitous and haphazard her poor sister's education in "the old Cambridge school," her escape from Kensington convention and hypocrisy to free speech and critical thinking in mixed-sex company seemed not just a revolution in manners but "a great advance in civilisation" (*MB* 196).

Even as Bloomsbury's intimate arena of uncensored speech, passionate debate, and rigorous argument provided a bridge from her solitary reading to the public world, Virginia brought to Bloomsbury her father's legacy: a fearless strength and clarity of mind that could "shock" young men fed on cold grouse and coffee. She was not blind to the advantages of her outsider's education. In August 1905 Thoby's Cambridge friends had privately issued a volume of unsigned poems, ironically titled *Euphrosyne* after the Grace "Joy"; it would have sunk without a trace, Bell remarks, had Virginia "not been careful to keep its memory green."[69] Thoby, writing anonymously in the *Cambridge Review*, had praised the poets' "originality of imagination, felicity of diction, skilful technique," and "audacious vocabulary," but Virginia was less impressed.[70] In an unpublished review dated 21 May 1906 she mocks these flowers of a Cambridge education. Their posturing authors "come from their University, pale, preoccupied & silent," as if burdened with "some awful communication," "a secret too dreadful to impart"; they disdain to "pass their Examinations, because . . . they despise success" and reserve "their most permanent & unqualified admiration . . . for the works which, unprinted as yet, 'unprintable' they proudly give you to understand, repose in the desks of their immediate friends." Recently "Some few songs

& sonnets" of "these gigantic works were graciously issued to the public"—songs "of Love & Death, & Cats, & Duchesses" such as "other
poets have sung before, & may, unless the race is extinct, sing yet again";
"But when taxed with their melancholy the poets confessed that such sadness had never been known, & marked the last & lowest tide of deca-
dence." Fine-tuning her phrasing, the reviewer concludes, "[There is certainly one advantage in] Among all the [dis]advantages of that sex which
is soon, we read, to have no [dis]advantages, there is much to be said
surely for that respectable custom which allows the daughter to educate
herself at home" and so "preserves her from the omniscience, the early
satiety, the melancholy self-satisfaction which a training at either of our
great universities produces in her brothers."[71]

Another episode in Virginia's rivalry with Thoby had occurred the
month *Euphrosyne* appeared. The Stephen children revisited their childhood summer home in Cornwall, and Virginia wrote an account of a
thrilling pilchard harvest—the one time in her experience when the
pilchards actually came into Carbis Bay, though each summer of their
childhood the fishermen had prepared the boats and waited. A newspaper
refused the piece, but on reading it Thoby confided to Vanessa that their
sister "might be a bit of a genius" (*MB* 130–31). A year later the Stephens
visited Greece and Turkey, and that November Thoby died of typhoid—
another "sledge-hammer" blow, more proof that life is a rearing, kicking
steed, a thing to be ridden (a figure revived in *The Waves*, dedicated in
spirit to Thoby) (*MB* 72). It remained for Virginia, once recovered from
the shock, to turn her [dis]advantages into literature. In 1907 she
embarked on her first novel, titled *Melymbrosia*; as it evolved into *The
Voyage Out*, Virginia renamed the ship that carries Rachel Vinrace
toward imaginary new lands and civilizations the *Euphrosyne*—putting
on the writer's mantle her beloved brother had laid down.[72]

Bloomsbury survived its founder Thoby and continued to evolve. In
1907 Vanessa married Clive Bell, and Virginia and Adrian moved to 29
Fitzroy Square, where they continued Thoby's "evenings." With Clive as
her astute and encouraging first reader, Virginia labored from draft to
draft of *Melymbrosia*. By April 1908 she had proceeded far enough to
dream that her dead father "snorted" at her manuscript and tossed it
aside—an anxiety that did not deter her from aspiring to "re-form the
novel and capture multitudes of things at present fugitive" (*L* 1:325, 356,
19 August). To Clive she confided that she found it "very difficult to fight
against" her "inkling of the way the book might be written by other people" and "to ignore the opinion of one's probable readers—I think I
gather courage as I go on. The only possible reason for writing down all

this, is that it represents roughly a view of one's own. My boldness terrifies me" (*L* 1:383, 7? February 1909).

In that watershed year 1910, the Bells befriended Roger Fry and Virginia's compositional labors reached a turning point. Woolf's resonant proclamation in her 1924 modernist manifesto "Mr. Bennett and Mrs. Brown"—"On or about December 1910 human character changed"—has long been linked with Fry's Post-Impressionist exhibition in that year of public crises great and small: the general elections of January and December; the famous *Dreadnought* hoax in February, when Adrian, Virginia, and friends masqueraded as "the Emperor of Abyssinia and his suite" and were honored with an official tour of His Majesty's battleship; King Edward VII's death and George V's accession, which in Woolf's essay marks the generational divide between the "Edwardians" Arnold Bennett, John Galsworthy, and H. G. Wells and the experimental "Georgians" Joyce, Eliot, Forster, Lawrence, and Woolf.[73] That year, too, suffrage demonstrations drew tens of thousands of women who defied middle-class decorum and turned the streets into festive public spectacles hung with striking banners and posters. On November 18 five hundred Women's Social and Political Union [WSPU] members marched to the House of Commons and met with six hours of physical and sexual brutality from East End police and bystanders, stirring public outcry far beyond the movement's constituents.[74] Out of the fray, Virginia addressed envelopes for the campaign and attended suffrage meetings (*L* 1:438, November 14). The 1910 suffrage battles reverberate in the leveling of social hierarchies—men over women, masters over servants, authors over readers—that "Mr. Bennett and Mrs. Brown" celebrates.

As the phrase "human *character*" suggests, 1910 also marks a breakthrough in Virginia's long travails (1907–13) to create her first novel and that as yet nonexistent author "Virginia Woolf."[75] Fry's championing of art that arouses "the conviction of a new and definite reality" appears to have influenced her transformation of *Melymbrosia* into the protomodernist *Voyage Out*, for Virginia's mid-November letter about the suffrage meetings announces, "next week I begin my work of imagination"—"begin," though she had been writing it for three years; that month too she first mentioned its new title, according to DeSalvo.[76] To Clive she wrote, "you will have to wait . . . to see what has become of it. . . . I should say that my great change was in the way of courage, or conceit; and that I had given up adventuring after other people's forms" (*L* 1:446, 29 December 1910). On or about December 1910, this letter and the novel's genetic text suggest, Virginia—stirred by London's street-theatre political conflicts, inspired by Post-Impressionist aesthetics, fortified by Fry's "moral courage" in promoting contemporary art to a volubly outraged British public—devised a new strategy to maintain her "boldness" in face of the censor and the public.[77] By staging her probable readers' probable reactions to volatile social issues *within the novel*, Woolf at once mirrors their passivity and rips through her fiction's symbolic boundaries to let in familiar but suppressed actualities.

In one scene added after 1910, for example, St. John Hirst tells Helen Ambrose about a letter from his mother "describing the suicide of the parlormaid":

> She was called Susan Jane, and she came into the kitchen one afternoon, and said that she wanted cook to keep her money for her; she had twenty pounds in gold. Then she went out to buy herself a hat. She came in at half-past five and said that she had taken poison. They had only just enough time to get her into bed and call a doctor before she died.
>
> "Well?" Helen inquired.
>
> "There'll have to be an inquest," said St. John.
>
> He shrugged his shoulders. Why do people kill themselves? Why do the lower orders do any of the things they do do? Nobody knows. They sat in silence. (*VO* 306)

With a clue to the mystery ("Why had she done it?") dangling before them like the purloined letter ("she had twenty pounds in gold"), the characters retreat from this sad news into their class position ("Why do the lower orders do any of the things they do do?"), displaying the obliviousness that ("Mr. Bennett and Mrs. Brown" argues) modernist formal experiments seek to disturb. Neither wonders how a parlormaid came by that large sum *in gold* or why, with such a fortune, the generically named Susan Jane should have entrusted her wealth to the cook, gone out to buy a hat, and returned having poisoned herself. Helen and Hirst are paragons of free and truthful speech; indeed—and perhaps not irrelevant to the matter at hand—Hewet earlier smoothly interrupts Hirst, a vicar's son, when he brings up in mixed company his father's observation of country gentlemen's free, frank passions (*VO* 202). Yet neither Hirst nor Helen mentions the glaring possibility of a domestic servant "ruined" by a gentleman who purchases her body and/or silence.[78] Even as it ostensibly observes Edwardian decorum, with its "interested" policing of talk about sex, gender, class, convention, labor, and value, Woolf's scene calls readers to see what the characters do not—thereby enacting the "death" of the author and the "birth" of the reader that "Mr. Bennett and Mrs. Brown" (and Barthes) celebrate.[79]

One character in *The Voyage Out* aspires to write "a novel about

Silence, . . . the things people don't say."[80] In revising *Melymbrosia* into *The Voyage Out*, Woolf dramatizes censorship and self-censorship within the narrative by staging socially enforced silences that function as speech acts. Framing the things people don't say, the narrative shows silence performing ideological work more deftly than words could ever do.[81] Not the text or characters but the reader becomes the potential locus of social transformation—of that change in human character that *The Voyage Out* does not so much depict as solicit, much as "Mr. Bennett and Mrs. Brown" calls its audience to embody—to substantiate—the change it proclaims. "Read the *Agamemnon*" and see whether you don't identify with Clytemnestra. Contemplate Jane Carlyle's death by marriage. Observe the swift evolution of cooks and maids, who once dwelt "like leviathans" in the "lower depths" of Edwardian houses and now breeze in and out of Georgian parlors, borrowing newspapers, modeling hats. Consider how "All human relations have shifted—those between masters and servants, husbands and wives, parents and children" (*CDB* 96). Make reality, not convention, the measure of art. Join in debating a changing *sensus communis* as a great age of literature dawns. On or about 1910 Virginia Stephen began experimenting with taking Bloomsbury's free speech public by means of a "re-form" of the English novel inseparably ethical and aesthetic, feminist and modernist. Overtaking the complacently "unprintable" *Euphrosyne*, the vessel that carries Rachel Vinrace away from England ventures beyond the censor's patrolled waters toward a future its framed silences invoke.[82] Formally conservative though it may appear beside her later novels, *The Voyage Out* is a Woolf in sheep's clothing—a leap beyond its probable readers' probable opinions toward a collaborative modernist art.

In 1911, while Virginia Stephen was in the midst of writing *The Voyage Out*, Leonard Woolf returned from Ceylon. Leonard—who revered Pericles' funeral oration on civilization's "unwritten laws"—privately named her Aspasia, after Pericles' beautiful, learned mistress, famed like him for eloquence and said to be his political adviser.[83] In an homage titled "Aspasia," he pictures Virginia as "the most Olympian of the Olympians," her room a snowy, windy "mountain top" floating in "illimitable space" amid "precipices & bottomless gulfs"; her thoughts "torn from reality" by a mind "so astonishingly fearless, there is no fact & no reality which it does not face."[84] While Virginia's part in Bloomsbury did not depend on marriage (after all, she and Leonard saw each other daily in their communal household), their marriage in 1912 helped her realize her public voice as the figure he portrays: a poet of reality and a political thinker in a democracy descended from Periclean Athens.

In conversation with Bloomsbury, Woolf/Aspasia developed a sense of Europe's Enlightenment ideal that underwrites her critique of its historical failures and her vision of its possible future. As chapter 2 argues, *The Voyage Out* launches Rachel on a quest for an enlightened civilization and frames her death as a symbolic sacrifice at the threshold of a modernist vision. After its publication, eighteen months into the war, Woolf noted of Bertrand Russell's lectures on pacifism, "Bertie . . . thinks he's going to found new civilisations," adding, "I become steadily more feminist, owing to the Times, . . . and wonder how this preposterous masculine fiction keeps going a day longer . . . I feel as if I were reading about some curious tribe in Central Africa" (*L* 2:76, 23 January 1916). In 1920, in an effort to "'rais[e] the moral currency of civilised nations,'" she publicly attacked the everyday misogyny at play in a dispute on the Plumage Bill and in her Bloomsbury friend Desmond MacCarthy's favorable review of Arnold Bennett's *Our Women* (*CS* 121, 6 August 1920). Hinting that men's confidence in their innate superiority might seem reckless without "more evidence than the great war and the great peace supply," she likens modern Englishwomen's new intellectual, social, and political freedoms to those of Aeolian women such as Sappho and predicts that when women enjoy education, "liberty of experience," and freedom to "differ from men" fearlessly and openly (as she does in Bloomsbury and, owning a press, in public), their cultural contributions will equal men's. Until then, she concludes, "we shall remain in a condition of half-civilised barbarism," of male "dominion" and female "servility"—the slave's "degradation" equalled by the master's (*CS* 123, 126–127).

Two stories of the 1920s depict women students entering and changing the public sphere. In "A Society" (1921), women students survey what men have done to civilize the world that women have "populated" and experiment with sperm banks, artificial insemination, and other reproductive techniques until the 1914 war and the botched Peace derail their work, after which one of their daughters weeps to find herself nominated "President of the Society of the future" (*CSF* 125, 136). In "The Introduction" (1925), Lily Everit inwardly gazes on parliaments, churches, telegraph wires, and Shakespeare and, in a grammatical tour de force, wrests speech and agency from a civilization that would reduce her to feminine passivity: "she felt like a naked wretch who having sought shelter in some shady garden is turned out and made to understand . . . that there are no sanctuaries, or butterflies, and this civilisation . . . depends on me" (*MDP* 43). Parlaying her fortuitous education in the old Cambridge school into a springboard to the public sphere, Woolf enters modern Europe's Enlightenment project skeptical of "this 'civilization' in which we find ourselves," prospecting for new lands, new civilizations.

Becoming "One"

> Oh, she is out of it—completely. They—the women, I mean—are out of it—should be out of it. We must help them to stay in that beautiful world of their own, lest ours gets worse.
>
> —Charlie Marlow, in Joseph Conrad's *Heart of Darkness*, 1899

> Woman finds herself forced into the background by the claims of civilization and she adopts a hostile attitude towards it.
>
> —Sigmund Freud, *Civilization and Its Discontents*, 1930

> One is not born but becomes a woman. No biological, psychological, or economic fate determines the figure that the human female presents in society: it is civilization as a whole that produces this creature.
>
> —Simone de Beauvoir, *The Second Sex*, 1949

At once a hereditary insider in English letters and a woman "forced" outside, Woolf casts off from Bloomsbury's Aeolian island toward a future unimagined by Conrad and Freud. In 1932 she appropriates Russell's vision of founding new civilizations for women's emancipation, hailing women embarking on the professions and public life as "explorers" in quest of "new lands, . . . new civilizations" (*P* 6). Before we track her own adventures in this long quest, let us first consider two moments in *A Room of One's Own* that show how Woolf's project emerges from and contributes to Bloomsbury's fight for "civilization."

A Room of One's Own reformulates Marlow's proposition in the following terms: "if one is a woman one is often surprised by a sudden splitting off of consciousness, say in walking down Whitehall, when from being the natural inheritor of that civilization she becomes, on the contrary, outside of it, alien and critical" (*RO* 97). That sentence cost its author some pains, particularly in respect to the pronouns. In *Women & Fiction* (the manuscript version) she feels her way: "not only did the whole of civilisation say These things are important & these trivial {often} against her own ([barely?]) [conception]; but [also] She had no Tradition {behind} {("For we think back through our mothers if we are women;) . . . there was no common sentence ready for her use}" (*WF* 109). Woolf's *she* and *we* extend her own case to the woman novelist as such. Her next try advances further from *I* to *one*:

[I] {one} can think [back] through [my] ones mothers, as through [my] {ones} fathers; [I can think] one can think of [civilisation] creating as the [inheritors of] {as a part} civilisation; or as an alien. . . . when I walked down Whitehall, {there had been} a distinct break in my consciousness; [had] From being the natural inheritor of civilisation, its statues, its government buildings, its triumphal arches, I had suddenly become an alien, a critic: & {as if I had thought back through a different universe to a woman in a tree; who had denied that this civilisation was any of her doing} (WF 142–43)

The move from I/she/we to the universal pronoun *one* extends the woman novelist's claim, even as this passage displays rhetorical symptoms of the dilemma of becoming *one* "if one is a woman" (especially, as it were, "a woman in a tree"). There is no common pronoun ready for her use. In a limited sense, *one* posits common ground: it asks or presumes assent that whatever is predicated applies to any "one," although to appeal to such assent is not to produce it. To be outside "civilisation" is to be, in effect, outside *one*—to be an anomaly, incapable of representing and of being represented. To renounce *one*—to speak as *I*, *she* (the feminine third person representative), or *we*, if "we" are women—risks acquiescing in this alienation and perhaps even abnegating any claim upon or responsibility for the public world.

Yet to submerge *I* in *one* risks assenting to common values that are none of "her doing" and so muting the critical force of her speech—unless, as in the next draft, the speaker at once flags her sex and undertakes to debate those values:

Then, [when one is in the attitude of a writer if one is writing, the a woman (*if one is a woman*,) so I have as I] if one is writing one thinks back [unconsciously?] through one's mothers; & if one is a woman, one [cannot] ([when] in writing)[we] is often surprised, say in walking down Whitehall, to find oneself splitting off from civilisation, & from being the [unconsci] natural inheritor of all [these] {the} [streets triumphs of] electric light & locomotion to becoming on the contrary outside government buildings & triumphal arches, [their] an alien, a critic. (WF 146, my emphasis)

The phrase *if one is a woman* has it both ways: it lays claim to "civilisation" on behalf of a woman who feels herself now its "[unconsci] natural inheritor" (alongside the unmarked sex that, to echo Irigaray, *is* "one"), now thrust outside, "an alien, a critic."[85]

In dismantling the opposition between woman and civilization that Marlow and Freud seek to naturalize, this *one* escapes Houdini-like the female-complaint genre; for ultimately not "woman" but "reality" grounds "one's" questioning of so-called common values:

> (One must be something then one is not) & many forces conspire to hold ones head in it—civilisation in many ways requires it—one must be civil— one must be tolerant & so on—So on the contrary those who . . . live at enmity with unreality, whether they fight it with the pen or the paint brush, or . . . the piano, or by sitting up till three o'clock talking about— anything under the sun, . . . [those are the people who get most from] . . . life . . . & give meaning to other peoples lives. (WF 171, cf. RO 110)

Here *one* is any subject, irrespective of sex, of a civilization that "hold[s] ones head" in convention. In the "fight" against that "unreality," the battle to transform the *sensus communis*, artists and thinkers are allies, civilization's subjects its beneficiaries.

Room's "one," then, subsumes feminism within the Enlightenment struggle for the rights and freedoms of *all* and, by the same token, makes women's emancipation representative of the move from personal oppression to political claims that any oppressed group must make.[86] As far from Marlow's "beautiful world" as from Freud's impotent outcast, this *one* claims for women public voice—the voice of the people, the demos, the human—and the right to participate in negotiating common values and shaping the common world. This "one" is not prescriptive; it posits but cannot effect a universal predicate. It is a gambit, an offering, an effort to think beyond personal interest to common ground, always subject to contesting claims. Against the mindless herd Fry thought civilization's doom, against totalitarian longings for "a new god," it bespeaks the commitment to think for "oneself" in common with others (*LK* 42–43, 115). Just as *Women & Fiction* evolves into *A Room of One's* (not *Her*) *Own*, *Three Guineas*' epistolary persona proposes, in the cause of "disinterested culture and intellectual liberty," to burn the "vicious," "corrupt" word "feminist"—often deployed to contain and pillory the women's movement as a special interest, when in fact that movement has historically advocated "the rights of all" and as such is "the advance guard" of 1930s England's antifascist, antiwar movements.[87] As *Room* urges a woman to write in "freedom" instead of "resenting the treatment of her sex and pleading for its rights," *Three Guineas*' heuristic bonfire illumines "men and women working together for the same cause": to fight for Europe's democratic principles and institutions against totalitarian threats within and without; and to advance Europe beyond "half-civilized barbarism" toward universal economic, cultural, and social rights, democratic institutions, and peace (*GR* 80, *TG* 155).

"But, you may say"

> But, you may say, we asked you to speak about women and fiction. What has that got to do with a room of one's own?
>
> —Opening sentence, Woolf, *A Room of One's Own*

Room's first word—"But"—belongs to its audience. This gesture at once preserves the book's occasion—live "talks to girls," the students of the Cambridge women's colleges Newnham and Girton who invited the lectures from which it grew—and hails every reader to debate common values in the public arena. In doing so, it affirms, with Jacques Rancière, that politics *is* disagreement and opens what Slavoj Žižek terms "the properly traumatic dimension of the political."[88] It enacts in small what Žižek evokes as democracy's founding moment when "Something emerged in ancient Greece under the name of the demos demanding its rights." Historically ("from Plato's *Republic*" to "liberal political philosophy"), the "established powers" play deaf, so that the "political struggle proper" is not "a rational debate between multiple interests" but a struggle "to be heard and recognized as . . . a legitimate partner" (989). *Room*'s "But" marks women's entry into public speech as neither Conrad's idealized and idealizing Intended nor Freud's hostile malcontent but as the people, the demos, fighting for precisely an idea of a *whole* society.[89] Like *The Voyage Out*'s parlormaid scene, this dialogic "But" ruptures the textual boundary, presses passive reading toward public voice, and makes *Room* not merely "about" but actively part of the struggle for civilization.

Having symbolically opened the floor to her readers even before she begins, Woolf piles on de-authorizing tactics, first, by averring that "lies will flow from my lips" and readers must judge for themselves whether they contain "some truth"; second, by donning the symbolic "veil" imposed on Western women in public from Pericles and St. Paul to Charlotte Brontë/"Currer Bell," Mary Ann Evans/"George Eliot," and Aurore Dupin/"George Sand": "Here then was I (call me Mary Beton, Mary Seton, Mary Carmichael, or by any name you please—it is not a matter of any importance)."[90] But why should this now famous public author veil herself in the Marys of the old Scots ballad "Mary Hamilton"?[91] If it's of no importance, why can't we just call her Virginia Woolf? As a sign of women's anonymity in public life, Woolf's "veil" at once mimics and transvalues the female burden of "chastity"—"a fetish invented by certain societies for unknown reasons" that has "even now, a religious importance" in women's lives, so that to "bring it to the light of day demands courage of the rarest"—that effectively polices the borders of a masculinized public sphere (*RO* 49–50). Like Judith Shakespeare's suicide, the women novelists' masculine pseudonyms attest to

> the convention which, if not implanted by the other sex was liberally encouraged by them (the chief glory of a woman is not to be talked of, said Pericles, himself a much-talked-of man), that publicity in women is detestable. Anonymity runs in their blood. The desire to be veiled still possesses them. They are not even now as concerned about the health of their fame as men are, and, speaking generally, will pass a tombstone or a signpost without feeling an irresistible desire to cut their names on it, as Alf, Bert or Chas. must do in obedience to their instinct, which murmurs if it sees a fine woman go by, or even a dog, Ce chien est à moi. (*RO* 50)

Parodying the "fetish" of chastity that has excluded women from participation in public life since Periclean Athens and early Christian Rome, Woolf deconstructs the veil and transvalues its [dis]advantage, making it the sign of an anonymity associated with Shakespeare, the balladmaker "Anon" (often perhaps a woman), and artistic freedom as such.[92] In modeling her authority on a Shakespeare so little concerned with his name that posterity never ceases trying to ascribe his plays to someone else, Mary/Woolf sacrifices none of her artistic ambition to the enforced modesty that renders the term *public woman* oxymoronic and obscene.[93] At the same time, rather than reify Woolf or anyone as "women's" representative, this strategically fictional and plural persona submits representativeness as such to the real differences she calls actual readers to debate. Embodying rather than silencing differences, whether of sex, gender, education, culture, politics, or economic status, *Room*'s open persona ("any name you please") poses the question of that "creature" woman who, Beauvoir writes, is not born but made by "civilization as a whole."[94]

Not a few readers take *Room* at its first word. Its rhetorical interlocutor becomes flesh, for example, in Alice Walker, who augments *Room*'s outline of Englishwomen's literary history with African-American women artists from Phillis Wheatley to creators of quilts and gardens; and in Jane Marcus, who sees in these sentences that continue the passage above a betrayal of Woolf's great-grandfather James Stephen's abolitionist legacy: "And, of course, it may not be a dog, remembering Parliament Square, the Sièges Allée and other avenues; it may be a piece of land or a man with curly black hair. It is one of the great advantages of being a woman that one can pass even a very fine negress without wishing to make an Englishwoman of her" (*RO* 50). Whereas Stephen battled racialized slavery in the British West Indies and, when he passed a "very fine negress, was moved to set her free," Marcus writes, Woolf "turn[s]her back on" her to "walk[] toward her own freedom."[95] In *Room*'s speaker's claim that women ("speaking generally") do not wish to enslave other women—to "mark" them as "one"'s own—Marcus finds a culpable *dis*owning of a woman presumed subject to racialized slavery. She judges that Woolf does not "claim equality or recognize a common humanity with her negress" but, rather, coopts her great-grandfather's arguments for "feminist claims for freedom and citizenship without relating racial subjectivity to gender" (7). Woolf "does not extend her concept of gender to include a black woman or to imagine her as a fellow exile," Marcus writes. "Like other feminist rhetoricians of genius, she steals the tropes of slavery to mark the oppression of women, a category that does not include blacks."[96]

Joining this debate, "one" would surely agree with Marcus's critique of Woolf's patronizing irony. Even if Mary/Woolf pictures the negress as free, how convenient for a white Englishwoman, however unfree herself, to idealize her existence as outside imperialism, untouched by colonialism. *L'Impérialisme, ce n'est pas à moi, Room*'s speaker says of herself and other women, essentializing the barbarous imperialist "instinct" as male; forgetting, too, her own notorious banknote-breeding purse, bequeathed by a colonial aunt in "Bombay," which plainly implicates her cherished freedom in racialized imperialist exploitation (*RO* 37). This moment seems all the more puzzling when we remember that Woolf had helped Leonard research *Empire and Commerce in Africa*.[97] Indeed, it was very likely she who—taking notes on books in French—found and copied out the thought from Pascal that Leonard chose for the epigraph of his book's first part, and that Woolf's passage above echoes: "*Ce chien est à moi, disoient ces pauvres enfants; c'est là ma place au soleil: voilà le commencement et l'image de l'usurpation de toute la terre.*"[98] Does this provenance—from Pascal to [Virginia] to Leonard to *Room*—suggest that *Room*'s speaker affiliates herself with anti-imperialism in a way that, however clumsy, patronizing, and self-serving, is perhaps as consistent with Stephen's castigation of racialized slavery as is Marcus's position? If *Room*'s speaker imagines the non-European woman ethnographically, as an autonomous subject of another civilization on whom she has no imperialist designs, Marcus imagines her ethnocentrically, as a postcolonial subject whose emancipation depends on the Eurocentric concept of rights Marcus accuses Woolf of restricting to white Englishwomen.

In this light, the passage and the objections it calls out point to the fraught question of the geopolitical scope, limits, and borderlands of Europe's Enlightenment project in the early twentieth century and beyond. It is historically much too late, Marcus suggests, for an Englishwoman liberated from labor by the spoils of racialized imperialism to pretend that her freedom has nothing to do with women of other races; too late to imagine an African woman as free or, like herself, subject only to men of her own race and class. Yet even as Mary/Woolf displays egregious blindness to her own complicity with imperial domination, *Room*'s "But" invites objection and dialogue. It hails this and any woman (or man) to join in public debate of the *sensus communis*; it sets the stage for her claim to be heard, recognizes her right to protest with Marcus, demand her rights alongside Mary/Woolf, toss *race* and *negress* on the bonfire along with *feminist*, or otherwise speak for herself.[99] As *Room*'s first word opens the door to a public arena and calls women-as-civilization's-creatures to speak on equal terms, unveiled and unmarked (a room of *one's* own), in the struggle to forge common values and common cause, the last word too belongs to its audience.

Were we ever to see such a bonfire as *Three Guineas* proposes, *Room*'s "But" might cease to reverberate. As it is, Walker and Marcus join Kant, Pascal, James Stephen, Josephine Butler, Leslie Stephen, Conrad, Freud, Keynes, Woolf, *Room*'s now global public, and countless others in struggling toward an ideal of civilization born in the time of Solon and Pericles (that much talked of man), for the sake of a sociability *Room*'s "But" keeps perpetually in play.[100] *Room* opens with a call that sounds through Woolf's oeuvre: to become "one," to enter history, to think in public and with others about the barbarity and no less the potential of "this 'civilization' in which we find ourselves," to imagine what it might mean to make it "one's" own.

I think a great deal of my future, and settle what book I am to write—
how I shall re-form the novel and capture multitudes of things at
present fugitive. . . .
—Virginia Stephen to Clive Bell, *Letters*, 19 August 1908

To explain what brought the English across the sea it would be
necessary to write much about modern life which has not yet been
written. . . . [T]he cause was neither love of conquest, love of rule or
love of money. . . . The English were dissatisfied with their own
civilisation.
—Woolf, *Melymbrosia*

That's what will strike our children as the least civilised thing about
us—that there was a time when women didn't like women.
—Rachel to Terence, Woolf, Later Typescript, *The Voyage Out*

TWO

Rachel's Great War

Civilization, Sacrifice, and the Enlightenment of Women in *Melymbrosia* and *The Voyage Out*

efore anyone dreamt of World War I, Virginia Woolf sailed her first heroine, Rachel Vinrace, through a gap in empire to fight a "Great War."[1] That gap is opened by Joseph Conrad's 1899 *Heart of Darkness* as Marlow voyages back from King Leopold's Congo to tell a lie that tastes of death to Kurtz's Intended. *The Voyage Out* (1915) also explores an uncharted darkness within a civilization that Rachel—like Marlow and unlike Kurtz's Intended—discovers as if for the first time. As she propels her heroine from a cloistered late-Victorian girlhood with her Richmond aunts to a fictional English colony in South America, Woolf makes Rachel's voyage out into the "great world" a first foray in her own "re-form"—at once ethical and aesthetic—of the English novel (*VO* 32).

Conrad, Woolf, and the Gender of Truth

It's queer how out of touch with truth women are!
—Charlie Marlow, in Joseph Conrad, *Heart of Darkness*

"It's the burden of lies" she thought. . . . "We carry the burden of lies."
—Rachel Vinrace, in Woolf, *Melymbrosia*

The Voyage Out originates in dialogue with Conrad's inaugural modernist voyage toward European imperialism's hidden "truth."[2] In Marlow's eyes, that "truth" is "a flabby, pretending, weak-eyed devil of a rapacious and pitiless folly," "redeem[ed]" only by "an idea; and an unselfish belief in the idea—something you can set up, and bow down before, and offer a sacrifice to."[3] Conrad's staging of the gender of this truth in his novella's last scene provides Woolf's point of departure. For Marlow truth is masculine. In Kurtz he witnesses the ghastly incarnation of Europe's murderous rapacity in Africa under cover of its ideals; he hears the deathbed whisper that sums up and judges Kurtz's life: "The horror! the horror!" (68). But Marlow finds this truth "too dark altogether" to tell Kurtz's Intended in Brussels when he visits her after Kurtz's death (76). He substitutes a lie, "your name"—even though, he tells his comrades on the *Nellie*,

> You know I hate, detest, and can't bear a lie, not because I am straighter than the rest of us, but simply because it appals me. There is a taint of death, a flavour of mortality, in lies—which is exactly what I hate and detest in the world—what I want to forget. It makes me miserable and sick, like biting something rotten would do. (68, 75, 29)

It is presumably Marlow's aversion to lies that compels him to relate Kurtz's savage maxim—"Exterminate all the brutes!"—instead of burying it "in the dustbin of progress" with "figuratively speaking, all the dead cats of civilisation" (51). Only gender, it seems, can induce him to lie. Kurtz's Intended "is out of it—completely," he says, and women "should be out of it. We must help them to stay in that beautiful world of their own, lest ours get worse" (49). Both this philosophy and Marlow's interview with the Intended echo the allegorical scene in Kurtz's oil sketch of "a woman draped and blindfolded carrying a lighted torch," the background "sombre—almost black," her movement "stately," the torchlight on her face "sinister," which Marlow studies at the Central Station (27–28). No mere coda to Marlow's tale but its climax, the interview with the unnamed Intended bathes the civilization that Kurtz, with his "gorgeous eloquence" and horrific acts, so splendidly epitomizes in the "sinister" light of an erotic sublime. She embodies at once the Enlightenment ideal that Kurtz "intended"—by contrast with the unspeakable violence that this white man playing god in the jungle actually commits and at last, for a moment, sees himself commit—and Marlow's lie, "your name." In his eyes "a soul as translucently pure as a cliff of crystal," the Intended is at the same time Marlow's unwitting yet unconsciously purposeful collaborator, his lie made flesh (70).

In an astonishing sentence abandoned in the manuscript, Marlow figures the idea that women are and should be "out of it—completely" as a "monster-truth" hungry for lies: "That's a monster-truth with many maws to whom we've got to throw every year—or every day—no matter—no sacrifice is too great—a ransom of pretty, shining lies—not very new perhaps—but spotless, aureoled, tender" (49n). This suppressed image reanimates the six-headed Skylla into whose voracious maws the goddess Kirkê instructs Odysseus to throw six of his sailors as he passes: "Better to mourn six men than lose them all, and the ship too."⁴ The allusion casts Marlow as the heroic voyager forced to propitiate this permanent monster with "pretty" lies—not once, as a foul-tasting exception to his rule of truth, but *every year*, or even *every day*. If Marlow's idea of women's "beautiful world" justifies his supposedly exceptional lie, the canceled sentence represents it as entirely unexceptional. The lie that tastes of "mortality" and leaves Marlow stirred by "anger," chilled by "infinite pity," shaking with fear that the heavens will fall is an offering to a social system that feeds on lies and lets no ship pass without a sacrifice (75).

In her otherwise excellent discussion of Marlow's lie, Juliet MacLaughlan argues that "Without Marlow's lie, all 'light of visionary purpose,' any 'slender ray of light' would be extinguished and, with these, the whole concept of humanity's upward potential."⁵ In light of Conrad's Skylla metaphor, the incoherent, near-hysterical language in which Marlow recounts his lie, and *The Voyage Out*, it would be truer to say that each novel in its different way endeavors to expose the fiction that "humanity's upward potential" demands men's lies to and idealization of women; and that this insight is crucial to its modernity. Marlow's ultimate revelation—legible in the bodily symptoms of rage, pity, and fear that become a hero throwing fellow voyagers into Skylla's maws as he sails by—is not that "the truth" is "too dark altogether" for a man of his otherwise truth-loving sensibility to reveal to women. It is that men and women collaborate in history's lies and delusions, which persist under the sign of Eros more durably than any truth. The Intended appears from her portrait "ready to listen without mental reservation, without suspicion, without a thought for herself"; and Marlow registers her "mature capacity for fidelity, for belief, for suffering" (71, 73). Nonetheless, he chooses not to trust this "soul . . . neither rudimentary nor tainted with self-seeking" with the truth; he bows—stoops to a lie—"before the faith that was in her" (74). For her part, she is no victim of his chivalry but elicits and embraces the lie that stokes her illusion with her leading questions and passionate desire: "I want—I want—something—something—to—to live with," she implores him, and confirms the lie: " 'I knew it—I was sure!' . . . She knew. She was sure."⁶

Neither Kurtz's Other nor "outside" civilization, the Intended is his double and mirror. Entombed in domestic seclusion, she lives the "truth" she is not permitted to know. For a woman of her qualities, to know the truth would be not just to "survive[]," as she tells Marlow she has done, but actually to begin to live in the world (73). Alongside the vortex of savagery that sucks Kurtz in despite his ideals and aspirations, redoubled in the compound stare of Kurtz's and Marlow's reflections in the "glassy panel" of the Intended's "mahogany door," the tale unveils a further horror in her impassioned blindness, itself redoubled in the twinned gestures of mourning by the desolate African woman on the river and this white woman in the "sepulchral city" of Brussels (72). Kurtz is dead yet alive, on the street and in the room where Marlow "s[ees] him clearly enough," hears his last words echo "in a persistent whisper all around us," and—more prosaic but no less important—learns that "Kurtz had been disapproved by her people. He wasn't rich enough or something" (75, 74). As he stands in Kurtz's place, Marlow's interview with the Intended evokes the enigmatic force of Eros behind a river of desire and lies that flows "into the heart of an immense darkness" and enacts the "monster-truth" of gender as their civilization's founding lie (75–76).

A reader of *The Voyage Out* can only wonder how Conrad's suppressed figure of Skylla might have fired the imagination of one of his deepest admirers, Virginia Woolf. In any case, Marlow's enmeshment in the economy of lies that binds gender into the heart of civilization was not lost on her. "We carry the burden of lies," reflects Rachel Vinrace as she sails out in Marlow's wake, leaving the not so beautiful world that immures her because of her sex (*M* 14). When she exclaims, "Nothing! I was taught nothing, nothing but lies," Rachel speaks as a woman who would batter down the walls that imprison her; when she expostulates "Lies! Lies! Lies!" after listening to an unconsciously manipulative servant, she extends the monster-system's everyday hunger for lies to class (*M* 183, *VO* 29). What happens when Rachel too must sail by Skylla? Can a woman uneducated in all but music hope to elude the "monster-truth" that even Marlow propitiates?

When Rachel's aunt Helen Ambrose remarks that she "would rather my daughter told lies than believed in God; only they come to the same thing," she flashes promising credentials as a mentor for the motherless Rachel (*M* 12). But Helen, for all her iconoclasm, is a far less radical thinker than Rachel herself on the subject of women and civilization. In a conversation cut from the late typescript, Rachel complains, "She doesn't care enough about women," and Terence banters, "She values the superior integrity of men."[7] It is Rachel who, talking with Terence, envisions a future when women's complicity with masculine domination "will strike our children as the least civilised thing about us," and who vows to teach her daughter that the "virtue she sees in women" is the "virtue she has in herself—a very profound truth." Rachel adds,

> "I always suspect a woman who doesn't like women. . . . Helen herself would be much better"—

"You can't expect a woman who's as beautiful as she is and as attrac-
tive to the other sex"—

"I manage—"

"Yes, but you're comparatively ugly."

"But, Terence, men and women—"

" . . . [D]on't let's talk theories, Rachel, let's talk about the things that
really matter."

"You're disgustingly lazy."

"No. . . . I'm sensible. Don't you see, Rachel . . . directly you begin
talking about men and women you're talking about things that don't
exist. I exist; you exist; and Evelyn and St. John—but that's all. Yet people will go on arguing and arguing as though there were hard and fast
laws, and they get so angry, and make themselves so unpleasant, and all
the time they're arguing about what doesn't exist, and the really important things are escaping them. . . . Besides, if there are laws, let's leave it
to the old fogeys to find them. . . . " (*VO* Heine 445–46)

Uneducated and naïve as she is, Rachel alone seeks to discover and grapple with the "laws"—natural and social—that shape the lives and destinies of men and women, and to battle against rather than propitiate civilization's many-mawed hunger for lies.

But Rachel has neither adequate weapons nor any very clear cause. She
struggles to put her predicament into words, "conscious of what with her
love of vague phrases, she called, 'The Great War.' It was a war waged on
behalf of things like stones, jars, wreckage at the bottom of the sea, trees
stars and music, against the people who believe in what they see. It was
not easy to explain, supposing Rachel knew what she meant" (*M* 21).
What she means is illustrated by a remembered talk with her aunts, when
she tried in vain "to find out what they thought. She had wanted to say
that there must be some kind of structure in the backg[r]ound which kept
them all living together, . . . though—she meant to wind up—'we seem to
be dropped about like tables or umbrellas' " (*M* 23). Thwarted in her
quest for an underlying "structure" by the unthinking acquiescence of
everyone around her, Rachel takes refuge in "symbols. Let all people be
images; worship spirits; wage the great war. . . . Music was real; books . . .
all things that one saw . . . all that one thought. . . . The war was waged
chiefly at meals, when one had to keep on knowing that the things that
were said were all misfits for ideas" (*M* 23).

This makeshift philosophy sets Rachel at a tangent to the talk swirling
around her in this protomodernist novel of manners: "Reality dwelling in
what one saw and felt, but did not talk about, one could accept a system
in which things went round and round quite satisfactorily to other people"

(*VO* 37). Encumbered though *The Voyage Out* is with the "appalling narrative business of the realist: getting on from lunch to dinner" that Woolf later repudiates as "false, unreal, merely conventional," producing "[w]aste, deadness," the novel's resistance to its own literalism foreshadows her modernist art (*D* 3:209, 28 November 1928). For example, when Mr. Pepper urges Rachel's father, Willoughby Vinrace—"a sentimental man who imported goats for the sake of the empire"—to fund a ship to study "the great white monsters of the lower waters," Willoughby replies, "the monsters of the earth are too many for me!" Rachel sighs, "Poor little goats!" and her father chides, "If it weren't for the goats there'd be no music, my dear: music depends upon goats."[8] Even as the narrative frames the *Euphrosyne*'s voyage and Rachel's music within the economy of empire, it overleaps conventional realism with Mr. Pepper's surreal evocation of "white, hairless, blind monsters lying curled on the ridges of sand at the bottom of the sea, which would explode if you brought them to the surface, their sides bursting asunder and scattering entrails to the winds" (*VO* 23). Rachel's war "on behalf of" sea wrecks against "people who believe in what they see" draws such moments of narrative extravagance into an allegorical force field where these marine monsters suffer a sea change and eventually resurface in her fevered thoughts as she lies ill: "While all her tormentors thought that she was dead, she was not dead, but curled up at the bottom of the sea. There she lay, sometimes seeing darkness, sometimes light, while every now and then some one turned her over at the bottom of the sea" (*VO* 341). Incarnating Mr. Pepper's monsters, Rachel becomes in her delirium a living allegory of realities drowned by the exigencies of empire, of submerged truths that will explode if brought too quickly to the surface.

As Rachel's fantasies of death-in-life compete with the plot of her death, we glimpse behind the novel's Edwardian facade its deeper affinity with modernism's great revolution of the social imagination, its contestation of reality. While Rachel, even as she dabbles in "misfits" herself, dreams "of saying what one thought, and getting it answered," the narrator ominously observes,

> Although these were symptoms of a war to come far subtler than any she had yet engaged in, she did not rise and go to meet it consciously. Uneducated, in the sense that no one had ever required her to know anything accurately, she was ill-fitted to keep her eye upon facts; correspondingly tempted to think of the bottom of the sea. "Why should I go bothering about my feelings, or other people's feelings," her meditations ran, " . . . I live; I die; the sea comes over me. . . . " [F]ortified

by the presence of the spirits, she floated; her soul was like thistle-down kissing the sea, and rising again, and so passing out of sight. (*M* 23, 24).

Woolf, who judged Conrad "a much better writer than all of us put together," also proposed that "there are no women in his books"; his "beautiful ships" are "more feminine than his women, who are either mountains of marble or the dreams of a charming boy over the photograph of an actress" (*L* 3:62, 3 August 1923; *CDB* 81). Named first the *Sarah Jane*, then the *Euphrosyne* (Joy, one of the three graces), Willoughby's imperial merchant ship too is a very vessel of femininity, if different in character from Marlow's *Nellie*: "a bride going forth to her husband, a virgin unknown of men; in her vigour and purity . . . likened to all beautiful things, worshipped and felt as a symbol" yet taken at a distance for "a tramp, a cargo-boat, or one of those wretched passenger steamers where people rolled around among the cattle on deck"; or again "a ship passing in the night—an emblem of the loneliness of human life," a "lonely little island" (*VO* 32, 87). As "she" voyages away from England—that "very small," still "shrinking island in which people were imprisoned"—the *Euphrosyne* takes on "an immense dignity": "she was an inhabitant of the great world, which has so few inhabitants, travelling all day across an empty universe, with veils drawn before her and behind"—the "great world" of reality and possibility, beyond the "prison" of appearances and conventions (*VO* 32).

Carrying its women voyagers, the *Euphrosyne* makes for the fictional South American colony Santa Marina—founded, we are told, not to serve the interests of the British Empire but, on the contrary, because "The English were dissatisfied with their own civilisation" (*M* 70). As Mr. Pepper can tell anyone who likes to know (though "history books" do not), an Elizabethan colony on the site succumbed after a century or so to hostile native populations, rival European imperialists, and disease. After the last boatload of English people departed, there remained no bastion of empire but a "happy compromise" of populations where "Portuguese fathers wed Indian mothers, and their children intermarry with the Spanish"—a backwater of both "civilisation" (which "shifted its center to a spot four or five hundred miles to the south") and modernity ("in arts and industries . . . still much where it was in Elizabethan days") (*VO* 89). This multicultural settlement where "Love and friendship and happiness with all the sorrows they bring, flourished . . . unrecorded" attracted the founders of a tiny new English colony, who wished to escape the Christian civilization of Europe's "older countries," with their

> enormous accumulations of carved stone, stained glass, and rich
> brown painting. . . . The movement in search of something new was . . .
> infinitely small, affecting only a handful of well-to-do people. It began
> by a few schoolmasters serving their passage out to South America as
> the pursers of tramp steamers. . . . [T]heir stories of . . . the marvels of
> the place delighted outsiders. . . . The place seemed new and full of new
> forms of beauty, in proof of which they showed handkerchiefs which
> the women had worn round their heads, and primitive carvings
> coloured bright greens and blues. . . . [A]n old monastery was quickly
> turned into a hotel, while a famous line of steamships altered its route
> for the convenience of passengers. (M 70, VO 90)

The new colony's name might almost be New Bloomsbury: "A single little group then, an infinitely small conspiracy . . . began to seek out what
they felt"—such as delicious sensations of nakedness outlawed in England, where if "One cried for Pan . . . startled women fled shrieking at the
sight of a man without trousers."[9] Rachel's suggestion that Helen embroi-
der "a troupe of naked knights" into her scenic tapestry allies her with
untrousered men against shrieking women, but her own desire is not to
disrobe herself but to strip the social body of the conventions that clothe
and hide it (M 129).

The Enlightenment of Women: The Education of Rachel Vinrace

> St. John did not agree. He said that . . . few things at the present time
> mattered more than the enlightenment of women.
> —Woolf, *The Voyage Out*

When St. John Hirst—at twenty-four a Cambridge mathematician and
"one of the three, or is it five" most distinguished young men in England—endorses "the enlightenment of women" as one of the things that
matter most to the modern world, the question of why, how, and to whom
it should matter, and what form that enlightenment ought to take, situates
Rachel's education within a vast social transformation in the early part of
the century (VO 144, 164). "Laugh at her and enlighten her," Helen
encourages Hirst when he wonders whether he can talk freely to Rachel;
"That's your duty" (M 188). But what does it mean to enlighten a
woman? No one in Rachel's purview quite knows, though everyone
makes efforts. For her part, she struggles to understand, articulate her
own perspective, and make herself heard. *The Voyage Out* counterposes
the question of women's enlightenment to the question of whether women
can or should be educated at all—whether, as Hirst and Hewet sometimes
wonder, women are "stupid" or "have a mind," suffer from "native inca-

pacity" or only lack training, whether they "reason," "feel," "really think," and can be talked to or are an alien subspecies (*VO* 107, *M* 118, 154, 156–57, *VO* 172).

From the outset, Rachel's education is entangled in the contradictions and conflicts surrounding the gender of truth and lies. At twenty-three, Rachel is no tabula rasa. She has been educated

> as the majority of well-to-do girls in the last part of the nineteenth century were educated. . . . [T]here was no subject in the world which she knew accurately. . . . [S]he would believe practically anything she was told, invent reasons for anything she said. The shape of the earth, the history of the world, how trains worked, or money was invested, what laws were in force, which people wanted what, and why they wanted it, the most elementary idea of a system in modern life—none of this had been imparted to her by any of her professors or mistresses. . . . All the energies that might have gone into languages, science, or literature, that might have made her friends, or shown her the world, poured straight into music. (*VO* 33–34)

Although she has failed to teach herself German—"which [her father] said, is the foundation of all knowledge"—Rachel excels as a pianist (*M* 19). Both her advanced sensibility and her fine musicianship emerge as she communes with the "spirit" of Beethoven's strikingly modern, ferociously difficult Opus 111 and, practicing, climbs "Up and up the steep spiral" of this "very late Beethoven sonata . . . like a person ascending a ruined staircase" (*VO* 37, 291). Music permits Rachel to be simultaneously highly accomplished and unworldly, even otherworldly; to dwell amid invisible "Spirits," the dead, "the things that aren't there . . . drowned statues, undiscovered places, the birth of the world, the final darkness, and death" (*M* 21).

The voyage brings Rachel abundant mentors. Finding Rachel thus adrift in her businessman father's wake, her aunt Helen intervenes in hope of teaching her "how to be a reasonable person" (*VO* 83). At first sight Helen seems an ideal mentor: a wife and mother, yet outside conventions, unsentimental, repelled by falsity and humbug. With G. E. Moore's *Principia Ethica* propped beside her as she embroiders, Helen is a fictional Vanessa, a paragon of Bloomsbury modernity and an antagonist of those proud "citizen[s] of the Empire" the worldly, glamorous Dalloways, who board the *Euphrosyne* in Lisbon by "special arrangement" (*M* 49, *VO* 40). Like Helen, Clarissa too finds Rachel appealing and would like to "rake her out before it's too late."[10] During her short stay she does what she can to counteract the influence of these "very oddest" of people: "literary people—they're far the hardest of any to get on with. The worst of it is," they "might have been . . . just like everybody else, if they hadn't got swallowed up by Oxford or Cambridge or some such place and been made cranks of" (*VO/E* 49). Answering Rachel's declaration "I shall never marry," Clarissa extols marriage and presses Jane Austen's *Persuasion* upon her (*VO* 60).

Meanwhile, the genial former M.P. Richard scoffs at "the equality of the sexes" and confides to the infatuated Rachel both his fervid hope to be in his grave before an Englishwoman has the right to vote and his categorical conviction that "no woman has what I may call the political instinct" (*VO* 43, 69). Rachel perseveres in her quest for enlightenment. "Please tell me—everything," she wants to say, convinced that "if one went back far enough, everything perhaps was intelligible"; that she might discover how "the mammoths . . . in the fields . . . had turned into paving stones and boxes full of ribbon, and her aunts" (*VO* 56, 67). While Rachel longs to trace the evolution of the modern "system" that shapes individual lives all the way back to nature and so unravel the perplexities of social laws and conditions, Richard looks forward to securing England's global empire: "He ran his mind along the line of conservative policy . . . as though it were a lasso that . . . caught . . . enormous chunks of the habitable globe. . . . 'we've pretty nearly done it,' he said; 'it remains to consolidate.' "[11]

Richard's own contribution to Rachel's enlightenment is of another order entirely. The two great "revelations" of his life, he tells her, are

> "The misery of the poor and"—(he hesitated and pitched over) "love"!
> Upon that word he lowered his voice; it was a word that seemed to unveil the skies for Rachel.
> "It's an odd thing to say to a young lady," he continued. "But have you any idea what—what I mean by that? No; of course not. I don't use the word in a conventional sense. I use it as young men use it. Girls are kept very ignorant, aren't they. Perhaps it's wise—perhaps—You *don't* know?"
> He spoke as if he had lost consciousness of what he was saying.
> (*VO* 68)

As Rachel waits breathless for his revelation about love as young men use it, Clarissa calls them to look at British warships lying like "eyeless beasts seeking their prey" on the waters: "Aren't you glad to be English!" (*VO* 69). When they next meet alone, Richard picks up more or less where he left off and suddenly kisses Rachel with a melodramatic "You tempt me" (*VO* 76).

The kiss puts an end to talk. Rachel is assailed that night by terrifying dreams of "gibbering . . . barbarian men" harassing the ship, which she confides to Helen after the Dalloways debark the next day (*VO* 77). Puz-

zled by Rachel's terror, Helen, who finds Richard "pompous," "sentimental," "silly," and "secondrate," explains lightly, "Men will want to
kiss you, just as they'll want to marry you" and advises her to forget it
(*VO* 80–81, 83). But Rachel, with her truth-seeking if uneducated mind
and her fierce curiosity about the "structure" of things, vows, "I shall
think about it all day and night until I find out exactly what it does
mean" and arrives at an epiphany far beyond Helen's comprehension
(*VO* 80):

> "Tell me," she said suddenly, "what are those women in Piccadilly?"
> "In Piccadilly? They are prostitutes," said Helen.
> "It *is* terrifying—it *is* disgusting," Rachel asserted, as if she included
> Helen in her hatred.
> "It is," said Helen. "But—"
> "I did like him," Rachel mused, as if speaking to herself. "I wanted
> to talk to him; I wanted to know what he'd done. The women in Lan-
> cashire—"
> It seemed to her as she recalled their talk that there was something
> lovable about Richard, good in their attempted friendship, and strangely
> piteous in the way they had parted.
> . . . [Helen] said, "you must take things as they are; and if you want
> friendship with men you must run risks. Personally," she continued,
> breaking into a smile, "I think it's worth it; I don't mind being kissed;
> I'm rather jealous, I believe, that Mr. Dalloway kissed you and didn't kiss
> me. Though," she added, "he bored me considerably."
> Rachel did not return the smile or dismiss the whole affair, as Helen
> meant her to. Her mind was working very quickly, inconsistently and
> painfully. Helen's words hewed down great blocks which had stood
> there always, and the light which came in was cold. After sitting for a
> time with fixed eyes, she burst out:
> "So that's why I can't walk alone!"
> By this new light she saw her life for the first time a creeping hedged-
> in thing, driven cautiously between high walls, here turned aside, there
> plunged in darkness, made dull and crippled for ever—her life that was
> the only chance she had—the short season between two silences.
> "Because men are brutes! I hate men!" she exclaimed.
> "I thought you said you liked him?" said Helen.
> "I liked him, and I liked being kissed," she answered, as if that only
> added more difficulties to her problem.
> Helen was surprised to see how genuine both shock and problem
> were. . . . [Helen] wanted . . . to understand why this rather dull, kindly,
> plausible politician had made so deep an impression on her, for surely at
> the age of twenty-four this was not natural. (*VO* 81–82)

By the stark "new light" that floods Rachel's mind in this scene, "a thousand words and actions bec[o]me plain to her" (*VO/E* 87). Her epiphany arrays the kiss, prostitutes, her own constricted, virginal life, and Helen herself—wife, mother, friend (especially of men), and complaisant mentor who would have her "take things as they are"—within a social system that sequesters women behind "great blocks" of ignorance, "high walls" of chastity, domesticity, and poverty, in seclusion from the great world appropriated by men and driven by male desire. If Richard's first impression is that Rachel is "conscious of her virginity" ("he could not suppress a smile"), he himself occasions a colder, brighter enlightenment than he or Helen has any notion of (*M* 29).

Although Rachel refuses to "take things as they are," Helen's insistence that she "be a person on your own account" leaves her "profoundly excited at the thought of living" (*VO* 84). This excitement puts her at odds with the "system" as she begins to grasp the social forces that imprison women, not just physically but economically, intellectually, emotionally, and morally. Rachel, "brought up with excessive care . . . for what it seems almost crude to call her morals," has "never troubled her head about . . . censorship" (*VO* 34–35). In her new awareness, her liking for Richard and her pleasure in the kiss do not contradict her hatred of "men" in the abstract. She has had "[n]o adventures," she tells Terence, unless one counts nightmarish visions of being "chased by men" after seeing "the women . . . under lamps in Piccadilly": "Suppose anyone had forbidden you to walk down Bond Street alone when you were eighteen! because of the women! It made me feel robbed of my life . . . you have only one life—just for a second and all that waste behind you and before you . . . I shall never never never have all the feelings I might have because of you" (*M* 150–51). Terence—nicknamed "Monk" in allusion to his sexual adventures—takes freedom for granted: "Have you ever walked about London at night, or been to a music hall, or talked to old men in the street—I forgot . . . you've never done any of these things, because of me," he says moments later. "I'm very sorry. It seems monstrous when one comes to think of it" (*M* 152, 154, 198).

As Rachel confronts the "monstrous" sex/gender system in the cold new light of her ongoing education, "what it seems almost crude to call" women's "morals" is unmasked as the oppressive code of female chastity that in effect makes the great world a masculine preserve and cripples women with fear. Like Conrad's "monster-truth," this system exacts everyday tribute of lies from men and women. "I would have told a lie, if you'd given me time," Rachel tells Terence, because of her fear "of you— not of you but of the world" and its ridicule; the fact that men "suspect one" and the fact that "women are kissed." "It's a pity that you should tell lies," Terence answers; "Nothing in the world would make it possible for me to tell a lie" (*M* 105–7). Hirst credits Cambridge with teaching him "to speak the truth," and Helen responds, "Practically no woman speaks the truth" without noting that virtually no woman has Hirst's education; Hirst adds, "And very few men" (*M* 155). When Hirst tells Rachel that he thinks it "quite possible" that she has a mind but doubts whether she can "think honestly because of your sex you see," she feels "as if a gate had clanged in her face" (*VO* 156). Terence, after talking with Evelyn Murgatroyd, mutters, "Why is it that they *won't* be honest?" (*VO* 194). As in Conrad, truth is a masculine prerogative, although men may choose to lie, especially when they talk with women.

What is it that makes it not just possible but necessary that women lie, and not impossible but at least unnecessary that men should? Terence comforts Rachel when she expostulates, "It is insolent to say that women can't be honest, to condescend to me because I am a woman. . . . if I had a gun I would shoot him!" (*M* 119). When she complains, "It's no good; we should live separate; we cannot understand each other; we only bring out what's worst," he answers that he is "bored" by "generalisations" about the sexes, which seem to him "generally untrue" (*VO* 156). Yet he later contradicts himself, treating Rachel like a specimen of an exotic race: "'I've often walked along the streets where . . . one house is exactly like another house, and wondered what on earth the women were doing inside,'" he says.

> "Doesn't it make your blood boil? . . . I'm sure if I were a woman I'd blow someone's brains out. But . . . how does it all strike you? . . . "
>
> His determination to know made it seem important that she should answer him with strict accuracy; but . . . Why did he make these demands on her? Why did he sit so near and keep his eye on her? No, she would not consent to be pinned down by any second person in the whole world. She . . . sighed, and waved her hand almost with a gesture of weariness towards the sea. (*VO* 215)

Rachel's wordless wave at the sea—as if being a "woman" were some natural fatality and not a socially induced condition—recalls the illustrations of "young women with their hair down pointing a gun at the stars" on the piano pieces she plays in the hotel (*VO* 165).

Along with other virtual guns pointed by women at Hirst, at "someone," at Terence ("now you look as if you'd blow my brains out"), these images pose the question of how far being a woman is a natural, how far a social, condition (*VO* 298). Once engaged, Rachel tries to put that question aside, considering it "reserved for a later generation" to discuss sex differences "philosophically" (in fact years will pass before Woolf tackles it in *A Room of One's Own*) (*VO* 292). But as Rachel tries to quit the social battlefield for the "reality" of Opus 111, Terence, busy at his novel, pesters her: "it's the fashion now to say that women . . . have . . . no sense of honour; query, what is meant by masculine term, honour? what corresponds to it in your sex?"—as if indeed he has "no conception what it's like—to be a young woman," though she has told him of its "terrors and agonies" and of a certain compensatory "freedom . . . like being the wind or the sea" in the fact that "No one cares" and "people don't listen" (*VO* 291, *VO/E* 247–48). Terence's obtuseness calls Rachel back to the "destiny" of her Great War, for *The Voyage Out* does not permit its heroine a merely personal salvation but subordinates her individuality to the "structure" of things—even as that destiny keeps in play Hirst's proposition that few things matter more at present than the enlightenment of women.[12]

Upstream on the Amazon: To See Things New

> "We have no poet" said Rachel. . . . "The world I know is made of good people, but not one who sees things new."
>
> "We must go to Shakespeare you mean" said Hewet. "And Shakespeare's . . . dead. . . . We must be our own Shakespeares. We must see things new."
>
> —Woolf, *Melymbrosia*

South America's "profusion of leaves and blossoms and prodigious fruits" puts Hewet in mind of Shakespeare: "That's where the Elizabethans got their style" (*VO* 268). Founded to explore and invent a new world, the modern English colony promises an adventure that it does not deliver. "If I were a man," Evelyn Murgatroyd goads one of her many hapless suitors, "I'd raise a troop and conquer some great territory. . . . I'd love to start life from the very beginning—as it ought to be. . . . It's the idea, don't you see? We lead such tame lives" (*VO* 136–37). While Rachel yearns for explorers and visionaries who "see things new," Santa Marina's English—"people with money, . . . given the management of the world"—are, in Terence's eyes, "not satisfactory," "ignoble" and, in Helen's estimation, not so different from the conventional Dalloways: "Think of his attitude to her—to all women. She has daughters to bring up. He rules us. A fine mess they'll make of it! Still . . . they're very nice people" (*VO* 134, *M* 65).

At nineteen, Virginia Stephen, on the premise that the "only thing in this world is music—music and books and one or two pictures," conceived "a colony where there shall be no marrying—unless you happen to fall in love with a symphony of Beethoven—no human element at all except what comes through Art" (L 1:41–42, 23 April 1901). In Santa Marina's monastery-turned-hotel, radical fantasy bows to realism and marrying comes to the fore. Yet in this specular English colony founded to "see things new," the conventional marriage plot is overborne by a daring surrealism, an intricate network of figures that transforms the novel of manners through a Post-Impressionist freedom of formal invention (M 151). Consider this conversation between Evelyn, with her ineffectual spirit of adventure, and Rachel. The love child of a farmer's daughter and "the young man up at the great house," who provided for Evelyn and her mother when his "people" blocked the marriage and was killed in the war, the self-dramatizing Evelyn collects proposals like scalps and longs to join "a revolution," found a colony, "cut down trees," "make laws," make a "splendid" world, stop prostitution, reform "inebriate women," fight and die for a cause, whether freedom, God, or the Russians.[13] When Evelyn suspects that Rachel has "no cause you'd die for," Rachel's oddly unconscious response frames the marriage plot as the "cause" that conscripts unwitting women to "die" for it:

> "If I thought that by dying I could give birth to twenty—no thirty— children, all beautiful and very charming, I'd die for that. . . . Perhaps." Candour forced her to consider the extreme horror of feeling the water give under her, of losing her head, splashing wildly, sinking again with every vein smarting and bursting, an enormous weight sealing her mouth, and pressing salt water down her lungs when she breathed. (M 179)

As if to bridge the gap that Rachel leaps from fantastically fertile maternity as a cause possibly worth dying for to *physical* drowning, the narrator explains that "a recent ship wreck suggested drowning as the form her death would take" (ibid.). But that Rachel imagines this "cause" as a deadly "horror" and not a glorious destiny passes unremarked as Evelyn replies incongruously, "That's just why one must marry" (ibid.).

Although Rachel tells Evelyn that she does not know who she is or what she wants, or even quite believe she exists, she too wants "to explore," to envision life from the beginning as it ought to be, to live with purpose if not to die for a cause (VO 251). Lent the first volume of Gibbon's *Decline and Fall of the Roman Empire* by Hirst, Rachel takes it with her on a walk in "this land where . . . it was possible to lose sight of civilisation in a very short time" and opens it to read of resistance to Roman colonization. The hot climate of "Aethiopia and Arabia Felix" protected "the unwarlike natives of those sequestered regions" from invaders; the northern European countries, peopled by "a hardy race of barbarians, who despised life when it was separated from freedom," "scarcely deserved the expense and labour of conquest" (*VO* 173–75). The words stir her imagination:

> Never had any words been so vivid and so beautiful—Arabia Felix— Aethiopia . . . hardy barbarians, forests, and morasses. They seemed to drive roads back to the very beginning of the world, on either side of which the populations of all times and countries stood in avenues, and by passing down them all knowledge would be hers, and the book of the world turned back to the very first page. Such was her excitement at the possibilities of knowledge now opening before her that she ceased to read. (*VO* 175)

Walking fast, "her body trying to outrun her mind," Rachel (in what only seems a non sequitur) confirms her "suspicion" that she is in love, "much as a person coming from a sickroom dreads to find the signs of infection" (*M* 132, *VO* 175–76). At the very moment when she exults to see for the first time "how the earth lived" and that "she herself was alive," Rachel finds herself "awed by the discovery of a terrible possibility in life" and makes her way back to the villa "much as a soldier prepared for battle," as if she has found a cause worth fighting for: to turn "the book of the world" back to the beginning so as to see things new in the light of "knowledge," "freedom," and (not least) "love" (*M* 132, *VO* 176).

To paraphrase Richard Dalloway, Rachel's cause is "love" as young women use it. But since the love most women live for makes Rachel fear death, as if by drowning or "infection," her cause is to see "love" new. The English colony teems with women who, however dissatisfied with their civilization, hold motherhood to be "the crown . . . of a woman's life" (*VO/E* 127). Such knowledge as the literary historian Miss Allan possesses, though enviable, is "not what women want"; unmarried women lead "the hardest life of all"; even the longsuffering family servant Mrs. Chailey expects to forget her tribulations when Rachel's child is placed in her arms (*VO* 115). Mrs. Thornbury, still bursting with vitality after helping her eleven children climb "infallibly to the tops of their trees," avers that "we can learn a great deal from the young. . . . I learn so much from my own daughters" (*M* 91, *VO* 116). And Susan Warrington rejoices, on becoming engaged to Arthur Venning, at the prospective reassignment of her familial servitude from her aunt Paley to her own children: " 'I am a woman with children too—one of the great company,' the regiment which toils all through middle life in the heat" (*M* 113).

At the dance celebrating Susan's engagement, Rachel makes a spontaneous intervention in the social rituals of mating and marriage that leads the whole company momentarily to see things new.[14] Early in the evening she announces, "This is my idea of Hell"; stung by Hirst's condescension, she longs to "be a Persian princess far from civilisation" and "the strife and men and women"; then Terence sweeps her off, and soon, Arthur reports, she has changed her mind: "she'd no idea dances could be so delightful" (*M* 117, *VO* 155, 163). At two in the morning, when the musicians, deaf to the dancers' appeals, hold up a watch and depart, Rachel is importuned to play, and she swirls the company beyond waltzes and polkas into the free-form expressionism of modern dance. Beginning with "some music that's really happy"—a Gluck melody, Mozart—she commands, "Invent the steps," and they do. Helen whirls Miss Allan about the room in a sequence of minuet steps, curtseys, spins, and darts "like a child skipping in a meadow"; Hirst hops first on one foot, then the other; Terence sways "like an Indian maiden . . . before her Rajah"; Miss Allan executes an elaborate bow to Susan and Arthur; Mr. Pepper adapts an "ingenious" figure-skating step; Mrs. Thornbury dances a one-woman quadrille; the Elliots "gallopad[e]" across the room with alarming "impetuosity" (*M* 125, cf. *VO* 166f). At last Rachel strikes into "The Mulberry Tree" for "the great round dance!" and the dancers join hands and whirl "faster and faster" until the chain breaks, flinging them every which way and leaving "Arthur and Susan sprawling back to back upon the floor" (*M* 125).

The scene recalls Virginia's reflections in a 1903 diary-essay, "A Dance in Queens Gate," on the unique power of dance music to "stir[] some barbaric instinct" so that

> you forget centuries of civilisation in a second, & yield to that strange passion which sends you madly whirling round the room—oblivious of everything save that you must keep swaying with the music—in & out, round & round—in the eddies & swirls of the violins. *It is as though some swift current of water swept you along*. It is magic music. Here the bars run low, passionate, regretful, but always in the same pulse. We dance as though we knew the vanity of dancing. We dance to drown our sorrows—but dance, dance—If you stop you are lost. This one night we will be mad—dance lightly—raise our hearts as the beat strengthens, grows buoyant—careless, defiant. What matters anything so long as ones step is in time—so long as one's whole body & mind are dancing too—what shall end it? (*PA* 165, my emphasis)

As Rachel looses the dancers from ritual patterns of coupledom, she opens the conventional mating dance to innovations of every kind—same-sex partners, individual expression, mime, invention, vagaries of speed and pace—as if the dance were mirroring profuse, prodigious forms of life and social relations, real and potential. This freedom, this forgetting of "centuries of civilisation" inspired by Rachel's musical imagination, culminates in a collective vision. After the round dance has ended, Rachel goes on playing Bach, and the "younger dancers" drift in from the garden to sit on "deserted gilt chairs round the piano"; as the music stills them, they seem to see "a building with spaces and columns . . . rising in the empty space" and then "to see themselves and their lives, and the whole of human life advancing" (VO 167). Seeing things new by the light of the impromptu Post-Impressionist spectacle Rachel's playing conjures, the community, on what Susan declares the "happiest night of my life," celebrates both her future and a revelatory vision of its own (VO 167).

Rachel's own engagement scene during a river voyage up the Amazon departs yet more daringly from the conventional novel of manners. As *Melymbrosia*'s narrator waxes poetic, we know we're not in Kansas anymore: "To find the sources of the river, you must be the first to cut through the thongs of creepers; the first who has ever trodden upon the mosses by the river side, or seen trees which have stood since the beginning of the world" (M 193). What is this river whose sources we ("you") are seeking? "It is as though some swift current of water swept you along," muses young Virginia on the "barbaric instinct" awakened by dance music, while Terence sees in the heroically maternal Mrs. Thornbury "a kind of beauty, . . . like a . . . river going on and on and on" (VO 294). That the novel's Amazon is not the actual river but the rushing current of Eros and generation we understand from its peculiar visibility to young couples during the picnic on the mountaintop: "Susan and Arthur had seen it as they kissed," Terence and Rachel as they "sat talking," Evelyn and Mr. Perrott as they "strolled" (VO 264). The river whose sources Rachel voyages upstream to seek is exotic not because it is a geographical feature of South America but because it allegorizes the tremendous hidden currents, natural and social, that sweep individuals along, not least the torrents of desire and life that society channels through marriage. The expedition, after all, is neither "dangerous nor difficult," indeed "not even unusual"; "Every year" English people steam upriver and return unharmed (VO 264). Yet this same river voyage carries Rachel to a specular, mythic locale, the "beginning of the world": at once a "garden of Eden" watered by natural and cultural "sources" and the "country of the future" where she and Terence would see their lives new (M 208).

If Susan's joyous engagement dance loosens the "tight plait" of Jane Austen's marriage plot, Rachel's engagement scene has a darker forebear in George Eliot's *The Mill on the Floss*.[15] When Terence remarks of Hirst's sister, "No one takes her seriously, poor dear. She feeds the rabbits," Rachel, instead of joining the world in not taking Miss Hirst seriously, identifies with her: "I've fed rabbits for twenty-four years; it seems odd now" (*VO* 213). In *The Mill on the Floss* Maggie Tulliver neglects to feed her brother, Tom's, rabbits while he's away at school, with fatal consequences, not only for the rabbits. Deborah Gorham notes that this feminine rabbit-feeding in support of brothers' education had an earlier, wider currency in popular children's literature. As Maria E. Budden's *Always Happy!! Anecdotes of Felix and his Sister Serena. A tale. Written for her Children, by a Mother* puts it, "In feeding his rabbits, and arranging his garden, [Serena] felt she was preparing a pleasure for her dear brother."[16]

Helen's "presentiments of disaster," her fear that desire has but "a moment's respite" before "again the profound and reasonless law asserted itself, moulding them all to its liking," again aligns Rachel with Maggie Tulliver (*VO* 285, 263). Called to look at jewelry in the jungle village, Helen sees instead "a boat upset on the river in England, at midday," as if the Amazon were the Floss in flood and their steamer the boat that Maggie, in a feat of will and strength, steers over the raging river to the mill to rescue Tom before they are capsized by wreckage on the rushing stream (*VO* 285). Through Mrs. Thornbury's likeness to "a river going on and on and on," Woolf shifts the symbolic course of the English river that destroys Maggie Tulliver—rather arbitrarily, Eliot's readers often feel—to figure not the wrath of the "World's Wife" (the quasi-sexual scandal over Stephen Guest that drives Maggie out of the community) but the "drowned" lives of the World's Mother—the female destiny of marriage and maternity that Rachel wishes not to "die" for.

What is that "profound and reasonless law"? In *Melymbrosia*'s version of the engagement scene, Terence calls their love "the most wonderful thing in the world"; Rachel feels it "Something terrible" (*M* 197). Terence loves her, he says, for her "free soul," which neither time nor "marriage" will alter; "That's why our life together will be the most magnificent thing in the world" (*M* 199). Contracting to remain independent and autonomous, Rachel tells Terence that she loves him as a woman, not a child; hence their marriage must be "a battle." He agrees: "You fight; and I shall fight! We'll have something better than happiness" (*M* 200). They celebrate their informal vow of mutual strength in their life's adventure not by a dance but by Terence's reading from Whitman's "Passage to India": "Voyage to more than India!/O secret of the earth and sky!/Sail forth—steer for the deep waters only,/Reckless O soul, exploring, I with thee, and thou with me,/For we are bound where mariner has not yet dared to go,/And we will risk the ship ourselves and all./O my brave soul!/O farther, farther sail!" (M 206–7). Despite Rachel's initial "terrible," her will to "fight" rather than submit, and the great "risk" of this voyage to "more than India" that will be their marriage, it is far from clear in this exalted moment that Rachel is destined to die.

In *The Voyage Out,* the engagement scene assumes a peculiarly literary fatality as the lovers seem to turn back the book of the world to the very first page, a Post-Impressionist Genesis. Even before they embark on the river voyage, Helen's fear for Rachel evokes the Fall: "great things were happening—terrible things, because they were so great. Her sense of safety was shaken, as if beneath twigs and dead leaves she had seen the movement of a snake" (VO 263). While the others rest on the journey, Rachel and Terence walk like a new Adam and Eve alone into a surreal jungle as Hirst calls after them "Beware of snakes" (VO 270). It is as if they cross from a Constable landscape into an Eden that Henri Rousseau might have painted. Larger than life, their figures move through great spaces full of strange light, vast and green, where butterflies circle and settle amid creaking, sighing sounds that make them feel they are "walking at the bottom of the sea" (VO 270). Strangest of all is the silence that weighs them down. Neither can "frame any thoughts," yet

> something between them . . . had to be spoken of. One of them had to begin, but which . . . ? Then Hewet picked up a red fruit and threw it as high as he could. When it dropped, he would speak. They heard the flapping of great wings; they heard the fruit go pattering through the leaves and eventually fall with a thud. The silence was again profound. (VO 271)

This silence may seem to augur a new genesis as Rachel journeys back to the world's symbolic beginning to see things new. But she and Terence scarcely speak, their words so bare and few that their conversation sustains itself as if by echo:

> "Does this frighten you?" Terence asked. . . .
>
> "No," she answered, "I like it." . . . There was another pause.
>
> "You like being with me?" Terence asked.
>
> "Yes, with you," she replied.
>
> He was silent for a moment. Silence seemed to have fallen upon the world.
>
> "This is what I have felt ever since I knew you," he replied. "We are happy together." He did not seem to be speaking, or she to be hearing.

"Very happy," she answered.

They continued to walk for some time in silence. . . .

"We love each other," Terence said.

"We love each other," she repeated.

The silence was then broken by their voices which joined in tones of strange unfamiliar sound which formed no words. . . . Sounds stood out from the background making a bridge across their silence. . . .

"We love each other," Terence repeated. . . . She said "Terence" once; he answered "Rachel."

"Terrible—terrible," she murmured . . . thinking . . . of the persistent churning of the water. . . . On and on it went in the distance, the senseless and cruel churning of the water. (*VO* 271)

Where *Melymbrosia*'s engagement scene moves past Rachel's "terrible" to envision an adventurous voyage toward a "magnificent" future, here "terrible" is the dialogue's last word, uttered as if in unconscious homage to the overwhelming force of that symbolic "river." Trying to speak a new beginning in the silences of an unwritten world, Rachel and Terence find themselves sucked into a maelstrom of unconscious repetition, as if an ancient cultural script were asserting itself with the force of nature. "I don't want to be late," says Terence. "We're so late—so late—so horribly late," he repeats "as if he were talking in his sleep" as he seeks the way back to the broad path that resembles "the drive in an English forest"— Rachel following, "ignorant of the way, ignorant why he stopped or why he turned" (*VO* 272).

As the characters fail to break into new speech, their bodies enact the ancient story of the Fall in which they seem entangled and lost, so that the social is infused with the surreal and even the sublime. Back with Helen and the others, Rachel hardly knows that she is "engaged." (Indeed the words are never spoken. On the other hand, can a young Edwardian man and woman emerge from the jungle without being engaged?) "Are we to marry each other?" she asks. "Marriage?" she repeats. "It will be a fight" (*VO* 281, 282). As she and Terence walk ahead, "sunk" beneath "the waters" of their "happiness," Helen comes up unheard and, with an iron blow like a "bolt from heaven," tumbles Rachel to the ground and rolls her in the grass until, "speechless and almost without sense," Rachel sees looming against the sky "the two great heads of a man and a woman, of Terence and Helen," who "kissed in the air above her. She thought she heard them speak of love and then of marriage," then "realised . . . happiness swelling and breaking in one vast wave" (*VO* 283–84).

But whose happiness? As if translating the Fall of Genesis into Rachel's physical fall, Helen's blow almost seems to knock Rachel's desire and happiness out of her own body and into the abstract man and woman kissing in the air above her (VO 284). " 'Who are they?' " Rachel, momentarily disoriented, wonders of the "human figures" awaiting them in the distance (VO 284). The company walks on to the Amazon village that is "the goal of their journey," as the Inner Station is Marlow's. Here Rachel and Terence flinch under the village women's strong gazes in an ethnographic encounter that makes Rachel feel her world as strange and inexplicable in their eyes as in her own. As she arrives at the "sources of the river," as it were, this flowing maternal life-world "far beyond the plunge of speech" yields a subdued yet momentous analogue to Marlow's epiphany: in this civilization as in her own, to be a woman is to be inscribed in and circumscribed by natural cycles of birth and death. "It does make us seem insignificant, doesn't it?" Terence sighs; to Rachel it seems that the women, the trees, and the river will "go on forever"; and Helen, as we have noted, involuntarily sees a boat capsized on an English river, as if Rachel's fate were now mysteriously revealed (VO 285). In short, the scene intercuts realism with a sublime apprehension of a nature "in comparison with which everything else is small": "Nature" as phenomena betokening "infinity"; the consciousness "that we are superior to nature within, and . . . without us"; "pain" that is "at the same time . . . purposive."[17] Journeying upstream on the Amazon to find "the sources of the river"— that powerful current of maternal destiny—Rachel confronts a femininity bound into nature, before which she is silent, insignificant, horribly late, or perhaps only terribly early.

Marriage and Sacrifice: The Death of Rachel Vinrace

> "I want to write a novel about Silence," [Terence] said; "the things people don't say. But the difficulty is immense. . . . [T]he whole conception, the way one's seen the thing, felt about it, made it stand in relation to other things, not one in a million cares for that. And yet I sometimes wonder whether there's anything else in the whole world worth doing. These other people," he indicated the hotel, "are always wanting something they can't get. . . . What you said just now is true: one doesn't want to be things; one wants merely to be allowed to see them." (VO/E 249)

How does Rachel Vinrace's death "stand in relation to other things"? In *Melymbrosia* Rachel falls into a delirium in which she "pushe[s] her voice out as far as possible until it became a bird and flew away," doubting "whether it ever reached the person she was talking to"; "each face" hovering over her reminds her "that she ought to fight for something"; she "wished for a moment to fight for something, and then forgot" (*M* 230–31). Rachel dies, it seems, when she ceases to fight; and once her life ebbs away, Terence feels "triumph and calm": " 'It is only to us two in the world that this could have happened. . . . Because we loved each other. Therefore we have this.' . . . This death was such a little thing. It seemed that they were now absolutely free, more free more entirely united than they had ever been before . . . the most wonderful thing in the world" (*M* 231–32).

Terence's eerie gladness parodies with shocking force his relief as the battleground of marriage gives way to what only he is left to describe as a perfect union of wills, freed "absolutely" from contingency and struggle by Rachel's "little" death. "I really don't advise a woman who wants to have things her own way to get married," says Katherine Hilbery's aunt Charlotte in Woolf's next novel, *Night and Day* (*ND* 212). To this homespun wisdom that marriage entails the sacrifice of a woman's desire and will, Rachel opposes her vow that her marriage will be a "fight." She does not go like a lamb to the slaughter but (like Gibbon's "hardy barbarians") takes up arms against the system and dies a soldier's death in the "cause" of seeing women, men, and marriage new. In this light, we can read Rachel's death as a sacrifice to a "cause" that conscripts her from the moment of her mingled pleasure and rage in response to Richard's kiss. Legally, economically, and socially, the Victorian marriage system enforces the sacrifice of women by constricting female destiny within the "profound and reasonless law" of desire, generation, and death. As Rachel foresees life with Terence as a fight to resist that sacrificial death-in-life (of which Evelyn says glibly, "That's just why one must marry"), her *actual* death—*before* the marriage—forecloses that fight and subtly alters her death's sacrificial meaning. Instead of marrying and fighting the system from within, Rachel dies a weary soldier's death ("she ought to fight," "wished for a moment to fight") on the threshold of marriage, outside the "structure" of things, in the midst of her greater war to speak "the truth."

Even before Rachel falls ill, *The Voyage Out* shows her vanquished in one everyday skirmish when Terence deliberately interrupts her practice of Beethoven's Opus 111. Deaf to its unearthly beauty—what she calls its "reality"—he describes it as "an unfortunate old dog going round on its hind legs in the rain" (*VO* 292). He then accuses her of reading "trash" and of being "behind the times" while she compares his industrious, domineering self-importance with "the ants who stole the tongue" at the picnic:

> "I thought you and St. John were like those ants—very big, very ugly, very energetic, with all your virtues on your backs. However, when I talked to you I liked you—"

> "You fell in love with me," he corrected her. . . .
>
> "No, I never fell in love with you," she asserted.
>
> "Rachel—what a lie—didn't you sit here looking at my window—
> didn't you wander about the hotel like an owl in the sun—?"
>
> "No," she repeated, "I never fell in love, if falling in love is what peo-
> ple say it is, and it's the world that tells the lies and I tell the truth. Oh,
> what lies—what lies!"
>
> She crumpled together a handful of letters from Evelyn M., from Mr.
> Pepper, from Mrs. Thornbury and Miss Allan, and Susan Warrington. It
> was strange, considering how very different these people were, that they
> used almost the same sentences . . . to congratulate her upon her engage-
> ment. (*VO* 293)

In condemning the world's conventional "lies" about love and marriage,
Rachel wages her Great War for "the truth." But Terence, a fearsome
opponent, has the lies and allies of gender in his arsenal. If their marriage
is to be a battle for "truth," the question is, whose truth? Helen wonders
whether Rachel is "a person ever to know the truth about anything" and
how Terence will stand "the sordid side of intimacy" (*M* 207). Hirst's con-
gratulations take form as a smug calculus that precisely calibrates the
empire's dependence on the fertility rate and his own dependence on the
economy of empire: "if every man in the British Isles has six male children
by the year 1920 . . . we shall be able to keep our fleet in the Mediter-
ranean; if less than six, the fleet disappears; if the fleet disappears, the
Empire disappears; if the Empire disappears, I shall no longer be able to
pursue my studies in the university of Cambridge" (*M* 218).

Though Mrs. Thornbury's sly wish that Hirst might "be the next"
deflates him, his reading of maternity as the pillar of England's imperial
economy illuminates Rachel's earlier subliminal identifications with
Willoughby's traffic in goats and Mr. Pepper's great white monsters of the
lower waters. Her "truth" resonates within his, though submerged in
images, unable to surface lest it "explode." Thus when Rachel and Terence argue about how to raise their prospective son and daughter, whether
their son should be like Hirst, and whether Hirst or Rachel speaks the
truth, Terence sides with Hirst, deaf to Rachel's truth claims: "with all
your virtues you don't, and you never will, care with every fibre of your
being for the pursuit of truth! You've no respect for facts, Rachel; you're
essentially feminine" (*VO* 295). Terence's presumptive masculine superiority beats her. Laying down her arms, she kisses him and, when he says,
"I ought to be writing my book, and you ought to be answering these,"
she obediently takes up her pen, only to be interrupted again as he reads
to her from a bad novel: "Perhaps, in the far future, when generations of

men had struggled and failed as he must now struggle and fail, woman would be, indeed, what she now made a pretence of being—the friend and companion—not the enemy and parasite of man" (*VO* 295, 297).

Wondering what their marriage will be like, Terence shakes his fist in Rachel's face and says, "now you look as if you'd blow my brains out. There are moments . . . when, if we stood on a rock together, you'd throw me into the sea" (*VO* 298). But he is mistaken, for it is herself Rachel suddenly sees "flung into the sea, . . . washed hither and thither, and driven about the roots of the world—the idea was incoherently delightful" (*VO* 298). As they act out this alarming fantasy, he dominates and she escapes: she swims about the room and he catches her saying, "our marriage will be the most exciting thing that's ever been done!"; then they "f[ight] for mastery, imagining a rock, and the sea heaving beneath them" until Rachel is thrown to the floor, still insisting, "I'm a mermaid! I can swim" (*VO* 298). On hearing of their engagement, Mrs. Flushing, like "a child" pouncing on "what its elders wish to keep hidden," observes that "if the boat ran upon a rock," neither Terence nor she herself would "care for anythin' but savin' yourself . . . One reads a lot about love. . . . But what happens in real life, eh? It ain't love" (*VO* 274). In the fight she imagines as marriage, Rachel saves herself by vanishing into her earlier imaginary underwater existence. This moment prefigures her death as a death-in-life, an escape from mentors and "tormentors" who think her dead when "she was not dead, but curled up at the bottom of the sea" (*VO* 341).

Earlier Terence has expressed amazement that "it's the beginning of the twentieth century, and until a few years ago no woman had ever come out and said things at all" (*VO/E* 245). He wonders at the "respect that women, even well-educated, very able women, have for men" in terms that foreshadow *A Room of One's Own* and *Three Guineas*:

> "They see us three times as big as we are or they'd never obey us. For that very reason, I'm inclined to doubt that you'll ever do anything even when you have the vote. . . . It'll take at least six generations before you're sufficiently thick-skinned to go into law courts and business offices. Consider what a bully the ordinary man is, . . . the ordinary hard-working, rather ambitious solicitor or man of business with a family to bring up and a certain position to maintain. . . . [T]he daughters have to give way to the sons; the sons have to be educated; they have to bully and shove for their wives and families, and so it all comes over again. . . . Do you really think that the vote will do you any good?" (*VO* 212–13)

Many "civilized" men *are* brutes, Terence insists. As she fights and "dies" for "truth," "reality," a new civilization, Rachel might well wonder whether, in the far future, when generations of women have struggled and failed as she must now do, men might not be what they now pretend to be—the friend and companion, not the enemy and parasite, of women.

For now, the fearsome "river" engulfs Rachel (as it nearly did Woolf), overwhelming "her own body . . . the source of all the life in the world, which tried to burst forth here—there—and was repressed" by "the weight of the entire world"—"churches, politicians, misfits, and huge impostures." [18] Yet in refusing to propitiate the "monster-truth" of gender, in making a final, mysterious retreat "Under the glassy, cool, translucent wave" where drowned women live among "drowned statues, undiscovered places, the birth of the world, the final darkness, and death," Rachel "dies" a sacrificial death on the threshold of Woolf's modernism. [19] Even as Woolf embraces modernity's ideal of civilization on women's behalf—that enlightenment project than which "few things matter more"—she designs a destination and a "destiny" for her heroine that bear witness, alongside Conrad and Marlow, to the great river of Eros that runs beneath civilization's barbarities and to the "terrible" fight to slay rather than propitiate a "monster-truth" that lives on women's bodies and sacrificial lies. Conrad evokes—and Woolf confronts—the "monstrous" system of gender in ways that render problematic the very terms *male modernism* and *female modernism*. [20]

Rachel's "fight" rescues the meaning of her sacrificial "death." No mere lie thrown in despair to a monster-truth, her death recaptures *Melymbrosia*'s suggestion of a modern fertility myth, oriented toward the future. "To the one man who had yet asked her to marry him she had said that it seemed to her ridiculous," Rachel reflects early on, for she "half expected to come up next year as a bed of white flowers" (*M* 21). Her education and engagement interrupt this lonely life among spirits and drowned things. Congratulating Terence and Rachel, Miss Allan lays on them "the burden of the new generation"; Mrs. Thornbury applauds their future:

> "You've a much better time than we had. . . . I can hardly believe how things have changed . . . And the things you young people are going to see! . . . in the next fifty years. . . . They're going to be much better people than we were. . . . All around me I see women, young women, women with household cares of every sort, going out and doing things that we should not have thought it possible to do." (*VO* 317–19)

After Rachel dies, a violent thunderstorm crashes and booms all around the hotel, and when it is over, the inmates' spirits seem watered and replenished. While the moth that evokes Rachel's soul or psyche dashes "from lamp to lamp" they talk of the future (*VO* 370). Miss Allan's "imaginary uncle"—"a most delightful old gentleman" who is "always giving me things" like a gold watch, a "beautiful little cottage in the New Forest," a ticket to a place she dreams of seeing—makes them all think of "the things they want[]": Mrs. Elliot, a child; the Flushings, Mrs. Thornbury, and Miss Allan, to "go on for a hundred years" so as to see the "changes, the improvements, the inventions—and beauty" and to find out whether there is "life in Mars"; Hirst, to see "the pattern" formed by movements and voices in the room (*VO* 371).

The reader, too, is led to think of "the whole conception, the way one's seen the thing, felt about it, made it stand in relation to other things."[21] For example (as we saw in chapter 1) not one but two women die in *The Voyage Out*: the good ship *Sarah Jane* sails back transformed into the Hirsts' parlormaid Susan Jane, who poisons herself after asking the cook to hold her twenty pounds of gold—the price of a woman's silence and a modernist strategy for calling readers to witness a civilization founded on the sacrifice of female desire. Through its postimpressionist stress on forms in relation, Woolf's first experiment to "re-form the novel and capture . . . things at present fugitive" projects a re-formed reader whose aesthetic pleasure in formal relations is inseparable from the ethical imperative to see things new. Long after surviving her own battle to make Rachel's death not "an accident" that "need never have happened" but a "destiny" whose meaning derives from its relation to other things, Woolf figured the sheer pleasure of reading (pace Richard Dalloway) as the most potent of forces in humanity's long struggle toward civilization, sociability, and peace:

> Reading has changed the world and continues to change it. When the day of judgement comes therefore and all secrets are laid bare, we shall not be surprised to learn that the reason why we have grown from apes to men, and left our caves and dropped our bows and arrows and sat round the fire and talked and given to the poor and helped the sick—the reason why we have made shelter and society out of the wastes of the desert and the tangle of the jungle is simply this—we have loved reading.[22]

THREE

The Death of Jacob Flanders

Greek Illusion and Modern War in *Jacob's Room*

fter Leonard read the manuscript of *Jacob's Room* (1922),
Woolf wrote,

> We argued about it. He calls it a work of genius; he thinks
> it unlike any other novel; he says that the people are ghosts;
> he says it is very strange: I have no philosophy of life he says; my peo-
> ple are puppets, moved hither & thither by fate. He doesn't agree that
> fate works in this way. . . . he found it very interesting, & beautiful,
> . . . & quite intelligible. . . . Neither of us knows what the public will
> think. There's no doubt in my mind that I have found out how to
> begin (at 40) to say something in my own voice. (*D* 2:186, 26 July
> 1922)

Reaching rough waters while composing *The Voyage Out*, Woolf had
worried that her young woman "will not speak, and my ship is like to
sink" (*L* 1:341, 4 August 1908). If *The Voyage Out* swims or sinks on
conversation, in *Jacob's Room* Woolf's "own voice"—ventriloquized
through a newly invented essayist-narrator—carries a radically free fictional form that subordinates plot and character to the social forces that
drive modern life and modern war. Seeing but unseen, this essayist-
narrator frames a kaleidoscopic array of private and public scenes with a
city-dweller's anonymity and freedom. The novel's vitality lies less in what
its characters say than in the essayist-narrator's angle of vision, as when
"she" (for reasons discussed below) notes that Clara Durrant with her
"young woman's language" is "not one to encroach upon Wednesday" in
her shilling diary (*JR* 71). As for Jacob Flanders, he is at once an elusive
being no net of words can capture and—delivered by his education to a
modern war that overwhelms individual will—a puppet moved hither and
thither by fate, one of the war dead, a ghost. As Rachel Vinrace dies in a

battle to bring to light civilization's hidden "truth," Jacob dies in the gap between a founding ideal of European civilization—summed up as the "Greek myth" or "illusion"—and modern barbarity (*JR* 137, 138). Through the deaths of their young protagonists, these companion pieces of the modernist bildungsroman suggest that to learn to read the modern novel is to become aware of the hidden forces that drive modern lives; that to witness the life and death of the puppet or ghost its pages pursue may be in some sense to save one's own.

The Battered Ulysses

Toward the end of *Jacob's Room*, Clara Durrant and Mr. Bowley stroll past the statue of Achilles in Hyde Park Corner:

> " 'This statue was erected by the women of England . . . ' " Clara read out with a foolish little laugh. "Oh, Mr. Bowley! Oh!" Gallop—gallop—gallop—a horse galloped past without a rider. The stirrups swung; the pebbles spurted.
> "Oh, stop it, Mr. Bowley!" she cried, white, trembling, gripping his arm, utterly unconscious, the tears coming. (*JR* 167)

In an England just embarked on a senseless war that would inflict a staggering number of casualties on the European nations over four years, two characters pause by a statue that links the violent conflicts of ancient Troy and contemporary Europe.[1] Beside the ancient war hero, the modern characters appear unheroic, bathetic, "foolish." As the riderless horse charges by, the "utterly unconscious" Clara turns in hysterical tears from the statue's inscription—"erected by the women of England"—to the kindly, ineffectual Mr. Bowley, who is the furthest thing from an Achilles and can do nothing to save her from that "unseizable force" or horse that is galloping toward war (*JR* 156).

But this little prose stanza (or room) opens onto other vistas that elucidate Clara's unconscious habitation of modernity. In the course of her random-walk investigations of the social system that drives Jacob toward his fate, the essayist-narrator observes the shaping influence of the classical heritage or "Greek myth" inculcated in public-school English boys from childhood (*JR* 137). "We have been brought up in an illusion," she remarks, fostered not only by the masculine education system and professions but by hero-worshipping "women of England": the statue's nameless sponsors; governesses who compare little boys like Jacob to Greek statues; mothers like Betty Flanders who hand them over to surrogate fathers to be taught Greek and Latin; prostitutes and lovers such as

Florinda, who tells Jacob, "You're like one of those statues . . . in the British Museum," and Fanny Elmer, who consoles herself while Jacob is away in (yes) Greece with daily visits to the "battered Ulysses" of the Elgin marbles; and strangers like Madame Lucien Gravé who, catching sight of him on the Acropolis, parodies the covert aggression of the European female passion for noble, "eyeless" war heroes by pointing her camera (the social machine writ small, an instrument of this female gaze) at Jacob's head (*JR* 138, 80, 170).

If Clara suffers unconsciously from the Greek "illusion," the essayist-narrator of *Jacob's Room* gauges the cost of this hero worship, as do other modernist writers in the aftermath of the First World War. In a small, bitter elegy in *Hugh Selwyn Mauberley* (1920), for example, Ezra Pound's litany of the illusions and "lies" that sacrificed a generation of young men memorializes in a few spare, carved lines his dead friend, the young sculptor of genius Henri Gaudier-Brzeska:

IV
These fought in any case,
and some believing,
        pro domo, in any case . . .

Some quick to arm,
some for adventure,
some from fear of weakness,
some from fear of censure,
some for love of slaughter, in imagination,
learning later . . .
some in fear, learning love of slaughter;

Died some, pro patria,
        non "dulce" non "et decor" . . .
walked eye-deep in hell
believing in old men's lies, then unbelieving
came home, home to a lie,
home to many deceits,
home to old lies and new infamy
usury age-old and age-thick
and liars in public places.

Daring as never before, wastage as never before
Young blood and high blood,
fair cheeks, and fine bodies;
fortitude as never before

frankness as never before
disillusions as never told in the old days,
hysterias, trench confessions,
laughter out of dead bellies.

V
There died a myriad,
And of the best, among them.
For an old bitch gone in the teeth,
For a botched civilization.

Charm, smiling at the good mouth,
Quick eyes gone under earth's lid,

For two gross of broken statues,
For a few thousand battered books.[2]

As in Pound's negation of Horace's *dulce et decor*, Woolf and many other war elegists ironically invoke the classical tradition that endows English public life to strip war of the glory these myths bestow. Unlike the Homeric bards who over many generations wrought the events of the Trojan war into a tragedy willed by the gods—so that, in Helen's words, "we might live in song for men to come"—the modernists do not invoke divine powers in hope of redeeming "wastage as never before." Where Homer paints warring gods and humans suffering war as fate divinely ordained, the modernists see "liars in public places," "disillusions as never told in the old days." Whereas the Homeric poems transform a ten-year war into the making of a people and a cultural identity that reaches from ancient Greece to modern London, Pound condemns a "botched" civilization—the "broken statues" and "battered books" that lured young blood, fine bodies, quick eyes to destruction.

"Only when a nation becomes a fiction does it go to war," Elaine Scarry proposes—a fiction of difference, boundaries, collective identity that underwrites the scapegoating of the other as the enemy. The First World War inspired the modernists not to heroic mythmaking but to a critical unmaking.[3] Pound's refrain *as never before* marks this break with "the old days," with "disillusions . . . never told." Whereas the *Iliad* endows human slaughter with tragic grandeur even as it captures war's sorrow, the modernists sought to expose the fictions or "lies" of nation and civilization imprinted upon the collective unconscious that bore millions of Jacobs, Jimmys, and Septimus Warren Smiths to their deaths. Allowing that "No doubt we should be, on the whole, much worse off without our astonishing gift for illusion," the essayist-narrator yet subjects the Greeks' seductive realism to skeptical regard. Because they "could paint fruit so that birds pecked at it," she observes, one first reads "Xenophon; then Euripides. One day—that was an occasion, by God—what people have said appears to have sense in it; 'the Greek spirit'; the Greek this, that, and the other; . . . The point is, however, that we have been brought up in an illusion. . . . it all seemed to [Jacob] very distasteful" (*JR* 137–38). The Greeks who paint fruit that attracts real birds paint the heroic fictions of Ulysses (that "liar in public places" par excellence) that his society projects onto Jacob—body ("statuesque, noble, and eyeless," the type of "manly beauty") and soul ("the flavour" and "love of Greek"—just enough to "stumble through a play") (*JR* 170, 137, 76). As birds peck at paint and canvas, nations make war over illusions. In postwar England Homeric illusion becomes disillusion; story, questioning; divinely sanctioned lies, the private and public deceits that strangle the young lives of Jacob, Jimmy, Florinda, Clara; epic tragedy, the struggle for an international civilization in which *non dulce non et decor pro patria mori.*

The Death of the War Story

> If any question why we died,
> Tell them, because our fathers lied.
>
> —Rudyard Kipling, "Common Form"

Literary historians of the First World War emphasize the abyss between the soldiers' agonizing experiences at the battlefront and the sunny heroic rhetoric that prevailed at home—sometimes felt to be "the enemy at the rear."[4] Modernist literature and art had to get rid of such stories as Kipling's "fathers" tell—"lies," "illusions," "common forms" oblivious to war's horrors—unless, as Walter Benjamin thought, modern war did it for them.[5] In the war's aftermath, wrote Benjamin, "the art of storytelling is coming to an end":

> One reason for this phenomenon is obvious: experience has fallen in value. . . . [O]ur picture, not only of the external world but of the moral world as well, overnight has undergone changes which were never thought possible. . . . Was it not noticeable at the end of the war that men returned from the battlefield grown silent—not richer, but poorer in communicable experience? What ten years later was poured out in the flood of war books was anything but experience that goes from mouth to mouth. . . . For never has experience been contradicted more thoroughly than strategic experience by tactical warfare, economic experience by inflation, bodily experience by mechanical warfare, moral experience by those in power. A

generation that had gone to school on a horse-drawn streetcar now stood under the open sky in a countryside in which nothing remained unchanged but the clouds, and beneath these clouds, in a field . . . of destructive torrents and explosions, was the tiny, fragile human body.[6]

Benjamin attributes the story's demise to the impossibility of any moral commensurate with the experience of modern war: "It is as if something that seemed inalienable to us, the securest among our possessions, were taken from us: the ability to exchange experiences" in a "moral world" (83–84). In an era in which manmade technological, economic, and political orders— far from extending the powers of body and mind as a tool or weapon extends the hand's ability to make or destroy—turn the human creature into an alienated instrument of remote interests and purposes, war stories disintegrate into briefs from hell, notes on incomprehensible slaughter and suffering. Thus Gaudier-Brzeska described trench warfare as "a sight worthy of Dante, there was at the bottom a foot deep of liquid mud in which we had to stand two days and two nights, rest we had in small holes nearly as muddy, add to this a position making a V point into the enemy who shell us from three sides, the close vicinity of 800 putrefying German corpses, and you are at the front in the marshes of Aisne."[7] But in this modern inferno, vacated by Dante's divinities hardly less than Homer's, there was no guide, no way out, and no moral reason for being there in the first place.

Two years after the armistice and the year she began *Jacob's Room*, Woolf reflected on the psychic wound that the war and its historical conditions had inflicted upon her generation, laying down beneath individual circumstance and personal happiness an ineradicable awareness of the precariousness and pain of human existence:

> Why is life so tragic; so like a little strip of pavement over an abyss. I look down. I feel giddy. I wonder how I am ever to walk to the end. But why do I feel this? . . . its life itself, I think sometimes, for us in our generation so tragic—no newspaper placard without its shriek of agony from some one. . . . And with it all how happy I am—if it weren't for my feeling that its a strip of pavement over an abyss. (D 2:72–73, 25 October 1920)

Breaking down conventional story and storytelling "to say something in my own voice," Woolf registers her generation's postwar apprehension of life as a narrow strip of pavement flung over an abyss.

Benjamin locates the novel's "significance" in the fact that it offers up to readers a "stranger's fate," which "by virtue of the flame which consumes it yields us the warmth which we never draw from our own fate. What draws the reader . . . is the hope of warming his shivering life with a death he reads about."[8] But, as readers began complaining from the moment it appeared,

Jacob's Room does not offer Jacob's story—his fate or death—as a flame at which to warm ourselves. Many early reviewers faulted its lack of a story; some denied it was a novel at all. One judged it mere "notebook entries" out of which "no true novel can be built"; another (Rebecca West) thought the lack of a plot in so accomplished a work proved Woolf "at once a negligible novelist and a supremely important writer"; another, disappointed that it had "no particular story to tell," confessed that the "old craving for a plot still remains in our unregenerate breasts"; another found "no more than the material for a novel," which the author "has done hardly anything to put . . . together"—"no narrative, no design, above all, no perspective"; another concurred that "little flurries of prose poetry do not make art of this rag-bag of impressions."[9] The novel's early readers, in short, mistook the dismantling of the story for neglect "to put it together," its strategic abandonment of storytelling for narrative failure, its paratactic analytic method for an impressionist "rag-bag."[10] In throwing out storytelling along with "character-mongering"—a move facilitated by the fact that Jacob's story in some way touched virtually every European's in 1922—Woolf not only re-forms narrative perspective and authority but in doing so challenges our "unregenerate" hunger for stories, calling us to modernism's critique of deadly "illusions" and its creative drive toward new civilizations (*JR* 154).

In deconstructing Jacob's story—not offering his fate as a flame at which to warm one's shivering life but beckoning us out onto the narrow pavement over an abyss that is modern life—*Jacob's Room* unwrites the novel (to paraphrase Woolf's 1920 story "An Unwritten Novel") to pose the question of how to live, what to do, when "illusions" fail. Earlier we noted the conjoined ethical and aesthetic dimensions of Woolf's resolve to "re-form the novel and capture multitudes of things at present fugitive" (*L* 1:356, 19 August 1908). This first work in her "own voice" re-forms the novel not by sacrificing historical consciousness to formal concerns— as critics from Lukács to Jameson mistakenly claim high modernism does—but by inventing a form to bring to the light of day the illusions a "botched" civilization imprints on the collective unconscious.[11]

Male Initiation

> Vous travaillez pour l'armée, madame? a Frenchwoman said to me early
> in the Vietnam War, on hearing I had three sons.
> —Adrienne Rich, *Of Woman Born*

Woolf does not tell Jacob's story but unwrites it to expose the social forces that initiate him into masculinity and leave him dead on the battlefield.

What facilitates this deconstructed bildungsroman is the fact that the war story evoked by Jacob Flanders' very name did not have to be told in 1922, for (as Lucrezia Warren Smith says) "Every one has friends who were killed in the War" (*MD* 66). Leaving "character-mongering" to the "gossips," the essayist-narrator frames Jacob's life and death not as a unique and personal story but as that of a generation. He is far more like than unlike those anonymous "dozen young men in the prime of life" who "descend with composed faces into the depths of the sea; and there impassively (though with perfect mastery of machinery) suffocate uncomplainingly together" (*JR* 154–55). As several critics note, Jacob's portrait anticipates Woolf's musings on the autobiography of her first cousin Herbert Fisher, who served in Lloyd George's cabinet during World War I:

> What would have been his shape had he not been stamped and moulded by that great patriarchal machine? Every one of our male relations was shot into that machine at the age of ten and emerged at sixty a Head Master, an Admiral, a Cabinet Minister, or the Warden of a college. It is as impossible to think of them as natural human beings as it is to think of a carthorse galloping wild maned and unshod through the pampas.[12]

What would have been Jacob's shape without Mr. Floyd's Latin lessons, Cambridge, the de rigueur continental tour, the war? Woolf's plan "to criticise the social system, & to show it at work, at its most intense" in *Mrs. Dalloway* only continues *Jacob's Room*'s critique of the modern social machine through which young men were "shot" like so much war materiel (*D* 2:248, 19 June 1923).

As the social molding of Rachel Vinrace's female body and mind moves her toward a destiny that she at once evades and fulfills, *Jacob's Room* traces an inexorable yet reasonless reduction of masculine subjects to dead bodies as first Jimmy, then Jacob "feeds crows in Flanders" (*JR* 97). Judith Lewis Herman compares rape and combat as "complementary social rites of initiation into the coercive violence . . . of adult society" and as "paradigmatic forms of trauma for women and men respectively."[13] Like Rachel's voyage to Santa Marina, Jacob's voyage to Greece—"the only chance I can see of protecting oneself from civilization," which he hopes to repeat "every year so long as I live"—offers only a fantasy of escape from a civilization that delivers him not to adulthood but to death (*JR* 146). As in *The Voyage Out*, initiated subjects and initiatory agents are diffused through the novel's social world. The essayist-narrator's striking refrain—"It was none of her fault"; "It was none of their fault"; "It seems that men and women are equally at fault"—punctuates a quest for causes that leads beyond individual responsibility or conscience (*JR* 30,

34, 35, cf. 71, 72, 82, 92). Something is wrong, someone must be accountable, yet no one is; social forces move people to think and act unconsciously, without knowledge or will.

Septimus is not mad to suppose that it "must be the fault of the world then—that he could not feel," nor Clarissa to conclude that "there were no Gods; no one was to blame" (MD 88, 78). How then does a society shape men to make war? How does it socialize women to raise sons for war? The traumatic aspects of many male initiation rituals suggest that war is no aberration from boys' induction into the modern Western social order. In anthropologists' broad descriptions of male initiation paradigms, the male child undergoes a painful separation from the mother and the early "green" (or natural) world that his culture identifies with her, followed by his symbolic death as his mother's child and a second birth as his cultural fathers' son.[14] The "death" of his early self and the birth of a new one may unfold through actual or symbolic violence: a wounding or scarification of the body, or rituals involving a renaming, secret lore, a new identity. The question of agency, Bruce Lincoln argues, is crucial to interpreting whether a given rite effects a deforming violation or a transformative fulfillment of its subject.[15]

In Jacob's case, his father Seabrook's accidental death leaves a vacuum quickly filled by the surrogate fathers who take over his education: Mr. Floyd, who teaches the Flanders boys Latin, and Captain Barfoot, whose battle-maimed body foretells Jacob's sacrificial destiny. Sailing with Timmy Durrant, young Jacob bathes naked in the sea, feels the boat's hot seat, "gnaw[s] ham from the bone," smells wildflowers on mainland breezes, gazes at the Scilly Isles, hears a faraway cry (JR 57). Captain Barfoot—Betty Flanders's authority on how to educate her three sons—models masculinity as a culturally inflicted wound, his lame leg and missing fingers evidence that he has "served his country," paid his dues to empire, earned his place as a representative of "law" and "order" who makes women feel "we must cherish this man" (JR 28). The counterpart of Seabrook as of Betty's vanished (and aptly named) brother Morty ("lost all these years—had the natives got him, was his ship sunk"[JR 91]), the survivor Captain Barfoot displays the violated—and violating—male body as, in Scarry's words, "a source of reality" that gives the sacrifice demanded by nation, empire, and war "force and holding power" (124, 128). He represents the long history of collective violence into which Jacob will be conscripted—the history that soon darkens the child's originally transparent "pane of glass," so that "to escape is vain" (JR 49). As Rachel Vinrace's resistance brings to light the sacrificial dimensions of normative female initiation (here reprised in Ellen Barfoot, "civilization's prisoner" in her bath chair), Jacob's second birth from fathers fuels the perpetual unconscious reproduction of a war-making society's "cultural fictions" and "cultural frauds," which the sons' bodies must *substantiate* (*JR* 25; Scarry, 124, 128).

Septimus's amazement at his own living death—"I have been dead, and yet am now alive"—registers the violating suppression of feeling and connection that masculinity exacts and war intensifies. So, too, his hallucination of his friend Evans emerging from the trees in Regent's Park wishfully misapprehends Evans's war death as temporary and symbolic: "in Thessaly . . . they waited till the War was over" (*MD* 70). In the vignette on Jacob's boyhood butterfly collecting, butterflies and moths—emblems of Greek Psyche or soul—flutter like free spirits in fields and gardens until caught, mounted, and labeled in boxes. One, eluding all published descriptions, evokes Jacob himself: "A tree had fallen the night he caught it. There had been a volley of pistol-shots suddenly in the depths of the wood. And his mother had taken him for a burglar when he came home late" (*JR* 23). Like the unclassified moth, the crashing tree allegorizes a dire initiatory moment when a natural being is sacrificed to culture (as Septimus urgently perceives, "Trees [a]re alive," "Men must not cut down trees," "do not cut down trees").[16] An "old cottage woman" who tells Jacob "of a purple butterfly which came every summer to her garden" stirs premonitions of male combat: "at dawn you could always see two badgers. Sometimes they knocked each other over like two boys fighting, she said" (*JR* 24).

But society is a mother as well as "a father" (*TG* 206). What induces women to give up their sons to masculinity and war making? Or, as Adrienne Rich asks, "How *does* the male child differentiate himself from his mother"; and must he " 'join the army,' . . . internalize patriarchal values?"[17] Male initiation symbolically removes the boy from his mother's world by shaming his early identification with her so-called feminine traits, producing masculinity dialectically from that early, suppressed identification as the "emotional disengagement and uncontrolled aggression" that war demands.[18] *Jacob's Room* anticipates *Three Guineas*' analysis of an early twentieth-century English public sphere that excludes women/mothers, leaving fathers to create public culture and values and to induct male children into that culture. In this society, the mother's role is to produce the son and give him up to a public world in which fathers control law, political economy, and cultural representation.

To refuse to work for the army, a woman with three sons would have to be "somehow heroic," as Betty Flanders has no thought of being (*JR* 154). Carrying on "the eternal conspiracy of hush and clean bottles," she assuages her sons' anxiety by denying danger: "What's all that water rushing in?" worries little Arthur. " 'It's only the bath water running away,' said Mrs. Flanders. . . . 'I thought he'd never get off—such a hurricane,' she whispered to Rebecca" (*JR* 12). This "conspiracy" of mothers and nurses fosters the illusion that the domestic sphere has nothing to do with the public sphere of "storms" and wars; is entirely safe from the troubles at home and abroad from which women like Clara and Betty wish men to protect them. By contrast, Mrs. Jarvis, far from cherishing men like Captain Barfoot, feels, "it's the man's stupidity that's the cause of this [war], and the storm's my storm as well as his" (*JR* 28). No less under the sway of illusion than those women of England who erect statues of Achilles to inspire their sons, Betty soothes her sons' fear of the storm/war—the militaristic society into which they are already being initiated—so that, lulled into unconsciousness ("Think of the fairies"), they will not lie awake questioning but grow up to play their parts "uncomplainingly" (*JR* 12, 155). So Betty does herself, murmuring when awakened by the roar of guns, "Not at this distance . . . It is the sea . . . as if nocturnal women were beating great carpets. There was Morty lost, and Seabrook dead; her sons fighting for their country. But were the chickens safe?" (*JR* 175).

Betty Flanders dutifully hands Jacob on to Mr. Floyd (who teaches him the Latin language of men), Captain Barfoot, and the Cambridge dons—the "elderly of the race" who initiate him into their militaristic culture by a "muster" of ideas that "march" in "procession," "orderly, quick-stepping, and reinforced," in cities that "show[] like . . . barracks and places of discipline" (*JR* 40, 36). Yet despite Betty's conspiratorial mothering and his status as civilization's inheritor, Jacob has his doubts. "Bloody beastly!" he expostulates after lunching with a don and his family; an essay with the skeptical title "Does History consist of the Biographies of Great Men?" lies on his writing table; faced with lovely but uneducated Florinda, "He had a violent reversion towards male society, cloistered rooms, and . . . the classics; and was ready to turn with wrath upon whoever it was who had fashioned life thus" (*JR* 35, 39, 82). Still, he "grow[s] to be a man" who is "about to be immersed in things," disciplined by the "great machine" (*JR* 139). As the "utterly unconscious" Clara subliminally senses when the runaway horse gallops past Achilles' statue, Jacob well learns the lesson crooned over him in the cradle—to substantiate in body and mind his civilization's illusions.

The Essayist-Narrator

It is not primarily Jacob who pursues the novel's critical enterprise but the essayist-narrator. Edward L. Bishop observes that this narrator "is characterized more fully as a mimetic character, as an autonomous self, than the ostensible focus of the text" and explores the ways she and Jacob are "hailed" ("Hey, you there!") as Althusserian subjects.[19] Yet if she seems to us more "there" than Jacob, that is less because she is a "mimetic character" than because she is (as Bishop also observes) the novel's "voice"— its breath and spirit, its sensibility and intelligence, its soul/psyche, the "hawk moth" that "hum[s] vibrating" over "the cavern of mystery" that is Jacob (Bishop 166, JR 73).

Barry Morgenstern argues that this "self-conscious" narrator must be distinguished from Woolf, and as a textual effect so she must.[20] Yet Jacob's Room, we noted, marks Woolf's discovery of how "to say something in my own voice." Woolf began her career as an essayist and reviewer, honing her "voice" in many early unpublished pieces and publishing "more than half of her 500-plus articles, essays, and reviews" in the eighteen years preceding Jacob's Room.[21] Further, while writing "An Unwritten Novel" (1920), she conceived "a new form for a new novel" based on the loose, light method she had devised for it and "Kew Gardens"—stories that cleave close to the border between short story and personal essay (D 2:13–14, 26 January 1920). In short, the modernist form Woolf invented "more or less by chance" for Jacob's Room is a hybrid of the essay, the short story, and the novel, carried by a breakthrough in narrative "voice." Though her "own," that voice is also freely impersonal, abstracted from "the damned egotistical self" that she felt "ruins" Joyce and Richardson (D 2:13–14, 26 January 1920). "Is one pliant & rich enough to provide a wall for the book from oneself without its becoming, as in Joyce & Richardson, narrowing & restricting?" Woolf wondered—her impersonal pronoun suggesting an answer by manifesting a self, a voice, that escapes the "thick little ego" to speak as "we" or "one."[22]

Unlike the third-person omniscient narrator of The Voyage Out, this essayist-narrator is at moments explicitly embodied. At times she seems simply a human presence, on a level with the people she observes and with her implied readers: an operagoer who laments that, in choosing a seat, she exiles herself from every other vantage; a traveler in Italy with dust on her shoes (an autobiographical traveler, familiar with Woolf's travel notebooks) who marvels at how recently she was riding an omnibus in Piccadilly; a passenger in a carriage following Clara and her mother in Long Acre who interrupts herself in mid-sentence so as not to block the way (JR 136, 174). At other moments she seems female, as when she registers a "difference of sex" on watching Jacob's dawning recognition of Florinda's infidelity: "Granted ten years' seniority and a difference of sex, fear of him comes first" (though the grammar makes the referent of this difference less than certain) (JR 94–95). Such moments strategically shatter any illusion of narrative omniscience and invite the engaged, writerly reading that—Woolf "venture[s] to remind" modern readers—is their "dut[y] and responsibilit[y]": "in the course of your daily lives this past week you have had far stranger and more interesting experiences than the one I have tried to describe," yet "you" make the "fatal mistake" of supposing "that writers are different blood and bone from yourselves; that they know more . . . than you do" (*CDB* 118). Or, as the essayist-narrator puts it, "fill in the sketch as you like" (*JR* 96).

By the same token, the crucial feature of this modernist essayist-narrator who invites collaboration is less her interpellation as a cultural subject than her Houdinilike escape from convention.[23] If, as Beauvoir says, one is not born a woman, the essayist-narrator is a "woman" only as it suits her—as when she presses her nose to the window of Jacob's Cambridge world to describe the don within slipping words that are at once coins and communion wafers into young men's minds, where they "dissolve . . . like silver." Whereas, thus infused with sacralized "manliness," the students "respect" this sacred cultural coin until they grow old, when "the silver disks would tinkle hollow, and the inscription read a little too simple, and the old stamp look too pure, and the impress always the same—a Greek boy's head," a "woman, divining the priest, would, involuntarily, despise" (*JR* 40–41). Here the essayist-narrator embraces interpellation as "feminine" only to turn it into a critical outsider's perspective (adumbrating those later outsiders, *Three Guineas*' epistolary persona and the playwright/director La Trobe). She does not passively submit to the "feminine" position assigned her but mimes it (in Irigaray's sense), parodies it, exploits its potential for resistance and critique, takes it apart and discards it like the social masquerade it is, like those "parts of a woman" she sees "shown separate" in "Evelina's shop off Shaftesbury Avenue": "In the left hand was her skirt. Twining round a pole in the middle was a feather boa. Ranged like the heads of malefactors on Temple Bar were hats—emerald and white, lightly wreathed or drooping beneath deep-dyed feathers. And on the carpet were her feet—pointed gold, or patent leather slashed with scarlet."[24] One is not born a "woman": the accoutrements in the window comically mirror the deconstructed femininity the narrator puts on and steps out of at will to become a naked soul, all eyes, seeing but not seen.[25]

As the essayist-narrator who isn't born a "woman" both parodies and eludes social·embodiment, she plays out the stakes of such consciousness through Julia Hedge, Clara Durrant, and Miss Umphelby, who aren't born women either but don't know it, at least not with such freedom. Miss Umphelby, despite her melodious, accurate Virgil, is plagued by worries over what she would wear were she to meet the immortal poet. Clara's is, Bonamy marvels, "an existence squeezed and emasculated within a white satin shoe," so that "to speak" is "unnatural to her" (*JR* 152, 166). "Unfortunate Julia!" (as the narrator characterizes her) waits for books that don't come, pile up, fall over, distracted by the all-male pantheon inscribed around the brow of the old British Library reading room and by young men like Jacob who swim effortlessly with the current in their intellectual endeavors while she labors arduously upstream, "Death and gall and bitter dust" dragging on her pen-tip (*JR* 106). Resenting his slightly "regal and pompous" bearing, his air of being one of the "six young men" on whom "the flesh and blood of the future" depend, "Julia Hedge disliked him naturally enough" (*JR* 107).

Like the woman crying, "Let me in!" all night in the mews while the oblivious Jacob is engrossed in the *Phaedrus*, Julia Hedge is part of the essayist-narrator's critique of the civilization Jacob inherits to his cost. But whereas Julia's feminist consciousness is reactive, a contingent, negative artifact of "the great patriarchal machine," the essayist-narrator roams freely between society's self-display and its hidden cracks and crevices. The narrator who cries "Unfortunate Julia!" is at one level utterly in sympathy with her; but rather than wait for and react to other people's books, she casts off a virtual self in Julia while herself eluding body, sex, and gender. The essayist-narrator exists not as a socially constructed "woman" but as a supple, open, analytic sensibility who explores postwar public and private worlds with unimpeded curiosity and desire. Observing not just civilization's dead monuments but the life that teems around them, she writes the books that Julia Hedge is almost too oppressed to know she is waiting for.

This is not to say that the essayist-narrator's "difference of sex" is immaterial to her social investigations. In late 1920, while writing *Jacob's Room*, Woolf wrote two high-spirited letters to the editor of the *New Statesman* to rebut "Affable Hawk"/Desmond MacCarthy's review of Arnold Bennett's *Our Women: Chapters on the Sex-Discord*, in which he complacently asserts that no amount of education will ever entirely overcome women's innate intellectual inferiority. Comparing "the Duchess of Newcastle with Jane Austen, the matchless Orinda with Emily Brontë, Mrs Heywood with George Eliot, Aphra Behn with Charlotte Brontë, Jane Grey with Jane Harrison," Woolf argues that

> the advance in intellectual power seems not only sensible but immense; the comparison with men not in the least one that inclines me to suicide; and the effects of education and liberty scarcely to be overrated. In short, though pessimism about the other sex is always delightful and invigorating, it seems a little sanguine of Mr Bennett and Affable Hawk to indulge in it with such certainty on the evidence before them.

In the same vein, she drily adds, however tempted women might be to conclude from the spectacle of mindless slaughter "that the intellect of the male sex is steadily diminishing, it would be unwise, until they have more evidence than the great war and the great peace supply, to announce it as a fact" (CS 123). Citing J. A. Symonds on the civilization that produced Sappho—" 'highly educated,' " accustomed to free association with men and free expression " 'to an extent unknown elsewhere in history—until, indeed, the present time,' " Woolf argues that in any civilized society women must have education, "liberty of experience," and freedom to "differ from men" openly and without fear (CS 125–26). Indeed Woolf makes women's freedom the index of civilization's degree and quality: until women can think, speak, and create fearlessly, she writes, "we" (men and women) "shall remain in a condition of half-civilised barbarism. At least that is how I define an eternity of dominion on the one hand and of servility on the other. For the degradation of being a slave is only equalled by the degradation of being a master" (CS 127).

Granting the essayist-narrator's difference from "Woolf," her musings on the Greek "illusion" suggest that she would not take exception to this criterion of civilization. By this standard, neither Achilles' war culture nor the modern England that keeps it alive by erecting heroic statues and molding little boys in their images ranks very high. In the *Iliad*, after all, it is not just Achilles' divine anger or the Homeric gods that reshape reciprocal slaughter into a plot of sacralized tragedy. Both the great conflict between Greeks and Trojans and the quarrel between Greek leaders Agamemnon and Achilles hinge on a pervasive violence against women, who are indeed enslaved to men as sexual and domestic labor and, not least, trophies of their "dominion." Thus Helen is an object of mimetic rivalry between Paris and Menelaus; Khrysêis, between Khrysês and Agamemnon; Brisêis, between Agamemnon and Achilles. Within the poem this violence is not merely unexamined but so deeply naturalized that Achilles can make peace with Agamemnon on returning to battle by offering up a symbolic human sacrifice of Brisêis: "Agamemnon, was it better for us/in any way, when we were sore at heart,/to waste ourselves in strife over a girl?/If only Artemis had shot her down/among the ships on the day I made her mine . . . !"[26]

While mimetic rivalries, kept women, and sexual triangles endure from Homer to *Jacob's Room*, they now come under the essayist-narrator's skeptical gaze. If women provide the "illusion" that undergirds the *Iliad*'s tragic and glorious war story, *Jacob's Room* at once exploits and deconstructs this illusion, excavating the prostitute from the unexamined collective unconscious and bringing "public" women and sexual triangles into the light of day. Not coincidentally, the essayist-narrator sandwiches her meditation on the "strange . . . love of Greek" shared by Timmy and Jacob between viewings of the prostitute Florinda. Florinda sits on Jacob's knee as "did all good women in the days of the Greeks"; then he sees her "turning up Greek Street on another man's arm" (*JR* 76, 94). Her name— bestowed by a painter "who wished it to signify" the "unplucked" "flower of her maidenhood"—frames Florinda as an artifact (or "illusion") of masculine fantasy and, further, makes her an ironic synecdoche of women's sexual enslavement in both ancient Greek and modern European civilizations—an emblem, like ancient Greece itself, of young men's "dominion":

> Civilizations stood round them like flowers ready for picking. . . . [T]he two young men decided in favour of Greece.
> "Probably," said Jacob, "we are the only people in the world who know what the Greeks meant." (*JR* 77, 76).

As she ponders Florinda's sexuality, the essayist-narrator dwells with sibylline delicacy on the obsession with chastity in Western life and art. "Whether or not she was a virgin seems a matter of no importance whatever," she proposes, "Unless," she adds, "indeed, it is the only thing of any importance at all":

> All plays turned on the same subject. Bullets went through heads in hotel bedrooms almost nightly on that account. When the body escaped mutilation, seldom did the heart go to the grave unscarred. Little else was talked of in theatres and popular novels. Yet we say it is a matter of no importance at all.
> What with Shakespeare and Adonais, Mozart and Bishop Berkeley— choose whom you like—the fact is concealed and the evenings for most of us pass reputably, or with only the sort of tremor that a snake makes sliding through the grass. But then concealment by itself distracts the mind from the print and the sound. If Florinda had had a mind, she might have read with clearer eyes than we can. (*JR* 79)

What clear-eyed readings of her culture would Florinda have produced if she had had a mind? If the "great patriarchal machine" has molded Florinda to use her head less to critique modern civilization than to uphold it, like the caryatids of the Erechtheum, the mere idea of her prostitute's-eye view illuminates a deep structural continuity between the male desire that drives the *Iliad*'s plot and the unconscious forces that fuel the modern social machine. Looking virtually at modern civilization through Florinda's clear eyes, the essayist-narrator brings its seamy underside, its barbaric unconscious, into view.[27]

The essayist-narrator—who is, as we have noted, anything but an exemplary subject—resists the cultural police ("Hey, you there!"). She ignores her culture's hailings into the proper, conventional, normative feminine positions so impeccably mastered by Clara Durrant and instead hails back from such out-of-the-way places as Florinda's mind if she had had one and other byways to which her curiosity about criminals, women, and other "outcast[s] from civilization" takes her (*JR* 96). If Florinda herself cannot articulate the prostitute's perspective on civilization's "illusion" that she so valuably marks, it is indirectly elaborated by the other women the essayist-narrator brings out of civilization's woodwork: the widow Betty Flanders (recalling the case of "the widow" that Rachel poses to Richard Dalloway), "civilization's prisoner" the crippled Ellen Barfoot, the trammeled Clara, the prostitute Laurette, the artist's model Fanny Elmer, the narcissist Sandra Wentworth Williams, the old English woman who sings "not for coppers, no, from the depths of her gay wild heart—her sinful, tanned heart" outside the Bank, and the old Greek woman who condemns "the whole of civilization" in "refus[ing] to budge" to let a tram pass beneath Jacob's hotel window in Patras (*VO* 66, *JR* 67, 138).

Although the male desire that shapes the *Iliad*'s plot plays through the Greek illusion of *Jacob's Room*, women sing their desire in every crevice of the social structure the essayist-narrator explores. Julia Hedge wants an expanded canon, Mrs. Jarvis dreams of joining the storms and wars of the public world, and a whole gamut of women want Jacob, even creating (with Bonamy) sexual triangles around him: Clara in mute longing, Sandra by compulsive seduction, Fanny with idealizing passion, Florinda in dumb affection as she embarks on an ambitious reading program in hope of winning his love. Whether these women's knowing yet complicit yearnings are of no importance whatever or the only thing of any importance at all remains an open question. If women's desires are never proposed as the cause of the Great War, there is still that curious scene in which Clara, Achilles, "the women of England," the riderless horse, and the ominously absent Jacob converge as if fortuitously under the essayist-narrator's gaze.

For his part, Jacob suffers from "modern gloom" as he plays the "diligent" tourist in Greece, duly following his guidebook's directive to observe "the slight irregularity in the line of the steps 'which the artistic sense of the Greeks preferred to mathematical accuracy' " (*JR* 149). Having discovered that, wherever he goes, there he is—never more so than in the presence of those ruined monuments his education teaches him to revere—he begins "to think a great deal about the problems of civilization, which were solved, of course, so very remarkably by the ancient

Greeks, though their solution is no help to us" (*JR* 149). As with Florinda, who does as "all good women" in the days of the Greeks, the more things change the more they remain the same. Civilization's problems devolve upon women as Jacob reverts to Achilles' age-old "solution": " 'Damn these women . . . How they spoil things . . . It is those damned women,' said Jacob, without any trace of bitterness, but rather with sadness and disappointment that what might have been should never be." (Here the essayist-narrator comments helpfully, "This violent disillusionment is generally to be expected in young men in the prime of life, sound of wind and limb, who will soon become fathers of families and directors of banks" [*JR* 151].) Only momentarily does Jacob follow youth's mandate, "Detest your own age. Build a better one" (*JR* 107). Would he have pursued a better one had he lived to father a family and direct a bank? In any case, it is not lost on the essayist-narrator that Jacob "never read modern novels."[28]

A Disconnected Rhapsody

How to address the "problems of civilization" is a question that the essayist-narrator also poses to her readers—one kept rigorously open in the novel's final gesture, Betty Flanders's deferential query about Jacob's empty shoes: "What am I to do with these, Mr. Bonamy?" (*JR* 176). As Bishop notes, Woolf cut the two closing lines of an earlier draft:

> They both laughed.
> The room waved behind her tears.[29]

The revision sharpens Woolf's modernist "re-form" of the novel by shifting the accent from feelings to questions, from the dead to the living, from the past to the future, and from a conventional story to "a disconnected rhapsody"—her own description of the novel as she wondered what reviewers might say, one that inscribes *Jacob's Room* within the Western epic tradition begun by the ancient bards or rhapsodes (*rhapsōidoi*) who developed the materials of the Homeric poems through oral performance.[30]

In tossing out those earlier closing lines, Woolf broke the graceful circle back to the opening scene of Betty Flanders's tearful letter writing and Jacob's stubborn insistence on dragging home his memento mori, the sheep's jaw found on the beach. She disrupts formal symmetry and closure to leave questions echoing in the air. "Did he think he would come back?" (*JR* 176). And now that his body feeds crows in Flanders, who will step into his shoes—put on his authority, write his essays on civilization, inherit the public world and build its "better" future, as he once expected to do? The tone of these questions is not, to my ear, despair or even grief. By contrast with Pound's bitter mourning in *Hugh Selwyn Mauberley* and T. S. Eliot's desolate melancholy in *The Waste Land*, Woolf's essayist-narrator has put mourning behind her and writes a "disconnected rhapsody" for those who are still here—the war's survivors, for whom life is a narrow pavement over an abyss. Permanently changed by a catastrophic war but all the more urgently alive for her experiences of loss, she leaves off the "intolerable weariness" of "looking at monuments" through guidebooks, stories, illusions, and calls her readers to venture with her onto that narrow pavement over an abyss that is modern consciousness (*JR* 136). Like that of *Between the Acts*, the ending of *Jacob's Room* symbolically delivers us to the first moment of all future historical time.

Adventurous, curious, free, yet attuned to the tragedy and agony of life for her generation, the essayist-narrator models a modernist soul or psyche for whom there are no stories nor any divinities on whom to blame a "botched civilization"; and for whom life is, in any case, a horse that will eventually throw you, whether your civilization is botched or not. Even if you could silence the guns of Western Europe, let the clocks of modern time run down, free the spirit from its bondage to civilization, there would still be the sheep's jaw. Or, as the narrator observes, "It's not catastrophes, murders, deaths, diseases, that age and kill us; it's the way people look and laugh, and run up the steps of omnibuses" (*JR* 82). Life, marked off by death before, between, and beyond the shaping powers of civilization and culture, remains an "unseizable force" that even a modern novel can't capture or still. Holding out not a story at which to warm ourselves but Jacob's shoes, *Jacob's Room* wordlessly mirrors the modern condition of walking out on a little strip of pavement over an abyss.

In the same spirit, *Jacob's Room*'s demystification of narrative authority makes it less a "sketchbook artist"'s work than an epic canvas on which its essayist-narrator paints civilization's "problems" in modernity's disillusioning yet revelatory light.[31] Like *The Waste Land* and *The Cantos*, *Jacob's Room* registers its epic ambition through allusion. The essayist-narrator weaves echoes of classical texts into her own, as if mirroring fragments of the Parthenon in the British Museum; but while Fanny seeks "Jacob's presence" in "the battered Ulysses," the essayist-narrator highlights significant differences of time and place (*JR* 170). Consider, for example, her turn on perhaps the most famous of all epic similes, which likens a thousand Trojan campfires arrayed across the plain to a starry sky:

> . . . As when in heaven
> principal stars shine out around the moon
> when the night sky is limpid, with no wind,
> and all the lookout points, headlands, and mountain
> clearings are distinctly seen, as though
> pure space had broken through, downward from heaven,
> and all the stars are out, and in his heart
> the shepherd sings: just so from ships to river
> shone before Ilion the Trojan fires.
> There were a thousand burning in the plain,
> and round each one lay fifty men in firelight.
> Horses champed white barley, near the chariots,
> waiting for Dawn to mount her lovely chair.
> (*Iliad* 8, 198–99)

Whereas the Homeric bard poses the spectacle of war against the peaceful natural and agricultural orders signaled by stars, moon, and shepherd, Woolf's rhapsodic essayist-narrator compares the strife and strivings of everyday life to the spectacle of war:

> Sunlight *strikes* in upon shaving-glasses; and *gleaming brass* cans; upon all the jolly *trappings* of the day; the bright, inquisitive, *armoured*, resplendent, summer's day, which has long since *vanquished* chaos; which has dried the melancholy mediaeval mists; drained the swamp and stood glass and stone upon it; and *equipped* our brains and bodies with such an *armoury of weapons* that merely to see the *flash and thrust of limbs engaged* in the conduct of daily life is better than *the old pageant of armies drawn out in battle array upon the plain.* (*JR* 163, my emphases)

In keeping with its tragic war plot, the *Iliad* celebrates making within unmaking, natural and cultural orders within the spectacle of reciprocal violence. By contrast, the rhapsode of *Jacob's Room* celebrates human battles against not an "enemy" people but the destructive forces of nature and time. Her staging of everyday life as a splendid battleground at once registers the violent work of nature, time, and death and celebrates the tragic beauty of their given order. For her the violence of everyday life is heroic enough, a spectacle on a par with Homer's sublime panorama of warriors' campfires under the stars: she sings a conflict in which humans oppose chaos and those absolute, unvanquishable enemies, "time and eternity," glimpsed through the "skirts and waistcoats" of social time (*JR* 168). Under her gaze life reveals itself as mortal combat against these most awesome of all forces, an inescapable contest that, no matter how bravely fought, must always be lost—as the "always punctual" Julia

Eliot, herself watching the runaway horse gallop past Achilles' statue, is made aware, involuntarily seeing in her mind's eye all "people passing tragically to destruction" (*JR* 168).

To return to Achilles' statue at Hyde Park Corner, what we notice now is not only Clara's unconscious, hysterical, helpless grief but how the statue is draped all around with domestic objects—how the social life of people and things counterpoints the Greek illusion: "The loop of the railing beneath the statue of Achilles was full of parasols and waistcoats; chains and bangles; of ladies and gentlemen, lounging elegantly, lightly observant" (*JR* 167). If the riderless horse suggests the "unseizable force" of social history, that galloping allegory of England's unconscious plunge toward the war that brings Jacob's death also recalls that "wild horse in us," the sheer animal life force, and, through Thoby (Woolf's model for Jacob and Percival), the horse that throws Percival in *The Waves* (*JR* 141).

Even as this darker revelation shadows Clara's white-knuckled confrontation with the existential modernity contingently brought home to a whole generation by the war, it is also profoundly independent of it. War or no war, death is the enemy of a life poised on the abyss, even in Homer.[32] In the *Iliad*, the greatest war story and the greatest antiwar story ever told, even Achilles must choose between going to war to make a hero's name inseparable from the fiction of Greece he defends and going AWOL to lead a long contented life at home. Nor does the great name he chooses over long life—the honor and glory that Odysseus extols when he meets Achilles' shade in Hades among "the after images of used up men"—assuage death's pain or repay his lost years of life, as he bitterly attests: "Let me hear no smooth talk/of death from you, Odysseus, light of councils/Better, I say, to break sod as a farm hand/for some poor country man, on iron rations,/than lord it over all the exhausted dead."[33]

In "On Not Knowing Greek" (1925), Woolf links the Greek war stories' underlying awareness of death as the unvanquishable enemy with her generation's experience of modern war:

> In the vast catastrophe of the European war our emotions had to be broken up for us, and put at an angle from us, before we could allow ourselves to feel them in poetry or fiction. . . . But the Greeks could say, as if for the first time, "Yet being dead they have not died." They could say, "If to die nobly is the chief part of excellence . . . we lie possessed of praise that grows not old." . . . With the sound of the sea in their ears, vines, meadows, rivulets about them, they are even more aware than we are of a ruthless fate. There is a sadness at the back of life which they do not attempt to mitigate. Entirely aware of their own standing in the shadow, and yet alive to every tremor and gleam of existence, there they

endure, and it is to the Greeks that we turn when we are sick of the vagueness, of the confusion, of the Christianity and its consolations, of our own age. (CR 34, 38)

This consciousness of an immitigable sadness at the back of life reaches from Achilles' tent to Jacob's room and underlies not only the *Iliad*'s story but the virtual stories that Achilles and Jacob foreclose by choosing war.

Writing to the aspiring novelist Gerald Brenan on Christmas 1922, two months after *Jacob's Room* appeared, Woolf described her generation's experiments with literary form in terms that anticipate the modernist manifesto "Mr. Bennett and Mrs. Brown": "The human soul it seems to me orientates itself afresh every now & then. It is doing so now. No one can see it whole therefore. . . . life has to be faced: to be rejected; then accepted on new terms with rapture" (L 2:598–99). In the same spirit, *Jacob's Room*'s disconnected rhapsody seeks not only to re-form the novel but to orient the reader afresh, not by offering a story's warmth but by modeling a skeptical, critical, analytic, life-loving sensibility—a subject who resists the hailings of the "social machine," who refuses to "suffocate uncomplainingly" (JR 155). If, as Marshall Berman contends, "we don't know how to use our modernism," if we have "missed or broken the connection between our culture and our lives," "lost the art of putting ourselves in the picture, of recognizing ourselves as participants and protagonists in the art and thought of our time," *Jacob's Room* recalls its readers to that "art."[34] It gives itself up to be read only as we abandon our unregenerate longing for stories and illusions to embrace its disconnected rhapsody. For, as Adorno observed, modernist art is no more obscure than traditional art.[35] It's just that—like Clara, or like Jacob, who "never read modern novels"—we would sometimes rather not face what it reveals.

The moderns had never written anything one wanted to read about death . . . "and now can never mourn, can never mourn, . . . From the contagion of the world's slow stain" . . . for there are moments when it seems utterly futile . . . simply one doesn't believe, thought Clarissa, any more in God.

—Woolf, "Mrs. Dalloway in Bond Street"

Thou thy worldly task hast done, Mrs. Dalloway read. Tears unshed, tears deep, salt, still, stood about her for all deaths & sorrows.

—Woolf, *The Hours*

When once the mourning is over, it will be found that our high opinion of the riches of civilization has lost nothing from our discovery of their fragility. We shall build up again all that war has destroyed, and perhaps on firmer ground and more lastingly than before.

—Sigmund Freud, "On Transience" (1916)

FOUR

Mrs. Dalloway's Postwar Elegy
Women, War, and the Art of Mourning

ix weeks after *Mrs. Dalloway* appeared, its author speculated on "a new name" for her novels: "A new ——— by
Virginia Woolf. . . . Elegy?" (*D* 3:34, 27 June 1925). In mod-
ernizing the elegy by adapting its poetics to prose fiction and
its work of mourning to postwar London's post-theological cosmos in
Mrs. Dalloway, Woolf moves beyond the "satiric elegy" of *Jacob's Room*
to explore the genre's full profundity, complexity, and power.[1] This communal elegy unseals "a well of tears"—for the survivors no less than the
war dead—and enters into colloquy with the pastoral elegy from the
Greeks through Shakespeare to Shelley in search of consolations for "This
late age of the world's experience" (*MD* 9). In making Clarissa Dalloway
its central elegiac consciousness and transposing certain conventions to
feminine registers, furthermore, the novel embraces the terrible losses that
the war inflicted on "poor devils, of both sexes," and critiques the war-
making society that *Three Guineas* figures as "a father" (*TL* 159, *TG*
206). But *Mrs. Dalloway*'s distinction as a war elegy arises from its discovery of the genre's deep resources for dramatizing and mediating violence both psychic and social: the violence of war and of everyday death;
the violence of everyday life; and the violence intrinsic to mourning, the
grief-driven rage that threatens to derail the mourner's progress toward
acceptance and consolation. In making the elegy a field for confronting
the violence that had devastated Europe and still loomed as a threat to its
future, *Mrs. Dalloway* joins the internationalist contributions of Woolf's
Bloomsbury contemporaries John Maynard Keynes and Sigmund Freud
to postwar debates about Europe's future. Its characters' struggles animate Keynes's prophetic castigation of the Peace as war by other means
and anticipate Freud's arguments against class oppression, and for the
consolations of science, philosophy, and art over "religious illusion," for

a civilization that must manage but can never eradicate the aggression that imperils it from within.[2]

In approaching *Mrs. Dalloway* as a communal postwar elegy, I rely on Peter Sacks's psychosocial analysis of the classical elegy as a dynamic, eventful working through of loss, fraught with real dangers. Sacks shows how the genre's conventions mediate the mourner's arduous journey from loss, grief, and rage to the renewed life and hope epitomized in the last line of Milton's "Lycidas," "Tomorrow to fresh woods, and pastures new."[3] Three features stand out in *Mrs. Dalloway*'s exploration of mourning. First, with roots in ancient fertility rites, the classical pastoral elegy figures the work of mourning through ceremonies surrounding the death and rebirth of a vegetation god such as Adonis, and its dialectical movement toward consolation (always necessarily symbolic) recalls the funeral games and contests through which a community of mourners negotiates its inheritance from dead father figures or paternal deities. Mourning, then, has an oedipal dimension as an immediate loss reawakens old crises of loss and brokenness, early wounds to narcissism and sexuality that psychoanalysis figures as castration. To mourn is to relive every loss back to the first loss of the mother and to suffer again the anguish of submitting to the reality principle figured as the law of the father.[4] As we shall see, the accidental death of Clarissa's sister Sylvia—caused, it seems, by their careless father—feminizes the vegetation myth as Sylvia becomes the matrix of Clarissa's homemade consolation. Moreover, Clarissa herself "survives" her historical prototype Kitty Maxse's death to body forth the "divine vitality" that the elegy seeks to recover, while her double, the (partly autobiographical) war veteran Septimus, suffers a death that enacts a potentially redemptive "message" of witness to social violence (*MD* 7, 83). In exploring its characters' conflicts with a society that is "a father," *Mrs. Dalloway* analyzes a civilization founded, as Freud shows, on the sacrifice of female desire and lends critical substance to his prediction that the war's survivors will perhaps rebuild their shattered civilization "on firmer ground and more lastingly."

Second, in correlating the elegy's formal conventions with the painful work of mourning, Sacks contrasts the elegy with its bad other, revenge tragedy. The poetic elegy submits mourning's formidable psychic turbulence to the rigorous formal mechanics of elegiac temporality. Meter, rhyme, repetition, refrain, repeated questions, procession, and ceremony: all serve to divide, order, pace, tame, channel the mourner's chaos of feelings. This finely elaborated order indirectly attests to the dangers that threaten the mourner's progress: on one side, melancholia—the refusal to relinquish the lost one, to submit to reality, to attach one's desire to a substitute object; on the other, the rage that may explode the genre's bounds, veer from symbolic expression to actual murder or suicide, pervert symbolic consolation into sacrificial violence in the failed mourning of revenge tragedy. In *Mrs. Dalloway*, as looser structures of repetition and refrain (Big Ben's striking of the hours, "Fear no more the heat o' the sun") mark their progress through the day, the characters battle psychic perils that write small the great crisis of loss, grief, and anger facing postwar Europe. Miss Kilman, impoverished because of her German ancestry, is beset by violent rage; Septimus's experience of his society's disavowed violence is labeled madness; Clarissa feels almost annihilated by existential doubt. Through them *Mrs. Dalloway* poses the great question of Europe's future after what was not yet the First World War (the novel calls it "the European war") as the fate of collective mourning—a *historic* question of genre for a traumatized Europe poised between elegy and revenge tragedy (*MD* 129).

Third, in keeping with the pastoral elegy's eclogic division of mourning voices, *Mrs. Dalloway* projects the dialectic of mourning into urgent social critique and contestation of the future.[5] The funeral games and "apparently innocent" singing matches of elegiac tradition, Sacks observes, channel grief into skilled performances that contest and carry on those virtues of the dead "deemed important for the community's survival" (36). In the novel's depiction of a great European capital five years after the war, an intricate tournament of such "poetry contests" pits Clarissa's "atheist's religion" against Miss Kilman's allegiances to God and Russia; Septimus's prophetic witness against his prosperous doctors' policy of "Conversion" to social norms; the furtively sexual Hugh Whitbread against the telling silences of Sally Seton and Milly Brush (*EE* 36, *MD* 78, 100). I shall first trace Clarissa's emergence as an elegiac consciousness from *The Voyage Out* to *Mrs. Dalloway* and then locate the novel's intramural poetry contests within public debates in and beyond Bloomsbury over postwar Europe's inheritance and future. Addressing the communal task—not yet negated by events—of navigating beyond anger and revenge toward peace, *Mrs. Dalloway* conjures from the "beautiful caves" of its characters' grief-ravaged psyches vistas of fresh woods and pastures new (*D* 2:263, 30 August 1923).

Life Drawing After Death

Set on a June day in 1923, *Mrs. Dalloway* emerged amid an outpouring of art after a war that military historian John Keegan describes as a "tragic and unnecessary conflict," which mobilized sixty-five million,

killed over eight million, left twenty-one million physically and/or psychically wounded or disabled, and blighted the lives and hopes of
uncounted loved ones.[6] A voice in Eliot's 1922 *Waste Land* marvels of a
crowd streaming over London Bridge, "I had not thought death had
undone so many"; to Lucrezia Warren Smith it seems that "Every one has
friends who were killed in the War" (*MD* 66). The war not only shattered
millions of lives but unleashed virulent nationalisms that rent the economic and cultural fabric of what had been becoming an increasingly
international civilization. As we saw in chapter 1, for Keynes, Leonard
Woolf, Clive Bell, Einstein, and others, it was a "Civil War" that threatened "the end of a civilization."[7] Yet even as it seemed to negate even the
idea of Enlightenment, it also dismantled four ancient empires, swept
away an outworn social and political order, and left Europe " 'a laboratory atop a vast graveyard' " in which communism, fascism, and liberal
democracy vied to promise the suddenly enfranchised masses "a New
Order," a "state of their own"; and, as Mark Mazower reminds us, "it
was not preordained that democracy should win out over fascism and
communism."[8]

By 1923 Freud's early confidence that Europeans would rebuild and
perhaps improve their democratic and internationalist civilization after
the war was losing ground to the totalitarian political orders that, fostered
by the Versailles Treaty, were already beginning to form.[9] On visiting
postwar Austria, British diplomat Harold Nicolson reported, "Everyone
looks very pinched and yellow: no fats for four years. The other side of
the blockade. . . . I feel that my plump pink face is an insult to these
wretched people."[10] A few years later Peter Walsh returns from India to a
civilization that seems a "dear . . . personal possession," a London puls-
ing with the resurgent creativity ("design, art, everywhere") and com-
mercial prosperity of the 1920s (*MD* 55, 71). Through the great and small
events that befall its characters this June day, *Mrs. Dalloway* portrays a
postwar civilization fraught with agonizing social contradictions yet
vibrating with the vital force of the future.

Could the elegy rise to this historic moment—mourn war losses of
unimaginable magnitude yet everywhere suffered as local, capture contending social forces, work through communal grief toward consolation
and hope? The "moderns" Clarissa rejects in "Mrs. Dalloway in Bond
Street" suggest not ("The moderns had never written anything one
wanted to read about death" [*CSF* 155]). In the war poets' harrowing
turns on the genre, savage ironies all but eclipse consolation: Wilfred
Owen's nightmarish "Dulce et Decorum Est"; the proleptic self-elegies of
Rupert Brooke ("The Soldier"), Isaac Rosenberg ("Break of Day in the

Trenches"), and Yeats's Major Robert Gregory ("An Irish Airman Foresees His Death"); Siegfried Sassoon's "Everyone Sang," with its stunning
reversal of the mourner's progress from anguished grief to solacing
vision.[11] On the home front, Ezra Pound's bitter epitaph on soldiers
slaughtered "for a botched civilization" in *Hugh Selwyn Mauberley*
(1920) and Eliot's monumental allegory of postwar Europe as a waste
land where parched spirits strain toward "dry thunder without rain"
memorialize a blasted civilization in which no consolation survives
beyond the art of the poem.

The "tinselly" Clarissa, who has lost no one very close to her in the
war, seems an unlikely candidate for renovating the elegy, yet her three
major portrayals—*The Voyage Out* (1915), "Mrs. Dalloway in Bond
Street" (1923), *Mrs. Dalloway* (1925)—link her intimately with the
genre.[12] The 1915 Clarissa tells Rachel Vinrace that as a girl she "sobb[ed]
over" "Adonais": " 'He has outsoared the shadow of our night,/Envy and
calumny and hate and pain— . . ./Can touch him not and torture not
again/From the contagion of the world's slow stain,' " she recites. "How
divine!—and yet, what nonsense! . . . I always think it's *living*, not dying,
that counts" (*VO* 58, cf. *M* 42–43). If every loss awakens every earlier loss
back to the first loss of the mother, the glamorous Clarissa—a substitute
for Rachel's dead mother—embodies the elegy's very principle: the necessity of relinquishing the dead and of forming new attachments in order to
carry on with life.[13] Rachel's death dramatizes this lesson's failure, but
Clarissa's deft critique reclaims the earthly solaces that "Adonais" sacrifices in its uncannily prophetic, near-suicidal closing ecstasy to urge
Rachel toward fresh woods and pastures new.[14]

In "Mrs. Dalloway in Bond Street," Clarissa steps into the glorious
June morning to Big Ben's "solemn," "stirring" strokes and reflects that
her fellow Londoners are "not all bound on errands of happiness. . . .
How people suffered" (*CSF* 152). Again "Adonais" is her touchstone as
she thinks of one friend's son, killed in the war, and another's death: "And
now can never mourn—how did it go?—a head grown grey . . . From the
contagion of the world's slow stain . . . have drunk their cup a round or
two before" (*CSF* 154, ellipses in original). But now she herself fights
despair as she quests for perfect gloves through London's glittering "contagion." She almost weeps to see, upright and immobile in her carriage,
her idol, ancient Lady Bexborough, said to be "sick of it all"; later she
quells an impulse to send the shopgirl, who looks "tired" and "twenty
years older," on holiday: "Selling gloves was her job. She had her own sorrows quite separate, 'and now can never mourn, can never mourn,' the
words ran in her head. 'From the contagion of the world's slow stain,' . . .

for there are moments when it seems utterly futile" (*CSF* 156–58). The floating predicate "and now can never mourn" dissolves the shop girl's "separate" sorrows in the submerged pool of common, unconsoled grief beneath Clarissa's thoughts:

> Lady Bexborough, who opened the bazaar, they say, with the telegram in her hand—Roden, her favourite, killed—she would go on. But why, if one doesn't believe? For the sake of others, she thought. . . . For one doesn't live for oneself. . . . Fear no more she repeated. There were little brown spots on her arm. And the girl crawled like a snail. Thou thy worldly task hast done. Thousands of young men had died that things might go on. At last! Half an inch above the elbow; pearl buttons; five and a quarter. (*CSF* 158–59)

Asking why go on, how go on, and for what—what sort of going on is possible after so many senseless deaths—Clarissa, even while enjoying the worldly luxuries of her class, expresses a communal grief and desolation and a longing for solace assuaged by neither Shakespeare's "Home art gone" (from an earlier age of the world's experience) nor Shelley's "divine . . . nonsense."

As the 1923 Clarissa marks the elegiac place vacated by "the moderns," *Mrs. Dalloway*'s working title, *The Hours*, announces its aspiration to public elegy (A New Elegy by Virginia Woolf) by echoing Shelley's apostrophe to the "sad Hour" of Keats's death:

> rouse thy obscure compeers
> And teach them thine own sorrow, say: with me
> Died Adonais; till the Future dares
> Forget the Past, his fate and fame shall be
> An echo and a light unto eternity![15]

Materializing these compeer hours in Big Ben's mundane strokes, Woolf adapts Shelley's figure to prose fiction's modernist-realist world through the novel's technical innovation: her "discovery" of how to light up her characters' psyches from within by arraying their interior monologues as a system of "beautiful caves" linked by passageways of common memories and experiences, in which each character's past meets "daylight at the present moment" (*D* 2:263, 30 August 1923). Translating Shelley's personified hours schooled by the Hour of loss into her characters' memory-haunted present, Woolf jettisons plot for the elegy's inward work of mourning and voices communal loss as a polyphony of private griefs: a tapestry of thought and feeling that interweaves all the characters' separate sorrows. Septimus's sublime hallucination of Evans, Rezia's poignant memories of Italy, Doris Kilman's consuming rage, Peter's anguish at losing Clarissa, Clarissa's grief for Sylvia: all summon Hours of loss that present and future cannot, or dare not, forget.

The 1925 Clarissa is first among equals in the compound elegiac subject formed by these "beautiful caves," privileged especially as the mourner of Septimus's death; but through this technique she now represents "all deaths & sorrows" in a way not limited by her limitations.[16] *Mrs. Dalloway*'s genesis in the death of Clarissa's original—a friend of Virginia's youth, Kitty Lushington Maxse (1867–1922)—dramatizes the referential diffusion and psychic mobility by which the elegy makes the death that occasions it encompass "all deaths & sorrows," including the elegist's own (QB 2:87). After Julia Stephen died in 1895, the glamorous and vivacious Kitty had exerted herself to conduct her friend's two young daughters into "good" society and marriages until, after their father's death in 1904, Vanessa and Virginia escaped to Bloomsbury to invent their modern lives and arts. Kitty was particularly severe on Virginia Stephen's artistic ambitions: she "scream[ed] against Bloomsbury," dismissed her writings, condemned her friends ("oh darling, how awful they do look!"), disliked her memoir of her father, and moaned, "Virginia might marry an *author* and they always talk about themselves!"[17] Safe beyond Kitty's Kensington, Virginia recalled having felt herself "a kind of slug" in that "unreal Paradise," with Kitty "like salt" on that "very sensitive snail" (L 1:209, 1 October 1905). But Kitty still animated her memory and imagination. The 1915 Clarissa "is almost Kitty verbatim; what would happen if she guessed?" (L 1:349, 10 August 1908); and when Woolf read of Kitty's death in October 1922, she was at work on the short story sequence begun with "Mrs. Dalloway in Bond Street."[18]

The news brought a flood of ambivalent memories of her old antagonist:

> the day has been spoilt for me—so strangely. . . . I hadn't seen her since, I guess, 1908—save at old Davies' funeral [in 1916], & then I cut her, which now troubles me—unreasonably I suppose. I could not have kept up with her; she never tried to see me. Yet yet—these old friends dying without any notice on our part always . . . saddens me: makes me feel guilty. I wish I'd met her in the street. My mind has gone back all day to her. . . . She got engaged at St Ives. . . . I keep going over this very day in my mind. (D 2:206, 8 October 1922)

Six days later the stories "branched into a novel" as Woolf, instead of attending the memorial service, remembered Kitty from afar:

> now Kitty is buried & mourned by half the grandees in London; & here I am thinking of my book. Kitty fell, very mysteriously, over some

bannisters. Shall I ever walk again? she said to Leo. And to the Dr 'I shall never forgive myself for my carelessness.' How did it happen? Someone presumably knows, & in time I shall hear. . . . I adumbrate here a study of insanity & suicide: the world seen by the sane & the insane side by side. Septimus Smith?—is that a good name?—and to be more close to the fact than Jacob.[19]

Two days later she elaborated this idea: "Sanity & insanity. Mrs D. seeing the truth. S. S. seeing the insane truth. . . . The pace is to be given by the gradual increase of S's insanity. on the one side; by the approach of the party on the other" (*H* 412).

Woolf's curiosity about Kitty's "mysterious" fall persisted: "there's Kitty Maxse falling over the bannisters and killing herself"; "I've heard nothing about Kitty, and couldn't face the memorial service—my black being incomplete. How on earth did it happen?" (*L* 2:573–74, 22, 29 October). Her later recollection that Clarissa "was originally to kill herself, or perhaps merely to die at the end of the party" while "Septimus, who later is intended to be her double, had no existence" may refer to this doubt, since she invented Septimus almost immediately, and nothing in *The Hours* suggests that Clarissa was to die or kill herself.[20] About November 9 Woolf devised the double design that displaces Kitty/Clarissa's death onto Septimus: "All must bear finally upon the party at the end; which expresses life, in every variety & full of conviction: while S. dies" (*H* 415). If Woolf ever settled whether Kitty threw herself downstairs or "merely" died, she did not record it; but in keeping with Sacks's point that the death the elegy mourns is always the elegist's own, her fantasy casts Kitty—hence Clarissa and Septimus—as her doubles. Kitty stands to Woolf (who had twice tried to kill herself) in much the same specular and sacrificial relation as Septimus stands to Clarissa; "S." substitutes for Kitty, Clarissa, and not least, Woolf—the seventh/septimus of eight Duckworth/Stephen children.[21]

Once Kitty died Clarissa could not go on "living" in quite the same way, despite her fictional status and the displacement of her death onto Septimus. Kitty's death shadows the fictional counterpart who survives her:

> did it matter that she must inevitably cease completely; all this must go on without her . . . or did it not become consoling to believe that death ended absolutely? but that somehow in the streets of London, on the ebb and flow of things, here, there, *she survived, Peter survived*, lived in each other, she being part . . . of people she had never met; being laid out like a mist between the people she knew best, who lifted her on their branches as she had seen the trees lift the mist, but it spread ever so far, her life, herself. (*MD* 9, my emphasis)

As her fear that *she must cease* swerves from the normative future condi-
tional (*somehow she would survive*) to the declarative past (*somehow . . .
she survived*), it is as if Clarissa (like Kitty) were already dead, or as if
Kitty were speaking through her; as if Kitty's actual death were converg-
ing grammatically with her afterlife in the 1925 Clarissa; or as if death
were scarcely to be distinguished from life's moment-by-moment vanishing into the past. Or, since *somehow . . . Peter survived* too, as if any ontological distinction between life and death were obscured by the ontological resemblances between absence and death, and between life and its
afterlife in memory, imagination, art. Clarissa and Peter have, after all,
borne each other like mist on their branches through their long mutual
absence, just as one would carry the other if one of them should die, and
just as Woolf carried Kitty in life and after death, in memory and art, in
stories that "branched" upon her death into this elegiac novel. In bringing Kitty back to "life" on a radiant June day that *in fact she never lived*,
Woolf flaunts the elegist's power, invisibly flourishing Clarissa herself in
Escher-like proof of Clarissa's own vision of life-after-death. Through her
art Kitty symbolically survives, spreads ever so far, her life, herself, borne
on in time by those who knew her (including Woolf, who had not seen her
for years and whose art Kitty scorned) and by people she never met,
including the novel's ever widening circles of readers.[22]

But the "beautiful caves" poetics that the 1925 Clarissa bodies forth
transcends sentimental memorial. At once portrait and persona (originally a facial image of the dead as well as a mask through which one
speaks, *EE* 126), she is no longer Kitty verbatim, an object drawn by
Woolf-as-writing-subject, but an image of the deeper, more complex ways
people survive—*or not*—in and through one another. For Woolf can raise
her old antagonist Kitty from the dead only by breathing her own life into
her. Books, she observes in her 1928 Introduction, are "flowers or fruit
stuck here and there on a tree which has its roots deep down in the earth
of our earliest life," so that "the truth" behind fiction's "immense
facades"—"if life is indeed true, and if fiction is indeed fictitious"—would
require "a volume or two of autobiography" (I 197). But is life "true" and
fiction "fictitious"? Is Kitty the inaccessible real behind Clarissa's mar-
moreal "facade"? Or does the novel's modernist poetics, continuous with
its symbolic consolations, debunk the distinction between subject and
object such propositions assume? *How* exactly does Kitty survive transfigured in art, her counsel "it's *living*, not dying, that counts" revived from
beyond the grave?

At stake in these questions is, first, a composite modernist self/other-
portraiture that weaves biography and autobiography, "Kitty verbatim"

and "invented" memories, observed surface and imagined depths, into fiction's "truth," Clarissa. An interfused Kitty/Woolf, dead yet living, absent yet present, a psyche unbounded by even a fictional body, Clarissa is a symbolic subject/object entity that captures as in a hologram the way the historical Woolf lifted the historical Kitty on the branches of her life and art.[23] But its postwar context gives this modernist portraiture deeper resonance. In 1918 Woolf saw her brother Adrian talking with a German prisoner of war and reflected, "The reason why it is easy to kill another person must be that one's imagination is too sluggish to conceive what his life means to him—the infinite possibilities of a succession of days which are furled in him, & have already been spent" (*D* 1:186, 27 August). In this light, her resurrection of Kitty—whom in Julia's stead she had, in a sense, fought for her life—as a Clarissa who somehow survives, blooming on the tree of her author's "earliest life," her infinite possibilities unfurling through the book of her day, marks not just a technical breakthrough but an elegiac act of imagination that intrinsically opposes violence.[24] Against the still unvanquished violence of its postwar moment—everyday death, everyday life, as well as the murderous ethos of war—this modernist narrative poses a counterforce ontological, aesthetic, and ethical, writ small in Clarissa's thoughts on the death of a young man she has never met, writ large in the narrative's luminous divinations of its characters' unfurling lives.

Who Is Sylvia? The Tree of Life/Death/Art

> Hang there like fruit, my soul,
> Till the tree die!
>
> —Shakespeare, *Cymbeline*

> Odd affinities she had with people she had never spoken to, some woman in the street, some man behind a counter—even trees, or barns.
>
> —Woolf, *Mrs. Dalloway*

If Kitty's symbolic resurrection dramatizes a daughter-artist's victory over Conversion-worshipping mothers, Clarissa's dead sister Sylvia figures not the contingent opposition of a Julia, a Kitty, or a German POW but the absolute antagonist death. This feminine vegetation deity, at once naturalized and mythified in Clarissa's figure of consolation, modernizes the pastoral elegy and opposes to the objectifying metaphysics of a war-making society an ontology, or theory of being, that locates being in "Odd affinities"—not discrete "subject and object" (*MD* 153, *TL* 38). Feminine in origin and history but not essence, this metaphysics frames the novel's intersubjective character drawing as a consolation for "poor devils, of both sexes."

Dropping the 1923 allusions to "Adonais," *Mrs. Dalloway's* opening pages follow Clarissa's thoughts from Sylvia (from Latin *silvanus*: forest) to the figure of survival as mist-bearing branches. The phrase *somehow she survived* thus condenses Clarissa with Sylvia, to whose death Peter Walsh traces Clarissa's "atheist's religion"—an aberration from the nationalist religion proper to her "public-spirited, British Empire, tariff-reform, governing-class spirit." Possibly, Peter speculates,

> she said to herself, As we are a doomed race, chained to a sinking ship
> . . . , as the whole thing is a bad joke, let us, at any rate, do our part;
> mitigate the sufferings of our fellow-prisoners . . . be as decent as we
> possibly can. Those ruffians, the Gods, shan't have it all their own
> way,—her notion being that the Gods, who never lost a chance of hurt-
> ing, thwarting and spoiling human lives were seriously put out if, all
> the same, you behaved like a lady. That phase came directly after
> Sylvia's death—that horrible affair. To see your own sister killed by a
> falling tree (all Justin Parry's fault—all his carelessness) before your
> very eyes, a girl too on the verge of life, the most gifted of them,
> Clarissa always said, was enough to turn one bitter. Later she wasn't
> so positive perhaps; she thought there were no Gods; no one was to
> blame; and so she evolved this atheist's religion of doing good for the
> sake of goodness. (*MD* 77–78)

If Peter is right, Clarissa took no solace in providential father-gods or promises of heaven but blamed malevolent "ruffians" and her inept father (if the parenthetical condemnation is hers too), later abandoning this childlike fantasy for a stoic ethics of decency. As her disillusion with father figures originates with Sylvia's death, so do the consolations of her "athe-ist's religion," whose figurative expression seems to have influenced Peter's earlier reverie in Regent's Park. There, longing "for solace, for relief, for something outside these miserable . . . craven men and women," he too imagines a sylvan feminine apotheosis:

> if he can conceive of her, then in some sort she exists, he thinks, and
> advancing down the path with his eyes upon sky and branches he rap-
> idly endows them with womanhood; sees with amazement how . . .
> majestically . . . they dispense with a dark flutter of leaves charity, com-
> prehension, absolution, and then, flinging themselves suddenly aloft,
> confound the piety of their aspect with a wild carouse. (*MD* 57)

Symbolically reborn in Clarissa's and Peter's metaphysical trees of life/death, the Adonis-like Sylvia opposes to sacrificing fathers and father-gods a "figure of the mother whose sons have been killed in the battles of the world"—everyday conflicts and the Great War alike (*MD* 58).

Sylvia, of whom we learn almost nothing, is less a character than a figure of death itself. She is the specter of Clarissa's, the harbinger of Septimus's, the ghost of Kitty's, and also, in this book that flowers on the tree of its author's earliest life, of Julia's and Leslie Stephen's, and (as shocking as Sylvia's) of Stella's at twenty-eight and Thoby's at twenty-six. As the vegetation god of this public elegy, she is also the deaths of the millions destroyed by the war and the prospective deaths that shadow the survivors. Sylvia—all dead sisters, brothers, fathers, mothers, friends, soldiers known and unknown, lost companions of war and peace—is death as the "life" or "truth" behind *Mrs. Dalloway*'s fictional "facade," the mystery of mortality: death as reality, necessity, Ananke, intrinsic to life and nature, to thrushes breaking snails on stones and to the falling tree that fells her.

As death transfigured, Sylvia is also art. As Clarissa transmutes her death and proper name into mist-bearing branches, Sylvia figures consolation's necessarily purely symbolic nature without losing her meaning of natural death. Her name condenses the work of mourning, at once memorializing her and dissolving her into nature's generic matrix: *silvanus* to Sylvia to figural mist-laden branches; dust to Dust to an urn filled with ashes. Her literary name also resonates with Woolf's memory of how Julia Stephen's death "unveiled and intensified . . . perceptions, as if a burning glass had been laid over what was shaded and dormant . . . as if something were becoming visible," "quickening" her thirteen-year-old self so that, desultorily perusing Palgrave's *Golden Treasury* in Kensington Gardens, she was startled to find a poem "instantly and for the first time . . . intelligible. . . . No one could have understood from what I said the queer feeling I had in the hot grass, that poetry was coming true. . . . It matches what I have sometimes felt when I write. The pen gets on the scent."[25] Sylvia is death as the alpha and omega of poetry, art, writing; the *sign* of Julia's, Kitty's, and all the past and future deaths that coalesced to transform stories of shopping, prime ministers, and "Cut flowers" into this modern pastoral elegy.[26]

It is no accident that Sylvia's memory sparks a reverie that takes Clarissa to Hatchard's bookshop window, where, on seeing Shakespeare's "Fear no more" from *Cymbeline*, she wonders, "What was she trying to recover? What image of white dawn in the country" (*MD* 9). The posthumous Kitty/Clarissa evokes the Posthumus (so named because he survived his mother's death at his birth) of *Cymbeline*—the play that inducted the nineteen-year-old scoffer Virginia into the bard's "company of worship-

pers." What she thought the "best lines" in this or perhaps any play, "Imogen says—Think that you are upon a rock, and now throw me again! and
Posthumous answers—Hang there like fruit, my Soul, till the tree die," find
echo in Clarissa's mist-laden branches and Woolf's tree of life hung with
flowers/fruit/books (*L* 1:45–46, 5 November 1901). Envisioning himself as
a tree embraced by his soul Imogen—or perhaps faithful Imogen as a tree
on which his soul hangs "like fruit" till death—Posthumus rejoices in Imogen's awakening from what turns out to be only a sleep, and in his own
release from suicidal despair at the mistaken thought that he has destroyed
her, his "only jewel." Imogen's "Why did you throw your wedded lady
from you?/Think that you are upon a rock, and now/Throw me again"
gently mocks his *fort/da* game. He has foolishly tested and accidentally
"killed" her, discovered his error and wished to die, only to find her miraculously restored: will he throw her again? Literalizing loss restored as only
the romance can, *Cymbeline* reunites Posthumus and Imogen as living
"tree" and "fruit" in deferral ("till the tree die"), if not defiance, of death.[27]

The modernist-realist character Clarissa cannot literally "recover"
what she has lost, but her longing for some "white dawn in the country"
summons pastoral memories of Bourton that recur throughout the day.
The most striking, Sally Seton's kiss—"the most exquisite moment of her
whole life"—she compares to "a present, wrapped up," hers to keep but
not to look at; an indestructible "diamond, something infinitely precious," a "revelation" imbued with "radiance" and "religious feeling"
(*MD* 35–36). Only through memory does Clarissa "recover" her lost
love, burnished with such metaphoric richness as young Virginia found in
Cymbeline. This "present," a gift too precious to unwrap or look at—a
moment once present now past, yet preserved in memory and symbolically "present" again—bespeaks memory's power to conjure lost "jew-
els," make them "present" in dazzling splendor. In other words, *Mrs. Dalloway* adapts Posthumus's consolation for a later age of the world's
experience by rescuing love-lost-and-recovered from the romance's unreal
paradise and relocating it in the symbolic realms of memory, imagination,
and art—where it defeats time and loss more securely than does the
romance of presence Posthumus's very name belies, even as it enacts the
mourner's necessary submission to the reality of loss.[28]

The young Virginia's query as to why *Cymbeline*'s characters "aren't
. . . more human?" foreshadows the mature Woolf's translation of Imogen's survival to Clarissa's realist world (*L* 1:45). Peter recalls how, riding
atop an omnibus, young Clarissa consoled herself for "how little one
knew people" and allayed her "horror of death" by theorizing that
human lives are not bounded in time and space but indefinitely dispersed

through a space/time continuum that extends beyond the organism's apparent life and death:

> she felt herself everywhere; not "here, here, here"; and she tapped the back of the seat; but everywhere. . . . She was all that. So that to know her, or any one, one must seek out the people who completed them; even the places. Odd affinities she had with people she had never spoken to, some woman in the street, some man behind a counter—even trees, or barns. It ended in a transcendental theory which, with her horror of death, allowed her to believe, or say that she believed (for all her scepticism), that since our apparitions, the part of us which appears, are so momentary compared with . . . the unseen part of us, which spreads wide, the unseen might survive, be recovered somehow attached to this person or that, or even haunting certain places after death . . . perhaps—perhaps. (*MD* 152–53, last ellipsis Woolf's)

Clarissa's "transcendental theory" extends Posthumus's tree hung with soul/fruit into a vast arboreal metaphor that augments conscious and/or bodily presence with unconscious experience, memory, and perception—of and by others—such that one's "unseen part" "spreads wide" in space and "might survive" in time, "be recovered somehow attached to this person or that."[29]

The apposition of *survive* with the passive *be recovered* finesses the question of *who* survives, *who* recovers, as it answers Clarissa's longing for some lost "image of white dawn in the country." How can this theory of being palliate a "horror of death" when it renders Clarissa alive scarcely different from Clarisssa dead; confounds life and death, self and other, presence and absence; values memory and imagination over actualities, one's unconscious "unseen part" over conscious "apparition"? Like Clarissa's branches and Peter's arboreal goddess, the passage embeds the theory in its practice. Clarissa's unseen part *already* spreads wide as she rides the omnibus with Peter; *already* she is not (just) "here" where she seems to be, for, as she speaks, her disavowed apparitional "here" detaches itself from accidents of time and place to endure in Peter's memory, "haunting" him in her absence, as now in the narrative present. Her assertion that she is not (only) "here" survives to make her "present"—*here*—to Peter decades later while, on this June day, her apparition busies itself elsewhere with party preparations, thinking of her life's moments as "buds on the tree of life, flowers of darkness" (*MD* 29). The Clarissa who was once (not) "here" on the bus with Peter "survives" "attached" to his later self; is "recovered" in his memory and by the narrative, a diamantine "present" preserved from time, death, loss, absence.

Does it matter that it is Peter, not her apparition, for whom her unseen part survives, or that her apparition must die as surely as Posthumus's tree? Does it matter that their shared moments, once "buds on the tree of life, flowers of darkness," are now memory's "fruits" on the tree of life and *death*? And of art, for the narrative structure on which Peter and Clarissa hang like souls or fruits is founded on this theory of being that branches beyond one's apparition in all directions, indeterminate and unseen. It is not plot that connects Clarissa with Septimus but such odd affinities with "people she had never spoken to" as exist between, say, Adrian—or Woolf—and the German POW. As theorized by Clarissa and practiced in the novel's intersubjective character drawing, odd affinities lift elegiac consolation out of the register of the sentimental to counter the "death of the soul": the atrophy of imaginative powers presupposed, Woolf thought, in the murderousness of war (*MD* 58).

What then of the odd affinity between two strangers and *semblables* at the heart of the book: "Mrs D. seeing the truth. S. S. seeing the insane truth" (*H* 412)? What is its nature and how does it console? One source of Clarissa's feeling "somehow very like" Septimus is her own everyday battle against despair (*MD* 186). Her ontology does not permanently allay her "horror of death" but itself forms part of a rich web of imagery, a very garment of consolation, that she spins out moment by moment as her mind tosses up metaphors (and genius, says Aristotle, is metaphor) that show what life is literally "like" for her.[30] As Peter observes, she "enjoy[s] life immensely"; it is "her nature to enjoy," to be "all aquiver" and "such good company, spotting queer little scenes, names, people from the top of a bus"; she possesses an "indomitable vitality," "a thread of life which for toughness, endurance, power to overcome obstacles, and carry her triumphantly through he had never known the like of" (*MD* 78, 152, 155). Yet her "gift . . . to be; to exist; to sum it all up in the moment as she passed" ceaselessly contends with her dread of death, her feeling that it is "very, very dangerous to live even one day," her everyday fight to affirm that "it's *living*, not dying, that counts" (*MD* 174, 8). This familiar "horror," highlighted in the draft, attacks Clarissa when she hears of Septimus's suicide and imagines his

> dread, that horror, the terror; she felt it too; horror filling her . . . the incapacity to withstand, the overwhelming hostility of the race . . . its vast loneliness, its entire feebleness, . . . so that if Richard had not been there, merely to read the Times aloud; so that listening one could recoup . . . could hear him breathing in the room; could wait like a crouched bird under a leaf; could gradually recover . . . her [?belief[31]]; not in Gods & power, but only in the breath, in the Times, in the fire; & so fanning this little flame, could feel rise within once more the imperious thing. But he had not recovered.[32]

Doubles and mirrors, exemplars of "Sanity & insanity," these two who meet at a party as if death were no unbridgeable divide see the "truth" and alike fight despair. But whereas Clarissa fans her wavering flame back to life, Septimus "had not recovered." Almost nothing separates the suicide displaced onto Septimus from Kitty/Clarissa/Woolf (and perhaps Shelley, with his divine nonsense) from the "divine vitality" Clarissa adores (*MD* 7). In Clarissa, life triumphs; in Septimus, death; but in their redoubled reflection, death-in-life mirrors life-in-death. She, like him, battles despair; he, like her, basks—moments before he leaps—in sanity, happiness, hope.

This is why death comes to Clarissa's party, of all the parties in London: because she can admit it; because she lets it in. Clarissa, that "thoroughgoing sceptic," recognizes the death that arrives uninvited, like Sally Seton, as surely as if Wilkins had intoned its name. Death comes to her party because she (the perfect hostess) can entertain it, a guest and a familiar. Its only seemingly fortuitous arrival clinches the novel's "idea," "*the contrast between life & death*," in an odd affinity: resemblance and difference attenuated, infinitesimal, yet absolute, momentous (*H* 414). He is somehow very like her, borne on her branches with Sylvia and Peter, barns and trees, *a man behind a counter* ("To look at, [Septimus] might have been a clerk," *MD* 84), *a woman in the street.*

We shall return to Clarissa's impromptu elegy for Septimus and the poetry contest it stages between her ontology of odd affinities and the objectifying positivism of the doctors who would "forc[e his] soul," sacrifice him to their "Goddess[es]" Proportion and Conversion (*MD* 184, 100). But first it will be helpful to consider a more vexed affinity between Clarissa and that woman in the street Miss Kilman. Through their contending metaphysics—Clarissa's "atheist's religion" and ruling-class nationalism against Doris Kilman's turn to God and Russia—this postwar elegy stages competing truths and values in a post-theological cosmos in which communities and nations must grapple with their differences and their aggression. Their conflict displays the nationalism and class antagonism that, Keynes warned, threatened Europe's hope of a democratic civilization as it prefigures Freud's postwar writings on the dangers of class oppression and religious "illusion" to Europe's future.

All the Commodities of the World: Miss Kilman *v.* Clarissa Between Keynes and Freud

> I want to criticise the social system, & to show it at work, at its most intense.
>
> —Woolf, *Diary*, 23 June 1923

Miss Kilman . . . got up, blundered off among the little tables, rocking slightly from side to side, and somebody came after her with her petticoat, and she lost her way, and was hemmed in by trunks specially prepared for taking to India; next got among the accouchement sets, and baby linen; through all the commodities of the world, perishable and permanent, hams, drugs, flowers, stationery, variously smelling, now sweet, now sour she lurched; saw herself thus lurching with her hat askew, very red in the face, full length in a looking-glass; and at last came out into the street.

—Woolf, *Mrs. Dalloway*

Hunted out of existence, maimed, frozen, the victims of cruelty and injustice (she had heard Richard say so over and over again)—no, [Clarissa] could feel nothing for the Albanians, or was it the Armenians? but she loved her roses (didn't that help the Armenians?).

—Woolf, *Mrs. Dalloway*

"With another throw of the dice," Clarissa "would have loved Miss Kilman! But not in this world. No" (*MD* 12). Here the "brutal monster" of involuntary hatred lumbers in "that leaf-encumbered forest, the soul," although she knows what she really hates is "the idea of her, which undoubtedly had gathered in to itself a great deal that was not Miss Kilman; had become one of those spectres with which one battles in the night; . . . who stand astride us and suck up half our life-blood, dominators and tyrants" (ibid.). The feeling is mutual. Doris Kilman thinks Clarissa not kind but "merely condescending," from "the most worthless of all classes—the rich, with a smattering of culture," and pictures her turned out of her sofa and installed "in a factory; behind a counter; Mrs. Dalloway and all the other fine ladies!" She violently envies her beauty, elegance, charm, domestic luxury, glamorous social life, adoring husband, and lovely daughter: "If she could have felled her it would have eased her. . . . If only she could make her weep; could ruin her; humiliate her; bring her to her knees crying, You are right! But this was God's will, not Miss Kilman's. It was to be a religious victory" (*MD* 123, 125).

Clarissa's intuition that she hates not Miss Kilman but a "spectre" comprised of "a great deal" else provokes us to inquire into that abstraction of domination and tyranny and so to grasp their class antagonism as a microcosmic cross section of the nationalist conflicts in which Europe's future is indeed at stake. This poetry contest indicts postwar nationalisms that, while pretending to battle external threats to peace and security, in fact *produce* enemies, dominators, and war by an unacknowledged violence within. The dominator-tyrant that Clarissa projects upon Doris Kilman, whose family (then Kiehlman) came from Germany in the eighteenth century, evokes a defeated and still belligerent postwar Germany, thrust like a pariah outside the Allies' international community, while the decadent Clarissa, whom Miss Kilman would reeducate, personifies an England tyrannical in victory and heedless of the political consequences of the international class oppression instituted at Versailles. In facing these women off, *Mrs. Dalloway* explores the competition, envy, hatred, and aggression between classes and nations that had already engulfed Europe in war and would slowly rise to a boil again in the 1920s and 1930s.

Doris Kilman, indeed, bodies forth Keynes's warning that the economic sanctions imposed by the Peace could only provoke another war. By the time Woolf wrote *Mrs. Dalloway*, her old friend Maynard had gained world fame by his critique of the Allies' war reparations policy as a punitive, barbaric, and self-destructive holdover of nationalism.[33] Participating as a British Treasury officer in the Paris Peace talks, he had resigned in protest in May 1919 and retreated that August to Vanessa Bell's country house (near Monks House, which the Woolfs had just taken), to write *The Economic Consequences of the Peace*, published that December. Keynes had urged the Allied leaders to embrace internationalist policies that would promote Europe's welfare as a whole, not enrich some nations at others' expense. Instead they instituted what he diagnosed as the "abhorrent and detestable" policy of a backward-looking "old man" who sees only the rivals France and Germany, not "European civilization struggling forwards to a new order" nor "humanity . . . at the threshold of a new age" (*ECP* 225, 36). An instrument of nationalist rivalry, the Versailles Treaty would, he predicted, "sow the decay of the whole civilized life of Europe" by "reducing Germany to servitude for a generation," "degrading the lives of millions of human beings," and "depriving a whole nation of happiness" (*ECP* 225).

Keynes, in short, prophesied not just the economic consequences of the Peace—"actual starvation" of "the European populations"—but their social, psychic, and political consequences: social unrest, revolution, and ultimately another "civil war" (*ECP* 228, 268). Since Germany's starving peoples would resist a foreign tax not compelled by "their sense of justice or duty" (282), the reparations would incite "vengeance," a "final civil war between the forces of Reaction and the despairing convulsions of Revolution, before which the horrors of the late German war will fade into nothing, and which will destroy, whoever is victor, the civilization and the progress of our generation" (*ECP* 282, 268). Condemning a treaty that violated both "human nature" and "the spirit of the age" and would foment political revolution as surely as Russia's "bloodthirsty philosophers," Keynes urged that "expediency and generosity agree": "the policy which will best promote immediate friendship between nations" would also favor "the permanent interests of the benefactor"—peace, prosperity, the security of Europe's democratic civilization (*ECP* 282, 238).

"Had Keynes's 1919 programme been carried out," Robert Skidelsky writes, "it is unlikely that Hitler would have become German Chancellor."[34] Ignored at Versailles, Keynes dedicated his book to "the new generation," which he sought to influence through "those forces of instruction and imagination which change *opinion*": the "assertion of truth, the unveiling of illusion, the dissipation of hate, the enlargement and instruction of men's hearts and minds" (*ECP* 298, 296–97). In pacifist Bloomsbury, opinion was already with him. *The Economic Consequences of the Peace*, Woolf mused, was "a book that influences the world without being in the least a work of art: a work of morality, I suppose" (*D* 2:33, 24 April 1920).

Works of art too may hope to influence the world. Not for nothing does Miss Kilman possess "a really historical mind" (*MD* 11). Despite her commanding "knowledge of modern history"—"thorough in the extreme"—Doris Kilman has lost her teaching post because of her German ancestry.[35] Deprived of her livelihood, she is a walking allegory of the aggressively aggrieved postwar Germany Keynes tried to forestall. She enters Clarissa's orbit through the kindness of Richard, who has found her "working for the Friends"—presumably, for peace—and, pained by her misfortune, has engaged her to tutor Elizabeth.[36] Miss Kilman reflects on how wartime nationalist paranoia has blighted her life:

> she had never been able to tell lies. Miss Dolby thought she would be happier with people who shared her views about the Germans. She had had to go. It was true that the family was of German origin; spelt the name Kiehlman in the eighteenth century; but her brother had been killed. They turned her out because she would not pretend that the Germans were all villains—when she had German friends, when the only happy days of her life had been spent in Germany! (*MD* 123–24)

An Englishwoman whose brother has, it appears, fought and died for England, Doris Kilman nonetheless finds herself a racialized outcast. Unjustly deprived of her livelihood, she feels "cheated" of her "right to some kind of happiness"—the one kind she can hope for, "what with being so clumsy and so poor" (*MD* 123). Too homely to find happiness in "the opposite sex" (men being in short supply in any case after the war) and too poor to buy "pretty clothes" (anyway, "No clothes suited" her "unlovable body"), she does not hope to "come first with anyone."[37] Still, she might have had the modest happiness of her teaching post—a vital social world, a secure if small income, the intellectual satisfactions and social place for which her degree and "more than respectable" expertise in "modern history" qualify her—had not her fellow English, anticipating both Versailles and Hitler's racialized violence, impoverished and degraded her in her own country (*MD* 132). The spelunking narrator, in short, traces her near-murderous envy of Clarissa not to an essentially tyrannical personality but to a natural resentment of social injuries. Her psychic "cave" illuminates her rage and self-righteousness not as isolated character faults but as a case study of the dynamics of nationalism and class in collective aggression—a fictional animation of Keynes's prophecy that an impoverished Germany would avenge itself on the Allies.

Miss Kilman's history anticipates the theory of human aggression that Freud read out of the "atrocities" and "horrors of the recent World War":

> The . . . truth . . . which people are so ready to disavow, is that men are not gentle creatures who want to be loved, and who at the most can defend themselves if they are attacked; they are, on the contrary, creatures among whose instinctual endowments is to be reckoned a powerful share of aggressiveness. . . . [T]heir neighbour is . . . someone who tempts them to satisfy their aggressiveness on him, to exploit his capacity for work without compensation, to use him sexually without his consent, to seize his possessions, to humiliate him, to cause him pain, to torture and to kill him. [Man is a wolf to man.] Who, in the face of all his experience of life and of history, will have the courage to dispute this assertion?[38]

Aggression and the death instinct, Freud argued, are not pathological aberrations but inherent in human nature and incradicable. Civilization demands that individuals renounce instinctual aggression (murder, cannibalism, incest) as well as submit to moral strictures against lust, avarice, lies, fraud, calumny, and so on; hence every individual is "virtually an enemy" of civilization.[39] Although civilization disarms this hostility with various forms of recompense, its economy of aggression renounced in exchange for benefits is inherently unstable, easily disturbed by social and economic inequities that exacerbate this fundamental discontent.[40] As we noted in chapter 1, Freud, like Keynes, saw class oppression as a formidable threat to Europe's democratic civilization, which could pacify its citizen-enemies only by reasonably equitable sociomaterial rewards.

One especially effective form of recompense, Freud notes, is identification with "cultural ideals," which consoles both oppressed and privileged classes, "since the right to despise the people outside it compensates them for the wrongs they suffer within": "No doubt one is a wretched plebeian, harassed by debts and military service; but, to make up for it, one is a Roman citizen, one has one's share in the task of ruling other nations and dictating their laws" (*FI* 17). So it is for the Londoners ("poor people all of them") who wait swelled with pride by Buckingham Palace for "the Proime Minister's kyar" while dreaming of "the heavenly life divinely bestowed upon Kings" no less than for the already "upright" Clarissa, who "stiffen[s]" further at any manifestation of Empire and sees "character," "something inborn in the race; what Indians respected," in the Palace's "foursquare" architecture (*MD* 12–19, *CSF* 153). So it is for the imperial Lady Bexborough, who "opened a bazaar" with the telegram informing her of her youngest son's death in her hand, and for Mr. Bowley, in whose "British breast" the breeze ruffles "some flag flying" (*MD* 5, 20). And so it ought to be but is not for Doris Kilman. When she loses her livelihood because she cannot pretend that all Germans are villains, England's cultural ideal ceases to be hers (as it has ceased to be international); and her aggression, which the civilization that subjects her is supposed to reward her for renouncing, erupts in a "violent grudge against the world" (*MD* 129).

What prevents Miss Kilman (an "outlaw" and "brigand" in the draft) from acting on her urge to "fell" Clarissa, if not that she is civilized, that she has a conscience (*H* 202)? In Freud's analysis, self-policing "conscience," not external police, is civilization's most powerful weapon against aggressive instincts, which civilization can frustrate but never destroy (*CD* 70). The repository of civilization's prohibitions, conscience absorbs forbidden aggression and redirects it against the self, producing unconscious guilt.[41] By this means civilization transforms its enemies into agents: it restrains each individual's "aggression by weakening and disarming it and by setting up an agency within him to watch over it, like a garrison in a conquered city"—though at the cost of "a loss of happiness" (*CD* 71, 81). While Miss Kilman takes pride in her virtue, "out of her meagre income set[ting] aside so much for causes she believed in," her civilized state—her conscience—has obviously not been bought and paid for by her society (*MD* 125). Even the London poor, the vagrant woman who grins at Richard, the servants to whom Clarissa sends "love" at her parties, let alone the ruling-class Bexboroughs, Dalloways, and prime minister, are better compensated than she (*MD* 165). Yet conscience forbids her to "ease" her "hot and painful" rage and redirects her aggression against herself (*MD* 124). In precise proportion to the fact that she *is* civilized, she is wracked by suppressed and thwarted appetites, envy, self-pity, self-reproach.

For consolation and hope, the aggrieved Miss Kilman turns to "Russia," which helps her to manage homicidal rage without veering into suicidal despair by converting violent envy into ideological aggression against Clarissa and her kind. "With all this luxury," she thinks, looking at Clarissa's Reynolds engraving while imagining a communized Mrs. Dalloway laboring in a shop or factory, "what hope was there for a better state of things?" "She could not help being ugly; . . . Clarissa Dalloway had laughed—but she would . . . think of Russia; until she reached the pillar-box" (*MD* 124, 128–29). "Russia"—an alternative civilization, a more just cultural ideal—sanctions her contempt for such emblems of the old order as Clarissa. Her career "absolutely ruined" by the England for which her brother died, Miss Kilman stands like a powder keg near Russia's still-smoldering revolution (*MD* 130). Her socialist fantasies illustrate Keynes's warning that to bring "economic ruin" upon "great countries" by "political tyranny and injustice" is to foment revolution—thus far forestalled in Central Europe only by its failure to offer any "prospect of improvement whatever" (indeed, for all her misery, Miss Kilman is still in London).[42]

When "Russia" fails, Miss Kilman "th[inks] of God," parodying Marx's attack on religion as palliating the masses' suffering without curing its economic causes (*MD* 124). Her religious practice amounts to a strenuous effort to fortify her conscience against her violent outrage, for "two years three months" after "Our Lord had come to her," her "Bitter and burning" anger remains unappeased. Thoughts of God bring not peace or mystical ecstasy but a holy warrior's righteousness: "Rage was succeeded by calm. A sweet savour filled her veins, her lips parted, and, standing formidable upon the landing in her mackintosh, she looked with steady and sinister serenity at Mrs. Dalloway," savoring imminent "religious victory" (*MD* 124–25). Although her vow to "fight; vanquish; have faith in God" restrains her violence, neither Russia nor religion soothes her "hot and turbulent feelings" or the worldly desires she is too poor, homely, and oppressed to satisfy ("It was the flesh that she must control") (*MD* 124–29).

Abandoned by Elizabeth and assailed by "shocks of suffering," Miss Kilman remains suspended between those strange bedfellows God and Russia as she makes her lonely way through "all the commodities of the world" out of the Army and Navy Stores and into "that other sanctuary, the Abbey," where she kneels in dogged prayer among "reverent, middle class, English men and women, some of them desirous of seeing the wax works" (*MD* 133). The narrative pointedly declines to dissociate God and the soul from commodities, nationalism, and class. Whereas better-fed Londoners find "God . . . accessible and the path to Him smooth," Miss

Kilman, hiding her face in twitching hands, "struggle[s]" "to aspire above the vanities, the desires, the commodities, to rid herself both of hatred and of love, . . . so rough the approach to her God—so tough her desires" (*MD* 133–34). So laboring, she "impresse[s]" the well-fixed Londoners with "her largeness, robustness, and power"—Mr. Fletcher, Mrs. Dalloway, the Rev. Edward Whittaker, "and Elizabeth too" (*MD* 134). Religious warrior, communist sympathizer, unwitting prophet of a humiliated and downtrodden Germany's working-class hero, Miss Kilman in her starved longing "for a better state of things" is a casualty of the nationalist hatreds against which Keynes inveighed. She stands as a small, ominous emblem of the economic ruin of great countries and a portent of revenge tragedy, counterposed to the effaced German elegy—an "ancient song" of "love which prevails"—sung by another "battered woman" in the street at the Regent's Park Tube station.[43]

More striking, finally, than the differences between Clarissa's ineffectual noblesse oblige and Miss Kilman's odious righteousness are their odd affinities. "Miss Kilman would do anything for the Russians, starved herself for the Austrians," thinks Clarissa, in whom luxury has bred a lighter, freer, if not more honest or noble conscience; "she was never in the room five minutes without making you feel her superiority, your inferiority; how poor she was; how rich you were; how she lived in a slum without a cushion or a bed or a rug or whatever it might be, all her soul rusted with that grievance sticking in it, her dismissal from school during the War— poor embittered unfortunate creature!" (*MD* 12). Unlike the aptly named Miss Kilman, who must be very, very good in order not to be positively criminal, the pampered Clarissa has no need of a heavy-duty conscience. She takes her privilege for granted, confuses Armenians with Albanians, tosses threadbare cushions to her servants "in gratitude . . . for helping her to be like this, . . . gentle, generous-hearted," and rides the coattails of Richard's social conscience from the haven of her sofa.[44] Claiming to wish "everybody merely to be themselves," she yet finds the idea of praying shut up in a room "nauseating," and she is "really shocked" by the glowering Miss Kilman: "This a Christian—this woman! This woman had taken her daughter from her! She in touch with invisible presences! Heavy, ugly, commonplace, without kindness or grace, she know the meaning of life!" (*MD* 125–26, 117). Yet hardly does she project on her "the power and taciturnity of some prehistoric monster armed for primeval warfare" than "hatred (which was for ideas, not people) crumble[s]" and Clarissa laughs in relief to see her "los[e] her malignity" and become "merely Miss Kilman, in a mackintosh, whom Heaven knows Clarissa would have liked to help" (*MD* 126).

For her part, Miss Kilman's conscience is weighty in proportion to the mass of rage it has had to absorb and find some nominally civilized alibi for. In truth she would far rather resemble than despise Clarissa, and if she did, she would not need the righteousness that weighs her down: "she minded looking as she did beside Clarissa. . . . But why wish to resemble her? . . . She despised Mrs. Dalloway. . . . Her life was a tissue of vanity and deceit. Yet Doris Kilman had . . . very nearly burst into tears when Mrs. Dalloway laughed at her" (*MD* 128). As the ur-Clarissa reflects, "All men were brothers. For that very reason, one must hate some of them, as one hated part of oneself" (*H* 271). As Clarissa glimpses her role in creating the monster she mistakes for Miss Kilman, Miss Kilman admits her secret wish to be like this woman she pretends has no virtues. No one wins this contest, but it shows that insofar as Miss Kilman is a monster, she is one created by the social system—a casualty of an economic war between the wars, a mute witness to Britain's unacknowledged tyranny.

Bringing the War Home: Message, Madness, "The Birth of a New Religion"

> Was there, after all, anything to make a passer-by suspect here is a young man who carries in him the greatest message in the world, and is, moreover, the happiest man in the world, and the most miserable?
>
> —Woolf, *Mrs. Dalloway*

Is Septimus Warren Smith mad or does he have a message? That he is mad would seem indisputable; even sympathetic discussions cast him as a war victim not a prophet.[45] Yet *Mrs. Dalloway's* postwar world of multifarious and contested realities pits Septimus's reality against that of his doctors to frame "madness" as censored truth. If, as Michel Foucault argues, civilization disciplines madness to suppress its truths, art recaptures truths branded madness to confront the world with the necessity of change: "by the madness which interrupts it, a work of art opens a void, a moment of silence, . . . where the world is forced to question itself. . . . [T]he world finds itself arraigned by that work of art and responsible before it for what it is."[46]

Mrs. Dalloway's opening scenes frame this contestation of a multiplicitous reality as an outworn monotheism confronts an immanent modernist cosmos. Clarissa's cutting-edge metaphor "another throw of the dice" is way ahead of Einstein's mistaken objection, "God does not play dice," in the 1926 controversy over Born and Heisenberg's quantum theory.[47] In *Mrs. Dalloway's* cosmos God does not play dice, for God does not exist. Fate plays dice. As the infinite possibilities that ride the crest of time collapse moment by moment into events, fate is arbitrary, time irreversible, disaster, suffering, and death inevitable if also unpredictable, and promises of heaven obsolete. Old transcendences metamorphose into an airplane swooping "like a skater . . . or a dancer" to leave an advertising slogan in a melting trail of smoke.[48] No two groundlings whose caves meet "daylight" at this moment read this celestial sign in quite the same way. " 'Glaxo,' said Mrs. Coates in a strained, awe-stricken voice"; " 'Kreemo,' murmured Mrs. Bletchley, like a sleep-walker"; "It's toffee," murmured Mr. Bowley; "So, thought Septimus, . . . they are signalling to me"; "Hadn't Mrs. Dempster always longed to see foreign parts?"; "a bright spark; an aspiration; a concentration; a symbol (so it seemed to Mr. Bentley, vigorously rolling his strip of turf at Greenwich) of man's soul; of his determination . . . to get outside his body, beyond his house, by means of thought, Einstein, speculation, mathematics, the Mendelian theory" (*MD* 20–28). Meanwhile, the earthbound counterpart of this heavenly sign, the inscrutable state motorcar ("probably the Queen, thought Mrs. Dalloway"), stops traffic in Bond Street with a loud backfire—a parodic "voice of authority" that rouses "the spirit of religion," "her eyes bandaged tight and her lips gaping wide" (*MD* 16, 14). Stirring nationalist piety in bystanders of every class, this blind spirit of monarchy and monotheism constellates an aleatory community of spectators marveling at manmade miracles, even as transcendence falls into immanence, revelation into high-tech marketing stunts, cathedrals into waxworks, divinely invested monarchs into a blank though "enduring symbol" of England's "majesty" (*MD* 16). Loss of monovocal authority becomes gain as the weird enchanting harmonies of irreducible differences surround and displace the totalizing "spirit" in their midst.

Freud's meditations on Europe's future in *The Future of an Illusion* and *Civilization and Its Discontents* illuminate the contending poetries, or metaphysics, of Miss Kilman's religious belief, England's nationalist religion, Clarissa's stoic atheism, and, not least, Septimus's war experience. Consigning religion—"perhaps the most important item in the psychical inventory of a civilization," without which many feel life would be intolerable—to humanity's childhood, Freud advocates an "*education to reality*" (*FI* 18, 81). Such an education would teach that sexuality and aggression are profound and ineradicable human instincts; that civilization must continually be fought for in the unceasing "battle of the giants" Love and Death for "world-dominion"; and that creative endeavors to make life "tolerable for everyone and civilization no longer oppressive to anyone" console for the renunciations civilization demands better than can illusions of a heavenly afterlife (*CD* 69, *FI* 82). The European religions, he complains, depict a cosmos so lacking in rationality and realism as to reduce believers to childish credulity. They falsely soothe an infantile "need for a father's protection" from sufferings inflicted by nature and humanity, exacerbate unconscious aggression and guilt by holding up impossible ethical ideals such as the Golden Rule, and foster hopes of "Heaven" that promote passivity and dissipate creative energies (*CD* 19, *FI* 82n). An "education to reality," by contrast, would emphasize science, which subjects its accounts of reality to empirical verification, and art, which claims no transcendent authority. People so educated would find consolation in scientific understanding of the world and in such pleasurable pursuits as relationships, thought and creativity, power to act in and change the world, nature, beauty, and art. Freed from religion's "bitter-sweet . . . poison," humanity would grow up: it would abandon fantasies of a beneficent Providence, accept its helpless and insignificant place in the cosmos, resign itself to fate (those aspects of life not susceptible of change), and direct its "liberated energies" toward improving life for all here and now, leaving "heaven to the angels and the sparrows" (*FI* 81–82 and n).

When Freud speculated that the "experiment of an irreligious education" might yield "hope for the future," a "treasure" to "enrich civilization," his English publisher—a daughter of agnostics educated at home not in institutions long steeped in Church sponsorship—had already created such treasures.[49] The skeptic Clarissa and the scapegoat Septimus dramatize the power of art, thought, and imagination to grapple with reality and console for loss in this late age of the world's experience when "simply one doesn't believe . . . any more in God"; and the novel's odd-affinities ontology and immanent cosmos anticipate Freud's this-worldly philosophy (*CSF* 153). At the crossroads between modern Europe's (first) civil war and its uncertain future, Freud's meditations on the aggression that threatens civilization from within resonate with Septimus's message; and his advocacy of art, philosophy, and science over religious "illusion," with Clarissa's arduous belief that "life"—though poised over an abyss, unwatched by any Providence, unredeemed by any heaven—is "enough" (*MD* 121–22).

Never spoken in so many words, Septimus's message exists as a depth charge in his character, story, and fate. A prophetic witness to the aggression instinctive in human nature and ineradicable from European civilization, he brings the war home in his very person. He not only exposes his fellow citizens' "really fearful . . . 'settling down' " as if the war had never been, as Katherine Mansfield put it; he brings the war home as *their war, their violence,* which they disavow in a contestation of reality to the death.[50] Tortured by the memory of Evans blown to bits before his eyes, confessing that he has "committed a crime," besieged by guilt at being alive but unable to feel, Septimus entertains the possibility "that the world itself is without meaning" (*MD* 88). To salvage its *meaning*, he tries to attest to the collective murder his civilization has commissioned from him, to offer a "truth" on which to rebuild civilization more lastingly. While Sir William Bradshaw and Dr. Holmes—gatekeepers of a society strategically blind to its own violence—pathologize his reality as "the deferred effects of shell shock," he tries to "tell the whole world"; when that fails, he acts out his "astonishing revelation" through his sacrificial death (*MD* 183, 70). Although Septimus loses his life in this poetry contest, *Mrs. Dalloway* captures his "truth" for the real-world contest between Love and Death that art, like Keynes's "moral book," may aspire to influence.

Septimus too is an elegiac consciousness. Despite his overwhelming grief, he is not inconsolable but struggles in his own way to survive his message—to communicate it without going insane in the elegiac progress toward life and the future that his suicide interrupts. Since his "brain [i]s perfect"—he can read the *Inferno* and add up his bill—he surmises that "it must be the fault of the world" that "he could not feel" (*MD* 88). Yet he does feel extremes of ecstasy and pain as his wavering gaze takes in the ravishing phenomenal world, its breathtaking beauty intensified in proportion to his devastation. He is amazed to tears by the mysterious "smoke words languishing and melting in the sky and bestowing upon him in their inexhaustible charity and laughing goodness one shape after another of unimaginable beauty and signalling their intention to provide him, for nothing, for ever, for looking merely, with beauty, more beauty!" (*MD* 21–22). Everything sings to him: Evans sings "from behind the tree," sparrows sing in Greek, the word *time* "split[s] its husk," Rezia's voice lapses into "contented melody," sounds make "harmonies with premeditation," even silence sings, "the spaces between . . . as significant as the sounds" (*MD* 70, 69, 146, 22). His rushing thoughts tumble out revelation after revelation. "Scientifically speaking," he theorizes, "the flesh was melted off the world," his body "macerated until only the nerve fibres were left," "spread like a veil upon a rock"; "I have been dead and yet am now alive," he hazards (*MD* 68–69). To his "ode to Time," a pastoral, symbolically reborn Evans sings antiphonally that the dead wait in Thessaly for the war's end when they will return, then suddenly materializes as Peter Walsh on the path: " 'for God's sake don't come!' . . . But the branches parted. . . . It was Evans! But no mud was on him; no wounds. . . . I must tell the whole world, Septimus cried . . . (as the dead man in the grey suit came nearer)" (*MD* 70). Where his insupportable memories meet "daylight," the everyday world splinters into the incandescent visions, music, and poetry that hold him to life.

Paul Fussell documents the chasm between the incommunicable reality experienced by the English soldiers at the front and the sentimental jingoism of civilians in England.[51] Back "home" ("avoid the use of the word home," notes Bradshaw), Septimus's boss, Mr. Brewer, applauds his distinguished war service and promotes him "to a post of considerable responsibility"; Septimus, appalled and revolted by the patriotic lies by which his fellow Londoners transform collective murder into "pleasurable . . . emotion" and himself into a war hero, is diagnosed as mad (*H* 138, *MD* 88). Sir William inquires,

> "You served with great distinction in the War?"
> The patient repeated the word "war" interrogatively.
> He was attaching meanings to words of a symbolical kind. A serious symptom, to be noted on the card.
> "The War?" the patient asked. The European War—that little shindy of schoolboys with gunpowder? Had he served with distinction? He really forgot. In the War itself he had failed.
> "Yes, he served with the greatest distinction," Rezia assured the doctor; "he was promoted."
> . . .
> He had committed an appalling crime and been condemned to death by human nature.
> "I have—I have—," he began, "committed a crime—"
> "He has done nothing wrong whatever," Rezia assured the doctor.
> . . .
> "I—I—" he stammered.
> But what was his crime? He could not remember it.
> "Yes?" Sir William encouraged him. (But it was growing late.)
> Love, trees, there is no crime—what was his message?
> . . .
> "I—I—" Septimus stammered.
> "Try to think as little about yourself as possible," said Sir William kindly. Really, he was not fit to be about.
> . . .
> "Trust everything to me," he said, and dismissed them. (*MD* 96, 98)

Captured and stilled in the work of art, Septimus's stammer interrupts the tanklike momentum of the heroic social script ventriloquized by Rezia and Sir William. Like a vulnerable body before their smoothly rolling sentences, his broken utterances mark a buried reality, the *appalling crime* of war, beside which their supposedly transparent "sane truth" appears unreal and insane.[52]

Septimus's doctors act as agents for a society that scapegoats him for bringing home the murderous aggression it would disavow, that projects its aggression upon him and expels him, its symbolic embodiment, so that he seems to bear it away. But the scapegoat who does not suffer silently turns victimage into prophecy.[53] While Rezia, following doctors' orders, exhorts Septimus to "Look" at the everyday sights in Regent's Park, a different reality absorbs him:

> Look the unseen bade him, the voice which now communicated with him who was the greatest of mankind, Septimus, lately taken from life to death, the Lord who had come to renew society, . . . the scapegoat, the eternal sufferer, but he did not want it, he moaned, putting from him with a wave of his hand that eternal suffering, that eternal loneliness. . . . "Oh look," she implored him. But what was there to look at? A few sheep. That was all. (*MD* 25–26)

What are a few sheep to a scapegoat "come to renew society"?—

> the lord of men . . . called forth in advance of the mass of men to hear the truth, to learn the meaning, which now at last, after all the toils of civilisation—Greeks, Romans, Shakespeare, Darwin, and now himself— was to be given whole to . . . "To whom?" he asked aloud. "To the Prime Minister," the voices which rustled above his head replied . . . these profound truths which needed, so deep were they, so difficult, an immense effort to speak out, but the world was entirely changed by them forever. (*MD* 67)

From his scapegoat's perspective, Septimus's premonition of the "birth of a new religion" (or an old one always in need of rebirth) is sane (*MD* 23). If the world could avow its violence, would it not be radically altered, redeemed from its lies, filled with the power to atone for and even renounce it? Meanwhile, his doctors—civilization's well-compensated disciplinarians—seek to ensure that the scapegoat stays a victim: "when a man . . . says he is Christ . . . & has a message, . . . society appoints the doctor to shut him up till he is cured. . . . Sir William not only prospered himself but saw to it that England should prosper too" (*H* 149–50, cf. *MD* 99). Making rounds in his sleek motorcar with his wife nestled in silvery furs, Bradshaw is "the judge, the saviour, the super man, in whose hands powers of life & death were lodged, torture, isolation; the great gaoler; the heavy compassionate man, who had seen so much of this sort of thing, made an excellent after dinner speech, & was at the top of his tree" (*H* 142). As Bradshaw lists reasons why Septimus must not kill himself ("King George . . . duty, & self-sacrifice, & humour & courage & the family"), Septimus muses on the oil portrait of Lady Bradshaw over the mantelpiece and Bradshaw's income of "£10,000 a year" and objects, "But life . . . offers no such bounty to us . . . And perhaps there is no God. [Sir William] shrugged his shoulders" (*H* 154). Having "devour[ed] "Shakespeare, Darwin, *The History of Civilization*, and Bernard Shaw," Septimus grasps his meaning: the "whole world was clamouring: Kill yourself, kill yourself, for our sakes" (*MD* 85, 92).

Back "home," in short, Septimus is fated to know "everything," to grasp "the meaning of the world," and to bear the burden of witness to his civilization's unimaginable violence without being driven mad (*MD* 66). "The War had taught him," for example, "the message hidden in the beauty" of even Shakespeare's words, sacred text of the civilization he went to war to "save":

> The secret signal which one generation passes, under disguise, to the next is loathing, hatred, despair. Dante the same. Aeschylus (translated) the same. . . . [H]uman beings have neither kindness, nor faith, nor charity. . . . They hunt in packs . . . scour the desert and vanish screaming into the wilderness. They desert the fallen. . . . Brewer at the office, . . . brutality blared out on placards; men were trapped in mines; women burnt alive; and once a maimed file of lunatics . . . ambled and nodded and grinned past him. . . . And would *he* go mad? (*MD* 86, 88–90)

Lone witness to a reality that everyone around him denies, Septimus fends off madness even as this incommunicable reality consumes the mundane world. Beckoning airplanes, whispering trees, birds speaking Greek, Evans cleansed and whole—all threaten to "sen[d] him mad. But he would not go mad. He would shut his eyes; he would see no more" (*MD* 22).

Septimus's "insane truth" is still truth, in face of which "not to be mad would amount to another form of madness."[54] He suffers, owns, and tries to bear witness to his civilization's "appalling crime" but is finally forced to reenact it through a death that he *expects to be read*—a death that he offers as a gift and that the narrative insulates from dismissal as madness. Bathed in the light of his last afternoon, he tests his sanity, looking cautiously at objects in his room and finding with relief that "None of these things moved. All were still; all were real"; "He would not go mad" (*MD* 142). He does "not want to die":

> why should he kill himself for their sakes?. . . . Besides . . . there was a luxury in it, an isolation full of sublimity; a freedom which the attached can never know. Holmes had won of course. . . . But even Holmes . . . could not touch this last relic straying on the edge of the world, this outcast, who gazed back at the inhabited regions, who lay, like a drowned sailor, on the shore of the world. (*MD* 92–93)

The sun feels hot, life good, the future full of possibilities that emerge in miniature in the hat he and Rezia, laughing together "like married people," create for Mrs. Peters (*MD* 143). Now the world's found order ("Mrs. Peters had a spiteful tongue. Mr. Peters was in Hull") seems not so "terrible"; his writings and drawings seem "insane. all about death, nightingales"; his fear of "falling down, down into the flames!" ("Actually [Rezia] would look for flames, it was so vivid") momentarily abates: "Miracles, revelations, agonies, loneliness, falling through the sea, . . . all were burnt out, for he had a sense, as he watched Rezia trimming the straw hat . . . of a coverlet of flowers" (*H* 313, *MD* 141–43). He foreknows that he must sacrifice his elegiac progress, perform the revelation no one heeds. But, feeling "Every power pour[] its treasures on his head" as his heart sings "Fear no more," he delays "till the very last moment" the death in which two realities converge: the suicide his society demands and, as Clarissa somehow divines, "an attempt to communicate" (*MD* 139, 149, 184). He is pushed, yet he also jumps. He frames his death as the antithesis of madness, "an immense effort to speak out" difficult, "profound truths", an offering, a sacrifice, a gift to "human beings": "what did *they* want? . . . 'I'll give it you!' he cried" (*MD* 149). Might recognition of his gift not help refound his civilization on firmer, more lasting ground? If so, is he mad to think that he dies for the sins of the world, dies so that others may live?

Through the artwork that reclaims his death from obscurity, Septimus bequeathes his message to the future. His suicide, pathologized by Sir William and Richard to promote the shell shock bill, is received by Clarissa precisely as a message: "defiance," a breathtaking escape from soul-destroying doctors, a Shelleyan "plunge[] holding his treasure" (*MD* 184, cf. *H* 386, where Shelley's name appears). In her spontaneous private elegy for him, his death inversely mirrors her life. Echoing "Adonais," she reflects that the living "would grow old," he never. By flinging his life away he has preserved "a thing . . . that mattered," something "defaced, obscured in her own life," lost "every day in corruption, lies, chatter" (*MD* 184). In opposing truth/treasure/death to lies/corruption/life, Clarissa confronts her own Conversion—her compromised treasure, Sally's kiss. Channeling her own rage and grief into social contestation, she indicts Sir William as Conversion's agent—"a great doctor yet to her obscurely evil, without sex or lust, extremely polite to women, but capable of some indescribable outrage—forcing your soul"; such men "make life intolerable" (*MD* 184–85).

We shall return in a moment to the sexual crises Clarissa's language evokes. Now her anger turns inward as existential "terror," an "awful fear" of having wasted her life, seizes her: "it was her disaster—her disgrace . . . her punishment. . . . She had schemed; she had pilfered. She was never wholly admirable. She had wanted success. Lady Bexborough and the rest of it. And once she had walked on the terrace at Bourton" (*MD* 185). At last she makes peace with her own defection from love's "sublimity" as the price of the life with Richard that she simply likes and, accepting this reality, glimpses her survival and future in the old woman in the window opposite (*H* 186). Rising like a sylvan goddess in her green dress, Clarissa concludes her small elegy with Septimus's fate and her own in equipoise:

> she did not pity him. . . . Fear no more the heat of the sun. . . . She felt somehow very like him . . . glad that he had done it; thrown it away. The clock was striking. The leaden circles dissolved in the air. He made her feel the beauty; made her feel the fun. But she must go back. (*MD* 186)

Elegy's brutal principle of substitution dictates the emotional logic by which the unknown young man's death helps Clarissa to embrace life, beauty, fun, her party, all her consolations in face of time and inexorable loss—"That's what I do it for" (*MD* 121). Her elegiac progress repeats in small her navigation from Sylvia's death through perilous grief and rage to the existential consolation simply "that one day should follow another," that she should "wake up in the morning; see the sky; walk in the park; meet Hugh Whitbread; then suddenly in came Peter; then these roses; it was enough" (*MD* 122).

If Clarissa's elegy for Septimus is inadequate to arraign the world before the truths it brands madness, *Mrs. Dalloway* captures his message within its fictional bounds for the actual world beyond them. Not Clarissa but we readers receive (or not) the message of Septimus's death, the costs of the war he names a "crime," the measure of what his life means to him, the infinite possibilities of his unfurling days. Meanwhile, Clarissa reflects on her Conversion, acknowledges loss, and affirms the consolations that reward the elegist's exigent bowing to reality. Let us now return to Clarissa's brief flare of rage at Sir William, which illuminates the protagonists' elegiac doubling as a splitting of authorial voice into the sane survivor and the insane war veteran whom Woolf created partly out of herself: "S's character. founded on R[upert Brooke?]? . . . or founded on me? . . . might be left vague—as a mad person is . . . so can be partly R.; partly me" (*H* 418). The novel's genetic text illuminates Woolf's transmutation of her own harrowing "madness," and of the losses, grief, and rage that fueled it, into an elegiac work of art that might influence the world. The

Septimus who is partly Woolf, these manuscript traces suggest, dies not only for his society's "crime" of war but also for the violence that its ruling "father[s]" visit upon women.

Sex, Lies, and Selling Out: Women and Civilization's Discontents

> (a delicious idea comes to me that I will write anything I want to write).
>   The truth?—was Harley Street founded on the truth? . . .
>   . . .
>   . . . [S]he was almost inclined to tell him about her brother, except
> that she was almost killed her brother [denied once that she] told a lie
> once about her brother. & would have done so, had it not seemed *mar-*
> *gin*: never let on that her brother was not
> —Woolf, *The Hours*

These words belong to a draft sequence that leads from Rezia's despairing thoughts in Harley Street to Lady Bruton's luncheon. The London medical establishment's "truth" forcibly embraces a "miserable rag & relic" of a soul who comes "fluttering . . . bereft of shelter, shade, or refuge, naked, defenceless," to suffer "the terrific stamp of Sir Williams rage. He swooped; he devoured. . . . Such decision, combined with humanity, . . . endeared Sir William greatly to the relations of his victims" (*H* 155, cf. *MD* 99–101). No reader of Woolf's letters about her incarceration in a home for the insane could fail to sense here the remembered "mad . . . me" on whom she drew for Septimus nor the "raging furnace" of feelings about "madness and doctors and being forced" that she "kept cooling in [her] mind" for years before she could "touch it without bursting into flame all over."[55] Refracting Septimus's war traumas through her experiences of the social system in action, Woolf discloses and disguises the tangled sources of "madness" in familial and societal dynamics, including her Duckworth half brothers' incestuous abuse, the reactions of family, friends, and doctors to this history, her relations' power over her incarceration, and the pressures of "Proportion" and "Conversion" (*MD* 100). In *The Hours* Septimus, like Woolf's "mad . . . me," hears nightingales sing Greek, Philomela's incestuous violation retooled to his war experience: "Evans was a Greek nightingale . . . & now sang this ode, about death . . . 'And so I reached Greece'; where he joined the poets, in Thessaly" (*H* 66). In *Mrs. Dalloway* nightingales become sparrows singing "in voices prolonged and piercing in Greek words, from trees in the meadow of life beyond a river where the dead walk, how there is no death" (*MD* 24–25). Yet Septimus never ceases to be "partly" the ghost of that "me" who signed herself "Sparroy" to Violet Dickinson—one friend who could grasp a "truth" that might as well have been Greek to the society that exalted George Duckworth.[56]

In creating a war veteran "partly" out of that former "me," Woolf foreshadows *Three Guineas'* analysis of the war at home, the abuses of women under the social law of masculine and heterosexual privilege. In *The Hours* and *Mrs. Dalloway*, women's telling of truth and lies dramatizes their negotiations of elegiac inheritance, sexuality, and social law in a civilization being rebuilt, perhaps, on firmer ground. As Sacks observes, the critical question of communal inheritance from the dead implicates the mourners' sexuality psychically and legally. The old crises of narcissism and sexuality that mourning awakens, inheritance must somehow resolve. Through same-sex attractions, intimations of incest and madness, and conversion dramas, *The Hours* and *Mrs. Dalloway* expose the systemic social violence that governs inheritance, dictates the mourner's sexuality, and provokes the violent energies that the elegy diverts from tragic enactment into social critique. More specifically, women must choose between challenging social law and submitting to it in exchange for socioeconomic rewards. Submission to the Goddess of Conversion, as Clarissa knows, entails lies—silences, omissions, censorship. Thus Lady Bradshaw has "gone under" fifteen years earlier: "a nervous twitch" signals something "really painful to believe—that the poor lady lied"; and Clarissa contrasts Septimus's uncorrupted "treasure" with her youthful passion for Sally, renounced and now obscured by "lies, corruption, chatter," as she consoles herself with the pleasures her bargain has bought her (*MD* 100–1). This recognition—her legacy from Septimus—weighs conversion's advantages against its costs: "she did not pity him"; she too has felt, "if it were now to die 'twere now to be most happy' "; still, life is enough (*MD* 186, 184, 35).

Mrs. Dalloway depicts a social system in which sexual desire and practice often diverge from law and publicity. Founded, as Freud points out, on the suppression of women's desire, civilization *sanctions*—punishes yet permits—incest and same-sex desire: "incest is anti-social and civilization consists in a progressive renunciation of it" (1897); "we may justly hold our civilization responsible for the spread of neurasthenia" (1898).[57] As Freud explains the contradiction, the incest taboo imposes "perhaps the most drastic mutilation" of erotic life that civilization exacts; for this reason it is incompletely renounced in modern society. Although civilization polices sexuality as if it were a subject people—it fears revolt, enacts strict precautions, and inflicts "serious injustice" by dictating "a single kind of sexual life for everyone"—it cannot actually enforce its prohibitions and so must "pass over in silence many transgressions which, according to its own rescripts, it ought to have punished" (*CD* 51–52). When Clarissa judges Sir William "obscurely evil, without sex or lust, extremely polite to women, but capable of some indescribable outrage," her specific exclusion of "sex or lust" in a context that has not raised any such issue invisibly flags a ghost of Woolf's "mad . . . me" who survives the doctor's dead patient. In *The Hours* Clarissa's owning of Septimus's death as her disaster and disgrace leads to a vehement vow to "fight Sir William Bradshaw. . . . She must go back; breast her enemy. . . . Never would she submit—never, never!" (*H* 398–99). Later excised, this rather uncharacteristic flare-up of social conscience alerts us to other scattered and muted deflections of violated sexuality in both texts, traces of Woolf's own negotiation of social law in the course of writing the novel.

Hard on the heels of the doctor so esteemed by his victims' relations, *The Hours* portrays Hugh Whitbread, who regularly brings his wife, Evelyn (frequently visited by Clarissa "in a nursing home"), to London "to see doctors" (*MD* 6). A freehand portrait of the incestuous George Duckworth, the "admirable Hugh" captures his smug prosperity, sartorial magnificence, "little job at Court," and the "scrupulou[s] little courtesies & old fashioned ways" that have kept him "afloat on the cream of English society for fifty-five years"—just George's age in 1923.[58] Although Hugh is one of the few characters into whose psychic cave the narrator does not venture, the ur-narrator hints sardonically at what his impeccable facade conceals: "a little information about the subconscious self & Dr Freud had leaked into him"; "He had heard of Freud & Stravinsky. . . . His affections were understood to be deep"; "one or two humble reforms to his credit" include his undersigning of many long "letters on girls & stamp out . . . nuisances [*sic*]," "nor did any girl lose her place in his household without being kept sight of" (*H* 156–57). *Mrs. Dalloway* leaves all this on the cutting-room floor, substituting a double entendre ("malicious" rumors that Hugh "now kept guard at Buckingham Palace, dressed in silk stockings and knee-breeches, over what nobody knew") and an oblique note that "servant girls had reason to be grateful to him" (*MD* 103).

The ur-narrator now hands off Hugh, swathed in innuendo, to Lady Bruton's secretary, Milly Brush, who is so irritated by his inquiries after her brother that "she was almost inclined to tell him about her brother, except that she was almost killed her brother [denied once that she] told a lie once about her brother. & would have done so, had it not seemed *margin*: never let on that her brother was not" (*H* 157). Was the ur-Milly Brush almost killed [by] her brother, or did she almost kill him—or, as her self-interfering grammar suggests, both? What does she deny/lie about, deny lying about, and/or never let on about? Who or what was or is her brother, or was/is he not? *Mrs. Dalloway's* narrator affects not to know, indeed, tells us less: Hugh always asks after her "brother in South Africa, which, for some reason, Miss Brush . . . so much resented that she said 'Thank you, he's doing very well in South Africa,' when, for half a dozen years, he had been doing badly in Portsmouth" (*MD* 103). As the narrative screws down the lid over a site of near-fatal sibling violence, Milly Brush silently mocks her interlocutor with the subaltern's lie.

Nothing in *The Hours* or *Mrs. Dalloway* suggests scattered cinders from Woolf's furnace of white-hot memories more vividly than the narrative convergence of this brother, Milly's incoherent lies, and the George-like Hugh—so solicitous, as it were, of servant girls—in a scene that covertly links the gender dynamics surrounding revelations of sexual violence to women's public speech. The specter of gender-marked "madness" (and familially engineered incarceration) as implements in the social control of "truth" hovers over the ur-Miss Brush, who seems to survive her separate sorrows by sheltering under her powerful employer's wing—a shadowy, diminished double of Lady Millicent Bruton. For her part, Lady Bruton "should have been a general of dragoons" but exhibits her own crippled relation to truth, speech, and social power in her "battle" to compose a letter to the *Times*, for which, feeling "the futility of her own womanhood as she felt it on no other occasion," she finally commandeers the expertise of none other than Hugh (*MD* 105, 109).

Hugh's sleaziness emerges more explicitly in the drama of truth and lies surrounding a rumor that he once kissed Sally Seton in the smoking-room at Bourton. (Innocuous as it sounds, the furor around this incident suggests that, like Richard's kiss in *The Voyage Out*, it stands in for sexual transgressions ruled unspeakable by actual and internalized censors.) Having fled her "intolerable" home for Bourton, the brilliant young rebel Sally educated the "sheltered" Clarissa in "sex . . . social problems . . . life, how they were to reform the world" and "abolish private property" (*H* 43, *MD* 33). In *The Hours* Peter recalls a heated debate on women's suffrage, he and Sally pro, Richard and Hugh con:

> Prostitutes . . . came in; & "the poor women in Piccadilly" she called them; & Hugh flushed, & hitched his trousers up. . . . He said nobody could tell what his mother meant to him. . . . & Sally was down right rude & echoed "your mother of course your mother["] . . . she told Hugh that he represented all that was most detestable in the British middle classes. She considered him responsible for the state of those poor girls. (*H* 76, 86)

Sally, it seems, taxed Hugh with complicity in a social system in which middle- and upper-class men exploit lower-class women to preserve the supposed purity of their disenfranchised mothers, wives, and daughters, and he retaliated by forcing himself on her sexually.[59] Peter's memory is hampered by the fact that "nobody ever knew what happened—it was considered too awful—whether he kissed her or not, merely brushed against her, . . . it had to be hushed up . . . Clarissa murmured something mysterious—but nobody could believe a word against the admirable Hugh, . . . always a perfect gentleman" (*H* 79). At the party Sally confirms the story and adds that Clarissa "Simply laughed" when she went to her "in a rage" (*H* 403). In *Mrs. Dalloway* Clarissa sees "her old friend Hugh, talking to the Portuguese Ambassador," and recalls how Sally accused him "of all people . . . of kissing her in the smoking-room" (that male preserve), so that Clarissa had

> to persuade her not to denounce him at family prayers—which she was capable of doing with her daring, her recklessness, her melodramatic love of being the centre of everything and creating scenes, and it was bound . . . to end in some awful tragedy; her death; her martyrdom; instead of which she had married, quite unexpectedly, a bald man . . . who owned . . . cotton mills at Manchester. And she had five boys! (*MD* 181–82)

Nowhere to be found in the suffrage debate, Clarissa defended Hugh "of all people" by silencing Sally at family prayers, of all places—family piety the cornerstone of a social system that protects men like Hugh by hushing up "truth" in the name of a hypocritical propriety.

Yet in her own mind Clarissa is not simply protecting Hugh but saving Sally from her own reckless idealism—from "awful tragedy," "death," "martyrdom." Her reaction stages the question of what genre shall govern Sally's life: the revenge tragedy that denouncing Hugh to an unjust society that is a father might set in motion? a martyrdom like Septimus's? or an elegiac conversion narrative like her own? Notwithstanding the ur-Clarissa who vows to fight her "enemy" and never submit, Clarissa *has* submitted to social law for the sake of life, beauty, fun. She recoils from the danger of fighting for truth and dictates conversion—lies—for Sally, too. And her influence takes. Sally, "that romantic, that brilliant creature" whose kiss ("a sudden revelation," "an illumination," "the religious feeling!") holds out a protestant alternative to the patriarchal religion of family prayers, and who shares Clarissa's "obscure dread" of marriage ("catastrophe," "doom," "going out to be slaughtered"), marries "a rich . . . cotton spinner" and has "five enormous boys"—a generic outcome that strikes Peter as "a little off the mark" (*H* 80, 47; *MD* 32, 34–35, 171).

The Goddess of Conversion could display no prouder trophy than Lady Rosseter. The bold and visionary Sally suppresses her passion for truth to become a very paragon of conventional prosperous matronhood, amply rewarded by social position, the sexual fulfillment her teeming progeny suggest, and a leisurely country life in which she rarely reads a newspaper. Her conversion affirms Freud's gendered divide between a "civilization" that "has become increasingly the business of men," who sustain it through "instinctual sublimations of which women are little capable," and women's familial and sexual domain, which civilization "force[s] into the background" (*CD* 50–51). Whereas the penniless Sally would "reform the world" on behalf of women and the poor, the complacent Lady Rosseter has converted this claim on her civilization's future into individual salvation through a marriage that indeed spells doom for Sally's "Radical" politics (*MD* 154).

Lady Rosseter's conversion attests to civilization's deep pockets in buying off witnesses to the barbarities within—to some extent, the lying Milly Brush suggests, even that seventh child Virginia, who hid truth behind fiction's "immense facades" in forging her former "mad . . . me" into Septimus. Yet the sibylline testimony of *The Hours* and *Mrs. Dalloway* intimates the ways Woolf's elegiac art mediated the memories of incest, madness, and social law that threatened to immolate her. The genres open to that remembered "me" would seem to correspond roughly to the fates Clarissa pictures for Sally: a tragic death by unjust social law; unsung martyrdom; suicide as an "embrace" or "attempt to communicate"; revenge, or the eruption of grief into murderous rage; elegiac conversion. In transforming that fluttering, bereft, naked, miserable, defenseless rag and relic of a soul into Septimus—one of the most astonishing characters in all of modern literature—Woolf wrests from her losses, grief, and life-threatening rage this work of art: a symbolic inheritance that lays her old self to rest (at least for a time) by bringing her to "life." As Clarissa's small elegy for Septimus is also an elegy for a buried self, Woolf's great postwar elegy for "all deaths & sorrows" enfolds a secret elegy for a self her art resurrects from ignominious death for something like tragedy or martyrdom, barely legible as she is in the work's palimpsest.[60] Septimus—not just his death but the life of suffering and witness that endows its gift—is her monument, a fictional facade over autobiographical truth in a work of art that arraigns its civilization and holds it responsible to itself for what it is. In ventriloquizing her "mad . . . me" through Septimus, Woolf heeds yet eludes the censors—Dr. Savage, Kitty, Julia, George, even perhaps Vanessa—that her fluttering relic of a soul must have heard cry, Kill yourself, for our sakes.

In vanquishing the life-threatening forces that beset her, Woolf, like Clarissa, emerges as an elegist-hero who fights death and the void and returns from the battlefield bearing trophies of consolation, flaunting her powers of survival: "A new [elegy] by Virginia Woolf"; "This is what I have made of it!" (*MD* 43, cf. *EE* 226). A triumph of elegiac conversion, *Mrs. Dalloway* transforms a destroyed "mad . . . me" into a symbolic consolation in which she, disguised as Septimus, poor devil of both sexes, dies for the sins of the world, dies so that others may live. He does not want it. Why "rage and prophesy? Why fly scourged and outcast?" (*MD* 142). Why indeed? Not because he is insane but because the world is; only because the sins and wounds of the world, and its consequent madness and art—not least, this postwar elegy with its arduous celebration of "life"—demand it. No guiltier than anyone else, his only "crime" to have tried to bear (in both senses) witness, Septimus dies for Harley Street's "terrific" institutionalized violence against defenseless souls, for the admirable Hugh's less admirable acts, for Milly Brush's suppressed history, Clarissa's defection, and Lady Rosseter's conversion as well as the Great War and the violent Peace.

But if no one in the novel fully claims the symbolic legacy evoked in Septimus's last words, and if *The Hours* preserves smoldering "truths" that even *Mrs. Dalloway* cannot openly explore, how can anyone think that art might influence the world? What force can art exert toward change, when to fight is out of character for Clarissa, conversion so far the norm that even Sally succumbs, and Septimus's death a silent testimony that leaves even the fictional world unchanged—while the actual world grinds on toward the revenge tragedy for which Versailles set the stage, horrendously enacting Hitler's 1922 vow: "It cannot be that two million Germans should have fallen in vain. . . . No, we do not pardon, we demand—vengeance!"[61]

As powerless as the eloquence of Keynes and Freud to forestall another civil war, Woolf's elegiac art battles alongside them on the side of Love for a future that history had not, in 1925, yet foreclosed. Further, and in keeping with the expansive web of conscious and unconscious being that Clarissa theorizes on the bus, the novel does depict a changing world even if no one seems to be directly changing it. To Peter his dear old civilization seems freer, less repressed and much improved, especially for women. "Newspapers seemed different. Now for instance there was a man writing quite openly in one of the respectable weeklies about water-closets. That you couldn't have done ten years ago" (*MD* 71). As a young man on whose "abstract principles" "the future of civilization" rests, he advocated women's suffrage; now "women's rights" are an "antediluvian topic" (*MD* 50, 73). As he strolls to the party on an evening marvelously lengthened by that postwar innovation "summer time," he delights in the spectacle of beautiful, well-dressed young people and (unlike fellow Anglo-Indians devoted to "biliously summing up the ruin of the world") "more than suspect[s] from the words of a girl, from a housemaid's laughter—intangible things you couldn't lay your hands on—that shift in the whole pyramidal accumulation which in his youth had seemed immovable" and "weighed them down, the women especially" (*MD* 162). Echoing "Mr. Bennett and Mrs. Brown" (1924), which proves by cooks borrowing newspapers and parlormaids trying on hats that "human character" has changed, Peter senses an exhilarating forward motion in postwar civilization that no single life—not his, Sally's, Clarissa's, Septimus's, nor even that of Elizabeth, who would like a profession but is "rather lazy"—can account for.[62] Yet there it is.

Lady Rosseter's conversion, moreover, represents no *final* defeat of Sally's reformist hopes, since *Mrs. Dalloway* also immortalizes Sally, ever streaking Bourton's corridor after her sponge like a modern successor to Keats's beleaguered maiden. And of course art may inspire readers to act upon their social worlds not just by depicting change but by exposing the social system in action. Precisely because its characters defect, convert, fail of speech, die, lie, and "go under," *Mrs. Dalloway* carries the "fight" to rebuild civilization on firmer ground into a future that is always becoming in the wake of the work of art: the future of its readers, whose myriad-minded creativity the skywriting airplane's beholders only suggest. Woolf, meanwhile, triumphed over loss, grief, and maddening rage to reach fresh woods and pastures new—to write her books, found her press, and persevere into the next war as "the only woman in England free to write what I like"—and felt, on finishing her great communal elegy, no longer "inclined to doff the cap to death": "More & more do I repeat . . . 'Its life that matters' " (*D* 3:43, 7–8 and n. 5, 22 September, 8 April 1925). If water closets in respectable weeklies now, perhaps Milly Brush's brother soon? For the moment, *Mrs. Dalloway* embraces the world as it is, letting Milly, Clarissa, Hugh, and Lady Rosseter live while Septimus dies for his civilization's barbarities—the sexual violence buried in this novel's news of the day no less than the war on its front page.

"That's my mother," thought Prue. . . . That is the thing itself.

—Woolf, *To the Lighthouse*

Beautiful pictures. Beautiful phrases. But what she wished to get hold of was that very jar on the nerves, the thing itself before it has been made anything.

—Woolf, *To the Lighthouse*

Hamlet or a Beethoven quartet is the truth about . . . the world. But there is no Shakespeare, there is no Beethoven; certainly and emphatically there is no God; we are the words; we are the music; we are the thing itself.

—Woolf, *Moments of Being*

FIVE

Picture the World
The Quest for the Thing Itself in *To the Lighthouse*

o *the Lighthouse* launches the modernist artist Lily Briscoe on a quest for what she calls "reality," "the thing itself before it has been made anything" (*TL* 193). Impossible on the face of it, this quest ends with the simultaneous completion of Lily's painting and the novel itself—each a portrait of "father & mother & child in the garden" (*D* 3:36, 20 July 1925). In what sense can these family portraits in paint and words fulfill a quest for reality, the thing itself? One answer lies in the way the narrative integrates the modernist aesthetics of painting and novel with the family history and "cosmogony" they capture and dramatize through Lily's creative labor (*TLhd* 24–25). As time passes, the late-summer idyll that enraptures Lily proves to be a fragile world floating above an abyss. The daughter-artist's unfinished painting of "Mrs. Ramsay reading to James" in "The Window" leads to a new struggle to grasp, through thought and memory, the "truth" about this now vanished world founded on loss (*TL* 52). In an abstract composition that mirrors the novel's stark and lovely vision, Lily pictures the world's vast emptiness defied by every creative "attempt": Mr. Ramsay's philosophy, William Bankes's botany, Shakespeare's sonnets, Scott's novels, Augustus Carmichael's poems, the enduring memories Mrs. Ramsay creates—with her servants' help—in those around her, Mrs. McNab's laborious rescue of the neglected house from ruin, the eight Ramsay children ("the best token," their father reflects, "they could give—his wife & himself—that they did not damn the poor little universe entirely"), and Lily's own "vision" (*TL* 147, 208, 80, *TLhd* 115).

In accord with the aesthetics of abstraction that transformed European art in the early twentieth century, Lily's modernist painting aims to depict realities beneath appearances. In seeking such "truth," painting and novel abstract the Western quest romance from the figures of gender that have historically shaped the genre. If Lily seems to be painting Mrs. Ramsay, her daughter's madonna finally reveals neither a fetishized feminine object—a Penelope, Beatrice, Dulcinea, or Molly Bloom—nor a masculine counterpart. Beneath the sexual difference that drives the traditional quest romance, Lily's creative process discloses the ontological difference—the difference of being—that impels her quest for "the thing itself." "Time Passes" abstracts this poetics of loss into a formal "crystal of intensity" with affinities to Wilhelm Wörringer's and others' theories of abstract art; and "The Lighthouse" tracks Lily's work of mourning and painting in quest of "revelation" alongside her inward apprehension of Mr. Ramsay's sail to the lighthouse as a voyage to death (*TL* 132, 161). Before turning to the novel, let us consider its tacit critique of the traditional (sexualized, masculinized) oedipal paradigm of quest romance and the sources, in family documents, of its master metaphor, the voyage.

Gender and the Quest Romance

As Northrop Frye sums up the quest romance from Homer to Joyce, woman "achieves no quest herself, but . . . is clearly the kind of being who makes a quest possible."[1] *To the Lighthouse* intervenes in this tradition that casts women as the quest's object, not as questing subjects, but it neither reverses the masculine paradigm by casting men as the objects of female desire nor sacrifices Lily's different perspective. In her art Lily Briscoe departs from Western culture's pervasive masculinization of desire and symbolic creativity, figured in the Raphaelesque Madonnas revered by William Bankes and doubly enforced by Charles Tansley's "Women can't paint, women can't write" and Mrs. Ramsay's complementary admonition that an unmarried woman has "missed the best of life" (*TL* 48, 49). But even as she strikes out on her own, in violation of masculinized representations masquerading as universal, Lily rejects the word "feminist" in its hostile contemporary usages: as the ur-Lily puts it—feeling a fleeting "horror of masculinity," then backtracking—"it was too difficult to know quite what one meant about all this"; "Oh but she was not a feminist! That was a silly thing to say. Think of Shakespeare" (*TLhd* 138–39). Difficult as it is to say "quite what one meant," Lily's pronoun "one" asserts her imaginative freedom from gender.[2]

Lily's (and Woolf's) art implicitly abandons the masculine model of quest romance, generalized in the psychoanalytic account of desire, language, and representation. Like Frye, Freud makes the quester presumptively male when he quips that women need not trouble about his query "what do women want?" since "you are yourselves the problem"; his bizarre answer—a baby symbolizing a penis—confines woman's desire to maternity, narrowly conceived as symbolic compensation not for lack as such but for lack of the male anatomy.[3] Lacan amplifies Freud's rhetorical masculinization of desire and representation, even as he protests that his theoretical vocabulary ("the law represented by the father," the "phallus," "castration") is merely figural. Positing the oedipal crisis as the origin of language and subjectivity, he overwrites the bodily mother/child origin with a symbolic paternal origin, the father's name and law.[4]

Lily's quest, by contrast, exposes gender as an "ontological impossibility," a social construction that can only obscure the "reality" she seeks.[5] To grapple with "this formidable ancient enemy . . . this truth, this reality, which suddenly laid hands on her, emerged stark at the back of appearances and commanded her attention," Lily has to "subdu[e] all her impressions as a woman to something much more general" (TL 158, 53). Rather than fix her gaze along masculine sight lines, she seeks a perspective beyond limiting "impressions" as a woman or indeed a man. If "Mrs. Ramsay reading to James" is her ostensible subject, her search for a "truth . . . at the back of appearances" leads from the child's wish to merge with the mother as "the thing itself" through a struggle to grasp difference and loss as the very condition of being toward a world-embracing "intimacy" mediated by art and, finally, to the convergence of desire's object with the world as "the thing itself."[6]

To the Lighthouse alters the "ideal order" of the quest romance's "existing monuments," as T. S. Eliot argues "really new" works do.[7] Whereas Frye highlights the genre's historic reliance upon figures of femininity, Lily's quest makes sexual difference accidental to being and meaning. Against the psychoanalytic view that "there is no subjectivity without sexual difference," To the Lighthouse makes ontological difference—the difference of being—the matrix of subjectivity and opens dynamics of maternal and paternal identification to both sexes.[8] Like the son's, this daughter's quest begins with the mother's loss. But whereas oedipal theory superimposes sexual difference on ontological difference, dictating that the son renounce the mother not as a mirror of himself but as the object of his love, the daughter loses the mother to the difference of being that intervenes at birth between the mother and the child of either sex. The traditional quest romance tracks the hero's desire for an idealized feminine object—a symbolic stand-in for the maternal body—through theoretically endless adventures of displacement and substitution. By contrast, Lily's (and Woolf's) quest subsumes the mother's loss within the difference intrinsic to being as such and leads through adventures of mourning and creativity past mere substitutes for the lost mother to things in themselves.

Whereas in *Ulysses* the artist-hero's aesthetic theory and practice symbolically mime female procreativity and fetishize femininity as the quest's end, *To the Lighthouse* tracks a daughter's quest from a symbolic attempt to merge with the mother (Lily's first portrait of Mrs. Ramsay) to an abstract painting that figures "something much more general": beneath sexual difference, a substrate of ontological difference.[9]

In this sense, Lily's modernist quest challenges the oedipal psychodrama that prevails even in strong feminist criticism of the novel.[10] If we blame the daughter's independence for the mother's death, limit feminist aesthetics to pre-oedipal murmuring, discount James's bond with his mother in favor of Lily's, do we not risk sustaining the fictions of gender that the novel critiques (and perhaps a sentimentality that Woolf was at pains to avoid)? Acknowledging the power of these readings, I suggest that the daughter-artist's quest moves beyond its (accidental) feminine origins toward universality, for neither the difference of being that impels it nor the adventures of loss and creativity that comprise it nor the picture of the world that concludes it is specific to female desire. As Lily quests toward the thing itself—no "thing" at all but a work of art created in freedom—she forgets traditional Madonnas to paint from life. As she thinks of her picture while "pretending to comb her hair" before the looking glass, she paints autobiographically not her outward appearance but "what had been in her mind as a baby"; "the deposit of each day's living mixed with something more secret than she had ever spoken or shown in the course of all those days"—"something" that belongs to her, to women, and to human consciousness (*TLhd* 255, 92, *TL* 52).

As Lily and James experience the loss of early plenitude, they contravene any claim that being is essentially bound up with sexual difference. The loss and desire that drive Lily's quest—the difference that exiles her from the mother as from every other being—preexist any figural "father"'s intervention and any mother's death, actual or symbolic. Seeking "the thing itself before it has been made anything," Lily discovers loss as the very condition of being and art as a bridge between mind and mind, mind and world.[11] In quest of an intimacy that embraces the island world and the world beyond, Lily voyages beyond oedipal desire, sexual love, fetishized femininity, gender masquerade, and the nostalgic and limited truism that an "original lost object—the mother's body" propels "the narrative of our lives, impelling us to pursue substitutes for this lost paradise in the endless metonymic movement of desire."[12] Discovering that nothing can bridge the gap between the thing itself and any representation, she quests from loss and grief through regressive longing, anguished mourning, and near despair toward a "vision" of the immanent world, not as a substitute for maternal plenitude (in the sense that what is possessed is never as good as what is lost) but in and as itself (*TL* 209).

A Family Legacy: Shipwreck, Salvage, New Voyage

Woolf's stories, diaries, letters, and memoirs document the rich autobiographical sources of *To the Lighthouse*. Drawn from her memory of childhood summers in Cornwall, it was to have "father's character done complete in it; & mother's; & St. Ives; & childhood; & all the usual things I try to put in—life, death, &c. But the centre is father's character, sitting in a boat, reciting We perished, each alone, while he crushes a dying mackerel."[13] James's thwarted dream of sailing to the lighthouse and its long-deferred fulfillment have obvious roots in Woolf's memories of those summers—a "perennial, invaluable" gift from her parents, "the best beginning to life conceivable."[14] That expedition embodies the novel's shaping metaphor of life as a voyage toward death, a tremendous adventure fraught with peril, possibility, trial, failure, triumph, and discovery on the way to that absolute end.

The novel's metaphor of life as a risky voyage was also a family legacy. Leslie Stephen and Julia Duckworth both had earlier families, and each lost a spouse in 1870. Family friends for years, and now fellow sufferers, they consoled each other as friends but did not marry until 1878. Left a widow with three small children at twenty-four, Julia was "numbed and petrified by her grief" and accepted "a life of sorrow . . . as her permanent portion." Leslie, "though plunged into deep melancholy," fought against grief's "dominion"; still, only in February 1877, when he realized that he loved Julia, did he feel "something like joy and revival."[15] In an undated letter gently declining his first marriage proposal, Julia recalled the shock of losing her adored husband Herbert Duckworth, which plunged her into "abiding sadness":

> You see, dear, though I don't feel as if life had been hard or as if I had not a great deal in it, still it has been different from yours and from most people's. *I was only 24 when it all seemed a shipwreck*, and I knew that I had to live on and on, and the only thing to be done was to be as cheerful as I could and do as much as I could and think as little. And so I got deadened. I had all along felt that if it had been possible for me to be myself, it would have been better for me individually; and that I could have got more real life out of the wreck if I had broken down more. But there was Baby to be thought of and everyone

around me urging me to keep up, and I could never be alone which sometimes was such torture. So that by degrees I felt that though I was more cheerful and content than most people, I was more changed. (*MBk* 40–41, my emphasis)

Like Macalister pointing out shipwreck sites to Mr. Ramsay, Julia points to the rocks where her vessel broke up, one man "drowned," and she too as good as perished ("I got deadened") (*TL* 206). Documenting the later Stephen family's precarious origin in the catastrophe from which these two castaways salvaged a future at first unimaginable, her letter shows her hesitating before a new world voyage that needed strength, hope, and courage she felt were beyond her resources.[16]

When Julia "had saved a life from the deep waters," Leslie wrote, borrowing her nautical metaphor to contrast their responses to grief, "she sought at once for another person to rescue, whereas I went off to take a glass with the escaped" (*MBk* 41). Elaborating her parents' metaphor, Woolf shipwrecks the Ramsays in the storms of time and traces the survivors' slow emergence from shock and grief to recreate their world. Danger and disaster do not wait until "Time Passes" to make themselves felt. In the first pages James's hope of sailing to the lighthouse is summarily quashed by his father, "who was incapable of untruth; never tampered with a fact" for "any mortal being, least of all . . . his own children, who, sprung from his loins, should be aware from childhood that life is difficult; facts uncompromising; and the passage to that fabled land where our brightest hopes are extinguished, our frail barks founder in darkness . . . one that needs, above all, courage, truth, and the power to endure" (*TL* 4).

Like the Stephens, the Ramsays are sailors on life's unpredictable, unmasterable seas. Mr. Ramsay not only possesses but cultivates in his children "qualities that would have saved a ship's company exposed on a broiling sea with six biscuits and a flask of water—endurance and justice, foresight, devotion, skill" (*TL* 34). The tempest-tossed Mrs. Ramsay has suffered a sea change into something rich and strange, "a figure that had dredged the depths of the sea of bitterness & sorrow & had come to the surface again with eyes pearl encrusted with tears and brows starred with immortality . . . with stars in her eyes and purple veils about her hair" (*TLhd* 22–23). At dinner (where the company only seems safely moored) she resembles "a fading ship" nearly "sunk beneath the horizon" until she rouses herself—"as a sailor not without weariness sees the wind fill his sail and yet hardly wants to be off again and thinks how, had the ship sunk, he would have whirled round and round and found rest on the floor of the sea"—to beam at Mr. Bankes "as if the ship had turned and the sun had struck its sails again"; later Lily remembers her "unable to surmount the tempest calmly" (*TL* 84, 199). She signals Lily that "life will run upon the rocks" unless Lily flatters Mr. Tansley; when Lily complies, asking whether he is "a good sailor," his reply ("he had never been sick in his life") conceals, "like gunpowder, that his grandfather was a fisherman . . . he had worked his way up entirely himself . . . he was Charles Tansley— a fact that nobody there seemed to realise" (*TL* 91–92).

In the draft Mrs. Ramsay turns back to Mr. Bankes to ask about mutual friends only to find the opportunity lost, that "island floated away" (*TLhd* 150). Beside Paul Rayley, newly engaged and "bound for adventure," Lily feels "moored to the shore"; she longs to join "the sailors and adventurers" and ever after remembers the "flare" sent up by Paul's engagement, his "glory" burning like "a signal fire on a desert island" (*TL* 101–2, 176, *TLhd* 299). After dinner the men confer as if "taking their bearings" on "the bridge of the ship"; then Mr. Ramsay reads chapter 29 of Scott's *Antiquary*, in which news arrives of Steenie Mucklebackit's death when his father's boat is swamped at sea (*TL* 112). In "Time Passes" an "ashen-coloured ship" crosses the horizon when Andrew dies; Mrs. McNab "lurche[s]" and "roll[s] like a ship at sea"; the derelict house nearly "plung[es] to the depths to lie upon the sands of oblivion"; war losses stain the sea "purplish . . . as if something had boiled and bled, invisibly, beneath," for "every one had lost some one these years" (*TL* 130–39). "The Lighthouse" abstracts life's voyage into Mr. Ramsay's sail with his children, "their heads . . . pressed down by some remorseless gale" this sunny day as they follow him down to the dock. Thus to Cam it seems "as if they were doing two things at once; . . . eating their lunch here in the sun and . . . making for safety in a great storm after a ship-wreck. Would the water last?" (*TL* 163, 205). Lily goes with them in spirit as her painting draws her "Out and out . . . further and further" onto "a narrow plank, perfectly alone, over the sea" or forces her to plunge and leap through "steep gulfs, and foaming crests" (*TL* 172, 157). Nearby Mr. Carmichael "sail[s] serenely through a world which satisfied all his wants" (*TL* 179).

To Woolf, "writing a novel in London"—this novel—felt like "nailing a flag to the top of a mast in a raging gale" (*D* 3:64, 3 March, *L* 3:244, 2 March 1926). Blown and buffeted by distractions, she saw her work-in-progress "glowing like the island of the Blessed far far away over dismal wastes, and cant reach land" (*L* 3:276, 18 June 1926). More than an anchor for the book's design, a mast to which to nail its story, the voyage to the lighthouse parlays a family legacy—a history and a metaphor—into a picture of the world. Herself and her vision born of shipwrecked survivors who salvaged life from the wreck and voyaged on together to create a new world, the daughter-artist launches her characters on their many courses toward a common destination.[17]

A Cosmogony of Doubt

> She asked him what his father's books were about. "Subject and object and the nature of reality," Andrew had said. . . . "Think of a kitchen table . . . when you're not there."
>
> —Woolf, *To the Lighthouse*

> I seem to make people think the Stephen family was one of insane gloom. I thought it was a cheerful enough book.
>
> —Woolf to Vanessa Bell, *Letters*, 22 May 1927

In Mrs. Ramsay's "cosmogony," the ur-narrator observes, "nature . . . had long supplanted . . . the hierarchy of Heaven" (*TLhd* 24, cf. *TL* 27–28). The doubting Mrs. Ramsay, who hears nature now murmuring, "I am guarding you," now warning of life's "quick passage . . . into the abyss, & the shattered race of risen waters afterwards," is soul mate to a husband who ponders whether a table exists when no one is there.[18] "He must have had his doubts about that table," Lily speculates—whether it was "real," or "worth the time he gave to it; whether he was able after all to find it" (*TL* 155). Of such skeptics Wittgenstein asks, "Couldn't we let him quietly doubt, since it makes no difference at all?"[19] Although Mr. Ramsay's skepticism leaves everyday belief (as in the earwig in his soup plate) intact, doubt makes all the difference in *To the Lighthouse*. Doubt is the "truth" of a world founded on the void, in which "the only desirable thing was truth," the "rock" to which he seeks, with a desire "consistent, inviolable, powerful beyond any other emotion," to "anchor his childrens minds, in the waste & turmoil of life" (*TLhd* 286). James remembers his father in lecture halls "prov[ing] conclusively that there is no God"; Mr. Ramsay consults his wife on how the story that "Hume stuck in a bog & an old woman rescued him on condition he said the Lords Prayer" will "go down" with "the young men at Cardiff": will Mrs. Bowley "be shocked (they were staying with the Bowleys . . .)".[20]

The narrator gently satirizes Mr. Ramsay's muscular doubt as "his natural appetite for pleasure" clashes with his philosophical devotion to "the august theme of human fate" (*TLhd* 82). When he clucks "Pretty— pretty" over a hen with chicks, William Bankes foresees their friendship's decline (*TL* 21). Even when he abandons "all trophies of nuts and roses" as he strains from Q toward R, finding at the furthest verge of thought only "a spit of land" edging "the dark of human ignorance," he never ceases to crave the "reverence, and pity, and gratitude" of the watchers on the shore, especially women (*TL* 44). Still, the narrator asks, who

> could blame the leader of that forlorn party which after all has climbed high enough to see the waste of the years and the perishing of stars, if before death stiffens his limbs . . . he does a little consciously . . . square his shoulders, so that when the search party comes they will find him dead at his post, the fine figure of a soldier? Mr. Ramsay squared his shoulders and stood very upright by the urn. (*TL* 35–36)

Mr. Ramsay's doubt paradoxically anchors a faith of his own. In Mrs. Ramsay reading to James he sees "wife & child—the holiest heart of life— (& her divine worn beauty with the boy on her knee, her lips resting lightly on his head, her arm encircling him, & such an expression of tenderness on her that she looked like the profound spirit brooding over the waters of life"); "Robbed of all detail," "this divinity," this madonna inspires his "splendid mind" as it does Lily's painting.[21] For him, she—not God—has "gallantly created the whole world," "braced herself" "to put forth" "that great venture," their life with its "welter of children," whom he loves without forgetting the vast ignorance no effort can enlighten (*TLhd* 71, 75, *TL* 21).

Like her husband, Mrs. Ramsay believes in the "truth" of this godless world. Despite recklessly encouraging James's hope of fine weather, she too is "impatient when people trifled with the truth of things . . . & threw veils [of] plausibility & optimism over what was sheer as a cliff & black as the sea" (*TLhd* 59). She too feels life "pour[ing] terrifyingly over an abyss into unknown lands" (*TLhd* 150). Hearing herself murmur, "We are in the hands of the Lord," she minds "saying something she did not mean," letting an "insincerity slip[] in among the truths," and disavows it: "Who had said it? Not she" (*TL* 63–64). While her Swiss maid's father lies dying of cancer, she reflects that there is "no escape," "No happiness lasted"; she says nothing of how "she too . . . had been ruined," but her tragic aura makes people imagine a lover who has "blown his brains out or . . . died in India."[22] And, like Mr. Ramsay, she has her consolations: the children ("she would have liked always to have had a baby"); the dinner party, where she conjures "love" like "a smoke, an incense, or a fume." "Of such moments," she thinks, "the thing is made that endures"; at such times "The insincerity, the sentimentality of words was for her divinely satisfactory . . . & partook . . . of eternity . . . here tonight was the heaven for such as her" (*TL* 58, 105, *TLhd* 172).

When the Ramsay children call Charles Tansley "the little atheist," what they mock is not that he does not believe in God (neither do they) but that he doesn't believe in life, at least not theirs (*TL* 5). In his contempt for women, children, circuses, and "nonsense," he doubts their very world, though even he falls under Mrs. Ramsay's sway, feeling proud "for the first time in his life" to be "walking with a beautiful woman" (*TL* 14). Still, here tonight is not heaven for such as Tansley, who sits mentally composing satires on " 'staying with the Ramsays' " to be "read aloud, to one or two friends": "It was worth while doing it once, he would say; but not again" (*TL* 90).

The skeptical creator-god Mrs. Ramsay strives to inculcate belief in the world she has made in her daughters. She directs remarks on the light-keeper's lonely existence "particularly" to them, chides them for laughing at Tansley, and models the Victorian feminine ideal:

> Indeed she had the whole of the other sex under her protection; for reasons she could not explain, for their chivalry and valour, for the fact that they negotiated treaties, ruled India, controlled finance; finally for an attitude towards herself which no woman could fail to feel or to find agreeable, something trustful, childlike, reverential . . . and woe betide the girl—pray Heaven it was none of her daughters!—who did not feel the worth of it, and all that it implied, to the marrow of her bones! . . .
>
> She was now formidable to behold, and it was only in silence . . . that her daughters, Prue, Nancy, Rose—could sport with infidel ideas . . . of a life different from hers; in Paris, perhaps; a wilder life; not always taking care of some man or other; for there was in all their minds a mute questioning of deference and chivalry, of the Bank of England and the Indian Empire, of ringed fingers and lace. (*TL* 6–7)

Mrs. Ramsay's vehement sermon to her "infidel" daughters even in their absence (as here, where she knits and ruminates while James cuts out pictures) bears out Lily's sense that she is a "prime force" "like a wave of the sea" that "took one up & flung one down."[23] Yet the daughters doubt. Nancy "desires of all things freedom," not "deference and chivalry," and laughs at her father's rage over Mr. Carmichael's second helping of soup; "Cam the Wicked" refuses to give Mr. Bankes a flower—"No! no! no! she would not!" Minta's torn stocking foretells her unraveling marital fidelity; Lily paints and does not marry.[24] And the narrator—that unseen daughter in the garden who ventriloquizes Mrs. Ramsay's fierce defense of femininity and her daughters' tacit demurrals—deftly portrays a mother-god who herself secretly harbors infidel doubts, hoping in an unguarded moment that her daughters will "find a way out of it all"—some "simpler," "less laborious way."[25]

In *Mimesis: The Representation of Reality in Western Literature*, which famously exemplifies modernist narrative by Mrs. Ramsay's stocking-knitting scene, Erich Auerbach foregrounds this doubting daughter-narrator. With one foot in a nineteenth-century cosmogony, he notes that the "narrator of objective facts has almost completely vanished," displaced by one "who doubts, wonders, hesitates, as though the truth about her characters were not better known to her than it is to them or to the reader."[26] Measuring her against a conventional omniscient narrator who "ought to know how matters stand with her characters," Auerbach momentarily misses the "objective fact" that, notwithstanding her practice of doubt, the narrator does, impossibly yet realistically, exactly render her characters' thoughts and feelings, even as the novel's twentieth-century cosmos founded on the void dispels illusions of objectivity.[27] Indeed his own hackneyed sketch of Mrs. Ramsay ("the wife of an eminent philosopher, . . . very beautiful and definitely no longer young") reinstates an "objective" perspective that the narrator subjects to "mute questioning," as his description of the narrator's "feminine . . . irony, amorphous sadness, and doubt of life" (as well as "good and genuine love") overlooks her comic, generous, joyful deployment of doubt's emancipatory and creative powers (528, 552, 531).

Among the infidel daughters, the autobiographical Lily was slow to appear. Woolf's first plan to portray her father in a boat reciting "We perished each alone" while crushing a dying mackerel soon led to a formal triptych: "father & mother & child in the garden: the death; the sail to the lighthouse," which she hoped to "enrich" and "thicken" with "branches & roots which I do not perceive now" (*D* 3:36, 20 July 1925). Ten days later her "single & intense character of father" had broadened into "a far wider slower book"; by August 6 "Mrs. R's character" was to be the "dominating impression" (*D* 3:37, *TLhd* 2). Only in the writing did the book's actual center emerge: the *child* in the garden, first James, then Lily, canted away from childhood by her age (thirty-three) and from family life by her status as friend. Lily sidles belatedly into the draft as "Miss Sophie Briscoe," "a kindly rosy lady who spent much of her life sketching" and is "glad, at 55," to have refused all suitors and so "retained her right to view male eccentricity from a distance."[28] Namesake of the goddess Wisdom, this eccentric and skeptical outsider morphs into the aspiring painter Lily, twenty-two years younger, whose battle to translate her vision into the language of form is all before her (*TLhd* 31). As Lily moves "the tree further in the middle," Woolf eventually plants Lily at the center of the novel's "roots" and "branches."

Surprisingly, the ur-Lily is a Roman Catholic who sees "the Ramsay world shrewdly enough from her own corner, where, she worshipped God" (*TLhd* 34). While traveling in Sicily over Easter 1927, Woolf wrote Vanessa of her fascination with Catholic ritual, which seemed to her more art than religion:

> I like the Roman Catholic religion. I say it is an attempt at art; . . . We burst into a service of little girls in white veils this morning which touched me greatly. It seems to me simply the desire to create gone slightly crooked, and no God in it at all. Then there are little boys brandishing palms tied in red ribbon and sugar lambs everywhere—surely rather sympathetic, and to me more attuned than those olive trees which the old gentlemen are for ever painting at street corners in Cassis. (*L* 3:360–61)

As Lily evolves into a secular painter, liturgical echoes solemnize her own "attempt at art" as well as Mrs. Ramsay's dinner party and Lily's commemoration with Mr. Carmichael of Mr. Ramsay's landing at the lighthouse. In fact art itself becomes for Lily an "august God" that summons her into the presence of "some apparition of truth behind appearances"—"whatever it is that rules the world & compels our allegiance; or exacts our submission." "Intolerant of acquiescence," this "old enemy" or "God—shape, form, mass bulk—unlike other Gods, roused her to perpetual combat" (*TLhd* 257). Not unlike the white-veiled girls, brides of the Church, Lily enters into an "awful marriage; forever" with this divine "lover" and "formidable enemy—space" with a devotion that subsumes and surpasses "bodily human love": "their union, could it be achieved, was immortal" (*TLhd* 280).

Lily's god of form, an absolute unmediated by any church, befits a world in which life pours terrifyingly over an abyss. To paint is to be called to witness "some apparition of truth behind appearances"; to see phenomenal "things" in "Everlasting & undeniable relationship," as when the Ramsays seem to Lily of "gigantic stature—Crucified, & transcendent, blessing the world with symbolical meaning" (*TLhd* 257, 280, 120). The struggle to paint spirits Lily to a plane of existence beyond even doubt, a realm of freedom: "How could she doubt it? She was extended, & freed . . . cut loose from the ties of life" to experience the "intensity & freedom of life" (*TLhd* 280). Escaping everyday entanglements, she engages in "perpetual combat" to wrest enduring forms from nature's flux, much as Mr. Ramsay perseveres from *P* and *Q* toward *R*[eality]. In defense against such contingent threats as Mrs. Ramsay's Angel in the House and Tansley's bogey (women "can't paint, can't write"; "man has Shakespeare . . . & women have not"), Lily possesses herself of "the whole secret of art": "To care for the thing not for oneself: what does it matter whether I succeed or not?" (*TL* 91, *TLhd* 136).

As to paint is, for Lily, to quit trivial conflicts for "immortal" battle, caring only for "the thing," so an early plan for *To the Lighthouse* lists under "Topics" "The great cleavages in to which the human race is split, through the Ramsays not liking Mr. Tansley"; and "How much more important divisions between people are than between countries. The source of all evil" (*TLhd* Appendix A/11–12). When her children mock the little atheist, Mrs. Ramsay laments that "Strife, divisions, difference of opinion, prejudices twisted into the very fibre of being . . . should begin so early. . . . such nonsense—inventing differences. . . . The real differences . . . are enough, quite enough" (*TL* 8–9). Among "real differences," the novel seeks a common "truth": though the dinner party is not heaven for Mr. Tansley, Lily, or Mr. Ramsay, each has a heaven—some "thing." Art, moreover, seeks to bridge real differences by what Clive Bell calls "significant form": "Art is the most universal and the most permanent of all forms of religious expression, because the significance of formal combinations can be appreciated by one race and one age as another, and because that significance is as independent as mathematical truth of human vicissitudes."[29] With Bell's proposition in mind, we turn to Lily's combat with "the hidden apparition of truth" in the formal language of her first composition (*TLhd* 257).

A Daughter's Madonna: The Triangular Purple Shape

> The jacmanna was bright violet; the wall staring white. She would not have considered it honest to tamper with the bright violet and the staring white, since she saw them like that, fashionable though it was, since Mr. Paunceforte's visit, to see everything pale, elegant, semitransparent.
>
> —Woolf, *To the Lighthouse*

When William Bankes and Lily turn from talking about the Ramsays to look at her picture, they zero in on the significant form at the heart of her work-in-progress. With disinterested curiosity William asks, "What did she wish to indicate by the triangular purple shape, 'just there'?" (*TL* 52). Her vision almost eclipsed ("it was bad! . . . infinitely bad!") a moment earlier by William's worshipful gaze at Mrs. Ramsay, Lily invokes reference—"It was Mrs. Ramsay reading to James"—and so opens a dialogue on those rival gods realism and abstraction (*TL* 48, 52). William's conventional realism presumes and values visible resemblance; Lily's impromptu modernist manifesto links her composition's formal abstraction to a psychic and metaphysical quest in a world founded on loss.

As William has a moment before gazed rapturously on Mrs. Ramsay, now he ponders how mother and child, "objects of universal veneration . . . might be reduced . . . to a purple shadow without irreverence." In response Lily retreats from referential claims and deflects "reverence" from the object to that august god form:

> She knew his objection—that no one could tell it for a human shape. But she had made no attempt at likeness. . . . the picture was not of them. Or, not in his sense. There were other senses too in which one might reverence them. By a shadow here and a light there, for instance. Her tribute took that form if, as she vaguely supposed, a picture must be a tribute. A mother and child might be reduced to a shadow without irreverence. A light here required a shadow there. (*TL* 52–53)

More exactly, Lily does not abandon referential claims but shifts them to a different register, a reality behind appearances. If her picture is not of them "in his sense," it presumably is in hers. What is her sense?

As Lily looks at her apparent subject, Mrs. Ramsay and James, her thoughts turn to a hidden reality, primal and subjective: "what had been in her mind" from infancy, the "residue of her thirty-three years," "something more secret than she had ever spoken or shown" (*TLhd* 92, *TL* 52). Not—or not only—"of them," her picture is also a self-portrait that neither depicts her outward appearance nor eradicates the visible world but captures relations in the language of form. Behind the traditionally revered mother and son, Lily sees and paints a daughter's madonna, which (like Lily herself) only gradually becomes visible. Her occlusion in her picture is reflected in her sidelong entrance into the narrative, not as subject and seer but as an object—almost knocked over by Mr. Ramsay, who "glare[s]" at her and William "without seeming to see them" as he gallops over the lawn shouting "The Charge of the Light Brigade," and patronized by Mrs. Ramsay when she looks up to see who has witnessed his "ridiculous" and "alarming" performance:[30]

> Only Lily Briscoe, she was glad to find; and that did not matter. . . . she was supposed to be keeping her head as much in the same position as possible for Lily's picture. Lily's picture! Mrs. Ramsay smiled. With her little Chinese eyes and her puckered-up face, she would never marry; one could not take her painting very seriously; she was an independent little creature, and Mrs. Ramsay liked her for it; so, remembering her promise, she bent her head. . . .

Indeed, he almost knocked her easel over, coming down upon her
with his hands waving shouting out, "Boldly we rode and well," but,
mercifully, he turned sharp, and rode off, to die gloriously she supposed
upon the heights of Balaclava. (*TL* 17)

Mrs. Ramsay, supposedly the object of Lily's gaze, dominates Lily's own
first appearance while Mr. Ramsay's "merciful" near miss allegorizes
Woolf's conviction that her writing life required her father's death: "He
would have been [1928 1832] 96, 96, yes, today; & could have been 96,
like other people one has known; but mercifully was not. His life would
have entirely ended mine. What would have happened? No writing, no
books;—inconceivable" (*D* 3:208, 28 November 1928).

Like the Ramsays' looks, William's adoring gaze at Mrs. Ramsay
almost annihilates Lily as subject. About to criticize Mrs. Ramsay, she
stops as his gaze makes her comment "entirely unnecessary," even makes
her "forget entirely" what she wants to say (*TL* 47–48). William, who has
viewed paintings all over Europe, reveres this flesh-and-blood mother and
child with a "rapture" that Lily tries to find "helpful," "exalting": "nothing so solaced her, eased her of the perplexity of life, and miraculously
raised its burdens, as this sublime power, this heavenly gift, and one would
no more disturb it, while it lasted, than break up the shaft of sunlight, lying
level across the floor" (*TL* 47–48). But "no woman could worship another
woman" as he does; and Lily pays a price in taking vicarious "shelter from
the reverence which covered all women" as, acquiescing, she slips from
seeing subject to feminized object. Turning to "steal a look at her picture"
she finds it "infinitely bad!" and, involuntarily thinking of how Paunceforte would have done it, struggles to salvage her vision: "But . . . she did
not see it like that. She saw the colour burning on a framework of steel; the
light of a butterfly's wing lying upon the arches of a cathedral . . . and there
was Mr. Tansley whispering . . . 'Women can't paint, women can't write' "
(*TL* 48). To paint from life rather than follow Raphael or Paunceforte, Lily
has to brave "demons" that make her "passage from conception to work
as dreadful as any down a dark passage for a child"; "against terrific
odds," she must "maintain her courage," fight "to clasp some miserable
remnant of her vision to her breast, which a thousand forces did their best
to pluck from her"—among them, the "masses of pictures she had not
seen," though "perhaps it was better not to see pictures: they only made
one hopelessly discontented with one's own work" (*TL* 19, 72).

Groping to recover her vision, Lily aligns her "different ray" with
William's eyebeam. Wondering "why" and "how" her gaze differs from
his, she seeks "the essential thing" about Mrs. Ramsay—the glove's

"twisted finger," by which anyone would have known it "hers indisputably" (*TL* 49). Lily finds this essence in a memory of how Mrs. Ramsay used to come in late at night to talk, beguilingly insisting that "she must, Minta must, they all must marry," while Lily "would urge her own exemption from the universal law; plead for it; she liked to be alone; she liked to be herself" (*TL* 49–50). At this memory's crux, the indefinite past tense ("would urge") modulates to past perfect, a singular event: "she had laid her head on Mrs. Ramsay's lap and . . . laughed almost hysterically at the thought of Mrs. Ramsay presiding with immutable calm over destinies which she completely failed to understand" (*TL* 50).

With this memory of clasping Mrs. Ramsay's knees while laughing "almost hysterically," Lily's daughter's madonna emerges. The triangular purple shape pictures not just James at Mrs. Ramsay's knee but Lily too, though "not in his sense." But we must pursue her sense further. Often framed as an oedipal triangle—in Abel's words, one of those "abstractions that universalize masculinity"—the triangular purple shape also figures the ontological loneliness that Lily's longing for Mrs. Ramsay dramatizes.[31] Absorbing the son's sexualized oedipal triangle within the daughter's ontological triangle, the triangular purple shape abstracts separation and loss as every subject's condition and expresses the universal necessity of triangulating desire so that, no longer bound within the mother/child dyad, it flows out toward the world. The triangular purple shape is "of them" not in his sense—mother and son—but in her more abstract sense: mother and child.

As Lily is the child in the garden, the purple triangular shape is the site of a human drama of separation and loss. Struggling to paint "what had been in her mind as a baby," the "residue" of her days and years, Lily is torn between the indomitable Mrs. Ramsay (who "never did submit: did not find it easy to give way") and her own desire.[32] Even as she urges her exemption from the "universal" law of marriage, her "almost" hysterical laughter contradicts her regressive and impossible desire to merge with the adored mother with the simple fact that she is already "herself." Capturing the glove's twisted finger, Lily's madonna expresses a daughterly worship as profound as William's, but more dangerous and ambivalent. Pressing "close as she could get," Lily imagines "treasures" hidden as in "the tombs of kings" "in the chambers of the mind and heart of the woman who was, physically, touching her," "tablets bearing sacred inscriptions, which if one could spell them out, would teach one everything" (*TL* 51). At the same time, she senses her fantasy's fallacy—"the deceptiveness of beauty" that tangles "one's perceptions, half-way to truth, . . . in a golden mesh"—and gropes toward some more effective "art" or "device":

What art was there, known to love or cunning, by which *one* pressed through into those secret chambers? What device for becoming, like waters poured into one jar, inextricably the same, one with the object *one* adored? Could the body achieve, or the mind, subtly mingling in the intricate passages of the brain? or the heart? Could loving, as people called it, make her and Mrs. Ramsay one? for it was not knowledge but unity that she desired, not inscriptions on tablets, nothing that could be written in any language known to men, but intimacy itself, which is knowledge.[33]

William's query about the triangular purple shape brings to light a hidden "truth": at once a crucial difference between a daughter's and son's experiences of separation, loss, and growing up and (as her pronoun *one* asserts) a fundamental sameness. If, for the son, sexual difference overwrites ontological difference as the oedipal prohibition sharply separates him from his mother and frames heterosexual love as a consoling substitute, a purely ontological difference separates mother and daughter. Sexual difference drops out of the picture and, although sexual desire briefly remains, it too is soon abandoned, less in obeisance to taboos against same-sex love, it appears, than because even sexual love cannot "make her and Mrs. Ramsay one." Indeed, Lily's fantasy is hardly sexual at all, so urgently does it evoke an unbridgeable abyss: "Nothing happened. Nothing! . . . And yet, she knew knowledge and wisdom were stored up in Mrs. Ramsay's heart."[34] Even as it preserves the memory of the maternal within sexual love for every subject, Lily's fleeting fantasy of union through "loving" overleaps oedipal dynamics to the ontological difference and desire that preexist sexual difference and desire.

While the abstract purple shape expressively merges mother and daughter, Lily is also struggling to "triangulate" her desire—to break the impasse between a self-annihilating longing to merge and the necessary pain and thrill of self-differentiation. Mrs. Ramsay remains Lily's first object of desire, bearing "the sound of murmuring" about her "For days . . . as after a dream some subtle change is felt in the person one has dreamt of" and wearing an "august shape . . . of a dome" (*TL* 51). But already she is not the only object, or even the privileged one. Already Lily is ranging beelike through "wastes" of air and "countries of the world alone," haunting "hives, which were people" (*TL* 51). As that august dome becomes multitudinous "hives," Lily extends the originary mother/child relation out into the world in quest of an "intimacy" that is and is not "knowledge," an art to bridge the gap between herself and every other being.

Abstract Form and the Thing Itself

How does Lily's art mediate this intimacy? Illuminated by her associations and memories, her semantically rich and elastic "purple triangular shape" expresses a complex reality: mother and child; the child merged with the mother; and the difference of being that unfolds in the triangulation of desire for every subject—including the mother, herself "a wedge-shaped core of darkness," "invisible to others" (*TL* 62). This figure of Mrs. Ramsay foreshadows Woolf's later remark that "It would be as difficult" to portray her mother's personality "as it should be done, as to paint a Cézanne" (*MB* 85). As the abstract purple shape captures a psychic predicament—the solitariness of being and the desire for intimacy—in the language of form, so Lily's difficulty is to solve the troubling emptiness at the center of her canvas. It is a question, she explains to William, of "how to connect this mass on the right hand with that on the left. She might do it by bringing the line of the branch across so; or break the vacancy in the foreground by an object (James perhaps) so. But the danger was that by doing that the unity of the whole might be broken" (*TL* 53). To introduce an "object" ("James perhaps," or a "branch") would banish vacancy but risks disrupting the "unity" or "whole" to which the triangle "reduce[s]" distinct bodies (Mrs. Ramsay, James, Lily). Yet as the triangle's purple—color of mourning—acknowledges loss as the origin of consciousness, so Lily expresses ineluctable difference in painterly chiaroscuro: "A light here required a shadow there" (*TL* 53). The problem of connecting masses at left and right dramatizes any subject's need to accept and mitigate separation and loss, while the branch, auguring extension and growth, suggests the "tree" Lily later resolves to center and finally abstracts into the "line . . . in the centre" that completes her vision (*TL* 209).

As Lily's composition brings realist elements (Mrs. Ramsay, James, purple jacmanna, white wall) under the rule of abstract form, the narrative foregrounds her divergence from conventional realism. William considers, "scientifically in complete good faith," how a "purple shadow" can represent that sacred cow of Western art, a madonna and child:

> The truth was that all his prejudices were on the other side. . . . The largest picture in his drawing-room, which painters had praised, and valued at a higher price than he had given for it, was of the cherry trees in blossom on the banks of the Kennet. He had spent his honeymoon on the banks of the Kennet, he said. (*TL* 53)

Picturesque, haloed in sentimental memory, appreciating in value, William's "largest painting" would have pleased the British public that derided Fry's 1910 "Manet and the Post-Impressionists" exhibition, with its Cézannes, Gauguins, Van Goghs, Picassos, Signacs, and Derains. His *Cherry Trees on the Kennet* and Lily's unfinished *Daughter's Madonna* illustrate opposite poles of the aesthetic continuum described in Wilhelm Wörringer's groundbreaking *Abstraction and Empathy* (1908): at William's end, the aesthetics of empathy, the organic, naturalistic, mimetic realism of Western European art from the Hellenic period through the nineteenth century; at Lily's end, the turn to abstraction in early twentieth-century European art, to a new formal language inspired by encounters with non-Western—Chinese, African, Ocean Island—abstract art.

Wörringer's interpretation of these formal modes resonates with both Lily's abstract form and the Ramsays' austere "cosmogony." For Wörringer, mimetic forms express human existence as at home in the natural world, whereas abstract forms express humanity's fragile contingency in face of nature and time and its dread of nature's arbitrariness. Abstraction (for Wörringer as for Bloomsbury a relative term, neither superficially mimetic nor purely nonrepresentational) arises from "great inner unrest at outward phenomena," a "spiritual dread of space" that no science puts to rest, since even the most intense thought cannot grasp the "unfathomable entanglement of all the phenomena of life."[35] Attuned to realities beyond reach of Western rationalism and positivist science—behind appearances and "*above* cognition"—an abstract aesthetics creates a tranquil refuge from unfathomable nature in forms felt as "necessary and irrefragable" (16–17). For Wörringer, both organic and abstract aesthetics seek deliverance from the self, the former from individual being, the latter from the arbitrariness and vulnerability of organic existence; but the "primal artistic impulse" tends to "pure abstraction," which does not copy nature but creates an ontological realm independent and apart.

Wörringer posits abstract form as the "consummate"—even the "only"—expression of freedom from "contingency and temporality." In contemplating an abstract form the spectator enjoys not "cognate-organic" resemblance but the form's "independen[ce] both of the ambient external world and of the subject" (44). Both kinds of art rescue the object from time; but rather than copy nature, abstraction strives to evoke the (imperceptible, unrepresentable) "thing itself" as it exists beyond the organic world of time, death, and decay. Whereas mimetic art cultivates resemblance, abstraction seeks a reality behind appearances—the thing purged of its dependence on life and death, nature and time, and "approximate[d] to its absolute value" (17). Organic forms give "happiness" to their creators and spectators by mimesis; abstract forms, by evoking an invisible reality (13). Thus the "talisman" or "trophy" that protects Lily from "horror & despair; annihilation; nonentity" is that "things themselves matter, nothing else." In painting she becomes "part of eternity," attuned to an unseen "presence" awkwardly evoked in the draft: "the thing she felt pressing out upon her & out of the visible world, this messenger who seemed to wait starkly & calmly & . . . to assert its rights & recall her from her strayings into a world that was more terrible & more intense than the world of affections . . . where failures were more terribly punished but success . . . hard rock" (*TLhd* 138, 144, 268).

Neither Roger Fry (a prime influence on Woolf's modernist art, to whom she thought of dedicating *To the Lighthouse*) nor Clive Bell directly cites Wörringer, but T. E. Hulme's 1913–1914 lectures had introduced his ideas to London, where abstraction had been in the air since 1910.[36] Of Fry's influence on modernist writers Woolf wrote in 1925, "Cézanne and Picasso had shown the way; writers should fling representation to the winds" or else seem "victims of the art of painting" who describe "apples, roses, china, pomegranates, tamarinds, and glass jars as well as words can paint them, which is, of course, not very well" (*RF* 172, "Pictures," *E* 4:243). While *To the Lighthouse* paints the visible world—its blue and silver evenings with flamingo clouds—it does not copy appearances for their own sake but, like Lily, seeks a "truth behind appearances": a wedge-shaped core of darkness, treasures hidden as in kings' tombs beneath Mrs. Ramsay's "deceptive" beauty, a white deal table suspended in a pear tree. When Woolf later compares the difficulty of portraying her mother to that of painting a Cézanne, she emphasizes that she, like Lily, seeks something behind the visible world's apples, roses, and glass jars. So does Mr. Ramsay in his "progress" from "nuts" and "roses" to "some turn on the road" where he "dismounted, tied his horse to a tree, & proceeded on foot alone" to face an apprehension like that which Wörringer finds expressed in abstract art:

> that the problem of human existence remains insoluble: our ignorance is complete, we know nothing; we never shall know anything . . . all diversions & excursions having been made we have to face the fact of our ignorance, . . . our powerlessness in the face of the greatest problems of life. [W]e come out on to a spit of land which the sea is slowly eating away & there we stand each alone, contemplating . . . lonely as a stake driven into the bed of a channel.[37]

Through an abstract aesthetics that turns away from mimetic representation—from the Madonnas of Michelangelo, Raphael, and Titian, Paunceforte's translucent landscapes, William's *Cherry Trees on the Kennet*—Lily (and Woolf) picture a hidden "truth" of the world. Like Mondrian with his progressively more abstract tree, Lily's formal adventure from "branch" to "tree" to "line . . . in the centre" moves from copying nature to composing forms that express something invisible to the eye alone.

Lily's abstract art has much in common with Mr. Ramsay's progress from P to Q toward an ever elusive R[eality], despite a crucial difference. Whereas he "never look[s] at things," Lily looks at and through them, seeking "a side of things . . . she looked at the jacmanna, the wall, the starlings—something spontaneous—immediate—which . . . these great men who saw kitchen tables in pear trees & lectured, worked & exhibited . . . neglected" (*TL* 71, *TLhd* 84). Indeed, he disparages art as if to assuage his class guilt for nuts, roses, "the pleasure he took in it all"—"as if to be caught happy in a world of misery was for an honest man the most despicable of crimes"; and he lectures on how "the arts are merely a decoration imposed" on life (*TLhd* 82, *TL* 43). Still, Lily shares his sense of nature's unfathomable violence and mystery, and her artistic practice—a labor of thought and feeling, "love" and "cunning"—is in its own way a quest for subject ("the residue of her thirty-three years"), object ("Mrs. Ramsay reading to James"), and the nature of reality ("the glove's twisted finger"). As Mr. Ramsay seeks truth in "angular essences," Lily seeks formal revelations of "things in themselves" (*TL* 23).

In light of Wörringer's theory, Lily's picture that is not "of them" in Mr. Bankes's sense condenses Mrs. Ramsay reading to James, Lily at Mrs. Ramsay's knee, and the hiddenness of Mrs. Ramsay herself in an abstract form—the triangular purple shape—that seeks a truth behind appearances: the grief of a daughter still partly merged with the mother; the loss of "the whole" that is the sine qua non of birth, being, language, art; the mystery of the mother's or anyone's being; and any subject's triangulated desire, reaching for the world. Her unfinished composition seems less a failure or false start than a statement of an existential problem that gestures toward its own solution, at once formal and developmental. For, seeking not "decoration" but "intimacy," Lily is suddenly startled to find her longing provisionally fulfilled by William's viewing of her work:

> It had been seen; it had been taken from her. This man had shared with her something profoundly intimate. And, thanking Mr. Ramsay for it and Mrs. Ramsay for it and the hour and the place, *crediting the world with a power which she had not suspected*—that one could walk away down that long gallery not alone any more but arm in arm with somebody—the strangest feeling in the world, and the most exhilarating—she nicked the catch of her paint-box to . . . and the nick seemed to surround in a circle forever the paint-box, the lawn, Mr. Bankes, and that wild villain, Cam, dashing past. (*TL* 53–54, my emphasis)

As William's critical, open-minded, curious scrutiny—"an agony" yet "immensely exciting"—takes Lily's painting out into the world, her effort to "have" her vision and make it visible to another validates her existence in its difference and freedom (*TL* 52, 209). In this small way, her unfinished picture already mediates the intimacy she desires: through William—no sexual object but a friend loved in himself—her art does not merely substitute for the broken "unity of the whole" but turns loss into gain—the strangest, most exhilarating feeling in a world whose "power" she now begins to sense.

Hunger for Art: Mildred's and Shakespeare's Masterpieces

The dinner party that fortuitously celebrates Minta and Paul's engagement intermingles domestic and fine arts and artists. Lily buffers Mrs. Ramsay's voiceless call to feminine self-sacrifice, her manipulative threat to drown "in seas of fire" unless Lily is "nice" to Charles Tansley, by thinking of her painting (*TL* 92). Lily finds Charles not at all pitiable, since he has his work, then remembers "as if she had found a treasure, that she had her work": "I shall put the tree further in the middle; then I shall avoid that awkward space. . . . She took up the salt cellar and put it down again on a flower . . . in the table-cloth, so as to remind herself to move the tree" (*TL* 84–85). As Lily outwardly complies, abandoning her experiment to see "what happens if one is not nice to that young man," her plan for her autobiographical tree buoys her spirits and she "laugh[s] out loud at what Mr. Tansley was saying" (*TL* 92–93). Later, "scorched" by "the heat of love" radiating from Paul Rayley, "its horror, its cruelty, its unscrupulosity," she sees the salt cellar and rejoices, "she need not marry, thank Heaven . . . She would move the tree rather more to the middle" (*TL* 102).

The salt-cellar not only shields Lily from becoming one of those "victims" Mrs. Ramsay leads "to the altar" but frees her to "reverence" Mrs. Ramsay's domestic art of orchestrating connections among people as Lily connects masses in her composition (*TL* 101, 52). Feeling her own life shrunk to an "infinitely long table and plates and knives" beside Minta and Paul's open future, Mrs. Ramsay wonders, "But what have I done with my life?" and wearily faces her intractable medium of human relations: "Nothing seemed to have merged. They all sat separate. And the whole of the effort of merging and flowing and creating rested on her. . . . if she did not do it nobody would" (*TL* 82–83). Mrs. Ramsay does it, gradually drawing these "scraps and fragments" all at cross-purposes into a candlelit "party round a table," making "common cause" against the darkness outside, until "Everything seemed right," joy ascending from husband and children and friends . . like a fume rising upwards, holding them safe together. . . . It partook . . . of eternity; . . . there is a coherence in things, a stability; something . . . is immune from change, and shines out . . . in the face of the flowing, the fleeting, the spectral, like a ruby; . . . Of such moments, she thought, the thing is made that endures. (*TL* 90, 97, 104–5)

Priestess of a secular communion that consecrates ephemeral moments into an experience that survives time and loss, Mrs. Ramsay ladles out "Mildred's masterpiece," the *boeuf en daube*, while voices abstracted from identity and meaning seem to cry "Latin words of a service in some Roman Catholic cathedral . . . as if . . . they had come into existence of themselves" (*TL* 80, 110). Embodying the company's "we" as the words, the music, the thing itself, these voices dissolve as if commingling separate lives in the fluid medium of sound: "And all the lives we ever lived and all the lives to be are full of trees and changing leaves," recites a voice that issues from her husband but seems "their own voice speaking."[38] As Mrs. Ramsay creates through her domestic art the intimacy Lily adores, even Augustus Carmichael wakes from his poet's dream to bow "as if he did her homage" (*TL* 111).

Yet this scene ends not with Mrs. Ramsay's triumph but with her own hunger for art. A desire "so strong that she never even thought of asking herself what it was" impels her into the parlor, where her husband sits reading, "to get something she wanted" though she "could not think what it was" (*TL* 117). She picks up a book and, "not know[ing] at first what the words meant at all," is soon "swinging" and "zigzagging" through Shakespeare's sonnet 98 "as from one branch to another, from one red and white flower to another": " 'Nor praise the deep vermilion in the rose,' she read. . . . she was ascending, she felt, on to the top, on to the summit. How satisfying! How restful! . . . And then there it was, suddenly entire; she held it in her hands, beautiful and reasonable, clear and complete, the essence sucked out of life and held rounded here—the sonnet" (*TL* 119, 121). In *The Mausoleum Book* Leslie Stephen describes a photograph of himself and Julia reading in the parlor at St. Ives with young Virginia behind them, gazing at the camera.[39] Here Lily (whose work Mrs. Ramsay dismisses) and the daughter-narrator (who lays the Victorian mother's ghost in order to write) seem invisible spectators of a scene that exalts art as life's "essence." In her unconscious thirst for art's elixir, Mrs. Ramsay dispels Lily's fantasy of her plenitude—her secret, sacred "tablets" inscribed with "everything"—and becomes herself a desiring, searching subject. Even as its words sound inconsolable depths, the sonnet's exquisite music and form—rhythm, rhyme, imagery, the climbing, branching syntax of its enclosed garden, immune to time and change—lift her "to the top . . . the summit." Demystifying the omnipotent maternal antagonist, the scene tacitly affirms both the daughter's art and desire's organic drive to branch out from originary "roots."[40]

The Shakespeare scene that endorses Lily's artistic quest contrasts another daughter's fate with Lily's branching desire. Watching her mother come downstairs, Prue thinks,

> That is *the thing itself,* . . . *as if there were only one person like that in the world; her mother.* And, from having been quite grown up, a moment before, talking with the others, she became a child again. . . . And thinking . . . how *she would never grow up and never leave home,* she said, like a child, "We thought of going down to the beach to watch the waves." (*TL* 116, my emphasis)

Prue—in the draft her mother's "slave"—becomes a child again as the "exhilarating" three-dimensional world collapses into the mother/child dyad.[41] As this scene deflects onto Prue Lily's dangerous longing to lose herself in the idealized mother, "Time Passes" records Prue's death as Lily quests on for forms that endure "like a ruby" or "a diamond in the sand" (*TL* 105, 132).

A Diamond in the Sand: Abstraction and Empathy in "Time Passes"

> I have some restless searcher in me. Why is there not a discovery in life? Something one can lay hands on & say 'This is it'? . . . Then . . . I have a great & astonishing sense of something there, which is 'it'—It is not exactly beauty that I mean. It is that the thing is in itself enough: satisfactory; achieved. . . . I do fairly frequently come upon this 'it'; & then feel quite at rest.
>
> —Woolf, *Diary,* 27 February 1926

On Wörringer's continuum "The Window" tends toward empathy, "Time Passes" toward abstraction. "Time Passes" was "the most difficult abstract piece of writing" Woolf had ever attempted: "I have to give an empty house, no people's characters, the passage of time, all eyeless & featureless with nothing to cling to" (*D* 3:76, 18 April 1926). The word "abstract" flags this ten-year "corridor of years" that her friends "dared" her to do as a Fry-inspired experiment in "fling[ing] representation to the winds."[42] Jettisoning the narrative conventions that "The Window" adapts to modernist psychological realism—event, plot, character, dialogue, and especially the empathic narrator who depicts the characters' psychic dramas—"Time Passes" delivers a shock of loss even before we learn of the three deaths. The narrator's new detachment marks the turn from empathy to abstraction. As if brutally heedless of our readerly investment in the characters' fates, she brackets events that would rivet a conventional narrator's attention. The sentences that float passing things into view and away on the river of time in "The Window"'s September idyll are here all but emptied of human forms. Faced with mindless nature's fecundity, indifferent violence, and mysterious, solitary beauty, she quests for some such symbolic refuge from time and death such as Wörringer theorizes and "Time Passes" in its formal abstractness offers (*TL* 132).

Of course, "The Window" foretells the destruction "Time Passes" records. In the midst of their "gaily spinning world," the Ramsays feel keenly the doomed stay human effort makes against inexorable time and death, he perched like a "desolate sea-bird" on "a spit of land which the sea is slowly eating away," she shedding secret tears, "bitter and black" (*MB* 84, *TL* 28, 44). "Time Passes"' abstract narrator—a voice "all eyeless & featureless with nothing to cling to"—abandons sentiment and tragedy to trace the dissolution of a world that foreknows its own vanishing.[43] At the same time this voice echoes with the ghostly presence of the daughter-subject (Lily, Woolf, the earlier narrator), felt in the (historical) past tense ("slept") that breaks through the fictional present in this early sketch:

> The Seasons./The Skull/The gradual dissolution of everything/This is to be contrasted with the permanence of—what?/Sun, moon & stars./ Hopeless gulfs of misery./Cruelty./The War./Change. Oblivion. Human vitality. Old woman/Cleaning up. The bobbed up, valorous, as of a principle/of human life projected/We are handed on by our children ?/ Shawls & shooting caps. A green handled brush./The devouringness of nature./But all the time, this passes, accumulates./Darkness./The welter of winds & waves/What then is the medium through wh. we regard human beings?/Tears. [di?]/[*Sleep th*] *Slept through life* (*TLhd* Appendix B, my emphasis)

Even as this dark passage between two days and two versions of a painting evokes a world emptied of life, its abstract forms retain human shape ("Old woman," "we," "human beings") and feeling ("Hopeless gulfs of misery," "Human vitality").[44] The narrator's quest through a sleeping world spans the ten-year night—an oblivion of grief—between Lily's falling asleep at the beginning and her waking at the end. Abstracted into a shattered seeker in a world lapsed out of meaning, a shadowy presence within the narrative voice, a daughter-subject undone by loss eyelessly watches the house fall into decrepitude and its slow restoration before awakening as Lily Briscoe in a recreated world. The eyeless, featureless quester for some diamond-hard stay against time and loss finds revelation not in any idea but in the organic vitality, will, and spirit of the aging caretakers who labor painfully to save the summer house from ruin.

The sleep that descends with "Time Passes" foreshadows death's oblivion. The last spoken words of the day seem inconsequent yet portentous: "Well, we must wait for the future to show"; "One can hardly tell which is the sea and which is the land"; "Andrew, . . . just put out the light in the hall" (*TL* 125). Nightfall heralds death's absolute destruction in the temporary unmaking of day by darkness, waking life by dreaming sleep, mimetic narrative replete with character and event by nature's abstract force: "Nothing, it seemed, could survive" the "downpouring of immense darkness" that engulfs the house before the narrator's eyes (*TL* 125). Sleep strips away identity and relation, leaving "scarcely anything . . . of body or mind by which one could say, 'This is he' or 'This is she' "; a hand takes on a life of its own, rising "as if to clutch something or ward off something"; "somebody laugh[s] aloud as if sharing a joke with nothingness" (*TL* 126). With the vivid life of "The Window" extinguished, the narrator imagines the house animated by "questioning" sea "airs" creeping among letters and books (*TL* 126). Seeing them waft upstairs where Mr. Carmichael blows out his candle, she would forbid them to "touch" or "destroy," make them "cease"; but if she prevails, it is only for "one night." A winter of ruinous nights follows, the trees like "tattered flags" signaling "death in battle," "gold letters" flashing from the "marble pages" of cathedral tombs (*TL* 126–27). Helpless to slow this destruction, she quests for what remains.

"Time Passes" deepens "The Window" 's picture of a world founded on loss. Night anticipates death; death in the abstract preexists any particular death. The "changing leaves" painted by Lily, sung by the poet, and gazed on by Mrs. Ramsay are storm-tossed by lengthening autumn nights. As trees "plunge and bend and their leaves fly helter skelter," the bodiless floating subject who seeks a "sharer of . . . solitude" finds the world's mirror shattered: "no image . . . comes . . . bringing the night to order and making the world reflect the compass of the soul. . . . Almost it would appear that it is useless in such confusion to ask the night those questions as to what, and why, and wherefore, which tempt the sleeper from his bed to seek an answer" (*TL* 128). Rendered abstractly by the dispassionate narrator, the seeker briefly takes on flesh, identity—"[Mr. Ramsay, stumbling along a passage one dark morning, stretched his arms out, but Mrs. Ramsay having died rather suddenly the night before, his arms . . . remained empty]"—before human fatality again engulfs particularity.[45]

As "great armies" follow the "advance guards" of sea airs into a house of unresisting things, the subject thins to nothingness (*TL* 128–29). Earlier, as we saw, Lily mirrors an inchoate self in an idealized mother, longing to merge with a fantasized plenitude that she knows to be an illusion. Now death shatters the mother's mirror, and Mrs. Ramsay's empty looking glass reflects the eyeless, featureless, imageless subject, precariously suspended over a void.[46] Whereas it once held "a face," "a world hollowed out in which a figure turned, a hand flashed, the door opened, in came children rushing and tumbling; and went out again," the looking glass is now a "pool" in which "light bent to its own image in adoration," as if reflecting her ethereal afterimage: "So loveliness reigned and stillness, and together made the shape of loveliness itself, a form from which life had parted"; "the clammy sea airs . . . scarcely disturbed the peace, the indifference, the air of pure integrity" (*TL* 129–30). As Mrs. Ramsay earlier feels "sopped full" of other people's emotions, now this silent "form" "w[eaves] into itself" bird cries, ships' horns, "a dog's bark, a man's shout" (*TL* 32, 129–30). As she earlier looks up in fear because the children are late, now "one fold" of her green shawl loosens and falls "with a roar, with a rupture, as after centuries of quiescence, a rock rends itself from the mountain and hurtles crashing into the valley" (*TL* 130). Unbroken by any human form, light reflects light, emptiness emptiness, questions questions in dizzying infinity. Confronted with this radical ungrounding of being and meaning that precedes and is laid bare by the mother's death, the subject loses substance, voice, identity: "Nothing it seemed could break that image, corrupt that innocence, or disturb the swaying mantle of silence."[47]

As if to interrupt this infinite regress, the effaced subject with nothing to cling to quests "hither and thither" for "some absolute good, some crystal of intensity, remote from the known pleasures and familiar virtues" of "domestic life, single, hard, bright, like a diamond in the sand" that "would render the possessor secure" (*TL* 132). While the looking glass and the mirroring world hold out the promise of a "face," the hope of an absolute ground is illusory: nothing can render the quester secure. But a treasure does materialize to rescue her from "Oblivion": Mrs. McNab comes "tearing the veil of silence with hands that had stood in the washtub, grinding it with boots that had crunched the shingle . . . to open all the windows, and dust the bedrooms" (*TL* 130). A flesh-and-blood survivor of vicissitudes both natural and social, this "bobbed up" and "valorous" paragon of "Human vitality" embodies the very "principle/of human life" (*TLhd* Appendix B). A grotesque parody of Mrs. Ramsay (as is Lily in her littleness and insignificance), Mrs. McNab proves that the world that remains is enough to break the silence, to bring a house back from ruin or an effaced daughter from the edge of madness. Mrs. McNab rubs the looking glass and—her own face appearing where once was Mrs. Ramsay's—performs a Marie Lloyd music-hall number for her own pleasure:

> something that had been gay twenty years before on the stage . . . but now, coming from the toothless, bonneted, care-taking woman, was robbed of meaning, was like the voice of witlessness, humour, persistency itself, trodden down but springing up again. . . . [S]he seemed to say how it was one long sorrow and trouble. . . . How long, she asked, creaking and groaning on her knees under the bed, . . . shall it endure? but hobbled to her feet . . . and again with her sidelong leer which slipped . . . from her own face, and her own sorrows, stood and gaped in the glass, aimlessly smiling . . . as if, after all, she had her consolations, as if indeed there twined about her dirge some incorrigible hope. . . . some channel in the depths of obscurity through which light enough issued to . . . make her . . . mumble out the old music hall song. The mystic, the visionary, walking the beach on a fine night . . . asking . . . "What am I," "What is this?" had suddenly an answer vouchsafed them (they could not say what it was) so that they were warm in the frost and had comfort in the desert.[48]

Interrupting the mirror's ricocheting reflections with her impromptu song, Mrs. McNab "vouchsafes" an "answer" to the disembodied seeker stranded on the shores of being.[49] This answer is all the more incontrovertible for being "robbed of meaning," abstracted from signification like the grin that slips from her face. A lurching, leering survivor singing of pain and trouble and sorrow, Mrs. McNab kicks the stone in living proof that the world goes on, the matrix of meaning holds, the human world now again visible in the mirror remains and consoles, life, even toothless, creaking, groaning, is "enough" (*TLhd* 236).

With this answer the mother's image is broken, multiplied, and scattered through the mirroring world in a profusion of metaphors that figure life inseparable from death, loss from meaning. Prue's wedding in a springtime "bare and bright like a virgin fierce in her chastity" stirs forebodings in the now "wakeful," "hopeful" wanderer on the shore:

> imaginations of the strangest kind—of flesh turned to atoms which drove before the wind, of stars flashing in their hearts, of cliff, sea, cloud, and sky brought purposely together to assemble outwardly the scattered parts of the vision within. In those mirrors, the minds of men, in those pools of uneasy water, . . . dreams persisted, and it was impossible to resist the strange intimation which every gull, flower, tree, man and woman, and the white earth itself seemed to declare (but if questioned at once to withdraw) that good triumphs, happiness prevails, order

rules. . . . softened and acquiescent, the spring . . . threw her cloak about her, veiled her eyes, averted her head, and . . . seemed to have taken upon her a knowledge of the sorrows of mankind. (*TL* 131–32)

Like an apotheosis of "The Window"'s madonna who foreknows Prue's, Andrew's, and her own death ("Never did anybody look so sad"), a nature veiled in maternal pathos binds beauty to destruction (*TL* 28). As Lily once longed to question Mrs. Ramsay, the restless seeker asks "sea and sky what message they reported or what vision they affirmed" and finds "among the usual tokens of divine bounty . . . something out of harmony with this jocundity and this serenity. . . . It was difficult . . . as one walked by the sea, to marvel how beauty outside mirrored beauty within" (*TL* 133–34). Peering into the abyss of language, she finds the "dream, of sharing, completing, of finding in solitude on the beach an answer, . . . but a reflection in a mirror, and the mirror itself . . . but the surface glassiness which forms in quiescence"; again "to pace the beach" is "impossible; contemplation . . . unendurable; the mirror . . . broken" (*TL* 134). Yet desire survives even war's "gigantic chaos," which hardly perturbs an "eyeless," "terrible" nature (*TL* 134–35). Mr. Carmichael's elegiac poems meet acclaim; Mrs. McNab picks flowers ("Thinking no harm, for the family would not come") and stands before the glass remembering bygone days: "She could see her . . . she could see her. . . . Yes, she could see Mrs. Ramsay. . . . She could see her now" (*TL* 135–37).

Entering Mrs. McNab's mind, the narrator is borne back toward empathy:

> She sighed; there was too much work for one woman. She wagged her head. . . . This had been the nursery. Why, it was all damp in here; the plaster was falling. Whatever did they want to hang a beast's skull there? gone mouldy too. And rats in all the attics. The rain came in. But they never sent; never came. . . . She didn't like to be up here at dusk alone neither. (*TL* 137)

In equipoise between abstraction and empathy, the narrator and Mrs. McNab make stay against destruction and beckon the seeker back to a life that is enough, an art that arrests nature's flux. Like Mrs. Ramsay's looking glass, the narrator's mirror, once animated with people, then stilled in inhuman loveliness, now reflects Mrs. McNab's vitality and the new life her work brings to "rusty laborious birth" (*TL* 139). With the house on the verge of pitching forever "downwards to . . . darkness," the narrator wonders, "What power could now prevent the fertility, the insensibility of nature? Mrs. McNab's dream of a lady, of a child, of a plate of milk soup?" (*TL* 138). Then a message announces the family's return, and Mrs.

McNab enlists her son and Mrs. Bast in a Herculean labor of deferred maintenance. Her humble arts suffice: the "power" of dream and memory stops the ruinous sea airs, guides the workers' toil, and enlivens their respite as, in a homely replay of the dinner party, they regale each other with tales of the Ramsays over tea.

Mrs. McNab and Mrs. Bast throw the eyeless, featureless daughter-subject something to cling to. Arduously recreating the material world, they anticipate Lily's own creative effort. Midwives to her rebirth at the end of "Time Passes," they bring a lost world back through memory's ordering power so that the "voice" of its "beauty" murmurs like a lullaby over the restored house, "too softly to hear exactly what it said—but what mattered if the meaning were plain?" (*TL* 142). An ethereal echo of the mother's voice, the murmuring world entreats the sleeper to see "how . . . a child might look" in the sceptered night's mirroring "eyes" and reawakens desire by "half-heard melody," "intermittent music," waves sounding "messages of peace" (*TL* 141–42). As a domesticated nature "sing[s] its song," the rebirth accomplished by Mrs. McNab culminates in the abstract seeker's fall back into organic body and identity: having "slept through life" all these years, "Lily Briscoe . . . clutched at her blankets as a faller clutches at the turf on the edge of a cliff. . . . Here she was again, she thought, sitting bolt upright in bed. Awake."[50] Lily wakes with a shock, thrown into being in the lap of a world that recalls but exceeds the lost mother—a world that, for her, is not yet enough. Refusing its soothing murmur—"why not accept this, be content with this, acquiesce and resign?"—Lily quests on to make "Life stand still" in the mirror of her art, to forge a diamond from the sands of time (*TL* 142, 161).

"The Lighthouse": Mourning, Painting, Revelation

> Until I was in the forties . . . the presence of my mother obsessed me. . . . Then one day . . . I made up . . . *To the Lighthouse*; in a great, apparently involuntary, rush. . . . I wrote the book very quickly; and when it was written, I ceased to be obsessed by my mother. I no longer hear her voice; I do not see her.
>
> I suppose that I did for myself what psycho-analysts do for their patients. I expressed some very long felt and deeply felt emotion. And in expressing it I explained it and then laid it to rest.
>
> —Woolf, *Moments of Being*

> I used to think of [father] & mother daily; but writing The Lighthouse, laid them in my mind. . . . (I believe this to be true—that I was obsessed by them both, unhealthily; & writing of them was a necessary act.) He

comes back now more as a contemporary. I must read him some day. I
wonder if I can feel again, I hear his voice, I know this by heart?

—Woolf, *Diary*, 28 November 1928

Just after *To the Lighthouse* bubbled up in her mind, Woolf sketched three
stories of guests at Mrs. Dalloway's party whose memories of lost child-
hoods resonate with her own expression of an old, deep emotion to dispel
an "unhealthy" obsession.[51] In "Ancestors," a "trivial" party evokes Mrs.
Vallance's Scottish childhood, peopled by "really dignified simple men and
women" like her parents (*CSF* 181). Prefiguring Cam, she recalls running
"wild among the currant bushes" and hearing "the most wonderful talk of
her time" from her father's friends; later, her widowed mother sat "among
her flowers by the hour," seeming "more with ghosts than with them all,
dreaming of the past . . . so much more real than the present" (181–82).
Through tears that carry a lifetime's sorrow ("she had suffered abominably . . . life was not what it had seemed then—it was like this party"),
she sees herself, "that little girl who was to travel so far, picking Sweet
Alice," reading in the pine attic, reciting Shelley to her father (182). Only
these people "had known . . . what she had it in her to be"; "with them she
was so pure so good so gifted that she had it in her to be anything"; could
she have stayed "for ever" in that garden, "always starlit, and always summer," then "none of this" would exist, and "she would have been oh perfectly happy, perfectly good" (182–83). Charged with loss and failed hope,
Mrs. Vallance's melancholy nostalgia turns her present to dust.

In "The Introduction," the aspiring writer Lily Everit (foreshadowing
Lily Briscoe) remembers lost childhood freedoms on being pinned like a
butterfly into the feminine role by Shakespeare's presumptive heir Bob
Brinsley. In "Together and Apart" two guests veer away from intimacy on
discovering a mutual love of Canterbury: "To be asked if he knew Canterbury—when the best years of his life, all his memories, things he had
never been able to tell anybody, but had tried to write (and he sighed) . . .
it made [Mr. Serle] laugh" (*CSF* 190). As a stranger "touche[s] the
spring," releasing "silver drops" of memory like those in which Lily
Briscoe dips her brush ("With such an image his poems often began"), he
feels that he has "never done a tenth part of what he could have done, and
had dreamed of doing as a boy in Canterbury" (190–91). Abruptly he
departs, pained like Mrs. Vallance by his "untapped resources"; "dissatisfied with his life, with himself, yawning, empty, capricious" (192).

Mrs. Vallance and Mr. Serle set the stage for Lily's struggle to recover
the past's lost plenitude in a work of art, freeing the present from its
shadow. Through mourning made visible as painting/writing, Lily/Woolf

lays the parents' ghosts, stills their voices, transforms obsession into memory, and delivers herself to the present, as Mrs. Vallance and Mr. Serle are powerless to do. In this light, the object of Lily/Woolf's quest for "the thing itself before it has been made anything" is a subject: herself, freed of the idealized mother who laughed at her desire to make art and the father whose long life would have made her work "inconceivable" (*TL* 193). If her picture/novel begins as an elegiac portrait of "father & mother & child in the garden," its final brushstroke completes a portrait of the daughter-artist grown up and into powers that both carry on and make new the parents' gifts—one who, by mourning and working through her memories of the past, wrests from her dead parents a vital inheritance (*D* 3:36).

The problem of getting beyond loss and substitution to the thing itself—from obsession with an irretrievable past to a present at once ordinary and miraculous—troubles Lily as she wakes, still questioning like the seeker of "Time Passes" in a "house full of unrelated passions": "What does it mean then, what can it all mean? . . . what did she feel, come back after all these years and Mrs. Ramsay dead? Nothing, nothing—nothing that she could express at all" (*TL* 145, 148). The "beautiful still day" seems "unreal," "as if the link that usually bound things together had been cut"; overhearing broken bits of Mr. Ramsay's recitation of Cowper's "The Castaway" as he passes the window ("Alone" and "Perished") makes her want to mend the syntax in "some sentence" that gets at "the truth of things" (*TL* 146–47). The "early morning hour" seems "frightening" and "exciting": "anything might happen" (*TL* 179, 191, 147, 146). As if "The Window"'s vanished paradise endows its "extraordinary unreality," Lily remembers her unfinished picture, "borne . . . in her mind all these years," with its "problem about a foreground. . . . Move the tree to the middle, she had said. . . . She would paint that picture now. . . . the solution had come to her: she knew now what she wanted to do" (*TL* 147–48).

Hardly has Lily picked up her brush when the Victorian parents loom into view, dead and alive. Mr. Ramsay descends on her demanding sympathy; Mrs. Ramsay rises up, an Angel on the Lawn modeling a "rapture of sympathy, of delight in the reward [women] had," Lily thinks sourly, "evidently . . . the most supreme bliss of which human nature was capable" (*TL* 150). Lily obstinately withholds: "Giving, giving, giving, she had died—and had left all this. Really, she was angry with Mrs. Ramsay. . . . It was all Mrs. Ramsay's doing" (*TL* 149). Facing off the Victorian father and the modernist daughter, the narrator sees them through to comic conciliation as Lily blurts out, "What beautiful boots!" then recoils in fear: "To praise his boots when he asked her to solace his soul; when he had

shown her his bleeding hands, his lacerated heart, . . . then to say, cheerfully, 'Ah, but what beautiful boots you wear!' deserved, she knew, and
she looked up expecting to get it, in one of his sudden roars of ill-temper,
complete annihilation" (*TL* 153). Not at all: he forgets self-pity, shows off
his magnificent footwear, praises their maker (England's finest), and bends
to knot and unknot Lily's laces "three times" in a mock-epic rite that
delivers them to the "blessed island of good boots" (*TL* 154). When Mr.
Ramsay leaves her to go down to the boat, the sympathy he no longer
demands wells up, "torment[ing] and "troubling her for expression" as he
recedes out of range into "some other region," "salut[ing]" her as he
passes with James and Cam, whose morose bearing annoys Lily on his
behalf (*TL* 154–56).

Through this unexpressed sympathy, "cast back on her, like a bramble
sprung across her face," Mr. Ramsay enters Lily's picture (*TL* 156). As her
brush flicks across the canvas, her mind moves between remembering
Mrs. Ramsay in the garden and imagining Mr. Ramsay's voyage. Her gaze
out to sea introduces all the boat scenes, choreographing her inward voyage and his sail to the rhythmic dance of her brushstrokes. His voyage,
further, is not the simple event it seems, for the force of Lily's thought crys-
tallizes the mimetic narrative of a long-deferred "great expedition" into
an abstract figure of life as an adventurous voyage toward death (*TL* 10).
Through a work of art that is also a work of mourning, Lily grapples with
her "formidable ancient enemy . . . this truth, this reality" to grasp the
"angular essences" of mother and father, past and present, self and world
(*TL* 158).

With Mr. Ramsay launched, Lily rides a "current[]" of brushstrokes,
her mind tossing up "scenes, and names, and sayings, and memories and
ideas, like a fountain spurting over that glaring, hideously difficult white
space, while she modelled it with greens and blues" (*TL* 159). Amid the
flotsam of associations, Tansley's bogey bobs up, his monitory voice
releasing a raft of memories that carry her past their old antagonism. Lost
in thought and intent on "truth," Lily recalls a windy morning when Mrs.
Ramsay, writing "letters by a rock," glimpsed something in the sea and
asked, "'is it a lobster pot? Is it an upturned boat?'" Suddenly Lily and
Charles were skipping stones

> and getting on very well. . . . That woman . . . resolved everything into
> simplicity; made these angers, irritations fall off like old rags; she
> brought together this and that and then this, and so made out of that
> miserable silliness and spite . . . something—this scene on the beach for
> example, this moment of friendship and liking—which survived, after all
> these years complete, so that she dipped into it to re-fashion her mem-

ory of him, and there it stayed in the mind affecting one almost like a work of art. (*TL* 160)

Epitomized in her ardent letter-writing (the "miracle" of "speech attempted" [*JR* 93]), Mrs. Ramsay's gift of banishing petty differences, bringing this and that together, inspires a solution to Lily's compositional problem and to her "old question" "What is the meaning of life?":

> *The great revelation had never come. The great revelation perhaps never did come.* Instead there were little daily miracles, illuminations, matches struck unexpectedly in the dark; here was one. This, that, and the other; herself and Charles Tansley and the breaking wave; Mrs. Ramsay bringing them together . . . making of the moment something permanent (as in another sphere Lily herself tried to make of the moment something permanent)—*this was of the nature of a revelation.* In the midst of chaos there was shape; this eternal passing and flowing . . . was struck into stability. Life stand still here, Mrs. Ramsay said. "Mrs. Ramsay! Mrs. Ramsay!" she repeated. She owed it all to her. (*TL* 161, my emphasis)

Putting aside Tansley's misogyny and her equally "grotesque" abuse of him as a "whipping-boy," Lily comes upon that "reality" she seeks, that "intimacy, which is knowledge"—something in "the nature of a revelation" (*TL* 197). Brushing on red and gray, she feels "as if a door had opened, and one went in and stood gazing silently about in a high cathedral-like place"—as if she has entered Mrs. Ramsay's "sanctuary" and beholds her sacred "tablets."[52]

No worshipper like William, Lily modernizes this revelation in making it her own. As she dips her brush in memory's silver drop to "illumine[] the darkness of the past," the "shortsighted" Mrs. Ramsay ("Is it a boat? Is it a cork?" "Is it a cask?") seems to defer to Lily's "vision" (*TL* 160, 171–72). Her thoughts leap from Mrs. Ramsay's "mania . . . for marriage" and vision of her life continuing in Paul and Minta's to the actual Rayleys, deviant Ramsays who have sailed choppy seas to end as "excellent friends" in an open marriage (*TL* 175, 174). Lily imagines telling Mrs. Ramsay that their "marriage had not been a success," feeling "a little triumphant" since she had only "escaped by the skin of her teeth" the scheme to make her marry William (*TL* 174, 176). Still, she has escaped:

> Mrs. Ramsay has faded and gone, she thought. We can over-ride her wishes, improve away her limited, old-fashioned ideas. . . . Mockingly she seemed to see her there at the end of the corridor of years saying, of all incongruous things, "Marry, marry!" . . . And one would have to say to her, It has all gone against your wishes. They're happy like that; I'm happy like this. Life has changed completely. At that all her being, even

her beauty, became for a moment, dusty and out of date. For a moment
Lily, standing there, with the sun hot on her back . . . triumphed over
Mrs. Ramsay. (*TL* 174–75)

Lily now recalls her "enormous exultation" at the dinner party when it
"flashed upon her that she would move the tree to the middle, and need
never marry anybody. . . . She had felt, now she could stand up to Mrs.
Ramsay—a tribute to the astonishing power that Mrs. Ramsay had over
one. Do this, she said, and one did it. Even her shadow at the window
with James was full of authority" (*TL* 176). She remembers too how
William, "shocked by her neglect of the significance of mother and son,"
pondered her original yet "not cynical" rendering of "a subject which,
they agreed, Raphael had treated divinely," his "disinterested intelligence" fortifying her in her struggle to paint what she sees (*TL* 176).

Seeing the empty step through William's remembered gaze, Lily conjures his Raphaelesque Madonna, Mrs. Ramsay as fetishized mother in
a symbolic economy ruled by masculine desire: "the shape of a woman,
peaceful and silent, with downcast eyes. . . . She would never lift
them."[53] Under the spell of this endless tradition of feminine substitutes,
Lily is momentarily overwhelmed by an "emotion[] of the body," a longing so intense that it empties the world of substance, turning steps and
chair and garden into mere "curves and arabesques flourishing round a
centre of complete emptiness. 'What does it mean? How do you explain
it all?' " she wants to ask Mr. Carmichael (*TL* 178–79). Lily can no
more bring Mrs. Ramsay back than she could possess her while she
lived, but her desire for "truth," "reality" carries her past substitutes
and empty simulacra. Almost miraculously, the emptiness where once
was the maternal plenitude with which she longed to merge "like waters
poured into one jar" slowly fills to become "a pool of thought, a deep
basin of reality" in which "the whole world seem[s] to have dissolved,"
so that "had Mr. Carmichael spoken . . . a little tear would have rent the
surface pool. . . . A hand would be shoved up, a blade would be flashed"
(*TL* 179). Lily spells out his wisdom: art is a magic sword that cuts both
ways. On the one hand, " 'you' and 'I' and 'she' pass and vanish; nothing stays," no art can capture the thing itself. On the other, "words" and
"paint," memory, imagination, and art, endure, so that, basking,
"gorged with existence," "sailing serenely through a world which satisfied all his wants," he has "only to put down his hand where he lay on
the lawn to fish up anything he wanted" (*TL* 178–79). Looking at her
picture, Lily too feels something of this serenity: "it would be hung in
the attics" yet one might say "even of a picture like that"—"of what it

attempted" if not of the "actual picture"—"that it 'remained for ever'" (*TL* 179). Art makes stay against time and death, not for the things it depicts but for the makers and beholders possessed of its double-edged sword.

Now, "without being aware of any unhappiness," Lily feels her eyes overflow with "a hot liquid" she does not recognize as tears (*TL* 179–80). As if welling up from a source deeper than grief—that "pool of thought," that "deep basin of reality" that is the world—this liquid seems at first about to drown her in irreparable loss, anguished grief, "bitter anger," mourning and the ever receding mirage of mourning's end ("to be called back, just as she thought she would never feel sorrow for Mrs. Ramsay again") (*TL* 181). Floundering in these "waters of annihilation," this "reality" in which she must now learn to breathe and swim, Lily momentarily resembles the mutilated fish Macalister's boy throws back into the sea, interpolated just here in the text (*TL* 181). If only she and Mr. Carmichael "demanded an explanation," she thinks, "those empty flourishes would form into shape; if they shouted loudly enough Mrs. Ramsay would return" (*TL* 180). Now, as if conjured by Lily's longing, Mrs. Ramsay does "mysteriously" return only to depart, "staying lightly" by Lily's side before being borne away on the flood of time: "raising to her forehead a wreath of white flowers . . . stepping with her usual quickness across fields among whose folds, purplish and soft, among whose flowers, hyacinths or lilies, she vanished" (*TL* 181).

As this apparition recedes in mourning's fields of purple and white, revelation deepens. Feeling an "instinctive need of distance and blue," Lily gazes over the bay toward what she imagines is the Ramsays' boat, taking its course among signaling ships and cliffs while Cam "murmur[s], dreamily half asleep, how we perished, each alone" (*TL* 182, 191). This moment answers Lily's earlier wish to join *perished* with *alone* in a sentence that captures the truth of things. Translating this sentence into her visual language, Lily surfaces from watery annihilation to find herself a little boat sailing among the others on the bay:

> One glided, one shook one's sails . . . between things, beyond things. Empty it was not, but full to the brim. She seemed to be standing up to the lips in some substance, to move and float and sink in it, yes, for these waters were unfathomably deep. Into them had spilled so many lives. The Ramsays'; the children's; and all sorts of waifs and strays of things besides. A washerwoman with her basket; a rook, a red-hot poker; the purples and grey-greens of flowers: some common feeling held the whole. (*TL* 192)

This epiphany transforms and fulfills Lily's old fantasy of merging like waters in one jar as she sees herself taking her course among the other boats—each separate, yet voyaging together through time's unfathomable waters, the bay replete with "so many lives" and "things." Afloat on being's flowing "substance," she finds the empty world suddenly "full." The wound that loss has cut in her side is salved by Mr. Ramsay's vision of life as a voyage each makes "Alone." With everyone in the same boat, so to speak, these waters of life and death comprehend all beings, as in Cowper's paradoxical refrain—"We perished, each alone"—in which aloneness is a "common feeling," a predicate of "We," and voices live to tell the tale of perishing.

Pondering this "common feeling," Lily envisions artists as "lovers" who give nature's "elements" "a wholeness not theirs in life," composing "globed compacted things over which thought lingers, and love plays" (*TL* 192). But her picture still eludes her, until she asks desperately, "if one can neither think nor feel . . . where is one?" only to reach a further epiphany. "*Here on the grass, on the ground*," she suddenly understands: "*Here sitting on the world*," she thinks, feeling "that everything this morning was happening for the first time. . . . The lawn was the world; they were up here together, on this exalted station . . . Mr. Carmichael . . . seemed . . . to share her thoughts" (*TL* 193–94, my emphasis). *On the ground, on the world* as if "for the first time," Lily breaks the vise of the past and arrives "Here," now, in a world teeming not with ghosts but with grass, ants, plantains, canvas, brush, so many lives—the everyday world of things in themselves.

Lily consecrates this arrival in unspoken communion with Augustus Carmichael, her silent mentor in how to live, what to do in a world in which everything perishes but words and paint. Now old and famous, said to have "lost all interest in life" when Andrew died, he too has made an elegist's journey: his poems say "something about death," "very little about love" (*TL* 194–95). Scarcely wanting "other people," he "did not much like" Mrs. Ramsay, Lily remembers, thinking of her "masterfulness," "positiveness," reserve, "monotonous" beauty, and devotion to the poor and sick—"a little distressing to people" like themselves, who doubt the efficacy of action, believe in "the supremacy of thought," and feel "the care of the world more truly theirs than hers": "one could not imagine Mrs. Ramsay standing painting, lying reading, a whole morning on the lawn. . . . Her going was a reproach to them."[54] Her defense of art steeled by Mr. Carmichael's presence, Lily still longs for "some secret sense" by which "to steal through keyholes and surround" Mrs. Ramsay, "which took to itself and treasured up . . . her thoughts, her imaginations, her desires" (*TL* 198). But the shift of tense in the very articulation of this wish (not *which might take and treasure* but *which took and treasured*) registers her dawning recognition that what she desires she already possesses: "What did the hedge," the garden, a wave breaking, mean to Mrs. Ramsay?—"(Lily looked up, as she had seen Mrs. Ramsay look up; she too heard a wave falling on the beach)" (*TL* 198). Without losing her critical difference, the modernist daughter at once continues and transforms the Victorian mother in body, spirit, gesture, art.

From her vantage "Here sitting on the world" Lily at last lets Mrs. Ramsay's ghost go: "Down fields, across valleys, white, flower-strewn— that was how she would have painted it. . . . They went, the three of them together, Mrs. Ramsay walking rather fast in front, as if she expected to meet some one round the corner."[55] Now things in themselves can appear, unclouded by obsession. Lily sees a flutter of white at the window as someone settles in a chair and throws "an odd-shaped triangular shadow over the step. It altered the composition of the picture a little. It was interesting. It might be useful" (*TL* 201). This fortuitous real shadow obviously recalls the "triangular purple shape" of the first painting, yet Lily does not think of that. Mourning's purple has faded; obsession subsides, unveiling a new picture of the world. If this triangular shadow stands in for the now missing bodies in Lily's composition, she apprehends it as a fresh discovery, something not seen before, "interesting," possibly "useful." It makes her feel that "the problem"—her longing "to be on a level with ordinary experience, to feel simply that's a chair, that's a table, and yet at the same time, It's a miracle, it's an ecstasy"—"might be solved after all" (*TL* 202). Gazing at this shadow—an emblem of things in themselves in their hiddenness, their unseen reality, an intimation of miracle and ecstasy amid everyday tables and chairs—Lily glimpses a life no longer consumed by longing for a lost past. What she once felt only Mrs. Ramsay could give, the world now casually, prodigally, provides. The daughter's madonna, that parable of triangulated desire, reveals itself in the white light of the everyday.

With this central element of her abstract composition in place, Lily invokes Mrs. Ramsay one last time, then is finally released from unquiet obsession into ordinary experience:

> " . . . Mrs. Ramsay!" she cried, feeling the old horror come back—to want and want and not to have. Could she inflict that still? And then, quietly, as if she refrained, that too became part of ordinary experience, was on a level with the chair, with the table. Mrs. Ramsay—it was part of her perfect goodness—sat there quite simply . . . , cast her shadow on the step. There she sat. (*TL* 202)

Separation is accomplished. Subject and object exist distinct in space-time, Lily "here . . . on the world," Mrs. Ramsay "There" in the past.[56] No daughter clasps her knees. The odd-shaped triangular shadow has shed the color of loss, of mutilating obsession, and signals everyday experience—a chair, a lawn, a shadow, a table—in all its mysterious possibility. With this revelation, "as if she had something she must share, yet could hardly leave her easel, so full her mind was of what she was thinking, of what she was seeing," Lily, the lost mother safe within her, looks out to the great world in which Mr. Ramsay is voyaging from P to Q toward Reality: "Where was that boat now? And Mr. Ramsay? She wanted him" (TL 202).

The Voyage to Death

> Life is as I've said since I was 10, awfully interesting—if anything, quicker, keener, at 44 than 24—more desperate I suppose, as the river shoots to Niagara—my new vision of death; active, positive, like all the rest, exciting; & of great importance—as an experience.
>
> —Woolf, Diary, 23 November 1926

"So much depends . . . upon distance," Lily reflects, propelled to the lawn's edge in search of the Ramsays' boat; "whether people are near us or far from us; for her feeling for Mr. Ramsay changed as he sailed further and further across the bay" (TL 191). At last the novel approaches its original "centre," her father's character, memorably summed up by his reciting "We perished, each alone" while crushing a dying mackerel. The boat scenes—sections 4, 8, 10, and 12 of "The Lighthouse"—fill out this caricature, portraying Mr. Ramsay's love for and gifts to his children along with his emotional tyranny. Having wrestled obsession to the "ground" of ordinary experience, Lily can paint him now because—distant in time and space, free of the rage that blinds his children—she can see him, not physically but with that "trick of the painter's eye" that seeks reality, truth, the thing itself behind apparently random and contingent appearances (TL 181). The daughter's portrait of the father pays homage to his legacy even as it bestows the sympathy he has ceased to compel.

Each framed by Lily's gaze, the boat scenes refract the portrait of "father & mother & child in the garden" through a temporal prism, with effects not unlike cubism's spatial simultaneity. Mr. Ramsay is seventy-one in "The Lighthouse," just Leslie Stephen's age at his death, which "mercifully" liberated his young daughters from those "Greek slave years" when his grief and self-pity engulfed them.[57] Transmuting two distinct phases of an autobiographical father/daughter relation into simultaneous events distant in space rather than time, "The Lighthouse" alternates self-portraits of the daughter-artist as she was and as she is: the seventeen-year-old Cam/Virginia, besieged by her father's demands; and the adult Lily/Woolf, freed by "distance" (time become space) to paint the whole picture: the needy father who threatens to overwhelm her; her love and sympathy as he teaches her his failure-proof knot; the children's bad grace as they troop down to the boat; her compassion for them too ("this was tragedy—not palls, dust, and the shroud; but children coerced, their spirits subdued"); his arrival at the lighthouse, which she paints as the death that not only freed her but left her the priceless legacy of his "character," no longer a burden but the very inspiration of her art.[58] Seen from Lily's distant (and Woolf's retrospective) vantage "here" on the world, the great expedition to the lighthouse transcends the belated fulfillment of James's childhood dream to capture life's adventure, a voyage—fraught with peril and loss, rich in possibility, pleasure, and discovery—toward death.

One "angular essence" Lily's composition captures is Cam and James's oppression under their father's will. Their "great compact—to resist tyranny to the death"—bespeaks the pathos of their subjection (*TL* 163). Their only weapon, sullen silence, avails little, for his moods shadow their every thought: "He would be impatient in a moment," they fear. "He hated hanging about . . . would never be content until they were flying along. . . . In their anger they hoped that the breeze would never rise . . . that he might be thwarted in every possible way, since he had forced them to come against their wills" (*TL* 162–63). Their subjection blots out the present, the thing itself; they see nothing clearly, least of all him. Cam feels involuntary pride in him as Macalister tells of three ships sunk in a storm: their father, "so brave," "so adventurous, . . . would have launched the lifeboat," "reached the wreck." Then she guiltily remembers her pact with James: "Their grievance weighed them down. . . . He had borne them down once more with his gloom and his authority, making them . . . take part in these rites he went through for his own pleasure in memory of dead people, which they hated, so that they lagged after him, and all the pleasure of the day was spoilt" (*TL* 164–65). The father who crushes a dying mackerel in the diary here crushes his children. To James he seems an oblivious wheel rolling over "his foot," "Cam's foot," "anybody's foot"; Cam, paralyzed with love and hate, is metonymically linked with a "kicking," suffocating fish:[59]

For she thought . . . (and now Macalister's boy had caught a mackerel, and it lay kicking on the floor, with blood on its gills) . . . looking at James . . . you're not exposed to it, to this pressure and division of feeling. . . . For no one attracted her more; his hands . . . and his feet, and his voice, and his words, . . . and his saying straight out before every one, we perish, each alone, and his remoteness. . . . But what remained intolerable, she thought, . . . watching Macalister's boy tug the hook out of the gills of another fish, was that crass blindness and tyranny of his which had poisoned her childhood and raised bitter storms, so that even now she woke in the night trembling with rage and remembered . . . his dominance: his "Submit to me." (*TL* 169–70)

While Lily/Woolf quests alongside Mr. Ramsay toward "reality," Cam/Virginia, who can't tell north from south or find their house on the island, makes her father impatient with women's "hopeless" "vagueness" (*TL* 167). While Lily/Woolf paints and writes, Cam/Virginia loses herself in daydreams and stories ("So we took a little boat") of "adventure about escaping from a sinking ship. But . . . she did not want to tell herself seriously a story; it was the sense of adventure and escape that she wanted," to make "her father's anger about the points of the compass, James's obstinacy about the compact, and her own anguish" all "stream[] away" (*TL* 188–89). Her "numbed and shrouded" mind wanders in a borderland between poetry and death, a watery "underworld . . . where the pearls stuck in clusters to white sprays, where in the green light a change came over one's entire mind and one's body shone half transparent enveloped in a green cloak" (*TL* 183). Looking "doggedly and sadly" at the shore where Lily and Mr. Carmichael engage in "immortal" battle with form, Cam sees only a "mantle of peace," "as if the people there had fallen asleep, . . . were free like smoke . . . to come and go like ghosts. They have no suffering there, she thought" (*TL* 170).

Even as the novel counterposes Cam/Virginia's death-in-life to Lily/Woolf's creative freedom, its temporal collage captures their autobiographical continuity. When Cam feels a "fountain of joy at the change, at the escape, at the adventure (that she should be alive, that she should be there)," she echoes Woolf's early memory of waking in St. Ives in ecstatic wonder "that I should be here."[60] When Cam remembers her father's library where she can think what she likes and not "fall over a precipice or be drowned, for there he is, keeping his eye on me," she recalls young Virginia, whose father "lugged home" from the London Library the Elizabethan travelogues that fired her imagination.[61] That Lily/Woolf paints/writes "what had been in her mind since she was a baby" while Cam/Virginia's visions dissipate in "shapes of a world not realised but turning in their darkness, catching here and there, a spark of light; Greece, Rome, Constantinople" measures the adult Lily's "distance" from—and young Cam's subjection to—the father's desire.[62] If Cam/Virginia figures the life Woolf feared to have led had her father lived on ("no writing; no books; inconceivable"), Lily, Cam's future self, pursues her quest in the freedom of her art.

So much, then, depends upon distance. In the family portrait that death and distance free Lily/Woolf to paint, these voyagers never return. "Distance had an extraordinary power; they had been swallowed up in it," Lily thinks; "they were gone for ever, *they had become part of the nature of things.* . . . The steamer itself had vanished, but the great scroll of smoke still hung in the air and drooped like a flag mournfully in valediction" (*TL* 188, my emphasis). As the little party in the boat comes in to land—an event Lily witnesses in imagination—James's vision of his father in "a waste of snow and rock very lonely and austere" recalls Mr. Ramsay's own thoughts of his death: "now that the snow has begun to fall and the mountain top is covered in mist . . . he would not die lying down; he would find some crag of rock, and there, his eyes fixed on the storm, trying to the end to pierce the darkness, he would die standing" (*TL* 184, 35). Approaching the lighthouse, he seems like "some old stone lying on the sand . . . as if he had become physically what was always at the back of both of their minds—that loneliness which was for both of them the truth about things" (*TL* 202–03). Father and son share a "knowledge" of the "stark tower on a bare rock," "glaring white and black" with "waves breaking in white splinters like smashed glass upon the rocks"; " 'We are driving before a gale—we must sink,' " says James, "exactly as his father said it" (*TL* 203). Like Lily, Cam, her rage quenched, tries to grasp her father's spirit: "he escaped. . . . You might try to lay hands on him, but then like a bird, he spread his wings, he floated off to settle out of your reach somewhere far away on some desolate stump" (*TL* 203–04).

When they pass the place where Macalister says three men drowned (evoking Mrs. Ramsay, Andrew, Prue), Mr. Ramsay refrains, to his children's surprise and relief, from bursting out, "*But I beneath a rougher sea [/And whelmed in deeper gulfs than he]*," "as if he thought . . . why make a fuss about that? Naturally men are drowned in a storm, but it is a perfectly straightforward affair, and the depths of the sea . . . are only water after all" (*TL* 206). Instead he praises James's handling of the boat. The son he once sheltered against life's all too real storms—while his wife, shocked at his "astonishing lack of consideration for other people's feelings," "flew in the face of facts, made his children hope what was utterly out of the question, in effect, told lies"—has possessed himself of his father's legacy: courage, truth, endurance, the justice, foresight, devotion, skill to save a ship's company exposed on a broiling sea with six biscuits and a flask of water.[63] As Cam, James, and Lily strain to watch, he reaches the lighthouse:

> Mr. Ramsay buttoned his coat, and turned up his trousers. He took the large, badly packed, brown paper parcel which Nancy had got ready and sat with it on his knee. Thus in complete readiness to land he sat looking back at the island. . . . What could he see? Cam wondered. . . . What was he thinking now? . . . What was it he sought, so fixedly, so intently, so silently? They watched him. . . . What do you want? they both wanted to ask. They both wanted to say, Ask us anything and we will give it you. But he did not ask them anything. He sat and looked at the island and he might be thinking, We perished, each alone, or he might be thinking, I have reached it. I have found it; but he said nothing. . . . He rose and stood in the bow of the boat, very straight and tall, for all the world, James thought, as if he were saying, "There is no God," and Cam thought, as if he were leaping into space, and they both rose to follow him as he sprang . . . on to the rock. (*TL* 207)

With Nancy's awkward parcel on his knee, Mr. Ramsay sails in memory of his wife and in the wake of her death toward his own, as if drowning (or dying) were "a perfectly simple, straightforward affair; & we all come to it; & the depths of the sea . . . have no terror for me" (*TLhd* 362). Leaping onto the rock of death—the absolute ground of being, and the granite of art—Mr. Ramsay concludes an "extraordinary adventure," the great expedition his children must take not because he forces them to but because it is life (*TL* 204).

Perishing alone as "We" must, Mr. Ramsay reaches the vanishing point of the revelation that separates subject from object, self from world.[64] But it is life that his adventure illuminates, not death. As he sets off Lily thinks, "There was no helping Mr. Ramsay on the journey he was going," and her portrait commemorates his landing without pretending to divine his thoughts (*TL* 154). Through James and Cam, Lily/Woolf from her necessary "distance" bestows her sympathy as she accepts his legacy of her own life, a little boat voyaging "between things, beyond things" toward the same destination. As Mr. Ramsay reaches *R*, death's Reality, Lily reaches *L*, the Lighthouse, revelation in the abstract:

> "He must have reached it." . . . [T]he effort of looking at it and . . . of thinking of him landing . . . had stretched her body and mind to the utmost. Ah, but she was relieved. Whatever she had wanted to give him, when he left her that morning, she had given him at last.
>
> "He has landed," she said aloud. "It is finished."[65]

Lily's liturgical echo abstracts Mr. Ramsay's quest into "something much more general," and the "old pagan god" Mr. Carmichael assists in these last rites on the "cathedral-like" lawn:

> He stood there as if he were spreading his hands over all the weakness and suffering of mankind; she thought he was surveying, tolerantly and compassionately, their final destiny. Now he has crowned the occasion, she thought, when his hand slowly fell, as if she had seen him let fall from his great height a wreath of violets and asphodels which, fluttering slowly, lay at length upon the earth. (*TL* 53, 171, 208)

Mourning's purple and white return in the wreath he seems to lay upon the dead, but now they lie on the earth instead of dominating Lily's picture. With the past laid to rest, her picture shimmers in "all its greens and blues," colors of earth and sky and the bay brimming with things and lives, voyagers and sea-changed wrecks. Turning to her canvas with "sudden intensity, as if she saw it clear for a second," Lily paints "a line there, in the centre," abstracting tree and lighthouse as Mondrian abstracts the organic tree: "It was done; it was finished. Yes, she thought, laying down her brush in extreme fatigue, I have had my vision" (*TL* 208–09). With this final brushstroke Lily marks her place in this portrait of father and mother and child in the garden, "here" in the ordinary, miraculous present. Her picture of the world, and the novel that mirrors it from genesis to completion, connect abstraction and empathy in a vision and a theory (Greek *theōrein*: vision, contemplation) of subject, object, the nature of reality.

To the Lighthouse appeared on May 5, Julia Stephen's death day. On reading it, Vanessa Bell affirmed its extraordinary—for her, "shattering"—realism:

> you have given a portrait of mother which is more like her to me than anything I could ever have conceived of as possible. It is almost painful to have her so raised from the dead. . . . *It was like meeting her again with oneself grown up and on equal terms and it seems to me the most astonishing feat of creation to have been able to see her in such a way.* You have given father too I think as clearly . . . it seems to me to be the only thing about him which ever gave a true idea. So you see as far as portrait painting goes you seem to me to be a supreme artist and it is so shattering to find oneself face to face with those two again that I can hardly consider anything else. . . . I am excited and thrilled and taken into another world as one only is in a great work of art. (*L* 3:572–73; 11 May [1927], my emphasis)

Vanessa alights exactly on the work her sister's art performs, its arduous quest—through a labor of mourning inseparable from growing up, though magnified and intensified by their mother's death—not to recover a lost childhood but to see the past "face to face," as one "grown up and on equal terms," on a level with ordinary experience.[66] Recreating "The Window"'s fleeting idyll, its devastation in "Time Passes," and the lives that open into the future in "The Lighthouse," Lily/Woolf navigates past the nostalgia on which Mrs. Vallance and Mr. Serle run aground to depict the great expedition that is anyone's life.

"By the way," Vanessa continues, "surely Lily Briscoe must have been rather a good painter—before her time perhaps, but with great gifts really?"[67] Painting her modernist picture of the world, Lily abandons "Beautiful pictures. Beautiful phrases" to voyage with the "sailors and adventurers" (TL 193, 102). No longer "moored to the shore" but "up to the lips" in being and life, grappling in her art with "whatever it is that rules the world," does she find the "risks" of her "perpetual combat" to capture "some apparition of truth behind appearances" rewarded by the "hard rock" of "success" (TL 101, 192, TLhd 257)? If the picture mirrors the novel, and if to bring the dead parents back to "life" is as difficult as to paint a Cézanne, has Lily too not created a masterpiece?

While Vanessa found herself face to face with her long-dead parents, Woolf reflected on her family inheritance. She felt "more like him than her, I think; and therefore more critical: but he was an adorable man, and somehow, tremendous" (L 3:374, 13 May 1927). Freeing desire from obsession and substitution, To the Lighthouse abstracts quest romance from gender and opens the genre's economy of desire to things in themselves: "She did not want Mrs. Ramsay now" but people and things, in and for themselves, here and now—the world that holds "so many lives" and "things besides" (TL 195). As Woolf's late "philosophy" that there is no Shakespeare, no Beethoven, no God, that "we" are the words, the music, the thing itself abstracts this revelation, so Lily, merging with a "we" who voyage and perish "alone" in the blue and green world, abstracts any voyager's quest toward subject, object, the nature of reality (MB 72).

"Rarely rarely comest thou, spirit of delight." That was I singing this time last year; & sang so poignantly that I have never forgotten it, or my vision of a fin rising on a wide blank sea. No biographer could possibly guess this important fact about my life in the late summer of 1926; yet biographers pretend they know people.

—Woolf, *Diary*, 4 September 1927

If we have the habit of freedom and . . . see human beings . . . and the sky, too, and the trees or whatever it may be in themselves . . . if we face the fact . . . that our relation is to the world of reality and not only to the world of men and women, then . . . Shakespeare's sister will put on the body which she has so often laid down.

—Woolf, *A Room of One's Own*

We are not slaves bound to suffer incessantly unrecorded petty blows on our bent backs. We are not sheep either, following a master. We are creators. We too have made something that will join the innumerable congregations of past time. We too, as we put on our hats and push open the door, stride not into chaos but into a world that our own force can subjugate and make part of the illumined and everlasting road.

—Bernard, in Woolf, *The Waves*

SIX

A Fin in a Waste of Waters

Women, Genius, Freedom in *Orlando, A Room of One's Own,* and *The Waves*

" utobiography it might be called," Woolf mused as she conjured a book titled first "The Moths/or the life of anybody," later *The Waves*.[1] As "books continue each other" (*RO* 80), *The Waves* (1931) culminates Woolf's middle series of self-portraits: *To the Lighthouse* (1927), *Orlando* (1928), and *A Room of One's Own* (1929). With related diary entries, letters, drafts, and essays, these comprise what I shall broadly consider as *The Waves'* genetic text.[2] To call these works self-portraits presumes a special notion of the genre such as Woolf implies in framing this "abstract mystical eyeless book: a playpoem" as her or "anybody" 's "life" (*D* 3:203, 7 November 1928). Loosed from objectivist notions of a singular, discrete individual, Woolf's self-portraiture abandons conventional ideas of resemblance between image and object (the subject as bounded identifiable entity; a recognizable body; its observable doings) to explore a more expansive and abstract concept of being, akin to Clarissa Dalloway's "transcendental theory" of a life, a self, that spreads "ever so far" beyond the organism's spatial and temporal bounds (*MD* 152–53, 9). By the same token, once we grasp that, as Derrida observes, an artist can designate "just about anything a self-portrait, not only any drawing . . . but anything that happens to me, anything by which I can be affected or let myself be affected" (as Clarissa does by claiming "odd affinities" with people, places, trees, barns), conventional criteria of resemblance fail. We cannot be sure by "*observing the work alone,*" apart from extrinsic visual or verbal clues, whether the artist is drawing the artist drawing the artist "or *something else*—or even [the artist] *as something else, as other.*"[3]

Or rather, given the gap between any life, any self, and its any and every representation, perhaps the one thing we can be sure of is that the artist is drawing the artist as something else, as other. Consider the seed of *The Waves*. On finishing the draft of *To the Lighthouse*, Woolf glimpsed what would become *The Waves*' signal icon and reflected "how it is not oneself but something in the universe that one's left with. It is this that is frightening & exciting. . . . One sees a fin passing far out."[4] A year later she remembers this apparition (an impersonal condition: "one sees," not a unique event: I saw) and underscores its auto/biographical import: " 'Rarely rarely comest thou, spirit of delight.' That was I singing this time last year; & sang so poignantly that I have never forgotten it, or my vision of a fin rising on a wide blank sea. No biographer could possibly guess this important fact about my life in the late summer of 1926; yet biographers pretend they know people."[5] After completing *Orlando* and *A Room of One's Own*, Woolf prepared to "attack this angular shape in my mind. . . . the Moths will be very sharply cornered"; on finishing *The Waves* she exulted, "I have netted that fin in the waste of waters which appeared to me over the marshes out of my window at Rodmell" (*D* 3:219, 28 March 1929, 4:10,7 February 1931).

What makes this apparition so "important" an auto/biographical "fact," years before it is "netted" in a work of art? What does it tell us about the "life" of a singing self thrice vanished—first into the remembering diarist, then into "one" (a pronoun that extends this singular vision to "anybody"), finally eclipsed ("not oneself") by "something in the universe"?[6] What is at stake in the transformation of an experience so private that (absent the diary entry) no biographer could guess it into "the life of anybody"? This chapter pursues these questions through the autobiographical trajectory from *Orlando* to *The Waves* by foregrounding two key features of these self-portraits as something other or more than oneself: *woman* and *freedom*. Each work depicts a woman artist entering the freedom arduously won by Lily Briscoe, who, defying the dictate "women can't paint, can't write," approaches her canvas as "an unborn soul," "reft of body," "drawn out of gossip," "living," "community . . . into the presence of this formidable ancient enemy . . . this other thing, this truth, this reality" (*TL* 159, 158). As Orlando evolves over centuries from callow scribbler to renowned English poet, s/he parodies and transcends the contingencies of gender while figuring the quest to capture truth, essence, life, body in words as (seriously enough) a wild goose chase. *A Room of One's Own* relates England's changing political economy of gender to its literary history and prophesies that in another century women writers will "put on the body" that the poet Judith Shakespeare "has so often laid down" (*RO* 114). In *The Waves*—a self-portrait as that fin whose elemental shape recalls the triangle Lily abstracts from "mother and father and child in the garden" to signal the difference of being—Woolf strives to bring *Room*'s prophecy to birth before its time.[7]

In highlighting the terms *woman* and *freedom* in the works leading up to *The Waves*, I seek to reconcile the tension between aesthetics and politics registered in the novel's curiously split reception. Formally the most original, ambitious, and adventurous of Woolf's books, *The Waves* has been widely acclaimed a "masterpiece" (however challenging or "elitist") on the one hand; avoided, dismissed, judged an "aesthetic failure," a mere "warehouse" of materials and ideas, on the other.[8] Even some admirers regard it as a modernist paragon of "mere" aestheticism, politically ineffective compared with realism.[9] Others rebut such dismissals by emphasizing the novel's engagement with gender or with "the submerged mind of empire."[10] I agree that *The Waves* is a masterpiece; but I question both the label of "mere" aestheticism and attempts to assimilate this "eyeless, mystical" book to political concerns, which tend to reify what its abstract form strips bare of substance. I propose instead that aesthetics converges with politics in the figure of the [woman] in *The Waves*—the subject as [woman], under erasure, there yet not there; bracketed in recognition of her vanishing, yet preserved in recognition of her status as bodily, natural, historical origin of this work of art. Approaching *The Waves* through its complex genesis, I frame it as a [woman] artist's modernist "story of the world from the beginning": a work of art that bodies forth the freedom manifest in creative genius by radically rethinking being, nature/physics, meaning, story, event, time, subjectivity, even grammar as rule, canon, law (*Wh* I 6, 9). As such, I argue, *The Waves* pursues a feminist politics' furthest goal: its own demolition (not to be confused with antifeminist projects toward the same end).

The feminist politics that produces *The Waves* is ultimately not an identity politics, marked by self/other oppositions and attendant scapegoat dynamics, but seeks women's freedom from identity and its politics.[11] It recognizes the importance of economic, political, and social freedoms to the conditions of aesthetic creation and fights for these freedoms, or rights, through strategies of resistance to the restrictive social identity "woman," constructed and imposed from without (as in Charles Tansley's mantra "women can't paint, can't write").[12] Yet it also seeks a greater freedom— a freedom that surpasses contingencies of politics and of identity—even as a woman artist's actualization of such freedom in a world in which it is said that women can't paint or write is implicitly political. In quest of this greater freedom, Woolf's autobiographical artist-figures play strategically with and against identity: Lily defies the identity Tansley predicates on her sex; Orlando calls some of her "many thousand" selves; *Room*'s speaker creates a persona of four legendary Maries in the spirit of an anonymous, androgynous Shakespeare; and *The Waves* ventriloquizes a [woman]'s vision through six lyric voices that tell a "life of anybody" (*O* 309).

The creative freedom that Woolf's self-portraits of 1927–1931 explore is allied with genius in ways not strictly governed by the history of women's contingent rights. If, as *Room* argues, Jane Austen could realize her gift as fully and freely as Shakespeare could his, then creative freedom intersects unevenly with political, social, and economic rights. Art may sometimes, and somewhat, reflect contingent rights or the lack thereof— as, Woolf finds, in the cases of "Judith Shakespeare," Margaret Cavendish, Lady Mary Wortley Montagu, Margaret Oliphant, Charlotte Brontë—but not always, necessarily, or neatly. Yet that Austen required no utopia to write as freely as Shakespeare does not invalidate *Room*'s socioeconomic critique of English literary history. Rather, it supports Woolf's argument that, while Judith Shakespeare could have written her brother's plays (for she too had genius), "it would have been extremely odd" had she done so, given sixteenth-century Englishwomen's economic, political, and social subjection (*RO* 46).

Freedom is already a key word for Lily Briscoe, who when she paints feels "cut loose" from contingent "ties" to experience life's "intensity & freedom," as it is in the Kantian aesthetics of Bloomsbury that she brings to life (*TLhd* 280). In chapter 1 we considered the disinterestedness of Kantian aesthetics, revived in Bloomsbury's "significant form." Here I shall argue that Kant's aesthetic theory helps elucidate the alliance of the terms *woman*, *freedom*, and *genius* in Woolf's texts.[13] For Kant, as we saw in chapter 1, the imagination's freedom exists in the noumenal realm, beyond nature's sensible, phenomenal realm and beyond human ken. Through the imaginative freedom that the artist exercises in creating "another nature . . . out of the material that actual nature gives it," art creates a bridge between nature and the supersensible realm of freedom. In contemplating a work of art—"something different which surpasses nature," which has a "completeness" not found in nature and which occasions thought to which "no concept can be fully adequate"—"we feel our freedom."[14] Whereas moral reason submits its judgments to moral law, and science submits its concepts to nature's law, art manifests a freedom subject to no rule but purposive in itself, for it is genius, or "nature in the subject"—an inborn gift that makes the artist one of "nature's favorites"—that alone "gives the rule to art" (*CJ* §46–49, esp. 150, 152, 162, *CPJ* 186, 188, 195–96). Thus, of the three "pure ideas of reason"—God, freedom, immortality—only freedom "proves its objective reality" by its effects in nature (*CJ* §91 327, *CPJ* 338). So Bernard paints human beings as neither "slaves" suffering "incessantly unrecorded petty blows on our bent backs" nor "sheep . . . following a master" but "creators" whose "force" transforms "chaos" into thought and art, "part of the illumined and everlasting road" (*W* 146).

By freedom, Kant writes, a human being actualizes "that worth which he alone can give to himself . . . not as a link in nature's chain but in the *freedom* of his faculty of desire" (*CJ* §86 293, *CPJ* 309). The masculine pronoun is accidental: we might just as well say, by freedom a human being actualizes "that worth which she alone can give to herself . . . in the freedom of her faculty of desire," where the pronoun "she" represents the human being as such.[15] Genius, moreover, is not a static attribute of the artist but a potential that the artist must struggle to realize: in this sense, freedom has its contingencies, as Kant notes in speaking of the artist's "slow and even painful" labor to give inspiration material form (*CJ* §48 156, *CPJ* 191). In the case of *The Waves*, these contingencies include the question of whether, and how far, a woman can represent—*and be understood to represent*—being as such; how far a woman—branded economically, politically, and socially with an identity that Monique Wittig names the "mark of gender," by contrast with the masculine identity generally taken as neutral, unmarked, universal—can aspire to represent the universal.[16] The oscillation between the marked pronoun *she* and the universal *one* in *The Waves*' genetic text rhetorically projects a free subject [woman] out of gender's contingency. The [woman] in *The Waves* wrests freedom from gender (an "ontological impossibility," as Wittig points out [66]) to actualize her genius in lyric prose that approaches poetry—the genre ranked highest by Kant (as by Woolf in *Room*) because it owes most to genius, least to rule; it "strengthens the mind by making it feel" itself "free, spontaneous, and independent of natural determination"; and it "plays with illusion" undeceived (*CJ* §53 170–71, *CPJ* 203–4).

The politics of *The Waves* is inseparable from its aesthetics insofar as it seeks to actualize genius, "nature in the subject," in a woman's body—thereby demonstrating not one woman's genius but women's equal, unremarkable likelihood of possessing inborn genius; and women's equal, unremarkable freedom to move from particular to universal, from "she" to "one." If this project seems dated to us, it had hovered in Woolf's future at least since 1920, when (as we saw in chapter 3) she publicly challenged her dear Bloomsbury friend Desmond MacCarthy's smug conviction that education could little compensate for women's inborn intellectual inferiority. Anticipating *A Room of One's Own*, Woolf invites MacCarthy to survey the history of English women writers to measure how immensely women have advanced in "intellectual power" with increasing access to education; and she contemplates with equanimity the thought of being herself compared with men—including, presumably, her elder and rival Bennett and MacCarthy himself, a brilliant conversationalist who never managed to write anything of moment.[17]

By keeping the body in the picture alongside genius and freedom, Woolf forestalls both the expulsion of politics from aesthetics implied by the judgment "mere" aestheticism and, equally, the displacing of aesthetic by political judgment. The female body is the site where aesthetics and politics converge: the locus of genius, "nature in the subject," and the target of the scapegoat dynamic that perpetually reproduces masculine domination.[18] In exploring the movement from *she* to *[she]/one*—from woman as particular to woman as universal—Woolf leaves open the question of whether its creator's sexed body and/or gender-inflected history necessarily register in the work of art, and if so, as an essential or a merely contingent feature, and in what sort of relation to the universal. Is *[she]* the purely political remainder of a historical *she* become *one*, or does *[she]* register the sexed body as a dimension of that nature-in-the-subject that is genius? Or, to take *Room*'s formulation, how exactly does a woman writing "as a woman who has forgotten that she is a woman" write (*RO* 93)? If, by actualizing genius in a woman's body, *[she]* exposes masculine privilege, gives the lie to essentialized constructions of genius and freedom, does *[she]* also disclose within the universal a corresponding *[he]*? Is *[she]* or *[he]* a merely accidental historical residue of the universal, or something more? What light do Woolf's depictions of women as creative subjects, freed from their traditional role as representation's objects in British aestheticism, cast on relations between embodied subjects (of either sex) and genius, freedom, art?

This chapter traces Woolf's exploration of the creative freedom won by Lily Briscoe ("so joyous in her freedom"), practiced as radical fantasy in *Orlando*, analyzed under the aegis of its socioeconomic conditions in *Room*, and pursued to the limit of her imagination in *The Waves* (*TLhd* 138). Throughout this long adventure Woolf keeps the sexed body in the picture even when the artist is "reft of body"—like Lily, like Woolf's anonymous, androgynous Shakespeare, like the [woman] in *The Waves*. On the watch for the ways Woolf draws the woman artist drawing the woman artist *"as something else, as other"* in these works, we turn first to *Orlando*.

Orlando and *The Oak Tree*: A Fantasia of Freedom

> I feel the need of an escapade after these serious poetic experimental books. . . . I want to kick up my heels & be off.
> —Woolf, *Diary*, 14 March 1927

Woolf's wish to kick up her heels and let her imagination race free launched an auto/biographical fantasia of a writing self in quest of poetry.

The ostensible subject of *Orlando: A Biography*—"the longest and most charming love-letter in literature"—is the writer and poet Vita Sackville-West, Woolf's intimate friend from 1923 and sometime lover between 1925 and 1928.[19] But there is a good deal of Woolf in Orlando too, particularly in the liberating theories of being, identity, biography, autobiography, and poetry that she infuses into Vita's aristocratic family history to create a character unbounded by sex, gender, even the ordinary human life span.[20] In *Orlando* Woolf sets out "to tell a persons life from the year 1500 to 1928. Changing its sex. taking different aspects of the character in different Centuries. the theory being that character goes on underground before we are born; & leaves something afterwards also" (*Oh* 2). She endows the androgynous Orlando with birth, wealth, rank, beauty, and that "rarer gift" glamour, which the Russian princess Sasha likens to "a million candles" burning without Orlando's having to light "a single one" (*O* 124). Yet Orlando aspires to be not society's favorite but nature's—a poet. The impressive circumstantial identity of this heir to 365 bedrooms pales beside Orlando's "ineffable hope" to be "by birth a writer, rather than an aristocrat"; to belong to the "sacred race" of poets "rather than to the noble."[21]

In pursuit of poetry, Orlando encounters gossiping, avaricious, social-climbing poets from Nick Greene to Alexander Pope, who, whatever their gifts, talk less of poetry than worldly *gloire* (or as Greene has it, "Glawr"). Indeed Orlando takes up the pen at sixteen in the Elizabethan period, ambitious to be "the first poet of his race," and she is crowned with laurels at thirty-six several centuries later—a utopian avatar of the [woman] poet who, Woolf predicts at the end of *Room*, will be born in "another hundred years" (*O* 104; *RO* 94). But Orlando's abiding role model remains Shakespeare, here portrayed as a genius whose imagination flourishes in obscurity; and Orlando's quest leads beyond literary prizes and the glory of a "name" toward freedom—from identity, gender, class, and every certainty, and on to the radical freedom and "terror" of "the present moment" (*O* 321–22).

Orlando famously begins with a pronoun: "He—for there could be no doubt of his sex." Emulating the barbaric, racist masculinity of his savagely imperial "fathers," "who had struck many heads of many colours off many shoulders," this Elizabethan boy "lunge[s] and plunge[s] and slice[s]" with his blade at a "head of a Moor" hung with others from the attic rafters (*O* 13). Having introduced his subject by parodying the violence that attends the formation and performance of identity, the biographer now undercuts contingencies of gender, class, race, nation, historical moment, age—all the self/other dynamics by which identity is formed and sustained—with a scene of writing.[22] Orlando drops his sword to hack about with his pen on "Aethelbert: A Tragedy in Five Acts," the latest of his "no more perhaps than twenty tragedies and a dozen histories and a score of sonnets," all bearing "the name of some mythological personage at a crisis of his career" and all failures—as, now, he throws down his pen in despair on catching sight of "the thing itself," in this case, a laurel bush whose precise shade of green eludes his net of words (O 16, 24, 76, 17).

Notwithstanding the biographer's conviction regarding the masculine pronoun (yet what rouses doubt more surely than denying doubt's possibility?), Orlando resembles that pronoun scarcely more than the laurel does "Aethelbert." As the laurel bush to the word "green," Orlando to the pronoun, the material world to language, the sexed body to gender. From the outset, gender is metaphor, poetry, fiction—a complex of figural meanings shaped by convention and attached to sexed bodies no more permanently or securely than clothes.[23] Bodies, meanwhile, stand aloof from language even when subjected to material investigation. If Queen Elizabeth—"who knew a man when she saw one, though not, it is said, in the usual way"—encourages confidence in the biographer's pronoun, the women who perch on Orlando's lap, "guessing that something out of the common lay hid beneath his duffle cloak" and "quite as eager to come at the truth of the matter as Orlando himself," parody the gulf between conceptual and carnal knowledge (O 26, 29). So too Orlando, bedazzled by a Russian "figure" flying by on the ice, can only guess at its sex ("alas, a boy it must be—no woman could skate with such speed and vigour"), even as amorous metaphors ("a melon, a pineapple, an olive tree, an emerald, and a fox in the snow") bubble up involuntarily in his mind (O 37). On the discovery that this "person" is "a woman," Orlando's own body broadcasts a lover's signs ("Orlando stared; trembled; turned hot and cold; longed to hurl himself through the summer air; to crush acorns beneath his feet; to toss his arms with the beech trees and oaks") (O 37–38). Yet even now something about Sasha seems "hidden," "concealed," keeping open the question not just of Sasha's sex but of what difference sex should make and why in this lesbian "love-letter" of a novel (O 47).

By aligning the sexed body with the laurel bush beyond the reach of language, Orlando sets the stage for its parody of gender, brought to the fore by Orlando's mysterious sex-change between his ambassadorship to Constantinople and her running away with the gypsies—an adventure that, like the expatriate Flush's Italian days, dismantles the English aristocrat's presumptive superiority. As the "woman" the biographer ceremoniously declares her to be, Orlando suffers the contingent bonds of gender, from skirts ("plaguy things to have about one's heels," she thinks,

"giving her legs a kick") to the forswearing of swearing and other masculine privileges; from lawsuits challenging her right to her property to
gender's mysterious power over bodies, as when a sailor nearly plummets
from a mast on sighting an inch of the very same leg so admired by Elizabethan eyes (O 137, 154). As Orlando assiduously learns to playact the
femininity that now befalls her ("La! . . . how you frighten me!" she cries
as the cross-dressing Archduchess Harriet drops her gown to reveal "a tall
gentleman in black"), she is "horrified to perceive how low an opinion she
was forming of the other sex, the manly, to which it had once been her
pride to belong"; " 'what fools they make of us—what fools we are!' "
she laments, "censuring both sexes equally, as if she belonged to neither;
and indeed, . . . she seemed to vacillate; she was man; she was woman; she
knew the secrets, shared the weaknesses of each," until, "uncertain
whether she was alive or dead, man or woman, Duke or nonentity," she
repairs to "her country seat, where, pending the legal judgment, she had
the Law's permission to reside in a state of incognito or incognita, as the
case might turn out to be" (O 178, 158, 168).

Whatever quandaries Orlando's sex causes sailors, language, the
Law—whatever its consequences for her social identity—the biographer
insists that Orlando's essence remains unchanged: "Orlando had become
a woman—there is no denying it. But in every other respect, Orlando
remained precisely as he had been. The change of sex, though it altered
their future, did nothing whatever to alter their identity," "their faces," or
(the masculine pronoun persisting in the face of facts) "his memory—but
in future we must, for convention's sake, say 'her' for 'his' and 'she' for
'he' " (O 138). If, as Gertrude Stein says, "I am I because my little dog
knows me," Orlando is Orlando because his/her elkhound Canute nearly
knocks him/her down in joy at his/her return (recalling Argos greeting the
disguised Odysseus). Although momentarily tripped up by linguistic gender, the staff knows Orlando too, Mrs. Grimsditch gasping, "Milord!
Milady! Milady! Milord!" (O 169).

Even with identity (in the sense of essence) preserved and the pronouns
tamed, sex eludes gender, as Orlando and her lover Shel discover. Each is
so astonished "that a woman could be as tolerant and free-spoken as a
man, and a man as strange and subtle as a woman," that each forms "an
awful   suspicion"—"You're   a   woman,   Shel!";   "You're   a   man,
Orlando!"—which drives them "to the proof" in scenes of "protestation
and demonstration" unknown "since the world began."[24] Although
Orlando thanks Shel for making her "a real woman, at last" (as if the category were purely relational), the biographer is silent on this "proof,"
undermined, in any case, by their frequent need to reverify it, as if gender

were a psycholinguistic condition that sex cannot finally cure (O 253). And, of course, a socioeconomic condition, for even after Orlando's sex is adjudicated by the court—"'The lawsuits are settled. . . . My sex . . . is pronounced indisputably, and beyond the shadow of a doubt (what was I telling you a moment ago, Shel?) Female"—the fact that her estates (much diminished after the lawsuits) are "tailed and entailed upon the heirs male of my body" leaves unclear whether a hypothetical daughter could inherit as Orlando evidently has (O 254–55).

In any case, Orlando's sex seems attested in the realm of nature (though her gender remains fluid) when she gives birth to "a very fine boy" on "Thursday, March the 20th, at three o'clock in the morning," an event the biographer swathes in such rhapsodic verbiage that a reader might almost miss it—the more so as this baby, like the sex change, alters Orlando's "future" not at all, by contrast with the nineteenth century when the "life of the average woman" was little more than a "succession of childbirths" (O 295, 229). Yet this event does not cancel Orlando's history ("She had been a gloomy boy . . . and sometimes she had tried prose and sometimes she had tried the drama. Yet through all these changes she had remained, she reflected, fundamentally the same") (O 237). Nor does it impede the biographer's rather self-contradictory theory that, "Different though the sexes are," every human being "vacillat[es] from one sex to the other . . . and often it is only the clothes that keep the male or female likeness, while underneath the sex is the very opposite of what it is above," producing such familiar "complications and confusions" as Orlando's cross-dressing adventures with the London prostitutes (O 189).

But if nothing can be predicated on gender, neither can the body, however its sex is adjudicated, limit or determine a life or self that (to return to Clarissa's theory) spreads "ever so far" beyond it. Orlando indeed resembles the laurel bush more closely than any pronoun. Abandoning "Aethelbert," Orlando walks his estate and ties his "floating heart" to an ancient oak tree that flourishes at its high point overlooking forty English counties. Its roots become "the earth's spine beneath him," "the back of a great horse he was riding," "the deck of a tumbling ship," until "all the fertility . . . of a summer's evening" seems "woven web-like about his body" (O 19). Hung in a tree, moved by "spiced and amorous gales every evening," Orlando's heart signals a life, a self, that overspills the body's bounds in time and space through sensation, thought, experience, metaphor, memory, history, and human connections into unbounded phenomenal and invisible worlds, illustrating *Orlando*'s "theory . . . that character goes on underground before we are born; & leaves something afterwards also."

The affinity of Orlando's body with the oak tree's roots, "running out like ribs from a spine this way and that beneath her," highlights the autobiographical status of "The Oak Tree," the one slender manuscript of Orlando's bloated juvenilia that survives and "the only monosyllabic title in the lot" (O 77, 324). Orlando labors over this poem through the centuries until, in the late-Victorian period, she finally publishes it at Sir Nicholas Greene's urging ("Really Orlando did not know what he meant. She had always carried her manuscripts about with her in the bosom of her dress," O 280). But by the time it goes into seven printings and wins prizes and critical acclaim—its author compared to "Milton (save for his blindness)" and given "a cheque for two hundred guineas"—Orlando cares nothing for Fame and Glawr (O 324). While she still hopes to belong to the sacred race of poets, it is not Milton who inspires her but the "rather fat, rather shabby" old poet Orlando once glimpsed as a boy, who sat in dingy ruff and hodden brown at the servants' table, "rolling some thought up and down, to and fro in his mind," then writing "half-a-dozen lines": "Was this a poet? Was he writing poetry? 'Tell me,' [Orlando] wanted to say, 'everything in the whole world'—for he had the wildest, most absurd, extravagant ideas about poets and poetry—but how speak to a man who does not see you? who sees ogres, satyrs, perhaps the depths of the sea instead?" (O 21–22).

Orlando's centuries-old memory of a poet she only belatedly guesses must have been " 'Sh—p—re' (for when we speak names we deeply reverence to ourselves we never speak them whole)" illuminates the stakes for women of the book's dismantling of gender: poetry, genius, the freedom of imaginative creation (O 313). *Orlando*'s Shakespeare dwells not in "the world of men and women" but in a "dark, ample and free" obscurity that "lets the mind take its way unimpeded."[25] While Greene deplores the Elizabethan playwrights' freewheeling methods ("Their poetry was scribbled down on the backs of washing bills held to the heads of printer's devils at the street door. Thus Hamlet went to press; thus Lear; thus Othello. No wonder, as Greene said, that these plays show the faults they do"), Orlando remembers being swept along with Sasha on a tide of "all the riff-raff of the London streets" to the Globe, where the world suffers the "strangest transformation": Othello's cries seem "torn from the depths of [Orlando's] heart. The frenzy of the Moor seemed to him his own frenzy, and when the Moor suffocated the woman in her bed it was Sasha he killed with his own hands."[26] While Nick Greene chases Fame and Glawr, Orlando muses on "the delight of having no name . . . like a wave which returns to the deep body of the sea"; on "how obscurity rids the mind of the irk of envy and spite" and "sets running in the veins the free waters of generosity and magnanimity"; and how Shakespeare, like "all great poets," wrote as the cathedral builders built—"anonymously, needing no thanking or naming."[27]

Orlando's enduring memory of Shakespeare inspires her to make good Milton's "blindness"—here, a masculine mark of gender, an imbalance in the naturally androgynous creative imagination that Woolf theorizes in *Room*—by uncoupling poetry from gender. As *Room* will exhort women poets to "look past Milton's bogey" and "the world of men and women" to see "reality; and the sky, too, and the trees or whatever it may be in themselves," *The Oak Tree* rewrites Milton's Eden, that garden of masculine universalism wherein dwell "He for God only, she for God in him."[28] Can it be accidental that the oak tree is sexually dimorphous, its male and female flowers mirroring the androgynous or "gunandros" poet (*Oh* 228 verso)? In any case, with Shakespeare as her model Orlando seeks not to invert Milton's hierarchy of "He" over "She" but to escape that metaphysical garden altogether by figuring in language a wilder, freer nature, bodied forth in the laurel bush ("the thing itself"), the oak tree, and Orlando's own fantastically free body; and further, in his/her "many thousand" selves and in the be-laureled little red book *The Oak Tree*. Parodying an old wish that his body might be granted "a grave among laurels," Orlando would bury *The Oak Tree* by the oak tree as a rather incongruous "tribute" to the land and a "return" of its gifts, except that she forgets her trowel and anyhow finds such "symbolical celebrations" "silly" (*O* 17, 104, 324).

Orlando, who has "no traffic with the usual God," rewrites Genesis and *Paradise Lost* as "a faith of her own," elucidated in her chapel as she repents her spiritual flaws, especially "The letter S"—"the serpent in the Poet's Eden":

> there were still too many of these sinful reptiles in the first stanzas of "The Oak Tree." But 'S' was nothing . . . compared with the termination 'ing.' The present participle is the Devil himself. . . . To evade such temptations is the first duty of the poet . . . for . . . poetry can adulterate and destroy more surely than lust or gunpowder. . . . A silly song of Shakespeare's has done more for the poor and the wicked than all the preachers and philanthropists in the world. . . . Thoughts are divine. Thus . . . she was back in the confines of her own religion . . . and was rapidly acquiring the intolerance of belief. (*O* 172–74)

The biblical scapegoating of women for sexuality and sin vanishes from Orlando's Eden, as do sexual hierarchy and even sexual difference for almost all practical purposes. Orlando and Shelmerdine embrace polymorphous androgyny and the end of gender in each other, proved as we saw by their joyful if inconclusive "demonstration[s]," unwritten "since the world began" (*O* 252). Playing with illusion undeceived, Virginia's "love-letter" to Vita strips bodies and poetic language down to mute materiality, disengaging sexual desire from sexual difference in an Edenic elsewhere in which laughter banishes divine law, oedipal protagonists, heterosexual plots and paradigms, and, not least, transcendent truth claims.[29]

In fact, "The Oak Tree," that slender manuscript that gets slenderer the longer Orlando works on it, rewrites Milton's Eden as a quest for "Life" (Vita) that never finds its goal or, rather, arrives, after centuries of searching, at the discovery that life (Latin: *vita*) has and can have no linguistic equivalent. "Life, life, what art thou?" sings Orlando at her worktable, echoed by the bored biographer, who (with a shot across Lawrence's bow) longs for her to stop writing and "think, at least, of a gamekeeper." A bird answers "Life, Life, Life!" moths "Laughter, Laughter!" until, "having asked them all and grown no wiser" in the quest "to wrap up in a book something so hard, so rare, one could swear it was life's meaning," they inform the expectant reader: "Alas, we don't know" (*O* 268–71). With this revelation of truth's utter illusoriness, Orlando pronounces "The Oak Tree" "Done!"—"only just in time" to prevent its "extinction" by incessant pruning (*O* 271). Its new Eden is an homage not to Milton but to a Shakespeare who signals freedom from gender, identity, class, every conviction, conclusion, fixed meaning—in Kant's terms, poetry's freedom to play with illusion undeceived. The boy who wishes Shakespeare to tell him "everything" matures into a [woman] poet who understands that genius is not knowledge but the imagination's pure freedom, elusive of concepts and conclusions.[30]

This revelation casts the supreme genius Shakespeare not as an obstructing presence whose words leave nothing more to say but as a benignly enabling exemplar of the poet's passion to transmute *the present moment* into language, as in the shock of Othello's words on Orlando's ear. While Sir Nicholas Greene pursues his antiquarian poetics, doles out honors for work "Done!" and makes Orlando feel that "one must never, never say what one thought. . . . one must always, always write like somebody else," Shakespeare inspires Orlando, with her far more modest gifts, to capture her own "present moment" (*O* 285). From Shakespeare Orlando learns that writing's possibility renews itself every moment as time and the world unfold past every act of writing, always beyond reach of language. Long after *The Oak Tree* appears, Orlando remains "Haunted!" as in childhood: "There flies the wild goose. . . . always I fling after it words like nets. . . . And sometimes there's an inch of silver—six words—in the bottom of the net. But never the great fish who lives in the coral groves" (O 313). Orlando follows *Orlando*'s Shakespeare in the impossible quest to net in language the world's green, the great fish, the wild goose, the thing itself, the present moment; and *Orlando* dramatizes this poet's succession when Orlando revisits her estate and—seeing roped-off antique chairs "holding their arms out . . . for Shakespeare it might be . . . who never came"—unhooks the rope and sits down herself.[31]

Orlando's tour de force ending evokes both the radical freedom and the annihilating "terror" of the present moment, whose contingency is redeemed only by the artist's power to create another nature (O 322). Exposed to "the shock of time" as present rushes into past, Orlando's "body quiver[s] and tingle[s] as if suddenly stood naked in a hard frost." "Braced and strung up by the present moment," she feels "strangely afraid, as if every time the gulf of time gaped and let a second through some unknown danger might come with it" (O 320–21). When a clock strikes in a carpenter's shop, time "hurtle[s] through her like a meteor, so hot that no fingers can hold it"; the sight of the carpenter's nailless thumb makes her faint. As she closes her eyes, she glimpses "something" that "one trembles to pin through the body with a name and call beauty, for it has no body, is as a shadow and without substance or quality of its own, yet has the power to change whatever it adds itself to" (O 321–22). This mothlike "shadow" (a foreshadow of *The Waves* and a figure of the aesthetic dimension) enables Orlando to compose the overwhelming moment into "something tolerable, comprehensible," and so to feel, "I can begin to live again. . . . I am about to understand. . . . " (O 322, latter ellipsis Woolf's).

Here the biographer observes that Orlando is "now a very indifferent witness to the truth of what was before her," her eyes fixed (like Shakespeare's) on a magical inward pool in which "everything was partly something else, and each gained an odd moving power from this union of itself and something not itself, so that with this mixture of truth and falsehood her mind became like a forest in which things moved; lights and shadows changed, and one thing became another" (O 322–23). Her consciousness once more sutured to the sensible world by thought, memory, language, her imagination infusing things in themselves with that transforming "something," Orlando "forg[ets] the time" and muses on "the secret transaction" that is poetry, "the thing itself—a voice answering a voice"; her "stammering answer . . . to the old crooning song of the woods, and the farms and the brown horses standing at the gate"; a "secret," "slow" speech "like the intercourse of lovers."[32] As *Orlando*'s last words ("Thursday, the eleventh of October, Nineteen Hundred and Twenty-eight"—its English publication date) deliver its first readers literally (and the rest of us symbolically) to the present moment, time's ferocious, uncapturable flight metamorphoses into the soaring goose that spells not just truth's impossibility but the freedom we feel in this wild bird's flight out of its natural body into "another nature" made by human art (O 329).

Originating in moments when "something useless, sudden, violent; something that costs a life" shatters certainty, Orlando's life drawing is as unfinishable and inexhaustible as Shakespeare's (O 287). As Orlando's freedom to be—and to love—man and woman rewrites the story of the world, her play with illusion gestures beyond every plot: "She had formed here in solitude . . . a spirit capable of resistance," observes the biographer. " 'I will write,' she had said, 'what I enjoy writing'; and so had scratched out twenty-six volumes" (O 175). Yet "for all her travels and adventures and profound thinkings," Orlando remains "in process of fabrication. What the future might bring, Heaven only knew. Change was incessant. . . . High battlements of thought; habits that had seemed durable as stone went down like shadows at the touch of another mind and left a naked sky and fresh stars twinkling" (O 175–76). Flinging herself on the oak tree's knoll, "the back of a great horse" that she spurs on in pursuit of a wild goose that flies faster than words, Orlando beholds in her mind's eye the changing skies over Constantinople—"another nature," like the sky over Milton's Sion—and the truth not that the world must change but that it is always changing, always different from what we think.

Freedom of Body, Freedom of Mind in *A Room of One's Own*

> As a matter of hard fact, the theory that poetical genius bloweth where it listeth, and equally in poor and rich, holds little truth. . . . [W]e may prate of democracy, but actually, a poor child in England has little more hope than had the son of an Athenian slave to be emancipated into that intellectual freedom of which great writings are born.
>
> —Arthur Quiller-Couch, *The Art of Writing*, cited in *A Room of One's Own*

> It is the freedom of it that remains overwhelming. One has been liberated; set free—one finishes Antony & Cleopatra feeling that.
>
> —Woolf, *Women & Fiction*

> One must have been something of a firebrand to say to oneself, . . . Literature is open to everybody. . . . Lock up your libraries if you like; but there is no gate, no lock, no bolt that you can set upon the freedom of my mind.
>
> —Woolf, *A Room of One's Own*

[Mary Carmichael] was no "genius". . . . But . . . she had . . . mastered the first great lesson; she wrote as a woman, but as a woman who has forgotten that she is a woman, so that her pages were full of that unconscious sexual quality which comes only when sex is unconscious of itself.

—Woolf, *A Room of One's Own*

The October that *Orlando* appeared, Woolf gave the "talks to girls" that inspired *A Room of One's Own* (*L* 4:102, 28 October 1929). Her now world-famous advice to the students of Newnham and Girton, the women's colleges at Cambridge, plunges the fantastic Orlando into an historical world in which women, it seems, are poor because men, it seems, are angry. As Orlando is Shakespeare's utopian sister, Judith Shakespeare is his realist sister, blocked from realizing her genius by the political economy of gender. As *Orlando* debunks essentialist justifications of women's exclusion from education, self-governance, and the public sphere, *Room* envisions the future of women's writing in light of advances in English-women's legal rights and the creative freedom they underwrite. In 1928, with "two colleges for women in existence since . . . 1866," married women's property rights established in 1880, suffrage won "a whole nine years ago," and economists urging a lower birth rate ("You must, of course, go on bearing children, but, so they say, in twos and threes, not in tens and twelves"), women writers at last have more than a " 'dog's chance . . . to be emancipated into that intellectual freedom of which great writings are born' " (*RO* 112–113, 108, citing Quiller-Couch). If, as Woolf contends, "Intellectual freedom depends upon material things" and "Poetry depends upon intellectual freedom," in 1928 a woman can earn five hundred pounds a year by her wits, have a room with a lock, and, like Orlando, pursue poetry, the "original" and "supreme" literary genre (*RO* 108, 66).

Woolf is alive not just to the freedom newly possible for women but to its continued limitation, as the multiple persona she fashions after the old Scots ballad "Mary Hamilton" attests: "Here then was I (call me Mary Beton, Mary Seton, Mary Carmichael or by any name you please—it is not a matter of any importance)."[33] In the ballad these three Maries survive the eponymous fourth, who bears a child by the queen's consort, casts it into the sea, and sings the last verses on her way to be hanged for this crime. As the lecturer Mary Beton, Woolf tracks the historical conditions of women's lives; consults Fernham's headmistress, Mary Seton, on their causes; contemplates the "safety and prosperity of the one sex" and "the poverty and insecurity of the other"; and projects the future of

Shakespeare's sister through the contemporary novelist Mary Carmichael (*RO* 24). As Mary Carmichael, Woolf places her own writing and its future on the line. And, though unnamed, Mary Hamilton too sur-vives (from Latin *super* above, beyond + *vivere* to live)—lives further and longer, beyond the original ballad—in *Room*. In the ballad it is she who names the other three Maries *in the act of memorializing herself*: "Last night there was four Maries," she sings as she climbs the scaffold. "The night there'll be but three;/There was Mary Seton, and Mary Beton,/And Mary Carmichael, and me."[34] When Woolf tells the students, "call me Mary Beton, Mary Seton, Mary Carmichael, or by any name you please," her "me" echoes Mary Hamilton's "me," as her "or" evokes that unspoken but (to her audience) familiar name.[35]

How does Woolf's "me" revive Mary Hamilton's? Jane Marcus suggests that Woolf "speaks *for*" both Mary Hamilton and Judith Shakespeare, William's (imaginary yet accurately historical, if not historically accurate) sister in *Room*'s speculative biography.[36] No less gifted, "adventurous," "imaginative," "agog to see the world" than her brother, Judith fled a hateful arranged marriage to London, where men guffawed at her until Nick Greene (him again) "took pity on her" and got her pregnant (as William did Ann Hathaway), so that, to end "the torture her gift had put her to," she took her life "one winter's night and lies buried at some cross-roads" by "the Elephant and Castle" (*RO* 47–49). Like Judith Shakespeare, Mary Hamilton, whose song sounds behind Woolf's guess that the ballad-maker Anon "was often a woman," possesses a "poet's heart . . . caught and tangled in a woman's body," and her life ends violently after she bears a child outside masculine law (*RO* 48–49). In speaking for these dead women poets, Woolf draws herself "as" a living body who resurrects history's lost Mary Hamiltons and Judith Shakespeares, and in particular terms. The woman's body in *Room* is at once a vessel of poetic genius, "nature in the subject," and a reproductive body sacrificed to and by laws that place sexuality and childbearing no less than cultural life under masculine legal, economic, and social control. It is a body subject not simply to the natural law of human reproduction but to the fatality of maternity in a political economy of gender that sets nature (the female reproductive body) at war with nature (genius). It is the body of a woman poet who can scarcely be said to have been forced to choose between procreation and creative labor, since human sexuality conjoins with man-made economy, law, and culture less to force a choice than to deprive her of choice.

There are other bodies in the woman poet's grave, for the children (who alter their mothers' futures as Orlando's child does not) also die. "Ye need nae weep for me," sings Mary Hamilton, "Ye need nae weep for me; / For had I not slain mine own sweet babe, / This death I wadna dee." If it seems incongruous to link the quasi-virginal, childless Woolf to this suffering maternal body, we remember how Vanessa sought to soothe their incestuous half brother George Duckworth's concerns about the propriety of the unmarried Virginia's sharing her Bloomsbury abode with men by reminding him coolly that "after all the Foundling Hospital was handy"—a modern escape hatch, before reliable contraception and abortion, from the fatality of female sexuality in a culture of man-made laws.[37] But given Mary's terms of endearment for her babe, these solutions would not lay the ghosts under *Room*'s floorboards. If contraception, abortion, and foundling hospitals help women survive their sexuality in an economy that keeps women poor and/or subject to masculine rule, they do nothing to alter that economy (again, a problem *Orlando*'s wealth finesses).

Woolf, in short, does not throw out the baby with the bathwater, the female reproductive body with man-forged manacles on women's freedom of mind. When Mary Beton and Mary Seton deplore their mothers' failure to make fortunes in trade to endow their futures, as their fathers have from time immemorial endowed those of their brothers, they confront the fact that had Mrs. Seton and her like "gone into business at the age of fifteen, there would have been—that was the snag in the argument—no Mary. What . . . did Mary think of that?" (*RO* 22):

> There . . . was the October night, calm and lovely, with a star or two caught in the yellowing trees. Was she ready to resign her share of it and her memories (for they had been a happy family . . .) of . . . Scotland . . . in order that Fernham might have been endowed with fifty thousand pounds . . . ? For, to endow a college would necessitate the suppression of families altogether. Making a fortune and bearing thirteen children— no human being could stand it. . . . If Mrs. Seton, I said, had been making money, what sort of memories would you have had . . . But it is useless to ask . . . because you would never have come into existence at all. Moreover, it is equally useless to ask what might have happened if Mrs. Seton and her mother and her mother before her had amassed great wealth and laid it under the foundations of college and library, because, in the first place, to earn money was impossible for them, and in the second, . . . the law denied them the right to possess what money they earned. (*RO* 22)

Mrs. Seton's dilemma that is not one—her choice between making babies or making money, colleges, libraries, wine cellars, and poetry, except that, of course, she has no choice—excavates the deeper, structural problem: the political economy of gender. Why didn't Judith Shakespeare write her brother's plays? because she was female, hence, poor, and subject not just to the world's indifference (like Keats) but to its hostility. And why are women poor? because women bear children in an economy whose violent appropriation of female labor to masculine control they are too busy and poor to protest. Thus Woolf pictures her audience "pointing to the streets and squares and forests of the globe swarming with black and white and coffee-coloured inhabitants," saying, "we have had other work on our hands. Without our doing, those seas would be unsailed and those fertile lands a desert. We have borne and bred and washed and taught . . . one thousand six hundred and twenty-three million human beings . . . and that, allowing that some had help, takes time" (RO 112).

Not content merely to have survived, Mary Beton discloses the structural binaries this economy produces: men, its sovereign subjects v. women, its circulating objects; wealth/poverty; education/ignorance; Stock Exchange/unpaid maternal labor. Although Room defers these issues in order to keep women's writing at center stage, the body stays in the picture. The deep question Maries Beton and Seton would pose to "an inscrutable society" that makes children the price of genius in a woman's body sounds insistently through the text: Lady Winchelsea and Margaret of Newcastle were childless; "four more incongruous characters could not have met" than Jane Austen, the two Brontës, and George Eliot, "Save for the possibly relevant fact that not one of them had a child" (RO 24, 66). Unable to solve the problems she articulates, Mary Beton, like a good academic adviser, tosses out topics for the students to pursue: Elizabethan women's education, literacy, privacy, fertility, "what, in short, they did from eight in the morning till eight at night"; "the history of men's opposition to women's emancipation," "more interesting perhaps than the story of that emancipation itself" though its author would need protective bars of "solid gold"; bolder still, an anthropology of chastity, that "fetish invented by certain societies for unknown reasons," which to "bring . . . to the light of day demands courage of the rarest" (RO 46, 55, 49–50).

For Judith Shakespeare to "have lived a free life in London in the sixteenth century . . . might well have killed her"; any work she did get done "would have been twisted and deformed" as well as "unsigned" (RO 50). Mary Beton tracks women's increasing access over the centuries to the education, discipline in the art, time to labor, peace, and the freedom of body and mind necessary "to write a work of genius"—"almost always a feat of prodigious difficulty" (RO 51). That by 1800 Jane Austen could express her gift as fully and freely as Shakespeare—without fear, bitterness, hatred, protest, preaching—seems to Mary a "miracle"; Charlotte Brontë, she judges, had "more genius" but felt with resentment "how

enormously her genius would have profited" had she had three hundred
pounds a year and freedom to travel, meet everyone, experience the world
(*RO* 68–70). As for Mary Beton herself in the year 1929, she is not poor
only by a fluke: an aunt's 1919 fall from her horse in Bombay has
endowed her freedom "to think for oneself" (*RO* 106). For, notwithstanding women's growing economic independence, merely earning one's
living does not in itself ensure "freedom of mind" (*RO* 99). Before that
fortunate fall, young Mary knew hard work, low pay, penury, and, worse,
"the poison of fear and bitterness" from "doing work that one did not
wish to do . . . like a slave, flattering and fawning."[38] Meanwhile,

> the thought of that one gift which it was death to hide—a small one but
> dear to the possessor—perishing and with it myself, my soul . . . became
> like a rust eating away the bloom of the spring, destroying the tree at its
> heart. However, as I say, my aunt died; and whenever I change a ten-
> shilling note a little of that . . . fear and bitterness go. . . . by degrees . . .
> modified . . . into pity and toleration; and then . . . the greatest release of
> all came, which is freedom to think of things in themselves. . . . Indeed,
> my aunt's legacy unveiled the sky to me and substituted for the large and
> imposing figure of a gentleman, which Milton recommended for my per-
> petual adoration, a view of the open sky. (*RO* 37–39)

It is too seldom remarked that Milton's gentleman in the sky is the
patriarchal god, made in man's image and historically invoked to authorize the economy of gender that keeps women poets poor, pregnant,
thwarted, and/or dead—"destroying the tree" (that recurring symbol of
freedom, reality, poetry, and the poet herself) "at its heart." What unveils
the sky—"things in themselves"—to Mary, what emancipates her from
being a "slave" to dull necessity into "that intellectual freedom of which
great writings are born," is the small inheritance that exempts her from
the rule that women are poor.

Woolf is often attacked for saying, in effect, that for women writers it is
not enough to be nature's favorite; one must also be one's aunt's. Failing
that, it is not enough to earn five hundred a year; you must earn it "by your
wits," like Aphra Behn, that bold pioneer of women's "freedom of the
mind, or rather [its] possibility."[39] It is true that Woolf's woman writer is
no better than she should be. The locale of Aunt Mary's fall emphasizes
that, in her modest degree, Mary Beton lives (like her brothers, fathers,
uncles, sons) on the "slave" labor of others in Britain's imperial and class
economy. Once Mary "ceases to speak," Woolf does not flinch at the Darwinian suggestion that her ambitions for women's writing may lead "to the
murder of one's aunts" and even urges her young listeners to get "By hook
or by crook" enough money to travel, idle, "contemplate the future or the

past of the world," dream over books, "loiter at street corners and let the line of thought dip deep into the stream," and to write travel, adventure, research, scholarship, history, biography, criticism, philosophy, and science—all fodder for future fiction and poetry (*RO* 105, 108, 109). Indeed, to be good writers women must renounce excessive virtue; why else does Woolf insist that "good writers, even if they show every variety of human depravity, are still good human beings"; and that women's writing benefits not women only but "the world at large" because writers "live more than other people in the presence of . . . reality" and help "the rest of us" to know it (*RO* 109–10)? No more a paragon of virtue than her male compeer, Woolf's woman writer, with her hook-or-crook methods and possible "depravity," is redeemed by what she reveals of "reality."

In the matter of what the world calls "depravity," *Room* practices what it preaches. Mary Beton evokes the obscenity trial of Radclyffe Hall's *Well of Loneliness* on 9 November 1928, at which Woolf stood ready to testify in the book's defense, when she lectures on Mary Carmichael's *Life's Adventure*, published "this very month of October"—like the similarly depraved *Orlando*, which escaped censorship and trial.[40] Mary Beton first compares reading this "last volume in a very long series" by English-women writers to "being out at sea in an open boat" (evoking *The Voyage Out*) and then considers how Mary Carmichael has struggled against tradition, breaking sentence and sequence to say something new (evoking *Jacob's Room, Mrs. Dalloway, To the Lighthouse*) (*RO* 80–81). Then

> I turned the page and read . . . I am sorry to break off so abruptly. . . . Do you promise me that behind that red curtain . . . Sir Chartres Biron is not concealed? We are all women, you assure me? Then I may tell you that the very next words I read were these—"Chloe liked Olivia" . . . perhaps for the first time in literature. Cleopatra did not like Octavia. And how completely *Antony and Cleopatra* would have been altered had she done so! As it is . . . the whole thing is simplified, conventionalised, if one dared say it, absurdly. Cleopatra's only feeling about Octavia is one of jealousy. Is she taller than I am? How does she do her hair? The play, perhaps, required no more. But how interesting it would have been if the relationship between the two women had been more complicated. (*RO* 82, first ellipsis Woolf's)

Mary Beton's comic precaution in case Sir Chartres Biron—the Chief Magistrate for the *Well of Loneliness* trial, who on November 16 ordered it seized and destroyed—might be lurking in the drapery flaunts a certain affinity between Hall's book and "Mary Carmichael's" *Orlando*, even as this scene anticipates Luce Irigaray's image of women as the "goods"—objects of exchange in an economy of masculine subjects—getting together in a lesbian economy that eludes and mocks masculine control of women's bodies and minds.[41] Mary Beton also recalls the escapades with prostitutes that Orlando's biographer glides over in silence: given time, she predicts, Mary Carmichael will depict "the courtesan, the harlot and the lady with the pug dog . . . as they are"—once she has struggled free of "that self-consciousness in the presence of 'sin' which is the legacy of our sexual barbarity," thrown off "the shoddy old fetters of class" (RO 88). While English literature has been immeasurably "impoverished" by the strictures on women's bodies and minds, the newly autonomous Mary— providing she "knows how to write"—can begin to repair those losses if she abandons a false and suffocating virtue for courage to "face . . . the world of reality" (RO 83–84, 114).

Mary Carmichael, though "no genius," not only treats characters and relationships that Shakespeare leaves untouched (as Chloe/Olivia's emergence from the matrix of Cleopatra/Octavia proves) but (like Shakespeare and Orlando) can explore the present moment's "caves" and "chamber[s] . . . where nobody has yet been" with a freedom that "women of far greater gift lacked even half a century ago" and coin into language the "feeling that is actually being made and torn out of us at the moment."[42] As for poetry, self-portraiture again undergirds Woolf's belief that the dead poet Judith Shakespeare "still lives . . . in you and in me, and in many other women" and her prophecy that she will soon be "knocking [the novel form] into shape for herself when she has the free use of her limbs" and inventing "some new vehicle, not necessarily in verse, for the poetry in her," as yet "still denied outlet."[43] Already "Fear and hatred" born of oppression have almost vanished from Mary's writing, felt only in "a slight exaggeration of the joy of freedom" as her "sensibility"—"wide, eager and free"—"respond[s] to an almost imperceptible touch on it," "feast[ing] like a plant newly stood in the air on every sight and sound" and bringing "buried things to light" (RO 92). No longer an economic "slave," Mary can write relatively unencumbered by impediments and grievances contingent on sex—in Kant's terms, by the "interest" that contaminates the free play of imagination and understanding requisite to "pure" aesthetic judgment (CJ §13 58–59, CPJ 107–8).

Indeed, Mary Carmichael has already "mastered the first great lesson; she wrote as a woman, but as a woman who has forgotten that she is a woman, so that her pages were full of that curious sexual quality which comes only when sex is unconscious of itself" (RO 93). At stake in this lesson is a disinterestedness that does not obliterate sex but renders it "unconscious of itself."[44] Insofar as "woman" signals a curtailment of human freedom—as in Charlotte Brontë's self-portrait as Jane Eyre—

Mary does not write as a "woman." Nor does she write like a man, since the "curious sexual quality" her writing exudes evidently differs from the dark bar of grievance the male professor's baleful *I* casts over his page; differs too from the androgynous Shakespeare's writing, as Chloe and Olivia demonstrate. If sex "unconscious of itself" signifies a living body and mind unburdened by grievances that bespeak "interest" and compromise freedom, does Mary's writing, like Orlando's baby, express sex as a pure fact of nature, apart from social law? In that case, is genius, "nature in the subject," inflected by sex as nature in the subject—sex as prior to the political economy of gender, unmarked by "interest"? If so, this "curious sexual quality" of writing, whether by Shakespeare, Austen, Proust, or Mary Carmichael, would not compromise the freedom art actualizes or the disinterested play of imagination and understanding by which, in Kant's terms, aesthetic judgments posit "subjective universal validity"— as if, in a figure from *Orlando* and *Room*, "*one* had gone to the top of the world and seen it laid out, very majestically, beneath" (*CJ* §8 49, *CPJ* 100, *RO* 93, my emphasis).

In drawing herself as Mary Carmichael, Woolf claims freedom of mind on her own behalf no less than her audience's. As her aunt's legacy underwrites Mary Beton's creative labor, so Woolf—who as a professional writer had just begun (in 1926, at the age of 44) to earn five hundred a year and more by her wits—was conscious of having "bought my freedom" to write *The Waves* by declining a two-thousand-pound commission: "A queer thought that I have actually paid for the power to go to Rodmell & only think of The Waves."[45] When Mary Beton closes Mary Carmichael's book saying, "give her a room of her own and five hundred a year, let her speak her mind . . . and she will write a better book one of these days. She will be a poet . . . in another hundred years' time," Woolf is thinking toward the lyric prose of *The Waves* (*RO* 94). Not for nothing does she urge Mary Carmichael to "catch those unrecorded gestures, those unsaid or half-said words, which form themselves, no more palpably than the shadows of moths on the ceiling, when women are alone, unlit by the capricious and coloured light of the other sex" as she approaches the novel as yet titled *The Moths*.[46] Enjoining Mary to "illumine your own soul with its profundities and its shallows," Woolf moves toward her own "Autobiography" of the soul or psyche, that moth whose wings cast angular shadows on the ceiling of the mundane world, as her anonymous, androgynous Shakespeare elucidates the sense in which *The Waves* is "the life of anybody."[47] Above an angry roar of bishops, deans, doctors, professors, patriarchs, and pedagogues, she exhorts Mary, "Think only of the jump, . . . as if I had put the whole of my money on her back; and she went over it like a bird" (*RO* 94). So Woolf will over-leap the "naturalist-novelist"'s world of men and women to contemplate things in themselves and declare jubilantly, on finishing *The Waves*, "I felt the pressure of the form—the splendour & the greatness—as—perhaps, I have never felt them. . . . I have taken my fence" (*RO* 88, *D* 3:298, 28 March 1930).

In her "peroration" Woolf prophesies that in a hundred years, if "we" (like Shakespeare, Orlando, Mary Carmichael) "have the habit of free-dom and . . . see human beings . . . in relation to reality; and the sky, too, and the trees or whatever it may be in themselves . . . if we face the fact . . . that we go alone and that our relation is to the world of reality and not only to the world of men and women, then . . . Shakespeare's sister will put on the body which she has so often laid down" (*RO* 113–14). But if Judith Shakespeare "lives in you and me"—if in *Room* the body so often laid down (Mary Hamilton's, Judith Shakespeare's) is reborn as Mary Beton, Mary Seton, Mary Carmichael, Woolf's audience ("you") and herself ("me")—why must a century pass before "she will be a poet" (*RO* 94)? Even as Woolf claims "the free use of her limbs" to invent a new form for the "poetry in her," she keeps the woman poet's realist body in the picture: sexual, maternal, still subject to the political econ-omy of gender, not yet transparent to the freedom that poetry, the high-est genre, makes felt. But Woolf—herself a "firebrand" in claiming "the habit of freedom"—cannot wait a century. Without denying the social struggles that remain before women poets can truly put on freedom's body, she strives to break history's "lock" on her mind's force; to put on freedom's body to create the [woman] who writes the children of *The Waves* (*RO* 76).

Another Nature: Abstract Form, Modern Physics, and the Garden of *The Waves*

> I dont want a Lavinia or a Penelope: I want 'She.'
>
> —Woolf, *Diary*, 28 May 1929
>
> I am telling myself the story of the world from the beginning.
>
> —Woolf, The Waves: *The Two Holograph Drafts*
>
> With intermittent shocks, sudden as the springs of a tiger, life emerges heaving its dark crest from the sea. . . . it is to this we are bound, as bod-ies to wild horses.
>
> —Rhoda, in Woolf, *The Waves*

> I see far out a waste of water. A fin turns. . . . Now . . . when a pretty woman enters . . . I shall say to myself, Look where she comes against a waste of waters. A meaningless observation, but to me, solemn, slate-coloured, with a fatal sound of ruining worlds and waters falling to destruction.
>
> —Bernard, in Woolf, *The Waves*

In observing that Mary Carmichael's writing betrays her former oppression only by a slightly exaggerated "joy of freedom," does Woolf frame this joy as an asset or a liability (*RO* 92)? Does this excess joy inspire art, or does it risk a new kind of contingency: the kind of "interest" that compromises freedom; an agenda, personal or social, that taints the "purposiveness without purpose" essential to "pure" aesthetic judgments (*CJ* §22 78–79, *CPJ* 125)? The oscillation between the marked pronoun *she* and the unmarked *one* in *The Waves'* genetic text suggests that Woolf felt this risk and—paradoxically—*practiced* writing "as a woman who has forgotten that she is a woman" to banish it. Wittig observes that, whereas the pronoun *she* marks women as aberration from the normative *he*, *I* speaks dominion over the world, and *one* parlays *I* into the voice of the universal, the human.[48] Woolf sets out to unmark *she*, to free it for representativeness, normativity, universality.

Thus, two months after she/"One" first sights the fin ("One sees a fin passing far out"), Woolf preserves her autobiographical subject's feminine origin but abstracts it from any particular mind: "I am now & then haunted by some semi mystic very profound life of a woman, which shall all be told on one occasion; & time shall be utterly obliterated; future shall somehow blossom out of the past. One incident—say the fall of a flower—might contain it. My theory being that the actual event practically does not exist—nor time either" (*D* 3:118, 23 November 1926). Later she imagines "a new kind of play" starring "Woman": "Woman thinks: . . ./He does./Organ Plays./She writes./They say:/She sings:/ Night speaks:/They miss" (*D* 3:128, 21 February 1927, ellipsis Woolf's). Again, she poses "*A man & a woman* . . . sitting at table talking" only to foreground the woman: "It is to be a love story: *she* is finally to let the last great moth in. . . . *she* might talk, or think, about the age of the earth: the death of humanity: then moths keep on coming. *Perhaps the man could be left absolutely dim*" (*D* 3:139, 18 June 1927; emphases added). Returning to *The Moths/The Waves* after *Orlando* and *Room*, Woolf again abstracts her "I" into a neutral "mind thinking" while insisting that this abstract mind should be a [woman's]:

> I am not trying to tell a story. . . . A *mind thinking*. . . . *Autobiography*
> it might be called. . . . One must get the sense that this is the beginning:
> this the middle; that the climax—when *she* opens the window & the
> moth comes in. *I* shall have the two different currents—the moths flying
> along; the flower upright in the centre; a perpetual crumbling & renew-
> ing of the plant. In its leaves *she* might see things happen. But who is *she*?
> I am very anxious that *she should have no name*. I dont want a Lavinia
> or a Penelope: *I want 'She.'* (D 3:229–30, 28 May 1929, my emphases)

In specifying who this abstract, nameless, autobiographical "She" is not,
Woolf removes her from literary tradition's "capricious" light: she does-
n't "want" a woman like Virgil's Lavinia, a pawn in Aeneas's empire-
building, Shakespeare's violated Lavinia, writing her story in sand with
bloody stumps, or Homer's Penelope, stuck at home during life's adventure. Instead, the grammatically impossible yet perfectly comprehensible
"I want 'She' " momentarily gives English a new rule (if *Caesar non est
supra Grammaticos*, poets are another matter). To "want 'She' " is to
want woman as subject not object, woman as free; to want [woman] in
the abstract, as not women's but freedom's representative—woman as
"oneself," She (not He) writ large as One.

Woolf continues to abstract this [She] from personality, time, event,
and gender without relinquishing her sex:

> The beginning. Well, all sorts of characters are to be there. Then the *per-
> son* who is at the table can call out any one of them at any moment; &
> build up by that person the mood, tell a story; . . . Childhood; but it must
> not be *my* childhood; . . . unreality; things oddly proportioned. Then
> another *person* or *figure* must be selected. . . . The Moth must come in:
> the beautiful single moth. . . . *She* might have a book—one book to read
> in—another to write in—old letters. . . . there must be great freedom
> from "reality." (D 3:236, 23 June 1929; emphases added except "*my*")

Here *she* seems to slip in unawares, as if Woolf were indeed writing as a
woman who has forgotten that she is a woman. Yet Woolf has not done
with remembering, to judge by this explicit unsexing of the thinking subject ten days later:

> The *lonely mind, mans or womans, it does not matter which*, & in this
> early light the form was inscrutable, the power that crystallises, collect-
> ing, rather at random, what would otherwise be lost & from many frag-
> ments attempting to make a whole: here brooding over the napkin and
> the glass, thought
>   *I* am telling myself the story of the world from the beginning. *I* am
> not concerned with the single life, but with lives together. *I* am trying to

> find, in the folds of the past, . . . such fragments as time having broken
> the perfect vessel still keeps safe[.] The perfect vessel? But . . . it was only
> when . . . the violence of the shock was over that *one* could understand,
> or really live.[49]

Scarcely has Woolf forged this abstract *I/one*, this representative sufferer of the brokenness of being, than a formal problem "cries out at once to be solved. Who thinks it? And am I outside the thinker? One wants some device which is not a trick" (*D* 3:257, 25 September 1929). Here Woolf writes as a woman ("am I outside the thinker?") who has forgotten she's a woman ("One wants some device"). Her solution is to refract the lonely mind through the "playpoem"'s mixed chorus, the six *I*'s—not characters but voices, translucent to being and to each other—who soliloquize one by one.[50] Although these voices attach to sexed bodies in a gendered social world, no hierarchy of being obtains among them.[51] Each speaks its subjective dominion over the world; meanwhile, the lonely mind's *I* ("I am telling myself . . . ") disappears in the impersonal omniscient voice of the lyric interludes, which transcribes and attributes each speaker's words.

In this subliming of *she* into *one* and thence into the lonely mind's omniscient voice, the subject of the genetic text both registers and surmounts freedom's contingency. It is as if, in the interest of disinterestedness, Woolf labors to master freedom's "first great lesson": to write as a woman who has forgotten that she is a woman, or perhaps (a century ahead of her time by *Room*'s prophetic reckoning) to write as a woman who has forgotten that she is a woman *might write*, despite remembering. In other words, the [woman] in *The Waves* is still there, in the *one* and the omniscient voice: as woman unmarked and/or as woman simulating the condition of being unmarked. The oscillating *She/one*, further, registers an oscillating temporality, the prophetic future that this work of art strives to embody symbolically in the present. Evoking Kant's concept of genius as that aspect of "nature in the subject" that "give[s] the rule to art," [she]— sexual difference as nature not culture, or nature *and* culture, insofar as culture enables her to cultivate her art in freedom—actualizes herself as nature's favorite; manifests freedom's "objective reality" by creating "another nature," this work of art.

In creating the [woman] of *The Waves* (*she* as *one*), Woolf creates "another nature" that throws a bridge from the realm of nature (or physics) to the realm of freedom; a new story of the world that rethinks being, nature, time, subjectivity, and indeed event and the story itself from the beginning in light of modern physics. Telling "the story of the world," [she] throws off the gender-bound law inscribed in Genesis to create a rival representation of nature, which Woolf labors through successive drafts to sign in the white ink of Kantian disinterestedness. In a passage later cut, the draft's thinking mind animates the suppressed maternal aspect of the waters over which the Western father-god broods to bring forth the world, figuring "waves that were of many mothers, & again of many mothers, & behind them many more, endlessly sinking and falling, . . . each holding up . . . a child" (*Wh* I:9–10). The draft, that is, "forgets" the legislating deity of a story of the world that symbolically exiles women from material and cultural creativity, replacing that solitary, singular, monotheistic origin and author with a feminized figure of the manifold, inexhaustibly proliferating creativity that sounds through *The Waves'* voices. But in inverting the original myth's gender hierarchy, does this figure perhaps betray a slightly excessive "joy of freedom"—sign, in effect, she, not [she]? The final text, in any case, forgets Genesis and gender altogether: "In the beginning, there was the nursery, with windows opening on to a garden, and beyond that the sea" (*W* 239). Disentangling ontology not from sex but from gender as contingent hierarchy, *The Waves* privileges neither sex as creator, witness, or namer at the world's origin.

Yet [She] persists, there and not there, in the waves, no longer mothers, that recur through the interludes; in the opening figure (first simile, then metaphor) of day dawning "*as if the arm of a woman couched beneath the horizon had raised a lamp,*" which refigures the Western father-god's "Let there be light"; and in her phantasmal Self-Portrait as Woman Writing at Elvedon—this other nature's spectral author, free to create the children or to nail them "like stoats to the stable door"; or so they fear, fleeing her gaze as if to escape into the real, the thing itself no writing can capture (*W* 7, 17). Most strikingly, [she] persists in the forgetting of sexual hierarchy in this transfigured Garden and Fall. Whereas in Eden death is not natural but metaphysical, "caused" by a sequence of events within a logic of divine law, transgression, and punishment, in *The Waves* nothing separates death and decay from the life that feeds on them: thus the draft's "lonely mind" sees "the snail slime, the sticky fluid in the hollow stalk & the [thin] rat heaving with maggots . . . in the hearts of those . . . unfortunate children" (*Wh* I:6). No story, no authority, domesticates nature's violence or mitigates death's horror; no telos redeems human suffering. The Fall is a fall into being that has always already happened; the garden in which the children wake is a stage for a "playpoem" of pure being, where (as in Orlando's Eden) no mother or father, divine or human, walks.

Not a mother but "Old Mrs. Constable"—a nurse remote from the originary authority with which Lily invests Mrs. Ramsay—presides over the children's first consciousness, their apprehension of ontological separateness. She " 'lifted her sponge and warmth poured over us,' said Bernard. 'We became clothed in this changing, this feeling garment of flesh' " (W 124). The sensations of this "garment of flesh" mediate between being and language; like the birds of the interludes, pecking at snail shells, the children have their being in nature, their bodies part of "the thing itself" that language can fashion into "anything" (TL 193). Thus Louis imagines himself a "stalk," camouflaged, "unseen," "green as a yew tree," with "hair . . . made of leaves," "rooted to the middle of the earth," until "an eyebeam" strikes him and Jinny, chasing butterflies, calls him to the human, sexual, social world: " 'I am a boy in a grey flannel suit. . . . She has kissed me. All is shattered' " (W 12–13). The kiss that destroys Louis's primordial fantasy and awakens Susan to lonely "anguish" arises not from sexual desire or transgression but from Jinny's fear of his absented state: " ' "Is he dead?" I thought, and kissed you' " (W 13). In this version of the Fall it is not sin that causes desire, suffering, death; rather, "eyebeam" and kiss materialize the desire inherent in the "anguish" of ontological difference, the shattered "perfect vessel." Originating outside cultural law in this garden, this kiss—of life not death—engenders sorrow but not hierarchy, jealousy but not gender.

In place of the ancient deity of Genesis, school and church authorities with feet of clay preside over a travesty of the real, natural world. Susan " 'would bury the whole school; the gymnasium; the classroom; the dining-room that always smells of meat, and the chapel' " (W 44). As the mystic Rhoda—pure psyche, a bodiless "small butterfly"—voices the soul, Dr. Crane's sermon (like Reverend Bax's in The Voyage Out) " 'mince[s] the dance of the white butterflies . . . to powder' "; " 'The words of authority are corrupted by those who speak them,' " Neville says; they " 'fall cold on my head like paving-stones, while the gilt cross heaves on his waistcoat' " (W 22, 36, 35). Dr. Crane's Christian tradition transforms history's chaos into a teleological "procession" that "erects" Louis, the Australian poet-clerk modeled on the St. Louis poet-clerk T. S. Eliot: " 'by his authority, his crucifix, . . . I recover my continuity. . . . I become a figure in the procession, a spoke in the huge wheel that turning, at last erects me.' "[52] Yet even Louis glimpses the metaphysical violence of the tradition that upraises him: " 'How majestic is their order, how beautiful their obedience!' " he marvels of Dr. Crane's schoolboys. " 'But they also leave butterflies trembling with their wings pinched off' " (W 47).

Against schoolroom and church, the children's garden world is a liminal space between nature and culture: on the one hand, laid with "paving-stones," the tradition that (as in *Jacob's Room*) soon occludes the children's transparent consciousness; on the other, scene of a nature (or physics) that eludes the gardener's hand, in which Woolf grounds this "story of the world from the beginning" (or metaphysics). Whereas Eden's father-god binds sexuality to sin, sorrow, and death through a narrative that opposes female desire to divine authority, the children of *The Waves* awaken in a nature inherently violent. No authority shapes their suffering into a story of sexual hierarchy, divine law, female transgression, and death as punishment at the hands of divine justice; here suffering arises not from desire framed as sin but from the originary shattering of the "perfect vessel"—from difference as such.

As metaphysics precedes the "other nature" of Genesis, the new physics of the novel's modernist moment informs the other nature of *The Waves*—in which "the actual event practically does not exist—nor time either"—as well as its abstract form and the narrative procedures that displace the Newtonian either/or logic of common sense with the both/and logic of the quantum universe. One critic proposes that the "crucial problem" facing the reader of *The Waves* is to find "a way to think that seems definite and common-sensical, rather than abstract, imagistic, philosophically 'distant' from—what? Life as we know it?"[53] To read *The Waves* in light of quantum physics is to find a ground and logic *in nature* for the challenge to common sense posed by its abstract form; and indeed to confront the limits of nineteenth-century realism. The discoveries of the new physics—the wave/particle paradox, the uncertainty principle, the dissolution of the subject/object duality, the phenomenon of entities mutually interacting at a distance without apparent physical mediation, governed by probability waves—contradict the common sense not just of Newtonian physics but even of Einstein's relativistic universe.[54] The quantum universe in fact exposes what we ordinarily think of as "common sense" as quite *un*natural, revealing the real, profound ungroundedness and illusoriness of substance, identity, event, and time.[55] As unfathomable as the nature that impels abstract art in Wörringer's theory, the strange nature disclosed by particle physics illuminates both *The Waves'* depiction of being as radically ungrounded, accidental, insubstantial, and the ephemeral voices that trace the border between a commonsensical but unreal world of bounded bodies and an intuited, mysterious but real world of things or (nonthings) in themselves. If *The Waves* seems distant from "life as we know it," it seeks to capture something of life, or (in *Room*'s word) "reality," as it is, beyond what our "definite and commonsensical" thinking can know of it.

Three features of *The Waves'* story or non-story of the world—the wave, the "perfect vessel," and the both/and logic that challenges either/or common sense—find analogues in quantum physics. The 1927 Davisson-Germer experiment demonstrated that the motion of electrons is governed simultaneously by wave functions and Newtonian mechanics, proving that, just as "an elementary particle is not an independently existing, unanalyzable entity" but "a set of relationships," the physical world "is not a structure . . . of independently existing unanalyzable entities" but "a web" of aspects that change "with their relationship to the whole."[56] It is not that there *might* not be a "substantive physical world" but that "there definitely is not" one, for the probability wave "describes not one world but an infinity of worlds"; of this "stupendously infinite superspace," the sensible world is but "a single, three-dimensional element" in which what is not "there" conditions what is.[57] As if to reveal freedom's "objective reality" by its effects in nature, *The Waves* allies its experimental form—and its metaphysical positing of "another nature" beyond illusions of substance, time, event—with the unseen reality disclosed by quantum physics.

How, then, describe the "real" world? The Copenhagen interpretation regards as "real" only the actual path that the electron selects from the wave function's infinity of possible paths: possibility perpetually collapses into event to create the world we perceive. Bernard's intuition that " 'We have destroyed something by our presence . . . a world perhaps' " fits with this view that a throw of the dice does indeed abolish chance, canceling other possible worlds (*W* 232). The (Aristotelian) "Many Worlds" interpretation regards as "real" *all* the worlds given by the wave function; the universe perpetually "split[s] into a stupendous number of branches," only one of which we perceive.[58] So Bernard doubts the truth of story (" 'a mistake, . . . a convenience, a lie' "); regrets the myriad thoughts that " 'slip through [his] fingers' " whenever he makes a sentence; finds " 'nothing one can fish up in a spoon; nothing one can call an event' " when he casts his net of words; and feels himself " 'not one person' " but " 'many people,' " " 'many Bernards' " (*W* 255–56, 276, 260).

So too Rhoda, the figural quintessence of *The Waves'* poetics of indeterminacy, haunts the borderland between being and nonbeing, rendering the vexed question of her suicide redundant: a possibility that cannot be fixed as an event—definite, scrutinizable, incontrovertible—in the ordinary sense appropriate to the realist novel or even the modernist-realist *Mrs. Dalloway*. Rather, Rhoda's life and death seem inseparable, insubstantial reflections in an ephemeral stream of language that tracks a continual becoming and dissolution of body, being, and time. Thus she remembers arriving, "holding an envelope in my hand," carrying "a message," at a "cadaverous, awful . . . grey puddle in the courtyard" to find that

> "I could not cross it. Identity failed me. We are nothing, I said, and fell. I was blown like a feather. I was wafted down tunnels. Then very gingerly, I pushed my foot across. . . . I returned very painfully, drawing myself back into my body over the grey, cadaverous space of the puddle. This is life then to which I am committed."[59]

The "life" that emerges "sudden as the springs of a tiger, . . . heaving its dark crest from the sea," and that binds *The Waves'* voices like "bodies to wild horses," is inseparable from death not only for Rhoda but for Percival, the questing knight, fertility god, and wounded fisher-king whose life/death tears the veil of illusory appearances (*W* 64). An Apollonian figure of ambition and action who exerts violent force over an unreal world, Percival is at the same time an antithetical Dionysus who enables the six friends to " 'see India' ": " 'who makes us aware that these attempts to say, "I am this, I am that" . . . are false'," and that " 'these roaring waters . . . upon which we build our crazy platforms are more stable than the wild, the weak and inconsequent cries that we utter . . . Speech is false' " (*W* 135, 137–38). The six worship Percival in a primal "communion" that intimates the "perfect vessel" and so partakes of death: "savage," "ruthless," they seem to "dance in a circle," "flames leap[ing] over their painted faces, over the leopard skins and the bleeding limbs which they have torn from the living body"—their hatred, as Jinny says, " 'almost indistinguishable from our love' " (*W* 126, 140, 138). Through their (imaginary) breaking of the vessel that is Percival's body, the six transcend their confining boundaries. On the silent, radiant Percival, nothing in himself, they project their longing for wholeness, for death, for the "perfect vessel" whose fragments they are: " 'They throw violets. They deck the beloved with garlands and with laurel leaves' " (*W* 140).

Metaphorically partaking of their god at the celebratory dinner, the six voices momentarily create a " 'globe whose walls are made of Percival, of youth and beauty and something so deep sunk within us that we shall perhaps never make this moment out of one man again' " (*W* 145). This metaphysical breaking and consuming of the vessel that is the god's body binds Percival's life to his deferred death, his fall from a horse that is nothing more or less than a fall from " 'this curious steed, life.' "[60] Abstract, arbitrary, accidental, unheroic, Percival's death, like his life, illuminates the world for the living, who like Clarissa feast on death to reconcile themselves to life. Grappling with " 'what death has done to my world'," Bernard sees in the midst of desolation something " 'abstract, facing me eyeless at the end of the avenue, in the sky' " and asks, " ' "Is this the utmost you can do? . . . Then we have triumphed" ' " (W 153, 154).

For Rhoda, bound so precariously to existence, Percival's death brings a stark "gift"—a hunger for "publicity and violence," a desire to "fling [her]self fearlessly into trams, into omnibuses" in quest of the real:

> " 'Like' and 'like' and 'like'—but what is the thing that lies beneath the semblance of the thing? Now that lightning has gashed the tree and the flowering branch has fallen and Percival, by his death, has made me this gift, let me see the thing. There is a square; there is an oblong. The play- ers take the square and place it upon the oblong. They place it very accu- rately; they make a perfect dwelling-place. Very little is left outside. The structure is now visible; what is inchoate is here stated; we are not so var- ious or so mean; we have made oblongs and stood them upon squares. This is our triumph; this is our consolation." (W 159, 163)

Not stories but structures console, Rhoda says: oblongs on squares, angu- lar shapes, a fin in a waste of waters, the perpetual "fight" that is life against the vanquisher death, abstracted from particular forms and set, in *The Waves*, against the infinite void. Human endeavor and authority find no ground in *The Waves'* abstract cosmos: " 'how strange it seems to set against the whirling abysses of infinite space a little figure with a golden teapot on his head. Soon one recovers a belief in figures: but not at once in what they put on their heads' " (W 227). Bernard reflects that " 'the earth is only a pebble flicked off accidentally from the face of the sun and that there is no life anywhere in the abysses of space' " (W 225). " 'Lis- ten,' " Louis says, " 'to the world moving through abysses of infinite space. It roars; the lighted strip of history is past and our Kings and Queens; we are gone; our civilisation; the Nile; and all life. Our separate drops are dissolved; we are extinct, lost in the abysses of time, in the dark- ness' " (W 225). Imagining annihilation, Bernard hears " 'for one moment the howling winds of darkness as we passed beyond life,' " then recalls himself: " 'I rise; "Fight, . . . fight!" ' " Neville urges, " 'Oppose ourselves to this illimitable chaos, . . . this formless imbecility.' " From his post with Rhoda by the cold urn, Louis observes them saying, " 'My face shall be cut against the black of infinite space' " (W 225–26). Jinny exults, " 'We have triumphed over the abysses of space, with rouge, with powder, with flimsy pocket-handkerchiefs' " (W 228). Bernard feels " 'the huge black- ness of what is outside us, of what we are not. The wind, the rush of wheels became the roar of time, and we rushed—where? And who were we? We were extinguished for a moment, went out like sparks in burnt paper and the blackness roared. Past time, past history we went. For me this lasts but one second' "; as always, " 'I jumped up, I said "Fight." . . . It is the effort and the struggle, it is the perpetual warfare, it is the shattering and piecing together—this is the daily battle, defeat or victory, the absorbing pursuit.' "[61]

In its quest for a "reality" beyond the accidental and momentary meanings with which each character invests the abstract condition they share, *The Waves* counterposes oblongs upon squares, a fin in a waste of waters, to the story—inevitably false, incomplete, arbitrary in its belief in time and event. Bernard says, " 'I have made up thousands of stories; I have filled innumerable notebooks with phrases to be used when I have found the true story, the one story to which all these phrases refer. But I have never yet found that story. And I begin to ask, Are there stories? . . . why impose my arbitrary design?' " (*W* 187–88). Elaborating Woolf's 1926 self-portrait, he sees

> "far out a waste of water. A fin turns. This bare visual impression is unattached to any line of reason, it springs up as one might see the fin of a porpoise on the horizon. Visual impressions often communicate thus briefly statements that we shall in time to come uncover and coax into words. I note under F., therefore, 'Fin in a waste of waters.' I, who am perpetually making notes in the margin of my mind for some final statement, make this mark, waiting for some winter's evening.
>   "Now I shall go and lunch somewhere . . . and when a pretty woman enters . . . I shall say to myself, Look where she comes against a waste of waters. A meaningless observation, but to me, solemn, slate-coloured, with a fatal sound of ruining worlds and waters falling to destruction."
> (*W* 189)

The fin has been taken to mark the "end of writing"—"division, difference and death."[62] But it would seem equally to signal the beginning of writing: the thing itself before it has been made anything; the abstract life force that human endeavor transforms into oblongs on squares, perfect dwelling-places—and its absence the ebb of life. Thus at his deadly school Bernard remembers, " 'Nothing, nothing, nothing broke with its fin that leaden waste of waters' "; when he dines with Neville and a silence descends, broken by a few words, it is " 'as if a fin rose in the wastes of silence; and then the fin, the thought, sinks back into the depths spreading round it a little ripple of satisfaction, content' "; approaching his own death, he calls to a self who no longer comes: " 'Now there is nothing. No fin breaks the waste of this immeasurable sea. Life has destroyed me' " (*W* 245, 273, 284).

The voices of the eyeless, mystical, abstract *Waves*, in which neither time nor event exists, perpetually sense other worlds beyond the phenomenal one and—aware that they partly create the world they do perceive—utter thoughts unfathomable to common sense, yet quite at home in the irreducibly strange " 'dwelling-place' " that quantum physics reveals to be our own.[63] *The Waves* captures moments of being within this nature in which all forms are insubstantial abstractions, every representation a dwelling-place founded on nothingness, and the perfect vessel a figure of an unfathomable cosmos, real yet absolutely unknowable. As one physicist puts it, what we ordinarily regard as "separate objects have interacted at some time in the past with other objects" in "an indivisible whole. Perhaps in such a world the concept of an independently existing reality can retain some meaning, but it will be an altered meaning and one remote from everyday experience."[64] So discrete events and enduring separate objects vanish from the "constant idea" behind Woolf's modernist autobiography, the "semi mystic very profound life of a woman" that is also a "life of anybody": "that behind the cotton wool is hidden a pattern; that we—I mean all human beings—are connected with this; that the whole world is a work of art; that we are parts of the work of art. . . . It proves that one's life is not confined to one's body and what one says and does" (*MB* 72–73).

The "silver-grey flickering moth-wing quiver of words" that is *The Waves* tracks a "life," an autobiographical subjectivity, that eludes the bounds of body, identity, time, event, not just in the mystic Rhoda and the poet Louis ("conspirators" by "the cold urn") but in everyday life, as when Bernard hears " 'deep below' " his ordered hours and days a " 'rushing stream of broken dreams, nursery rhymes, street cries, half-finished sentences and sights—elm trees, willow trees, gardeners sweeping, women writing' "; hears, as it were, a stream of being that carries things known and unknown, present and absent, remembered and forgotten—a figure of all time captured and stilled in the linguistic vessel of this work of art, this other nature (*W* 215, 141, 255). This unseen being, this life unconfined to one's body, recasts metaphysics in the image of a nature of infinite interpenetrating energies wherein, since every observation is an interaction, "subject and object and the nature of reality" are fundamentally inseparable (*TL* 23).

The both/and quantum logic of Woolf's modernist autobiography— her self-portraits as "something else, something other"—keep "she" and "one," "she" *as* "one," simultaneously in play.[65] As for freedom's "first great lesson," the genetic text quests for a voice that is female not in *what* it says ("many mothers") nor in style or rhythm, since these are conventional and imitable (à la Molly Bloom), but simply in itself: a unique event, precipitated by infinite throws of the dice from infinite possibilities, yet an irreducible actuality; an autobiographical voice that tells no story but contemplates a world inseparable from its contemplation, in doing so creating another nature; a voice heard by another as "hers."[66] Bernard, summing up, finds story false and discursive language useless: he needs " 'nothing consecutive but a bark, a groan' "; " 'a little language such as lovers use, words of one syllable such as children speak. . . . I need a howl: a cry. . . . I need no words' " (W 251, 295). There is nothing of sex or gender in this longing for a voice expressive beyond words. But in its abstract form, *The Waves* is, or strives to be, that cry; and we seem to glimpse the [woman] in *The Waves* in the "sea-green woman" whose cry lifts the stranded Rhoda after Percival's death and carries her back to the waves. In the concert hall Rhoda says,

> "we cluster like maggots on the back of something that will carry us on. . . . [W]e settle down, like walruses stranded on rocks, like heavy bodies incapable of waddling to the sea, hoping for a wave to lift us, but we are too heavy, and too much dry shingle lies between us and the sea. . . . Then . . . the sea-green woman comes to our rescue. She sucks in her lips, assumes an air of intensity, inflates herself and hurls herself precisely at the right moment as if she saw an apple and her voice was the arrow into the note, 'Ah!'
>
> "An axe has split the tree to the core; the core is warm; sound quivers within the bark. 'Ah,' cried a woman to her lover, leaning from her window in Venice, 'Ah, Ah!' she cried, and again she cries 'Ah!' She has provided us with a cry. But only a cry. And what is a cry? Then the beetle-shaped men come with their violins; wait; count; nod; down come their bows. And there is ripple and laughter like the dance of olive trees and their myriad-tongued grey leaves when a seafarer, biting a twig between his lips where the many-backed steep hills come down, leaps on shore." (W 162–63)

In this virtuoso Self-Portrait as Sea-Green Woman, "She" is the signature in white—or green—ink of nature's favorite, one who in her freedom turned the "sledgehammer blows" of being into these words never heard in nature—this voice of another nature, whose existence intimates freedom's reality.[67] "She" is the natural, bodily origin of the unbodied cry, the "Ah" that pulses through these words that belong to "one" and no one—the voice of a being split to the core to release a song of herself beyond phenomenal sound—a song of oneself, inseparable from "the singing of the real world, as one is driven by loneliness & silence from the habitable world . . . bound on an adventure."[68]

I have this moment, while having my bath, conceived an entire new book—a sequel to a Room of Ones Own—about the sexual life of women: to be called Professions for Women perhaps—Lord how exciting!

—Woolf, *Diary*, 20 January 1931

[You women] who are trying to earn your livings in the professions, are making an experiment. . . . You call out . . . all those sympathies which, in literature, are stimulated by the explorers who set out in crazy cockle shells to discover new lands, and found new civilisations.

—Woolf, *The Pargiters*, "First Essay," 1932

I think this will be a terrific affair. I must be bold & adventurous. I want to give the whole of the present society—nothing less: facts, as well as the vision.

—Woolf, *Diary*, 25 April 1933, on *The Pargiters*

Absolutely floored. . . . I think, psychologically, this is the oddest of my adventures. . . . Oh if only anyone knew anything about the brain. . . . This will be the most exciting thing I ever wrote, I kept saying. And now its the stumbling block.

—Woolf, *Diary,* 5 and 6 September 1935, on *The Years*

The difficulty wh[ich] now faces me is how to find a public, a way of publishing, all the new ideas that are in me?

—Woolf, *Diary*, 19 February 1937

"Can I mention erection?" I asked. . . . [Keynes:] No you cant. I should mind your saying it. Such revelations have to be in key with their time. . . . Is he right, or only public school?

—Woolf, *Diary*, 6 January 1940

■ ■ ■ SEVEN

The Sexual Life of Women

Experimental Genres, Experimental Publics from
The Pargiters to *The Years*

 hile finishing *The Waves*, Woolf was called back to the public voice of *A Room of One's Own* by an invitation to
address the London/National Society for Women's Service, a
professional organization newly evolved from the first
women's suffrage committee. Scarcely two years after she had urged the
Cambridge women whose invitation inspired *A Room of One's Own* to
earn their livings and so insure their freedom of mind—and only twelve
years after the 1919 Sex Disqualification Removal Act had opened the
professions to women—a society of professional Englishwomen had
materialized. Addressing this unprecedented audience in a "Speech of January 21 1931," Woolf launched a decade of experimental projects on the
intersections of gender, power, and public speech that explored new directions for women's private and public lives, the civilization their thought
and labor might transform, and her own writing.

The emergence of this new audience initiated dynamic interactions
with real and imagined publics as Woolf battled taboos on speech—and
thought—about "the sexual life of women." It was a subject ahead of its
time, and Woolf's negotiations with internal and external censorship produced a series of Portraits of the Artist with Her Publics in an array of
genres: the "Speech of January 21 1931"; the experimental "essay-novel"
The Pargiters (1932–33), which branched into the realist novel *The Years*
(1937) and the epistolary essay *Three Guineas* (1938); the memoir "A
Sketch of the Past" (1939–40); the pageant-within-a-novel *Between the
Acts* (1941); the late essay "Professions for Women" (1942); and related
notes, letters, and diary entries.[1] Building on earlier studies of *The Years*
as a defensive "pargeting" (plastering-over, whitewashing) of sensitive
autobiographical material—and, in Woolf's judgment, a "deliberate"
"failure"—this chapter explores the dialectical interdependence of artist

and audience in public speech about women's sexuality as Woolf strives to bring a female unconscious policed by internalized censors to public voice.[2]

Focusing on crucial textual sites in this unfolding project, I examine Woolf's experiments with the address to her audience through what Bakhtin conceives as "speech genres"—diary entry, notes, speech, essay-novel, realist novel, epistolary essay, private letter, memoir/"sketch," even a hypothetical police blotter. The "concept of the speech addressee (how the speaker or writer senses and imagines him) is of immense significance in literary history," Bakhtin observes; every "epoch," "literary trend," "style," and "literary genre within an epoch or trend" implies a particular concept of "the addressee," "a special sense and understanding of its reader, listener, public, or people":

> When speaking I always take into account the apperceptive back-ground of the addressee's perception of my speech: the extent to which he is familiar with the situation, whether he has special knowl-edge of the given cultural area of communication, his views and con-victions, his prejudices (from my viewpoint), his sympathies and antipathies—because all this will determine his active responsive understanding of my utterance. These considerations also determine my choice of a genre . . . , of compositional devices, and . . . the *style* of my utterance.[3]

Although Woolf first addressed a new audience of professional women and experimented with genres, publics, and external and internal cen-sorship at what seemed an auspicious moment, she ultimately trans-formed *The Pargiters*' collective "talking cure" into *The Years*' talking symptoms. Hardly had she announced her subject than repression intervened in what she found "psychologically" the "oddest" of adven-tures: what begins as a history of women's sexual life ends veiled in enigmatic allegory, as if in an involuntary hystericization of her text.[4] Against the view that Woolf's revisions betray a simple failure of courage, anger, or truth telling, I suggest that her actual and imagined audiences—and the gaps between them—were critical to this project's successes and failures from the outset. In a sense, then, this chapter is about a book that does not exist: Woolf's unwritten book about "the sexual life of women." Yet in its very "failure," this experiment illumi-nates gender as, for women, a realm of unconscious loss and forbidden or alienated desire.

From Private Cry to Public Voice: Portraits of the Artist with Her Publics, 1931–1932

> What is a cry independent of the population it appeals to or takes as its witness?
>
> —Gilles Deleuze and Felix Guattari, *A Thousand Plateaus*

"Lord how exciting!" cries Woolf in her bathtub as, on the eve of her Speech, she has a sudden epiphany of "an entire new book—a sequel to a Room of Ones Own—about the sexual life of women: to be called Professions for Women perhaps."[5] Without a witness a cry vanishes; but even in the solitude of the diary, which mirrors the privacy of the bath, this cry is in dialogue with the social world that occasions it. Already it has witnesses: the diary's documentary witness, its future readers, and in a sense the "population" of professional women whose invitation elicits it, and who will materialize next day in the Millicent Fawcett lecture hall as the newly empowered women whom *The Pargiters* hails as "explorers" setting out "in crazy cockle shells to discover new lands, and found new civilisations." Each speech genre—invitation, the diarist's epiphany, Speech, essay— "senses and imagines" its addressee in ways conditioned by the two-hundred-year epoch Woolf ranked with the Crusades and the Wars of the Roses: European women's gradual entry into public speech (*RO* 65).

What has women's sexual life to do with transforming public culture— with discovering new lands, new civilizations? Naked in her tub, Woolf conceives a book whose high-spirited title marks women's historic transition from "the oldest profession," prostitution—the then current connotation of "public women"—and marriage (continuous with prostitution in a socioeconomic system that excludes women from public life) into professions until recently restricted to men. This change challenges the political economy of gender that institutes, sanctions, and sustains the masculine appropriation of the public sphere. Sexuality is intimately implicated in this economy of dominance and submission. In a 1907–8 memoir ("Reminiscences") she recalls her own experience of women's systemic oppression during the "seven unhappy years" between her half sister Stella's death in 1897 and Leslie Stephen's in 1904, when she and Vanessa endured their father's tyranny and their older, richer, "seducing half brother" George Duckworth's social and sexual interference (*MB* 136, *L* 4:382, 18 September 1931). Dressed in white and amethysts at her first party, Vanessa seemed to Desmond MacCarthy "a Greek slave" (*porne*); had either their mother, Julia (d. 1895), or Stella lived, Woolf writes, "how different 'coming out' and those Greek slave years . . . would have been!" (*MB* 106). Quentin Bell wrote that "George had spoilt her life before it had fairly begun"; though his "public face was amiable, . . . to his half-sisters he stood for something horrible and obscene. . . . He came to pollute the most sacred springs, to defile their very dreams" (QB 1:44). At twenty-four Virginia took a "snub" from George's new wife as occasion to proclaim their emancipation: "now we are free women! Any form of slavery is Degrading—and the damage done to the mind is worse than that done to the body!!" (*L* 1:228, 29 June 1906).

Besides playing with new senses of "public women," Woolf's bathtub epiphany broached, as she later put it, the problem of "how to find a public, a way of publishing, all the new ideas that are in me" (*D* 5:57, 19 February 1937). How to move from her self-selected private audience—the "two hundred . . . well dressed, keen, & often beautiful young women" who found the Speech a "delicious entertainment"—to the much wider, indeed international public she now enjoyed as England's preeminent novelist?[6] What speech genre, what "special sense and understanding" of her readers—men and women, some deeply invested in the system, others reformists or radicals—could take Woolf's cry public? What could be said on the controversial, taboo-riddled matter of women's sexual and socioeconomic lives, and how, and by whom, and to whom? This vital question animates Woolf's portraits of the artist with her audience in the four texts related to the Speech.[7] Following on the diary's "Bathtub Epiphany, 20 January 1931," these self-portraits depict reciprocal hailing, external censorship, conscious and unconscious self-censorship, and the experimental speech genre Woolf invents in response to the professional women's question about what "obstacles" and "barriers" she has met in her "professional experiences" (*P/MN* 163).

Woolf's preparatory Manuscript Notes for the Speech fall between the diary and the Speech on the private/public continuum. At first Woolf can recall no obstacles, especially compared with the composer Ethel Smyth, with whom she was to share the podium. Her forebears from Sappho to Austen have "broken down most of the barriers long ago," and paper, ink, even publication come cheap compared to orchestras, concert halls, and assembled audiences (*P/MN* 163). Although she does not mention it here, Woolf had earlier pronounced herself, as co-owner of the Press, "the only woman in England free to write what I like" and famously declared that aspiring women writers need five hundred pounds a year and rooms of their own (*D* 3:43, 22 September 1925). Yet it now appears that not even owning the means of production, let alone mere personal economic independence, can ensure a woman artist's freedom of speech, for obstacles—censorship, self-censorship—swim into view. As a reviewer, Woolf felt constrained by her editors and public to pay lip service to prevailing values. She "always knew what I was expected to say" and felt "pressure . . . to say what was agreeable. Dear old Henry James—he must be praised. One must not attack the crass stupidity of Carlyle. . . . To say what one thought—that was my little problem—against the prodigious Current; to find a sentence that could hold its own against the male flood." A woman journalist can easily "make money"; her "excruciating difficulty," Woolf warns, is "to say what you think—and make money"; "to stand up for your own point of view": if, for example, one were to condemn war as "a stupid and violent and hateful and idiotic and trifling and ignoble and mean display. . . . Of course, none of this would be printed" (P/MN 163–64).

The author and publisher of *A Room of One's Own* who has stood up for her values *and* made money falls outside the frame of this monitory self-portrait as Journalist Battling the Current.[8] But in broaching the subject of gender, publics, and money, Woolf uncovers a far more treacherous obstacle: the unconscious self-censorship that constrains women writers, unlike "Mr. Joyce or Proust" with

> their honesty, their openness, their determination to say everything. For women, the prudery of men is a terrible bugbear. Dr. Johnson said, "We were shocked to see a woman cross her legs." So until the year 1850 (I daresay), women never crossed their legs. Now men are shocked if a woman said what she felt (as Joyce does). Yet literature which is always pulling down blinds is not literature. All that we have ought to be expressed—mind and body—a process of incredible difficulty and danger. . . . I found my angle incessantly obscured, quite unconsciously no doubt, by the desire of the editor and of the public that a woman should see things from the chary feminine angle. (P/MN 164–65)

Here a woman artist who desires "the naked contact of a mind" lapses "quite unconsciously" into decorous tea pouring while her male contemporaries defy the "conventions" and censorship of actual and imaginary "men."[9] Woolf's tangled verbs evoke an audience of men who "are shocked" even though she has refrained from saying "what she felt," in deference not to an actual public but to an imaginary internalized audience of censorious men. A part of her mind has gone over to the other side and performs the work of censorship from within. This unwitting self-censorship illuminates the "incredible difficulty and danger" she faces: not editors, publics, and conventions (whose power Woolf with her press can trump), nor even an imaginary public of censorious men, but a quite unconscious wall of repression that obscures "what she felt" even from herself.

Dropping Dr. Johnson, Proust, and Joyce, the Speech depicts the woman artist's battle against repression in self-portraits as Angel-Slayer, Silenced Critic, and Ambivalent Fisherwoman. Woolf famously personifies female self-censorship as the internalized specter of Coventry Patmore's Angel in the House, that watchdog of dependent femininity who tolerates only opinions "pleasing to men." Although this ostensibly obsolete Victorian feminine ideal arose at a historical moment when "a real relationship" between the sexes was "unattainable" due to "the British Empire, our colonies, Queen Victoria, Lord Tennyson, the growth of the middle classes and so on," Woolf still had to fight her to the death, a victory she justifies as self-defense ("If I had not killed her, she would have killed me") and attributes not to any prowess but to a small independent income: "if one has five hundred a year there is no need to tell lies and it is much more amusing to tell the truth" (*P/S* xxx–xxxi).

Yet this Angel-Murderer who has ostensibly "rid herself of falsehood" and can now "be herself and write" still finds it hard to publish opinions that might offend men. For example, she writes, she came across a glowing review of a history of Clare College, Cambridge, by an unnamed "very celebrated economist"—her old friend John Maynard Keynes—while browsing in the *Nation*. It seemed to say that Clare's fellows "had given in pious memory of their founder the lady of Clare six thousand pounds to a woman. 'Clothed in the finest dress . . . armed with intellect and learning, adorned with curiosity and fancy' . . . Who is this woman I asked myself; and . . . discovered that it was not a woman"; they had "spent six thousand pounds upon a history of their college."[10] On the next page, Vera Brittain writes of the poverty of Somerville, a women's college at Oxford (*P/S* xxxvi). Had Woolf been the reviewer,

> O you old humbugs. I should have begun. . . . who profess devotion to the lady of Clare . . . would it not be better to spend your six thousand pounds not upon a book, clothed in the finest dress of paper and buckram, but upon a girl, whose dress allowance is very meagre, and who tries to do her work, as you will read if you turn the very next page in the Nation, in one cold gloomy ground floor bedroom which faces due north and is overrun with mice. . . . If the members of Clare college handed over the six thousand pounds . . . to Girton . . . I am sure that the lady of Clare would rise from her grave and say Gentlemen you have done my will. (*P/S* xxxiv–v)

Woolf doubts that her opinion "would be printed," since her "values" are not the celebrated economist's; perhaps she could not easily utter it even in freethinking Bloomsbury, since Keynes owned the *Nation*, and Leonard had until recently been its literary editor (xxxvi). Yet in *Three Guineas* she eventually publishes more or less what she says here she cannot, even extrapolating from this Self-Portrait as Muzzled Critic a comic vision of the Lady of Clare, appearing over Cambridge as "a cloud in the sky" in "the shape of a woman; who, being supplicated for a sign, let fall in a shower of radiant hail the one word 'Rats' " (*TG* 230 n. 18, *P/S* xxxiii–xxxv & n). Although women's values will put them at "logger-heads with some respected chiefs" of their "innumerable professions," she tells her audience, their "most amusing and exciting experiences will be" to bring their "ancient and privileged professions"—law, architecture, medicine, finance—"more in touch with human needs" and to "adapt" them to "your sense of values, your common sense, your moral sense[,] your sense of what is due to humanity and reason" (*P/S* xxxvi).

Woolf's challenge to her friend Maynard's complacent masculine privilege dramatizes her increasingly oppositional stance within Bloomsbury and the difference an audience makes.[11] The professional women called out more radical speech than even Bloomsbury did, or so Woolf's observation that her Speech left Leonard "slightly exacerbated" ("interesting . . . if . . . true") suggests (*D* 4:7, 23 January 1931). In the Speech's third self-portrait, Woolf revisits Bloomsbury's Cambridge origins and reworks *Room*'s "Portrait of the Artist Rebuked by a Beadle" into a drama of *self*-censorship. As in *Room*, the woman artist is lost in reverie, "letting her imagination sweep unchecked round every rock and cranny of the world that lies submerged in our unconscious being." But now, with no beadle in sight, she wakes with a jolt from this deep world, this collective ("our") unconscious, as her fish—women's sexual life—gets away:

> The imagination has rushed away . . . into what dark pool of extraordinary experience. The reason has to cry "Stop!" . . . The imagination comes to the top in a state of fury. . . . how dare you interfere with me! . . . And I—that is the reason—have to reply, "My dear you were going altogether too far. Men would be shocked." Calm yourself, I say, as she sits panting on the bank . . . with rage and disappointment. . . . In fifty years I shall be able to use all this very queer knowledge . . . But not now. . . . I cannot make use of what you tell me—about womens bodies for instance—their passions—and so on, because the conventions are still very strong. If I were to overcome the conventions I should need the courage of a hero, and I am not a hero. . . . [T]here are conventions, even for men; and if a man like Lawrence . . . runs against convention he injures his imagination terribly. . . . you would not like to become shrivelled and distorted . . . It is your nature to understand and to create.
>
> Very well says the imagination, dressing herself up again in her petticoat and skirts. . . . We will wait another fifty years. But it seems to me a pity. (*P/S* xxxviii–xxxix)

In this allegory of a woman's imagination beleaguered by her reason in the guise of common sense, internal censorship forces that rapt explorer of the depths into Victorian petticoats. Loath to shock men, fearful that flouting convention will ruin her work, she discovers in herself a secret agent of the femininity she thought to have murdered. As her reason is found to be in bed with the public policing of women's intellectual "chastity," Woolf's imaginary audience splits into a public that includes the Bloomsbury to whom she could once "say everything" and the professional women whose invitation unseals a female unconscious—a realm of "extraordinary experience" fraught with "fury," "rage," "disappointment."[12]

In short, revising *Room*'s argument that a woman who earns her living buys freedom of speech, Woolf offers herself as evidence that a woman who lives by her pen must possess a finely calibrated if largely unconscious "special sense and understanding" of her public. At the same time, this dynamic self-portraiture performs a kind of divestiture, bringing unconscious constraints and censors to light. As in *The Waves* she set out to become the poet *Room* prophesies, so she no sooner pictures her bound and gagged imagination ("We will wait") than she sallies forth on this hero's adventure. As she does, she reconfigures her imaginary public in the image of professional women, and she appeals to them not just to constitute an alternative public for women artists' uncensored speech but to liberalize the mainstream public: whether "men can be educated to stand free speech in women"— whether, that is, they can be "civilised"—"lies on the lap of the Gods, no . . . upon your laps, upon the laps of professional women."[13] Rather than trust "the future of fiction" to the public sphere's masculinized gods, Woolf urges her immediate audience to form a radical public to whom women artists, like Joyce and Proust, can "say everything."

The Speech ends with three pictures. In one, professional women encourage a paterfamilias struggling to reconcile his belief that "nature had meant women to be wives, mothers, housemaids, parlourmaids, and cooks" with the fact that they are "doctors, civil servants, meteorologists, dental surgeons, librarians, solicitors' clerks, agricultural workers, analytical chemists," and so on. In another, women "live in perfect freedom, without any fear," with "civilised" men who have "triumphed over" a "very lopsided education" and are open to change (*P/S* xliv). In the third Woolf pictures women at work in their own rooms as a "situation of extraordinary interest and amazing possibilities" for new social and cultural scripts, exciting private and public "conversation":

> I predict that the next step will be a step upon the stair. You will hear
> somebody coming. You will open the door. And then—this at least is my

guess—there will take place between you and some one else the most interesting, exciting, and important conversation that has ever been heard. But do not be alarmed; I am not going to talk about that now. My time is up. (*P/S* xliv)

At once private and public, this unprecedented conversation figures a future for women, men, and fiction just short of utopian fantasy.[14] The Speech that begins with censorship ends by playfully hailing adventurous, "civilised" women and men into exciting conversations that the artist leaves wordless in the air—anticipating La Trobe, who listens telepathically in the pub for Giles and Isa to speak next year's play's first words. Like La Trobe's mirrors, the Speech calls its audience to a collaborative project, positing the revolutionary potential of women's public speech. Like La Trobe herself, a "slave to her audience," Woolf figures her freedom of speech as dependent on her public. Seeking to catch their desire as it breaks into words, she aligns her art's future with their as yet unimagined conversations on modernity's horizon (*BA* 94). If her public's conventionality impedes her, their struggles toward freedom inspire her. The Speech, then, moves beyond Bloomsbury toward a newly imaginable public, a new collective freedom of speech. As the professional women hailed Woolf to the verge of new speech, she in turn hails them as a new public whose stories she will write as they live them.

The Speech's momentum carried Woolf toward a striking experimental "speech genre": the unfinished, posthumously published *The Pargiters: A Novel-Essay based upon a paper read to the London/National Society for Women's Service* (October-December 1932). In this hybrid work six essays on the changing conditions of middle-class Englishwomen's lives bracket five purported "short extracts" from a "faithful and detailed" historical novel about "a family called Pargiter," which spans the generations from 1800 to 2032.[15] The novel-essay not only depicts but enters into a progressive social history as Woolf, with "a certain sense and understanding" of her addressee, seeks to engage her reader's "actively responsive understanding." Bakhtin notes the role of the "familiar and intimate genres and styles" of the Renaissance in transforming "the official medieval picture of the world" and, more generally, the "very significant" power of such genres to dismantle "traditional official styles and world views" that have become "faded" and "conventional" (97). So in *The Pargiters* Woolf crosses realist narrative with the "familiar and intimate" essay to hail the new public the Speech envisions: "civilised," civilizing, tolerant, independent-minded, politically conscious, adventurous, and creative.

The opening Essay, a revision of the Speech, preserves its familiar, intimate scenario ("When your Secretary asked me to come here tonight") and evokes its original audience: women "trying to earn your livings in the professions," whom the Essayist hails as comrade "explorers" in an "experiment" toward new lands and civilizations (*P/E1* 5–6). Professional women remain the Essayist's explicit (albeit rhetorical) addressee as, speaking from within the work in a persuasive mode that anticipates, mirrors, and answers her imagined audience's differences and objections, she models the "actively responsive understanding" she seeks. As the Novelist explores "the situation" in light of women's "special knowledge," the Essayist prods readers to reflect on their "views and convictions," "prejudices," "sympathies and antipathies."

But something deeper is at stake in the dialogic essay-novel's familiar and intimate scenario. Several of *The Pargiters*' early titles—"The Open Door," "Opening the Door" (23 & 26 January 1931), "The Knock on the Door" (28 May 1931, 20 July 1931), and "my Tap at the Door" (3 September 1931)—foreground the Speech's portrait of a woman at work in a room she has paid for, the scene of that "most interesting" future conversation.[16] But these rooms, doors, knocks, and taps echo certain more ominous taps and opening doors in Woolf's autobiographical writings. In "22 Hyde Park Gate" (1920), Woolf recalls taking off her satin dress and climbing into bed in the "dark," "silent" house after a tedious social evening with George, ready to "fall asleep and forget them all!":

> Then, creaking stealthily, *the door opened*; treading gingerly, someone entered. "Who?" I cried. "Don't be frightened," George whispered. "And don't turn on the light, oh beloved. Beloved—" and he flung himself on my bed, and took me in his arms.
>
> Yes, the old ladies of Kensington and Belgravia never knew that George Duckworth was not only father and mother; brother and sister to those poor Stephen girls; he was their lover also. (*MB* 177, my emphasis)

A year or two later, Woolf rewrote this scene in "Old Bloomsbury": "There would be *a tap at the door*; the light would be turned out and George would fling himself on my bed, cuddling and kissing and otherwise embracing me in order, as he told Dr Savage later, to comfort me for the fatal illness of my father" (*MB* 182, my emphasis). Here Woolf drily notes that 46 Gordon Square "could never have meant what it did had not 22 Hyde Park Gate preceded it"; for there, in the Stephens' first Bloomsbury house, she herself first had a "room with a lock on the door" that she makes a condition of a woman's creative freedom (*MB* 182, *RO* 105). Displacing the bathtub epiphany's title, "Professions for Women," these titles transfigure the sexual trauma that, Woolf told Ottoline Morrell soon after beginning *The Pargiters*, had "sent me mad" as a world in which a woman can lock as well as open her door—the sine qua non of her independent work, thought, speech, and sexual life.[17]

Echoing (perhaps unconsciously) the personal history touched on in Woolf's memoirs, *The Pargiters*' early "Door" titles locate this experimental genre at a historic threshold where gender as an unconscious realm of deprivation, vulnerability, and loss gives way to gender as a visionary font of the "most interesting" conversation ever heard. But Woolf could scarcely explore the sexual life of women without reawakening her own, and these double-faced doors signal the perils of this adventure along with its great expectations. Woolf's experimental speech genre seeks to bring women's censored sexual life into public speech to make way for those unprecedented conversations between free, civilized women and men. But if, as Virginia proclaimed in 1906, "the damage done to the mind is worse than that done to the body," the "incredible difficulty and danger" of transgressing censorship barriers gauges the power—and hidden costs—of repression in her own case as in women's history.

In this light, *The Pargiters*' experimental genre attempts something like a collective "talking cure."[18] In *Studies on Hysteria* Freud and Breuer emphasize the primacy of feeling in the talking cure: the analysand does not just recollect a trauma but relives the associated "psychical process" while giving "verbal utterance" to feelings "in the greatest possible detail" (57). Woolf did not use the term *talking cure*, but her remark that in writing *To the Lighthouse* she did for herself "what psycho-analysts do for their patients"—"expressed some very long felt and deeply felt emotion," "explained it and then laid it to rest"—registers an artist's working experience of unconscious symbolic process.[19] The familiar, intimate essay-novel projects the analytic scenario into the public arena, where it engages its audience in a critique of the unconscious taboos that enforce the "traditional world view." As the Novelist narrates the characters' private experiences, the Essayist—or, as she once calls herself, "the analyst"—"examine[s]" them in light of socioeconomic forces to trace (1800-) and inspire (-2032) social change (*P* 108). Speaking what the characters cannot, Woolf's dialogic novelist-analyst brings to light psychosocial forces behind the characters' symptomatic strangulations, dissimulations, and "double conscience" in order to break their hold on social institutions and the future.[20]

Woolf had many times confided her experiences with her "incestuous brother" George to Violet Dickinson, Janet Case, Vanessa, Vita, Ethel Smyth, Ottoline Morrell, and the Bloomsbury Memoir Club (*L* 6:56, 14 July 1936). But taking these revelations public was another story. In seeking to name the violence of gender for a resistant public, the novelist/analyst seeks public recognition not for a personal history but for an untold collective history. But if *The Pargiters* was to be a progressive and visionary history of the sexual life of women, how to document that history? And who is its addressee—the professional women to whom she appeals to authorize difficult, dangerous revelations about women's private and public lives or the greater public whose resistance women must dismantle?

In *The Pargiters'* very First Essay, Woolf's fight against censorship, self-censorship, and repression runs aground on a crisis of verification that arises with these questions. Embarking with her imagined public upon a radical social critique leading toward "new civilizations," the analyst soon finds herself defending the novelist's "history," and on somewhat peculiar terms. Rather than distinguish its truth claims from those of history by virtue of its genre (part fiction, part analysis), she asserts its basis in "fact" and "truth," verifiable in *memoirs*:

> If you object that fiction is not history, I reply that though it would be far easier to write history . . . that method of telling the truth seems to me so elementary, and so clumsy, that I prefer, where truth is important, to write fiction. . . . 'The Pargiters' . . . is not a novel of vision, but a novel of fact . . . based upon some scores—I might boldly say thousands—of old memoirs. . . . [T]here is scarcely a statement in it that cannot be [*traced to some biography, or*] verified, if anybody should wish so to misuse their time. I hope that I am not making an empty boast if I say that there is not a statement in it that cannot be verified. (*P/E*1 9)

Even as she claims that her fiction captures a "truth" that eludes conventional histories, the analyst projects—and mirrors—an audience skeptical of that "truth." Confronting the problem of how to ground a collective (hi)story of women's sexual life, she *hopes* it is no *empty boast* to say that *almost* every statement *could* be verified in "memoirs" or "biography"— documents she *boldly* supposes exist in *scores* or even *thousands*, though she has not *misused* her time in research.

But do memoirs and biographies support her truth claims? And what sort of "truth" do these forms of life writing offer? The analyst's boast is not empty: after all, her own unpublished memoirs of 1907–8 and 1920–22 existed (no wonder she need not bother with research)—potential material, Woolf well knew, for biographers, who were already beginning to write her "life."[21] Further, as her notebooks, scrapbooks, diaries, letters, and *Three Guineas* show, she did read "scores" of memoirs during the thirties. Yet these did not document the "truths" about "women's bodies" and "passions" that her essay-novel sought to explore.[22] Within a month of embarking on the First Essay, the analyst complains that no novel of the 1880s treats subjects such as little Rose Pargiter's fright on encountering an exhibitionist in the street and blames "biographers and autobiographers," who "also ignore it, and thus reduce" the novelist's "material." For verification, she ironically directs readers to the "Police Court news"—as if this impersonal, objective record of alleged infractions of the law for a collective addressee, the community itself, might redress the omissions of memoirists and biographers and make up for the loss of subjective voice and testimony she deplores (*P/E3* 50–51).

The Pargiters fractures along this fault line; this crisis of verification is also a crisis of audience. To whom, for whom, with whom does Woolf speak? After three more essays Woolf drops the analyst, with her bold, insupportable claims, to develop the chapters into *The Years* and the essays (buttressed by extensive research) into *Three Guineas*. But the quest for verification did not end in 1932. Failing to document her fiction's "truth" in published memoirs and biographies, Woolf urged women friends—Victoria Ocampo, Ottoline Morrell, Ethel Smyth, Violet Dickinson, Vanessa, and others—to write about their lives, as if willing the stories she sought into existence. Already in February 1932 she promised to send Ethel "22 Hyde Park Gate," "an old memoir that tumbled out of a box when I was looking for something else that I wrote ten years ago about our doings with George Duckworth when we were so to speak virgins" (*L* 5:13). In July 1933 she was "writing memoirs" "to refresh my mind for P's."[23] By May 1934 Vanessa must have complied, for, Woolf wrote, reading her manuscript memoir of George "so flooded me with horror that I cant be pure minded on the subject."[24] By late 1934 Woolf concludes, "Very few women yet have written truthful autobiographies"; and a year later, she seems resigned to constraints on women's public speech, including her own: "one always lies when one speaks in public" (*L* 5:356, 451, 22 December 1934, 6 December 1935).

As for biography, in 1936 Woolf learns with distress that her old confidante Violet Dickinson has burned her memoir of the Stephen family: "Why, in Heavens name . . . Your view would have been fascinating— George, Gerald, Father—Hyde Park Gate. Cant you re-write it and send it me? . . . as a little defence against the flood."[25] Some weeks later she is still lamenting this lost memoir, worth "£100 in gold" (by contrast with "Poor Miss Holtby"'s "wildly inaccurate" biography), and urges Violet to put down "a few plain facts" to "get a nib between the ribs"—signing her old convalescent's moniker as if to jog Violet's memory.[26] In 1939, as Roger Fry's biographer, she is "thinking about Censors. How visionary figures admonish us"; "All books now seem to me surrounded by a circle of invisible censors" (D 5:229, 7 August). In 1939–40 she resumes her effort to fill the memoirists' documentary gap by her own late memoir, "A Sketch of the Past." Still, angels and beadles haunt her mind and materialize even in Bloomsbury, as when she recounts asking Maynard, "Can I mention erection?"—who replied, "No you can't. I should mind your saying it. Such revelations have to be in key with their time"—and wonders, "Is he right, or only public school?" (D 5:256, 6 January 1940). Since *The Pargiters* positions memoir and biography as prior to fiction, let us consider, before turning to *The Pargiters* and *The Years*, what light "A Sketch of the Past" may shed on the problem of keeping revelations about women's sexual life in key with the times.

Self-Portraits with Beast: "Sketch" (Memoir), Letter, Essay, 1939–1941

Woolf began "A Sketch of the Past" on 18 April 1939, added to it intermittently eleven times over the next eighteen months, once retrieved it from her wastebasket, and left it unfinished at her death among the papers her last note asked Leonard to destroy. The "Sketch" begins with her first memories of her mother, St. Ives, and an infant self who exists as pure sensation, a "container" of "ecstasy" and "rapture" (MB 67). These first pages highlight her memoir's two central themes: the importance of capturing feeling in life drawing and the question "how far I differ from other people" (MB 65). "I feel that strong emotion must leave its trace," Woolf writes, "and it is only a question of discovering how we can get ourselves again attached to it, so that we shall be able to live our lives through from the start" (MB 67). Then, to show how feelings soon become "more complex . . . less isolated, less complete," Woolf describes a feeling "about the looking-glass in the hall," into which, at six or seven, she often looked, but only when alone, and with "a strong feeling of guilt" that makes her wonder whether she inherited her father's puritanism along with her mother's beauty (MB 67–68). Realizing that she could feel "ecstasies and raptures spontaneously and intensely and without any shame or the least sense of guilt, so long as they were disconnected with my own body," brings her to the memory of her half brother Gerald Duckworth—twelve years older than she—"explor[ing] my private parts" before the mirror at Talland House when she was "very small":

> I can remember the *feel* of his hand going under my clothes; going firmly and steadily lower and lower. I remember *how I hoped that he would stop*; how I *stiffened and wriggled* as his hand approached my private

parts. But it did not stop. His hand explored my private parts too. I remember *resenting*, *disliking* it—what is the word for *so dumb and mixed a feeling?* . . . This seems to show that a *feeling* about certain parts of the body; . . . how it is wrong to allow them to be touched; must be *instinctive*. It proves that Virginia Stephen was not born on 25th January 1882, but was born many thousands of years ago; and had from the first to encounter instincts already acquired by thousands of ancestresses in the past. (*MB* 68–69 my emphases)

Within a few pages Woolf narrates an incident of molestation unmentioned in the 1920–22 memoirs, not half-hidden in a reticent paragraph ("Old Bloomsbury") or imparted as a brief concluding flourish ("22 Hyde Park Gate") but with a strong emphasis on feeling. Like the analyst, the memoirist values feeling's "truth," however partial and uncertain, over such " 'lives' of other people" as merely "collect a number of events, and leave the person to whom it happened unknown" (*MB* 69). Moreover, the analyst's anxious search for a *collective* history of women's sexual life recurs in the memoirist's emphases on an ancestral legacy of instinctive modesty and on "truth": "Witness the incident of the looking-glass. Though I have done my best to explain" her feeling, "I have only been able to discover some possible reasons; there may be others; I do not suppose that I have got at the truth; yet this is a simple incident; and it happened to me personally; and I have no motive for lying about it" (*MB* 69).

Woolf now turns to a second memory—or perhaps dream—that "may refer" to the first:

> I was looking in a glass when a horrible face—the face of an animal—suddenly showed over my shoulder. I cannot be sure if this was a dream, or if it happened. Was I looking in the glass one day when something in the background moved, and seemed to me alive? I cannot be sure. But I have always remembered the face in the glass, whether it was a dream or a fact, and that it frightened me. (*MB* 69)

Directly following the memory of Gerald's invading hands, the beast in the mirror in this dream or memory has been read as expressing young Virginia's fear of predatory male sexuality and her "horror" at being reduced herself to an "animal, a body without a self, a body that devours selves."[27] The Self-Portrait with Beast, then, is also a Self-Portrait *as* Beast: a picture of the child's fear of "my own body" as a vessel of animal desire, in all its susceptibility to others' desires. Associative memories link the baby in the nursery who felt herself a "container" of the "ecstasy" and "rapture" that flowed in through her body's senses with the same body's unspoken potential for sexual desire, ecstasy, rapture—perverted, her memoir suggests, by a sentimental education to "shame," "guilt," and fear. The Self-Portrait with/as Beast pictures a traumatic break between that infant body and its animal desire, stolen, in effect, by Gerald's hands and "all Georges malefactions"—rendered bestial, split off from the self and repudiated.[28] The looking-glass reflects a divided being whose split and doubled gaze confirms her alienated desire, its face no longer hers.

Reticently and sporadically, the "Sketch" pursues its author's sexual life. On May 2, instead of taking up where she left off, Woolf disclaims any hope of wresting that slippery fish "truth" away from contingency: "this past is much affected by the present moment"; "What I write today I should not write in a year's time"; what she writes she leaves to "chance," having "no energy at the moment to spend upon the horrid labour" required "to make an orderly and expressed work of art; where one thing follows another and all are swept into a whole" (MB 75). The next three entries recall her mother's life, especially her two marriages, and her death, which made her "unreal" and her children "hypocritical," caught between "what we ought to be and what we were," "immeshed in the conventions of sorrow," in "foolish and sentimental ideas" (MB 95). Approaching the July 19 entry on Stella's engagement to Jack Hills, Woolf pictures herself as "a child advancing with bare feet" to peer into the "depth" of memory's "cold river" (MB 98). On 8 June 1940, after a ten-month lapse, she retrieves the "Sketch" from the wastebasket to recount how Jack "opened my eyes on purpose, as I think, to the part played by sex in the life of the ordinary man"—shocking her "wholesomely" (MB 103–4).

The July 1940 entry on 22 Hyde Park Gate revisits an important scene in The Years, as we shall see: "In the hall lay a dog, beside him a bowl of water with a chunk of yellow sulphur in it"; over the mantel hung the legend: " 'What is to be a gentleman? It is to be tender to women, chivalrous to servants' "; Woolf comments, "What innocence, what incredible simplicity of mind it showed—to keep this cardboard quotation—from Thackeray I think—perpetually displayed, as if it were a frontispiece to a book—nailed to the wall in the hall of the house" (MB 117). Then she describes her own room after Stella married and she and Vanessa "were promoted to separate bed sitting rooms" and recalls mistaking a mating cat for "an obscene old man gasping and croaking and muttering senile indecencies" as she lay in bed. Her room had a "living half" and a "sleeping half," which "were always running together":

> How they fought each other; that is, how often I was in a rage in that room; and in despair; and in ecstasy; how I read myself into a trance of perfect bliss; then in came—Adrian, George, Gerald, Jack, my father; how it was there I retreated to when father enraged me; and

paced up and down scarlet; and there Madge came one evening; and I
could scarcely talk for happiness; and there I droned out those long
solitary mornings reading Greek . . . And it was from that room Gerald fetched me when father died. There I first heard those horrible
voices. . . . (MB 123)

Instead of fleshing out these scenes, Woolf imagines her old room revealing "its ghosts" to its current guesthouse lodgers—an imagined public
for the memoir's half-suppressed revelations—and their response:
"amused; also pitiful; and perhaps one of them would say what an odd,
what an unwholesome life for a girl of fifteen," adding, "Such a life is
quite impossible nowadays," and if familiar with *Lighthouse, Room*, or
The Common Reader, "This room explains a great deal" (MB 123–24).
She led the "two lives that the two halves symbolized," Woolf writes,
with "the muffled intensity, which a butterfly or moth feels when with
its sticky tremulous legs and antennae it pushes out of the chrysalis . . .
and sits quivering beside the broken case . . . its eyes dazzled, incapable
of flight" (MB 124). Too young at thirteen to take in her mother's death,
she remembers thinking, "'But this is impossible; things aren't, can't be,
like this'" when "the second blow"—Stella's death—"struck on me . . .
with my wings still creased, sitting there on the edge of my broken
chrysalis" (MB 124). As much as this chapter of 22 Hyde Park Gate's
"book" censors of its inmate's turbulent "two lives," the lodgers'
bemused reception of its ghostly reenactments evokes a young woman
as yet "incapable" of the flights of mind that created Rachel Vinrace,
Rhoda, and *The Waves*.

The next entry, 18 August, focuses on the deep bond formed among the
four young Stephens by these two deaths. Since, Woolf writes, she can
describe herself only by describing her siblings, she begins by sketching
Thoby. On 22 September, she decides to "write about St Ives" to "lead up
to Thoby" (MB 126–28). On 11 October she finds in her previous entry
only "one actual picture of Thoby; steering us round the point without
letting the sail flap" and sketches herself hesitating at the threshold of her
old room. Why, she wonders, should she

> shirk the task, not so very hard to a professional . . . of wafting this boy
> from the boat to my bed sitting room at Hyde Park Gate? It is because
> I want to go on thinking about St Ives. . . . But it is true, *I do not want
> to go into my room at Hyde Park Gate*. I shrink from the years
> 1897–1904, the seven unhappy years [after] those two lashes of the ran-
> dom unheeding, unthinking flail that brutally and pointlessly killed the
> two people who should have made those years normal and natural, if
> not "happy."

> *I am not thinking of mother and of Stella; I am thinking of the dam-*
> *age that their deaths inflicted. I will describe it more carefully later. . . .*
> That is why I do not wish to bring Thoby out of the boat into my room.
> (MB 136, my emphasis)

In earlier memoirs, only Gerald and George transgress her bodily and psychic boundaries. Does this moment implicate Thoby too—omitted, like Vanessa, from the above list of visitors to her room? Deferring explanation, Woolf now describes how "genuinely, though dumbly, bound to us" Thoby became after the deaths, how their "numbing, mutilating" impact created "a passionate fumbling fellowship" among the Stephen children; and how she sought to redeem disaster by making living itself a daring, heroic feat: "a force" had "respected me sufficiently to make me feel myself ground between grindstones" (MB 137). After explaining that her relationship with Thoby became more "serious" and that they were "naturally attracted to each other," Woolf does bring him into her room, where, she recalls, they argued "about Shakespeare; about many many things; and often lost our tempers; but were attracted by some common admiration," though "reserved" in expressing it:

> Brothers and sisters today talk quite freely together about—oh everything. Sex, sodomy, periods, and so on. We never talked much about ourselves even; I can recall no confidences, no compliments; no kisses; no self analysis. . . . As for sex, he passed from childhood . . . to manhood under our eyes, in our presence, without saying a single word that could have been taken for a sign of what he was feeling. (MB 138–39)

Beneath Thoby's silence, she felt his "great pride in us whose photographs were always on his fireplace at Cambridge"; his tenderness toward women, "already distinctly sketched though so submerged"; how "astonishingly handsome" he looked, formally dressed, with his pipe and Cambridge friends (139–40). Woolf portrays him, in short, as a romantic, heroic youth idealized by his young sister; one who, far from having any part in such "doings" as George's and Gerald's, "had he been put on, would have proved most royally" (MB 139, 140).

The next entry illuminates the psychically incestuous life of 22 Hyde Park Gate. "Rushing too far ahead," Woolf forces herself back "to the year that Stella died—1897": "I could sum it all up in one scene": "a leafless bush, a skeleton bush, in the dark of a summer's night," outside a garden house where she sits with Stella's widower, Jack Hills, who grips her hand and moans that she cannot understand how "It tears one asunder."

> "Yes I can," I murmured. Subconsciously, I knew that he meant his sexual desires tore him asunder . . . at the same time as his agony at Stella's

> death. Both tortured him. And the tree outside in the August summer half light was giving me, as he groaned, a symbol of his agony; of our sterile agony; was summing it all up. Still the leafless tree is to me the emblem, the symbol, of those summer months. (*MB* 140–41)

This skeletal tree that symbolized the young survivors' "sterile" sexuality put forth "little red chill buds" when Jack and Vanessa fell in love and contemplated an "illegal" marriage, condemned by George because people would talk but not forbidden by Leslie (Vanessa "must do as she liked"). The memoirist describes how she "wobbled" between Vanessa and George, who took "my arm in his" and put "pressure on my hand" as he exhorted her to dissuade Vanessa (*MB* 141–142). Again Woolf flags this tree to exemplify her use of scenes to capture "reality." As we shall see, she had earlier written of this tree and the incestuous desire it summed up in a 1903 essay, *The Pargiters*, and *The Years*.

Woolf's next and final entry of mid-November 1940 returns to the seven unhappy years when the sisters in "close conspiracy" "did battle for that which was always being snatched from us, or distorted": painting, writing, autonomy. "Explorers and revolutionists," they fought for their lives against their tyrannical, explosive, self-pitying father, whose elaborate household they now had to manage, since "woman was then (though gilt with an angelic surface) the slave." They fought a femininity imposed by their mother's and Stella's "dead hand"; by the jealous, controlling, sentimental gaze of the "almost brainless" George, with his strong "physical passions"; by the "patriarchal" world they were "asked to admire and applaud"; by the London society George attempted to force them to join ("a perfectly competent, perfectly complacent, ruthless machine" in which a "girl had no chance"); and by the gulf between "convention" and "intellect" at 22 Hyde Park Gate (*MB* 143–59).

Although the "Sketch"'s inconclusive end suggests that Woolf meant to return to it, five months later she had swum to her death. Did she judge that even her own memoir failed to tell the truth about her body, her passions? On 24 December she seems to pass the torch to Ethel Smyth, who, urged on by Woolf, was writing her autobiography:

> there's never been a womans autobiography. Nothing to compare with Rousseau. Chastity and modesty I suppose have been the reason. *Now why shouldn't you be not only the first woman to write an opera, but equally the first to tell the truths about herself?* . . . I should like an analysis of your sex life. As Rousseau did his. More introspection. More intimacy. *I leave it to you.* (*L* 6:453, my emphases)

Her next letter to Smyth continues,

> I'm interested that you cant write about masturbation. . . . But as so much of life is sexual—or so they say—it rather limits autobiography if this is blacked out. It must be, I suspect, for many generations, for women; for its like breaking the hymen . . . a painful operation, and I suppose connected with all sorts of subterranean instincts. I still shiver with shame at the memory of my half-brother, standing me on a ledge, aged about 6, and so exploring my private parts. Why should I have felt shame then? (*L* 6:459–60, 12 January 1941)

This private letter, a coda to her Self-Portrait with/as Beast that registers a vivid somatic "shiver" of "shame," circles back to the "Sketch"'s first entry. Closer to the verbalized feeling of the talking cure than the earlier memoirs' sang-froid, this letter invites dialogue: why should she have felt, and feel, shame? At the same time, as if expecting no answer, these letters sound a covert valediction to Woolf's decade-long experiment with telling truths about women's bodies and passions. Her child-self's ancient "instinct" of privacy, chastity, modesty resurfaces as an impediment to truth, realigning publicity with violation, not cure. If a life like hers is "'quite impossible nowadays,'" as the lodger murmurs of the ghosts at Hyde Park Gate, what is the point of publicity? As Woolf retreats from the intimate, familiar memoir genre to the still more intimate and familiar private letter, her public shrinks to the one old comrade with whom she had ten years earlier sailed out in crazy cockle shells toward new horizons for women's lives.[29]

Was it about this time that Woolf revised the Speech into "Professions for Women"?[30] So its retrospective, valedictory stance (like that of these letters) and echoes of the "Sketch" suggest. Angel and fisherwoman still figure the "two very genuine" challenges of her professional life, but now she looks not forward toward new adventures but backward, assessing her career (*DM/PW* 241). No longer does she "kill" the angel once and for all; now she emphasizes the prolonged struggle, the less than certain victory, the frustration of battling a "phantom," "far harder to kill . . . than a reality" (*DM/PW* 238). The Angel "died" (as *Three Guineas* proves), but the fisherwoman failed to tell "the truth about my own experiences as a body." Here Woolf generalizes her pessimistic forecast to Ethel:

> I doubt that any woman has solved it yet. The obstacles against her are still immensely powerful—and yet they are very difficult to define. . . . Outwardly, what obstacles are there for a woman rather than for a man? Inwardly, . . . she still has many ghosts to fight, many prejudices to overcome. Indeed it will be a long time still, I think, before a woman can sit down to write a book without finding a phantom to be slain, a rock to

be dashed against. And if this is so in literature, the freest of all professions for women, how is it in the new professions which you are now for
the first time entering?

. . . Even when the path is nominally open—when there is nothing to
prevent a woman from being a doctor, a lawyer, a civil servant—there
are many phantoms and obstacles. . . . [I]t is necessary also to discuss the
ends and the aims for which we are fighting, for which we are doing battle with these formidable obstacles. (*DM/PW* 241–42)

Abandoning the Speech's new world vision, "Professions for Women"
teems with unvanquished "obstacles" that defer and obscure that future.
As before, Woolf enlists her audience in an ongoing "battle," but no victory is in sight. Again she vests the future in them, but now the artist who
awaits their words and acts vanishes. When Woolf confesses that she does
"not think I solved" the problem of "telling the truth about my own experiences as a body," she seems to foreclose any further attempt. Her own
image drops out of her picture of the future, replaced by "a woman"
writer and an audience who will "decide for yourselves" how to "fur-
nish," "decorate," and "share" "rooms of your own in the house hitherto
exclusively owned by men," and how to answer the great questions "you"
can ask for "the first time in history" (*DM/PW* 241–42). When she replaces
the Speech's playful closing prophecy of an "exciting" conversation that
she won't alarm them by talking about because "My time is up" with the
stark "My time is up; and I must cease," her voice seems to cross from the
historic occasion of the Speech into real time, as if what is "up" were her
lifetime, what "must cease" not the Speech but her speech (*P/S* xliv, *DM/
PW* 242). Did Woolf revise the Speech with her death in view? It almost
seems so as she takes leave of the partly real, partly imaginary audience
who inspired her last decade of work: "Willingly would I stay and discuss
those questions and answers—but not tonight" (*DM/PW* 242). A subdued return to the bathtub epiphany that broached its title with such
excitement, "Professions for Women" paints the artist as a battle-weary
veteran who has "done my share, with pen & talk, for the human race"
and hands on the fight for civilization to a future beyond her own (*D*
5:276, 29 March 1940).

"A Sketch of the Past" must have lain near Woolf's writing table when
she wrote her last words to Leonard on 28 March 1941: "Will you
destroy all my papers" (*L* 6:487). Unfinished and somehow unfinishable,
it survives its brushes with oblivion as a "sketch" not just of the past but
of the "difficulty and danger" Woolf encountered in writing of women's
bodies and passions—not a completed picture but one last effort to tell
"the truths about herself." Woolf's adventurous imagination could not

keep her fifty-year bargain with her temporizing reason, yet she could devise no genre intimate and familiar enough to convey those "truths." The late letters' Self-Portrait with A Public of One—of Ethel alone—depicts a memoirist who has given up hope of calling out a public who will join in collaborative truth telling through "actively responsive understanding"; who will play, in Bart Oliver's words, that "very important part" the audience (*BA* 58). Let us turn now to the interplay of speech genres, imagined audiences, and repression as Woolf reworks several key scenes of *The Pargiters* for *The Years*: Rose's adventure, Elvira/Sara's 1907 scene with the leafless tree, and scenes of siblings North (earlier George) and Peggy Pargiter.

From Talking Cure to Talking Symptoms: Rose Pargiter

In judging that she did not tell the truth about her bodily experiences but did publish an analysis of the sex/gender system that the Angel would have censored, Woolf echoes her views on the two works she continued to think of as "one book": *The Years*, a "deliberate" "failure"; *Three Guineas*, "morally, a spine: the thing I wished to say, though futile" (*D* 5:65, 130, 148; 7 March 1937, 12 March, 3 June 1938). But how far was *The Years'* "failure" deliberate, how far an involuntary function of repression? To what extent can we distinguish the art of *The Years* from the internalized censorship and repression that are, in a sense, its secret subject?

These questions foreground the enforcement of gender by language and silence in everyday life as in speech genres. Woolf anticipated public resistance as she sought to expose sexual and gender domination in the private house and public life; an even more formidable obstacle was the hidden force of repression.[31] As Woolf turns the essay-novel's chapters into *The Years*, the collective talking cure vanishes in the characters' talking symptoms, rendered in a realist narrative shot through with allegorical moments that veil a deeper story. In the analyst's absence, the audience is left to guess at the story behind these clues, which appeal to what Bakhtin calls the reader's "apperceptive . . . knowledge." With its characters' stories submerged in somatic speech, *The Years* in its allegorical dimension addresses an audience whose recognition would confirm its "truth." Putting aside memoirs and biographies, *The Years* draws its readers into its portrait of a society struggling toward self-transformation, so that they become at least passive witnesses of—at most active participants in—the novelist's vision of society's "old fabric insensibly changing without death or violence into the future."[32] As its realist dimension voices the characters' longing for social transformation,

its allegorical dimension calls readers to play an active role in that transformation by sensing its untold stories—in keeping with Bakhtin's concept of the speech addressee in all its "immense significance in literary history." As in *The Voyage Out*, "the special sense and understanding of its
. . . public" solicited by *The Years*' melding of modernist realism and allegory allows for a range of readers, some "familiar with the situation," some with "special knowledge," all with views, convictions, prejudices, sympathies and antipathies that shape their "active responsive understanding" of the book. The partly real, partly imaginary audience conjured by the Speech and First Essay now becomes an actual public cast as potential agents of historical change and creators of the future beyond the novel's end.

The revision of *The Pargiters*' opening sections reveals a certain tension between *The Years*' realistic and allegorical dimensions. The novelist of *The Pargiters* depicts the fright and shame of a late-Victorian child, Rose Pargiter, on being accosted by an exhibitionist in the street; the analyst reflects on how the taboo against telling the truth about this experience engenders a specifically female unconscious.[33] Rose's story dramatizes a child's fall into a femininity that forces her to repress desire and give up freedom—to relinquish claims to autonomy, domestic space, educational resources, public streets, adventure, authority, creativity, full participation in public and private life; in short, to comply with the masculine appropriation of the private and public worlds.[34] Rose's foreclosed speech illuminates the function of repression in instituting and maintaining gender while occluding its nature as loss.

The analyst first highlights the Victorian taboo against unaccompanied middle-class women's freedom to walk in the public streets by noting the absurdity of "three healthy" Pargiter daughters "sitting round a tea table with nothing better to do" than manage the linens and peep through blinds at young men calling next door (P/E2 33, 38). This division of public spaces that men traverse freely from private spaces such as the Abercorn Terrace house—a very fortress of female chastity—effects a masculinization of public culture, policed by aggressive male sexuality, that constrains the daughters' freedom of movement, association, earning power, and speech. The contradiction between their culturally imposed, ostensibly "passionless" femininity and their natural curiosity and desire forces them into guilty dissimulation. Instead of desiring freely, the analyst writes, they become "ashamed, indignant, confused"; their sexual "feeling, since it was never exposed, save by a blush, or a giggle, wriggled deep down into their minds, and sometimes woke them in the middle of the night with curious sensations, unpleasant dreams, that seemed all to come from this one fact—that Abercorn Terrace was besieged on all sides by what may be called street love" (P/E2 38).

In the Second Chapter, little Rose takes back the night. Brushed off by her brother Bobby whom she asks to accompany her, she sneaks out to buy toys, pretending that she is a hero—"Pargiter of Pargiter's Horse"—carrying a secret message to English people "besieged in a fortress" (P/C2 42). When a man appears in the shadows, she incorporates him into her game: "the enemy!" Returning home, she sees him leaning against the pillar box "as if he were ill" and feels "the same terror again"; "There was nobody else anywhere in sight. As she ran past him, he gibbered some nonsense at her, sucking his lips in & out; & began to undo his clothes . . . " (P/C2 42–43). The analyst points to this ellipsis as a mark of censorship—a lie of omission, dictated by "a convention, supported by law, which forbids . . . any plain description of the sight that Rose, in common with many other little girls, saw"; "to illustrate this aspect of sexual life," the novelist can only "state some of the facts; but not all" and then "imagine the impression on the nerves," "the brain," "the whole being, of a shock which the child instinctively conceals . . . and is also too ignorant, too childish, too frightened, to describe or explain even to herself" (P/E3 51).

The ellipsis that protects the masculine aggression that makes public space dangerous to middle-class women by complying with the "unspeakability" of women's sexual experiences does not prevent the novelist from calling attention to a gender perversion that dissimulates "a primitive, vengeful aggression" behind an "erotic" scenario.[35] The novelist's public self-censorship is writ small in Rose's private muteness. The frightened child hopes someone will catch her out so that she will be forced to tell; but no one notices her absence, and her guilt for disobeying is compounded with fear and shame. Her nurse is strategically inattentive: since no one must know that Rose escaped her unwatchful eye, she overlooks the new toys and, when Rose wakes from a nightmare about a man in her room, blames "rich cake for tea" and tells her to go to sleep, "dream of fairies," and, in a surfeit of pargetings, not to lie on her back ("Thats what gives you bad dreams") (P/C2 45–46).

As Rose's caretakers silently urge her to repress "what she had seen," her experience engenders an unconscious populated by nightmare phantoms and hallucinations. When Eleanor finds her disturbed and sleepless, counting sheep that leer with the man's face, Rose's fear keeps her silent: "It was not only that she had been very naughty, running out alone. It was that she was terrified"; "somehow, it was horrid, nasty"; "she could not tell anyone: not even Eleanor. He had undressed . . . " (P/C2 48, ellipsis Woolf's). Despite her fear that they "would be very angry with her" if they knew "what she had seen," Rose ventures a half-truth—"I thought I saw a man in the room"—which their parting injunctions against rich cake ignore (P/C2 48). No sooner does she act out an adventure of freedom and desire in the public street than Rose involuntarily learns her vulnerability not just to dangers that court publicity such as her brother might encounter but to a sexual danger that harms her most by its unspeakability.[36] The taboo inculcates femininity as a loss of speech, voice, witness, never acknowledged as such and never mourned.

If talk makes for cure, repression makes for disease. Telling lies diminishes Rose mentally and morally and "distorts the relationship between the liar and the lied to, even if the lie is justified" (P/E3 52). Repressed, femininity-as-loss resurfaces masked as chastity, passionlessness, "virtue," which, by crippling women's freedom, sustains a system in which men control law, wealth, professions, policy, the public streets, children, and the future. The Pargiter daughters are given to understand

> that some convention was absolutely necessary for them, and not for their brothers; since plainly it was unthinkable for a middle- or upper-middle class woman to have a relation with a man which might lead to her bearing an illegitimate child—a disgrace which a woman could scarcely survive, socially, or practically either; for the whole cost of the child's upbringing (in 1880) would fall solely upon her; and she was disabled by law from earning enough money to provide for herself, let alone for another human being.
>
> The question of chastity was therefore complicated in the extreme, since it was influenced by so many feelings that could not be discussed and by so many facts that might be resented but could not possibly be altered. Had not the demand for the vote, which might ultimately lead to some right to earn one's living, been again dismissed in the House of Commons? (P/E3 52–53)

In the analyst's materialist account, chastity maintains women's social, legal, political, economic, and sexual subjection. In 1880, decades before women's suffrage, there was little hope of altering the conditions and laws that barred women from public schools and professions, enforcing their economic dependence. Not just law and economics but the very categories of the thinkable and speakable militated against an unwed woman's bearing a child—"illegitimate" by virtue of belonging to a mother, not a father. A powerful agent in the repression of "feelings that could not be discussed," middle-class femininity works against social change.

Women's loss is men's gain. When Rose's brother Bobby—Martin in *The Years*—is accosted on the street by a woman his friend tells him is a prostitute, he finds "nothing frightening . . . in her jeers and laughter" but feels "secure, and rather scornful, and . . . proud" that his friend "should, by using the word 'prostitute,' initiate" him into "a great fellowship" that grants him a "great many rights and privileges" in exchange for "certain loyalties and assertions; for example, it was essential to make it plain that the school room was his room"; "Rose should be kept out of it"—though "privately" Bobby prefers playing with Rose and compromises by casting her as "his assistant" or "the audience," fighting when she resists (*P/E3* 54). A "public woman" whose sexual services any man may rent, the prostitute confirms Bobby's effortless inheritance at his sisters' expense, reinforcing his autonomy, sexual superiority, and entitlement in the private/public continuum.

Grace Radin's view that Woolf judged the essays "a clumsy device that impeded the narrative flow" is surely right, but what do we lose with the analyst's talk?[37] In *The Pargiters*, the analyst speaks what Rose cannot, dissecting the everyday censorship that turns her adventure into a formative lesson in femininity. In *The Years*, the characters are no longer case studies but suffer unanalyzed private pain. Whereas the analyst frames Rose's experience as "a very imperfect illustration" of the "actual fact" that children "are frequently assaulted, and sometimes far more brutally than she was," *The Years* leaves Rose alone with her experience (*P/E3* 50). As Rose grows up, unconscious guilt, shame, rage, and fear fuel her distinguished career as a militant suffragist who survives imprisonment and force-feeding (while Martin dines on roast beef in the City) to gain, finally, the vote, a "decoration" from the state for her war work, and a toast from her cousin Sara (*Y* 359). Yet she never speaks of her private experiences. A childhood suicide attempt, her outrage when she is blamed for a microscope broken by Martin's friend, her secret misery at "a certain engagement"—all, barely glimpsed in the narrative, resonate in her sudden intense wish, while visiting her cousins Sara and Maggie, "to talk about her past; to tell them something about herself that she had never told anybody—something hidden" (*Y* 359, 161, 166–67). As no one listens, Rose says nothing. The reader is left to puzzle over a story that, absent an audience within the text, Rose herself hardly knows.

In the analyst's absence, the characters' talking symptoms grow more pronounced. Whereas *The Pargiters* moves from Rose's nursery to the Third Essay, *The Years'* narrative follows Eleanor out of the nursery and downstairs to ebb and pool in her surreal mindscape:

> "I saw," Eleanor repeated, as she shut the nursery door. "I saw . . . "
> What had she seen? Something horrible, something hidden. But what?
> There it was, hidden behind her strained eyes. She held the candle

slightly slanting in her hand. Three drops of grease fell on the polished skirting before she noticed them. She straightened the candle and walked down the stairs. She listened as she went. There was silence. Martin was asleep. Her mother was asleep. As she passed the doors and went downstairs a weight seemed to descend on her. . . . A blankness came over her. Where am I? she asked herself, staring at a heavy frame. What is that? She seemed to be alone in the midst of nothingness; yet must descend, must carry her burden—she raised her arms slightly, as if she were carrying a pitcher, an earthenware pitcher on her head. Again she stopped. The rim of a bowl outlined itself upon her eyeballs; there was water in it; and something yellow. It was the dog's bowl, she realised; that was the sulphur . . . the dog was lying . . . at the bottom of the stairs. She stepped carefully over the body of the sleeping dog and went into the drawing-room. (*Y* 42–43)

Asking herself the question she failed to ask Rose, Eleanor struggles to see "something horrible, something hidden" behind her own "strained eyes," as if Rose's fear has stirred some buried memory. A weighty blankness descends on her, the "burden" of an unconscious past, now slightly deranged by her temporary escape from her culture's "heavy frame."[38] For a moment her mind is suspended—out of body—between existential nothingness and her accustomed place in the human caravan.[39] Then, resealing the repression beneath her "pargeting" questions to Rose, the ordinary world reasserts itself: illegible shapes slowly resolve into familiar objects as Eleanor in this mute little allegory *lets sleeping dogs lie*.

Or is it allegory? Is it not simply realism? Everyone steps over this dog in *The Years*; other characters enter trancelike states. What would the analyst say of this passage that supersedes her? If the retreat from talking cure to talking symptom is a retreat from social criticism to realism, Eleanor's trance still captures her alienation from her experience, memories, and feelings and makes the working of repression visible as the force that keeps her from seeing what she sees, knowing what she knows. If this is realism, and surely it is, it dramatizes what is lost with the analyst as the new risk that Eleanor's dissociation may be read as "natural"; that it may normalize the systemic violence of gender rather than provoke critique.

Insofar as the sleeping dog becomes allegory, it marks not just Eleanor's halt on the threshold of memory but the novelist's, for the autobiographical "Sketch," as we saw, recalls the dog by his water bowl in the hall at 22 Hyde Park Gate, near the legend on gentlemanliness, with its astonishing "innocence" and "incredible simplicity of mind" (*MB* 117).

Without actually telling the characters' "hidden" stories, *The Years* unsettles this "simplicity" with such details as Eleanor's trance, Rose's "thin white scar just above the wrist joint" (sign of an inarticulate loss that overflows mourning's channels into self-mutilation or suicide), and other intimations of dashed hopes, thwarted ambitions, and unspeakable knowledge. Such signs also intimate the "immense difficulty and danger" that the novelist faced in attempting to transform memory and "truth" into narrative. Whether the retreat from talking cure to talking symptoms aggravated or averted the risk, the novelist sacrifices the analyst to frame the sleeping dogs of a Victorian childhood Rose's sister Delia sums up at the party: "It was Hell!" (*Y* 158, 417).

Instead of mourning losses they cannot see, feel, speak of, or remember, the characters of *The Years* found their adult lives on repression, as if to say that it is not the wounds and burdens of the past that matter but creativity in the present and hope for the future. Rose channels her unspoken grief into political activism, enduring imprisonment and force-feeding in the suffrage battle, and wants to live to be eighty "to see what's going to happen"; Eleanor, freed after almost thirty years of caring for her father, experiences a paradisal "feeling, not a dream," of happiness at the party—its price the sealing over of painful memories: "I do not want to go back into my past. . . . I want the present."[40] In a passage excised in galleys, Eleanor steps with a thrill of pleasure into a steaming tub in her pristine white-tiled bathroom under a moonlit skylight.[41] Successor to the cold, dank, dark Abercorn Terrace bathroom, the room mutely celebrates advances in the sexual life of women from that unspeakable past.

If a trauma is a psychic wound for which the words are lost, *The Pargiters* explores the ways gender is, for women, a loss of language imposed by the everyday censorship that thwarts hope of change or "cure." In *The Years*, the Pargiter daughters' tiled-over past parallels Woolf's public speech on the sexual life of women: as Rose threw a brick for suffrage, Woolf tossed that "revolutionary bomb of a book," *Three Guineas*; as Eleanor halts on the brink of memory, Woolf leaves it to her readers to divine their dramas of desire, speech, and loss, or not; to naturalize her realist rendering of gender's symptoms or to "read" them (*VW:CH* 402). As the novel-essay becomes modernist-realist narrative, gender as loss recedes into a sealed-off past, mourning into unconscious sadness, grief into a vision of society "insensibly changing without death or violence into the future." As talk gives way to hystericized silence, symptoms, allegory, *The Years* overwrites the Speech's visionary artist and audience with a realist portrait of a society whose painful truths remain choked in somatic speech, even as the characters transcend pain and isolation to affirm their lives, each other, and the future. Considered as realism, it is not failure, deliberate or not. Considered as an effort to tell truths about women's bodies and passions, its reticence attests to a losing battle against repression, as the Elvira/Sara scenes show.

Allegory as Lost History: Self-Portraits as the Prophet Elvira, 1903–1936

> It is an utterly corrupt society I have just remarked, speaking in the person of Elvira Pargiter, & I will take nothing that it can give me &c &c. . . . now, as Virginia Woolf, I have to . . . say that I refuse to be made a Doctor of Letters. . . . I hardly know which I am, or where: Virginia or Elvira; in the Pargiters or outside.

—Woolf, *Diary*, 25 March 1933

> And, even today, when I'm desperate, almost in tears looking at the chapter, unable to add to it, I feel I've only got to fumble & find the end of the ball of string. . . . Isn't it odd that this was the scene I had almost a fit to prevent myself writing? This will be the most exciting thing I ever wrote, I kept saying. And now its the stumbling block. I wonder why? too personal, is that it? Out of key? But I wont think.

—*Woolf, Diary*, 5, 6 September 1935, on *The Years'* 1907 scene

> The things one does not remember are as important; perhaps they are more important.

—Woolf, "A Sketch of the Past"

As Radin observes, *The Pargiters'* Elvira—Sara in *The Years*—originates as an autobiographical artist-figure. The "turn of the book" was to hinge on a scene, based on Virginia's 1903 diary-essay "A Dance in Queens Gate," in which the crippled Elvira/Sara discovers writing as a way to "authenticate" her existence as she lies in bed on a summer night while a dance goes on beneath her window.[42] Imagining this scene in 1933, Woolf veered between exhilaration and paralysis.[43] Her "bold," "venturous" plan was to make Elvira a prophetic consciousness in a society riding a wave of change, a switch point for "millions of ideas but no preaching—history, politics, feminism, art, literature—in short a summing up of all I know, feel, laugh at, despise, like, admire hate & so on" (*D* 4:152, 161, 25 April, 31 May 1933). But the scene's successive versions move the opposite way, from a critical modernist realism toward speechless allegory. Again Woolf posed the problem of genre: what could "hold together" "satire, comedy, poetry, narrative, . . . a play, letters, poems"?

She thought that it "tend[ed] to a play" (*D* 4:151–52, 162, 25 April, 13 June 1933). As a "feeling of having to repress; control" came to dominate her long labor, taking her nearer the dangerous "precipice to my own feeling" than she had been since 1913, she channeled ideas, analysis, prophecy, and "preaching" into *Three Guineas* and rewrote Elvira as *The Years'* eccentric, ineffectual Sara who drugs her pain with wine.[44] Ambitious in concept and baffling in execution, this self-portrait shows prophecy (intrinsically bound to history) yielding to allegory, which signals loss while suppressing its history.

At the heart of that scene Woolf envisioned as the book's "turn" stands a tree rather like the one that symbolizes the young Stephens' crisis of sexuality after Stella's death in the "Sketch." In all versions from 1903 to 1937, this tree figures an existential crisis that screens a crisis of sexuality and engenders a crisis of genre: a contest between thought and reality, vision and fact, symbol and story, allegory and history; a contest too between elegy and prophecy as genres to mediate the integration of past and future, loss and hope. In Elvira's scenes the losses and grief of women temporarily consoled in *Mrs. Dalloway* resurface.[45] Time has passed, more change has come; but if the leafless tree evokes the pastoral elegy's vegetation myth and the sexual crises attendant on loss, this project on the sexual life of women questions the adequacy of symbolic consolation. A symbol at once of blight and of potential rebirth, the leafless tree is a site of struggle between realism and allegory, a struggle that finally evades tragedy and elegy to end in the repression of history, the loss of loss.

With the leafless tree of the 1940 "Sketch" in mind, let us turn to the diary-essay of 29 June 1903, "A Dance in Queens Gate," composed the spring before Leslie died, when George was squiring Virginia to parties and embracing her at night in her room "to comfort me for the fatal illness of my father."[46] Alone in this room at the top of the house, Virginia hears waltz music from the mews below and looks down at "the leaves of a tree" against the bright skylight: "this incongruity—the artificial lights, the music—the talk—& then the quiet tree standing out there, is fantastic & attracts me considerably."[47] Aligning her gaze with the tree above the dancers, she observes that they seem "no longer masters of the dance—it has taken possession of them. And all joy & life has left it, & it is diabolical, a twisting livid serpent, writhing in cold sweat & agony, & crushing the frail dancers in its contortions" (*PA* 167). In the next entry (30 June), "A Garden Dance," Virginia has "just come back from a real dance" where, dressed in "fine clothes," she has watched dancers looking "like flies struggling in a dish of sticky liquid" while talking with a "Director of the Bank of England" "about the floor & the weather & other frivolities, which I consider platitudes in my nightgown": "Honestly, I enjoyed my window dance [of 29 June] the most" (*PA* 169–71). Having pressed her half brothers to depart at one and written this little essay, she placidly concludes, "Now I open my book of astronomy, dream of the stars a little, & so to sleep."[48]

These contrasting self-portraits as Contemplative Tree and Dubious Debutante say nothing of a tap at the door, the phrase that recurs in Woolf's memoirs of George's nocturnal visits and as an early title for *The Pargiters*. But in the First Holograph, dated 3 April 1933—the first sketch of the scene that was to be "the turn of the book"—a cryptic proto-tap, immediately suppressed, marks the place where the hinge was to be. Elvira lies in bed imagining herself "not a girl of 17 but the tree in the garden," surging with life beneath its "apparently iron-bound wood":

Behold—now it shakes! . . . She pulled herself up to look out of the window at the tree. Although it was the end of June, the tree was shadowed by the house opposite. She had imagined it pale green: it was black.

She lit the candle by her bedside. It was a quarter past twelve. On the table [stood a great] there was a litter of books, one open, full of pencil marks

She wrote the date. 25th June 1902.

And added At this moment of writing . . . the tree in the garden is like a flood of silver fish passing through black water. [I am waiting for Maggie to come home.] She looked at the time—it was 20 past midnight. She added the [date] hour to her observation. With her candle beside her she lay back again. Twenty minutes past twelve on the 26 of [July] June: here she was, ?writing so, in bed, *lying alone. [[But what about somebody] The thought ?as ?best she could make it had something ?stabilizing & yet terrifying. Here she was: a body with eyes in its ?head.* Laughing she sat up & noted everything in the room as if it were necessary to authenticate the moment with the greatest precision. "Now" she wrote. The candle is casting a ?little ?flower over the ceiling. There is nothing. She drew made a little square picture in pencil of the room.

At the same time, she added, under her drawing, nothing This is perfectly, exactly true to the best of my belief. She felt that she had made a mark, which in years to come she would still find there: that *she had asserted once and for all the fact of her existence.* Everything became extremely close, & solemn. She could hear a thousand things, very slight sounds that had been inaudible. It was extremely exciting. Her cheeks flushed. And yet owing to this slight hump that showed itself under her nightgown she would never look very young. Her face [never] had that curious twist which makes the face of [cripples] the deformed seem to ripple slightly. She would never be The long hands, hanging out far from the sleeves, [would]}[49]

When Elvira finds her tree/self not green but "black," she writes to affirm her existence against a world that threatens to negate it. Noting the date and hour as she waits for her sister Maggie to return from the dance, and likening her tree/self to silver fish in black water (echoing the underwater realm of "our unconscious being" in the fisherwoman image), Elvira laughingly asserts art's powers and consolations. But why should she need thus to "mark," "authenticate," and "assert" her existence? When she flushes with excitement, how is it that her "slight hump" contravenes ("And yet") this moment? Something seems to be missing; and Woolf's lament three days later—"I cant write it now"—flags the broken words that seem to mark a "turn," a crux or crossing, within this draft: the half-formed "terrifying" "thought" of "somebody."[50] Almost immediately repressed, this fleeting thought leaves another, nearly illegible "mark" of Elvira's existence, a textual scar of a crisis perhaps historical as well as existential, or so Woolf's memoirs and the vicissitudes of this project on women's sexual life suggest. Elvira's writing exerts a counterforce against the annihilation that this repressed "thought," like the black tree, threatens. Yet it does so not by witness (talking cure) but by repression (symptom). Hastening across this break, pushing under the "terrifying" thought, the narrator moves on to Elvira's flushed face and disfiguring "hump." It is as if the Woolf of 3 April 1933, recalling the Virginia of 29 June 1903, elaborates allegorically a "mark" of a history that she didn't write then and "cant" write now. Veiling something unthinkable, she paints Elvira (subject, seer, artist) as "Laughing Survivor, a Body with Eyes, Mysteriously Deformed"—but leaves what she has survived just outside the frame.

Elvira's deformity positions her outside the human mating dance she observes below. Protecting her from the invisibly crippling femininity imposed by the dance world—the desiring, sexualizing gaze, and the future it entails—her crooked spine preserves her as a subject, not object, of vision. As Teiresias is a seer who cannot see, Elvira is a seer "with eyes" who, as it were, cannot be seen. Her affliction removes her from conventional women's time ("never . . . [never] . . . never"); it transfigures a suppressed historical wound into a physical condition with no past or future. In rewriting a psychic trauma as a physical injury (Sara is said to have been "dropped" as a baby, Y 122), the passage buries history beneath allegory: the black tree, the crippled body, disguise historical loss as ontological lack, to be redeemed by art. Like the black tree, Elvira's crooked back condenses the mourner's loss, the victim's violation, the hysteric's symptom, the survivor's scar, and the sign of the prophet who—though she will never never never—affirms the gift and consolation of her art (MB 136).

As Elvira's first portrait parlays the victim's mark into the prophet's stigma, the suppression of her history begins a hystericization that proceeds from draft to draft.

The 1932 manuscript carries a trace of Elvira's lost history in the Pargiters' family tree, where Elvira and her sister, the significantly named Magdalena, are the youngest of seven children, including several brothers (*P* [2]). Was Elvira to have brothers like the Duckworths? If so (oddly, in a family chronicle), Woolf never wrote them in; except for two brief mentions they are absent from *The Years* and from all versions of this scene, the book's intended "turn."[51] Or are they? In her 1903 essay Virginia describes a sky "dark & tragic before," now "more terrible": "deathly pale—but alive: . . . very chaste, & very pure, & the breeze is ice cold" as the dawn "fold[s] the world in its pure morning kiss"—a white "radiance" that puts out lamps, an "awful silence" in which "no music can sound" (*PA* 167). This virginal aubade embraces a morning world that extinguishes dances, sexuality, the acquiescent femininity into which the "barbaric" waltz inducts women, taps at the door in the night, and possibly a "terrifying" thought of "somebody." In the Second Holograph, like a "wizard" uttering an "imprecation," Elvira takes poetic flight on this frigid breeze—"Oh if I could freeze the wind into ice and wear it next my heart"—within a realist prose shot through with poetry, art, myth, allusion.[52] As the brothers drop out of her family tree, magic spells, crying nightingales, and the *Antigone*, with its unburied brothers and sister buried alive by a father-tyrant, intimate what the realist narrator does not say.

The Second Holograph purges the frightening "thought" and translates any hint that a sexual crisis engenders Elvira's writing into allegorical trees and nightingales. Again, her arboreal sexuality—"iron-bound winter wood" hiding a vital core—is a site of conflict between desire and a reality that threatens to negate it. Lying in her room with arms upraised, Elvira first imagines her body as roots, branches, "gummy, glistening" sap, and unfurling leaves "now that the spring had come," then

> hauled herself up in bed to *verify* the picture. She was wrong. The tree was there, but since it stood in shadow, the leaves . . . were [black] completely black. It was after midnight. . . . the tree might have been made of shadow. . . . She lit the candle [by her bedside & saw that it was] [twenty minutes past twelve]. . . . [open now on the table] was a copybook . . . the pages . . . written across with pencilled lines. She [wrote], or drew here . . . & wrote "25th June 1901." . . . twenty minutes past twelve on the 26th June ?1931 I am at the moment [sitting up in bed writing.] [The tree is black."] She looked up "I am sitting up in my room writing. . . . My stockings have fallen on to the floor. There

are four books on the table beside me: also my watch: [also . . . four walls. She *verified* each statement] [also] two chairs & a X. This is the present moment. It was then she thought that one might stabilize the moment:[53]

Is Elvira's tree/self "black" and dead, insubstantial as a shadow, or sentient and alive, *verified* by her writing? Now the waltz, signaling the sexual initiation she escapes, intrudes: "She stopped writing, as if . . . the music made it impossible. . . . Under its influence the moment was no longer . . . to be pinned down satisfactorily by cataloguing chairs and tables. It was full of [sadness] grey, of [melancholy] other emotions: pleasure, yes: sadness: yes: and what else?" (Holograph M42, 348–49). Antagonized by the dance world of "strange passion" and "barbaric instinct" (*PA* 165), Elvira deflects her irritation into fantasies of being "not herself but something remote," like this "shadowcrossed sky" under a moon where "nothing" is heard "but the two nightingales who sang to each other night after [night], calling and answers . . . the voices came brokenly . . . her poems. Then replies. The mountains separated them. But [the question was of course . . .] at what intervals?" (Holograph M42, 350).

This "other tune, with its pauses and replies," evokes Ovid's nightingale and Philomela's broken-voiced song of violated sexuality.[54] As Elvira listens in the quiet between waltzes, another "horrible" waltz begins, "enrag[ing]" her, and "completely destroy[ing] her vision." To gain "power . . . over the . . . disturbance" she flings words "mangled from something she had read" against "its mechanical accuracy, its machinelike quality"; and with a sudden gesture spills milk over her books: Gaskell's *Wives and Daughters*, *Timon of Athens*, *Afloat in the Pacific*, and her cousin's translation of "Sophocles"—presumably the *Antigone* of later drafts.[55] Alongside the nightingales, the spilled milk (like the sleeping dog) heightens mundane accident into hyperreal allegory. An effect of anger and violence in a battle over the airwaves—a contest between waltz and poem and their conflicting stories of women's sexual life—the spilled milk parodies the circumlocutory distance at which allegory holds "terrifying" thought—as if to admonish against crying over spilled milk, inalterable events, lost maternal figures whose presence would have changed everything.

Is the Second Holograph's deepened allegory a "deliberate" solution to the problem of sexual violation, speech genres, and publics or a symptom of unthinkable historical truth (like the incoherent "thought" of the First Holograph and the Milly Brush passage in *The Hours*)? If the Second Holograph was composed later in April 1933—when Woolf was finding the book "fun," "a terrific affair"—its allegorical turn may have provided a refuge from translating painful memory into realist narrative ("I cant write it now"); from vulnerability not only to an actual public but to inward threats of annihilation, madness, suicide. Is the turn to allegory "deliberate" or simply necessary—a middle way between "terrifying" memory and repression, an averted mode of testimony?

Without judging these allegorical moments a failure of courage or truth telling, we can register their cost. As Elvira's sexual history vanishes into her crippled body, what is at stake in the black tree's contradiction of her fantasy of green, leafy sexuality and voice becomes abstract and obscure. The antipathetic waltz—full of "melancholy," "pleasure," "sadness," "what else?"—does not adequately motivate her impulse toward prophecy and the sublime. Although the Ovid allusion suggests sexual violation transformed into wordless song, Elvira's poetic "power" floats free of any such narrative as illuminates Ovid's nightingales; and its figural mode seems complicit with the repression that blocks Woolf's realist storytelling and banishes the brothers, symptoms of the incestuous history that blighted her budding sexuality and (in this book) voice. Confining violent fathers and brothers between the covers of Sophocles and Ovid, the Second Holograph registers "the damage done to the mind," "worse than that done to the body," by transgressions not just of the room's and body's boundaries but of desire's psychic boundaries. It intimates a sexual history drowned in "the world that lies submerged in our unconscious being" that disables witness, testimony, truth-telling, historical voice— Elvira's human tongue.

Both Antigone and Philomela seem treacherous models for Elvira/Sara. Antigone's familial loyalty in burying her dead brothers leads to her own fate of being buried alive by decree of vengeful Creon. In her rage at the brother-in-law who raped and mutilated her, Philomela embraces symbolic art—the speechless tapestry in which her sister reads her story—not as a consoling end in itself but as an instrument to visit on her destroyer a violence as horrific as his own. Borrowed from Ovid's narrative of sisters transfigured into unintelligible voices, Elvira's nightingales are a mute memorial to loss, a history frozen into image, speech transmuted into song without words. Counterposed to the terror of memory, the draft's allegorical speech at once sustains and betrays the realist project of bearing witness to a pervasive violence against women in a world where gender is enforced by psychic and social barriers that immure history in the unconscious.

The Third Holograph—thirty-nine pages, 2–18 June 1933—ends with Elvira's hope of redeeming her deformity by prophetic speech.[56] This version throws out the spilled milk, keeps the nightingales, aligns Elvira with

Antigone, buried alive on a moonlit night, and (as the scene's first full version) definitively lops the fraternal branches off the family tree.[57] Here Elvira longs for words "beautiful, passionate enough!" for the white and black shapes in the garden below (356), then contemplates her cousin Edward's cloistered life while browsing in his *Antigone* until Maggie and their mother, Eugénie, come in after the dance. Eugénie rebukes Maggie for calling her dinner partner a "bore," Maggie envies Elvira's freedom from the dance world with its mechanical music "full of sadness, defiance, splendour" (375, 355), and Elvira teases Eugénie to tell stories about ancestresses "falling passionately in love with gardeners, with stable boys; . . . shaking their bouquets when they got home at night" to find "a heart pierced with an arrow; or again nothing but a word of assignation" (383). When their father interrupts, Elvira sees Eugénie become suddenly "beautiful, insincere" and wants to ask, "Why did you marry him?" (385). Their mother is "a liar," she tells Maggie, speaking with "extraordinary bitterness, neither like a girl nor a woman but aged, drawn, sexless. And why can't she tell the truth? Because of that little man," she continues (386). Alone, Elvira reflects that "She was only 17"; perhaps at seventy, by "following with extreme daring each indication . . . she would have set free . . . the complete truth" (390).[58]

Revisiting Elvira—now "Sally in bed"—in September 1935 (the year after George's death), Woolf recorded her own hysterical symptoms in what had become "psychologically the oddest" of her "adventures" (*D* 4:338–39, 5, 6 September). She could not write the "turn of the book" in 1933 or since, and she cannot write it now. Worse, as she turns Elvira/Sally's scene into the "1907" chapter of *The Years*, she defaces the Third Holograph's self-portrait as the ambitious young Elvira by turning her into the cryptic, inconsequent Sara. Nightingales on an icy, virginal moon hint at the history condensed in her deformed body; a sister, not a brother, taps at her door; Eugénie's stories of pleasure vanish. More ominously, reality countermands prophetic desire as the "1907" scene restages the crisis of verification that interrupted the first Essay. Lying "straight and still" as the dance proceeds below, Sara muses on a philosopher's idea that "'the world is nothing but . . . thought.'" She imagines her body as "thought," then "a root," a "tree" putting forth branches with leaves; looking out to "verify the sun on the leaves," she is "contradicted" by a tree with "no leaves at all"; "the tree was black, dead black" (*Y* 133). As the black tree moves Elvira to write in order to assert her existence as a "body with eyes," Sara surveys the garden scene, imagines the nightingales, and, seeing a man pick up something from the grass, makes up a story: "And as he picks it up," she murmured, looking out, "he says to the lady . . . Behold, Miss Smith, what I have found on the grass—a fragment of my heart. . . . I have found it on the grass; and I wear it on my breast"—she hummed the words in time to the melancholy waltz music—"my broken heart, this broken glass, for love . . . is best" (Y 134–35). Then Sara reads, seeing Antigone whirl "out of the dust-cloud to where the vultures were reeling" to fling "white sand over the blackened foot" and be "buried alive" by Creon; soon Sara too has "laid herself out" to sleep like a living corpse (Y 136). The narrator reports a mundane conversation in the garden below; then Maggie comes in and Sara tests whether indeed "the world is nothing but thought," asking whether anyone gave her "a piece of glass . . . saying to you, Miss Pargiter . . . my broken heart?"; "No," Maggie replies, "why should they?" (Y 138).

As memoirs failed to verify the novelist's "truth," Maggie's experience contradicts and trivializes Sara's experiment with prophetic "thought." Elvira's existential crisis becomes an idle play of questions as Sara and Maggie ask, "Would there be trees if we didn't see them?"; " 'what's "I"? . . . "I" . . . ' She stopped" (Y 140). Where Elvira affirms her existence, Sara questions hers; in the contest between thought and reality, reality seems the victor: the crippled prophet in search of "the complete truth," becomes in effect a tree falling unheard, making no sound; a hysteric defined by her lack of an audience. "Hush!" Martin admonishes over lunch as Sara tries to respond to his query as to what she makes of religion ("'The father incomprehensible, the son incomprehensible'"); "Somebody's listening." Later, atop a bus, he says, "now, Sally, you can say whatever you like. *Nobody's listening. Say something . . . very profound*"; she is silent (Y 229, 236, my emphasis). Eugénie, rumored to have had an affair with *her* brother-in-law Abel, plays into Sara's frustrated desire for reality, history, truth: she puts a flower to her lips and promises to tell "the true story one of these days"—but Sara insists she never will (Y 143–44). Elvira's hope to "set free . . . the complete truth" is lost as Sara falls asleep, wrapped in her sheet "like a chrysalis"—anticipating Woolf's portrait of her young self emerging from the chrysalis, "its eyes dazzled, incapable of flight" (Y 144, MB 124). Her abstract, seemingly arbitrary, singularity unredeemed by prophetic speech, Sara does not so much critique her culture as secede from it, in company with her homosexual friend Nicholas (Y 322, 324).

If Sara's reality test reclaims the narrative from allegory, it also spells disaster for the artist-figure Woolf meant to be the hinge of the book. The black tree/disfigured body that was to burst into leafy speech is muted in Sara, nor did Woolf add "someone to look at" her who might have salvaged something of her revelations (as Peter remembers Clarissa's).[59]

Woolf's misery on confronting the scene in 1935 suggests that the unexpected direction the book's "turn" took was less "deliberate" failure, conscious pargetting, than unconscious, involuntary symptom. Is there relief as well as anguish as she buries not only the brothers but Elvira's prophetic ambition in Sara—who, although entombed alive like Antigone, embodies truths she can neither speak nor write? No less than Ovid's Philomela, Antigone seems an awkward model for Sara, her effort to honor her brothers at cross-purposes with Woolf's brother burying, her own live burial a parody of "the damage done to the mind" by brothers contingently associated with Antigone's.[60] By contrast with *Three Guineas*' courageous Antigone, who acts out of love and seeks not to break but to "find" the law, the Antigone of *The Years* highlights what appears to be the daughter's involuntary silencing by repression.

This textual history thus signals much more than "a failure of courage, a disappointing retreat."[61] Seemingly helpless against repression, Woolf expressed not fear but baffled desperation at having lost what she planned with such excitement to say. As late as 21 June 1936, she was still urging herself to revise "strongly daringly," with "immense courage & buoyancy," at the same time suffering "complete despair & failure[,] . . . living so constrainedly; so repressedly . . . Always with a feeling of having to repress; control" (*D* 5:24–25). As *The Years* foundered on repression, writing lapsed from remembering to repeating; from the visionary, liberating project Woolf envisioned in her bath to an ordeal that threatened to reawaken a "terrifying" past. It is perhaps no accident that the project came to resemble an "aggressive," unkillable reptile—an image to which Woolf made frequent recourse to describe the "unspeakably conventional" George and Gerald.[62] When Woolf gestured toward memoirs as touchstones of truth, she could not have foreseen that the fish the "conventions" forbade her to pursue would prove a "monster[] of the lower waters," as difficult to escape as George apparently was in the scenes that made Virginia's Greek tutor gasp "like a benevolent gudgeon."[63] Woolf's judgment—"I myself know why its a failure, & that its failure is deliberate"—belies the immense effort, courage, and will to "truth" against the force of repression that the genetic text makes visible (*D* 5:65, 7 March 1937).

"The leafless tree was behind our ostensible lives for many months," Woolf wrote in 1940. "But trees do not remain leafless. They begin to grow little red chill buds" of desire, as in the "illegal" marriage with her brother-in-law that Vanessa contemplated (*MB* 141). Budding only briefly in that incestuous house, Vanessa's desire changed direction to issue in children—her first arriving shortly before Virginia and *her* brother-in-law, Clive, began a flirtation. In a manuscript passage, Elvira speculates that her cousin Rose's "powers of expression have obviously been atrophied by some early & painful I should venture to say hideous experience [which she doesn't want to talk about] Just as a tree . . . if you put a ring round its root all the apples on one side are bitter [small] wrinkled . . . but on the other side dipped in golden lustre."[64] In Elvira's portrait of Rose we glimpse yet another authorial self-portrait as a tree partly blighted by a root unnaturally bound.

Woolf could not wrestle the alligator of women's sexual life to the ground, but the aura of Elvira's unwritten history clings to *The Years*, broken into cryptic images, dispersed among the characters, and passed on, as we shall see, to the next generation.[65] At the same time, the party in the "Present Day" chapter circles back to Elvira/Sara's 1907 scene and finesses the loss of history by founding the characters' hope for the future not on an arduous, elegiac working through of memories but on the repression of loss and the abnegation of violence.[66] At a crossroads that points one way toward reality, mourning, rage, submission, consolation, and the other toward murder, suicide, tragedy, repression takes a shortcut via oblivion to the Pargiters' final family portrait as people who have given up trying to speak, not because somebody's listening but because almost nobody is.

Dream Brother: The Flight to the Present

In *The Pargiters* there is a brother named George who is renamed North in *The Years*. The 1932 family tree stops short of this next generation, but George/North and his sister, Peggy, are children of Morris Pargiter, nephew and niece of Eleanor, Rose, Martin, and the rest, and first cousins once removed of Sara and Maggie. As in the original plan, this younger generation is an index of historical change. North returns from twenty years on an African farm, an "outsider" to English civilization (prefiguring *Three Guineas*' Outsider). Peggy, an unmarried physician and the novel's only professional woman, longs to "live differently" (*Y* 317, 323, 403). True to the adage that one generation's sins are laid on the next, the narrative hints at incest between North and Peggy, who seems to embody a symptomatic "truth" about women's bodies and passions.

When we first meet these children during Eleanor's visit to her brother Morris's family at Wittering in 1911, North is a "brown eyed cricketing boy" and Peggy, in a stiff blue dress, "sixteen or seventeen" (*Y* 202, 205). Summoned by her mother at bedtime, Peggy lingers "whispering with her brother in the hall." She comes "reluctantly" and kisses her mother "obediently; but she did not look in the least sleepy. She looked extremely pretty and rather flushed. She did not mean to go to bed, Eleanor felt sure" (Y 210). In bed, Eleanor hears a sound: "Peggy, was it, escaping, to join her brother? She felt sure there was some scheme on foot" (Y 212). At the party in the "Present Day" chapter, Peggy and North reminisce about "the night of the row" when she climbed down a rope and they "picnicked in the Roman camp"; a "pink-eyed boy" spied them "coming home that morning" and "told on them" (Y 395). Innocent as this escapade seems, Peggy's feelings point to more than a picnic:

> He looked at her again. And now he's comparing me with the girl I saw him talking to, she thought, and saw again the lovely, hard face. He'll tie himself up with a red-lipped girl, and become a drudge. He must, and I can't, she thought. No, I've a sense of guilt always. I shall pay for it, I shall pay for it, I kept saying to myself even in the Roman camp, she thought. She would have no children, and he would produce . . . more little Gibbses. (Y 396)

North remembers that "he used to read her his poetry in the apple-loft" and "as they walked up and down by the rose bushes. And now they had nothing to say to each other," though "She still knew certain things about him"; "they still had something very profound in common" (Y 395). Peggy masters her jealousy enough to ask North to bring a girl he has met to see her. Putting her hand on his arm, she feels "something hard and taut beneath the sleeve. . . . [T]he touch of his flesh, bringing back to her the nearness of human beings and their distance, so that if one meant to help one hurt, yet they depended on each other, produced in her such a tumult of sensation that she could scarcely keep herself from crying out, North! North! North!" (Y 397).

Does Woolf parget her past in George/North, or does she rehabilitate her half brother as a figure of healing change, a comrade in the quest for new civilizations? Unable to tell the "complete truth," does she overleap trauma to envision a future in which brothers might be allies and friends? In any case, what seems crucial here is that Peggy's desire is fully in play.[67] She is no victim nor North an abuser; they hatch their "scheme" together. It is her own desire for which she feels guilt and must "pay" by renouncing sexual and procreative pleasure. As if displaced from Elvira/Sara to Peggy, a history of a woman's sexual life subtly surfaces as Peggy's memories cast a gleam upon her present misery. Although she earns her living, her work is an escape from pain, a way "not to live; not to feel"; in her sexual life she fares no better than Sara or Eleanor and—for no apparent reason, unless that night in the Roman camp—is less happy, free, and fulfilled than Eugénie, Kitty, and Maggie (Y 355). The sight of her father Morris's "rather worn shoes" gives Peggy a "sudden warm spurt" of feeling, "Part sex; part pity. . . . Can one call it 'love'?"[68] Talking at cross-purposes with her hard-of-hearing uncle Patrick, she wonders whether, since "Pleasure is increased by sharing it," "the same hold[s] good of pain?" (Y 351–52). As Elvira/Sara stands at a tangent to the mating game, Peggy, "marooned" at the dance, picks up a book "to cover her loneliness," predicting, "He'll say what I'm thinking, . . . Books opened at random always did" and reads " *'La mediocrité de l'univers m'étonne et me révolte'*. . . . Precisely, she said" (Y 383).

At the 1937 party, no prophet, male, female, or "sexless," looks upon the scene. Sara is part of the common life, which includes conformists and outsiders, pillars of the system and rebels against the "conspiracy" that, in North's eyes, links family life to economic striving, class and gender oppression, war, and imperialism (Y 341). Several characters voice the longing for change that has sounded since the war: "to live differently—differently."[69] In the 1917 chapter, as they dine in Maggie's cellar during an air raid, Eleanor has wondered, "when will this New World come? When shall we be free? When shall we live adventurously, wholly, not like cripples in a cave?" (Y 297). Now, at seventy-nine, she enjoys travel, family, and new friends—a life salvaged from the wreck of her dutiful Victorian femininity; in Peggy's eyes "a fine old prophetess, a queer old bird, venerable and funny at one and the same time," Eleanor has visited India and wants before she dies to experience "another kind of civilisation. Tibet, for instance" (Y 328, 335). Meanwhile, she has moments of inexplicable joy: "She laughed. Her feeling of happiness returned to her, her unreasonable exaltation. It seemed to her that they were all young. . . . Nothing was fixed; nothing was known; life was open and free before them" (Y 382).

North returns from Africa with an ethnographic perspective on his native culture and joins the chorus in quest of new civilizations (Y 317, 323, 403). The English, he finds, talk of nothing but "money and politics"; of the class oppression that underwrites middle-class English domesticity he thinks, "Could nothing be done about it? . . . Nothing short of revolution." The ruling-class "conspiracy" forcibly strikes him: "they're not interested in other people's children . . . Only in their own; their own property; their own flesh and blood, which they would protect with the unsheathed claws of the primeval swamp. . . . How then can we be civilised . . . ?" (Y 318, 375, 378). That dark continent Europe entangles him in "a jungle; in the heart of darkness"; he tries "cutting his way towards the light" but has only "broken sentences, single words, with which to break through the briarbush of human bodies, human wills and voices, that bent over him, binding him, blinding him" (Y 411). When Peggy challenges him to reject the "conspiracy," he feels momentary hostility, then recognizes something "true" in "her feeling, not her words. He felt her feeling now; it was not about him; it was about other people; about another world, a new world" (Y 413, 422). Peggy, he realizes, expresses their generation's longing for "a different life. Not halls and reverberating megaphones; not marching in step after leaders, in herds, groups, societies caparisoned. . . . But what do I mean, he wondered—I, to whom ceremonies are suspect, and religion's dead; who don't fit" (Y 410). Like Rachel Vinrace, North seeks a new script, "a new word that was no word"—"the sweet nut. The fruit, the fountain that's in all of us" (Y 412).

The First Essay's vision of new civilizations recurs in North's dream of an antifascist "new word" to oppose to Europe's corrupt, barbaric heart, uncovered by Conrad at modernism's origin and gaining sway in the militant authoritarian regimes of the 1930s. Nicholas's attempted speech at the end of the evening—in which he tries to thank the house "which has sheltered the lovers, the creators, the men and women of goodwill" and to toast "the human race . . . now in its infancy, may it grow to maturity!"—at once founders and elicits this new word as the company cries him down and prophecy yields to polyphony. At Kitty's invitation ("Tell me, privately"), he modulates from oratory back to conversation's sweet nut: "It was to have been a miracle! . . . A masterpiece! But how can one speak when one is always interrupted?" (Y 425–26). Likewise, Edward, don and translator of Greek drama, declines to expatiate upon "the chorus" even as a chorus of the future materializes in the caretaker's children (as close as the novel gets to 2032), who sing for their cake in words their listeners find hideously unintelligible yet weirdly beautiful. Meanwhile, North longs for "someone, infinitely wise and good," to "think for him, . . . answer for him," and finds this desire met when Maggie laughs as if "possessed by some genial spirit . . . that made her bend and rise," like a "a tree . . . tossed and bent by the wind. No idols, no idols, no idols, her laughter seemed to chime as if the tree were hung with innumerable bells, and he laughed too" (Y 423, 425). The vital speech of Elvira's black tree bursts forth transfigured in polyphonic voices, the little choristers, and Maggie's wordless laughter. Heralded by these new words that are no word, the unforeknowable "new world" dawns.

Even though The Years scales back The Pargiters' historical ambitions to a meliorative realism shadowed by the Present Day political scene, hope for the future survives in its characters' private consciousness of being "happier . . . freer" than in the past and in their longing to "live differently" (Y 422–23). In the closing tableau the seven elderly Pargiters stand against the window, observed by Sara and Maggie, while "God Save the King" drifts from the gramophone, departing guests hear pigeons coo, and Eleanor sees a couple alight from a taxi and enter a house, as if to recall the exciting conversation prophesied by the Speech. As Eleanor holds out her hands to Morris—"And now?"—these survivors seem to shelter in the only possible paradise, the present, which Eleanor, Kitty, Delia and Rose insist *has* improved on the past and which breaks like a wave toward a future "open and free" (*Y* 435). On the other hand, there is a terrible disjunction between this dawn's illusory "peace" and the threat of war on the horizon; between the transformative energy that impelled Woolf's new speech genre, the essay-novel, and the impotence of any "new word" against the economic and political engines of fascism and war. Like Pound's radio speeches, Eliot's religious incantations, and Joyce's laminate dream-language, Maggie's laughter sounds at a moment of impending violence no word will forestall.

In this sense *The Years* almost seems to parget the very future it heralds—to strand us at the limit of modernism, beyond the agency of speech and vision, even as it clings to hope of a more civilized and humane future. For, in a way, Woolf's epiphany still echoes in this new word that is no word. Addressing its audience intimately, as Nicholas does Kitty; humbly, as Edward does North; with spontaneous joy, like Maggie's free-floating laughter; unintelligibly yet enchantingly, like the singing children; without prophecy, polemic, or preaching, *The Years* distills Woolf's experiment with speech genres into the freedom and surprise of everyday social practices. Insofar as its new word that is no word marks the place of a longing to "tell someone," it signals speech that would free the future from the wounds, scars, and losses of the past.

In the absence of *The Pargiters'* psychosocial analysis, the ground of that hope shifts from shared witness of the past to its repudiation. Eleanor ventriloquizes the flight to the Present Day for lack of an audience: "I do not want to go back into my past. . . . I want the present"; " 'My life . . . ' she said aloud, but half to herself. . . . But no, she thought, I can't find words; I can't tell anybody" (*Y* 336, 367). So Kitty sums up "the old days" as "bad days, wicked days, cruel days" (*Y* 350). As her essay-novel yielded to a leap of faith in the future, Woolf felt she had laid a heavy "paving stone of a book" over her "old fountains"; to Ethel Smyth she dismissed her effort at a historical narrative, saying the "Present day, the last chapter, has as much as one wants. And its all very bad, but well meant— morally" (*D* 5:31, 9, 10 November 1936, *L* 6:113, 17 March 1937).

If *The Years'* new dawn gives up the struggle to integrate past and present in hope of a future founded (in Freud's words) on firmer ground and more lastingly, its "failure" fed new hope as Woolf's unfulfilled vision became the impetus of new projects. She suffered through its publication, taking solace in Leonard's praise without changing her own opinion; she felt relief that, though not the book she had planned, it seemed "to come off at the end," and looked forward to *Three Guineas*: "even if The Years is a failure, I've thought considerably; & collected a little hoard of ideas."[70] When she sent off the last proofs, her mind "sprung up like a tree shaking off a load" (*D* 5:44, 30 December 1936). Publication day loomed like a "head lamp on my poor little rabbits body": she saw her own "positively terrified" eyes in the glass and felt "I'm going to be beaten, I'm going to be laughed at, I'm going to be held up to scorn & ridicule" (*D* 5:63–64, 1–2 March 1937). In the event, *The Years* was favorably reviewed on the whole and triumphed in the marketplace. As if reversing the black tree's negation of Elvira/Sara's leafy speech, her public heaped praise and pots of money upon the book she had feared would leave her "little reputation" "an old cigarette end": it outsold all her other books, was a bestseller in America, and brought her annual earnings to an all-time high.[71] As the reviews appeared, her dread diminished but her private opinion held: "to think then its *not* nonsense; it does make an effect. Yet of course not in the least the effect I meant" (*D* 5:67, 12 March 1937). Only Basil de Selincourt's review gave her hope that it would be not taken as a "death song of the middle classes" but "debated" as "a creative, a constructive book," so that "3 Gs. will strike very sharp & clear on a hot iron" and "my immensely careful planning won't be baulked."[72]

Woolf continued her quest toward new civilizations by means of new engagements with her public in *Three Guineas* and in *Between the Acts*, which grew from the seed of the village pageant in the 1911 chapter. With *The Years'* worldly success creating a wind at her back, she plunged ahead with the unfinished business of the 1931 Speech, reviving the idea of Elvira in the prophetic "St. Virginia" who answers St. Paul's epistle in *Three Guineas* and in Miss La Trobe, the visionary village playwright who stages a new revision of English history in *Between the Acts*. As Woolf began rethinking the analyst's essays for *Three Guineas*, she continued to experiment with finding "a public" for "all the new ideas that are in me," a genre and style to disarm her readers' probable resistance: "if I say what I mean . . . I must expect considerable hostility. Yet I so slaver & silver my tongue that its sharpness takes some time to be felt" (*D* 5:84, 30 April 1937). If her 1931 project of bringing the sexual life of women into public discourse was "too ambitious," *Three Guineas'* critique of the sex/gender system in modern England and *Between the Acts'* experimental pageantry are no less so (*L* 6:116, 7 April 1937). It's just that they stand at a safer distance from Woolf's own untold "experiences as a body."

Any man who prays or prophesies with his head covered dishonors his head, but any woman who prays or prophesies with her head unveiled dishonors her head. . . . For a man ought not to cover his head, since he is the image and glory of God; but woman is the glory of man.

—St. Paul's First Epistle to the Corinthians 11:4–7

We can see the educated man's daughter, as she issues from . . . the private house, and stands on the bridge which lies between the old world and the new, and asks, as she twirls the sacred coin in her hand, "What shall I do with it? What do I see with it?" . . . Let us . . . lay before you a photograph . . . of your world as it appears . . . through the shadow of the veil that St. Paul still lays upon our eyes; from the bridge which connects the private house with the world of public life.

—Woolf, *Three Guineas*

EIGHT

St. Virginia's Epistle to an English Gentleman

Sex, Violence, and the Public Sphere in *Three Guineas*

I n *Three Guineas* (1938) Woolf paints another portrait of the artist collaborating with her audience in the quest for "new civilisations." Abandoning *The Pargiters*' essay form, she devises an epistolary essay, a compound public letter, as "a way of publishing all the new ideas that are in me": a letter to an English gentleman who asks her to join his society "to prevent war" and "to defend liberty" and "culture," enclosing a second letter to an honorary treasurer who asks her help to rebuild a women's college, and a third to an honorary treasurer who asks her help for women entering the professions.[1] By specifying as addressees two professional women and one "civilized" man of her own class—established, prosperous, socially concerned, rather like one of her Bloomsbury friends—who can presumably "stand free speech in women," Woolf projects the mixed-sex professional public she envisioned in her 1931 Speech: "we speak with the same accent; use knives and forks in the same way; expect maids to cook dinner and wash up . . . ; and can talk during dinner without much difficulty about politics and people; war and peace; barbarism and civilization" (*P* xl, *TG* 4–5). She frames his appeal, and her own "free gift" of a guinea for the cause of preventing war and defending liberty and culture, as "a momentous . . . occasion in the history of civilization" and a milestone "in the history of human correspondence, since when before has an educated man asked a woman how in her opinion war can be prevented?" (*TG* 153–54, 3).

Woolf, as we saw, had been thinking about such questions since 1931. At work on *The Pargiters, The Years,* and *Three Guineas* between 1932 and 1937, a period of mounting social crisis in Europe and intensive social commentary by British intellectuals, she collected many such letters, circulars, manifestos, and appeals in three large scrapbooks, along with notes and cuttings from newspapers, journals, memoirs, biographies, social and intellectual histories, and *Whitaker's Almanac* containing facts and opinions "about women, men, law, sexuality, sports, religion, the Church, science, education, economics, politics, and social mores."[2] By 1935 she envisioned *Three Guineas*—whose working titles included *Answers to Correspondents*, *Letter to an Englishman*, and *Two Guineas*—as a public letter condensing "all the articles editors have asked me to write during the past few years—on all sorts of subjects. Shd. women smoke. Short skirts. War—&c. This wd give me the right to wander: also put me in the position of the one asked. And excuse the method: while giving continuity."[3] The scrapbooks' documentary cross section of British public life (the matrix of *Three Guineas'* 124 footnotes) supports Woolf's radical and much misunderstood argument that the institutionalized psychology of dominance and submission that shapes relations between the sexes on the private/public continuum bears fundamental similarities to the group psychology of fascism and war; that England's public institutions—its schools, professions, government, and Church—camouflage and mystify the collective violence that excludes women from the public sphere; and that the fight for civilization, peace, and freedom against war and tyranny entails disabling the mechanism of collective violence as such.

Three Guineas, in short, breaks through *The Years'* silences and evasions to expose the scapegoating of women as the structural act of barbarism that founds the masculine public sphere. Reflecting on women's exclusion from full and free participation in the society and culture that the English gentleman asks her to help defend, Woolf fashions a complex epistolary persona. First, speaking freely as civilization's "natural inheritor" (in the phrase from *A Room of One's Own*), she hails the English gentleman into dialogue on the terms given by his own Enlightenment rhetoric and their shared cause: the defense of peace and freedom, the fight against barbarism and tyranny (*RO* 97). Since her free speech is underwritten by her independent earnings, she "need not acquiesce; she can criticize," like the First Essay's analyst and the outsider North Pargiter (*TG* 24). At the same time, this newly emergent professional woman surveys a public world still largely barred to women "from the bridge which connects the private house with the world of public life," and Woolf signals this condition by "the veil that St. Paul still lays upon our eyes" (*TG* 26). Replying at once to the contemporary gentleman's letter and to St. Paul's epistle dictating the "veiling" or subordination of women in public life, this veiled St. Virginia revives the prophetic speech Woolf envisioned for Elvira/Sara and eloquently articulates the longing to "live differently."[4]

As Woolf's epistolary persona dons the public garb St. Paul mandates for women prophets, she also transvalues the Pauline veil to betoken not simply sexual difference parlayed into gender hierarchy but women's quasi-anthropological vantage on the civilization men have created. In analyzing the scapegoat psychology that masculinizes the public sphere, Woolf adopts an anthropological stance and vocabulary derived from Frazer's *The Golden Bough*: "scapegoat," "sex taboo," "sacred" (pervasively); of male professional plumage, "daubed red and gold, decorated like a savage with feathers"; of professional ceremonies, "Here you kneel; there you bow; here you advance in procession behind a man carrying a silver poker; here you mount a carved chair; here you appear to do homage to a piece of painted wood; here you abase yourselves before tables covered with richly worked tapestry."[5] This chapter seeks to bring out the deep coherence of *Three Guineas*' argument, and to explain its otherwise perplexing focus on the sacred, by aligning Woolf's analysis of women's scapegoat role with René Girard's extension to modern societies of the scapegoat economy that Frazer derives from "the savage mind."[6] Girard's theory illuminates *Three Guineas*' linking of violence and the sacred in modern British culture and its analysis of the scapegoat psychology that drives collective violence.

By 1931 (the year of Woolf's Speech), the 1919 Sex Disqualification Removal Act had opened the professions to women and made it possible to imagine a critical mass of Englishwomen exercising public power for the first time in history.[7] Now Woolf turns the English gentleman's historic request into a symbolic occasion to expose the structural role that violence and the sacred play in maintaining a masculinized public sphere that she traces ("to go no further back") to St. Paul (*TG* 253 n. 38). She had hardly begun her research, in fact, than she wrote that she had "collected enough powder to blow up St Pauls"—a fantasy that makes both London's Cathedral and the Church Father synecdoches for the public sphere's gender barrier, even as it prefigures what one reviewer would describe as "a revolutionary bomb of a book."[8]

In framing her letter as a reply to St. Paul's epistle requiring women who speak in public to veil their heads, and in making St. Paul the exemplary opponent of women's full and free participation in public life, Woolf deconstructs the social process of sacralization. The sacred pervades her meditation on violence. From her historic position on the bridge between the private house and the public world, her veiled woman holds the newly earned "sacred coin" that underwrites her free speech as she gazes at the "sacred edifices" of public architecture and the "sacred gates" of the universities and the professions (*TG* 23, 7, 39, 60, 99, 135, 213). From behind her "veil" (women's private clothes, in contrast to the "barbarous . . . spectacle" of men's hierarchic professional costumes, which invite "the ridicule which we bestow upon the rites of savages"), she can describe a civilization built on a sacralized masculine appropriation of the public world: men's schools, churches, professions, buildings, telegraph wires, governance, and indeed men's wars, each with its exclusive male "priesthood," all subsidized by women's unpaid labor (*TG* 26, 30–31, 194). Holding her "sacred sixpence" that, since the "sacred year 1919," Englishwomen can earn and own and spend, she can prophesy "a new religion based, it might well be, upon the New Testament, but, it might well be, very different from the religion now erected upon that basis."[9]

How could the Woolf who wrote "O you Christians have much to answer for!" to a correspondent about Christina Rossetti, who feared that her friend T. S. Eliot's religious conversion would render him "dead to us all from this day forward," who cheerfully roared "I hate religion" into the composer Ethel Smyth's deaf ear after a performance of her Mass—how could this apparent hereditary and lifelong atheist, daughter of the eminent agnostic Leslie Stephen, write anything but an agnostic gospel, a subversive epistle debunking such "sacred" letters as St. Paul's instructing the Corinthian women to veil their heads when prophesying?[10] Classifying *Three Guineas* as prophecy, Catherine F. Smith describes the genre as "a literary mode peculiar to cultural crisis"—a vision of "new culture, new history, new self" revealed through "the prophet's own irradiated consciousness."[11] With that description in mind, I suggest that Woolf not only discovers and exposes a violence at the heart of the sacred as it has been constructed from St. Paul to "St. Pauls" but offers a radical interpretation of the Gospels and the sacred. Analyzing women's role as the sacralized scapegoat of both England's state religion and a secular public sphere that derives its authority from the Church, Woolf's veiled woman is the modern incarnation of the women who prophesied alongside St. Paul—who, after all, insists not that women not prophesy and preach but that they veil themselves when doing so.[12] This veiled St. Virginia challenges St. Paul's interpretation of the Gospels from the perspective of the scapegoat at the heart of Paul's Church.

As St. Virginia's reply to St. Paul, *Three Guineas* recreates the scenario of the forgotten women prophets of early Christian history that Woolf sketches as she considers the recommendation that women be barred from that "highest of all" professions, the clergy, put forward by the Church of England's 1935 *Report of the Archbishops' Commission on the Ministry of Women* (*TG* 184). When "the daughters of educated men" asked to enter this profession in 1935, Woolf writes, its priests had to consult the New Testament, where the Christian religion "has been laid down once and for all by the founder . . . in words that can be read by all in a translation of singular beauty; and whether or not we accept the interpretation that has been put on them, we cannot deny them to be words of the most profound meaning" (*TG* 185). There these priests might have read: "There is neither male nor female: for ye are all one in Christ Jesus" (*TG* 186). Christianity's founder, Woolf concludes—whose disciples were working-class men like himself—demanded neither training nor sex in a prophet; the "prime qualification" was rather "some rare gift . . . bestowed . . . upon carpenters and fishermen, and upon women also. As the Commission points out there can be no doubt that in those early days there were prophetesses—women upon whom the divine gift had descended" (*TG* 186).

Only with the professionalization of religion—as Elaine Pagels describes it, the move from a gnostic to an orthodox notion of spiritual authority with the establishment of the Church and its all-male apostolic succession—were women driven outside the "sacred gates," where, however, they could still exercise spiritual authority by creating secular literature:

> In three or four centuries, . . . the prophet or prophetess whose message was voluntary and untaught became extinct; and their places were taken by the three orders of bishops, priests, and deacons, who are invariably men, and invariably, as Whitaker points out, paid men, for when the Church became a profession its professors were paid. Thus the profession of religion seems to have been originally much what the profession of literature is now. It was originally open to anyone who had received the gift of prophecy.[13]

In making early Christian prophecy continuous with literary creativity, Woolf aligns her own text with a gnostic understanding of spiritual authority, which views the Gospels not as fixing revelation for all time but as recording a spiritual message that remains, in Pagels's words, "spontaneous, charismatic, and open," unfolding through the creative speech of those who understand it. As the boundary between secular and sacred dissolves, my heuristic "gesture of deification" (St. Virginia) self-destructs.[14]

Adopting a gnostic stance toward the New Testament to expose the scapegoat psychology of the Church, Britain's public sphere, and European fascism, *Three Guineas* revives the lost dialogue between St. Paul and the veiled women prophets in the secular correspondence between Woolf and the English gentleman—St. Paul's inheritor by virtue of his privileged place in England's public sphere. Questioning the Church's monopoly on spiritual authority, St. Virginia/Woolf enters into epistolary dialogue with St. Paul/the English gentleman to deconstruct by the light of reason Paul's sacralization of masculine economic, social, and spiritual privilege.

Scapegoat Theory and the Veiled Woman

How exactly does the New Testament figure in Woolf's argument against war, fascism, and collective violence? In *Violence and the Sacred* and *The Scapegoat*, Girard spells out the scapegoat theory that underlies Woolf's reading of the New Testament and his own. For Girard, violence *is* the sacred.[15] Human cultures have historically been sacrificial in nature, producing rituals and myths that enable individuals to bind themselves into a society by sacrificing a scapegoat on whom they project their own differences, thereby channeling outside the community violence that would otherwise destroy it from within. The persecution of the scapegoat purifies the community of its violence through a collective displacement of aggression onto a victim, whom it marks with a sign of difference that symbolically externalizes differences that actually exist within and among the persecutors themselves. In this way, violence becomes the sacred: the collective crime that founds the society also founds the intrinsically paradoxical sacred (from Latin *sacer*: "holy" and "accursed").[16] As the etymology of "religion" (from Latin *religare*, *re* + *ligare*: to bind) suggests, the scapegoat's sacrifice binds the perpetrators together, whereas without this channeling of difference and violence they would be at war with one another.

In Girard's view, almost all mythologies tell the story of collective violence from the persecutors' self-justifying perspective and thereby manifest the scapegoat mechanism at the origin of the sacred as a structural principle. One exception is the Gospels, which decode and demystify the scapegoat mechanism by telling the story from the victim's perspective. Whereas a myth that tells the story from the persecutors' perspective makes the violence seem justified and necessary—in this sense, functioning as a microcosm of the society it represents—a myth that tells the story from the victim's perspective exposes rather than exploits the scapegoating mechanism.[17] Such texts, by revealing the violence to be unjust and unjustifiable, offer a revelation that enables human societies to move beyond magical thinking to reason, beyond arbitrary persecution ("hate without a cause") toward a "science" of justice.[18]

Similarly, *Three Guineas* decodes women's function as the scapegoat whose expulsion establishes bonds between men—thereby exposing women's hidden but crucial (and sacralized) structural role in the founding and perpetuation of a masculinized public sphere that dominates a feminized private house. As the persecutors must project a sign of difference upon the scapegoat, who in reality is not significantly different from themselves, Woolf's veiled woman wears the mark of the victim whose collective persecution has historically founded masculine public culture. At the same time, she transforms it into a sign of the outsider's anthropological perspective at the historic moment when she moves out of the scapegoat's role and into autonomous public speech. *Three Guineas*' veiled woman on the bridge joins the effort Woolf and Girard discover in the Gospels: to expose the scapegoat mechanism by telling the story of collective violence from the victim's perspective, thereby to advance humanity from tyranny and war toward peace and freedom; from persecutory societies to an open society that would dismantle not just the gender barrier but the social and national barriers on which fascism, Nazism, xenophobic nationalism, and war depend.

Girard does not fail to notice that male societies found and sustain themselves by making women their primary scapegoats. In *Violence and the Sacred*, he briefly wonders whether the taboo against menstrual blood in certain societies "respond[s] to some half-suppressed desire to place the blame for all forms of violence on women," since it effects "a transfer of violence" and establishes "a monopoly that is clearly detrimental to the female sex" (*VS* 36). In *The Scapegoat*, analyzing a Dogrib myth of a woman who "has intercourse with a dog and gives birth to six puppies" that turn out to be humans who shed their animal skins as soon as she leaves the house, he observes, "The fact that she is a woman is the stereotypical victim's sign. . . . The woman is certainly responsible for the crisis since she gives birth to a monstrous community. But the myth tacitly admits the truth. There is no difference between the woman criminal and the community" (*S* 49). As the persecutors purge themselves of their violence by directing it against a scapegoat who is in fact not different from themselves, so a masculinized public culture turns the biological sign of sexual difference—which in reality marks each sex in relation to the other—into a social sign of the victim.[19]

Girard does not pursue woman's role as scapegoat in modern societies, but *Three Guineas* illuminates this hidden and sacralized violence by telling the story from the perspective of its "stereotypical victim." The female body marks woman as the scapegoat for a society of men that, by "veiling" (or subordinating) her in a modern analogue to menstrual taboos, gains a monopoly of England's public sphere that is clearly detrimental to the female sex.[20] This scapegoat psychology, Woolf argues, not only accounts for women's subordinate socioeconomic position but drives the immediate social crises in Germany, Spain, and Italy. As the Gospels

tell a story of scapegoating from the victim's perspective to enable humanity to move beyond superstition and persecution toward reason and justice, Woolf's veiled woman uses the "sacred coin" of her free public
speech to illuminate scapegoat psychology within England, Europe, and,
not least, the self.

Violence and the Sacred in the War at Home

In attributing Englishwomen's exclusion from and subordination in the
public sphere to the same scapegoat psychology that was fueling Europe's
civil violence and its rising dictatorships, *Three Guineas* points to similar
structures and dynamics at work in these very different instances of collective violence.[21] On the strength of this analysis Woolf appeals for a
mutual recognition of vulnerability that would ally all victims of persecution in the fight against any and all such barbarity. You too, she tells the
English gentleman, now witness tyrants "making distinctions not merely
between the sexes, but between the races. . . . Now you are being shut out
. . . because you are Jews, because you are democrats, because of race,
because of religion. . . . The whole iniquity of dictatorship, whether . . .
against Jews or against women, in England, or in Germany, in Italy or in
Spain is now apparent to you" (*TG* 157). Her countryman's own vulnerability to tyranny and collective violence will, she hopes, enable him to
perceive the scapegoat mechanism that structures the whole panoply of
contemporary European social tyrannies and to join the fight against all.[22]

In Bloomsbury's vanguard spirit, Woolf affirms the principle that to
fight one form of tyranny is to fight them all. As we saw in chapter 1, she
points out that those nineteenth-century activists misleadingly labeled
"feminists" were doing so from the start, as Josephine Butler's words
attest: " 'Our claim was no claim of women's rights only; . . . it was a
claim for the rights of all—all men and women—to the respect in their
persons of the great principles of Justice and Equality and Liberty' " (*TG*
155). "The daughters of educated men who were called, to their resentment, 'feminists,' " Woolf tells her correspondent, "were in fact the
advance guard of your own movement" (*TG* 156). Woolf's military rhetoric frames the women's movement as a war at home, fought for the very
rights and freedoms at stake in the contemporary fight against European
fascism and Nazism, and makes women's battles for freedoms denied
them on the ground of their sex a paradigm for all such wars. In barring
women from full and free participation in public life, from its schools and
professions to its Stock Exchange, Parliament, and Church, the men of
England (like those of Germany, Spain, and Italy) in effect institute a mod-

ern equivalent of the menstrual taboo. Further, they have repeatedly banded together to enforce that taboo by violence, waging what *Three Guineas* describes as a civil war of "professional men *v.* their sisters and daughters," with its many local skirmishes: "the battle of Westminster," the fight waged with "fury and brutality" against women's suffrage; "the battle of Harley Street," the fight to keep women out of the medical profession; "the battle of equal pay for equal work"; "the battle of the Royal Academy"; "the battle of the Degree" at Cambridge (*TG* 96–97, 247–48 n. 17). Men's insistence on their prerogatives at women's expense, Woolf concludes, springs from "an emotion . . . of the utmost violence," which sometimes inflicts "flesh wounds" (as in the suffrage battles), always "timeshed" and "spiritshed" (*TG* 212, 247 n. 17, 97).

Three Guineas characterizes this war between the sexes as a holy war in which men fight to defend their sacred taboo against women's freedom, women to dismantle it. "Nothing," writes Woolf, "would induce the authorities encamped within the sacred gates [of the universities, the professions, the Church] to allow the women to enter" (*TG* 99). "Society it seems was a father," who, claiming that God, nature, law, and property were on his side, battled ferociously to keep daughters in the functional role of unacknowledged scapegoat for a public sphere appropriated by men (*TG* 206). The scapegoat economy is manifest in men's violent resistance to opening education and the professions to women, acted out on women who managed to breach those sacred gates or create alternative gates of their own.[23] Thus in the 1869 "battle of Harley Street," two hundred medical students attacked the first women students of the Royal College of Surgeons at Edinburgh: they "howled and sang songs," slammed the gate in their faces, and disrupted instruction by introducing a sheep into the lecture room, as if dramatizing their determination to keep women in the scapegoat role.[24] In "the battle of the Degree," Cambridge undergraduates—beneficiaries of "the finest education in the world"—overwhelmingly defeated the proposal that women who had passed the same examinations as the men might use the letters "B.A." to enhance their prospects of employment, and then "proceeded to Newnham and damaged the bronze gates which had been put up as a memorial to Miss Clough, the first Principal" (*TG* 43). In 1937 Cambridge still refused women students and faculty the status of members of the university and limited the number of women students by quotas: not more than five hundred women could study there in 1934–35, as against more than five thousand male undergraduates, subject to no quota (*TG* 234 n. 26).

If men's defense of their sacred gates channels against women aggression that might otherwise erupt among themselves, thereby strengthening the male community, such barbarity, Woolf observes, makes it seem "as if there were no progress in the human race, but only repetition" (*TG* 100). The "old and rich" universities teach domination and acquisition, not "human intercourse," "the art of understanding other people's lives and minds." Their "barriers of wealth and ceremony, of advertisement and competition," make them "uneasy dwelling-places—cities of strife" where "nobody can walk freely or talk freely for fear of transgressing some chalk mark, of displeasing some dignitary" (*TG* 50). The churches, far from offering women refuge from this cultural violence, perpetuate and indeed sacralize it: barred from the ministry (literally sub-ordinated) for almost two thousand years, women were also told that their desire for learning "was against the will of God" and denied "many innocent freedoms, innocent delights, . . . in the same Name."[25] The civil professions secularize this tyranny: in the 1930s the British civil service excluded women employees from the better jobs in practice if not in theory and dictated terms for their private lives, requiring them to "resign on marriage" yet prohibiting them from "cohabiting openly with men" (*TG* 246 n. 14).

Woolf's veiled woman questions whether professional life, which seems to encourage competitive greed, can be called civilized at all; whether it offers spiritual, moral, and intellectual value or only the inhumane "slavery" of which Woolf cites doctors, judges, and members of parliament complaining (*TG* 108, 169). The professions that seem to promise women freedom in fact impose some "very barbarous" duties; thus a "great bishop" laments his "awful mind- and soul-destroying life" (*TG* 106, 169). Yet traditional marriage and the duties of the private house offer no civilized refuge from the barbarity and tyranny of the masculine public sphere. Since wives have only a "spiritual and nominal share" in their husbands' incomes, "if he is in favour of force, she too will be in favour of force" (*TG* 87). In "the patriarchal system," the woman on the bridge observes, women stand less between "the old world and the new" than "between the devil and the deep sea": "the private house, with its nullity, its immorality, its hypocrisy, its servility" and "the public world, the professional system, with its possessiveness, its jealousy, its pugnacity, its greed" (*TG* 23, 113).

Woolf marvels at "how much criticism is still bestowed upon women" "even at a time of great political stress" like the nineteen-thirties and speculates, "the need for a scapegoat is largely responsible, and the role is traditionally a woman's. (See Genesis)" (*TG* 260 n. 41). Her exhibits of male contemporaries who blame the war on women include C. E. M. Joad, who recommends that women, having proven incapable of saving men from themselves by preventing war, return to the kitchen:

"Before the war money poured into the coffers of the W.S.P.U. in order that women might win the vote which, it was hoped, would enable them to make war a thing of the past. The vote is won . . . but war is very far from being a thing of the past. . . . Is it unreasonable . . . to ask that contemporary women should be prepared to give as much energy and money, to suffer as much obloquy and insult in the cause of peace, as their mothers gave and suffered in the cause of equality? . . . If it is, then the sooner they give up the pretence of playing with public affairs and return to private life the better. If they cannot make a job of the House of Commons, let them at least make something of their own houses. If they cannot learn to save men from the destruction which incurable male mischievousness bids fair to bring upon them, let women at least learn to feed them, before they destroy themselves." (*TG* 64–65)

Wondering how "even with a vote" women are expected to cure the masculine violence that "Mr. Joad himself admits to be incurable," Woolf moves on to H. G. Wells's complaint of women's failure to vanquish fascism: "There has been no perceptible woman's movement to resist the practical obliteration of their freedom by Fascists or Nazis"; and Cyril Chaventry's broad denunciation of women for not using their "indisputably different" values to improve the civilization that men have built (*TG* 65, 111). Though "a woman is at a disadvantage and under suspicion when in competition in a man-created sphere of activity," Chaventry writes, "today women have the opportunity to build a new and better world, but in this slavish imitation of men they are wasting their chance" (*TG* 111). Chaventry, Woolf drily observes, suggests that even "the enormous professional competence of the educated man has not brought about an altogether desirable state of things in the civilized world," since "those who have built that world are dissatisfied with the results." Yet, she marvels, if men "believe that, 'at a disadvantage and under suspicion' as she is, with little or no professional training and upon a salary of £250 a year [as against the archbishop's £15,000, the judge's £5000, the permanent secretary's £3000], the professional woman can yet 'build a new and better world,' they must credit her with powers that might almost be called divine" (*TG* 112). Woolf's irony suggests that it is anything but a contradiction that men should attribute "divine" powers to the women they scapegoat. As Girard observes, the scapegoat is sacralized precisely because it is the agent of community; it is holy because it was first accursed, deified because it was first crucified, and its function is all the more exigent in times of social crisis.[26]

Rather than despair that no civilized public world of peace and freedom exists, the veiled woman asks her women correspondents, "how can we enter the professions and yet remain civilized human beings . . . who wish to prevent war?" (*TG* 114). This question opens her argument that professional women can help humanity advance from barbarity to civilization by refusing to exchange the victim's role for the persecutor's on entering the professions, thereby undermining the scapegoat economy of public life. Taking seriously both the risk that women will fall in with those values (exchange the scapegoat's role for the scapegoater's) and Chaventry's hope that professional women might reform the public sphere through their historically different perspective and values, Woolf spends her three guineas: the first for a "new college" that would teach the arts not "of dominating other people; . . . of ruling, of killing, of acquiring land and capital" but "of human intercourse"; the second to help women enter and reform the professions; the third to support the English gentleman's society for the prevention of war (*TG* 50). Fearing that "in another century or so if we practise the professions in the same way," women will "be just as possessive, just as jealous, just as pugnacious, just as positive as to the verdict of God, Nature, Law, and Property as these gentlemen are now," Woolf attaches two strings to the second guinea, aimed at subverting scapegoat psychology and ending the holy wars waged to keep others, whether defined by sex, class, race or ethnicity, outside the professions.[27] First, "You shall swear that you will do all in your power to insist that any woman who enters any profession shall in no way hinder any other human being, whether man or woman, white or black, provided that he or she is qualified to enter that profession, from entering it; but shall do all in her power to help them" (*TG* 101). Second, putting aside any claim that women are "by nature" more disinterested and less violent than their brothers, Woolf urges professional women to adapt the values fostered by their different socialization to transform the public world.[28]

Woolf names the four "great teacher[s]" women's economic and political subordination has provided them: poverty (enough money to live in health and independence, not wealth for its own sake); chastity (not the physical chastity enforced for centuries by the patriarchal marriage system but resistance to the seductions of money); derision (the practice of a profession not for prizes and glory but for love of the work); and "freedom from unreal loyalties" to "old schools, old colleges, old churches, old ceremonies, old countries" and from "pride of nationality," family and sex.[29] By combining these values with "some wealth, some knowledge, and some service to real loyalties," Woolf writes, women can use the professions

> to have a mind of your own and a will of your own. And you can use
> that mind and will to abolish the inhumanity, the beastliness, the horror,

the folly of war. . . . [L]et the daughters of uneducated women dance round the new house, the poor house . . . in a narrow street [and] sing, "We have done with war! We have done with tyranny!" And their mothers will laugh from their graves, " . . . Light up the windows of the new house, daughters! Let them blaze!" (*TG* 121, 126–27)

This apocalyptic flight suggests that Woolf's prophecy that "We who now agitate these humble pens may in another century or two speak from a pulpit [as] mouthpieces of the divine spirit" might be coming true before its time (*TG* 93). Writing of Girard, Sandor Goodhart defines "the notion of the prophetic" as "elaborat[ing] for us the total picture of our implication in human violence, showing us where it has come from and where it is leading us, in order that we may give it up."[30] In this sense *Three Guineas* anticipates the Gospel according to Girard. One feature of a prophetic text is, Girard suggests, its transformation of scapegoating from a structural principle (a scapegoating that enables the text to exist) to a theme (a demystification of the scapegoat mechanism). *Three Guineas'* thematic treatment of scapegoat psychology and its strategic evacuation of the scapegoat position—its explicit refusals to substitute new scapegoats for old—make it a prophetic text in this respect, as does Woolf's exhortation to women not simply to join the public sphere but to use the "sacred coin" of their newly earned freedom of speech to renounce complicity with an aggressively patriarchal state, religion, and empire and to fight for "the rights of all."[31]

In *Three Guineas* not even the warrior, the dictator, the tyrant is a scapegoat; for, Woolf tells us, we are the warrior. Describing a photograph that displays a "figure of a man," his eyes glazed and glaring, his uniformed body covered with "several medals and other mystic symbols," his hand on a sword; a figure "called in German and Italian Führer or Duce; in our own language Tyrant or Dictator," against a background of "ruined houses and dead bodies—men, women and children," she writes:

we have not laid that picture before you in order to excite once more the sterile emotion of hate. On the contrary it is in order to release other emotions such as the human figure . . . arouses in us. . . . For it suggests . . . that the public and the private worlds are inseparably connected; that the tyrannies and servilities of the one are the tyrannies and servilities of the other . . . that we cannot dissociate ourselves from that figure but are ourselves that figure . . . that we are not passive spectators doomed to unresisting obedience but by our thoughts and actions can ourselves change that figure. A common interest unites us; it is one world, one life. How essential it is that we should realise that unity the dead bodies, the ruined houses prove. For such will be our ruin if you in the immensity of your public abstractions forget the private figure, or if we in the intensity of our private emotions forget the public world. Both houses will be ruined, the public and the private, the material and the spiritual, for they are inseparably connected.[32]

Woolf follows this picture of the warrior as "ourselves" with examples of women using free speech to challenge tyranny and transform this figure within their own communities, from Sophocles' Antigone challenging Creon's barbaric decree to such latter-day, street-theater Antigones as the English suffragist Emmeline Pankhurst, who, when women's speech fell on deaf ears, "broke a window and was imprisoned in Holloway," and Germany's Frau Pommer, who had been arrested by the Nazis and faced trial for slander for saying, " 'The thorn of hatred has been driven deep enough into the people by the religious conflicts, and it is high time that the men of today disappeared' " (TG 258 n. 39).

As we saw in chapter 1, Woolf aims her own free speech at transforming the warrior who is ourselves by offering to lay down arms in the battle of the sexes. Proposing to the English gentleman that they abandon "the old ceremonies" and "invent a new ceremony for this new occasion" of the veiled woman issuing into the public world, she suggests that they burn "an old word, a vicious and corrupt word that has done much harm in its day and is now obsolete": "feminist" (TG 154). This word, she observes, has been used to divide women and men and to obscure the fact that women have been fighting for full human and civil rights not just for themselves but, as Butler emphasized, for all. Insofar as it belies the revolutionary force of the women's movement by misrepresenting it as an exclusionary society of women founded on the scapegoating of men and other "others," it is a false and "vicious" word. When the smoke dies down, Woolf tells her correspondent, there will appear "men and women working together for the same cause," "fighting side by side" against all tyrannies, all barbarity (TG 155, 157).

Woolf deepens her insight that the warrior is "ourselves," hence that we can and must change that figure from within, in proposing that she and her correspondent also burn the words "tyrant" and "dictator," the complements of "feminist" (TG 156). This ceremonial sacrifice would enable men and women to reposition themselves, no longer opposing each other but fighting side by side, not against outsiders as embodiments and personifications of evil but against tyranny and collective violence wherever they occur—against the tyranny and violence within that make the warrior "ourselves" (Whitehall, St. Paul's, Cambridge, the civil service) no less than such external threats to peace and freedom as Franco, Hitler, Mussolini, Stalin. Even as she acknowledges that the words *tyrant, dictator,* and *feminist* are "not yet obsolete," Woolf, in her radical refusal to obscure the violence within the self and the community by focusing solely on external antagonists, invents a thought experiment that enacts a rejection of scapegoat psychology; a ritual renunciation of the sacrificial barbarism that underlies every "document of civilization," every human society.[33]

But even as she figures herself fighting beside rather than against her public brother and sends him a guinea—"given without fear, without flattery, without conditions"—in support of their common cause, Woolf declines to join his society precisely on the grounds that the words *tyrant* and *dictator* are not yet obsolete (*TG* 154). Societies, she notes, seem to be inherently barbarous, generating by their very existence a boundary that distinguishes insiders from outsiders and at least potentially functions to channel aggression against outsiders. Given the long history of public fathers' and brothers' tyrannical injunctions against their daughters and sisters ("You shall not learn; you shall not earn; you shall not own"), women must wonder whether there is not

> something in the conglomeration of people into societies that releases what is most selfish and violent, least rational and humane in the individuals themselves? Inevitably we look upon society, so kind to you, so harsh to us, as an ill-fitting form that distorts the truth; deforms the mind; fetters the will. Inevitably we look upon societies as conspiracies that sink the private brother, whom many of us have reason to respect, and inflate in his stead a monstrous male, loud of voice, hard of fist, childishly intent upon scoring the . . . earth with chalk marks, within whose mystic boundaries human beings are penned, rigidly, separately, artificially; where, daubed red and gold, decorated like a savage with feathers he goes through mystic rites and enjoys the dubious pleasures of power and dominion while we, "his" women, are locked in the private house without share in the many societies of which his society is composed. (*TG* 160)

So lately excluded herself, the veiled woman cannot "join your society" and "merge our identity in yours" without fearing to deepen "the old worn ruts" that lead to collective violence in modern societies hardly less (perhaps more) than in Frazer's "savage" cultures (*TG* 161). Nor can she uncritically join the many other "societies of which his society is composed," each defined by such "chalk marks" as divide nations, races, classes, religions, schools, and professions (ibid.). Since history teaches that women who propose to enter their brothers' societies "invite a shower of dead cats, rotten eggs, and broken gates," she will help to prevent war by remaining an Outsider (*TG* 134). Accepting the duties and risks along with the privileges of free speech, and experimenting toward a "new civilisation" founded on the subversion of the scapegoat mechanism, "the outsider will say, 'in fact, as a woman I have no country. As a woman I want no country. As a woman my country is the whole world' " (*TG* 166). As long as there are insiders and outsiders, she will stand with the outsiders, her patriotism taking form, in the spirit of Bloomsbury internationalism, as the desire "to give to England first what she desires of peace and freedom for the whole world" (ibid.).

The Outsiders' Society: Women Un/Veiled, Re-ligion Unbound

If every document of civilization is a document of barbarism, is it possible to imagine a civilization not founded on barbarism? Can the veiled woman use her "sacred coin" to unbind religion from scapegoating—to found, in the broadest sense, a revolutionary society? Does the Outsider's unexpected alliance with the Gospels pose a genuine challenge to the scapegoating ideology of England's Church and secular society, or does Woolf's ambition "to blow up St. Pauls," so to speak, not implicate her in the sacrificial violence she analyzes?

How, for example, can the oxymoronic Society of Outsiders offer a genuine alternative to existing antiwar societies when Woolf herself conjures "chalk marks" of sex and class in describing its members as "educated men's daughters working in their own class . . . and by their own methods for liberty, equality, and peace" (*TG* 162)? This, she asserts, they can do "much more effectively" as outsiders than by acting as "playboys and playgirls of the educated class who adopt the working-class cause without sacrificing middle-class capital, or sharing working-class experience" (*TG* 269 n. 13). If Woolf judges the middle-class fantasy of joining forces with the working class without giving up economic and social privilege hypocritical and escapist, her own proposal would seem not only to preserve class boundaries but to contravene both the spirit of the second guinea's condition that professional women help all other qualified aspirants to make their way and her scenario of fighting tyranny "side by side" with her public brothers.

On the other hand, since the "elastic," experimental Outsiders' Society has no dues, administration, or formal membership, it is in fact open to anyone; and since its members oppose collective aggression and affirm "equality" and "the rights of all," its sex and class criteria seem pragmatic rather than exclusionary in spirit. Woolf defends the necessity of this "clumsy term" "the daughters of educated men" for "the class whose fathers have been educated at public schools and universities": "Obviously, if the term 'bourgeois' fits her brother, it is grossly incorrect to use it of one who differs so profoundly in the two prime characteristics of the bourgeoisie—capital and environment" (*TG* 223 n. 2). If economic independence is a necessary precondition for the experimental work against barbarism and war for which women's experience as scapegoats especially prepares them, then it is professional women who can best afford to use their emerging social power to fight tyranny and collective violence. So, at least, Woolf was understood by the leftist writer and journalist Naomi Mitchison, who responded as one of the "250 'daughters' who are in such an economic position that they can answer your appeal."[34]

Yet even as she acts pragmatically within her own class position by urging "daughters of educated men" to think and act as outsiders—not excluding working-class women but recognizing that they can ill afford the Outsider's work—Woolf offers a critique that women in other class positions can adapt to their circumstances and ends. Agnes Smith, an unemployed textile worker (who received "two shillings less than her unemployed brother") and unsuccessful Labour candidate for the local council, admired *Three Guineas* but objected that Woolf wrote "only of and for the 'daughters of educated men,' when the problems with which you deal are those of the working woman also."[35] Smith wished to "help in making woman what she is yet far from being—a free citizen" and agreed that what Woolf calls the " 'infantile fixation' suffered by men prevents women from being a free citizen, and so retards civilisation" (99). But she pointed out the impracticability of Woolf's suggestion that working women might refuse work at munitions factories: "A working woman who refuses to work will starve—and there is nothing like stark hunger for blasting ideals" (99). Smith proposed to write "a similar book from the working woman's point of view" but wistfully remarked that the working woman lacks Woolf's "economic freedom" and her "access to books," stimulating "conversation, and living, with people who know how to follow a line of thought, and work out its implications" (99). Woolf encouraged Smith in this project and suggested that Smith send it to the Hogarth Press; Smith's *A Worker's View of the Wool Textile Industry* was published in 1944 by Hillcroft Studies (99).

Although Woolf declines to speak for working-class women and conceives Outsiders as educated men's daughters, *Three Guineas* envisions all women as an emerging economically independent collective that might conceivably exert diffuse social power against barbarism, tyranny, and war.[36] To increase the numbers of women who possess "a mind . . . and a will of their own with which to help you to prevent war," she tells the English gentleman, requires both helping women enter the professions and campaigning for wages for childcare and housework (*TG* 88). In arguing for the need to transform the unpaid domestic labor of women of all classes into paid work, Woolf conceives women not as a distinct economic class but as achieving economic equality with men across classes. If this argument does not directly propose to eliminate class differences, it neither precludes nor conflicts with Bloomsbury's democratic-socialist critique of class and war, suggested in the outsider's efforts to dissent from the "disastrous unanimity" of human nature's "old tune": "Here we go round the mulberry tree, . . . give it all to me, all to me. Three hundred millions spent upon war" (*TG* 89).

As the socioeconomic construction of the family is the linchpin of women's economic dependence, its reform is the key to any hope of women's collective power to fight tyranny and war. This project drives Woolf's critique of St. Paul and the Church, exemplary proponents of a state religion and public ideology founded on the scapegoating of the female body. Ranking the clergy as the "highest" profession, Woolf points to the Church's powerful authority in sustaining the scapegoat psychology of secular public culture (*TG* 184). To reform the Church would undo not only its own sub-ordination of women but its influence in women's exclusion from public life. To that end, Woolf urges Outsiders to "make it their business to have some knowledge of the Christian religion and its history" by attending services, analyzing sermons, and freely criticizing the clergy's opinions; to seek to "free the religious spirit from its present servitude" and, "if need be, to create a new religion" that would renounce this foundational scapegoating of the female body (*TG* 172).

Woolf finds expert authority for this critique in the appendix of the 1935 *Report of the Archbishops' Commission on the Ministry of Women* by L. W. Grensted, Professor of the Philosophy of the Christian Religion at Oxford. Dissenting from the *Report*'s general recommendation that the Church continue to bar women from the ministry, Grensted argues that this policy has no rational or theological ground but is an irrational holdover of infantile anxiety about the female body.[37] He attributes the Church authorities' "non-rational sex-taboo" against women's public authority to an unconscious "infantile fixation": "subconscious . . . infantile conceptions" that "betray their presence, below the level of conscious thought, by the strength of the emotions to which they give rise," such as the idea that woman is "man manque" or that admitting women to Holy Orders would be "shameful" (*TG* 191). Grensted finds "ample evidence of these unconscious forces" in various earlier mythologies; but because "the Christian conception of the priesthood rests not upon these subconscious emotional factors, but upon the institution of Christ, . . . there is

no theoretical reason why this Christian priesthood should not be exercised by women as well as by men and in exactly the same sense" (*TG*
193). The Gospel according to Grensted abandons the foundational
scapegoating of women depicted in some earlier mythologies and offers a
basis for founding a new society on the renunciation of scapegoating.

Emerging from behind the veil of Grensted's authority (itself "veiled,"
or relegated to the *Report*'s appendix), Woolf proposes that, in their common interest of preventing war, she and the English gentleman "grope our
way amateurishly enough among these very ancient and obscure emotions
which we have known ever since the time of Antigone and Ismene and
Creon at least; which St. Paul himself seems to have felt; but which the
Professors have only lately brought to the surface and named 'infantile
fixation,' 'Oedipus complex,' and the rest" (*TG* 198). To unpack Grensted's diagnosis, she returns to the mixed-sex dinner conversation she has
earlier invoked as evidence that she, earning her own living, can speak
freely and that her "civilized" correspondent "can stand free speech in
women." But now she judges that assumption premature. Educated men
and women may "meet privately and talk, as we have boasted, about 'politics and people, war and peace, barbarism and civilization,' " she tells the
English gentleman, "yet they evade and conceal" whenever such questions as "admitting, shall we say, the daughters of educated men to the
Church or to the Stock Exchange or the diplomatic service" arise (*TG*
183, 196). The dominance/submission model of heterosexual relations
prevails over reason. The women sense "some 'strong emotion' on your
side 'arising from some motive below the level of conscious thought' "
and respond by "a strong desire either to be silent; or to change the conversation; to drag in, for example, some old family servant, called Crosby,
perhaps, whose dog Rover has died . . . and so evade the issue and lower
the temperature" (*TG* 196–97).

As Grace Radin points out, Woolf alludes here to her own silences and
evasions in *The Years*' chapter "1913"—for her, a year of terrible suffering and attempted suicide, which the novel does not transpose into the fictional life of Elvira/Sara but deflects into Crosby's story.[38] Now Woolf
removes the muffling "veil" to put on the table the hidden barbarity that
founds the civilization she is asked to help defend and to envision what it
might mean to "live differently." First she attempts "to analyse both our
fear and your anger," the strong emotions that compel such evasions, by
considering the battles between three irrationally angry, quasi-incestuous
Victorian fathers and their rational, desiring daughters: Sophia Jex-Blake,
Elizabeth Barrett, and Charlotte Brontë (*TG* 197). Such private fathers
ultimately "had to yield" before their daughters' more powerful desire to

pursue knowledge, experience, "an open and rational love," "a rational existence without love"; "to travel; to explore Africa; to dig in Greece and Palestine," "to compose—operas, symphonies, quartets," "to paint . . . naked bodies"; before the whole "variety of the things that they wanted, and had wanted, consciously or subconsciously, for so long" (*TG* 210–11). So too must tyrannical public fathers eventually yield, Woolf predicts, framing her Victorian case studies within a vision of women's historical progress toward a rational and humane law to supersede the male dominance/female submission model of heterosexual relations. As the characters of *The Years* discuss "the psychology of great men . . . [b]y the light of modern science" in hope of discovering "how [to] make religions, laws . . . that fit—that fit," *Three Guineas* makes Antigone the epitome of the daughters' struggle to conquer irrational paternal force by reason and the emblem of women's desire "not to break the laws, but to find the law."[39]

It is finally the very irrationality of the subconscious hostility to women's freedom that leads Woolf to project a future in which men and women might speak freely together, an emancipatory history that belongs to the Enlightenment project for "the rights of all." Far from capitulating to domination, *Three Guineas* is a strong defense of the daughters' desire for freedom in all its forms.[40] In search of a rational law to replace the rule of shame, anger, and fear aroused by women's desire to participate in the public world, Woolf takes the Pauline veil as a figure of the chastity enjoined upon women in patriarchal cultures. She interprets the "Victorian, Edwardian and much of the Fifth Georgian conception of chastity," whose "skeleton fingers can be found upon whatever page of history we open from St. Paul to Gertrude Bell," and its obverse, shame, as an irrational barrier to women's public speech that institutes and perpetuates male control of female sexuality and reproduction (*TG* 252–58 n. 38).

In her longest footnote, Woolf analyzes Pauline chastity as "a complex conception, based upon the love of long hair; the love of subjection; the love of an audience; the love of laying down the law, and, subconsciously, upon a very strong and natural desire that the woman's mind and body shall be reserved for the use of one man and one only"; an ideology "supported by the Angels, nature, law, custom and the Church, and enforced by a sex with a strong personal interest to enforce it, and the economic means" (*TG* 255 n. 38). Interpreting chastity as a strategy for reserving a "woman's mind and body" for one man, Woolf counters Paul's strongly emotional, extravagantly incoherent argument:

> (For man was not made from woman, but woman from man. Neither was man created for woman, but woman for man). That is why a

woman ought to have a veil upon her head, because of the angels. (Nevertheless, in the Lord woman is not independent of man nor man of woman; for as woman was made from man, so man is now born of woman. And all things are from God.) Judge for yourselves; is it proper for a woman to pray to God with her head uncovered? Does not nature itself teach you that for a man to wear long hair is degrading to him, but if a woman has long hair, it is her pride? For her hair is given to her as a covering. If any one is disposed to be contentious, we recognize no other practice, nor do the churches of God.[41]

From "internal evidence" Woolf concludes that Paul "was a poet and a prophet, but lacked logical power, and was without that psychological training which forces even the least poetic or prophetic nowadays to subject their personal emotions to scrutiny," even as her focus on chastity finds the hidden logic of his text in his irrational fear of women's maternal power.[42] In her analysis, Paul's veil of chastity effects a cultural transformation of biological sexual difference into gender hierarchy and sexually grounded victimage. The veil signals the control of female sexuality by a masculinized public sphere, a gender barrier that fuels the civil war between the sexes on all fronts of British public life.

Woolf's illustrations of Grensted's infantile fixation chart a re-ligion of which St. Paul is but one apologist; a transhistorical and transcultural society encompassing secular and sacred authorities, "infected" mothers who zealously guard their daughters' chastity and irrational fathers, Greek, Roman, and English, as well as German, Spanish, and Italian (TG 206). To exemplify the state as a public father "afflicted" with this irrational anxiety and the scapegoating it engenders, Woolf paints Sophocles's Creon as

> an infant crying in . . . the black night that now covers Europe, and with no language but a cry, Ay, ay, ay, ay. . . . But it is not a new cry, it is a very old cry. . . . We are in Greece now; Christ has not been born yet, nor St. Paul either. But listen: . . . "We must support the cause of order, and in no wise suffer a woman to worst us. . . . They must be women, and not range at large." (TG 206, 215)

In modern England, scientists resort to the same illogic as Creon and St. Paul, displacing anxiety about women's sexuality upward to their brains in an effort to justify the "aggravated and exacerbated emotion to which the name sex taboo is scientifically applied." Here Woolf enlists the support of her Bloomsbury friend Bertrand Russell: "Anyone . . . who desires amusement may be advised to look up the tergiversations of eminent craniologists in their attempts to prove from brain measurements that women are stupider than men" (TG 212). Woolf comments:

> Science, it would seem, . . . is a man, a father, and infected too. . . . Many
> years were spent waiting before the sacred gates of the universities and
> hospitals for permission to have the brains that the professors said that
> Nature had made incapable of passing examinations examined. When at
> last permission was granted the examinations were passed. . . . Still
> Nature held out. The brain that could pass examinations was not the
> creative brain . . . that can bear responsibilities and earn the higher
> salaries. . . . [M]oreover, whatever the brain might do . . . , the body
> remained. . . . [T]he priests and professors . . . intoned: But childbirth
> itself . . . is laid upon woman alone. (*TG* 212–13)

Decoding anxiety about the maternal body as the buried emotion that
bends Paul's epistle and many other ancient and modern social scripts out
of logic, Woolf exposes an ideology far broader than the Church, one that
binds the sacred and secular professions into a common re-ligion. This
religion, or ideology, allays the "infantile fixation" by constructing
women as mothers within a feminized "lifeworld," as Habermas names
it, dominated economically and socially by a masculinized state.[43] By laying responsibility for privatized, unpaid childcare primarily upon women,
this system regularly reproduces the infantile fixation in its sons and
daughters, driving the vicious circle that links the scapegoating of women
to tyranny and war.[44]

Having analyzed unconscious anxiety about the maternal body as the
root of men's hostility toward admitting women into "it matters not . . .
which priesthood; the priesthood of medicine or the priesthood of science
or the priesthood of the Church"; and having argued that this originary
scapegoating is both paradigmatic and foundational ("the role is traditionally a woman's"), Woolf now envisions how women's unveiling could
lead to a revolutionary society *not* founded on a scapegoating at its heart
(*TG* 194, 260 n. 41). Her analysis leads to an effort to demystify and de-
essentialize the maternal role; to debunk what she elsewhere calls "the religion & superstition of motherhood," the other side of Paul's essentializing
sacred coin (*D* 4:264, 27 November 1934). To change the psychology that
leads from the maternal body to war, Woolf observes, women could, like
Lysistrata, refuse to bear the children who will be conscripted into a tyrannical, war-making society; refuse to play the scapegoat/mother without
whom "the State would collapse."[45] Better, women and men could under-
take to integrate the state with the lifeworld, sharing equally in both.
Since, under "modern conditions," "even a woman who has six children
is only necessarily laid up for twelve months out of her whole lifetime";
and since giving birth did not "incapacitate us from working in Whitehall,
in fields and factories, when our country was in danger," nothing need pre-

vent women from bearing children and taking part in public life—particularly if the "bold suggestion" that childcare "should be shared by both parents" were implemented, as illustrated by a member of parliament who "has resigned in order to be with his children" (*TG* 214, 282–83 n. 47).

To integrate the lifeworld with the state would be to refigure the body politic no longer as an arena of male *pubes* but as a two-sexed, parental body. In such a society, women and men would make new terms not only for motherhood (as paid labor within the state economy) but, more radically, for both the professions and parenthood, dissolving the gender barrier between the private and public spheres to enrich the lives of both sexes. "If the State paid your wife a living wage for her work which, sacred though it is, can scarcely be called more sacred than that of the [paid] clergyman," Woolf tells the English gentleman, "your own slavery would be lightened. . . . You could see the fruit trees flower [and] share the prime of life with your children. . . . the opportunity of freedom would be yours" (*TG* 169–70). And if men and women dismantled the division of labor by gender, "the half-man" and half-woman "might become whole" and relatively free: men could see "the pageant of the blossom" and share their children's upbringing; women would no longer be consumed by unpaid, unrecognized domestic labor but, without forfeiting family or neglecting children, could share the work, struggles, governance, and self-representation of the public world (*TG* 170, 107). With that economic and social integration, sexual hierarchy within the family would break down. Heterosexual relations would shift from the economically based dominance/submission model that characterized the Victorian prostitution/marriage continuum to the free (as opposed to paid) love that began to make "the oldest profession in the world (but Whitaker supplies no figures) unprofitable" when women's desire to participate fully in public life began winning out over men's efforts to privatize and own them.[46] Abandoning the most ancient, primal, and pervasive form of scapegoating, the new cooperative models of heterosexuality, the family, and the state would further peace not war.

To abolish the sacrificial foundations of the gender-marked division between private house and public world, *Three Guineas* proposes, would be to found a new civilization, one that would bind men and women to fight not only tyrants outside its borders but the tyranny within; one that would call the boundaries and borders of nation, empire, race, sex, and class into question by emphasizing a "unity that rubs out divisions as if they were chalk marks only"; a re-ligion, a society, that would enable men and women to live, as well as to fight tyranny, "side by side" (*TG* 218, 157). Framed not as a utopian fantasy but in the larger terms of humanity's slow advance from "the old world" to "the new," from magical thinking to reason and justice, this prospect indirectly fulfills Woolf's initial plan to track the changing "sexual life of women" through a historical novel about "a family called Pargiter, from the year 1800 to the year 2032," exposing institutionalized socioeconomic violence against women as one crucial key to the censorship, self-censorship, and repression that sustain "half-civilized barbarism" (P 8–9, CS 127). Woolf's Outsider spends her three sacred coins to further what is ultimately a single cause: to dissociate the idea of the sacred from collective violence and to dedicate economic and social power to the fight against scapegoating and tyranny as such. To the extent that money is intrinsically worthless—made of paper or debased metal—it is of course pure social credit, a form of belief that in some ways functions analogously to religious belief. In seeking to weight the coins women can now freely possess with a specific social value, to figure women's economic power as the currency of a "new [world]" founded on the renunciation of collective violence, Woolf seeks to reform the "priesthoods" of the public sphere by changing the belief, the social authority, that money mediates.

Although Woolf exposes St. Paul's mystification of male socioeconomic privilege, she does not throw out the baby with the bathwater. In rejecting "the arrogance and monopoly of Christianity" but affirming the Gospels as an exemplary challenge to scapegoat psychology, the a/gnostic Woolf aligns a heterogeneous (St. Paul v. the Gospels) New Testament with her critique of modern England's social system and the unconscious scapegoat psychology that implicates it in the fascist violence it consciously opposes (L 4:83, 25 August 1929). Like the protagonist of the Gospels, Woolf's un/veiled woman transcends the scapegoat role by exposing the arbitrariness and futility of collective violence. In keeping with Girard's view of the progress the Gospel revelation makes possible, she seeks a new "law" for a new society—a rational law, a "science of justice," purged of arbitrary violence through a collective transformation of unconscious aggression into shared consciousness. In this light, *Three Guineas'* dinner conversation scenario sets the stage in the everyday world for that "most interesting conversation that has ever been heard" forecast in the 1931 Speech (P xliv). Like the prophecies of Pagels's gnostics, this conversation in the "sacred coin" of free speech would create the Gospels' "profound meaning" anew, not bound to its letter but free to incarnate its spirit—a spirit betrayed by a Church that, until November 1992, still cherished the scapegoating of women at its heart.[47] In this sense, Woolf's challenge to St. Paul and "St. Pauls" revives the gnostics' challenge to the Church Fathers' claim to exclusive mediation of "the religious spirit."

Although Woolf does not mention it, the archbishops' *Report* contains a second dissent, by the dean of St. Paul's, W. R. Mathews, who sets aside what he calls his own "irrational prejudice . . . against any change in the traditional order" to argue that the "whole situation has been changed by the emancipation of women, which is a tardy consequence of the working of Christian principles in civilisation."[48] The Gospels, Enlightenment philosophy, and Woolf's modern feminism-under-erasure, which advocates a critical enlargement of "the rights of man" to encompass "the rights of all," speak for shared principles in this great conversation on civilization's future, as do the *Antigone*, the Hebrew Bible narratives that Girard discusses, Mary Astell, Josephine Butler, Sophia Jex-Blake, Elizabeth Barrett, Emmeline Pankhurst, Bertrand Russell, Frau Pommer, Naomi Mitchison, Professor Grensted, and Agnes Smith—the host of voices *Three Guineas* transcribes in its analytic cross section of this most interesting and important conversation.[49]

In light of this tradition, we might weigh the familiar criticism that *Three Guineas* pays too little attention to differences among women, whether of race, class, or nation, against its striving toward communication and community across barriers and differences—a politics to which contemporary escalating nationalism, tribalism, sexual violence, tyranny, and war around the world lend an urgency not unlike that which shaped this text in 1937–38. As in *A Room of One's Own*, Woolf practices what she preaches in *Three Guineas*' very address. Backed by a critical mass of educated, professional women (who may or may not agree with her), she brings to the arena of public debate a historically muted alternative to the dominant voices of public authority, even as her epistolary persona strategically subverts her own oppositional stance.[50] Addressing a contemporary inheritor of the masculine privilege that St. Paul helped institute, Woolf attempts to speak across the differences that divide her from her correspondent and to channel those differences not into hostilities but into a vision of a shared world, founded on "the living belief" that "now is in human beings" and not any orthodox Church—a shared belief in "the capacity of the human spirit to overflow boundaries and make unity out of multiplicity" (*L* 6:50, 29 June 1936, *TG* 218). Answering St. Paul's and her male contemporary's epistles, hailing her correspondent into dialogue as a public brother bound by the logic of his own Enlightenment political rhetoric to defend "the rights of all," Woolf enters the public sphere to envision with others a civilization made new.

In one of my classes on *Three Guineas*, a student, Diana Black, remarked that she thought as she read it, "Ah, so that's where feminist theory comes from." Breaking through the unconscious evasion and fear that dogged Woolf's work on *The Years*, *Three Guineas* resonates with contemporary voices forging a new common coin for an open society through conversations on reproductive rights, comparable worth, wages for housework, state-subsidized childcare, parental leave, equal pay for equal work, affirmative action, sex discrimination, sexual harassment, sex and gender in defense and war, the ongoing battles of women and other dominated groups for human rights, economic rights, and political representation, corruptions of and threats to democratic political structures and processes, and war. Opposing itself to all tyranny and collective violence, *Three Guineas'* visionary, unbounded feminism-under-erasure paves the way for contemporary feminism's alliance politics. Packing "enough powder to blow up St Pauls" into her letter to the world, Woolf charts many of the political, economic and social challenges that still confront women and men, races, religions, classes, and nations, in the world's continuing struggle to deal with differences by conversation rather than by violence.

"For," the outsider will say, " . . . As a woman my country is the whole world." And if [there remains] some love of England dropped into a child's ears by the cawing of rooks in an elm tree, by the splash of waves on a beach, or by English voices murmuring nursery rhymes, she will make [it] serve her to give to England first what she desires of peace and freedom for the whole world.

—Woolf, *Three Guineas*

Thinking is my fighting.

—Woolf, *Diary*, 15 May 1940

Look at ourselves, ladies and gentlemen! Then at the wall; and ask how's this wall, the great wall, which we call, perhaps miscall, civilization, to be built by (here the mirrors flicked and flashed) orts, scraps and fragments like ourselves?

—Megaphonic voice, Woolf, *Between the Acts*

Ambitious, ain't it?

—Mrs. Manresa, Woolf, *Between the Acts*

NINE

The Play in the Sky of the Mind

Between the Acts of Civilization's Masterplot

 hen Woolf began *Between the Acts* (first titled *Pointz Hall*) in April 1938, the second civil war predicted by Keynes seemed imminent every day. Her wartime diary captures the impact of world events on private life during the novel's composition. Hitler arms "his million men," invades Austria, looks ready to "pounce again" (D 5:132, 162, 26 March, 17 August 1938). Stalin stages show trials; the Allies sacrifice Czechoslovakia; Hitler invades Poland; England declares war; Hitler seizes Paris. German bombs fall on London, destroying the Mecklenburgh Square house the Woolfs have just taken and the Tavistock Square house they have just vacated. Government-issue gas masks arrive. Living at Rodmell between London and the Channel, under skies crossed by British and German bombers, the Woolfs black out their windows (and are once upbraided by the village warden for a crack of light); put up friends, family, and Hogarth Press staff; stretch food rations with fruit and honey from the garden. Virginia sees a hospital train, "grieving & tender & heavy laden & private," and hears bombs fall near Sissinghurst while talking on the telephone with Vita Sackville-West (D 5:289, 30 May 1940). She distrusts the "unity of hatred" bred by war but "instinctively" wishes luck to twelve Royal Air Force planes flying south in formation (D 5:213, 306, 11 April 1939, 26 July 1940). The Woolfs throw themselves to the ground during a sudden air raid—"a peaceful matter of fact death," Virginia muses, "to be popped off on the terrace playing bowls this very fine cool sunny August evening" (D 5:313, 28 August 1940). They debate who would most mind losing the other, each wishing to die first; Virginia decides "2 birds had better be killed with one stone" and walks two steps closer to Leonard (D 5:327, 6 October 1940). The Woolfs do not know that their names number 115 and 116 on the Nazis' secret arrest list for England, but they foresee "all Jews to be given up" and, sensing that "we are being led up garlanded to the altar," stow petrol in the garage for suicide in case Hitler should invade.[1]

Without abandoning their critique of violence, the Woolfs and their circle were anything but defeatist in this seemingly "necessary" war.[2] "It seems entirely meaningless—a perfunctory slaughter, like taking a jar in one hand, a hammer in the other. Why must this be smashed? Nobody knows," Virginia writes, and: "What do I do to help?" (D 5:235, 260, 6 September 1939, 20 January 1940). She doesn't want to die (or "go to bed at midday: this refers to the garage"); she imagines opening her diary in ten years to see "what was happening to the war" (D 5:293, 343, 9 June, 8 December 1940). Ethel Smyth says, "Oh of *course* we shall fight and win" (D 5:297 and n, 20 June 1940). Churchill rallies the British over the wireless after France falls and, during the Battle of Britain, evokes "Our majestic city—&c. which touches me," Woolf adds, "for I feel London majestic. Our courage &c." (D 5:317, 11 September 1940). In the Sussex countryside she feels "How England consoles & warms one" and reports that Keynes thinks "our victory certain" (D 5:346, 24 December 1940). Amid a din of "sinister sawing" planes, whistling, thudding bombs, flames, smoke, Hitler's "violent rant" on the wireless, and English broadcasts in "the usual highflown tense voice," she longs "for a speaking voice, once in a way"; she pictures "how one's killed by a bomb" and repeats, "I dont want to die yet."[3] Their tenant Mr. Pritchard is "calm as a grig" in face of an unexploded bomb in Mecklenburgh Square: " 'They actually have the impertinence to say this will make us accept peace—!' he said" (D 5:317, 10 September 1940). She visits the ruins "where I wrote so many books" and "we . . . gave so many parties" (D 5:331, 20 October 1940).

The diary captures the persistence of everyday life in face of the war's horrors. "These are the moments . . . for living," Woolf writes, "unless one's to blow out; which I entirely refuse to do"; she longs for "10 years more, & to write my book" (D 5:260, 285, 20 January, 15 May 1940). Inverting Faust's wager with the devil—"If ever I say to the passing moment,/Linger awhile, thou art so fair,/Then! that day—let it be my last"—she hopes her diary catches the fleeting moments that make her say to life, "Stop you are so fair," and muses, "Well, all life is so fair, at my age" (D 5:352, 9 January 1941). As the "echo" of England's war-distracted reading public fades (for a writer, "part of one's death") and the dark winter that would be her last descends, Woolf vows that "This trough of despair shall not . . . engulf me"; two weeks later she wonders, "why was I depressed?"[4] Then her fighting strength ebbs, and the diary— "travellers notes which I offer myself shd I again be lost"—falls silent as she leaves it with fair life (D 5:260, 26 January 1940).

It is sometimes said that *Between the Acts* cannot be read apart from Woolf's suicide, a claim any look at the criticism must find dubious.[5] Even supposing that her suicide on 28 March 1941, a few weeks after delivering the manuscript to the Hogarth Press, is an important fact about the novel, this profoundly illegible event resists the readings we try to impose on it. In any case, Woolf's last novel can no more be reduced to a "suicide note" than can the late diary, those traveler's notes on fair life to help her keep her path amid the glooms of war. Like the diary, *Between the Acts* is an arena of fighting by thinking, the final voyage in Woolf's long quest for new lands and civilizations, and her own last stand in the eternal battle of Eros and Thanatos. Fearing that *Three Guineas* would be like "a moth dancing over a bonfire—consumed in less than one second," Woolf animates that book's radical insight into the scapegoat psychology of the sex/ gender system, war, and fascism by mobilizing the outsider La Trobe to "attack Hitler in England" through an experiment in the public art of the theater (*D* 5:142, 24 May 1938). The narrative poses her daringly experimental play against the coming war to explore relations between the characters' everyday lives and their festival roles as director, actors, audience, and hosts; "real" life and art; history and spectatorship; insular nationalism and Europe's fate and future; embodied community and the collective violence of genocide and war. Answering its spectators' longing for a "new plot" at the edge of an unknowable future, the pageant-within-a-novel conjures an intermittent *we* from disparate *I*'s (*BA* 215). Far from a pure English pastoral or a retreat from Bloomsbury internationalism to insular, war-enforced nationalism, pageant and novel dissolve national, formal, and experiential boundaries to "give to England first" what their outsider-artists desire "of peace and freedom for the whole world."[6]

Outsider Patriotism

The pageant's earliest seed already escapes the "chalk marks" scored on the earth to divide nations and creeds (*TG* 160). In the "1911" chapter of *The Years* Eleanor Pargiter visits her brother's family at Wittering during the summer fête, when the villagers act Shakespeare in the garden to raise money for the church steeple. What could be more English? But it is Dante's *Purgatorio* that Eleanor opens that evening to read: "For by so many more there are who say 'ours'/So much the more of good doth each possess."[7] Woolf's first idea of *Pointz Hall* echoes this idea:

> Let it be random & tentative; . . . dont, I implore, lay down a scheme; call in all the cosmic immensities; & force my tired & diffident brain to

embrace another whole. . . . But . . . why not Poyntzet Hall: a centre: all lit. discussed in connection with real little incongruous living humour; & anything that comes into my head; but "I" rejected: 'We' substituted: to whom at the end there shall be an invocation? "We" . . . composed of many different things . . . we all life, all art, all waifs & strays—a rambling capricious but somehow unified whole. . . . And English country; & a scenic old house—& a terrace where nursemaids walk? & people passing—& a perpetual variety & change from intensity to prose. & facts—& notes; &—but eno'. (D 5:135, 26 April 1938; last two ellipses Woolf's)

Woolf envisions not "thick little egos" (in Clive Bell's phrase) but a loose, inclusive "we" composed of "all life, all art, all waifs & strays" in a modern English pageant re-formed in the image of the outsider's patriotism.[8]

In *Between the Acts*, the pageant's author and director, with her exotic name, La Trobe, is not "presumably pure English. From the Channel islands perhaps?"; her "eyes and something about her" remind one village matron of "the Tartars" (*BA* 57–8). Her possible "Russian blood" aside, her Russian soul is suggested when she transfigures the Pointz Hall terrace into an "open-air cathedral," its trees "columns . . . in a church without a roof . . . where swallows . . . danc[e], like the Russians, . . . to the unheard rhythm of their own wild hearts" (*BA* 64–65, 57–58). The narrator's figure of the pageant as a "play . . . in the sky of the mind—moving, diminishing, but still there" affiliates the poetics of this quasi-Russian Englishwoman with what Woolf elsewhere calls "the Tchekov method": "Everything is cloudy and vague, loosely trailing rather than tightly furled. The stories move slowly out of sight like clouds in the summer air, leaving a wake of meaning in our minds which gradually fades away."[9] This figure locates pageant and narrative at once in an English village and in the "whole world"—that open country of the mind, the unbounded regions of thought and feeling that are the outsider's dwelling place—and gestures with Chekhovian tenderness and inconclusion toward the possible consequence of this art of seeming inconsequence for a world at war.[10]

Although Woolf professed to have "no country" as a woman, an artist, and a Bloomsbury internationalist, an abounding love of England suffused her outsider's patriotism. "I expect I have it as strong in me as you," she told *Time and Tide*'s outsider editor the Viscountess Rhondda, though differently from the "unfortunate young men who are shot through the sausage machine of Eton—Kings or Christchurch" (*L* 6:236–37, 10 June 1938). When Hitler refused to leave Poland and Britain declared war, Woolf wrote, "Lord this is the worst of all my life's experiences. . . . Yes, it's an empty meaningless world now. . . . I repeat—any idea is more real than any amount of war misery." Wishing to use her "faculties patrioti-cally," she felt that thinking and writing were "the only contribution one can make—This little pitter patter of ideas is my whiff of shot in the cause of freedom" (D 5:234, 6 September 1939). Freedom's cause was antithet-ical to propaganda and jingoism: "its all bombast, this war. One old lady pinning on her cap has more reality" than the "feelings war breeds: patri-otism; communal &c, all sentimental & emotional parodies of our real feelings."[11] Nine months into the war she noted,

> We have now been hard at it hero-making. The laughing, heroic, Tommy—how can we be worthy of such men?—every paper, every BBC rises to that dreary false cheery hero-making strain. Will they be grind-ing organs in the street in 6 months? Its the emotional falsity; . . . not all false; yet inspired with some eye to the main chance. So the politicians mate guns & tanks. No. Its the myth making stage of the war we're in. "Please, no letters" I read this twice in the Times Deaths column from parents of dead officers. (D 5:292, 3 June 1940)

"Please, no letters" intimates grief no dreary false cheery hero-making can console. Facing "suicide shd. Hitler win," Woolf remarked "the odd incongruity of feeling intensely & at the same time knowing that there's no importance in that feeling. Or is there, as I sometimes think, more importance than ever?" (D 5:284, 13 May 1940).

Between the Acts opposes no system or program to the scapegoating and false sentiment bred by war. A novel, Woolf wrote, is "an impression not an argument"; and after *The Years* she had vowed "to write quick, intense, short books, & never be tied down"; "to flout all preconceived theories—For more & more I doubt if enough is known to sketch even probable lines, all too emphatic & conventional" (L 5:91, 16 August 1932; D 5:214, 11 April 1939). The key to her book's mise en scène is, rather, its attention to "random & tentative" moments. In the acts between the acts, and in the spectators' thoughts and feelings, pageant and novel seek a "natural law" by which to build civilization's broken "wall" (D 5:340, 18 November 1940). Erich Auerbach illuminates what is at stake in this poet-ics. A narrative procedure that treats small moments heretofore "hardly . . . sensed" as "determining factors in our real lives," he observes, reveals "something new and elemental," "nothing less than the wealth of reality and depth of life in every moment to which we surrender ourselves with-out prejudice." "The random . . . moment passes unaffected" by

> the controversial and unstable orders over which men fight and despair. . . . The more it is exploited, the more the elementary things which our lives have in common come to light. The more numerous,

varied, and simple the people are who appear as subjects of such random moments, the more effectively must what they have in common
shine forth. In this unprejudiced and exploratory type of representation
we cannot but see to what an extent—below the surface conflicts—the
differences between men's ways of life and forms of thought have
already lessened. The strata of societies and their different ways of life
have become inextricably mingled. . . . A century ago . . . Corsicans or
Spaniards were still exotic; today the term would be quite unsuitable for
Pearl Buck's Chinese peasants. Beneath the conflicts, and also through
them, an economic and cultural leveling process is taking place. It is still
a long way to a common life of mankind on earth, but the goal begins
to be visible.[12]

Eyes on the sky of the mind above their warring nations, Woolf and Auerbach affirm the "reality" of everyday moments against the political orders
over which men fight and despair.

In its wealth and depth of life, the "random & tentative" moment captures aggression and violence as well as "fair life" on the wing. For Woolf,
such moments offer both respite from conflict and glimpses of private,
everyday violence before it is harnessed by the state for political ends. The
acts between the acts in this only seemingly remote English pastoral disclose Hitler in England and abroad, everyday barbarism beside everyday
civility. Giles, who dresses for dinner, spurns one of his guests and stamps
on a snake swallowing a toad. Mrs. Chalmers cuts La Trobe while carrying flowers to the grave of a husband who (in the Early Typescript) used to
beat her. Lucy Swithin and the persecuted homosexual William exchange
disembodied smiles in a mirror as she shows him the house. Some spectators cover their eyes lest Albert, the "village idiot," do "something dreadful"; others talk of "common people" in Roman cafés who "hate Dicta-
tors," of German-Jewish refugees ("People like ourselves"), of friends'
visits to Italy and Russia (BA 86–87, 121). Far from idealizing English or
European civilization, Between the Acts fights Hitler in England by illuminating the interfused hate and love, aggression and peace in everyday
moments in the desire to give to England first the peace and freedom—civilization's sine qua non—its author wishes for "the whole world."

Civilization's Masterplot: Women Between the Acts

In search of a "cure" for her "raging tooth," Isa Oliver scans the shelves
in the Pointz Hall library—"the nicest room of the house," a guest once
gushed (BA 19). The Faerie Queene, Kinglake's Crimea, Keats, The
Kreutzer Sonata, Shelley, Yeats, Donne, lives of Garibaldi and Lord

Palmerston, *The Antiquities of Durham,* Eddington, Darwin, Jeans: "None of them stopped her toothache." As shy of books ("What remedy was there for her at her age—the age of the century, thirty-nine—in books?") as of guns, Isa picks up the London *Times* and chances on a report of a gang rape of a fourteen-year-old girl by soldiers in the heart of England's public sphere, the Horse Guard barracks in the government offices in Whitehall.

> "The guard at Whitehall . . . told her the horse had a green tail; but she found it was just an ordinary horse. And they dragged her up to the barrack room where she was thrown upon a bed. Then one of the troopers removed part of her clothing, and she screamed and hit him about the face. . . . "
>
> That was real; so real that on the mahogany door panels she saw the Arch in Whitehall; through the Arch the barrack room; in the barrack room the bed, and on the bed the girl was screaming and hitting him about the face, when the door (for in fact it was a door) opened and in came Mrs. Swithin carrying a hammer. (*BA* 16–20)

As Stuart N. Clarke discovered, this gang rape is not only "real"—an actual event in Isa's fictional world—but real, or historical.[13] It occurred on 27 April 1938, and the three soldiers were tried at the Old Bailey on June 27, 28, and 29, the *Times* reported. One was convicted of attempted rape, another of rape, a third of aiding and abetting rape. The rape impregnated the girl, and a London surgeon openly performed an abortion, for which he was tried on 18–19 July (defended by a Mr. Oliver) and acquitted on the grounds that the pregnancy endangered the girl's health.[14] In *A Room of One's Own,* Whitehall is the scene of an Englishwoman's sudden recognition that she is not her civilization's "natural inheritor" but "outside of it, alien and critical" (*RO* 97). Like the "real" swallows, rain, cows, and planes that traverse La Trobe's pageant, this news item about a rape of an English girl by English soldiers tears through the novel's illusion, linking Isa's "toothache" with "real"—and real—violence against women at the core of so-called civilization.

While composing *Between the Acts,* Woolf read Freud's theory of family structure as civilization's "germ-cell," which contributed to her thinking on the lines of force linking private life with the public world.[15] In Freud's "scientific myth," civilization originated with the marriage system after a horde of brothers murdered the primal father out of sexual jealousy. Then, since each, "like his father," wanted "all the women for himself," they instituted the incest taboo and exogamy to keep the peace: the brothers agreed to renounce the women ("their chief motive for dispatching their father"), and these objects of desire became objects of exchange between men in the marriage system.[16] Noting Freud's remark that "Sexual desires do not unite men but divide them," Girard observes that "Sexual prohibitions, like all other prohibitions, are sacrificial," and "all legitimate sexuality is sacrificial."[17] Marriage, in other words, does not banish violence but channels "the vicious and destructive cycle" of violence between men into the "generative violence" of the marriage system—a "sacrificial rite" that "protects the community" and "allows culture to flourish" (VS 93). The sacralized exchange of women forges bonds among men who might otherwise be at war, while the exogamous bride functions as a scapegoat whose expulsion from the community buys peace. Unlike such prohibitions as murder, to which all social subjects are in theory equal parties, the "brothers" ' renunciation of sexual objects within the community makes women objects of ritual exchange in a marriage system that— because it keeps peace between men—is civilization's cornerstone.

Freud's comment that "woman finds herself forced into the background" by civilization's claims and "adopts a hostile attitude towards it" does not contradict Woolf's observation that "if one is a woman one is often surprised" to find oneself not civilization's "natural inheritor" but "outside of it, alien and critical."[18] But whereas Freud identifies woman with the "nature" ("the family," "sexual life," unsublimated instinct) that civilization opposes, Woolf frames woman as civilization's *natural* inheritor, an insider "surprised" to find herself forced outside. For Freud civilization is *naturally* masculine; for Woolf it is *unnaturally* masculine. For Freud (and Girard), civilization originates when violent sexual rivalries are channeled into "legitimate" forms, and it demands women's sacrificial role. So, in Conrad's *Heart of Darkness*—invoked, as we saw, in *The Voyage Out*, *The Years*, and again on *Between the Acts'* last page—Marlow sees woman's outsider position as both a given and a sentimentalized moral imperative, a "monster truth" that demands everyday tribute: women are "out of it—completely" and "should be out of it. We must help them to stay in that beautiful world of their own, lest ours gets worse."[19] Whereas Freud casts masculine domination as nature's law, Marlow, as culture's law, Woolf—speaking as "a woman" and as an Enlightenment subject ("one")—looks beyond brute force to the reason and speech that distinguish the human species and lays claim to civilization.

When Woolf read Freud's theory in 1939, she was still pondering her 1931 project on the sexual life of women. By incorporating the real gang rape into her novel, she broaches the issue of civilization's violence against women in a way that tears not only fiction's veil but the boundary between (women's) private and (men's) public worlds; between Isa's private "toothache" and the state military, legal, and medical institutions involved in the rape and its aftermath; between Isa's silent thoughts and the girl's public speech; between women as scapegoat-victims and women as desiring subjects, speakers, and creators between the acts of civilization's masterplot.[20] The news report of the Whitehall gang rape animates the contradictions between Woolf's assumption that woman is civilization's "natural inheritor" and Freud's and Conrad's view that she is and must be kept "out of it—completely." If the rape brutally demonstrates a woman's structural position as an outsider within a society structured by male desire—and illustrates "Hitler in England"—the trials dramatize both her status as citizen and her public speech.[21] The girl's cries, shouts, screams, police witness, and trial testimony mobilize "her" civilization's juridical and medical institutions; and the soldiers' convictions and sentences, although they cannot right the wrong, publicly vindicate her speech acts.[22]

That the real girl refused acquiescent victimhood and marshaled the powers of the law, medicine, and the state to fight both violence perpetrated by government military personnel and state control of her body sets up the conflict at the heart of *Between the Acts*.[23] Isa seeks a "cure" for her silent pain in the newspaper (her generation's "book"), and the girl's speech acts, reported in the late June news items, beckon her toward the "remedy" of speech. In the Olivers' troubled marriage, which complicates Freud's masterplot, Giles the father-hero is, in Isa's unspoken slogans, "Our representative, our spokesman," "The father of my children, whom I love and hate"; she, his complicit counterpart, seethes with suppressed desire for the gentleman farmer Haines and rage at her philandering husband, whose infidelity "made no difference . . . but hers did" (*BA* 215, 110). Isa practices a furtive, symptomatic speech, murmuring escapist, even suicidal, prose poems in lyric antiphony to her "strained" marriage and writing them in account books to hide their existence from Giles (*BA* 106). "Tor[n] asunder" by love and hate, she feels it is "time someone invented a new plot, or that the author came out from the bushes" (*BA* 215).

This year the girl's screams pierce Isa's habitual performance as the marriage system's silent scapegoat. Isa breaks off reading at "she screamed and hit him about the face" when Lucy Swithin enters with a hammer. Like a Möbius strip the "real" rape twists and seamlessly joins Isa's suppressed anger in her paraphrase moments later: "Every summer, for seven summers now, Isa had heard the same words . . . only this year beneath the chime she heard: 'The girl screamed and hit him about the face with a hammer' " (*BA* 22). Like a Chekhovian gun that fires but misses its mark, this hammer only nails a placard announcing the pageant to the Barn. But as

Isa's fantasy embellishes the girl's resistance, the Pointz Hall family becomes not just a microcosm of civilization's "germ-cell" but a laboratory for small, everyday changes that may lead to greater ones. Echoing all day in Isa's mind, the news story initiates her private struggle toward speech and, by extension, calls women's desire and speech out from the crevices, the secret account books, of a civilization still mired in barbarism.

As in Chekhov, words strike with greater force than guns or hammers. In *Three Guineas* the mixed-sex company at the dinner table avert their gaze from the systemic violence of everyday heterosexual relations; but here Mrs. Swithin's entrance does not change the subject. On this festival day of the pageant "Words raised themselves and became symbolical," "ceased to lie flat in the sentence," "rose, became menacing and shook their fists at you" (*BA* 59, 71). The news story shakes its fist at Isa's paralysis, at fiction's evasions of half-civilized barbarism, with a vehemence neither "fantastic" nor "romantic" but real (*BA* 20). During a decade of exploring the sexual life of women, Woolf had uncovered not just women's scapegoat role but an opposing "force of tremendous power": women's desire and will, which had "forced open the doors of the private house," "Bond Street and Piccadilly," "cricket grounds and football grounds"; "shrivelled flounces and stays"; and made the world's "oldest profession . . . unprofitable"; a fighting force for "the rights of all" under "the great principles of Justice and Equality and Liberty" (*D* 4:6, 20 January 1931, *TG* 210–11, 155). *Between the Acts* zooms in on the acts between the acts, those unnoticed random moments that shape our real lives, and makes Isa, aching for a new plot, a sort of test case for the challenge of women's speech to civilization's masterplot. The girl's real screams not only foil Isa's silence but hail her to speech.

Outsider Art: Nature, History, Religion

> Nature had provided a site for a house; man had built his house in a hollow.
>
> —Woolf, *Between the Acts*

> Ah, but she was not just a twitcher of individual strings; she was one who seethes wandering bodies and floating voices in a cauldron, and makes rise up from its amorphous mass a re-created world.
>
> —Woolf, *Between the Acts*

> We're the oracles, if I'm not being irreverent—a foretaste of our own religion.
>
> —Woolf, *Between the Acts*

In *Between the Acts* the outsider allies her art with "Nature" against manmade chalk marks, schemes, systems, theories, forms social, architectural, and aesthetic—in a word, history as error, burden, constraint. Nature—variously figured as a splendid but overlooked site for a house, a lily pond whose depths conceal a great carp, the muddy springs of thought and feeling beneath civilization's "paving-stones," the prehistoric island once rife with rhododendrons and mastodons where now run the Strand and Piccadilly, a symbolic "night before roads were made, or houses," a rain shower that does not spoil but saves the pageant—is the heuristic ground for "a re-created world," a new beginning conjured by art's illusion (*BA* 153). Critics in search of a "matricentric" alternative to civilization's masterplot often frame *Between the Acts* as a fall from feminist utopia to patriarchal realism, from Lily Briscoe's empowering maternal garden to a world darkened and diminished in the mother's absence.[24] But Woolf, as we saw, had felt years earlier that writing *To the Lighthouse* freed her from her parents' ghosts; and *Orlando* and *The Waves* suggest not imaginative impoverishment but adventurous freedom and deepening vision.[25] In Woolf's last self-portrait, too, the artist is no longer a daughter but a woman of the world. Often discounted as a failed artist, an ineffectual village eccentric, even a parody of the fascist group leader, the outsider artist La Trobe, self-created and self-named, thinks not back through her mothers but forward with her community toward the future.

La Trobe's art has its wellsprings neither in a fantasy of the mother's body (as in those sacred "tablets" and "treasures" Lily pictures in Mrs. Ramsay's "mind and heart") nor in the father's culture but in the world, as it is and as it might be (*TL* 51). Early on Lucy Swithin traces the expression "Touch wood" to Antaeus, son of Terra (earth) and Neptune (water), who "touch[ed] earth" to replenish his strength (*BA* 24). So Woolf "touched ground" after the ordeal of *The Years* ("Whatever happens I dont think I can now be destroyed"); and after the pageant La Trobe voyages toward her next play on "green waters" rising from the "earth"—an elemental confluence that figures not fetishized *mater*, a psychohistorical extension of the mother's body, but nature as ground, as reality.[26] If Lily/Woolf draws inspiration from the maternally authored world that "spun so gaily in the centre" of that "great Cathedral space . . . childhood," La Trobe's experimental pageant reflects the spectators who inspire it, help create it, and see it floating in the sky of the mind (*MB* 81, 84).

For La Trobe rewriting history begins at home. In a biography left on the cutting-room floor, an ur-La Trobe overcomes painful origins by inventing a "past" (flying that red flag of doubt "she said") that opens into a widening future. As pageant master, her biographer notes, she is

"far more advanced than Miss Seers or Miss Gibbs and had more knowledge of life at first hand than the admirable Mr. Giddings." The biographer then hints at the sources of her "knowledge":

> Her name was not La Trobe. It was Trob. And if her life had been writ-
> ten instead of being expunged from time to time from a natural desire to
> hide her father, who had fallen and been in prison, truth, the biogra-
> pher's Goddess, would have forced the biographer to say: At the age of
> eighteen, through no fault of her own, Lilian had a baby; At the age of
> twenty-five, she kept a hat shop; at the age of thirty, she became La Trobe
> and sold cakes in Winchester from a recipe bequeathed her by her
> mother a widow, *she said*. Her father, *she said*, had been a clergyman,
> when she sold cakes at Winchester, home-made, on tables covered with
> check clothes; there she changed her name and called herself La Trobe;
> at the age of thirty-five, she was breeding spaniels; and so successfully
> that at the age of forty, she had a cottage with kennels attached; took sil-
> ver cups at shows; and was, according to the biographer's choice of epi-
> thets, the mainspring, the live wire, the pivot of all village activities.[27]

Triply "expunged"—by its subject, by a "biographer" "forced" to channel it direct from "Truth" who yet denies having "written" it, and by its
author, who abandons it in the draft—La Trobe's biography, like Mary
Hamilton's and Judith Shakespeare's, begins in the vicissitudes of female
sexuality. If "Lilian" with her virginal name had a baby at eighteen
"through no fault of her own," who *was* at fault?—an abandoning
seducer? a rapist? that narratively proximate, possibly likely (since
"fallen" connotes a sexual crime) suspect, her jailbird father, whose
crimes she has "a natural desire to hide"? a society that is "a father,"
whose law condemns and penalizes "fallen" women, unwed mothers,
"illegitimate" children (*TG* 206)? A modern, entrepreneurial Judith
Shakespeare, Lilian wrests fairytale successes from her fraught beginnings
to elude her forebears' fate, finessing her past, dodging the suicide's grave,
and spinning out her future as she goes. Experiencing something of
women's sacrificial position "at first hand," she survives so-called illegitimate childbearing and makes her way outside the political economy of
marriage, sharing her bed with an actress instead of a man and wielding
public authority in the annual village pageants.

La Trobe's "knowledge of life at first hand," her resourceful survival
and invention, her adventures outside marriage and family, and her unsettling of assumptions about law and propriety are key credentials for a
pageant master who strives to "re-create the world" for an audience that
longs for "a new plot." Her lesbianism categorically removes her from the
circuits of heterosexual desire and consolidates her outsider status.

Mocked yet tolerated by the villagers, she walks the edge of transgression: "One of these days she would break—which of the village laws? Sobriety? Chastity? Or take something that did not properly belong to her?"[28] With her exotic name, stormy affair with the actress, and gender-bending style—"swarthy, sturdy and thick set [she] strode about the fields in a smock frock; sometimes with a cigarette in her mouth; often with a whip in her hand; and used rather strong language—perhaps, then, she wasn't altogether a lady? At any rate, she had a passion for getting things up"— she at once parodies and transforms the group leader who, Freud argues, mirrors its members' identity (*BA* 58). As a leader, she opens her "advanced" consciousness to her community by reflecting back not an exclusive ideal but a "we" composed of "all waifs & strays," which the pageant gathers into "a rambling capricious but somehow unified whole."[29]

The ur-La Trobe who outdoes Miss Seers, Miss Gibbs, and "the admirable Mr. Giddings" also reminds us that in 1939 Woolf was negotiating between her philosophical and practical outsiderhood on the one hand, and her fierce ambition on the other, which surfaced in rivalries with such longtime friends as E. M. Forster and T. S. Eliot.[30] When *Three Guineas'* reception seemed cool ("my own friends have sent me to Coventry"), she estimated Eliot's and Forster's reputations "higher than my own." Yet she was, she affirmed, "fundamentally . . . an outsider": "I'm kicking my heels with P. H. . . . And I feel so free of any criticism; own no authority"; "I do my best work & feel most braced with my back to the wall."[31] Forster, she noted, enjoyed "praise . . . from the young" and had been "saluted" as England's "best living novelist."[32] Later she declined Forster's offer to nominate her for the London Library Committee, still furious at his report of how they had invoked her father to authorize their horror of women members when her name came up in 1935 (*D* 5:337, 7 November 1940). The Woolfs missed Forster's 1934 "Pageant of Trees" at Abinger and his 1938 pageant *England's Pleasant Land*—both far less advanced than La Trobe's.[33]

La Trobe's advantage over the admirable Mr. Giddings suggests Woolf's rivalry with the admirable Mr. Eliot, whose plays she set out to surpass in her pageant-within-a-novel.[34] While first sketching *Pointz Hall*, she complained of having to "represent[] also T. S. Eliot at his absurd command" at Ottoline Morrell's memorial service; afterward she teased him, "Yes, I murmured 'I'm Mrs Woolf,' at Ottolines funeral; then in a bold loud voice BUT I REPRESENT T. S. ELIOT—the proudest moment of my life; passing, alas, like spring flowers."[35] Eliot, she felt, was all too evidently "on the side of authority," even if his "humorous sardonic gift

. . . mitigates his egotism" (*D* 5:193, 19 December 1938). A week after *Three Guineas* appeared, in fact, Cambridge University gave this august personage an honorary degree, conferred by its Chancellor, Lord Baldwin—who was simultaneously to be seen marching in ceremonial robes in the pages of *Three Guineas* to illustrate "A University Procession." Woolf notes Eliot's honor beside *Three Guineas'* sales figures: "I think 10,000 will go off. And its hit the crest of the wave. Tom being given his degree at Cambridge: walking in procession with the other bigwigs: Trinity feast; Tattoo; honours List—if anyone reads it, the illustration is pat to hand" (*D* 5:149–50, 11 June 1938).

With *Pointz Hall* underway, Woolf felt "selfishly relieved" when Eliot's play *The Family Reunion* flopped in 1939: "why? Had it been a success would it have somehow sealed—my ideas? does this failure confirm a new idea of mine—that I'm evolving in PH about the drama?" She thought his characters "stiff as pokers. . . . And the chief poker is Tom: but cant speak out. A cold upright poker. And the Fates behind the drawing room curtain. A clever beginning, & some ideas; but they spin out: & nothing grips: all mist—a failure: a proof hes not a dramatist. A monologist. This is stated very politely by the papers this morning."[36] She recognized that her "growing detachment from the hierarchy, the patriarchy" made her "dislike, & like, so many things idiosyncratically"; and as Eliot's failure fed her hope of success, his success made her fear failure: "When Desmond praises East Coker, & I am jealous, I walk over the marsh saying I am I; & must follow that furrow, not copy another" (*D* 5:347, 29 December 1940). Having raised the question of dialogue in formally specific terms, Woolf covertly replies to Eliot's blank-verse drama with her "playpoem" (a generic hybrid as apt for *Between the Acts* as for *The Waves*): against the monologist Tom who "wont speak out," the dialogist La Trobe, who (no less paradoxically) hides in the bushes to harangue her audience through a megaphone, along with a dialogist narrator who writes this poetics large on the plane of the story.[37]

In contrast to the "monologist" Eliot, the dialogist outsider La Trobe brews a "we" from the spectators' "wandering bodies and floating voices" (*BA* 153). In her memoir "A Sketch of the Past" (1939–40), Woolf projects a lyrical image of this "we" in summing up what she calls her "philosophy": "*Hamlet* or a Beethoven quartet is the truth about this vast mass that we call the world. But there is no Shakespeare, there is no Beethoven; certainly and emphatically there is no God; we are the words; we are the music; we are the thing itself" (*MB* 72). Beside this idea that art (*Hamlet*, Beethoven) and "all human beings" are woven into nature's (the world's) great unfathomable "pattern," the "religion" or philosophical "systems" of "[Herbert] Read; Tom Eliot; Santayana; Wells" seemed to Woolf "queer little sandcastles": "weathertight, & giv[ing] shelter to the occupant" but finally "only word proof not weather proof" (*MB* 72, *D* 5:340, 18 November 1940). When she muses, "I am the sea which demolishes these castles" as she counsels herself to stay the outsider's course, she allies her art with nature against the force of history:

> We have to discover the natural law & live by it. . . . I am carrying on, while I read, the idea of women discovering, like the 19th century rationalists, agnostics, that man is no longer God. My position, ceasing to accept the religion, is quite unlike Read's, Wells', Tom's, or Santayana's. It is essential to remain outside; & realise my own beliefs. (*D* 5:340, 18 November 1940)

Woolf's view of the historian G. M. Trevelyan as "The complete Insider," "the perfect product of the Universities," similarly allies the outsider symbolically with nature: "Insiders are the glory of the 19th century. They do a great service like Roman roads. But they avoid the forests & the will o the wisps" (*D* 5:333, 337, 26 October, 5 November 1940). In *Pointz Hall*'s last pages, Woolf weaves imagery from his *History of England*, with its foldout frontispiece map tracing ancient roads through the forests and marshes of "Celtic and Roman Britain," into Lucy's "Outline of History," where she reads of a time when England was "'a swamp. Thick forests covered the land. On top of their matted branches birds sang.'"[38] From Trevelyan's imagined island Woolf conjures a heuristic new beginning, a "now" before roads or houses were made, paths still to be cut toward an uncharted future.

When La Trobe sets the pageant on a natural terrace overlooking the fields, with Bolney Minster's distant spire just visible, she seeks to free her re-created world from the burdens of the past symbolized in the house:

> It was a pity that the man who had built Pointz Hall had pitched the house in a hollow, when beyond the flower garden and the vegetables there was this stretch of high ground. Nature had provided a site for a house; man had built his house in a hollow. Nature had provided a stretch of turf half a mile in length and level, till it suddenly dipped to the lily pool. . . . There you could walk up and down, up and down, under the shade of the trees. (*BA* 57, 10)

The perfect site for a house becomes "the very place for a play" (*BA* 57). Like women discovering that "there is no God" but in the "we" who are the words, the music, the thing itself, La Trobe pursues the outsider's quest to "free the religious spirit" when she transforms this terrace into an "open-air cathedral, . . . a church without a roof" (*TG* 172, *BA* 64–65).

Taking her chances with the weather, setting the pageant's illusion amid fields where a cow's yearning bellow, a sudden shower, a wind that blows the actors' words away, birds on the wing, "twelve aeroplanes in perfect formation" play parts unscripted yet not uninvited, she releases the spectators from convention to contemplate the human world as part of nature. The "representatives of our most respected families," some "there for centuries, never selling an acre," become part of a immeasurably greater past and future; the "we" gathered in this cathedral under the sky overflows this small community to represent the human species, evoked by Lucy's prehistoric Piccadilly swarming with "monsters . . . from whom presumably . . . we descend" (BA 74, 8–10). Without ceasing to be themselves, the villagers are people on the earth come together in the sociability that Between the Acts, like Kant, sees as human beings' "true 'end' "; and, at the same time, human beings who belong to a nature that works with hidden purposes, beyond any single life and beyond human comprehension.[39]

Opening the pageant's borders to chance showers, swallows, wind, cows, and, most important, the audience, La Trobe lets nature in its beauty—its purposiveness without purpose—and its mysterious purposes shimmer through art's illusion as she blends the pageant, experientially and formally, into that unfathomably great work of art "the world." Staged outdoors, the pageant speaks on many planes and in different voices. Unlike Eliot's Family Reunion, its meaning, and that of the novel, are not to be sought in the words—the virtuosic interplay of utterance, conversation, silent reflection and communication, reported speech, citation, the written word in books and newspapers, talking objects and rooms, script, and performance, the animate web of spoken and unspoken words from all across the bandwidths that is Between the Acts. Rather—embodying the "very latest notion" that "nothing's solid," as a spectator says—the novel dissolves plot, story, event, and character into these myriad voices, seemingly random yet orchestrated, as if ordinary language were throwing off mundane functionality and aspiring to the condition of music (BA 199). Capturing ephemeral thought, speech, and performance on the wing, Between the Acts is a tour de force of listening to the words for the sake of a music that plays through and between them, beyond the reach of sound. We turn now to two crucial aspects of its dialogic art: beauty and change.

Dialogic Poetics: Beauty

Bodying forth the "death" of the author, La Trobe's advanced theatrical practice foregrounds the spectators as the play's coauthors.[40] As Bart informs his guests, "Our part . . . is to be the audience. And a very important part too" (*BA* 58). La Trobe does not invent this dialogic drama out of nothing. "One year we wrote the play ourselves," Lucy Swithin recalls at the family luncheon on which Mrs. Manresa and William Dodge have intruded with their picnic hamper. The blacksmith's son "had the loveliest voice," and that natural mimic Elsie at the Crossways "Took us all off," she remembers. "People are gifted—very. The question is—how to bring it out? That's where she's so clever—Miss La Trobe" (*BA* 59). In line with this job description, La Trobe (a. k. a. "Miss Whatshername") strives to bring out the community's voices, hidden and potential (*BA* 197).

And the villagers need her, for we glimpse the sort of thing they come up with when they write the play themselves when Colonel Mayhew wonders, "Why leave out the British Army? What's history without the Army, eh?" and his wife describes what La Trobe has probably planned for a finale: "a Grand Ensemble. Army; Navy; Union Jack; and behind them perhaps—Mrs. Mayhew sketched what she would have done had it been her pageant—the Church. In cardboard. One window looking east, brilliantly illuminated to symbolize—she could work that out when the time came."[41] La Trobe's part is not to execute their conventional visions, which arguably resemble them far less closely than does her mirror play at the end. Rather (like Orlando's Shakespeare and "the moderns" in the "Essay on Criticism"), she "rule[s] them, impose[s] her will," to bring out their mute thoughts and feelings. Her part is to be their "Bossy" leader ("someone must lead. Then too they could put the blame on her") and equally their "slave" ("O to write a play without an audience—*the* play") in the effort to call out voice, speech, and feeling they do not yet know they have.[42]

Between the Acts' narrator at once depicts La Trobe's dialogism and practices it herself. As La Trobe opens the pageant's borders to chance so that nature glints through art's illusion, the narrator records every event and voice with stenographic fidelity so that the pageant becomes but one voice among many, its first scene nearly lost amid other sounds and voices:

[1] "What luck!" [2]Mrs. Carter was saying. [1]"Last year . . . " [2] Then the play began. Was it, or was it not, the play? [3]Chuff, chuff, chuff [2]sounded from the bushes. It was the noise a machine makes when something has gone wrong. Some sat down hastily; others stopped talking guiltily. All looked at the bushes. For the stage was empty. . . . While they looked apprehensively and some finished their sentences, a small girl, like a rose-bud in pink, advanced; took her stand . . . and piped:

[4] *Gentles and simples, I address you all . . . .*

[2] So it was the play then. Or was it the prologue?

[4] *Come hither for our festival* [2](she continued)
[4] *This is a pageant, all may see*
  Drawn from our island history.
    England am I. . . .

[5+] "She's England," [2]they whispered. [5+]"It's begun." "The prologue," [2]they added, looking down at the programme.

[4] "*England am I,*" [2]she piped again; and stopped.

[2] She had forgotten her lines.

[6] "Hear! Hear!" [2]said an old man in a white waistcoat briskly. [6] "Bravo! Bravo!"

[7a] "Blast 'em!" [2]cursed Miss La Trobe, hidden behind the tree. . . .

[7b] "Music!" [2]she signalled. . . . But the machine continued: [3]Chuff, chuff, chuff.

[7c] "*A child new born . . .* " [2]she prompted. (*BA* 76–77)

Before the play has progressed six lines, we hear at least seven voices: Mrs. Carter, the narrator, the gramophone ("chuff"—the voice of the thing itself, mediating nothing), little Phyllis, whispering spectators, the kind old man, and the director in three vocal modes, cursing sotto voce, calling in vain for music, then prompting from the script, a sort of eighth voice. Like Mr. Erskine in *Jacob's Room*, who tells Charlotte Wilding that he can count "twenty different sounds on a night like this," the narrator records each one moment by moment as if it were a rolling camera pointed at the scene: " 'Sorry I'm so late,' said Mrs. Swithin . . . 'What's it all about? I've missed the prologue. England? That little girl? Now she's gone. . . . And who's this?' It was Hilda, the carpenter's daughter. . . . 'A cushion? Thank you so much' "; " 'O,' Miss La Trobe growled behind her tree, 'the torture of these interruptions!' " (*JR* 60, *BA* 79–80).

Who speaks? Together the spectators' unscripted comments, the faltering little actor, the exasperated director, the gramophone's scraping needle, the script, and the observant narrator create the rustling, glancing voice of the play in performance—and something more: a voice beyond all these voices, a metavoice that belongs to no one, not even the narrator, whose gaze and reportage more nearly resemble a documentary cinematographic apparatus than an omniscient, moralizing storyteller. Yet there is nothing mechanical about the quality of her attention, which suffuses this Chekhovian human comedy with aesthetic feeling. It is as if she at once attends to every moment for its own sake and listens, watches, for possible designs and refrains to appear—for that ephemeral "something" that *Orlando* calls "beauty" to transform into a "playpoem" the documentary field of human speech marked out by the novel's first sentence ("they were talking") and its last ("They spoke").

Or: it is as if, behind the narrative's quasi-documentary mode, a metavoice (the artist? the author? we'll come back to this question) were weaving everything, from the not very privileged script to the most trivial interruption, into an encompassing intention or design, an aesthetic whole that requires each element as a tapestry requires each thread or an orchestral composition every note, motif, and instrument. In the essay that describes Chekhov's stories leaving "clouds in the summer air, . . . a wake of meaning in our minds which gradually fades away," Woolf writes that "fictitious people" must not say what the narrator can say "more economically for them" (*E* 4:455). Recalling this caution, we begin to see that it is the very triviality of the characters' utterances that makes them transparent to this metavoice, Beauty, behind the voices. Triviality is indispensable to the aesthetic effect that lifts what they say "simply in their natural voices" out of the mundane and exceeds, yet does not violate, the director's plan (*E* 4:453). Although the "excruciated" La Trobe damns these interruptions to which the narrator gives equal time—these trivial, irrelevant voices that wander from the script, transgress the actor/audience divide, and (she fears) threaten to ruin the pageant—the playwright-director and narrator are not at cross-purposes (*BA* 203). Precisely because the narrator's wide-angle lens exceeds and even betrays La Trobe's local intention, it makes her radically dialogic art fully visible, even as it weaves it almost imperceptibly into that greater work of art, the world.

In keeping with the dissolving boundaries between the work of art and the world according to Woolf's "philosophy," between the real rape and the novel's fictional world, between nature and the pageant, the narrator writes the "real" spectators and the "real" world into the picture. The pageant provides an occasion and a temporal frame to hang the human voices on, a canvas for the narrator's documentary art. Its mere existence is drama enough: anticipation, preparations, acts, intervals, performance, and aftermath on this festival day engender the subtly eventful social panoply of the playpoem all around the pageant that the narrative exists to capture. The question, then, is less Who speaks than How, though thinking about How leads to a different understanding of Who. *Between the Acts* dissolves any notion of a divide between functional and poetic language. Like a stone chip in a mosaic, the most ordinary utterance brushes against, calls out, even becomes poetry through context and contiguity, as when at tea in the Barn a voice says, "A bit too strong? Let me add water," and Isa thinks, "That's what I wished . . . when I dropped my pin. Water, water" (*BA* 104). Speech is never naked. Like Lucy Swithin, the narrator constantly "increas[es] the bounds of the moment" through kaleidoscopic juxtapositions (*BA* 9). Every utterance is richly laden, nuanced, made strange by spatial and temporal resonances, reverberating with and against others like the strings of a piano, exceeding any speaker's intention. So too the play in performance exceeds the artist's intention without leaving the realm of the aesthetic. The pageant casts a spell over the world that surrounds it, drawing the "real" life around it under the sway of this mysterious beauty.

The spectators are taken with La Trobe's natural effects, part art, part chance. "Look, Minnie!" cries Etty Springett as birds flit across a fake pond. "Those are real swallows!" (*BA* 164). The audience sees double: dishcloths are silken headdresses, a painted sheet is a pond circled by green stakes for bulrushes, "Eliza Clark, licensed to sell tobacco," is Queen Elizabeth. The villagers show through their roles and costumes: "Who came? . . . Love embodied. . . . Sylvia Edwards in white satin" (*BA* 91). Conversely, the Intervals do not spill and waste the emotion La Trobe brews but refract it through life's translucent medium as spectators become impromptu players: "Hail, sweet Carinthia. My love. My life," William greets Isa at tea in the Barn, echoing the Elizabethan scene. "My lord, my liege," she returns with an ironic bow (*BA* 105, cf. 88). As in a hall of mirrors, illusion and the "real" world collide and intersect, unsettling hardened conventions to release a question that reverberates through the pageant's reception: "D'you think people change? Their clothes, of course. . . . But I meant ourselves . . . " (*BA* 120–21, ellipses Woolf's). Without forgetting beauty, let us look at the way the novel stages the question of change by tracking Isa from the scenes leading up to the pageant through her role as privileged spectator to the closing scenes where she becomes the unwitting protagonist of next year's play.

Dialogic Poetics: Change

> Every year it was either wet or fine. . . . it seemed impossible that any thing should change. . . . But she changed; it changed—the thing that was behind the wall: today "it" was "the girl screamed; and hit him about the face; they dragged her to the bedroom in the barrack and held her down."
>
> —Woolf, *Pointz Hall*

Prompted by the historical pageant, the question of whether people change, if so, how, and what art has to do with it goes to the heart of the dialogic poetics of play and narrative. The scenes that set the stage for the pageant and everything "between" establish Isa among the novel's dramatis personae through an array of domestic and psychic scenes involving sex, love, violence, infidelity, jealousy, money, class, and gender. This "real"-life documentary at the pageant's permeable borders introduces characters who will play the audience's "very important part": the Olivers chat with the neighbors about the cesspool, Lucy wakes with the birds, little George digs a flower, Bart scares him with his monster-beak, Isa muses on her two kinds of love for Haines and Giles and orders the fish. Isa's consciousness shapes the library scene with the newspaper, the hammer, the question of the weather, while luncheon preparations go on in kitchen and dining room and the scullery maid takes a break by the lily pond. The Olivers extend hospitality to the "strangers," Mrs. Manresa—a racy New Zealand-born "wild child of nature" married to a "disinterested" Jewish businessman whose initials imitate "a coronet" on his "great silver-plated car"—and the homosexual poet-clerk, William Dodge. Giles comes late from the city, the company sits uncomfortably over coffee on the hot terrace, Lucy shields William from Giles's contempt, and it gradually emerges that thirty-nine-year-old Isa is drawn to Haines, unhappy with her womanizing husband, tender with her two children though pinned unwillingly into domesticity, and teeming with suppressed thoughts and feelings that issue in the poems she hides in account books.

The news report of the rape challenges Isa's silence, as we have noted; and in *Pointz Hall* it has already changed Isa before the pageant begins. Although "it seemed impossible that any thing should change" these seven years, "she changed; it changed—the thing that was behind the wall: today 'it' was 'the girl screamed; and hit him about the face' " (*PH* 56). Once the pageant begins, the Intervals create broad arenas for performances of spectatorship through conversations and solitary reflections. Left "stranded" and "separate" at the first Interval as the gramophone wails "*Dispersed are we*," Isa follows "that old strumpet" Mrs. Manresa (who has been ogling Giles) toward the Barn for tea, murmuring a singsong of despair: "what wish should I drop into the well? . . . That the waters should cover me . . . of the wishing well. . . . Water. Water. . . . Should I mind not again to see may tree or nut tree?" (*BA* 95–96, 103–04). First William, then little George, interrupt her desolation; then Isa silently mocks Giles ("Silly little boy, with blood on his boots") and sweeps William (riveted by Giles's beauty, loath to go) off to the greenhouse, plucking "bitter herb" and "Old Man's Beard" on her way. There she picks up a knife and improvises for William a mock scene of love betrayed:

"She spake," Isa murmured. "And from her bosom's snowy antre drew the gleaming blade. 'Plunge blade!' she said. And struck. 'Faithless!' she cried. Knife, too! It broke. So too my heart," she said.

She was smiling ironically as he came up.

"I wish the play didn't run in my head," she said. (*BA* 113)

This melodramatic play-speech comes not from the pageant but from the "real" love-hate plot that tears her asunder, which the pageant brings bubbling up from her mind's "mud" through convention's "marble" pavements (*BA* 45). The play clears a psychic space that allows Isa to act out buried feelings for William without having to avow them. She is only playacting, and his discreet "Still the play?" does not intrude.[43] But suddenly they are talking "as if they had known each other all their lives," and when she wonders "why they could speak so plainly to each other," he gestures at "the doom of sudden death hanging over us" (*BA* 114). During the first Interval, in short, Isa moves from solitary singsong through improvised play-speech to "plain" speech. Meanwhile, as if confirming the dialogic interchange between pageant and spectators, the communal "inner voice, the other voice," takes on Isa's murmuring rhythms—"Working, serving, pushing, striving, earning wages—to be spent—here? Oh dear no. Now? No, by and by. When ears are deaf and the heart is dry"—as if the pageant has unstopped not just Isa's stifled speech but a common spring of hidden feeling (*BA* 119).

The pageant now depicts the Age of Reason, its advances, evils, and foibles declaimed (once Bart has urged her to speak up so the audience can understand her) by a superb Mabel Hopkins in the title role. "*Commerce*" pours out a "*Cornucopia*" of "*ores*," sweated out of the earth by "*savage[s]*" in "*distant mines*"; "*At my behest, the armed warrior lays his shield aside; the heathen leaves the Altar steaming with unholy sacrifice*"; music and the arts flourish in "*peace*." So do vanity, duplicity, and greed, the Congreve parody "*Where there's a Will there's a Way*" insists—no surprise to Cobbet of Cobbs Corner, who has "known human nature in the East" and finds it "the same in the West" (*BA* 123–24, 110). Still, "reason prevails," affirmed by the "triple melody" of music, cows, and view (*BA* 134). When finally the young lovers flee their elders' snares and a voice exclaims, "All that fuss about nothing!" everyone laughs and La Trobe "glow[s] with glory": "the voice had seen; the voice had heard" (*BA* 138–39). The voice sees more or less what Isa saw during act 1, the postimpressionist emphasis on abstract emotion: "Did the plot matter? . . . The plot was only there to beget emotion. . . . Perhaps Miss La Trobe meant that . . . ? Don't bother about the plot: the plot's nothing. . . . Love. Hate. Peace. Three emotions made the ply of human life" (*BA* 90–92).

Reason's proclamation of the end of "unholy sacrifice" seems lost on Isa, who, alone again in the second Interval, wavers from her wish "that the waters should cover me" to paint herself "the last little donkey" in history's "long caravanserai," stumbling under a burden of personal and cultural memory. As La Trobe calls for "The next tune! Number 10!" Isa wanders off, sees Haines vanish in the crowd, and stops in the stable yard by that ancient fertility symbol "the great pear tree" to soliloquize, as if she were already a shade,

> "Where do I wander? . . . Down what draughty tunnels? Where the eyeless wind blows? And there grows nothing for the eye. No rose. To issue where? In some harvestless dim field where no evening lets fall her mantle; nor sun rises. All's equal there. Unblowing, ungrowing are the roses there. *Change is not; nor the mutable and lovable; nor greetings nor partings*; nor furtive findings and feelings, where hand seeks hand and eye seeks shelter from the eye. . . . " (*BA* 154–55, my emphasis)

"Change"—greetings and partings, shifting light, blowing roses—holds Isa ambivalently to life through her despair and evokes dreams of life set free of possessions and memories:

> "How am I burdened with what they drew from the earth; memories; possessions. This is the burden that the past laid on me, last little donkey in the long caravanserai crossing the desert. 'Kneel down,' said the past. 'Fill your pannier from our tree. . . . Go your way till your heels blister and your hoofs crack.'
> . . . "That was the burden . . . laid on me in the cradle; murmured by waves; breathed by restless elm trees; crooned by singing women; what we must remember: what we would forget. . . . " (*BA* 155)

If it obliterated history's burden, even catastrophe—apocalyptic "lightning"—might herald "a good day":

> "Now comes the lightning . . . from the stone blue sky. The thongs are burst that the dead tied. Loosed are our possessions. . . .
> "It's a good day, some say, the day we are stripped naked. Others, it's the end of the day . . . But none speaks with a single voice . . . free from the old vibrations. Always I hear corrupt murmurs; the chink of gold and metal. Mad music. . . .
> "On, little donkey, patiently stumble. Hear not the frantic cries of the leaders who in that they seek to lead desert us, nor the chatter of china faces glazed and hard. Hear rather the shepherd, coughing by the farmyard wall; the withered tree that sighs when the Rider gallops; the brawl in the barrack room when they stripped her naked; or the cry which in London when I thrust the window open someone cries . . . "[44]

Tormented by "corrupt murmurs," Isa counsels herself to listen for other voices—a shepherd's cough, the withered tree's sigh, the girl's screams, the London street cry that plays both in her memory and on the gramophone, calling her back to act 3 and life.[45]

Seeing Giles emerge from the greenhouse with Mrs. Manresa, Isa follows them back unseen for the parodic Victorian scene. Mingling with Colonel Mayhew's call for "the Army," "who'll buy my sweet lavender" stirs the elderly widows Mrs. Lynn Jones and Etty Springett to an overture of reminiscences: "You couldn't walk—Oh, dear me, no—home from the play. Regent Street. Piccadilly. Hyde Park Corner. The loose women" (*BA* 157–58). No loose women appear onstage where "Budge the publican"'s truncheoned constable glares "eminent, dominant, . . . from his pedestal" while Mrs. Hardcastle poses the burning question "O has Mr. Sibthorp a wife?" on behalf of her four daughters to a top-hatted, side-whiskered "chorus" (*BA* 160, 163, 169). The widows feel vague indignation when the donkey's hindquarters, played by Albert, become "active" during Mr. Hardcastle's closing prayer and the young lovers take up "the white man's burden" "*To convert the heathen!*" "*To help our fellow men!*" while Budge praises "*'Ome, Sweet 'Ome*" (*BA* 172–73). But as the third Interval begins, change is on all the spectators' minds: Isa and Lucy discuss whether the Victorians were "like that" or "only you and me and William dressed differently"; Etty flings William "a vicious glance," as if blaming him for the empire's wane; Mrs. Jones admits, "Change had to come"; Giles, William, and Isa confide "(without words), 'I'm damnably unhappy' " as if yearning for change (*BA* 173–76).

While waiting for act 2, someone has remarked, "Perhaps she'll reach the present, if she skips," doubtless unaware of the Parkerian doctrine that "It is most unwise to include any episode more recent than, say, fifty years ago" when staging "History without Tears."[46] The Intervals already form a bridge to the present, sometimes confusingly, as when the last one segues into a finale that takes the Mayhews and everyone else by surprise. La Trobe's script reads, "try ten mins. of present time. Swallows, cows, etc." As Parker might have warned, "something was going wrong" (*BA* 179). The spectators await a spectacle: "How long was she going to keep them waiting? 'The Present Time. Ourselves.' They read it on the programme. . . . 'The profits are to go to a fund for installing electric light in the Church.' . . . Over there. You could see the spire among the trees." La Trobe watches in agony as her daring experiment, indispensable to the pageant's success, looks to be failing: "what could she know about ourselves? . . . Other people, perhaps. . . . But she won't get me" (*BA* 178).

This is not exactly what Barthes means by the death of the author, but La Trobe's anguish does implicate the spectators, passive before the empty stage (*BA* 180). " '*Reality too strong*,' she muttered. 'Curse 'em!' . . . Panic seized her. Blood seemed to pour from her shoes. This is death, death, death, . . . when illusion fails" (*BA* 178–80, my emphasis). Has La Trobe, like Woolf, been reading Freud? "One can try to re-create the world," Freud writes, but one "will as a rule attain nothing. *Reality* is *too strong* for him. He becomes a madman, who for the most part finds no one to help him in carrying through his delusion" (*CD* 28, my emphasis). But La Trobe is not a "madman," and as she struggles to re-create the world for her scattered, distracted audience, "reality" is on her side: a "sudden, pro-fuse" rain shower pours from a "black, swollen" cloud "like all the peo-ple in the world weeping. Tears. Tears. Tears. . . . all people's tears, weep-ing for all people . . . sudden and universal."[47] Wiping her cheeks, La Trobe sighs, "That's done it." Nature saves her experiment, bringing tears to the spectators' minds. The "risk" she has taken in acting outdoors, opening the pageant to nature and chance, pays off in a History with Tears that no Parkerian would have dreamt of, or dared.

Isa "helps" too, spontaneously making meaning of this moment: " 'Oh that our human pain could here have ending! . . . O that my life could here have ending'. . . . Readily would she endow this voice with all her treas-ure if so be tears could be ended. . . . On the altar of the rain-soaked earth she laid down her sacrifice" (*BA* 180–81). No "idle reader" but an active Barthesian spectator, Isa answers the "simple tune" that takes up where Nature leaves off—"the voice that was no one's voice, . . . the voice that wept for human pain unending"—with a fantasy of her death as no longer an escape but a sacrificial offering to end "all people's tears."[48] As the nar-rative weaves Isa's prose poems into the pageant's web of music, rain, and tears, the dialogic pageant now interrupts with a worldly tableau ("Crude, of course") that draws her from private fantasy to public utter-ance:

> "O look!" she cried aloud.
> That was a ladder. And that (a cloth roughly painted) was a wall. . . .
> Mr. Page the reporter, licking his pencil, noted: "With the very limited
> means at her disposal, Miss La Trobe conveyed to the audience Civiliza-
> tion (the wall) in ruins; rebuilt (witness man with hod) by human effort;
> witness also woman handing bricks. Any fool could grasp that. Now
> issued black man in fuzzy wig; coffee-coloured ditto in silver turban;
> they signify presumably the League of . . . "
> A burst of applause greeted this flattering tribute to ourselves [. . .]
> all liberated; made whole . . . (*BA* 181–83, bracketed ellipsis mine)

As the audience lapses into self-congratulatory Grand Ensemble complacency, Isa's "O look!" keeps in view this far from realized vision of a civilization created not by parricidal brothers but by an inclusive global brother/sisterhood, beyond national and racial "chalk marks" ("the League of . . . ").[49]

While they all "look," La Trobe's tour de force mirror scene begins. The actors leap out of the bushes flashing "Anything that's bright enough to reflect, presumably, ourselves," until the spectators glimpse their own faces onstage beside the broken wall (BA 183). "What's more," as the narrator says, they *hear* themselves—and even *see* their thoughts embodied—as each actor "declaim[s] some phrase or fragment from their parts," including that very important part, the audience (BA 185). Earlier in the day, Giles mutters, "I fear I am not in my perfect mind" watching Great Eliza come apart onstage; during the Victorian scene Mrs. Lynn Jones reflects on "something—not impure, that wasn't the word—but perhaps 'unhygienic' about the home"; Isa thinks of the rape, picks Old Man's Beard, and improvises ("Plunge blade!") for William in the greenhouse (BA 85, 174, 113). Now, in the play's last scene, the actors echo, mime, and embody these unscripted moments in a sound-collage as mysterious as Chekhov's breaking string: "*I am not* (said one) *in my perfect mind. . . . Home? Where the miner sweats, and the maiden faith is rudely strumpeted. . . . Is that a dagger that I see before me?*" (after *Lear*, sonnet 66, and *Macbeth*) while "the girl in the Mall" and "the old man with the beard" dance out from the bushes with the rest (BA 185).

How is this done? Has La Trobe, busy in the bushes during the Intervals, transcribed those "stray voices, voices without bodies, symbolical voices they seemed to her, half hearing, seeing nothing, but still, over the bushes, feeling invisible threads connect the bodiless voices" (BA 151)? Does she direct her actors to catch the spectators' utterances and freely repeat them in this scene—to make their secret voices sound in this final chorus of aural mirrors? Or—since "She felt everything they felt"—does she somehow divine their inward voices, just as she hears "the first words" of next year's play the moment Isa and Giles speak them? Whatever her method, it is writ large by the narrator, who not only hears the characters' unspoken thoughts but shows them overhearing each other's, soundlessly conversing in a hyperreal form of free indirect discourse—as when Giles hears Isa think "as plainly as words could say it, 'No, . . . I don't admire you . . . Silly little boy, with blood on his boots' " (in quotation marks, as if her feeling is so palpable she seems to have spoken) and silently wonders: "Whom then did she admire? . . . Some man, he was sure, in the Barn. Which man? He looked round him" (BA 111).

For the narrator as for La Trobe, it is a small step from rendering such silent, wireless talk to a collective "voice that was no one's"; from the characters' inner voices to the audience's and even the pageant's. Before the discomposed spectators can flee the "indignity" of their reflections, an impersonal amplified voice pins them to their seats, implicitly countering Hitler's exhortations to a "master race" with a "megaphonic, anonymous, loud-speaking affirmation" of humanity in all its variegated, interwoven vice and virtue:

> let's talk in words of one syllable, without larding, stuffing, or cant. . . . And calmly consider ourselves. Ourselves. Some bony. Some fat. . . . Liars most of us. Thieves too. . . . The poor are as bad as the rich are. Perhaps worse. Don't hide among rags. Or let our cloth protect us. Or . . . book learning; . . . Or . . . white hairs. Consider the gun slayers, bomb droppers, here or there. They do openly what we do slyly. . . . A tyrant, remember, is half a slave. . . . O we're all the same. Take myself now. Do I escape my own reprobation, simulating indignation, in the bush, among the leaves? . . . Look at ourselves, ladies and gentlemen! Then at the wall, and ask how's this wall, the great wall, which we call, perhaps miscall, civilization, to be built by (here the mirrors flicked and flashed) orts, scraps and fragments like ourselves? (BA 186–88)

The voice borrows Hitler's braying tactics only to insist (with *Three Guineas*) on the spectators' agency. As the war makers are "*Ourselves*" (including "*myself*"), so too "*civilization*" depends on "*orts, scraps and fragments like ourselves.*" But the voice seeks not just to exhort but to inspire: "*What? You can't descry it? All you can see of yourselves is scraps, orts and fragments? Well then listen to the gramophone affirming*" (*BA* 188). After the mirrors splinter their longing for heroic spectacle ("a Grand Ensemble. Army; Navy; Union Jack; . . . the Church") into scraps, orts and fragments while the braying megaphone urges them, even so, to build civilization's broken wall, La Trobe's cacophony of voices culminates in music. Sweating in the bushes, Jimmy fits a record on the gramophone—"Bach, Handel, Beethoven, Mozart or . . . merely a traditional tune?"—and fills the pageant's space with the music, the thing itself that "we" are: "Was that voice ourselves?" they wonder. "Scraps, orts, and fragments, are we, also, that?" (*BA* 189). Who speaks?—no thick little ego, no solitary, bounded mind, but the "we" who are the words, the music, the thing itself. The gramophone gestures toward a greater music of the human voice and of the world, a music not merely heard but felt and imagined as that great unfathomable "pattern" to which the narrative attunes us (*MB* 72).

In this voice too harmony and discord contend. In place of the hoped-for Grand Ensemble, the music bodies forth the "whole population of the mind's immeasurable profundity," and the community, with "the doom of sudden death hanging over" them, affirms itself not in its univocality but in the inexhaustible differences without which no "pattern," "music," or authentic "we" can exist (*BA* 189). The music's inner voices now "strain[] asunder," now are "solved; united," made "whole"; now sound "On different levels ourselves" going "forward; flower gathering some on the surface" or "descending to wrestle with the meaning; but all comprehending; all enlisted" (*BA* 189). Against the enforced univocality of totalitarianism, parodied and deconstructed by the megaphone, the music gathers up in its aural mirror a dialogic community, to which real differences, as Arendt says, are so much less dangerous than indifference; a community of spectators who enact a public "form of being together" where "no one rules and no one obeys," where people seek to "persuade each other."[50] It is almost as if the pageant conjures the "we" Churchill vowed would "fight in the fields" against the Nazis' scapegoating perversion of community, even as it bodies forth the outsider's wish to give to England first what she desires of peace and freedom for the whole world.[51] Ephemeral as a cloud or play, perpetually moving between unity and dispersal, pageant and novel together listen for the metavoice of that "rambling capricious but somehow unified whole," that *we* whose "hidden . . . pattern" connects "all life, all art, all waifs & strays" (*D* 5:135, 26 April 1938, *MB* 72).

"What's more" (to borrow the narrator's phrase), even as the narrative attunes us to this silent music, it also—like Reverend Streatfield— "speak[s] . . . in another capacity," to which the "distant music" of twelve aeroplanes in formation that cuts his word in two draws attention (*BA* 193). The "opp . . . portunity" (broken but mended with three ps) to "illuminat[e] . . . our dear old church" recalls the opp portunity to build civilization's broken wall on firmer ground and more lastingly. As the warplanes cut through a word that a human voice ("I speak only as one of the audience, one of ourselves") completes around them, the question voiced at the end of the pageant reverberates: How rebuild the wall, a world laid ruin by war (*BA* 192)? That question lingers and floats with the play in the sky of the mind, as when Lucy sees in the lily pond leaves a floating world of Europe, India, Africa, America and wonders whether "civilisation"'s fragile "blue thread," if broken here, might flourish elsewhere (*PH* 423, *BA* 205).

After the music ceases and Mrs. Manresa wipes her eyes, the audience's applause seems to make an end; and then another after Reverend Streatfield's proposed "vote of thanks to the gifted lady" fails for lack of an "object corresponding to this description" and "God Save the King" blares from the bushes (*BA* 194, 191). But as the mirrors and music finesse the moment when art leaves off and "real" life resumes, here again, with La Trobe nowhere in sight, the pageant prolongs itself in unscripted spectacle and applause:

> Was that the end? The actors were reluctant to go. They lingered; they mingled. There was Budge . . . old Queen Bess. And the Age of Reason hobnobbed with the foreparts of the donkey. . . . And little England, still a child, sucked a peppermint drop. . . . Each still acted the unacted part conferred on them by their clothes. Beauty was on them. Beauty revealed them. . . .
>
> "Look," the audience whispered, "O look, look, look—" And once more they applauded; and the actors joined hands and bowed.
>
> . . . *Dispersed are we; who have come together. But,* the gramophone asserted, *let us retain whatever made that harmony.*
>
> O let us, the audience echoed . . . , keep together. For there is joy . . . in company.
>
> . . . So . . . for the last time they applauded. (*BA* 195–97)

In this accidental tableau, the actors and spectators are the words, the music, the thing itself, beyond any Shakespeare, Beethoven, or La Trobe. The audience's "Look . . . O look, look, look" recalls Woolf's converse of Faust's bargain that the day he says "Stay" to a passing moment shall be his last: "If one does not lie back & sum up & say to the moment, this very moment, stay you are so fair, what will be one's gain, dying? No: stay, this moment. No one ever says that enough."[52] Struck by this "Beauty," the departing guests fulfill La Trobe's hope that they have "taken" her "gift"—come together in the sociability and community mediated by art ("O let us . . . keep together. For there is joy . . . in company") to find the world transformed once the illusion ends (*BA* 196, 209).

The spectators' spontaneous response to the postpageant tableau—"Oh look, look, look"—not only enacts Kant's understanding of aesthetic judgments as positing that anyone who looks in freedom, that is, without personal interest, would find this sight beautiful but materializes the social dimension always implicit in the act of judging. Further, it illustrates Arendt's view that a Kantian theodicy would have the "beauty of things in the world" at its heart (*LK* 30). Both this ending beyond the ending and the novel that captures it gesture toward beauty as a modernist theodicy, a belief that nothing holds people to life, community, and hope in face of history's horrors more surely than the beauty of things in the world. "I'd no notion we looked so nice," Lucy whispers between scenes. "Hadn't she?" William wonders. "The children; the pilgrims; behind the pilgrims the trees, and behind them the fields—the beauty of the visible world took his breath away"; the "entrancing spectacle (to William) of dappled light and shade on half clothed, fantastically coloured, leaping, jerking, swinging legs and arms" makes him "clap[] till his palms stung" (BA 82, 93). During the preparations, clothes, crowns, paper swords, turbans lie flung over the grass in "pools of red and purple," "flashes of silver," giving off "warmth and sweetness" that draw butterflies; now the dispersing "pilgrims" feast on the found beauty that trails in the pageant's wake (BA 62–3, 201).

"Beauty—isn't that enough?" William ponders. "But here Isa fidgeted. . . . 'No, not for us, who've the future,' she seemed to say. The future disturbing our present" (BA 82). "Little England"'s part in this tableau on the cusp between pageant and "real" world evokes the future no "Beauty" can forestall. "A child new born" at the pageant's beginning, she is "still a child" now, her future clouded by imminent war. As "little England" melts into this "real" child who, with George and baby Caro—glimpsed as a fist throwing a toy from a pram—embodies the unknown future, the spontaneous tableau sutures the pageant to a historical world that never ceases beginning (BA 11). Their scripted parts yield to their "unacted parts" as the actors carry the play's expectant aura into "real" life (BA 153). The pageant achieves its "end" as the spectators see themselves performing a script of their own making: " 'He said she meant we all act. Yes, but whose play?' " (BA 199–200). The play for which, Bart says, they must "'Thank the actors, not the author. . . . Or ourselves, the audience'" melts imperceptibly into a living theater, history in the making (BA 203).

For Isa, disturbed by the future, beauty is not enough. As the play yields the stage to "real" life, her question—"D'you think people change?" looms large in her own case. The novel's last two scenes depict Isa and La Trobe in mysterious dialogue. Alone in the darkening landscape, La Trobe feels triumph and despair: "She could say to the world, You have taken my gift! . . . But what had she given? A cloud that melted into the other clouds on the horizon," a "failure" that "meant nothing" (BA 209). Suddenly the tree that shelters her during the pageant bursts into activity, its boughs "pelted" by starlings like "winged stones," humming with natural music "as if each bird plucked a wire": "A whizz, a buzz rose from the bird-buzzing, bird-vibrant, bird-blackened tree. The tree became a rhapsody, a quivering cacophony, a whizz and vibrant rapture, branches, leaves, birds syllabling discordantly life, life, life, without measure, without stop devouring the tree. Then up! Then off!"[53] From feeling that she has "suffered triumph, humiliation, ecstasy, despair, for nothing," La Trobe suddenly finds herself standing (like Antaeus) on an earth that metamorphoses before her eyes into the setting of her next play:

There was no longer a view—no Folly, no spire of Bolney Minster. It was land merely, no land in particular. She put down her case and stood looking at the land. Then something rose to the surface.

"I should group them," she murmured, "here." It would be midnight; there would be two figures, half concealed by a rock. The curtain would rise. What would the first words be? The words escaped her.

Again she lifted the heavy suitcase to her shoulder. She strode off across the lawn. . . . It was strange that the earth, with all those flowers incandescent . . . should still be hard. From the earth green waters seemed to rise over her. She took her voyage away from the shore, and, raising her hand, fumbled for the latch of the iron entrance gate. (*BA* 210–11)

Buoyed and replenished by the earth's green waters, the dialogic artist sets off in her cockleshell toward new lands, new civilizations, the future potential in the "real" voices she weaves into art. Drinking alone in the "shelter" of the village pub, she drowses and nods and dreams in "oblivion" among "voices" until "Words without meaning—wonderful words" rise from her mind's "fertile" depths, "above the intolerably laden dumb oxen plodding through the mud"; she sees "the high ground at midnight; there the rock; and two scarcely perceptible figures. Suddenly the tree was pelted with starlings. She set down her glass. She heard the first words" (*BA* 212).

As La Trobe listens in the pub, Isa and Giles are about to speak in the private house. Over dessert Lucy asks what the play meant—"The peasants; the kings; the fool and . . . ourselves?" Each looks at the play that still hangs "in the sky of the mind—moving, diminishing," "drifting away to join the other clouds," and sees "something different" (*BA* 212–13). Remembering "not the play but the audience dispersing," the "looking-glasses and the voices in the bushes," Isa wonders, "What did she mean?"; as the play fades in the darkening sky she thinks of the girl who "had gone skylarking with the troopers," had "screamed" and "hit him. . . . What then?" (*BA* 213, 216). Reading of "mammoths, mastodons, prehistoric birds" in her Outline of History, Lucy unknowingly sets the stage for the scene La Trobe imagines by symbolically obliterating that "house in a hollow" Pointz Hall: " 'Prehistoric man, . . . half-human, half-ape, roused himself from his semi-crouching position and raised great stones' " (*BA* 218). Finally, Giles and Isa, left alone, become the "two figures, half concealed by a rock," in La Trobe's mind's eye, "enormous" against the window, about to speak:

Alone, enmity was bared; also love. Before they slept, they must fight; after they had fought, they would embrace. From that embrace another life might be born. But first they must fight, as the dog fox fights with the vixen, in the *heart of darkness*, in the fields of night.

. . . The window was all sky without colour. The house had lost its shelter. It was night before roads were made, or houses. It was the night that dwellers in caves had watched from some high place among rocks.

Then the curtain rose. They spoke. (*BA* 219, my emphasis)

Here Woolf restages Genesis for the last time, returning full circle to the jungle scene in *The Voyage Out*. Isa—who longs for change, for a new plot—is poised on the verge of speech. But whereas a fatal silence weighs down Rachel and Terence, Isa and Giles, abstracted into the first man and woman in a world always beginning, always to be created anew, face a future that despite the looming war remains unknown, "open and free."[54] Added very late to the last page of Woolf's adventure toward new civilizations, the Conrad allusion frames this scene as a challenge to Marlow's famous speech act, the mortal-tasting "lie" he throws to the sentimental idea that women must be kept "out of" the public world "lest ours gets worse."[55] Like a wave approaching this sandcastle, the scene brings a woman armed not with clubs or guns but with words—symbolic weapons that rise up menacingly all day, shaking their fists—out of a not so beautiful private world onto the public stage. Will Isa's speech—which is to say ours, since "Our part is to be the audience"—only repeat, as some critics hold, like Mrs. Haines's on the cesspool: "What a subject to talk about on a night like this!" . . . "What a subject to talk about on a night like this!" (*BA* 58, 3–4)? Or might she/we speak a new word, to whose infinite possibilities the myriad speech acts captured in the narrative attest? That Isa, thinking of the rape as the play floats in the sky of her mind, wonders "What then?"; that a new "life" may issue from their fight and embrace; that La Trobe awaits their words as she voyages away from the shore: all keep an unforeseeable future in play.

What does Isa say? Will her words join that "force of tremendous power" that is breaking through the private house to the public world? Like *Civilization and Its Discontents*, *Between the Acts* and Woolf's modernist quest close with the eternal battle of Eros and Thanatos; and like Freud she forbears to rise up before her fellow men and women "as a prophet."[56] We want to hear Isa, or think we do; we resist Woolf's dissolution of her art's objecthood. But while we await Isa's words we resemble the spectators staring blankly at the empty stage as "The Present Time. Ourselves" unfolds. "We're the oracles," as a departing spectator says (*BA* 198). Only in the real world can the pageant and novel in the sky of the mind water and replenish a fighting force for what "we call, perhaps miscall, civilization" (*BA* 188). Woolf's last ending beckons us over the edge of the page toward opp portunities that history's violence continually interrupts but can never foreclose.

The Spectator's Freedom

"People are saying the end of the world has come. But it hasn't."
—Woolf, *Pointz Hall*

"Next time . . . next time . . . "
—Woolf, *Between the Acts*

Overspilling its fictional bounds into a real future beyond its ending, *Between the Acts* is an eloquent capstone to Woolf's and Bloomsbury's thinking in public in the spirit of Enlightenment modernity. As Kant was hailed as the philosopher of the people—of the French Revolution, human rights, freedom, self-governance—the dialogic novel and the pageant created by a "we" of orts, scraps, and fragments address not a cult or an elite but the people, the demos, the community. Theater—the communal art par excellence, originating in public festival—calls out a "we" with roots in European democracy's Athenian origins. In 1939, with Europe under totalitarian threat, the experimental pageant master La Trobe stages in public the spectators' freedom to create, talk, judge, and differ in the sociability that is human beings' highest end.

As Arendt observes in pursuing the political implications of Kant's aesthetics, the spectators constitute the public realm in which the pageant appears. It is they who create the field of its possibility; even its makers and actors—even La Trobe with her blood, sweat, and tears—must exercise the spectator's judgment to make their vision intelligible. In this sense, spectators "exist only in the plural," as a "we" whose members are always imaginatively involved with each other, and who—by contrast with the univocal mass audiences of Nazi extravaganzas, and even the comparatively passive audiences of Parkerian pageants—at once preserve their individual judgment and enlarge it in communication and community with others (*LK* 63). As the example of Isa shows, *Between the Acts'* narrative zeroes in on perspectival shifts between the private person encumbered with interests and prejudices and the spectator who looks and judges in company with others ("O look!"); who, since the spectators' part is to have "no part," to be "impartial," "outside the game," engaged in contemplation, can, at least in theory (*theōrein*, looking), cast off prejudice to see and judge disinterestedly—freely (*LK* 55).

For Kant, as we saw, to judge is not simply to give one's opinion but to set aside "interested" sentiment and prejudice, merely private and personal criteria, to experience the imaginative freedom and pleasure that a work of art puts in play. It is to widen one's thinking by taking others into account so as to form a judgment one believes ought to command assent from other unprejudiced spectators, whether or not it does in practice—a judgment for which one posits "subjective . . . universal validity." This only seemingly paradoxical claim, we noted, is binding not on others but only on the one who judges. It posits not that everyone must agree in judgments of beauty but that, in judging, I think beyond my own interests, take into account "the possible, rather than the actual, judgments of others"; I consider people in general, not by empathy (exchanging my prejudices for what I imagine to be theirs) nor by going along with the crowd but by imagination: by thinking in my own identity where actually I am not.[57] To judge, Arendt observes, is neither to jettison critical thought for passive acceptance of others' views nor to "cut off" one's thinking from others'. It is to make others "present" by "force of imagination": "one trains one's imagination to go visiting," in the spirit of that "right to go visiting" Kant posits in *Perpetual Peace* (*LK* 43). For "One judges always as a member of a community," and ultimately as "a member of a world community," in "one's 'cosmopolitan existence' "; one "take[s] one's bearings from the idea, not the actuality, of being a world citizen," "a world spectator"—like the Outsider who would give to England first what she desires of peace and freedom for the whole world (*LK* 75–76).

"The idea, not the actuality": the gap between theory and practice guarded by the notion of subjective universal validity means that there is always room for disagreement. Against the totalitarian threat across the Channel, the difference and disagreement voiced in the pageant's wake become practical proofs of the spectator's freedom. The spectator promises nothing. "D'you get her meaning?" Lucy asks, adding when Isa demurs, "But you might say the same of Shakespeare" (*BA* 175). As the spectators disperse, their voices float in air, subsumed in the phrase "someone was saying," punctuated by pauses in a rhythm of talking and listening:

> "I do think," someone was saying, "Miss Whatshername should have come forward and not left it to the rector . . . After all, she wrote it. . . . I thought it brilliantly clever . . . O my dear, I thought it utter bosh. Did *you* understand the meaning? Well, he said she meant we all act all parts. . . . He said, too, if I caught his meaning, Nature takes part. . . . Then there was the idiot. . . . Also, why leave out the Army, as my husband was saying, if it's history? And if one spirit animates the whole, what about the aeroplanes? . . . Ah, but you're being too exacting. After all, remember, it was only a village play. . . . For my part, I think they

should have passed a vote of thanks to the owners. When we had our pageant, the grass didn't recover till autumn . . . Then we had tents. . . . That's the man, Cobbet of Cobb's Corner, who wins all the prizes at all the shows. I don't myself admire prize flowers, nor yet prize dogs . . . "
(*BA* 197–98, Woolf's ellipses)

The music of spectatorship sounds in this medley, a sort of vocal reprise *ad libitum* (Latin: at pleasure) of the instrumental voices that earlier strain apart, crash, solve, unite, advance on the surface or dive under to wrestle with meaning, "all comprehending; all enlisted" in the "mind's immeasurable profundity" (*BA* 188–89). The narrator who wonders of La Trobe's musical finale, "Was that voice ourselves? Scraps, orts and fragments, are we, also, that?" transcribes the spectators' talk as discord and harmony, ephemeral as a cloud or play, perpetually moving between unity and dispersal within that "rambling capricious but somehow unified whole" whose unseen "pattern" connects "all life, all art, all waifs & strays" (*BA* 189).

These voices, not judging in theory but talking in practice, end prospectively, like pageant and novel: " 'Next time . . . next time . . . ' " (*BA* 201). If the gap between the subjective universal validity of judgments and their actual practice of spectatorship seems all but unbridgeable, at least one spectator muses, "was that, perhaps, what she meant? . . . that if we don't jump to conclusions, if you think, and I think, perhaps one day, thinking differently, we shall think the same?" (*BA* 200). In its tentative aspiration the question enacts spectatorship as a public "form of being together" where "no one rules and no one obeys," where people seek to "persuade each other" (*LK* 141). Its abstractness registers the *sensus communis* or common understanding, the community sense, as alive, not written in stone but actively held and perpetually open to debate, critique, reaffirmation—change.[58] When La Trobe refuses thanks as the dialogic pageant's "author," when Reverend Streatfield doffs the authority of his office to speak "only as one of the audience," when the spectators who at first mockingly fold their hands as if in church later repeat and debate his remarks, each performs spectatorship as thinking in freedom and community with others.[59]

What is important is not that the orts, scraps, and fragments who compose this "we" should "think the same" (the totalitarian spectacle's aim) but that in their individuality and freedom they can imagine doing so "one day." Repeated in fractal relation from pageant to "real" world to real world, this prospective view points beyond story or event to "the truth about this vast mass that we call the world": meaning lies not in the event ("Don't bother about the plot: the plot's nothing") but in the way it opens into "new horizons for the future" (*MB* 72, *BA* 90–92; *LK* 56). So the pageant floats in the sky of the mind, "melt[ing] into the other clouds on the horizon," and the spectators carry it into the world, giving it meaning as only they can, in the myriad ways summed up by Lucy's postpageant vision by the fishpond of "speckled, streaked, and blotched . . . beauty, power, and glory in ourselves" (*BA* 205, 209). As the spontaneous tableau beyond the ending suggests, the pageant, like the novel, has its "end" (formal and teleological) in "Ourselves": the spectators who are in the largest sense its protagonist, whom art enables momentarily to escape their— our—thick little egos to see ourselves reflected in the future of the community and human species that little "England" embodies and evokes (*LK* 57). In Arendt's words, "the Beautiful teaches us to 'love without self-interest,' " "to *liberate* ourselves" from "private conditions and circumstances" so as "to attain that relative impartiality that is the specific virtue of judgment"; to find that we have "an 'interest' in disinterestedness," in thinking and feeling as (in Streatfield's words) "part of the whole."[60]

"And if we're left asking questions," someone says, "isn't it a failure, as a play? I must say I like to feel sure if I go to the theatre, that I've grasped the meaning . . . Or was that, perhaps, what she meant?" (*BA* 199–200, ellipsis Woolf's). Does the pageant fail "as a play"? The voice first assumes that there is one meaning, "the" meaning, then wonders whether La Trobe meant to dispel that idea. Is it not the pageant's freedom from fixed, ascertainable meaning that signals its success—indeed, its very nature—as art: beauty, purposive without purpose; a new form, another nature, which gives rise to concepts without end, yet to which no concept is adequate; which offers not singular, universal meaning but the "gift" of pleasure and sociability, of talk as changing, ephemeral, and free as clouds? Against the young poets Woolf addresses in "The Leaning Tower," who declare that art makes nothing happen, *Between the Acts'* study of spectatorship proposes that art makes something important happen, not despite but because its effects are as diffuse as the shower that rescues the pageant from incomprehension. Diverging from her monologist friend Tom, Woolf allies her "new idea . . . about the drama" with nature—and human nature—as change: with the sea that demolishes systems like sandcastles, rain like all people's tears, art like clouds in the sky of the mind that regenerate feeling and community, private thought and public speech. To fail would be to make nothing happen: to fail to create beauty and the pleasures—free, disinterested judging, talk, community, a sense of "the whole" that preserves the individual, hope for the future— that beauty in its freedom occasions.

In its focus on the spectator's freedom, *Between the Acts* reflects on

Woolf's long career of fighting by thinking in the intimate public that was Bloomsbury and the greater, ever widening public in which her voice continues to sound. Woolf belonged to that public as writer or *Schriftstellerin*—her profession on the Nazi list, stamped "*Geheim!*" (secret), that names the Woolfs among the first in England to be arrested—and until 1938 as publisher, disseminating others' voices along with her own.[61] Totalitarian regimes can exist only by suppressing the freedom and truth telling of public speech, filling the vacuum with propaganda and jingoism. For Kant, in fact, "the most important political freedom" is "the freedom to speak and to publish"; and publicity is the very key to political good and evil (*LK* 39). Publicity—as essential to a good state as censorship to a bad one—solves "the problem of organizing a state" "even for a race of devils, if only they are intelligent," for if rational, they must assent to "universal laws for their preservation," even if each is "secretly inclined to exempt himself"; and a constitution designed so that they "check each other" produces the same "public conduct" as if each were not so inclined.[62] Kant's "devils," Arendt notes, are simply "those who are 'secretly inclined to exempt' themselves'," which to do publicly would expose them as "enemies of the people, even if these people were a race of devils. And in politics, as distinguished from morals, everything depends on '*public* conduct' " (*LK* 17–18, emphasis in original).

When Woolf reflected that as co-owner of a press she was "the only woman in England free to write what I like," she identified her freedom with her public voice (*D* 3:43, 22 September 1925). Owning a press, she could attack and outmaneuver "Hitler in England," could think in public on the world stage—a feat possible only in a "good" state, one that in principle protects public speech, whatever its practical obstacles.[63] Throughout her writing life the outsider Woolf exercised the free speech protected by Britain's democratic state—a freedom invoked by Leonard when, in 1939, he discounted Hitler's and Mussolini's impact on "the future of civilization," since "Even a semi-civilized state like Britain or France" could vanquish any dictator "if it remained true to the principles and traditions of its semi-civilization."[64] A year later Virginia alone held out against the prospect of a fascist victory while talking "about Civilisation" one evening with Leonard, Eliot, Clive Bell, and Saxon Sydney-Turner: "All the gents. against me. . . . Said very likely . . . this war means that the barbarian will gradually freeze out culture. . . . Clive also pessimised—saw the light going out gradually. So I flung some rather crazy theories into the air."[65] Having fought to escape Marlow's "beautiful world" and to forge a public voice, as the Bloomsbury gents (even the Jewish Leonard, a Cambridge Apostle after all) had not had to do, Woolf held to faith in the power of free public speech to vanquish Hitler in England and abroad.

When Woolf swam to her death on 28 March 1941, perhaps it was not that she had ceased to believe in civilization's future but that she could fight no more. If, like La Trobe, she could re-create the world only in collaboration with her audience; if hearing no "echo" from the wartime public felt like part of her death, neither the madness to which she attributed her suicide nor her death negate the future that pageant and novel leave open.[66] " 'Let it blaze against the yew trees,' " says Bernard of the "One life" the six friends have made. " 'There. It is over. Gone out' " (W 229). Woolf's late writings voyage toward a "whole world" as beautiful in its unfathomable purposes as a work of art. Herself gone out, her work survives—lives beyond her own life, lives more and further and better—in the private and public conversations, the public thinking and fighting, it continues to inspire. Woolf's legacy and Bloomsbury's is the unfinished and unfinishable fight for civilization—peace, freedom, art, beauty, sociability—that they hand on to the later generations of the "whole world," figured "first" in "little England," little George, and baby Caro's fist.

Preface

1. See Hannah Arendt, *On Revolution* (1965; New York: Penguin, 1979), chap. 6 ("The Revolutionary Tradition and Its Lost Treasure"), esp. section 3, 249–55. "Permanent revolution": Marshall Berman, *All That Is Solid Melts into Air: The Experience of Modernity* (New York: Simon and Schuster, 1982), 95.

2. Perry Anderson, "Modernity and Revolution," *New Left Review* 144 (March–April 1984): 102.

3. Philippe Sollers, *Writing and the Experience of Limits*, ed. David Hayman, trans. Philip Bernard and David Hayman (1968; New York: Columbia UP, 1983), 40–41 (translation modified). See Hannah Arendt, *Lectures on Kant's Political Philosophy*, ed. with an interpretive essay by Ronald Beiner (Chicago: U of Chicago P, 1982), 115.

4. Berman, *All That Is Solid*, 95–96.

5. E. g., the extensive writings of Jürgen Habermas, which seek to preserve and extend the emancipatory dimension and successes of the Enlightenment project while criticizing new forms of domination produced by it; Roy Porter, *Enlightenment: Britain and the Creation of the Modern World* (London: Allen Lane/Penguin, 2000); Sankar Muthu, *Enlightenment Against Empire* (Princeton: Princeton UP, 2003); Pamela Cheek, *Sexual Antipodes: Enlightenment, Globalization, and the Placing of Sex* (Stanford: Stanford UP, 2003); *What's Left of Enlightenment? A Postmodern Question*, ed. K. M. Baker and P. H. Reill (Stanford: Stanford UP, 2001); Robert C. Bartlett, *The Idea of Enlightenment: A Post-Mortem Study* (Toronto: U of Toronto P, 2001); Neil Postman, *Building a Bridge to the Eighteenth Century: How the Past Can Improve Our Future* (New York: Knopf, 2000); Anthony Cascardi, *Consequences of Enlightenment* (Cambridge: Cambridge UP, 1999); *Geography and Enlightenment*, ed. D. N. Livingstone and C. W. J. Withers (Chicago: U of Chicago P, 1999); Marie Fleming, *Emancipation and Illusion: Rationality and Gender in Habermas's Theory of Modernity* (University Park: Pennsylvania State UP, 1997); *Race and the Enlightenment*, ed. E. C. Eze (Oxford: Blackwell, 1997); Karlis Racevskis, *Postmodernism and the Search for Enlightenment* (Charlottesville: UP of Virginia, 1993).

1. Civilization and "my civilisation": Virginia Woolf and the Bloomsbury Avant-Garde

1. "In the decade before the 1914 war there was a political and social movement in the world, and particularly in Europe and Britain, which seemed at the

time wonderfully hopeful and exciting. It seemed as though human beings might really be on the brink of becoming civilized" (Leonard Woolf, *Beginning Again: An Autobiography of the Years 1911–1918* [New York: Harcourt Brace Jovanovich, 1964], 36).

2. Immanuel Kant, "An Answer to the Question: What Is Enlightenment?" (1784) in *Kant: Political Writings*, rev. ed., ed. Hans Reiss, trans. H. B. Nisbet (Cambridge: Cambridge UP, 1991), 54–60.

3. Leonard Woolf, *Barbarians Within and Without* (New York: Harcourt, Brace, 1939), 65, hereafter cited as *BWW*. Roy Porter and others argue that Enlightenment thought began earlier in Britain than in France and Germany in reaction to the seventeenth century's bloody civil wars. Citing J. G. A. Pocock, who writes that "the historiography of enlightenment in England remains that of a black hole," Porter addresses this "blind spot" in *Enlightenment: Britain and the Creation of the Modern World* (London: Allen Lane/Penguin Press, 2000), xvii.

4. Bloomsbury's boundaries are notoriously unfixed; I list here the figures central to my argument, though other associates (e. g., E. M. Forster, T. S. Eliot, Katherine Mansfield, Bertrand Russell, Lytton Strachey) also come into play. Raymond Williams, "The Bloomsbury Fraction," in *Problems in Materialism and Culture: Selected Essays* (New York: Verso, 1980) also includes Freud, albeit playfully reduced to "Sigmund for sex" (166). See also S. P. Rosenbaum's *The Early Literary History of the Bloomsbury Group* (New York: St. Martin's P), vol. 1, *Victorian Bloomsbury* (1987) and vol. 2, *Edwardian Bloomsbury* (1994). "Civil War": see Clive Bell, *Peace at Once* (Manchester and London: The National Labour Press Ltd., [1915]), 53; J. M. Keynes, *The Economic Consequences of the Peace* (New York: Harcourt, Brace and Howe, 1920), 5, hereafter cited as *ECP*; Leonard Woolf, *BWW*, 131. From the other side, Freud shifted from jingoistic patriotism in 1914 to pacifism as war casualties mounted; he publicly advocated the League of Nations and joined Einstein, Russell, and other international intellectuals in petitions for disarmament and peace (Gabriel Jackson, *Civilization and Barbarity in Twentieth-Century Europe* [New York: Prometheus/Humanity Books, 1999], 115). A group of continental intellectuals, including Einstein, rebutted a manifesto proclaiming German militarism the guardian of German culture with an antiwar "Counter-Manifesto" (October 1914) that called all "good Europeans" to unite to defend "international relations" and "a world-embracing civilization," for "never has any previous war caused so complete an interruption of that cooperation which should obtain among civilized nations"; the "many sympathetic replies . . . revealed such diverse dogmatic stands that the task of reconciling these views seemed hopeless, and the project was abandoned" (Albert Einstein, *The Fight Against War*, ed. Alfred Lief [New York: John Day, 1933], 5–7).

5. As Menno Spiering and Michael Wintle observe, after 1914 "many were forced actually to think for the first time about the very concept of Europe. If 'Europeanness,' European civilization and European superiority were taken for

granted around 1900, they never would be again in the same way" in face of
"the appalling record of inhumanity over four years. . . . The new ideologies of
communism and fascism . . . spawned of the European war . . . were to challenge and modify the ascendant liberal democracy. The war and its settlement
cemented the supreme position of the nation in politics, allowing it to dominate
the state at the expense of the interests of minorities. . . . The class system and
gender relations in Europe were fundamentally altered: the Great War was truly
a watershed for European civilization" (*Ideas of Europe Since 1914: The
Legacy of the First World War*, ed. Spiering and Wintle [New York: Palgrave
Macmillan, 2002], 4).

6. *D* 4:298 (9 April 1935), *TG* 95, *P* 6. In Woolf's writings the word has
many senses—light, ironic, playful, casual, commonplace, serious, inventive; as
in amenities (electricity, omnibuses, telephones, gas fires and cookers, Mozart
on the gramophone, ambulances—"one of the triumphs of civilisation" *MD*
151); city life ("the ease & speed of civilization") *v.* the desire to "rusticate" (*D*
3:45, *L* 6:302); the civility whose "thin veils" Mr. Ramsay rends "wantonly"
and "brutally" (*TL* 32); national or historical cultures, as in "no sign of our
snug English civilisation," Americans "alien to our civilisation," Jacob's and
Timmy's sense that "civilizations stood round them like flowers ready for picking" (*PA* 330, *D* 3:95, *JR* 76); human culture, e. g., *The Waves'* vision of a
future when "we are gone; our civilisation; the Nile; and all life," "the canopy
of civilisation is burnt out" (*W* 225, 296). Brian W. Shaffer, with different
emphases, finds Bloomsbury's "theory of civilization" "more an individual than
a collective phenomenon, more a state of mind than a nation-state" (*The Blinding Torch: Modern British Fiction and the Discourse of Civilization* [Amherst:
U of Massachusetts P, 1993], 17, 99, 80).

7. *MD* 36. See Lucien Febvre, "*Civilisation*: Evolution of a Word and a
Group of Ideas," in *A New Kind of History: From the Writings of Febvre*, ed.
Peter Burke, trans. K. Folca (London: Routledge and Kegan Paul, 1973),
219–57, esp. 220, 227, 228, 230. Febvre notes two major senses: the material,
intellectual, moral, political, and social life of a group, irrespective of any value
judgment; and Western civilization ("ours") with its progress, failures, greatness, weakness, "a collective asset and an individual privilege" (220). He contrasts the "old concept of a superior civilization" of "the white peoples of
Western Europe and Eastern America"—the "moral idea" of that civilization as
a "something . . . nobler . . . than anything outside it—savagery, barbarity or
semi-civilization"—the *ethnocentric* conception—with the "almost contradic-
tory" *ethnographic* concept of a civilization as all the observable features of the
collective material, intellectual, moral, political, and social life of one human
group (247, 220).

The word originated in late eighteenth-century France and England to
denote reason's "triumph and spread" (228) against systemic violence within
and beyond Europe. Boswell returned from a continental tour in 1766, the year
the French word was first recorded, and in 1772 recommended the (rejected)

dynamic form *civilization* for Johnson's *Dictionary*, which identifies *civility* with "freedom" and opposes it to *barbarity*; "I thought *civilisation*, from *to civilise*, better in the sense opposed to *barbarity* than *civility*; as it is better to have a distinct word for each sense, than one word with two senses" (James Boswell, *The Life of Samuel Johnson* [New York: Modern Library, n.d.], 400 (re March 23, 1772). Condorcet's 1781 usage opposes it to "war," "conquest," "slavery," and "want," within Europe and later throughout the world (Febvre 233). The American and French revolutions engaged its connotations of "progress in human enlightenment," democratic institutions, science, and adjudication of disputes by reason (238). Gradually, its meaning shifted from an "ethnocentric" (racialized, imperialist) concept of a "superior" civilization destined for territorial expansion toward an ethnographic, value-neutral, scientific, relativistic concept of civilizations plural; by 1920 European imperialism had long manifested an irreconcilable clash between the ethnocentric and the "practical, radical, and in itself incontestable" ethnographic concepts, though the idea of a "general human civilization remain[ed] alive in people's minds" (247–48). Bloomsbury registers a convergence of ethnocentric self-critique with ethnographic recognition of civilizations plural.

8. E. M. Forster, "Bloomsbury, An Early Note," *BGMC* 79. Gerald Brenan saw Bloomsbury as a "splendid flower of English culture" attached to a "dying" class and mode of life; "They carried the arts of civilized life and friendship to a very high point, and their work reflects this civilization"; "two of them at least, Virginia Woolf and Maynard Keynes, possessed those rare imaginative gifts that are known as genius" ("Bloomsbury in Spain and England," *BGMC* 355).

9. In *Saving Civilization: Yeats, Eliot, and Auden Between the Wars* (Cambridge: Cambridge UP, 1984), McDiarmid argues that these poets tended to "despair" of civilization's prospects and maintain, with Auden, that "Poetry makes nothing happen"; such salvation as they imagined involved "communal identity based on inherited myths, legends, and religious truths" (x, xi, 123). "Saving civilization," she observes, was a "roomy expression" that carried "greater self-consciousness and even embarrassment . . . with each generation": "Yeats rarely uses the word without approbation, Eliot rarely without quotation marks, and Auden rarely without skepticism" (4, 10). Bloomsbury's responses to the post-1914 crisis also contrast with D. H. Lawrence's Spenglerian jeremiad against mechanization and his call for strong leaders to take nations toward the unity of "one vast European state" (*Movements in European History*, in *The Cambridge Edition of the Works of D. H. Lawrence*, ed. Philip Crumpton (Cambridge: Cambridge UP, 1989), 242).

10. Peter Bürger, *Theory of the Avant-Garde*, trans. Michael Shaw (Minneapolis: U of Minnesota P, 1984), 49–50. Bürger's analysis of Brecht's art as "enter[ing] into a new relationship to reality" would also describe Woolf's art; her last novel, *Between the Acts*, implicitly questions his premise that art inhabits "a realm . . . distinct from the praxis of life" and his pessimistic thesis that

"Art as an institution prevents the contents of works that press for radical change . . . from having any practical effect" (91–92, 95). See also Rosenbaum, *Victorian Bloomsbury* (see n. 4, above), esp. 3–4, 24–28.

11. Bürger, *Theory*, 43. Edel calls Keynes a "suprapolitical" thinker (*Bloomsbury: A House of Lions* [Philadelphia and New York: Lippincott, 1979], 47). See Hannah Arendt, *Lectures on Kant's Political Philosophy*, ed. with an interpretive essay by Ronald Beiner (Chicago: U of Chicago P, 1982), 8 (citing Kant's Geselligheit / "Sociability"), 141, cf. 40; hereafter cited as *LK*. Discussions of Kant's influence on Bloomsbury have emphasized G. E. Moore and prewar Bloomsbury's aesthetics without reference to the political; see, for example, Rosenbaum, *Victorian Bloomsbury*, part 3; and Andrew McNeillie, "Bloomsbury," in *The Cambridge Companion to Virginia Woolf*, ed. Susan Raitt and Sue Roe (Cambridge: Cambridge UP, 2000), 1–22. Renato Poggioli observes that "avant-garde art can exist only in the type of society that is liberal-democratic from a political point of view, bourgeois-capitalistic from a socioeconomic point of view" (*The Theory of the Avant-Garde*, trans. Gerald Fitzgerald [Cambridge: Harvard UP, 1960], 106). Gene H. Bell-Villada extends these conditions to "a liberalizing capitalism," "a libertarian-permissive social-ism," even, "in principle, absolute monarchies" such as Wilhelmine Germany, Hapsburg Vienna, and Czarist Russia (*Art for Art's Sake and Literary Life: How Politics and Markets Helped Shape the Ideology and Culture of Aestheticism, 1720–1990* [Lincoln: U of Nebraska P, 1996], 157). Raymond Williams differentiates modernism ("the alternative, radically innovating experimental artists and writers" with "their own facilities of production, distribution and publicity") from the avant-garde ("fully oppositional formations, determined . . . to attack . . . the whole social order"); whereas modernism "proposed a new kind of art for a new kind of social and perceptual world," the avant-garde envisioned "a breakthrough to the future, its members not the bearers of a progress already repetitiously defined, but the militants of a creativity which would revive and liberate humanity" (*The Politics of Modernism: Against the New Conformists*, ed. Tony Pinkney [London: Verso, 1989], 50–51). Following Bürger, Andreas Huyssen differentiates historical avant-gardes from mod-ernism, wherein "art and literature retained their traditional 19th century autonomy from everyday life" (*After the Great Divide: Modernism, Mass Culture, Postmodernism* [Bloomington: Indiana UP, 1986], 163). Astradur Eysteinsson rejects this rigid distinction and argues for a more supple and imag-inative recognition of the interpenetrating features of modernism and the avant-garde (*The Concept of Modernism* [Ithaca: Cornell UP, 1990).

12. Williams, "The Bloomsbury Fraction," 166.

13. Williams, 165–66, 156, 168. A version of his essay reads: "embarrass-ing, that is to say, to those many for whom 'civilised individual' is a mere flag to fly over a capitalist, imperialist, and militarist social order" ("The Signifi-cance of 'Bloomsbury' as a Social and Cultural Group," in *Keynes and the Bloomsbury Group*, ed. D. Crabtree and A. P. Thirlwall [London: Macmillan,

1980], 63). Whereas Williams contrasts Bloomsbury's "social conscience" to the " 'social consciousness' of a self-organizing subordinate class" (156), Patrick Brantlinger finds that Bloomsbury embraced a democratic socialism close to Williams's and held pacifist, anti-imperialist, internationalist, and feminist positions in some ways more radical than his (" 'The Bloomsbury Fraction' Versus War and Empire," in *Seeing Double: Revisioning Edwardian and Modernist Literature*, ed. Carola M. Kaplan and Anne B. Simpson [New York: Macmillan, 1996], 150). In the decades since Williams tamed Edel's Bloomsbury "lions" by positing consumer culture as their "legacy," Bloomsburies bedecked in the logos of a global capitalist culture in which corporations dominate government and the public sphere have proliferated. E. g., Jennifer Wicke argues that "lifestyle is what Bloomsbury was selling" ("*Mrs. Dalloway* Goes to Market: Woolf, Keynes, and Modern Markets," *Novel* [fall 1994]: 6); and Jane Garrity allies Bloomsbury's "calculated self-promotion and exposure" with British *Vogue*'s stylesetting designs on all "'civilized corners of the globe'" ("Selling Culture to the 'Civilized': Bloomsbury, British *Vogue*, and the Marketing of Modernity," *Modernism / Modernity* 6:2 [1999]: 29–58).

14. Williams 166, 167; with this notion he forecloses the question: "We do not need to ask . . . whether Freud's generalizations on aggression are compatible with single-minded work for the League of Nations, or whether his generalizations on art are compatible with Bell's . . . or whether Keynes's ideas of public intervention in the market are compatible with the deep assumption of society as a group of friends and relations" (167). The group's indefinite and shifting boundaries as well as their multidisciplinary works can make its intellectual coherence hard to discern, not least because undue attention is paid to Clive Bell's "elitist's credo" *Civilization* (Edel, *Bloomsbury* 253), which Leonard judged "superficial" while its dedicatee, Virginia, complained that it reduced civilization to "'a lunch party at No. 50 Gordon Square'" (*D* 3:184, 31 May 1928; Quentin Bell, *Bloomsbury* [London: Weidenfeld and Nicolson, 1968], 88).

15. *RF* 272, citing a letter by Fry: "I'm gradually getting hold of a new idea about the real meaning of civilisation, or what it ought to mean. It's apropos of the question of the existence of individuals. It seems to me that nearly the whole Anglo-Saxon race especially of course in America have lost the power to be individuals. They have become social insects like bees and ants. They just are lost to humanity, and the great question for the future is whether that will spread or will be repulsed . . . whether people are allowed a clear space round them or whether society impinges on that and squeezes them all into hexagons like a honeycomb." Woolf adds, " 'The herd' is the phrase that dominates the letters at this time. . . . The herd . . . is the adversary, swollen immensely in size and increased in brute power. The herd on the one side, the individual on the other—hatred of one, belief in the other. . . . A vast mass of emotional unreason seemed to him to be threatening not only England—that was to be expected; but France also. France, he lamented, had lost that 'objectivity which has been

the glory of its great thinkers.' And this emotionalism, this irrationality could only be fought by science. We must try to understand our instincts, to analyse our emotions" (*RF* 232). *Civilization* is a key word for Fry and in Woolf's biography.

16. Bloomsbury's fight against the violence within European civilization resonates with contemporary global debates; see, for example, Onuma Yasuaki, "In Quest of Intercivilizational Human Rights: Universal vs. Relative Human Rights Viewed from an Asian Perspective," in *The East Asian Challenge for Human Rights*, ed. J. Bauer and D. Bell (Cambridge: Cambridge UP, 1998), expanded as "Towards an Intercivilizational Approach to Human Rights—for Universalization of Human Rights through Overcoming of Westcentric Notion of Human Rights" (English manuscript summary of his *Jinken, kokka, bumei / Human Rights, States and Civilizations*, Tokyo : Chikuma Sobo, 1998); and *Human Rights in Cross-Cultural Perspectives*, ed. A. An-Na'im (Philadelphia, 1992).

17. Sigmund Freud, *Civilization and Its Discontents*, trans. and ed. James Strachey (New York: Norton, 1961), 69, 92; hereafter cited as *CD*. At once English and European, Bloomsbury internationalism contravenes Hugh Kenner's equation of high modernism with the specific internationalism of American and Irish expatriate art (Pound, Eliot, Joyce, Stein), in contrast to "provincial," "regional" authors such as Faulkner, Williams, and Woolf ("The Making of the Modernist Canon," *Chicago Review* 34 [spring 1984]: 49–61).

18. Jean-Francois Lyotard, *The Postmodern Condition: A Report on Knowledge*, trans. Geoff Bennington and Brian Massumi (Minneapolis: U of Minnesota P, 1984), xxiii–xxiv; Susan Stanford Friedman, "Definitional Excursions: The Meanings of Modern / Modernity / Modernism," *Modernism / Modernity* 8:3 (2001): 507.

19. Leonard Woolf, *Downhill All the Way: An Autobiography of the Years 1919–1939* (New York: Harcourt Brace Jovanovich, 1967), 48.

20. Clive Bell, Play-Reading Book, King's College, Cambridge, cited in HL 261. See also Samuel Hynes, *A War Imagined: The First World War and English Culture* (New York: Atheneum, 1991), 84f; and Q. Bell on Bloomsbury's Enlightenment discourse: "The hatred of Christian for Christian, of nation for nation, the blind unreasoning hatred that had hounded Oscar Wilde or killed Socrates . . . were all communal emotions that resulted from irrationality. The sleep of reason engenders . . . the monsters of violence. . . . The great interest of Bloomsbury lies in the consistency, the thoroughness and, despite almost impossible difficulties, the success with which this [the suppression of irrational forces] was done" (*Bloomsbury*, 105; cf. 78, 67). My own argument is that Bloomsbury believed not that reason could "cure" society's irrationality but that rational institutions are its best hope of managing ineradicable aggression in face of the real, looming specter of totalitarianism; Freud's vision of history as unending struggle between the immortal adversaries Love and Death corrects myths of Enlightenment as an achieved state and/or inevitable progress.

21. Arendt, "Thinking and Moral Considerations," *Social Research* 38 (1971): 417–46, cited by Beiner, *LK* 109–10. For Kant, Arendt notes, the role of critical thought is not diminished where it does not prevail; even war (" 'an unintended enterprise . . . stirred up by men's unbridled passions' "), though always vetoed by moral-practical reason, provides " 'a motive for developing all talents serviceable for culture to the highest possible pitch' " and in " 'its very meaninglessness' " prepares " 'for an eventual cosmopolitan peace' "— with respect to which " 'we must simply act as if it could really come about,' " whether or not it is " 'really possible' " (*LK* 53–54).

22. Quentin Bell, *Bloomsbury Recalled* (New York: Columbia UP, 1995), 33; *TG* 80. Clive Bell, Duncan Grant, Bertrand Russell, and Lytton and James Strachey were conscientious objectors; Russell was imprisoned and deprived of his Cambridge lectureship in 1916. Leonard condemned the "senseless and useless war . . . which our government probably could have prevented and should never have become involved in" but was not a "complete pacifist"; once war began, he felt "the Germans must be resisted and I therefore could not be a Conscientious Objector"; he was excused from service because of his congenital tremor (*Beginning Again* 177). As an important Treasury official, Keynes was exempt from conscription; at seventeen he had been a pacifist in the Boer War (Edel, *Bloomsbury* 51). *Peace at Once* nearly lost Clive his family income and inheritance (*Selected Letters of Vanessa Bell*, ed. Regina Marler [New York: Pantheon, 1998], 167). Fry was descended from eight generations of Quakers (*RF* 11).

23. Clive Bell, *Peace at Once* (Manchester and London: National Labour Press, [1915]), 5.

24. See Robert Skidelsky, *John Maynard Keynes*, vol. 1, *Hopes Betrayed 1883–1920* (London: Macmillan, 1983), 358.

25. See Leonard Woolf, *International Government* (1916), *Empire and Commerce in Africa* (1920), *Economic Imperialism* (1920), *Imperialism and Civilization* (1928), *The Intelligent Man's Way to Prevent War* (1933), *Barbarians Within and Without* (*Barbarians at the Gate* in the English edition) (1939), and *The War for Peace* (1940). On the contribution of Leonard's *International Government* to the League of Nations, see Edel, *Bloomsbury* 240–41; Alex Zwerdling, *Virginia Woolf and the Real World* (Berkeley: U of California P, 1986), chap. 10; Laura Moss Gottlieb, "The War between the Woolfs," *Virginia Woolf and Bloomsbury: A Centenary Celebration*, ed. Jane Marcus [Bloomington: Indiana UP, 1987], 242; Brantlinger, 153f, who cites Duncan Wilson's view of *International Government* as "a landmark in the study of international affairs" in *Leonard Woolf: A Political Biography* (New York: St. Martin's P, 1978), 67; and Wayne K. Chapman and Janet M. Manson, "Carte and Tierce: Leonard, Virginia Woolf, and War for Peace," in *Virginia Woolf and War*, ed. Mark Hussey (New York: Syracuse UP, 1991), 58–78.

26. John Keegan, *The First World War* (New York: Knopf, 1999), chap. 3.

27. Leonard Woolf, *Growing: An Autobiography of the Years 1904–1911* (New York: Harcourt Brace Jovanovich, 1961), 111, 113–14.

28. Leonard Woolf, *Empire and Commerce in Africa: A Study in Economic Imperialism* (London: Allen and Unwin, [1920]), 24, 10, 9, 356; hereafter cited as *ECA*. See Natania Rosenfeld, *Outsiders Together: Virginia and Leonard Woolf* (Princeton: Princeton UP, 2000), chap. 1. On rival European imperialisms as a cause of the war, see also Keegan, *The First World War*, chap. 7.

29. *ECA* 353, 69, 49. See Adam Hochschild, *King Leopold's Ghost: A Story of Greed, Terror, and Heroism in Colonial Africa* (Boston: Houghton Mifflin, 1998), esp. 273.

30. L. Woolf, *Imperialism and Civilization* (1928), 28; he calls for "the end of imperialism, the end of conflict, and the beginning of a synthesis of civilizations" (135). "The 'native' is no longer to be regarded as the 'live-stock' on Europe's African estate, as the market for the shoddy of our factories and our cheap gin, or as the 'cheap labour' by means of which the concessionaire may supply Europe with rubber and ivory and himself with a fortune, but as a human being with a right to his own land and his own life, . . . to be educated and to determine his own destiny, to be considered, in that fantastic scheme of human government which men have woven over the world, an end in himself rather than an instrument to other people's ends" (Woolf, *ECA* 356–57, 359); "Imperialism was rechristened the white man's burden, and imperialists who slaughtered Africans . . . said . . . that what they were really doing was civilising savages" (*BWW* 132).

31. See Sigmund Freud, *The Future of an Illusion*, trans. W. D. Robson-Scott, rev. and ed. James Strachey (New York: Doubleday Anchor, 1964), 2–3f, hereafter cited as *FI*; and Freud, *CD*, 23f. The Woolfs' Hogarth Press published *The Future of an Illusion* in 1928 and *Civilization and Its Discontents* in 1930. For fuller discussion see my chapter 4.

32. For Freud as for Keynes, civilization encompasses all the knowledge and capacity by which humankind controls destructive natural forces and uses natural resources to satisfy its needs as well as the regulation of human relations, "especially the distribution of the available wealth"; since social relations organize power and wealth, these material and social economies are interdependent: human relations are "profoundly influenced by the amount of instinctual satisfaction which the existing wealth makes possible," and some individuals function as wealth for others through labor or sexual attachment (*FI* 3).

33. *FI* 81, 88. Freud frames religion as the "universal obsessional neurosis of humanity," which protects against personal neurosis by writing neurosis large in the form of cultural myth (*FI* 70). See also my chapter 4.

34. *FI* 43–44 and 44 n; Freud argues that whereas a religious believer can only "despair" when its illusions collapse, those who live by "reason and experience . . . can bear it if a few of our expectations turn out to be illusions," for "our science is no illusion"; and our mental apparatus is "part of the world," equal to the challenge of exploring it (*FI* 89, 91–92). Against "an artist's joy in creating," he wants to argue, "fate can do little," though he acknowledges that art can no more than any other human endeavor provide an "impenetrable

armour" against fate (*CD* 26–27). Cf. Fry: "If religions made no claim but what art does—of being *a* possible interpretation without any notion of objective validity all would be well . . . but religions all pretend to do what science tries to do—namely discover *the* one universally valid construction and hence . . . religions have always obstructed the effort towards more universal validity" and "have stood in the way of the disinterested study (science) and vision (art) of the universe. I don't doubt they've had to because men couldn't straight away get the disinterested attitude, but I think they ought to go, and that one can't by reinterpreting . . . make them friends of man's real happiness" (*RF* 271–72).

35. *BWW* 68, 150; in subverting the dictatorship of the proletariat by a dictatorship of party rulers, he writes, they are "destroying with one hand the civilization which they are attempting to build with the other" (160).

36. Freud, "On Transience," *The Standard Edition of the Complete Psychological Works of Sigmund Freud*, trans. and ed. James Strachey, 24 vols. (London: Hogarth P, 1953–66), 14:307; hereafter *SE*. In light of Freud's postwar account of aggression, it is surely de trop to insist that irony colors his thinking on civilization and freedom, as it is blind to ignore his stress on science and art as he pursues the question of how to rebuild civilization "on firmer ground" in face of ineradicable human aggression in his later works.

37. *CD* 58; Freud considers that the Golden Rule "cannot be recommended as reasonable" and "jokingly" recommends as closer to "psychological truths" Heinrich Heine's fantasy of life's simple pleasures: a "humble cottage," "good food," fresh milk, butter, flowers, "a few fine trees," "and if God wants to make my happiness complete, . . . the joy of seeing some six or seven of my enemies hanging from those trees. Before their death I shall . . . forgive them all the wrong they did me in their lifetime. One must, it is true, forgive one's enemies—but not before they have been hanged" (*CD* 57 and n). Edel notes that Leonard demurred from Keynes's representation of early Bloomsbury thought as "ingenuous utopianism" with "no respect for traditional wisdom, or the restraints of custom"; Leonard "had always taken a dim view of society" and "argued that the very nature of their discussions showed they knew the world for what it was" (*Bloomsbury* 54); cf. Quentin Bell, "Maynard Keynes and His Early Beliefs," *Bloomsbury Recalled* 224. Joshua D. Esty argues that "My Early Beliefs" does not just "diagnose a youthful error" but "claims that rational individualism is historically obsolete" ("National Objects: Keynesian Economics and Modernist Culture in England," *Modernism / Modernity* 7:1 [2000]: 3).

38. *LK* 17–18 citing Kant, *Perpetual Peace*; for fuller discussion see my chapter 9.

39. *D* 3:207 10 November, cf. 3:201, 27 October 1928, where, having given the lectures that became *A Room of One's Own*, Woolf writes, "I think I see reason spreading" and wishes she had the intellectual training to "deal with real things"; on *Room*'s allusions to the trial see my chapter 6. Woolf's "fence" figure anticipates Hannah Arendt's etymological linking of the law with the

notion of a wall or boundary line that harbors and encloses political life (*The Human Condition* [Chicago: U of Chicago P, 1958], 65–66).

40. Shaffer, *The Blinding Torch*, n. 6 above.

41. Kathy J. Phillips, *Virginia Woolf Against Empire* (Knoxville: U of Tennessee P, 1994), 200; Phillips tends to identify civilization with imperialism.

42. See J. H. Willis, Jr., *Leonard and Virginia Woolf as Publishers: The Hogarth Press, 1917–41* (Charlottesville: U of Virginia P, 1992), 237, 396–99 and passim. Between the purchase of its first hand press in 1917 and Virginia's death in 1941, the Press published Eliot's *Waste Land*, *Poems*, and *Homage to John Dryden*, all of Virginia's books except the first edition of *Night and Day*, Katherine Mansfield's *Prelude*, five volumes of Rilke in translation, translations of Gorky's *Reminiscences of Tolstoi*, Chekhov, Dostoevsky, Andreyev and Bunin, eight volumes of Freud, Christopher Isherwood's *Goodbye to Berlin*, Henry Green's *Party Going*, E. M. Forster's *What I Believe*, and Roger Fry's *The Artist and Psycho-Analysis*. In economics, politics, and social theory, it published Keynes's *The Economic Consequences of Mr. Churchill*, *A Short View of Russia*, and *The End of Laissez-Faire*, Kingsley Martin's *British Public and the General Strike*, Kathleen Innes's pamphlets on the League of Nations for young people, many works on disarmament, international arbitration, and world peace, including H. G. Wells's *Democracy under Revision*, *The Common Sense of World Peace*, and *The Open Conspiracy* and Philip Noel-Baker's *Disarmament and the Coolidge Conference*, eight pamphlets on Russia, communism, and Marxism, and Mussolini's *The Political and Social Doctrine of Fascism* ("the only statement by Mussolini of the philosophic basis of fascism"), followed by Leonard's attack on "the savage quackery of modern totalitarianism" in *Quack, Quack!* and *The League in Abyssinia*. Its anti-imperialist list included Leonard's *Imperialism and Civilization* and *After the Deluge: A Study of Communal Psychology*, Norman Leys's *Kenya*, *The Colour Bar in Africa*, and *Last Chance in Kenya*, Lord Olivier's *The Anatomy of African Misery* and *White Capital and Coloured Labor*, Denis Ireland's *Ulster Today and Tomorrow*, Leonard Barnes's *The New Boer War* and *The Future of Colonies*, C. L. R. James's *The Case for West Indian Self-Government*, K. M. Pannikar's *Caste and Democracy*, W. G. Ballinger's *Race and Economics in South Africa*, and Parmenas Githendu Mockerie's *An African Speaks for His People*. On women and civilization Hogarth published Margaret Llewelyn Davies's *Life as We Have Known It*, Ray Strachey's *Our Freedom and Its Results*, Jane Harrison's *Reminiscences of a Student's Life*, Willa Muir's *Women: An Inquiry*, Viscountess Rhondda's *Leisured Women*, G. S. Dutt's *A Woman of India: Being the Life of Faroj Nalini (Founder of the Women's Institute Movement in India)* and Woolf's feminist classics, *A Room of One's Own* and *Three Guineas*.

43. Kant, "What Is Enlightenment?" (n. 2 above): "The guardians who have kindly taken upon themselves the work of supervision will soon see to it that by far the largest part of mankind (including the entire fair sex) should consider the step forward to maturity not only difficult but also highly dangerous. Now,

this danger is not so very great, for they would certainly learn to walk eventually after a few falls. But an example of this kind is intimidating and usually frightens them off" (54).

44. Arthur Power, *Conversations with James Joyce*, ed. Clive Hart (Chicago: U of Chicago P, 1974, 1982), 35.

45. Both Bloomsbury scholars and feminist theorists have been slow to take account of the Enlightenment terms of Woolf's feminism. Williams's "class fraction" analysis ignores Woolf's observation that the class of educated men "possesses . . . practically all the capital, . . . land, . . . valuables, . . . and patronage in England" (*TG* 25); he finds "the delay in higher education for women of this class" a factor in "the specific character of the Bloomsbury Group" and a "persistent sexual asymmetry" "an important element in [its] composition," its "effects . . . ironically and at times indignantly noted by Virginia Woolf" (161–62). (On Marxism's elision of men and women as political subjects whose interests cut across economic class boundaries, see Monique Wittig, "The Mark of Gender," in *The Poetics of Gender*, ed. Nancy K. Miller [New York: Columbia UP, 1983], 63–73). Brantlinger reduces *Three Guineas'* political argument to "an aestheticized anarchism in which personal relationships take precedence over politics, laws, and institutions," one that refuses "to be political in the standard, common sense of the term . . . because politics refuses to include women and . . . means empire and war" (157, 163).

In *Feminism as a Radical Humanism* (Boulder, Colo.: Westview, 1994), Pauline Johnson finds feminist thinkers in "bad faith" in respect to their Enlightenment inheritance: "contemporary feminism is itself dependent on . . . those ideals of civil and human rights which are inscribed in modern social institutions" and "is as much a specific articulation of the universalizing dimension of modern humanism as it is the inheritor and interpreter of the idea of self-determining individuality" (ix). Yet she charges Woolf with creating an "alternative vision" that separates "the polysemic artwork from the sphere of everyday social practices" and offers only "a compensatory, substitute gratification which siphons off and renders harmless the radical need for changed gender relations"; although Woolf posits an "ideal subjectivity" that "empowers her fiction with a strongly critical standpoint, the merely aesthetical character of this ideal means that her critique ultimately fails to project a practical imperative" ("From Virginia Woolf to the Post-Moderns: Developments in a Feminist Aesthetic," *Radical Philosophy* 45 [1987]: 29). For Rita Felski, Woolf and Stein represent "an artistic and intellectual—though not necessarily political—elite" (*The Gender of Modernity* [Cambridge: Harvard UP, 1995], 27–28) and, thus, a modernist "conception of the text as a privileged and subversive space" which "undermines truth and self-identity" and "has a potential tendency to limit direct political effects, precisely because it presupposes the separation of the polysemic artwork from the sphere of everyday social practices" (*Beyond Feminist Aesthetics: Feminist Literature and Social Change* [Cambridge: Harvard UP, 1989], 162–63).

46. Of the "explosion of genius" in eighteenth- and nineteenth-century Germany and Austria, Noel Annan writes, "No one can appreciate the nineteenth century, or indeed our own times, unless he realizes that we live in the shadow of a Renaissance as brilliant and dominating as the Italian Renaissance" (*Leslie Stephen: The Godless Victorian*, [New York: Random House, 1984], 165). On "Stephen's Rehabilitation of the Augustan Age" see Annan, chap. 8; René Wellek, *Immanuel Kant in England, 1793–1838* (Princeton: Princeton UP, 1931), cites Stephen's essay "The Importation of German" (*Studies of a Biographer*, 2:38–75). See also Rosenbaum, *Victorian Bloomsbury*, chap. 10 ("Moore"). If Kant and Freud—himself a great Enlightenment figure who intended psychoanalysis to help free human beings from the trammels of the unconscious as of superstition—seem yoked by violence together, I would emphasize the continuity between Freud's radical insights on postwar Europe's future, Kant's vision of Enlightenment as unending struggle, and both thinkers' deep ambivalence toward civilization and their stress on rational systems and institutions rather than individuals in their political thought; in short, their pessimism of the intellect, optimism of the will. The Freud Library in London and New York holds several titles by Kant.

47. S. P. Rosenbaum, "Wittgenstein in Bloomsbury," in *The British Tradition in 20th Century Philosophy: Proceedings of the 17th Annual Wittgenstein Symposium*, ed. Jaako Hintikka and Klaus Puhl (Vienna 1995), rpt. in Rosenbaum, *Aspects of Bloomsbury: Studies in Modern English Literary and Intellectual History* (New York: St Martin's P, 1998), 173. The word *disinterested* had of course long been in play in Britain, in the eighteenth-century writings of Alison, Shaftesbury, Addison, Hutcheson, and others and later in Matthew Arnold's understanding of the critic's obligation to make "a disinterested effort to learn and propagate the best that is known and thought in the world" (*The Complete Prose Works of Matthew Arnold*, ed. R. H. Super, 3:282), aspects of which resonate in I. A. Richards's systematic analytic method, T. S. Eliot's emphasis on "impersonality," and F. R. Leavis's analytic "laboratory-method." See also D. H. Lawrence's 1914 letter to Edward Garnett on the obsolescence of the literary character's "old stable *ego*" (*The Letters of D. H. Lawrence*, 8 vols., ed. James T. Boulton [New York: Cambridge UP, 1979–2000], vol. 2, ed. G. J. Zytaruk and J. T. Boulton, 183).

48. Immanuel Kant, *Critique of Judgment*, trans. J. H. Bernard (New York: Hafner, 1951), §8, 49; hereafter cited as *CJ* by section and page. Cf. *Critique of the Power of Judgment*, ed. Paul Guyer, trans. Guyer and Eric Matthews (Cambridge: Cambridge UP, 2000), §8, 100; hereafter cited as *CPJ*. "Subjective . . . universal validity"—on the face of it a contradiction in terms—is the key to art as a bridge between one mind and another, a point that challenges Pierre Bourdieu's relegation of Kant to a " 'high' aesthetic" and his claim that he (and not Kant) is at pains to "bestow worth on all others" (*Distinction: A Social Critique of the Judgment of Taste*, trans. Richard Nice [Cambridge: Harvard UP, 1984], 485). Kant distinguishes the "*common sense*" based in feeling, which

provides a "subjective principle" of "universal validity" in aesthetic judgments, from "common understanding, which people sometimes call common sense (*sensus communis*)" (*CJ* §20, 75, *CPJ* 122).

49. As we shall see in considering Lily Briscoe's abstract composition and *The Waves* in my chapters 5–6; and contra Bell-Villada, *Art for Art's Sake*, who attributes a failure of discipline to modernist art forms.

50. *CJ* Introduction IX, 32–34, §13 58–59; *CPJ* 35–38, 107–8; not to be confused with a lack of discipline in the art.

51. Clive Bell, *Proust* (New York: Harcourt Brace Jovanovich, 1929), 85.

52. *LK* 42–43; *CJ* §19–22 74–77 (*CPJ* 121–24) and passim. Cf. Benjamin Constant: "Art for art, without aim, since any aim denatures art. But art attains an aim it does not have" (cited by Bell-Villada, *Art for Art's Sake*, 26–27).

53. Virginia Woolf, "Women & Fiction" holograph manuscript, Fitzwilliam Museum, Cambridge, England. Rosenbaum transcribes *nobody* here; the handwriting is inconclusive.

54. Clive Bell, *Art*, ed. J. B. Bullen (1914; New York: Oxford, 1987), xi; note that Bell skips G. E. Moore's *Principia Ethica*. For a comparison of Fry's and Bell's aesthetic writings, see Bullen's introduction; for Bell's critique of Moore, see *Art* 87f. For Bell's argument that "good states of mind" arise from aesthetic contemplation see *Art*, chap. 3, esp. 114–117 in which he concludes that "there are no qualities of greater moral value than artistic qualities, since there is no greater means to good than art" (117). Woolf thought of dedicating *To the Lighthouse* to Fry, who had "kept me on the right path, so far as writing goes, more than anyone" (*L* 3:385, 27 May 1927) and wrote that his "simple gospel" was "that all decency and good come from people's gradually determining to enjoy themselves a little, especially to enjoy their intellectual curiosity and their love of art" (*RF* 291).

55. Fry, "An Essay on Aesthetics," in *Vision and Design*, ed. J. B. Bullen (1920; Mineola, N.Y.: Dover, 1998), 21. Kant's influence is felt in Fry's remarks on form's relation to the "aesthetic judgment proper"; his "Essay" distinguishes art from ordinary life by its presentation of "a life freed from the binding necessities of our actual existence"; speculates that "the fullness and completeness of the imaginative life may correspond to an existence more real and more important than any that we know of in mortal life" and "represent . . . what mankind feels to be the completest expression of its own nature, the freest use of its innate capacities"; and asserts that art's proper beauty is "supersensual" and "satisfies fully the needs of the imaginative life" (15–16, 21, 22). Bell similarly emphasizes Kantian disinterestedness, or "detachment from the concerns of life," in his "aesthetic hypothesis—that the essential quality in a work of art is significant form": "the formal significance of any material thing is the significance of that thing considered as an end in itself. . . . Instead of recognizing its accidental and conditioned importance, we become aware of its essential reality . . . that which lies behind the appearance of all things—that which gives to all things their individual significance, the thing in itself, the ultimate reality. . . .

Those who find the chief importance of art or of philosophy in its relation to conduct or its practical utility . . . will never get from anything the best that it can give" (*Art* 100, 68–70). The distinction, in other words, is not between art and everyday social practices but between aesthetic contemplation as an everyday social practice and the purposive, utilitarian concerns of everyday life.

56 . *A Roger Fry Reader*, ed. Christopher Reed (Chicago: U of Chicago P, 1996), 87–88.

57. Desmond MacCarthy, secretary for the First Post-Impressionist show, notes that his own share of the profits amounted to £460 but that Fry "did not make one penny" from it or later from the Omega Workshops (*BGMC* 79).

58. *RF* 153. E. g., an influential *Times* critic called it "a rejection of all that civilisation has done"; the artist Eric Gill found it a crux of "reaction and transition" (*RF* 154–55). The poet Wilfred Scawen Blunt saw "idleness and impotent stupidity, a pornographic show"; one Dr. Hyslop diagnosed the paintings as "the work of madmen"; Gauguin and Van Gogh were "too much" even for Forster (Christopher Hassell, *A Biography of Edward Marsh* [New York: Harcourt Brace, 1959], 168, cited by Hynes, 328). Virginia judged the paintings less good than books but (as a survivor of life with George Duckworth, perhaps?) was mystified that duchesses could take offense at such "modest" art, "innocent even of indecency" (*RF* 156–57; *L* 1:440, 27 November). To Fry the public's "outbreak of militant Philistinism" proved that, for the ostensibly "cultivated classes" who had lapped up his lectures on "Raphael, Titian, Botticelli, and the rest," art was "merely a social asset"; in sensibility and the capacity for disinterested aesthetic judgment, "one's housemaid 'by a mere haphazard gift of providence' might surpass one" (*RF* 157–58, 161). See also Samuel Hynes, *The Edwardian Turn of Mind* (Princeton: Princeton UP, 1968), 325–26, and Peter Stansky, *On or About December 1910: Early Bloomsbury and its Intimate World* (Cambridge: Harvard UP, 1996), chaps. 7–8.

59. See n. 45 above.

60. On her father's role in Virginia Woolf's education and the importance of her reading in history to her literary experiments, see Katherine C. Hill, "Virginia Woolf and Leslie Stephen: History and Literary Revolution," *PMLA* 96 (May 1981): 351–62. On Stephen's ambivalence toward women's education, see Lyndall Gordon, *Virginia Woolf: A Writer's Life* (New York: Norton, 1984), chap. 6.

61. Henry Sidgwick (who like Stephen resigned his Cambridge fellowship in protest against the condition that he sign the Thirty-Nine Articles) stipulated that the women's college he founded, Newnham, should have no chapel.

62. Annan, *Leslie Stephen* 42; see 43–47. Annan notes the irregularity of Stephen's being allowed to remain a fellow though not a tutor in those reformist days.

63. *CR* 39; *D* 3:271, 8 December 1929, 1:224, 7 December 1918. On Woolf's passion for Richard Hakluyt's *Voyages: The Principal Navigations Voyages Traffiques and Discoveries of the English Nation Made by Sea or*

Over-land to the Remote and Farthest Distant Quarters of the Earth at any time within the compasse of these 1600 Yeeres (1600), see Alice Fox, *Virginia Woolf and the English Renaissance* (Oxford: Clarendon, 1990), chap. 2, and "Virginia Woolf at Work: The Elizabethan *Voyage Out*," *Bulletin of Research in the Humanities* 84 (spring 1981): 65–84. Joanna Lipking pointed out in conversation that some of these were slave voyages. In *Step-Daughters of England: British Women Modernists and the National Imaginary* (New York: Manchester UP, 2003), Jane Garrity argues that modernist women writers reinscribe "the rhetoric of empire even as they resist it," "trading on the familiar British trope of geographical expansionism and conquest"; though she does not analyze Hakluyt's part in the discourse of imperialism that Woolf inherits and transforms, her book provides a useful point of departure for such a study (3).

64. "'Ginia is devouring books, almost faster than I like," *Sir Leslie Stephen's Mausoleum Book*, ed. Alan Bell (Oxford: Clarendon, 1977), 103 (journal entry, 10 April 1897).

65. On Woolf's self-fashioning after Shakespeare, see my "Virginia Woolf as Shakespeare's Sister: Chapters in a Woman Writer's Autobiography," in *Women's Re-Visions of Shakespeare: On Responses of Dickinson, Woolf, Rich, H. D., George Eliot, and Others*, ed. Marianne Novy (Urbana: U of Illinois P, 1990), 123–42.

66. Cf. Ann Banfield, *The Phantom Table: Woolf, Russell, Fry, and the Epistemology of Modernism* (Cambridge: Cambridge UP, 2000), 8f.

67. Bell, *Bloomsbury*, 24. On the social history of the Apostles' cultivation of friendship and moral authority, see W. C. Lubenow, *The Cambridge Apostles, 1820–1914: Liberalism, Imagination, and Friendship in British Intellectual and Professional Life* (Cambridge: Cambridge UP, 1998). Leslie Stephen, Clive Bell, and Thoby were not members; Leonard Woolf, Keynes, Lytton and James Strachey, Saxon Sydney-Turner, Roger Fry, Forster, MacCarthy, and Henry Lamb were, as well as G. E. Moore, Bertrand Russell, and Alfred North Whitehead. Clive Bell's Midnight Society (himself, Leonard, Thoby, Lytton, Saxon Sydney-Turner, and A. J. Robertson) at Trinity was also important to forming the friendships that led to Bloomsbury.

68. *MB* 54; Bell, *Bloomsbury*, 40. In her late memoir Virginia notes "the influence on me of the Cambridge Apostles" (*MB* 80). On the Apostles' 9–1 vote in favor of admitting women in 1894 (after Russell delivered a paper titled "Lövberg or Hedda?"), actually executed only in 1970, see Banfield, *The Phantom Table*, 20–21.

69. QB 1:98. The Three Graces Euphrosyne (Joy), Aglaia (Brilliance) and Thalia (Bloom), daughters of Zeus, inspire delightful conversation. *Euphrosyne*'s authors were Saxon Sydney-Turner, Lytton Strachey, Clive Bell, Walter Lamb, Leonard Woolf, and some others (QB 1:98, 1:205). Individual poems are unattributed in the book, but see Rosenbaum, *Edwardian Bloomsbury* (n. 4 above), chap. 3, esp. 63–64. A catalogued letter from Christabel

MacLaren, Baroness Aberconway, identifying the authors of particular poems was discovered to be missing from the British Library copy in May 2003.

70. "Euphrosyne," *Cambridge Review* 27 (2 November 1905): 49, cited by Rosenbaum, *Edwardian Bloomsbury*, 73.

71. QB 1.205–6 and n. Virginia teases, "they entered the College, young & ardent & conceited; pleased with themselves, but so well pleased with the world that their vanity might be forgiven them. They return not less impressed with their own abilities indeed, but that is the last illusion left to them."

72. *M* xv; Louise A. DeSalvo, *Virginia Woolf's First Voyage: A Novel in the Making* (Totowa, N.J.: Rowman and Littlefield, 1980), 29–31. The ship was earlier called *Sarah Jane*.

73. *CDB* 96, 95. Adrian Stephen, "The *Dreadnought* Hoax," *BGR* 16–17. George Duckworth was aghast at Virginia's recklessness of her reputation. See also QB 1:157–61, appendix E, passim; Peter Stansky, *On or About December 1910*, chap. 2; HL 278–83.

74. See Lisa Tickner, *The Spectacle of Women: Imagery of the Suffrage Campaign 1907–1914* (Chicago: U of Chicago P, 1988), 120–21; 139 women filed statements alleging acts of violence, twenty-nine "violence with indecency." Tickner notes that WSPU militancy from 1905 combined with the 1906 Liberal landslide to infuse new energy into the suffrage campaign (begun in 1867); by 1910 it encompassed " 'all classes, . . . every rank and grade,' " and it had " 'organised the arts in its aid' " (xii, citing Cicely Hamilton, *A Pageant of Great Women* [1909]). See also Stansky, *On or About December 1910*, chap. 6 and passim; Martha Vicinus, *Independent Women: Work and Community for Single Women, 1850–1920* (Chicago: U of Chicago P, 1985), esp. 253, 265; and my "Modernism, Genetic Texts, and Literary Authority in Woolf's Portraits of the Artist as the Audience," *The Romanic Review*, ed. A. Compagnon and A. Grésillon, 86:3 (1996): 513–26.

75. Long afterward, at work on *Roger Fry*, Woolf planned a "break in the book. A change of method" on reaching "the Post I[mpressionist]s. & ourselves" (*D* 5:160, 7 August 1938). Elizabeth Heine writes that "Fry's influence begins about the time of the first Post-Impressionist show . . . and may have been strongest . . . in the winter of 1912–13, when Leonard Woolf acted as secretary for the second Post-Impressionist exhibition and the idea of the Omega Workshop was coming to fruition" ("Virginia Woolf's Revisions of *The Voyage Out*," in *The Voyage Out*, ed. Heine, introduced by Angelica Garnett [London: Hogarth, 1990], 424), hereafter cited as *VO* Heine.

76. *L* 1:438. DeSalvo writes that by the end of December she was calling her novel *The Voyage Out* "at least part of the time" (*M* xvii, xx, citing "[Dec 25] and Dec 30 1910, Berg Collection," which may refer to "Vanessa Bell folder 18" cited two notes earlier).

77. As Woolf would later note, "Killing the angel in the house" was part of a woman writer's job description yet had to be accomplished without rousing the censor (*DM* 238). Based on physical evidence (type of paper used for Draft B,

letters of 14 November 1910 and 25 May 1911, and the early chapters of Draft C), DeSalvo posits that Extant Draft B, reconstructed, transcribed, and published by her as *Melymbrosia*, "was begun early in 1909," finished about March 1910, and revised "from late October to December 1910 and after"; and Draft C begun "in the later part of 1910 and . . . 1911" (*M* xix, xli, xxi). But, since "the next easily datable manuscript was the Holograph, volume I," dated 1912 in Woolf's hand, Draft B and most of Draft C could conceivably have been composed "any time between 1909 and 1912" (*M* xvi); e. g., chap. 21 of *Melymbrosia* is dated 1912. DeSalvo speculates that the greater part of Draft B / DeSalvo's *Melymbrosia* belongs to the period 1909–earlier 1910 and Drafts C and D to later 1910–1913, with *The Voyage Out* (finished in 1913, published in 1915) typeset from Draft D of 1913. Elizabeth Heine, however, finds *Melymbrosia* "misleading in much of its biographical dating of the drafts" (450). She dates the completion of DeSalvo's *Melymbrosia* draft from just before the Woolfs' wedding in August 1912 ("my novel is at last dying. O how sad when it's done!"; "the Novels are finished," *L* 1:506–07, [July] and 3 August 1912) and argues that the late 1912–1913 revision was "profound, a re-seeing, a re-creation" (*VO* Heine 426). See DeSalvo, "Sorting, Sequencing, and Dating the Drafts of Virginia Woolf's *The Voyage Out*," *Bulletin of Research in the Humanities* 82 (1979): 271–93; and Heine, "The Earlier *Voyage Out*: Virginia Woolf's First Novel," *Bulletin of Research in the Humanities* 82 (1979): 294–316, and "Virginia Woolf's Revisions of *The Voyage Out*," *VO* Heine (n. 74 above), 399–463.

78. The 1971–75 British television series *Upstairs / Downstairs* scripts a happier outcome of the servant Sarah's pregnancy by young Master Bellamy.

79. Other post-1910 pages also resound with the "smashing" and "crashing" of Edwardian decorum as the hotel "seeth[es] with scandals"—an affair between Evelyn and Mr. Perrott ("but that was told me in confidence"); Sinclair's suicide threats; trouble between the engaged couple Susan and Arthur over "a young female . . . from Manchester"; rumors that Mrs. Paley "tortures her maid in private" (*VO* 306–7). Woolf also expanded a passage about an alleged prostitute "hoofed out" of the hotel by elderly males, whose moral outrage somehow exempts members of their own sex and class seen wandering the corridors at night (*VO* 307, cf. *M* 220).

80. *VO* 216. The date of this passage is uncertain because the corresponding page of *Melymbrosia* appears to be missing (see *M* 153).

81. Critics differ in interpreting manuscript evidence of Woolf's fight against convention, fear of ridicule, anger, repression, censorship, and self-censorship; see, e. g., Brenda R. Silver, "Textual Criticism as Feminist Practice: Or, Who's Afraid of Virginia Woolf Part II," in *Representing Modernist Texts: Editing as Interpretation*, ed. George Bornstein (Ann Arbor: U of Michigan P, 1991), 193–222; DeSalvo, *Virginia Woolf's First Voyage*, who sees the revised novel as "a voyage *away from* the bluntness, the candor, the openness, and even the subtlety with which Woolf had handled her material in" *Melymbrosia* (66); and Celia Marshik, "Publication and 'Public Women': Prostitution and

Censorship in Three Novels by Virginia Woolf," *Modern Fiction Studies* 45 (Winter 1999): 853–86. In 1920, reading it for the first time since 1913, Woolf gave her first novel a mixed review: "such a harlequinade . . . an assortment of patches—here simple & severe—here frivolous & shallow—here like God's truth—here strong & free flowing as I could wish. What to make of it, Heaven knows. . . . Yet I see how people prefer it to N[ight]. & D[ay].—I dont say admire it more, but find it a more gallant & inspiriting spectacle" (*D* 2:17, 4 February).

82. After Rossetti's "Jenny," it is difficult to see what *Euphrosyne*'s young authors felt to be unprintable. In one amateurish dramatic monologue, "At the Other Bar," the speaker recounts meeting a woman he has ruined in a brothel (*Euphrosyne* [Cambridge: Elijah Johnson, 1905], 23–36).

83. Edel writes that the comic poets represented Aspasia as Pericles' political adviser and that he recognized his son by her as legitimate (*Bloomsbury* 174). Leonard does not cast himself as Pericles in "Aspasia"; see Rosenfeld, *Outsiders Together*, 64. Woolf read Landor's *Pericles and Aspasia* (1903) in 1906.

84. Monk's House Papers, Leonard Woolf Papers IID 7A; see George Spater and Ian Parsons, *A Marriage of True Minds: An Intimate Portrait of Leonard and Virginia Woolf* (New York: Harcourt Brace Jovanovich, 1977), 61 & n.

85. See Luce Irigaray, *This Sex Which Is Not One*, trans. Catherine Porter with Carolyn Burke (1977; Ithaca: Cornell UP, 1985).

86. A contemporary reviewer of *Room* predicted that "Future historians will place Mrs. Woolf's little book beside Mary Wollstonecraft's *The Rights of Women* and John Stuart Mill's *The Subjection of Women*. It does for the intellectual and spiritual liberation of women what those works did for the political emancipation" but "outshines them both in genius" (*Spectator* 143 [28 December 1929]: 985). Cf. Monique Wittig: "each new class that fights for power must . . . represent its interest as the common interest of all the members of the society"; it "must give the form of universality to its thought," "present it as the only reasonable" and "universally valid" position ("The Mark of Gender" 69, citing Karl Marx and Friedrich Engels, *The German Ideology*).

87. *TG* 155–56, citing Josephine Butler. That bonfire was utopian even in Bloomsbury: Woolf's "own friends . . . sent [her] to Coventry" for *Three Guineas* (*D* 5:189, 22 November 1938). Clive thought it her "least admirable production" (*Recollections of Virginia Woolf by Her Contemporaries*, ed. Joan Russell Noble [1971; Athens: Ohio UP, 1994], 72). Bell reports—as "hearsay"—Keynes's "angry and contemptuous" dismissal of its "silly argument"; "what really seemed wrong," opines Bell, "was the attempt to involve a discussion of women's rights with the far more agonising and immediate question of what we were to do in order to meet the ever-growing menace of Fascism and war" (QB 1:205).

88. Jacques Rancière, *Disagreement: Politics and Philosophy* (Minneapolis: U of Minnesota, 1999); Slavoj Žižek, "A Leftist Plea for 'Eurocentrism,' " *Critical Inquiry* 24 (Summer 1998): 992, 991.

89. Freud does acknowledge (recalling Woolf's 1920 letter on Bennett and MacCarthy) that no one can tell what women would be like if educated: "women in general are said to suffer from . . . a lesser intelligence than men. The fact itself is disputable and its interpretation doubtful. . . . So long as a person's early years are influenced" by "sexual," "religious," and "loyal" "inhibition[s] of thought . . . we cannot really tell what in fact [s]he is like" (*FI* 79).

90. *RO* 5. Here as in my chapter 8, I read Woolf's figure of the veil as referring not to Islamic or any other non-Western tradition but to Western women's exclusion from/subordination in the modern public sphere, formulated in such ancient dicta as St. Paul's instruction that women veil themselves in public and Pericles' rule that women be neither heard from nor "talked of" in public. Nineteenth-century European women authors' strategic self-"veiling" in masculine pseudonyms is a latter-day symptom.

91. These three Marys, like Mary Hamilton, are all servants to the queen (possibly Mary Stuart); Mary Hamilton is led to the gallows after she bears the king's child and casts it into the sea. See "Mary Hamilton: Versions A and B," *The Norton Anthology of Poetry*, 4th ed. (New York: Norton, 1996), 91–95.

92. There exists no document with a signature spelled "Shakespeare."

93. That Woolf remains visible behind her "veil" anticipates Wittig's observation that women must not "suppress our individual selves" to "become a class," for "no individual can be reduced to her/his oppression" and "one can become *someone* in spite of oppression"—"constitute oneself as a subject as opposed to an object of oppression." Moreover, "There is no possible fight for someone deprived of an identity," for "although I can fight only with others, first I fight for myself" ("One Is Not Born a Woman," *Feminist Issues* [Winter 1981]: 50–51). Wittig criticizes Marxism's erasure of individuality, its failure to account for men and women as both classes and subjects; her essay suggests a reading of *Room*'s ideal of androgyny as a strategy to align women with the universal without denying sexual difference.

94. Simone de Beauvoir, *The Second Sex*, trans. and ed. H. M. Parshley (1949; New York: Random House, 1989), 267.

95. Alice Walker, *In Search of Our Mothers' Gardens: Womanist Prose* (New York: Harcourt Brace Jovanovich, 1983), 231–43; Jane Marcus, "A Very Fine Negress," Modern Language Association, Toronto, 1997, 6–7, 5, 3. Stephen, Marcus observes, "did indeed want to make an English citizen, woman or man (legally) of the wronged slave"; he indicted the English colonists' invention of "a cause of slavery, additional to all those which lawgivers, civil or barbarous, have elsewhere recognized, or rapacious avarice explored; namely the having a black skin without a deed of manumission. They have thus contrived to effect, what human despotism never attempted or imagined before. They have attached slavery in the abstract to a large portion of the human species; so that it is no longer a particular private relation, requiring the correlative of a master, but a quality inherent to the blood of that unfortunate race, and redounding to the benefit of the first man-stealer who reduces it into

possession" (James Stephen, *The Slavery of the British West India Colonies Delineated* [1824–30], cited in Marcus). See also Marcus, *Hearts of Darkness: White Women Write Race* (Piscataway, N.J.: Rutgers UP, 2004).

96. Jane Marcus, "Registering Objections: Grounding Feminist Alibis," in *Reconfigured Spheres: Feminist Explorations of Literary Space*, ed. Margaret R. Higonnet and Joan Templeton (Amherst: U of Massachusetts P, 1994), 188.

97. See Wayne Chapman, "Leonard and Virginia Woolf Working Together," *Virginia Woolf Miscellanies: Proceedings of the First Annual Conference on Virginia Woolf* (New York: Pace UP, 1992), 210.

98. "That dog is mine, said those poor children; that's my place in the sun: behold the origin and image of the usurpation of the whole world" (Blaise Pascal, *Pensées* [London: J. M. Dent, 1908], no. 295 [85]; see *ECA* viii).

99. Wittig parallels *race* and *woman* as social constructs: "Colette Guillaumin has shown that before the socioeconomic reality of black slavery, the concept of race did not exist . . . in its modern meaning. . . . what we believe to be a physical and direct perception is only a sophisticated and mythic construction, an 'imaginary formation,' which reinterprets physical features (in themselves as neutral as any others but marked by the social system) through the network of relationships in which they are perceived. (They are seen *black*, therefore they *are* black; they are seen as *women*, therefore they *are* women. . . .)" ("One Is Not Born a Woman," 48–49, citing Guillaumin, "*Race et nature: Système des marques, idée de groupe naturel et rapport sociaux*," *Pluriel* 11 [1977]).

100. As of 1997 *A Room of One's Own* had been translated into at least twenty-four languages; see B. J. Kirkpatrick and Stuart N. Clarke, *A Bibliography of Virginia Woolf*, 4th ed. (Oxford: Clarendon P, 1997).

2. Rachel's Great War: Civilization, Sacrifice, and the Enlightenment of Women in *Melymbrosia* and *The Voyage Out*

1. *The Voyage Out* in its several draft versions was in progress from 1907-8 and in proofs by May 1913; its publication was delayed until 1915, after Woolf had recovered from a severe breakdown and suicide attempt, and it caused another breakdown. Woolf's use of the phrase "Great War" thus precedes World War I. DeSalvo's *Melymbrosia* (the novel's first title) is a reconstruction of the extant draft B, begun about 1910 and revised in 1912 (see my chapter 1, 21–24 and nn 72–82). On Woolf's manuscript revisions see Louise A. DeSalvo, *Virginia Woolf's First Voyage: A Novel in the Making* (Totowa, N. J.: Rowman and Littlefield, 1980), chaps. 2–4; on her revisions of the first American and second English editions, chap. 5. As I note in chapter 1, I agree with DeSalvo that Woolf muted much important material in transforming *Melymbrosia* into *The Voyage Out* (not least because her "boldness terrifie[d her]," *L* 1:383) and argue that she devised dialogic strategies to shift the burden of meaning at certain moments to the reader. Hence discarded passages often illuminate Woolf's first novel project as a whole. I therefore approach the novel as a multidimen-

sional work through its genetic text, using a palimpsestic (or variorum, or holo-grammatical) method, and cite the American text of *The Voyage Out* when possible and *Melymbrosia*, the 1915 English text (*VO/E*), or *VO* Heine (chapter 1, note 75) when necessary. See also Elizabeth Heine, "The Earlier *Voyage Out*: Virginia Woolf's First Novel," *Bulletin of Research in the Humanities* 84 (spring 1981): 294–316, and Beverly Ann Schlack, "The Novelist's Voyage from Manuscripts to Text: Revisions of Literary Allusions in *The Voyage Out*, *Bulletin of Research in the Humanities* 84 (spring 1981): 317–27.

2. On *Heart of Darkness* and *The Voyage Out*, see Marianne DeKoven, *Rich and Strange: Gender, History, Modernism* (Princeton: Princeton UP, 1991), chap. 4 ("The Vaginal Passage"); Rosemary Pitt, "The Exploration of Self in *Heart of Darkness* and *The Voyage Out*," *Conradiana* 10:2 (spring 1978): 141–54; Shirley Neuman, "*Heart of Darkness*, Virginia Woolf, and the Spectre of Domination," in *Virginia Woolf: New Critical Essays*, ed. Patricia Clements and Isobel Grundy (Totowa, N.J.: Barnes and Noble, 1983), 57–76; and Mark A. Wollaeger, "The Woolfs in the Jungle: Intertextuality, Sexuality, and the Emergence of Female Modernism in *The Voyage Out, The Village in the Jungle*, and *Heart of Darkness*," *Modern Language Quarterly* 64:1 (March 2003): 33–69.

3. Joseph Conrad, *Heart of Darkness*, ed. Robert Kimbrough, 3d ed. (1899; Norton, 1988), 20, 10. See Adam Hochschild, *King Leopold's Ghost: A Story of Greed, Terror, and Heroism in Colonial Africa* (New York: Houghton Mifflin, 1998), esp. chap. 9.

4. *The Odyssey of Homer*, trans. Robert Fitzgerald (New York: Vintage, 1989), 212. Kirkê charts Odysseus's course past the "cavemouth" that is "the den of Skylla, where she yaps / abominably, a newborn whelp's cry, / though she is huge and monstrous. / . . . Her legs— / and there are twelve—are like great tentacles, / unjointed, and upon her serpent necks / are borne six heads like nightmares of ferocity / with triple serried rows of fangs and deep / gullets of black death. . . . / And no ship's company can claim / to have passed her without loss and grief; she takes, / from every ship, one man for every gullet" (212).

5. Juliet McLaughlan, "The 'Value' and 'Significance' of *Heart of Darkness*," *Conradiana* 15 (1983): 21.

6. *Heart of Darkness*, 51, 75–76, Conrad's ellipsis. On the lie and the Intended see also Bruce R. Stark, "Kurtz's Intended: The Heart of *Heart of Darkness*," *Texas Studies in Language and Literature* 16 (1974): 535–55; Garrett Stewart, "Lying as Dying in *Heart of Darkness*," *PMLA* 95 (1980): 319–31; Nina P. Straus, "The Exclusion of the Intended from Secret Sharing in Conrad's *Heart of Darkness*," *Novel* 20:2 (winter 1987): 123–37; Johanna M. Smith, "Too Beautiful Altogether: Patriarchal Ideology in *Heart of Darkness*," in *Joseph Conrad, Heart of Darkness: A Cast Study in Contemporary Criticism*, ed. Ross C. Murfin (New York: St. Martin's P, 1989), 179–95; and Henry Staten, *Eros in Mourning: Homer to Lacan* (Baltimore: Johns Hopkins UP, 1995), chap. 7.

7. Heine quotes this passage from chap. 24 in the Later Typescript in *VO* Heine 445. In this conversation Terence speculates that Helen and St. John might have "founded a new society—a Society for the Protection of Prostitutes" and Rachel answers, "I don't think Helen will ever protect prostitutes" (444–45); in *The Voyage Out* Helen is incensed at the scapegoating of the prostitute in the hotel.

8. *M* 8, *VO* 22–23. In *The Voyage Out* the *Euphrosyne* takes "dry goods to the Amazon and rubber home again" (38). On the name *Euphrosyne* see my chapter 1.

9. *M* 71. The passage recalls Rupert Brooke and the Neo-Pagans, who, Brooke wrote, "don't copulate without marriage, but we *do* meet in cafés, talk on buses, go unchaperoned walks, stay with each other, give each other books, without marriage"; she "went to stay with Rupert Brooke at Grantchester, where she supplied a word for one of his poems and bathed naked with him by moonlight in the Granta"; "he, one may surmise, considered both these acts . . . sympathetic gestures; it was decent of her to help him to a simile and decent too not to be too prudish about stripping in mixed company" (QB 1:174 and n). Apparently Virginia's sensibility outdistanced her nephew's "not . . . too prudish" idea of her.

10. Here I cite Woolf's 1915 English text; see *The Voyage Out*, ed. Lorna Sage (Oxford: Oxford UP, 1992), 50; hereafter cited in the text as *VO/E*.

11. *VO* 51. The text silently mocks the sententious Richard when he picks up Helen's Moore and reads a sentence to the effect that the Cambridge ethicist Henry Sidgwick is the only philosopher to have stated that "'Good . . . is indefinable'" (*VO* 78, 74); as Richard mouths platitudes about scholars passing torches, the text inscribes the name of this activist reformer who not only wrote about ethics but (like Leslie Stephen) resigned his Cambridge fellowship to protest the criterion of religious faith and founded within that male bastion a women's college, Newnham, to pass learning's torch from woman to woman. On Sidgwick's reformist leadership see W. C. Lubenow, *The Cambridge Apostles, 1820-1914: Liberalism, Imagination, and Friendship in British Intellectual and Professional Life* (Cambridge: Cambridge UP, 1998).

Perhaps following Clive Bell's suggestion that "to draw such sharp & marked contrasts between the subtle, sensitive, tactful, gracious, delicately perceptive, & perspicacious women, & the obtuse, vulgar, blind, florid, rude, tactless, emphatic, indelicate, vain, tyrannical, stupid men, is not only rather absurd, but rather bad art, I think," Woolf makes Dalloway's finest legislative achievement a shortened workday for Lancashire women weavers, of which he owns being "prouder . . . than I should be of writing Keats and Shelley into the bargain!" (QB 1:209, VO 65).

12. *L* 1:345, 9 August 1908. Casting about for a name for her heroine (Rose, Cynthia, Rachel), Woolf rejected a suggestion of Clive Bell's in terms that suggest her ambitions for her heroine: "Belinda is perhaps a little too dainty for my woman, and what I conceive of as her destiny. But I talk grandly, feeling in my heart some doubt that she ever will have a destiny" (*L* 1.345, 9

August 1908). In an earlier study I question whether Woolf as yet foresaw
Rachel's death ("it seems doubtful that she would have spoken of Rachel's
death by jungle fever as a destiny that would tempt her to 'talk grandly'")
("Out of the Chrysalis: Female Initiation and Female Authority in Virginia
Woolf's *The Voyage Out*," *Tulsa Studies in Women's Literature* 5 [spring
1986]: 66–67).

13. VO 190, M 178, VO 192, 136, 248. In *Melymbrosia* Evelyn is the child
of the clergyman's daughter and "the handsome young son at the big house,"
who has provided them a good allowance, reluctantly married someone else,
and died in the war (*M* 140).

14. On the dance scene's Austenian provenance, see QB 1:210 and Wollaeger, "The Woolfs in the Jungle," 40f.

15. Here my argument overlaps with my earlier study, "Out of the
Chrysalis."

16. Maria E. Budden, *Always Happy!! Anecdotes of Felix and his Sister Serena. A tale. Written for her Children, by a Mother*, 4th ed. (London, 1820), 90;
cited in Deborah Gorham, *The Victorian Girl and the Feminine Ideal* (London:
Croom Helm, 1982), 45.

17. Immanuel Kant, *Critique of Judgment*, trans. J. H. Bernard (New York:
Hafner, 1951), §25–28 (88, 94, 104, 98); cf. *Critique of the Power of
Judgment*, ed. Paul Guyer, trans. Guyer and Eric Matthews (Cambridge: Cam-
bridge UP, 2000), 131–48.

18. VO 258. For a concise calendar of Woolf's illnesses as *The Voyage Out*
approached publication, see Bell's chronology; she attempted suicide on the
evening of 9 September 1913, after seeing two doctors (QB 1:197-201,
2:227–29).

19. VO 327, 329; M 21. In her delirium Rachel tries to remember the song
to Sabrina—the drowned virgin of Spenser's *Faerie Queene* whom Milton
brings back to "life" as a water-goddess with power to save the Lady from
sexual danger—from Milton's *Comus: A Mask*, which Terence is reading
aloud when she falls ill. For fuller discussion, see my "Out of the Chrysalis,"
83–85; and Lisa Low, "'Listen and Save': Woolf's Allusion to *Comus* in Her
Revolutionary First Novel," in Sally Greene, ed., *Virginia Woolf: Reading the
Renaissance* (Athens, Ohio: Ohio UP, 1999), 117–35. Milton's only surviving
manuscript, held by the Wren Library at Trinity College, Cambridge, has
"Lycidas" and *Comus*. Virginia might conceivably have looked at this manuscript in her brother Thoby Stephen's company during his years at Trinity; it is
the manuscript in the "famous library" that the speaker of *A Room of One's
Own* is barred from examining because women were not then admitted to the
library unless accompanied by a fellow or "furnished with a letter of introduction" (*RO* 8).

20. M 154. Here I depart from critics who argue that *Heart of Darkness* and
The Voyage Out "reinstate 'the patriarchal maternal,' a maternal principle not
yet strong enough to commit to an expression of its difference" (Wollaeger,

"The Woolfs in the Jungle," 64–65, citing DeKoven, *Rich and Strange*, 138).
On "male" and "female modernism" see Wollaeger, 64–69.

21. In his role as aspiring—and surviving—novelist, Karen R. Lawrence suggests, Terence functions as a kind of double for Rachel; see "Woolf's Voyages Out," in *Penelope Voyages: Women and Travel in the British Literary Tradition* (Ithaca: Cornell UP, 1994), 178.

22. *VO* 357, *BGR* 417–18. Woolf urges readers to read a book "as if one were writing it" in terms that recall Terence's ideal reader (*BGR* 415). This essay, "The Love of Reading," is an abridged version of "How Should One Read a Book?" made by Woolf for a booklist printed by the Hampshire Book Shop, Northampton, Massachusetts, in 1932. Other versions were published in the *Yale Review* and *CR2* (*BGR* 415).

3. The Death of Jacob Flanders: Greek Illusion and Modern War in *Jacob's Room*

1. "More than eight million men died as an immediate consequence of the fighting, and many millions more perished in the upheavals which followed the conflict, especially in eastern Europe and Russia. The permanently disabled and seriously wounded numbered a further 22 million. . . . Bereavement was almost universal" (Menno Spiering and Michael Wintle, *Ideas of Europe Since 1914: The Legacy of the First World War*, ed. Spiering and Wintle [New York: Palgrave Macmillan, 2002], 4).

2. Ezra Pound, *Hugh Selwyn Mauberley*, in *Selected Poems of Ezra Pound* (New York: New Directions, 1957), 63–64.

3. See Elaine Scarry, *The Body in Pain: The Making and Unmaking of the World* (New York: Oxford, 1985), 131 and chap. 2 passim. My analysis draws on Scarry's discussion of "civilization and its deconstruction" or "de-civilization" (145f) and on René Girard's analysis of mimetic desire, reciprocal violence, and scapegoating in *Violence and the Sacred*, trans. Patrick Gregory (Baltimore: Johns Hopkins UP, 1977), and *The Scapegoat*, trans. Yvonne Freccero (Baltimore: Johns Hopkins, 1986).

4. Michael Norman, *These Good Men: Friendships Forged from War* (New York: Crown, 1989), 141; see Paul Fussell, *The Great War and Modern Memory* (New York: Oxford, 1975), esp. chap. 3.

5. Rudyard Kipling, "Common Form," from *Epitaphs of the War*, in *The Norton Book of Modern War*, ed. Paul Fussell (New York: Norton, 1991), 194–95.

6. Walter Benjamin, "The Storyteller" (1936) in *Illuminations*, ed. Hannah Arendt, trans. Harry Zohn (New York: Schocken, 1969), 83–84.

7. Letter to Pound, in Ezra Pound, *Gaudier-Brzeska: A Memoir* (1916; New York: New Directions, 1960), 59. Fussell notes that soldiers of the Latin countries turned to Dante; the Protestant English, to *Pilgrim's Progress* (*The Great War*, 139).

8. Benjamin, "The Storyteller," 110.

9. *VW:CH* 99, 101, 103, 107, 108.

10. Aspects of the early reception persist: Michael Rosenthal dismisses *Jacob's Room* as juvenilia (*Virginia Woolf* [New York: Columbia UP, 1979]). Alex Zwerdling judges it a minor work of "the sketchbook artist": "Only on the small canvas . . . rather than on the grand frescoes of the heroic imagination, could Woolf allow herself to sketch—in a deliberately halting and fragmented style and a conspicuously impure tone—her vision of a permanently inscrutable young man" (*Virginia Woolf and the Real World* [Berkeley: U of California P, 1986], 63, 83). William R. Handley writes that the novel "represents an imaginative space in which Woolf would rewrite the story of modern civilization" but finds her efforts to "know" Jacob "problematic and even futile" ("War and the Politics of Narration in *Jacob's Room*," in *Virginia Woolf and War*, ed. Mark Hussey [Syracuse: Syracuse UP, 1991], 115, 110). Conversely, *The Voyage Out*'s early reception shows how the noise of a story can drown out a novel's critical energies. Not only do the characters within the novel "warm" themselves at Rachel's death; critics tended to do the same, at the expense of her radical quest for civilization's hidden "truth."

11. Thus Fredric Jameson, *The Political Unconscious: Narrative as a Socially Symbolic Act* (Ithaca, N.Y.: Cornell UP, 1981): "After the peculiar heterogeneity of the moment of Conrad, a high modernism is set in place. . . . The perfected poetic apparatus of high modernism represses History just as successfully as the perfected narrative apparatus of high realism did the random heterogeneity of the as yet uncentered subject. At that point, however, the political, no longer visible in the high modernist texts, any more than in the everyday world of appearance of bourgeois life, and relentlessly driven underground by accumulated reification, has at last become a genuine Unconscious" (280).

12. *MB* 153; cf. Zwerdling, *Virginia Woolf*, 74.

13. Judith Lewis Herman, *Trauma and Recovery* (New York: Basic, 1992), 61.

14. See, for example, Mircea Eliade, *Rites and Symbols of Initiation: The Mysteries of Birth and Rebirth*, trans. Willard R. Trask (New York: Harper and Row, 1958) and Sherry B. Ortner, "Is Female to Male as Nature Is to Culture?" in *Women, Culture, and Society*, ed. Michelle Rosaldo and Louise Lamphere (Stanford: Stanford UP, 1974), 67–87.

15. Bruce Lincoln, *Emerging from the Chrysalis: Studies in Rituals of Women's Initiation* (Cambridge: Harvard UP, 1984).

16. *MD* 22, 24, 148. Images of moths/psyches and falling trees recur in Woolf's works, notably in *Jacob's Room*'s Cambridge chapel scene, *Mrs. Dalloway*, in which Clarissa remembers her sister Sylvia, "killed by a falling tree," the short story "The Introduction," and the essay "Reading" (*JR* 32, *MD* 78).

17. Adrienne Rich, *Of Woman Born: Motherhood as Experience and Institution* (New York: Bantam, 1977), 197.

18. Herman finds these qualities already visible in the issues that three-year-old boys negotiate in play with war toys (*Trauma and Recovery* 64).

19. Edward L. Bishop, "The Subject in *Jacob's Room*," *Modern Fiction Studies* 38 (1992): 166. For Bishop the narrator exemplifies "female subjectivity" as defined by Teresa de Lauretis: "at once inside and outside the ideology of gender . . . at once 'woman' and 'women' " (163). I see her as enacting a more radical evasion of gender, beyond "woman" and "women."

20. Barry Morgenstern, "The Self-Conscious Narrator in *Jacob's Room*," *Modern Fiction Studies* 18 (1972): 351–61.

21. Beth Carole Rosenberg and Jeanne Dubino, eds., *Virginia Woolf and the Essay* (New York: St. Martin's P, 1997), 1.

22. *D* 2:13–14, 26 January 1920; Clive Bell, *Proust* (New York: Harcourt Brace Jovanovich, 1929), 85; cf. my chapter 1.

23. Bishop writes that the narrator "is of course in a room of her own, but she maintains a consciousness of the interpellated nature of that space . . . that Jacob and those educated like him at Cambridge lack" ("The Subject," 163).

24. *JR* 121. See Luce Irigaray, "Any Theory of the 'Subject' Has Always Been Appropriated by the 'Masculine,' " in *Speculum of the Other Woman*, trans. Gillian C. Gill (Ithaca: Cornell UP, 1985), 133–46.

25. See Simone de Beauvoir, *The Second Sex*, trans. and ed. H. M. Parshley (1949; New York: Random House/Vintage, 1989); and Monique Wittig, "One Is Not Born a Woman," *Feminist Issues* 1 (winter 1981): 47–54.

26. *The Iliad of Homer*, trans. Robert Fitzgerald (New York: Doubleday, 1974), 459 (bk. 19). Cf. my "The Daughter's Seduction: Sexual Violence and Literary History," *Signs* 11 (1986): 621–44.

27. *JR* 25, 138. Celia Marshik analyzes the depiction of Florinda and other characters in light of censorship issues and social purity campaigns in "Publication and 'Public Women': Prostitution and Censorship in Three Novels by Virginia Woolf," *Modern Fiction Studies* 45:4 (winter 1999): 853–86.

28. *JR* 122. Vara Neverow points out that Jacob may in fact have fathered a child, since Florinda is pregnant when he dies, though that question is undecidable given Jacob's sighting of Florinda "on another man's arm" (*JR* 94).

29. E. L. Bishop, "The Shaping of *Jacob's Room*: Woolf's Manuscript Revisions," *Twentieth Century Literature* 32 (1986): 130, citing the manuscript in the Berg Collection, New York Public Library, 3: 63; see *Virginia Woolf's Jacob's Room: The Holograph Draft*, transcribed and ed. Edward L. Bishop (New York: Pace UP, 1998), 275–76.

30. *D* 2:179, 23 June 1922. Zwerdling's generic classification—"satiric elegy"—foregrounds important features, but my reading diverges from his view that "the hesitation of her style and the impurity of her tone are manifestations of the impacted satiric impulse" (*Virginia Woolf and the Real World*, 83).

31. See n. 10 above.

32. Woolf read the first four books of the *Odyssey* during her 1906 tour of Greece; the rest in 1908. See Brenda R. Silver, *Virginia Woolf's Reading Note-*

books (Princeton: Princeton UP, 1983), XXXIV. B.4–5. Woolf asks Violet Dickinson whether she is reading the *Iliad*, remembers their 1906 visit to Mycenae (*L* 1:253, 28? November 1908), and refers to Pope's translation in an essay on Lady Elizabeth Holland (*Books and Portraits*, ed. Mary Lyon [New York: Harcourt Brace Jovanovich, 1977], 190); Edward Pargiter has read it with far more care than *Hamlet* or *Paradise Lost* (*P* 63); but she does not mention reading it herself.

33. *The Odyssey of Homer*, trans. Robert Fitzgerald (New York: Vintage, 1989), 201.

34. Marshall Berman, *All That Is Solid Melts into Air: The Experience of Modernity* (New York: Simon and Schuster, 1982), 24.

35. Theodor Adorno, *Aesthetic Theory*, trans C. Lenhardt, ed. Gretel Adorno and Rolf Tiedemann (London: Routledge and Kegan Paul, 1970), 262; "Conversely," he comments, "what our manipulated contemporaries dismiss as unintelligible secretly makes very good sense to them indeed" (262).

4. *Mrs. Dalloway's* Postwar Elegy: Women, War, and the Art of Mourning

1. Alex Zwerdling, *Virginia Woolf and the Real World* (Berkeley: U of California P, 1986), chap. 3.

2. The Woolfs' Hogarth Press took over publication of the International Psycho-Analytic Library in 1924, after which it published English translations of all Freud's works. *The Future of an Illusion* (1927) and *Civilization and Its Discontents* (1929/30) resonate with Bloomsbury's internationalist stance toward the war.

3. Peter Sacks, *The English Elegy: Studies in the Genre from Spenser to Yeats* (Baltimore: Johns Hopkins UP, 1985), 2, 1; hereafter *EE*. On the roots of elegiac conventions in "specific social and literary practices," see "Interpreting the Genre," 1–37. See also Maria diBattista, "Virginia Woolf's *Memento Mori*," in *Virginia Woolf's Major Novels: The Fables of Anon* (New Haven: Yale UP, 1980), chap. 2; J. Hillis Miller, *Mrs. Dalloway*: Repetition as the Raising of the Dead," in *Fiction and Repetition: Seven English Novels* (Cambridge: Harvard UP, 1982), chap. 7 (hereafter "RRD"); Claire M. Tylee, *The Great War and Women's Consciousness: Images of Militarism and Womanhood in Women's Writings, 1914–64* (Iowa City: U of Iowa P, 1990), 150–67; and Caroline Webb, "Life after Death: The Allegorical Progress of *Mrs. Dalloway*," *Modern Fiction Studies* 40:2 (summer 1994): 279–98.

4. *EE* 8f. I agree that there is "substantial overlap in men's and women's mourning" and that a woman's mourning recapitulates the loss of the mother and "her internalization and identification with the idealized parent figure"; but Woolf translates psychoanalytic theory's androcentric terms to the ontological loss and sexual wounding inherent in being, distinct from the systemic, socially inflicted losses women suffer through "male culture's establishment of an almost exclusive relation between masculinity and the figures of authority" (*EE* 13, 15, 321).

5. *EE* 34–3 5. Sacks interprets this ancient strategy of elegy as, first, a symbolic recapitulation of "the 'splitting' and self suppression that accompanied the self's first experiences of loss and substitution, its discovery of signs both for lost objects and for the self"; second, a "dramatizing strategy" that calls attention through ritual and ceremony to the mourners' " 'work' as survivors"; third, the "confrontational structure required for the very recognition of loss," which furthers mourning's "necessarily dialectical movement"; fourth, the "poetry contest" whereby survivors channel grief into skill in contending over the communal inheritance from the dead (*EE* 3 5–3 6).

6. John Keegan, *The First World War* (New York: Knopf, 1999), 3.

7. Leonard Woolf, *Barbarians Within and Without* (New York: Harcourt, Brace, 1939), 1 3 1; hereafter *B WW*; Clive Bell, *Peace at Once* (Manchester and London: National Labour Press, [1 9 1 5]), 53; J. M. Keynes, *The Economic Consequences of the Peace* (New York: Harcourt, Brace and Howe, 1920), 5, hereafter *ECP*; Leonard Woolf, *Downhill All the Way: An Autobiography of the Years 1919 to 1939* (New York: Harcourt Brace Jovanovich, 1967), 9; cf. Albert Einstein, *The Fight against War*, ed. Alfred Lief (New York: John Day, 1 9 3 3), 5–7.

8. Mark Mazower, *Dark Continent: Europe's Twentieth Century* (New York: Knopf, 1999), x–xii, citing Czech political philosopher Thomas Masuryk.

9. Mussolini came to power in 1 9 2 2; Hitler was arrested and imprisoned after the "beer hall putsch" of November 1 9 2 3.

10. Harold Nicolson, *Peacemaking 1 9 1 9: Being Reminiscences of the Paris Peace Talks* (New York: Harcourt, Brace, 1939), 293. Nicolson's diary tracks the "horrible" Treaty negotiations through the signing ceremony, which sent him "[t]o bed, sick of life" (3 7 0–7 1). See also John Maynard Keynes, "Dr Melchior: A Defeated Enemy," *Two Memoirs* (New York: Augustus M. Kelley, 1949), 1 1–7 1.

11. In her essay "On Not Knowing Greek" (1 9 2 5) Woolf elaborates: "In the vast catastrophe of the European war our emotions had to be broken up for us, and put at an angle from us, before we could allow ourselves to feel them in poetry or fiction. The only poets who spoke to the purpose spoke in the sidelong, satiric manner of Wilfr[e]d Owen and Siegfried Sassoon. It was not possible for them to be direct without being clumsy; or to speak simply of emotion without being sentimental" (*CR* 34). Jahan Ramazani pursues Owen's description of his war elegies as "to this generation in no sense consolatory" in a study that begins by positing "the modern elegy's repudiation of the traditional elegy" and ends in acknowledging "the persistence of the traditional elegy within the modern" (*Poetry of Mourning: The Modern Elegy from Hardy to Heaney* [Chicago: U of Chicago P, 1994], 69, 3 6 1). On Woolf's response to the death of her childhood friend Brooke in April, 1 9 1 5, and his subsequent "canonisation" see Karen L. Levenback, *Virginia Woolf and the Great War* (Syracuse: Syracuse UP, 1999), chap. 1.

12. *D* 3:3 2, 1 8 June 1 9 2 5. I differentiate the Clarissas by publication date; Woolf composed *The Voyage Out* between 1908 and 1 9 1 3, "Mrs. Dalloway in

Bond Street" in 1922, *Mrs. Dalloway* in 1923–24. In a draft of *The Voyage Out*, Clarissa answers Richard's view that "One has to make allowances" for "poets and artists in general": "Think of Shelley. I feel that there's almost everything one wants in Adonais" (*M* 30–31). As she approached *The Hours*, Woolf expressed dissatisfaction with the 1923 Clarissa ("Mrs Dalloway doesn't seem to me to be complete as she is," *L* 3:45, 4 June 1923). The ur-Orlando takes a last swipe at her: " 'There's that tiresome Mrs. Dalloway!' recognizing a lady she very much disliked looking in at a glove shop window" (*Orlando: A Biography*, ed. Andrew McNeillie [Oxford: Blackwell, 1998], Appendix A: 170 3Pr 1E 1A).

13. Elegies often figure the mother's symbolic loss (whether understood ontologically as differentiation contingent on birth or in sexual terms as oedipal prohibition) as her literal death; a guest brings tears to Clarissa's eyes by telling her that she looks "so like her mother as she first saw her walking in a garden in a grey hat" (*MD* 267). Sacks discusses Amy Clampitt's redressing of the elegy's "multiple exclusion or occlusion of figures representing the mother" in "Procession at Candlemas" (*EE* 325).

14. As Sacks remarks, "Adonais," completed the year before Shelley enacted its closing lines, drives the genre "to the brink of . . . ruin" (165). On 18 May 1933 Woolf described "sitting, by an open window, by a balcony, by the bay in which Shelley was drowned, wasn't he, 113 [actually 111] years ago, on a hot day like this . . . Mary Shelley and Mary Williams walked up and down the balcony of the house next door [Casa Magni] waiting while Shelley's body rolled round with pearls—it is the best death bed place I've ever seen" (*L* 5:186–87).

15. Percy Bysshe Shelley, "Adonais," in *Shelley: Poetical Works*, ed. Thomas Hutchinson and G. M. Matthews (New York: Oxford UP, 1970), 470, stanza 1, lines 4–9.

16. *H* 266. For some critics—e.g., Trudi Tate, *Modernism, History, and the First World War* (New York: Manchester UP, 1998), 165f, and Sharon Ouditt, *Fighting Forces, Writing Women: Identity and Ideology in the First World War* (London: Routledge, 1994), 189f—Clarissa's class privilege and snobbery overwhelm any elegiac sensibility; in Ouditt's words she is "a trivial woman who represents a dying age" and lacks "political vision and fortitude" (189).

17. *L* 1:134–35, 212, March 1904, 10 November 1905; *MB* 191; *HL* 214.

18. On 14 April 1922 Woolf told T. S. Eliot that she expected to finish this story in three to six weeks (*L* 2:521). In August she told Ottoline Morrell that she had finished two Mrs. Dalloway stories (teasingly referred to as "my Garsington novel") (*L* 2:543); on 28 August she planned to finish "Mrs Dalloway" on "Sat. 2nd Sept" and then to work on "the next chapter of Mrs. D. . . . the Prime Minister?" until "say Oct. 12th" (*D* 2:196). A plan dated 6 October lists eight titles: "Mrs. Dalloway in Bond Street," "The Prime Minister," "Ancestors," "A dialogue," "The old ladies," "Country house?," "Cut flowers," and "The Party" (*H* 411; cf. *MDP*). "Mrs. Dalloway in Bond Street" appeared in the *Dial* in July 1923; Woolf sent it and another story to Eliot on 4 June for the *Criterion*, but he published neither.

19. *D* 2:207–8, 14 October. Jacqueline E. M. Latham, "The Model for Clarissa Dalloway—Kitty Maxse," *Notes and Queries* 214 (July 1969): 262–63, finds no condolence letter from Woolf among the five hundred-odd in the Maxse papers at Chichester; she prints a letter from Virginia to Kitty, probably of summer 1905 when the Maxses visited the Stephen children at Carbis Bay in Cornwall (QB 1:195).

20. Virginia Woolf, "Introduction to the Modern Library Edition of *Mrs. Dalloway* (1928)," in *Mrs. Dalloway*, ed. Morris Beja (Oxford: Blackwell, 1996), Appendix C, 198, hereafter "I."

21. Daniel Ferrer makes this point but questions the importance of Kitty's death to the novel's genesis in *Virginia Woolf and the Madness of Language*, trans. Geoffrey Bennington and Rachel Bowlby (New York: Routledge, 1990), 154 n. 25.

22. For other interpretations of Woolf's remark in "I", see Edward Mendelson, "The Death of Clarissa Dalloway: Two Readings," in *Textual Analysis: Some Readers Reading*, ed. Mary Ann Caws (New York: MLA, 1986), 272–80; and Miller, "RRD," 176–201 passim. Mendelson makes (and rebuts) the case that Clarissa dies, citing her fear of death, the heart condition that makes her sleep alone in a narrow, coffinlike bed, Peter's vision of her "falling where she stood, in her drawing-room" on hearing St. Margaret's bells toll "for death that surprised in the midst of life" ("No! No! . . . She is not dead! I am not old, he cried, and marched up Whitehall, as if there rolled down to him, vigorous, unending, his future"), and her sudden vanishing from her party (*MD* 75). Miller frames Woolf's storytelling as "the repetition of the past" in the characters' memories and that of the narrator, who "remembers all" and "resurrect[s] the past": an "invisible mind . . . more powerful than their own," she "rescues them from the past," "registers with infinite delicacy their every thought and steals their every secret," and "speaks for them all," "'after' anything [they] think or feel"; thus "narration is repetition as the raising of the dead" (176–79) and Clarissa's return to her party, her "resurrection from the dead" ("RRD" 201).

23. For Lytton Strachey this compound Kitty / Woolf registered as a "discrepancy in Clarissa herself; he thinks she is disagreeable and limited, but that I alternately laugh at her, & cover her, very remarkably, with myself. . . . I think there is some truth in it. For I remember the night at Rodmell when I decided to give it up, because I found Clarissa in some way tinselly. Then *I invented her memories*. But I think some distaste for her persisted. Yet, again, that was true to my feeling for Kitty" (*D* 3:32, 18 June 1925, my emphasis). Woolf lent Clarissa her girlhood passion for Madge Vaughan ("I see myself now standing in the night nursery at Hyde Park Gate . . . saying . . . 'At this moment she is actually under this roof' " (*D* 2:122, 2 June 1921, cf. *MD* 51) and experience of "Constantinople" (a code word for lesbian love), and otherwise freed her from fact (e. g., Kitty had no children).

24. Woolf depicts Julia Stephen's antifeminism in Mrs. Ramsay and recalls

her stern rebuke when Kitty broke her first engagement in "22 Hyde Park Gate" (*MB* 165).

25. *MB* 93. In *Jacob's Room* someone sings "Who Is Silvia?": "She excels each mortal thing / Upon the dull earth dwelling. / To her let us garlands bring" (88). Virginia's beloved half sister, Stella Duckworth, died in 1897.

26. *H* 411. Sacks relates the elegy's cut and broken branches and flowers to the "vegetation god, whose death and rebirth governed the phases of the rites" and "allowed the devotees or survivors to . . . intensify their grief or gratitude regarding an otherwise manifold and ungraspable world of nature"; the withering vegetation also symbolically "reverses man's submission to nature," which becomes no longer "the *cause* of human grief but rather the mourner or even the effect of a human-divine loss" (*EE* 20–21). On Jane Harrison's influence on Woolf's vegetation imagery, see Beverly Ann Schlack, *Continuing Presences: Virginia Woolf's Use of Literary Allusion* (University Park, Penn.: Pennsylvania State UP, 1979), 52–53 and passim.

27. Miller aligns Imogen's return from "death" with Clarissa's return "from her solitary confrontation with death during her party" ("RRD" 200).

28. Posthumous derives from Latin *posthumus*: "erroneously (by association with *humus* earth, ground, as if referring to burial) for *postumus* last, superl. of *posterus*" (*OED*). As Sacks points out, Guiderius / Polydore and Arviragus / Cadwal first sang "Fear no more," their dirge for Imogen / Fidele, for their dead mother, Euriphile (*EE* 18).

29. Building on Elizabeth Abel's reading of *Mrs. Dalloway* as a "progression from a pastoral female world to an urban culture governed by men" (*Virginia Woolf and the Fictions of Psychoanalysis* [Chicago: U of Chicago P, 1989], 42), Joseph Allen Boone relates this passage to Nancy Chodorow's theories of female psychological development (*Libidinal Currents: Sexuality and the Making of Modernism* [Chicago: U of Chicago P, 1998], 187).

30. The narrator brings to daylight various treasures of Clarissa's psychic cave: e. g., kissing Peter in her drawing room stirs "the brandishing of silver-flashing plumes like pampas grass in a tropic gale in her breast"; when Elizabeth barges in, Big Ben strikes the half hour "with extraordinary vigour, as if a young man, strong, indifferent, inconsiderate, were swinging dumb-bells this way and that"; time is a roving, protean figure with multiple personalities: "Love—but here . . . the clock which always struck two minutes after Big Ben, came shuffling in with its lap full of odds and ends, which it dumped down as if Big Ben were all very well with his majesty laying down the law, so solemn, so just, but she must remember all sorts of little things besides" (*MD* 46–47, 69, 71).

31. Wussow transcribes "beauty" here; it seems likely that Woolf meant to write "belief." Her scribble is inconclusive (holograph manuscript, British Library).

32. *H* 388, cf. *MD* 185. In citing *The Hours* I make some silent elisions and corrections and do not differentiate its temporal layers.

33. Keynes had lived in the communal houschold at 38 Brunswick Square

with Virginia, Adrian, Duncan Grant, and Leonard Woolf. Before Versailles Woolf wrote rather satirically of his "prophecies" about Lloyd George and England's economic future (*L* 2:208, 1 January 1918); later she recorded his resignation from the Peace talks (*D* 1:280, 288; 10 June, 8 July 1919). In 1921 she praised his Memoir Club piece "Dr Melchior" (*L* 2:456, 3 February).

34. Robert Skidelsky, *John Maynard Keynes*, vol. 1: *Hopes Betrayed 1883–1920* (London: Macmillan, 1983), 399; he adds that Keynes's "case on reparations remains unshakeable" (400).

35. *MD* 125. The historical model for Miss Kilman was the classical scholar Louise Ernestine Matthaei (1880–1969), fellow and director of studies at Newnham from 1909, who was forced out in 1916 "under a cloud"; she explained to Leonard, "my father was a German. I find it makes a good deal of difference—it is a distinct hindrance commercially" (*D* 1:135–36 and n. 14, 9 April 1918). Woolf recorded Leonard's intention to hire her on the *International Review* at a salary of £200–250 (*D* 1:143, 21 April 1918). The belligerent Miss Kilman has nothing of Matthaei's "limp, apologetic attitude," her "odious" reluctance "to declare her opinions—as if a dog used to excessive beating, dreaded even the raising of a hand," but shares her "unattractive" person, blotchy complexion, "inconceivably stiff & ugly" dress, and "quick mind" (*D* 1:136).

36. *MD* 124. Masami Usui notes Miss Kilman's association with Quaker peace activism and relates her to international struggles for women's rights in "The Female Victims of War," in *Virginia Woolf and War: Fiction, Reality and Myth*, ed. Mark Hussey (New York: Syracuse UP, 1991), esp. 158–63; cf. Zwerdling, *Virginia Woolf and the Real World*, 133. Her work "for the Friends" apparently supplements her traditionally hierarchical Protestant denomination, with its "Reverend Whittaker."

37. *MD* 129. This wistful thought coexists with her passion for Elizabeth. Tylee, 165f, and Eileen Barrett ("Unmasking Lesbian Passion: The Inverted World of *Mrs. Dalloway*," in *Virginia Woolf: Lesbian Readings*, ed. Barrett and Patricia Cramer [New York: New York UP, 1997], 159–62), read Miss Kilman as a narrative and psychic locus of Clarissa's displaced and disavowed lesbian desire; cf. Abel, *Virginia Woolf* 20–44 and Boone, *Libidinal Currents* 172–203.

38. *Civilization and Its Discontents*, trans. and ed. James Strachey (New York: Norton, 1961), 58; hereafter *CD*.

39. Sigmund Freud, *The Future of an Illusion*, trans. W. D. Robson-Scott, rev. and ed. James Strachey (New York: Doubleday Anchor, 1964), 3; hereafter *FI*.

40. Forms of recompense include: protection against natural forces; material wealth and comfort, which accrue to individuals and classes in greater and lesser degrees; the "mental wealth" of cultural identity, political ideals, communal pride, art, religious ideas, and science; and such personal satisfactions as drugs, love, "cultivat[ing] one's garden," beauty, work, and the "pleasure principle" by which individuals adapt to their environment so as to gain from it all possible gratification (*FI* 16, *CD* 23f). For Freud as for Keynes, civilization

encompasses, on the one hand, all the knowledge and capacity by which humankind controls destructive natural forces and uses natural resources to satisfy its needs, and, on the other, the regulation of human relations, "especially the distribution of the available wealth"; these material and social economies are inseparable, since human relations "are profoundly influenced by the amount of instinctual satisfaction which the existing wealth makes possible" (*FI* 3). Through social relations that organize power and wealth, some individuals function as wealth for others through labor or sexual attachment, in Freud's view making class oppression a threat to civilization's stability.

41. Freud considers this unconscious guilt—a hidden reservoir of unacknowledged aggressive desire—"the most important problem in the development of civilization" (*CD* 81).

42. *ECP* 295–96. Cf. Freud on how "the narcissism of minor differences" (Spaniards *v.* Portuguese, North Germans *v.* South Germans, English *v.* Scots, Christians *v.* Jews) makes "intelligible" the fact that "the dream of a Germanic world-dominion called for antisemitism as its complement" and that "the attempt to establish a new, communist civilization in Russia should find its psychological support in the persecution of the bourgeois. One only wonders, with concern, what the Soviets will do after they have wiped out their bourgeois" (*CD* 61–62).

43. *MD* 81. Miller ("RRD" 189–90) identifies the song "*Allerseelen*" by Hermann von Gilm and Richard Strauss as the source of the beggarwoman's age-old "fertilising" song ("ee um fah um so / foo swee too eem oo"), which encompasses "the pageant of the universe" and makes the earth seem "green and flowery" as it issues from the archetype of all graves: "a mere hole in the earth, muddy too, matted with root fibres and tangled grasses, . . . soaking through the knotted roots of infinite ages, and skeletons and treasure, streaming away in rivulets over the pavement and all along the Marylebone Road, and down towards Euston, leaving a damp stain" (*MD* 81). Woolf's draft translation breaks off: "Lay by my side a bunch of purple heather / The last red aster of a" (*H* 98).

44. *MD* 39. Tate points out that Richard Dalloway, M. P., may that very day be orchestrating the Armenians' dire fate at Britain's hands (147–70).

45. On Septimus, war trauma, and shell shock, see Elaine Showalter (who aligns him with Sassoon), *The Female Malady: Women, Madness, and English Culture, 1830–1980* (New York: Penguin, 1985), chap. 7; Sue Thomas, "Virginia Woolf's Septimus Warren Smith and Contemporary Perceptions of Shell Shock," *English Language Notes* 25:2 (1987): 49–57; Judith Lewis Herman, *Trauma and Recovery* (New York: Basic Books, 1992), 49, 52; Ouditt, who sees Septimus as homosexual and attributes his death to "a civilian metonym of war, the logical corollary to the brutal imposition of a fixed gender identity" (*Fighting Forces* 197); and Karen DeMeester, "Trauma and Recovery in Virginia Woolf's *Mrs. Dalloway*," *Modern Fiction Studies* 44:3 (1998): 649–73.

46. Michel Foucault, *Madness and Civilization: A History of Insanity in the Age of Reason* (New York: Random House/Vintage, 1973), 288–89; cf. x–xi.

47. *MD* 12, cf. *H* 271 (MS dated 20 October 1924). See Paul Davies, *Other Worlds: . . . Space, Superspace, and the Quantum Universe* (New York: Simon and Schuster, 1980), 43.

48. On the emergence of this advertising technology in England, see John K. Young, "Publishing Women: Modernism, Gender, and Authorship" (Ph.D. Diss., Northwestern University, June 1998), chap. 4, and "Woolf's *Mrs. Dalloway*," *The Explicator* 55 (1999): 99–101. On Bloomsbury, marketing, and Keynes's theory of markets as inherently chaotic, see Jennifer Wicke, "*Mrs. Dalloway* Goes to Market: Woolf, Keynes, and Modern Markets," *Novel: A Forum on Fiction* 28:1 (fall 1994): 5–23.

49. *FI* 80. Freud's remarks on such "treasure" follow closely on his observation that no one can tell what women are like as long as sexual and religious inhibitions of thought are inculcated from childhood (*FI* 79). Although certain affinities between Freud's postwar works and Woolf's suggest that he may have read her, his library in the Freud Museum, London, has none of her books.

50. Letter to John Middleton Murry (10 November 1919), speaking of Woolf's *Night and Day*, in *The Collected Letters of Katherine Mansfield*, 3 vols., ed. Vincent O'Sullivan and Margaret Scott (Oxford: Clarendon, 1993), 3:82.

51. Paul Fussell, *The Great War and Modern Memory* (New York: Oxford UP, 1975), esp. 174f.

52. Cf. Gilles Deleuze's and Claire Parnet's idea that to have a style means "to stammer in one's own language"—a difficult feat "because there has to be a need for such stammering" (*Dialogues*, trans. Hugh Tomlinson and Barbara Habberjam [New York: Columbia UP, 1987], 4).

53. René Girard argues that the scapegoat mechanism, fueled by mimetic desire, shapes "the dynamics of all mythological and religious beginnings," which religions conceal "by suppressing or disguising collective murders and minimizing or eliminating the stereotypes of persecution in a hundred different ways" (*The Scapegoat*, trans. Yvonne Freccero [Baltimore: Johns HopkinsUP, 1986], 165).

54. Blaise Pascal, quoted in Foucault, ix.

55. *L* 3:180, 1 May 1925, to Gwen Raverat about Septimus; Woolf adds, "You can't think what a raging furnace it still is to me—madness and doctors and being forced. But let's change the subject." In a letter of 28 July 1910 to Vanessa / "Dark Devil," Woolf begs to be liberated from the home for female lunatics at Twickenham, where her family has installed her to undergo Dr. George Savage's version of S. Weir Mitchell's rest cure; she pays ritual homage to Vanessa and displays ostentatious good temper and reasonableness while trying to get across that the rest cure is driving her insane (*L* 1:430–31).

56. For example, on 22 September 1904: "You will be glad to hear that your Sparroy feels herself a recovered bird" (*L* 1:142). See Roger Poole, *The*

Unknown Virginia Woolf (Atlantic Highlands, N.J.: Humanities P, 1982), chap. 13 ("The Birds Talking Greek").

57. See Strachey, introduction, *CD* 6.

58. *MD* 5–6, 103; *H* 156–57. For Woolf's portraits of George Duckworth see *MB*, passim.

59. *H* 87. In *Mrs. Dalloway* Clarissa recalls that he did it "to punish her for saying that women should have votes" (181). On prostitution and class see Judith R. Walkowitz, *City of Dreadful Delight: Narratives of Sexual Danger in Late-Victorian London* (Chicago: U of Chicago P, 1992).

60. In 1915 Woolf recorded seeing "a long line of imbeciles," "every one . . . a miserable ineffective shuffling idiotic creature, with no forehead, or no chin, & an imbecile grin, or a wild suspicious stare"; her response, "It was perfectly horrible. They should certainly be killed," suggests disavowal of a suicidal self that she identifies with them, echoed in Septimus's memory of "a maimed file of lunatics" who "ambled and nodded and grinned past him. . . . And would *he* go mad?" (*D* 1:13, 9 January 1915; *MD* 90).

61. A. Bullock, *Hitler* (London: 1952), 79, cited by Keegan, 3.

62. *MD* 137. Cf. Tylee, *The Great War and Women's Consciousness*, 166.

5. Picture the World: The Quest for the Thing Itself in *To the Lighthouse*

1. Northrop Frye, *Anatomy of Criticism* (Princeton: Princeton UP, 1957), 323. Avrom Fleishman finds "the romance theme of a quest to restore a lost garden . . . played out in a comic conflict" that leads to "a restoration of family unity in the absence of . . . the mother" (*Virginia Woolf: A Critical Reading* [Baltimore: Johns Hopkins UP, 1975], 121). See also Harold Bloom, "The Internalization of Quest-Romance," in *Romanticism and Consciousness: Essays in Criticism* (New York: Norton, 1970), 3–23; Paul Zweig, *The Adventurer: The Fate of Adventure in the Western World* (Princeton: Princeton UP, 1974); and Dana A. Heller, *The Feminization of Quest-Romance: Radical Departures* (Austin: U of Texas P, 1990).

2. On the function of pronouns in inculcating gender, and the ontological power of the pronoun "one," see Monique Wittig, "The Mark of Gender," in *The Poetics of Gender*, ed. Nancy K. Miller (New York: Columbia UP, 1983), and my chapters 1 and 6.

3. "Femininity," *The Standard Edition of the Complete Psychological Works of Sigmund Freud*, trans. and ed. James Strachey, 24 vols. (London: Hogarth P, 1953–66; New York: Macmillan, 1953–74), 22:113, 124ff; hereafter cited as *SE*; cf. "Female Sexuality," *SE* 21: 223–31.

4. Thus "There is woman only as excluded by the nature of things which is the nature of words"; "There can be nothing *human* that pre-exists or exists outside the law represented by the father; there is only either its denial (psychosis) or the fortunes and misfortunes ('normality' and 'neurosis') of its terms" (Juliet Mitchell in *Feminine Sexuality: Jacques Lacan and the école freudienne*, ed. Mitchell and Jacqueline Rose [New York: Norton, 1977], 23, origi-

nal emphasis; cf. Rose, 55; Lacan in Mitchell and Rose, 144). That the father merely "represents" social law only highlights this rhetorical masculinization of "human" subjectivity; that "man" too exists only as excluded by the "nature" of things/words hardly mitigates Lacan's polemical exploitation of gender. Citing Winnicott, Ogden, Benjamin, Bach, Freud, Lacan, and Kristeva, Suzanne Juhasz argues that no third person's intervention but rather "the necessary presence of aggression within the relationship" fosters the "development of daughter's and mother's subjectivity"; "the space of the symbolic exists within the mother-infant relationship, rather than having to be constructed beyond it" ("Towards Recognition: Writing and the Daughter-Mother Relationship," *American Imago* 57:7 [2000]: 169).

5. Monique Wittig, "The Mark of Gender," 66.

6. *TL* 51, *MB* 72. Passages of Woolf's 1939–40 memoir, "A Sketch of the Past," revisit the autobiographical material of *To the Lighthouse*.

7. T. S. Eliot, "Tradition and the Individual Talent," *Selected Essays* (New York: Harcourt Brace Jovanovich, 1950), 5.

8. Rachel Bowlby, *Feminist Destinations and Further Essays on Virginia Woolf* (Edinburgh: Edinburgh UP, 1997), 57.

9. On *Ulysses'* quest romance see my *Modernism's Body: Sex, Culture, and Joyce* (New York: Columbia UP, 1996), chap. 2.

10. For example, Margaret Homans acutely analyzes Lacan's gender-bound rhetoric but implicates Lily in a "masculine" model of subjectivity and art that requires the mother's death: at best Lily "adopt[s] some of the son's strategies" even if she "at least refuses to victimize the mother actively"; at worst she risks "excluding and killing the mother for the sake of representation's projects." For Homans the novel's only alternative to masculine representation is Cam's dreamy echo of her mother's nonreferential murmuring, which "reproduces" the pre-oedipal mother/daughter relation in language the symbolic order devalues (*Bearing the Word: Language and Female Experience in Nineteenth-Century Women's Writing* [Chicago: U of Chicago P, 1986], 286–87; on Lacan, see 5–16). Patricia Moran counters that Mrs. Ramsay "devalues women's desires and talk" (*Word of Mouth: Body Language in Katherine Mansfield and Virginia Woolf* [Charlottesville: U of Virginia P, 1996], 141). Elizabeth Abel departs from the matricidal reading but keeps its gendered terms: Cam "thinks back through her father" in a story of "narrative imprisonment" while Lily "escape[s]" through a painting that preserves the mother/child bond James must sacrifice (*Virginia Woolf and the Fictions of Psychoanalysis* [Chicago: U of Chicago P, 1989], 67). Abel compares James's and Cam's "Freudian/Lacanian" developmental narratives (chap. 3) with Lily's "Kleinian challenge" (chap. 4) and finds in Lily's picture "the dual unity, mother and daughter, that has been the subject of Lily's narrative" (47, 83). See also Maud Ellmann on Lily's "matricidal painting" and the novel's oedipal economy in "The Woolf Woman," *Critical Quarterly* 35:3 (1993): 94. My reading agrees with Helen Storm Corsa that Lily's "grief over the loss of the

mother" long precedes Mrs. Ramsay's death ("*To the Lighthouse*: Death, Mourning, and Transfiguration," *Literature and Psychology* 21 [1971]: 123–24); even if we understand "Killing" as "the last outpost of mourning" (Brenda Wineapple, "Mourning Becomes Biography," *American Imago* 54:4 [1997]: 449), Lily's painting no more causes Mrs. Ramsay's death than do Mrs. McNab's labors. See Su Reid, *To the Lighthouse* (London: Macmillan, 1991), for a review of feminist and other debates.

11. Woolf uses this phrase in response to Vita Sackville-West's poems: "I was trying to get at something about the thing itself before its been made into anything: the emotion, the idea. . . . [O]ne ought to stand outside with one's hands folded, until the thing has made itself visible; . . . there are odder, deeper, more angular thoughts in your mind than you have yet let come out" (*L* 3:321, 2 February 1927).

12. Terry Eagleton's paraphrase of Lacan in *Literary Theory: An Introduction* (Minneapolis: U of Minnesota P, 1983), 185.

13. *D* 3:18–19, 14 May 1925; six weeks later Woolf wrote, "I am making up 'To the Lighthouse'—the sea is to be heard all through it" and proposed to substitute "Elegy" for "novel" (*D* 3:34, 27 June).

14. *MB* 128. *The Hyde Park Gate News* of 12 September 1892 (the family gazette, written and published by the Stephen children, chiefly Virginia, from 1891–94) posted this item: "On Saturday morning Master Hilary Hunt and Master Basil Smith came up to Talland House and asked Master Thoby and Miss Virginia Stephen to accompany them to the lighthouse as Freeman the boatman said that there was a perfect tide and wind for going there. Master Adrian Stephen was much disappointed at not being allowed to go" (*QB* 1:32). See also Jean MacGibbon, *There's the Lighthouse: A Biography of Adrian Stephen* (London: James and James, 1997).

15. *Sir Leslie Stephen's Mausoleum Book*, ed. Alan Bell (Oxford: Clarendon, 1977), 47; hereafter cited as *MBk*. Woolf told Vanessa that she had "specially refrained" from reading her mother's letters or "father's life" (F. W. Maitland's 1906 *The Life and Letters of Leslie Stephen*) while writing *To the Lighthouse* (*L* 3:379, 22 May 1927); but she certainly had read *The Mausoleum Book*— written "for Julia's children" after her death in 1895—even if her memories made "direct reference to the documents . . . superfluous" (xxix).

16. Julia later wrote (still refusing his proposal) that she loved Leslie "with my whole heart—only it seems such a poor dead heart" (*MBk* 53). The next January she accepted; they married on 26 March 1878 and, he wrote, "my own darling did come to life again" (*MBk* 58).

17. "Grief," Stephen wrote, "is of all things not to be wasted" (*MBk* 71). Elsewhere he described Julia as having suffered "one of those terrible blows which shatter the very foundations of life . . . and seem to leave for the only reality a perpetual and gnawing pain. . . . Yet the greatest test of true nobility of character is its power of turning even the bitterest grief to account . . . by slow degrees it undergoes a transmutation into more steady and profound love of

whatsoever may still be left" ("Forgotten Benefactors," in *Social Rights and Duties* [1896], cited in *MBk* xiv–xv).

18. *TL* 43, *TLhd* 25. Gillian Beer notes that Stephen summarized Hume's view that "The belief that anything exists outside our mind when not actually perceived is a 'fiction' " in his 1876 *History of English Thought in the Eighteenth Century* ("Hume, Stephen, and Elegy in *To the Lighthouse*," *Virginia Woolf: The Common Ground* [Edinburgh: Edinburgh UP, 1996], 36). Stephen's *An Agnostic's Apology and Other Essays* appeared in 1893. On the table debate in British empiricist philosophy see Ann Banfield, *The Phantom Table: Woolf, Russell, Fry, and the Epistemology of Modernism* (Cambridge: Cambridge UP, 2000). Betokening the question of the world's existence independent of human perception, "our familiar table," Russell writes, is "a problem full of surprising possibilities"—not least that there may be "no table at all," merely a sensory illusion that vanishes with the perceiver (*The Problems of Philosophy*, 16, cited in Banfield 50, 43).

19. Ludwig Wittgenstein, *On Certainty*, cited in Julia Annas and Jonathan Barnes, *Modes of Scepticism: Ancient Texts and Modern Interpretations* (Cambridge: Cambridge UP, 1985), 8. Annas and Barnes contrast the ancient skeptics' "practical doubt," which attacked not knowledge but belief, with modern skepticism, which "leaves all our *beliefs* intact: provided only that we do not claim to know anything"; "it does not affect our behaviour or mode of life, and it is to that extent unserious" (9, 7–8).

20. *TLhd* 315, 109, *TL* 43. As publication day neared Woolf worried, "People will say I am irreverent" (*D* 3:133, 1 May 1927). Michael Lackey notes that "there has been no extended analysis of Woolf's atheism, even though the topic appears in every novel and almost every short story" ("Atheism and Sadism: Nietzsche and Woolf on Post-God Discourse," *Philosophy and Literature* 24:2 [2000]: 359).

21. *TLhd* 69, 63–64. Cf. Genesis 1–3. According to Annan, Leslie "worshipped" Julia as "a living image before whom he could pour out the flood of devotion that could find no outlet in religion"; Leslie himself wrote, "To see her as she was is to me to feel all that is holy . . . in human affection"; after her death George Meredith wrote Leslie that he had never "reverenced a woman more" (*MBk* xviii, 33, 74). Although the final text drops the Genesis allusion, Mrs. Ramsay retains an aura of divinity, as does Woolf's later portrait of Julia: "there she was, in the very centre of that great Cathedral space which was childhood . . . from the very first . . . the creator of that crowded merry world which spun so gaily in the centre of my childhood. . . . it was herself. This was proved on May 5th 1895. For after that day there was nothing left of it" (*MB* 81, 84).

22. *TLhd* 56–8, *TL* 64. Mrs. Ramsay's sadness is sometimes misread as "depression," e. g., Martha C. Nussbaum, "The Window: Knowledge of Other Minds in Virginia Woolf's *To the Lighthouse*," *New Literary History* 26:4 (1995): 736.

23. *TLhd* 85. For excellent Lacanian studies of Lily's struggle to lay the mother's ghost, see Daniel Ferrer, *Virginia Woolf and the Madness of Language*, trans. Geoffrey Bennington and Rachel Bowlby (New York: Routledge, 1990), chap. 3, and André Viola, "Fluidity Versus Muscularity: Lily's Dilemma in Woolf's *To the Lighthouse,*" *Journal of Modern Literature* 24:2 (2000/2001): 271–89.

24. Whereas the beautiful Prue dies in childbirth, Rose excels in domestic arts, and willful Cam submits to her father and brother, Nancy is the paragon infidel—a "wild creature" who "scamper[s] about the country all day long," hides in her attic from "the horror of family life," and incorrigibly mocks Tansley. Her Constantinople fantasy in response to Minta's touch and her bafflement as to what Minta and people in general "want" anticipate *Orlando*'s lesbian sexuality. Like Rhoda in *The Waves* she contemplates "nothingness" in anemone pools; and she fails to carry on her mother's ministry, forgetting what one sends to the lighthouse (*TL* 58, 73, 76). Neither did the "Cathedral space of childhood" circumscribe Virginia: "I enclosed that world in another made by my own temperament; . . . from the beginning I had many adventures outside that world . . . and kept much back" (*MB* 84). Minta Doyle (based on Kitty Maxse, who "got engaged at St Ives," *D* 2:206, 8 October 1922) pursues "a wilder life" in her open marriage.

25. *TL* 6. Mrs. Ramsay herself envisions state-sponsored motherhood, anticipating *Three Guineas*; is unpleasantly reminded of herself in the Grimm tale's fisherman's wife; feels herself "nothing but a sponge sopped full of human emotions"; admits being "driven on, too quickly she knew, almost as if it were an escape for her too, to say that people must marry; people must have children"; and finds Rose's "deep," "buried," "quite speechless feeling" for her "quite out of proportion to anything she actually was" (*TL* 32, 60, 81).

26. *To the Lighthouse* culminates a series including the *Odyssey*, *Genesis*, the *Divine Comedy*, *Henry IV, Part 2*, *Don Quixote*, the *Decameron*; see "The Brown Stocking," in *Mimesis: The Representation of Reality in Western Literature*, trans. Willard R. Trask (1946; Princeton: Princeton UP, 1953), 534–35. The subtitle translates literally as "Represented Reality."

27. As Katë Hamburger points out, "subjective" and "objective" require each other to be meaningful; she argues that through free indirect discourse or "narrated monologue" (Woolf's "oratio obliqua") fiction achieves a realism that historical discourse "by its nature cannot attain" (*The Logic of Literature*, rev. ed., trans. Marilynn J. Rose [Bloomington: Indiana UP, 1973], 171–2; *D* 3:106, 5 September 1926). The narrator's "interpreting voice" binds "almost imperceptibly" with the characters' reproduced "conscious or unconscious thoughts," blending their "interior" voices with the narrator's "exterior," "objectifying interpretive acts" (ibid.). For J. Hillis Miller, Woolf's narrator lacks intrinsic characteristics, merely narrating what the characters know from the vantage point of their future ("Mr. Carmichael and Lily Briscoe: The Rhythm of Creativity in *To the Lighthouse,*" *Tropes, Parables, Performatives:*

Essays on Twentieth-Century Literature [New York, 1990]). On Auerbach, see also my chapter 9.

Many critics relate Woolf's multiperspectival stream of consciousness to Nancy Chodorow's psychoanalytic work on female development; e. g., Abel, *Virginia Woolf*, 71f; Joan Lidoff, "Virginia Woolf's Feminine Sentence: The Mother-Daughter World of *To the Lighthouse*," *Literature and Psychology* 32 (1986): 43–57; Ellen Bayuk Rosenman, *The Invisible Presence: Virginia Woolf and the Mother-Daughter Relationship* (Baton Rouge: Louisiana State UP, 1986), chap. 5.

28. *TLhd* 29. By September 5 Woolf had "made a very quick & flourishing attack" in which no Lily appears (*D* 3:39). Sophie mutates into "Kind old Mrs. Beckwith," whose sentimentality ("always saying how nice it was and how sweet it was and how they ought to be so proud and they ought to be so happy") gets on the children's nerves (*TL* 148, 203, cf. 142, 192). Diane Filby Gillespie discusses Woolf's 1904–15 sketches, drawings, and copies in *The Sisters' Arts: The Writing and Painting of Virginia Woolf and Vanessa Bell* (Syracuse: Syracuse UP, 1988), esp. 21–33.

29. Clive Bell, *Art* (1914; London: Chatto and Windus, 1931), 278. Bloomsbury's aesthetic formalism resonates with other London movements such as Vorticism.

30. *TL* 17–18. This moment marks a divide between Victorian father and modernist daughter that Tennyson's 1854 poem's broader reception also registers; see Jerome J. McGann, "Tennyson and the Histories of Criticism," *The Beauty of Inflections: Literary Investigations in Historical Method and Theory* (Oxford: Clarendon, 1988), 173–203. The poem commemorates the military debacle of the Light Cavalry Brigade in the Crimean War, when soldiers obeyed an order to rush toward certain death: though "All the world wonder'd" at the commanders' incompetence no less than the soldiers' blind devotion to duty, the poem exalts the heroic ethos, urging, "Honor the charge they made!"

31. For Abel this scene signals that "Lily discovers less a neutral language of form than abstractions that universalize masculinity"; she sees the triangle as a "cover-up" for "underlying issues of boundaries repressed by the Freudian domain," and Lily's memory as a pre-oedipal "unpainted scene" that displaces James with "a relation of the mother that is the *female* child's *enduring* legacy" (*Virginia Woolf* 73, 75–76, original emphasis). I argue that Lily's abstract triangle does not merely supplement the son's sexualized oedipal triangle with the daughter's ontological difference but universalizes that ontological difference by uncovering a stratum of loss inherent in being that preexists the oedipal triangle; thus it is if anything a universalizing *feminine* abstraction, though more accurately described as neutral. That both sexes suffer the mother's loss and must extend desire beyond the mother-child dyad to the world challenges the privileging of sexual difference in Freudian and Lacanian developmental narratives.

32. *TLhd* 108. Woolf later wrote that "rage alternated with love" in her family life; reading Freud she found "that this violently disturbing conflict of

love and hate is a common feeling; and is called ambivalence" (*MB* 108). See Jane Lilienfeld, "The Deceptiveness of Beauty: Mother Love and Mother Hate in *To the Lighthouse*," *Twentieth Century Literature* 23 (1977): 345–76, and, on the maternal fusion Lily partly desires, Nancy Chodorow, "Family Structure and Feminine Personality" in *Women, Culture and Society*, ed. Michelle Zimbalist Rosaldo and Louise Lamphere (Stanford: Stanford UP, 1974), 43–66.

33. *TL* 50–51, my emphasis. If Woolf's novel and Lily's painting are essentially the same work, that "art" or "device" is exemplified by the narrative voice that merges "almost imperceptibly" ("like waters poured into one jar") with those of the characters. See n. 27.

34. *TL* 51. Lily's fantasy also points to an oedipally configured lesbian desire. Woolf began *To the Lighthouse* and her affair with Sackville-West the same year; see Louise A. DeSalvo, "Lighting the Cave: The Relationship between Vita Sackville-West and Virginia Woolf," *Signs* 8 (1982): 195–214, and Suzanne Raitt, *Vita and Virginia: The Work and Friendship of Vita Sackville-West and Virginia Woolf* (New York: Oxford, 1993).

35. Wilhelm Wörringer, *Abstraction and Empathy: A Contribution to the Psychology of Style*, trans. Michael Bullock (1908; New York: International Universities P, 1953), 16–17.

36. See T. E. Hulme, "Modern Art and Its Philosophy" and "Romanticism and Classicism," in *Speculations: Essays on Humanism and the Philosophy of Art*, ed. Herbert Read, foreword by J. Epstein (London, 1924), and *Further Speculations*, ed. S. L. Hynes (Minneapolis: U of Minnesota P, 1955). Fry knew the work of the sculptor Henri Gaudier-Brzeska, killed at twenty-three in World War I; Gaudier, who frequented Hulme's salon and participated in Fry's Omega Workshop, had studied in Germany and had almost certainly read Wörringer. His work (like Woolf's) shows stronger affinity with Wörringer's organic / abstract continuum than with Hulme's rigidly geometric emphasis. On Woolf's abandoned plan to dedicate the novel to Fry, see *L* 3:385, 27 May 1927; *D* 3:127 ("Roger it is clear did not like Time Passes"), 3:129. See also Christopher Reed, "Through Formalism: Feminism and Virginia Woolf's Relation to Bloomsbury Aesthetics," *Twentieth Century Literature* 38 (spring 1992): 20–43; and Cheryl Mares, "Reading Proust: Woolf and the Painter's Perspective," in *The Multiple Muses of Virginia Woolf*, ed. Diane F. Gillespie (Columbia: U of Missouri P, 1993), 58–89.

37. *TLhd* 80–81, cf. *TL* 44. Cf. Thomas Hardy's portrait of Leslie Stephen in his sonnet "The Schreckhorn. With Thought of L. S. (June 1897)." An avid Alpine climber, Stephen was the first European to "conquer" the formidable Great Schreckhorn peak in 1861 ("frequently flattened out against the rock like a beast of ill-repute nailed to a barn"). In 1897, gazing at the Schreckhorn, Stephen's friend Hardy suddenly felt "a vivid sense of him, as if his personality informed the mountain—gaunt and difficult, like himself. His frequent conversations on his experiences in the Alps recurred to me, experiences always related with modesty in respect of his own achievements, and with high com-

mendation of the achievements of others, which were really no greater than his own. As I lay awake that night, the more I thought of the mountain, the more permeated with him it seemed . . . as if the Great Schreckhorn were Stephen in person":

> Aloof, as if a thing of mood and whim,
> Now that its spare and desolate figure gleams
> Upon my nearing vision, less it seems
> A looming Alp-height than a guise of him
> Who scaled its horn with ventured life and limb,
> Drawn on by vague imaginings, maybe,
> Of semblance to his own personality
> In its quaint glooms, keen lights, and rugged trim.
>
> At his last change, when Life's dull coils unwind,
> Will he, in old love, hitherward escape,
> And the eternal essence of his mind
> Enter this silent adamantine shape,
> And his low voicing haunt its slipping snows
> When dawn that calls the climber dyes them rose?

Hardy did not send Stephen this poem, fearing "he might not care for it" (Frederick William Maitland, *The Life and Letters of Leslie Stephen* [1906; New York: G. P. Putnam's Sons, 1908], 277–78).

38. *TL* 110–11. The poem is "Luriana, Lurilee," by Charles Elton (1839–1900), a relative by marriage of the Stracheys, published only in 1943; Philippa Strachey evidently sent it to Woolf, perhaps for consideration by Hogarth (see *L* 3:443, 21 December 1927). Elizabeth French Boyd notes that Woolf heard Leonard and Lytton Strachey recite it from memory (" 'Luriana, Lurilee,' " *Notes and Queries* 208 [1963]: 380–81).

39. This photograph is reproduced in *MBk* 90–91. Mrs. Ramsay's desire for composure and stability, projected onto the "stillness, and . . . superb upward rise . . . of the elm branches," mirrors Lily's for symbolic creation (*TL* 113). Jane Marcus contrasts Mrs. Ramsay's rapturous loss of self in the sonnet with Mr. Ramsay's self-interested reading of Scott in *Art and Anger* (Columbus: Ohio State UP, 1988), 242–46. Richard Maxwell provides a searching evaluation of Scott's achievement and reception in "Inundations of Time: A Definition of Scott's Originality," *ELH* 68:2 (2001): 419–68.

40. Woolf recalled her joy in watching her mother read the *Hyde Park Gate News*: "How excited I used to be when . . . she liked something I had written! Never shall I forget my extremity of pleasure—it was like being a violin and being played upon" (*MB* 95).

41. *TLhd* 192. Prue's model, Stella Duckworth, died of peritonitis after her marriage in 1897.

42. *RF* 172, *TL* 174; cf.: "It might contain all characters boiled down; & childhood; & then this impersonal thing, which I'm dared to do by my friends, the flight of time, & the consequent break of unity in my design. That passage . . . seven years passed . . . interests me very much. A new problem like that

breaks fresh ground in ones mind; prevents the regular ruts" (*D* 3:36, 20 July 1925).

43. *D* 3:76, 18 April 1926. This narrator and the visionary seeker prefigure *The Waves'* faceless Rhoda. My view of this eyeless, featureless, but not quite effaced narrator agrees with Miller that language has "an ineffaceable tendency . . . to project faces and bodies"; "Wherever there is language there will be personality" ("Mr. Carmichael and Lily Briscoe," 163–65); and with Randi Koppen that art is never "void of life because it is connected in so many ways with the experiencing body" ("Embodied Form: Art and Life in Virginia Woolf's *To the Lighthouse*," *New Literary History* 32:2 [2001]: 388).

44. Cf. Wörringer's argument that abstract art is impelled by, and mitigates, "great inner unrest at outward phenomena," "spiritual dread" of vast space and time (16–17).

45. *TL* 128. Susan Dick notes that the bracketed events—the deaths, Prue's marriage, Mr. Carmichael's poems, his and Lily's return to the house—were late additions in the third version of "Time Passes" ("The Restless Searcher: A Discussion of the Evolution of 'Time Passes' in *To the Lighthouse*," *English Studies in Canada* 3 [1979]: 311–329). See *TLhd* 198–238.

46. Object relations psychology posits the mother as the emerging subject's first mirror, in whom the child sees itself reflected whole and coherent while its inner experience remains unbounded, incoherent, unintegrated. In these terms, the still unrealized self whose place is marked by the salt cellar/tree temporarily dissolves into the liminal daughter-subject of "Time Passes," and its destroyed and remade world mirrors her disintegration and re-creation. See Susan Squier, "Mirroring and Mothering: Reflections on the Mirror Encounter Metaphor in Virginia Woolf's Works," *Twentieth Century Literature* 27 (fall 1981): 272–88; Lidoff, esp. 49–51; Lacan, "The Mirror Stage as formative of the function of the I," *Ecrits: A Selection*, trans. Alan Sheridan (New York: Norton, 1977), 1–7; and Abel, who invokes Winnicott's "intermediate zone in which subject and object are only partly distinct," where "we play, we make our symbols, we conduct our cultural lives" (*Virginia Woolf* 70).

47. *TL* 129. Jack F. Stewart sees the light as "Mrs. Ramsay's spirit" in "Light in *To the Lighthouse*," *Twentieth Century Literature* 23 (1977), 377–89, esp. 384–86; Gayatri C. Spivak, "Unmaking and Making in *To the Lighthouse*" in *Women and Language in Literature and Society*, ed. Sally McConnell-Ginet, Ruth Borker, and Nelly Furman (New York: Praeger, 1980), finds "a discourse of madness within this autobiographical roman à clef" (316).

48. *TL* 130–31. Mary Lou Emery, " 'Robbed of Meaning': The Work at the Center of *To the Lighthouse*," *Modern Fiction Studies* 38 (1992): 217–34, deplores the text's "theft and exclusion" of Mrs. McNab necessary to Lily's " 'birth' as an artist and . . . Woolf's achievement of aesthetic unity" and argues that Lily's painting "marks over and supplants" Mrs. McNab's work (228, 231). Yet Mrs. McNab, far from being "dehumanized" and "excluded," arguably affirms the essential ordering power of human effort, art, and memory

perhaps even more profoundly than does Mrs. Ramsay or Lily; indeed her
Marie Lloyd imitation acts out the consolation she finds in art. Woolf saw
Lloyd's charwoman turn at the Bedford Music Hall in 1921: "a mass of corruption—long front teeth—a crapulous way of saying 'desire,' & yet a born
artist—scarcely able to walk, waddling, aged, unblushing. She is beaten nightly
by her husband. I felt that the audience was much closer to drink & beating &
prison than any of us" (*D* 2:107, 8 April). On class tensions in readings of
Woolf, see Mary M. Childers, "Virginia Woolf on the Outside Looking Down:
Reflections on the Class of Women," *Modern Fiction Studies* 38 (1992): 61–79.

49. The draft reads: "The voice of the principle of life, & its power to persist; . . . & its courage, & its assiduity, & its determination, denied one
entrance, to [try] another—& its humour, & its sorrow, so that Mrs. McNab
seemed to have turned her old sprightly dance song into an elegy which . . .
long living had robbed of all bitterness. . . . it seemed as if a channel were tun-
nelled in the heart of obscurity, & . . . there issued peace, enough, when the
grind & grit returned . . . to make her lean her heart against the thorn & if she
was infinitely mournful, & dirgelike in her sidelong glance there was, account
for it as one may, the forgiveness of an understanding mind"; "Leaning her
bony breast on the hard thorn she crooned out her forgiveness" (*TLhd* 211,
213, 215). This "principle of life" that denied one embodiment (Mrs. Ramsay)
finds another (Mrs. McNab) confirms Mrs. McNab as figurative mother and
mirror; the Philomela allusion projects the daughter's suffering into the "elegy"
that celebrates her survival.

50. *TL* 142–43. Lily's awakening recalls Woolf's two "earliest" memories,
being held in her mother's lap on the train to St. Ives; and listening to the waves
and the breeze moving the blind cord across the floor, thinking, "it is almost
impossible that I should be here" and "feeling the purest ecstasy I can conceive"; she continues with a painterly vision of these "first impressions" (*MB*
65–66).

51. Woolf listed "Ancestors" in the plan for short stories about Mrs. Dalloway's party of October 1922 and again in "Notes for Stories," dated 14
March 1925, which has a plan for "The Introduction." She composed "Ancestors" during 18–22 May 1925. "The Introduction" and "Together and Apart"
(first titled "The Conversation") follow in the manuscript book; on 14 June she
noted, "I've written 6 little stories . . . & have thought out, perhaps too clearly,
To the Lighthouse" (*D* 3:29).

52. *TL* 171, 50–51. Phyllis Rose argues that Woolf fashions herself her
mother's heir and rejects Victorian femininity by transforming her mother into
an artist (*Woman of Letters: A Life of Virginia Woolf* [New York: Oxford,
1978], 169).

53. *TL* 177. On the psychic dangers of Lily's "triumph" over the lost
mother, see Viola.

54. *TL* 195–96, *TLhd* 334. Since "her dark days of widowhood," Leslie
wrote, Julia had felt "set apart to relieve pain and sorrow," her constant acts of

kindness "a kind of religious practice." After her death he established a fund in her name to endow a nurse at St. Ives (*MBk* 82–83, 103). The draft dwells on Lily's defense of art against Mrs. Ramsay, who "so infinitely prefer[s] life" and is compelled "to help desperate people": "Could [Lily] have painted that picture it would have done more to help the eternal dying woman . . . There is something better than helping dying women. Something . . . beyond human relations altogether . . . & loving and not loving one another, all this little trivial baseness of . . . marrying & giving in marriage, pales beside it. . . . Yet so terrible a doctrine could not be confessed. Tansley would have shot her. Mrs. Ramsay would never have understood. . . . Yet a society which makes no provision for the soul . . . the mind . . . swings its way out of turmoil here . . . reaching some more acute reality where it can rest" (*TLhd* 278–79). Cf. the Shakespeare scene; the liturgical language of Lily's defense of art in the final text; the ur-Mr. Carmichael who like Lily has "no needs. . . . She painted; he wrote"; and the essay "How Should One Read a Book?" (*TLhd* 276, *E* 4:388–400).

55. *TL* 201. Mrs. Ramsay, Prue, and Andrew correspond to Julia, Stella, and Thoby Stephen; the "some one," "her companion," suggests Herbert Duckworth (1833–1870), whose "sweetness of temper" Leslie remarked (*TL* 181, *MBk* 35).

56. Ferrer reads this vision as a hallucination that effects a shift from storytelling to an unconscious discourse as Lily "tunnel[s] her way into the past" by painting (*Virginia Woolf* 41f). Lily's prolonged oscillation between anguished mourning, in which the past overwhelms the present, and life "here" and now puzzled Woolf: "The novel is now easily within sight of the end, but this, mysteriously, comes no nearer. I am doing Lily on the lawn: but whether its her last lap, I don't know" (*D* 3:106, 3 September 1926). Cf. Freud's insight into mourning's interminability: "Although . . . the acute state of mourning will subside, we also know we shall remain inconsolable. . . . No matter what may fill the gap, even if it be filled completely, it nevertheless remains something else. . . . [T]his is how it should be, . . . the only way of perpetuating that love which we do not want to relinquish" (*The Letters of Sigmund Freud*, trans. Tania and James Stern [New York: Basic Books, 1960], 386).

57. *TL* 205. Of the seven "Greek slave years" between Stella's death in 1897 and Leslie's in February 1904, Woolf wrote, "Nessa and I were fully exposed without protection to the full blast of that strange character" (*MB* 106–7). Leslie comments on Stella's care of him after his wife's death (*MBk* 104n). Mark Spilka judges Lily's grief incomplete and inexplicable, "borrowed" from Woolf's "own buried fund of confused childhood feelings" (*Virginia Woolf's Quarrel with Grieving* [Lincoln: U of Nebraska P, 1980], 95–97).

58. *TL* 148–49. Jean-Jacques Mayoux, "Sur un livre de Virginia Woolf," *Revue anglo-américaine* 5 (1928): 438, and Ruth Z. Temple, "Never Say 'I': *To the Lighthouse* as Vision and Confession," in *Virginia Woolf: A Collection of Critical Essays*, ed. Claire Sprague (Englewood Cliffs, N.J.: Prentice-Hall, 1971), 94, touch on the "ironical antiphony" of Cam's and Lily's thoughts.

59. *TL* 185, 169. Cf. Abel, *Virginia Woolf*, 58, and see her chap. 3 on James's oedipal / crushed-foot narrative.

60. *TL* 189, *MB* 65; see n. 53 above; cf. *TLhd* 348, where Lily is astonished not at her own existence but at Mrs. Ramsay's: "the thought of her became slowly lit up—a miracle, an ecstasy—that she should exist, that she had lived."

61. *TL* 205, *D* 3:271, 8 December 1929; cf. my chapter 1.

62. *TL* 189. See n. 10 above on readings of Cam's relation to representation. In emphasizing Cam/Virginia's autobiographical continuity with Lily/Woolf, I locate the key to their different stances in their unequal access to the freedom necessary to create, not in pre-oedipal and oedipal relations to the mother.

63. *TL* 31–32. James's experience of this moment in the draft recalls Woolf's remark that her writing life began upon Leslie's death: "It seemed to him that one was now about to start on things for oneself. One had sixty, perhaps seventy years of living before one" (*TLhd* 349).

64. See Banfield, *The Phantom Table*, chap. 5 ("The Dualism of Death").

65. *TL* 192, 208. Lily echoes Christ's words at his death, *Consummatum est* (John 19:28)—the close of the Catholic Mass. "I'm casting about for an end," Woolf wrote. "The problem is how to bring Lily & Mr R. together & make a combination of interest at the end. . . . I had meant to end with R. climbing onto the rock. If so, what becomes [of] Lily and her picture? Should there be a final page about her & Carmichael looking at the picture & summing up R.'s character?" (*D* 3:206, 5 September 1926). Reading the finished novel, she found much of it "lovely," "Soft & pliable & I think deep, and never a word wrong for a page at a time"; "Lily on the lawn . . . I do not much like. But I like the end" (*D* 3:132, 21 March 1927).

66. Woolf replied, "But what do you think I did know about mother? It can't have been much"; and: "I'm in a terrible state of pleasure that you should think Mrs Ramsay so like mother. At the same time, it is a psychological mystery why she should be: how a child could know about her; except that she has always haunted me, partly, I suppose, her beauty; and then dying at that moment, I suppose she cut a great figure on one's mind when it was just awake, and had not any experience of life—Only then one would suppose that one had made up a sham—an ideal" (*L* 3:379, 383; 22 and 25 May 1927). Conceived not as an "objective" likeness but as a collage of insights from many remembered and imagined perspectives, Woolf's cubist portrait captures, among other things, her mother's radical otherness, apparent to the adult as it cannot be to a child.

67. *L* 3:573. Readers often accept Mrs. Ramsay's indulgent dismissal and Lily's own expectation that her picture will be hung in the attic; see Carolyn Heilbrun on early commentators, "*To the Lighthouse*: The New Story of Mother and Daughter," *ADE Bulletin* 87 (1987): 12–14. Contemporary reviews by Louis Kronenberger, Rachel A. Taylor, Arnold Bennett, Orlo Williams, Conrad Aiken and Edwin Muir overlook the centrality and drama of Lily's story; Jean O. Love accepts "Lily's acknowledgment that her painting has no value as a

work of art" (*Worlds in Consciousness: Mythopoetic Thought in the Novels of Virginia Woolf* [Berkeley: U of California P, 1970], 178); Lucio Ruotolo describes the painting as an "'attempt'" with "an empty center," "destined to rest unnoticed and unappreciated in someone's attic" (*The Interrupted Moment: A View of Virginia Woolf's Novels* [Stanford: Stanford UP, 1986], 141).

6. A Fin in a Waste of Waters: Women, Genius, Freedom in *Orlando*, *A Room of One's Own*, and *The Waves*

1. *D* 3:229, 28 May 1929; *Wh* I:1 and verso.

2. *RO* 84. To summarize this trajectory: while still at work on *To the Lighthouse*, Woolf glimpsed a new form, "prose yet poetry; a novel & a play" (*D* 3:128, 21 February 1927). A few weeks later she conceived *Orlando* as "an escapade after these serious poetic experimental books" (*D* 3:131, 14 March 1927). By October she was writing *Orlando*, published the month she delivered the lectures that led to *A Room of One's Own* (20 and 26 October 1928); she wrote *Room* the next spring and then began *The Waves*. I assimilate freestanding earlier works and ancillary writings as well as the holograph drafts to *The Waves'* genetic text to trace the emergence of what I call the [woman] in *The Waves* from relative confinement in the social category of "woman" toward gender's vanishing point in the practice of creative freedom, even as sex remains in the picture as a bodily attribute.

3. Jacques Derrida, *Memoirs of the Blind: Self-Portraiture and Other Ruins*, trans. Pascale Anne Brault and Michael Naas (Chicago: U of Chicago P, 1993), 65. Woolf's remarks that the "impulse toward autobiography may be spent" now that women are "beginning to use writing as an art, not as a method of self-expression," and that "one must strain off what was personal and accidental," are consistent with *The Waves'* transformed concept of autobiography (*RO* 83, 25).

4. *D* 3:113, 30 September 1926. Although Woolf does not remark on it, the "purple triangular shape" of "The Window" and the "odd-shaped triangular shadow" of "The Lighthouse" seem to prefigure this abstract fin. In the "Time Passes" draft of May 1926, a "black snout" erupts through the "purple, foaming sea," an allegory of the inexorable life/death force breaking the watery "mirror of sublime reflection"; later James recalls his father's belief that "they were all sinking in a waste of waters" (*TLhd* 222, 227, 352; appendix D 61). A diary entry of 15 October 1923 describes the "wet windy night" when Woolf went to meet Leonard at the train and, not finding him, was stunned to physical rigidity by fear: "as I walked back across the field I said Now I am meeting it; now *the old devil has once more got his spine through the waves*. . . . Reality, so I thought, was unveiled. And there was something noble in feeling like this; tragic, not at all petty"; when Leonard finally appeared she felt physical "lightness & relief & safety. & yet there was too something terrible behind it—the fact of this pain, I suppose . . . & it became connected with the deaths of the miners. . . . But I have not got it all in, by any means" (*D* 2:270, my emphasis).

5. *D* 3:153, 4 September 1927. Woolf cites Shelley's "CCXXVI: Invocation," included in one of her favorite anthologies, *The Golden Treasury of the Best Songs and Lyrical Poems in the English Language,* ed. Francis T. Palgrave (London: Macmillan, 1875); the poem's speaker fears desertion by the Spirit of Delight, who is "love and life," unless he sets his "mournful ditty / To a merry measure" and professes love of all things loved by the Spirit. The allusion glosses the fin as both desolation at the ebbing of "love and life" and the persistent life force that keeps summoning Delight.

6. "One" and the informal alternative "you" of course carry class connotations. Gillian Beer finds that Woolf's decision to abandon the draft's efforts at working-class speech limits *The Waves*' aspirations as "the life of anybody," though this judgment perhaps applies a nineteenth-century notion of resemblance that the novel eludes (*"The Waves*: 'The Life of Anybody,' " in *Virginia Woolf: The Common Ground* [Edinburgh: Edinburgh UP, 1996], 89–90).

7. Woolf read Shakespeare intensively while at work on *The Waves* and measured her writing against his; see my "Virginia Woolf as Shakespeare's Sister: Chapters in a Woman Writer's Autobiography," in *Women's Re-Visions of Shakespeare,* ed. Marianne Novy (Urbana: U of Illinois P, 1990), 123–42.

8. In *The Singing of the Real World: The Philosophy of Virginia Woolf's Fiction,* Mark Hussey titles his chapter on *The Waves* "Aesthetic Failure" and describes the novel as "a store-house of typical ideas, but not much more than this. It is a kind of warehouse in which are found the materials from which novels such as *To the Lighthouse* or *Between the Acts* may be created" (82). On the novel's reception see Beer.

9. E.g., for Pauline Johnson, "the merely aesthetical character" of the "ideal subjectivity" Woolf's fiction posits, despite its "strongly critical standpoint," "ultimately fails to project a practical imperative" ("From Virginia Woolf to the Post-Moderns: Developments in a Feminist Aesthetic," *Radical Philosophy* 45 [1987], 29). For Rita Felski, Woolf (like Stein) represents "an artistic and intellectual—though not necessarily political—elite" (*The Gender of Modernity* [Cambridge: Harvard UP, 1995], 27–28); and the modernist "conception of the text as a privileged and subversive space which undermines truth and self-identity" potentially limits "direct political effects," by presupposing "the separation of the polysemic artwork from the sphere of everyday social practices. In other words, prevailing conceptions of literature which make it possible to identify the literary text as a site of resistance to ideology by virtue of its formal specificity simultaneously render problematic attempts to harness such an understanding of literary signification to the necessarily more determinate interest of an oppositional politics" (*Beyond Feminist Aesthetics: Feminist Literature and Social Change* [Cambridge: Harvard UP, 1989], 162–63). Cf. my chapter 1, n. 45.

10. E.g., on gender see Makiko Minow-Pinkney, *Virginia Woolf and the Problem of the Subject: Feminine Writing in the Major Novels* (New Brunswick, N.J.: Rutgers UP, 1987), chap. 6; on "the submerged mind of

empire" (J. M. Coetzee's phrase, cited by Marcus, 136) see Jane Marcus, "Britannia Rules *The Waves*," in *Decolonizing Tradition: New Views of Twentieth-Century 'British' Literary Canons*, ed. Karen Lawrence (Champaign-Urbana: U of Illinois P, 1992), 136–162; and Patrick McGee, "The Politics of Modernist Form: Who Rules *The Waves?*" *Modern Fiction Studies* 38:3 (autumn 1992): 631–49.

11. I use politics here in Jacques Rancière's sense of "disagreement"; see *Disagreement: Politics and Philosophy* (Minneapolis: U of Minnesota P, 1999), vii–20. On the political vicissitudes of identity, see Charles Taylor, "The Politics of Recognition," in Amy Gutman, ed., *Multiculturalism and "The Politics of Recognition," An Essay by Charles Taylor* (Princeton: Princeton UP, 1992), 25–73; and Susan Okin, "Is Multiculturalism Bad for Women?" in *Is Multiculturalism Bad for Women?* ed. J. Cohen, Matthew Howard, and Martha Nussbaum (Princeton: Princeton UP, 1999).

12. These rights can be construed as negative freedoms from arbitrary and discriminatory social and political limits to autonomy, such as bars to education, work, enfranchisement, and property ownership.

13. Woolf probably did not read Kant's Third Critique but did read G. E. Moore's *Principia Ethica*, Roger Fry's historical and practical art criticism, and Clive Bell's *Art*; and through Leonard encountered the Kantian lingo of the Cambridge Apostles (e. g., "Apostles" versus "phenomenons," *D* 5:212, 30 March 1939). I argue not that Woolf derived her discourse and practice of aesthetic freedom directly from Kant but that Kant's theoretical link between art and freedom illuminates her writings and, conversely, that her work illuminates Bloomsbury's Kantian aesthetics. Moore wrote his dissertation on Kant, the philosopher whom, in his early writings, he "criticizes most strenuously, and yet, takes most seriously"; Baldwin adds, "no serious thinker now could agree with the totality of Moore's position" (*Principia Ethica* [1903], ed. Thomas Baldwin [Cambridge: Cambridge UP, 1993], xxxvi–xxxvii). Lytton Strachey descried in Moore's last two chapters an "indiscriminate heap of . . . the utterly mangled remains of Aristotle, Jesus, Mr Bradley, Kant, Herbert Spencer, Sidgwick, & McTaggart," in *Letters of Leonard Woolf*, ed. Frederic Spotts (New York: Harcourt Brace Jovanovich, 1989), 36. When Moore visited the Woolfs in 1940, Woolf found "less force & mass to him than I remembered. Less drive behind his integrity, unalloyed, but a little weakened . . . & not quite such a solid philosophic frame . . . so that our reverence is now . . . retrospective" (*D* 5:286, 20 May 1940). On the link between Bloomsbury aesthetics and Kant see also my chapters 1 and 9.

14. Kant, *Critique of Judgment*, trans. J. H. Bernard (New York: Hafner, 1951), §49 157–58; hereafter cited as *CJ* by section and page; cf. *Critique of the Power of Judgment*, ed. Paul Guyer, trans. Guyer and Eric Matthews (Cambridge: Cambridge UP, 2000), 192, 81, hereafter cited as *CPJ*. Kant's noumenal realm, of which we can know nothing, differs in its abstractness from the Platonic realm of ideal Forms. This abstractness allies Kant's critical aesthetics

with Woolf's abstract art in that each is concerned neither with represented phenomena nor with visible forms abstracted from appearances but with an inaccessible *reality* behind appearances that is linked to freedom.

15. Kant uses *Mensch/er* here.

16. Monique Wittig, "The Mark of Gender," in *The Poetics of Gender*, ed. Nancy K. Miller (New York: Columbia UP, 1983); see also Casey Miller and Kate Swift, *Words and Women: New Language in New Times* (Garden City, N.Y.: Doubleday/Anchor, 1977), esp. chap. 3.

17. *CS* 123. *Orlando*'s Preface thanks MacCarthy along with dozens of others dead and alive, including Eliot, Woolf's niece and nephews, her servant Nelly Boxall, Defoe, Sterne, and Pater (*O* viii). *Room* cites MacCarthy's opinion that "female novelists should only aspire to excellence by courageously acknowledging the limitations of their sex," from *Life and Letters*, August 1928 (*RO* 78 and n. 3); cf. *WF* xxx–xxxviii. For an afterimage of the famous talk of this "babbling . . . nightingale" (*D* 5:82) who could lunch till 8, see *D* 5:279–80, 20 April 1940.

18. See Pierre Bourdieu, *Masculine Domination* (Stanford: Stanford UP, 1991).

19. Nigel Nicolson, *Portrait of a Marriage* (London: Weidenfeld and Nicolson, 1973), 201.

20. On *Orlando*'s autobiographical dimensions, see my "Virginia Woolf as Shakespeare's Sister."

21. *O* 83. Conjuring the memory of Shakespeare's face, Orlando wonders, "but who the devil was he? . . . Not a Nobleman; not one of us"—betraying, the biographer notes, the "effect noble birth has upon the mind and incidentally how difficult it is for a nobleman to be a writer"; even the backbiting poetaster Nick Greene provides such lively relief from the aristocracy's prosaic materialism that Orlando is struck by "how active and valiant . . . in body; how slothful and timid in mind" English lords tend to be (*O* 79–80, 92).

22. Orlando's biographer assumes the masculine gender at the outset: "Happy the mother who bears, happier still the biographer who records. . . . Never need she vex herself, nor he invoke the help of novelist or poet" (*O* 14–15); but his gender seems as fluid as Orlando's, while bodily sex is disavowed altogether ("let us, who enjoy the immunity of all biographers and historians from any sex whatever . . . " *O* 220); among other things, his masculinity parodies the internalized censorship apparatus Woolf remarks in *Room* and elsewhere.

23. Sandra M. Gilbert, "Costumes of the Mind: Transvestism as Metaphor in Modern Literature," *Critical Inquiry* 7 (winter 1980): 391–417, sidesteps the relation of sex to gender by arguing that Orlando is "no more than a transvestite . . . not because sexually defining costumes are false and selves are true but because costumes *are* selves and thus easily, fluidly, interchangeable" (405).

24. *O* 252, 258. Cf. Woolf's comic reversal of Rochester's fall from his horse and his rescue by Jane Eyre in Orlando's rescue by Shelmerdine, as well as their

similarly unorthodox marriage: "She was married, true; but if one's husband was always sailing round Cape Horn, was it marriage? If one liked him, was it marriage? If one liked other people, was it marriage? And finally, if one still wished, more than anything in the whole world, to write poetry, was it marriage? She had her doubts" (O 247–50, 263–64).

25. RO 114, O 104. See " 'Anon' and 'The Reader': Virginia Woolf's Last Essays," ed. Brenda R. Silver, Twentieth Century Literature 25 (fall/winter 1979): 356–441, where, in "Notes for Reading at Random," Woolf ponders the paradox of Shakespeare's impersonality: "the person is consumed: S[hakespeare] never breaks the envelope. We dont want to know about him: Completely expressed" (375). On Woolf's construction of Shakespeare as a model of anonymous and androgynous poetic power, see Maria diBattista, Virginia Woolf's Major Novels: The Epic of Anon (New Haven: Yale UP, 1980), 134f, and Karen Lawrence, "'Shikespower': Shakespeare's Legacy for Virginia Woolf and James Joyce," MLA paper, Chicago, 1985.

26. O 91, 55–57. Woolf returns to this point in "Anon": "To the Elizabethans the expressive power of words after their long inadequacy must have been overwhelming. . . . There at the Globe or at the Rose men and women whose only reading had been the Bible or some old chronicle came out into the light of the present moment" and "heard their aspirations, their profanities, their ribaldries spoken for them in poetry. And there was something illicit in their pleasure. The preacher and the magistrate were always denouncing their emotion. That too must have given it intensity" (395–96).

27. O 104–5. Cf. the Shakespeare of "Anon," who sheds personal wants, grievances, anxieties to merge his imagination with the common life so that his plays, though "written by one hand," are "in part the work of the audience" who enabled the playwright's "great strides" and "vast audacities beyond the reach of the solitary writer" (395).

28. RO 114; John Milton, Paradise Lost, book 4, line 299.

29. Cf. the seed of The Jessamy Brides and Orlando: "The Ladies are to have Constantinople in view. Dreams of golden domes. My own lyric vein to be satirised. Everything mocked" (D 3:131, 14 March 1927). See Louise A. DeSalvo, "Lighting the Cave: The Relationship between Vita Sackville-West and Virginia Woolf," Signs 8 (1982): 195–214, and Suzanne Raitt, Virginia Woolf and Vita Sackville-West (Oxford: Clarendon, 1992). Vita lived in Constantinople in 1913–14 while her husband Harold Nicolson was ambassador; traveling in Turkey with her ambassador husband in the early 1700s, Lady Mary Wortley Montagu wrote that "the coldest and most rigid prude upon earth could not have looked upon" the women dancers without thinking of "something not to be spoken of" (Letters). On Woolf's "orientalizing" of lesbian sexuality see Karen R. Lawrence, "Orlando's Voyage Out," Modern Fiction Studies 38 (1992): 253–77.

30. In Kant's theory, "pure a priori imagination," unlike reason, operates by a "hidden art in the depths of the human soul, whose true operations we can

divine from nature and lay unveiled before our eyes only with difficulty" (*Critique of Pure Reason,* trans. and ed. Paul Guyer and Allan W. Wood [Cambridge: Cambridge UP, 1998], §180–181, 273–74).

31. *O* 318. Orlando's estate is based on the Sackville-Wests' ancestral estate Knole in Kent, granted by Elizabeth I to Thomas Sackville in 1566. Knole inspired Shakespeare fantasies in both Vita and Woolf. Vita's *Knole and the Sackvilles* (1922; Tonbridge, Kent: Ernest Benn, 1984), which Woolf reread as she began *Orlando,* notes that sketchy evidence that Shakespeare visited Knole gave the young Vita "wild dreams that some light might be thrown on the Shakespearean problem by a discovery of letters or documents at Knole. What more fascinating or chimerical a speculation for a literary-minded child breathing and absorbing the atmosphere of that house? I used to tell myself stories of finding Shakespeare's manuscripts up in the attics, perhaps hidden away under the flooring somewhere" (57–58). Visiting Knole in 1924, Virginia remarked "chairs that Shakespeare might have sat on" (*D* 2:306, July 5).

32. *O* 323, 325. From observing Pope, Orlando learns that genius ("now stamped out in the British Isles") is no steady flame that makes "everything plain" at risk of "scorching" its beholders "to death" but resembles the intermittent beams of a "lighthouse," only "more capricious," sometimes "laps[ing] into darkness for a year or forever," so that "To steer by its beams is . . . impossible" (*O* 207–8). The one positive lesson Orlando gleans from the eighteenth-century poets is that "the most important part of style" is "the natural run of the voice in speaking" (*O* 212).

33. *RO* 5. "Mary Hamilton" is also known as "The Four Maries." See Jane Marcus's "Sapphistry: Narration as Lesbian Seduction in *A Room of One's Own,*" in *Virginia Woolf and the Languages of Patriarchy* (Bloomington: Indiana UP, 1987), 163–87; and Alice Fox, "Literary Allusion as Feminist Criticism in *A Room of One's Own,*" *Philological Quarterly* 63 (spring 1984): 145–61. Mary Carmichael also recalls Lily Briscoe's silent mentor, the poet Augustus Carmichael.

34. *Norton Anthology of Poetry,* 4th ed., ed. Margaret Ferguson, Mary Jo Salter, and Jon Stallworthy (New York: Norton, 1996), 93.

35. Woolf also echoes the ballad's "me" in a letter of 27 April 1928 complaining that she telephoned Vita to find her "gone nutting in the woods with Mary Campbell, or Mary Carmichael, or Mary Seton, but not me—damn you" (*L* 3:487).

36. Marcus, "Sapphistry," 211 n. 10.

37. *MB* 201; Leonard, Adrian Stephen, John Maynard Keynes, and Duncan Grant shared 38 Brunswick Square with Virginia before her marriage. Woolf's childlessness was a decision made by Leonard and her doctors and a cause of deep regret.

38. *RO* 37. If genius and freedom have no gender, education and creative labor do in 1928 England, as the historicization of genius in *Room's* opening anecdotes emphasizes; cf. *RO,* 53–54, and see my "Modernism, Genetic Texts,

and Literary Authority in Woolf's Portraits of the Artist as the Audience," *The Romanic Review* 86:3 (1996): 513–26.

39. *RO* 66, 64. Woolf's inheritance enabled her to become the prodigiously productive professional writer and publisher she was; for a year-by-year record of the Woolfs' income and earnings see Leonard Woolf, *Downhill All the Way: An Autobiography of the Years 1919 to 1939* (New York: HBJ, 1967), 142.

40. *D* 3:206 n. 11 (10 November 1928); *RO* 80. Marcus, "Sapphistry," links the ballad "Mary Hamilton" to the 1928 trial of Radclyffe Hall's *The Well of Loneliness*; Celia Marshik discusses *Orlando* in light of British censorship law and Woolf's involvement in that trial in "Publication and 'Public Women': Prostitution and Censorship in Three Novels by Virginia Woolf," *Modern Fiction Studies* 45:4 (winter 1999): 853–86.

41. Luce Irigaray, "When the Goods Get Together" ("Les Marchandises entre Elles"), trans. Claudia Reeder, in *New French Feminisms*, ed. Elaine Marks and Isabelle de Courtivron (New York: Schocken, 1981), 107–110.

42. *RO* 84, 92, 14. For Mary Jacobus, that women's different perspectives undermine established fictions "makes 'the difference of view' a question rather than an answer" ("The Difference of View," *Reading Woman: Essays in Feminist Criticism* [New York: Columbia UP, 1986], 27–40).

43. *RO* 113, 77. Woolf's 1927 essay "The Narrow Bridge of Art" is a manifesto for *The Waves*: "the lyric cry of ecstasy or despair, which is so intense, so personal, and so limited, is not enough. The mind is full of monstrous, hybrid, unmanageable emotions. That the age of the earth is 3,000,000,000 years; that human life lasts but a second; that the capacity of the human mind is nevertheless boundless; that life is infinitely beautiful yet repulsive; that one's fellow creatures are adorable but disgusting; that science and religion have between them destroyed belief; that all bonds of union seem broken, yet some control must exist—it is in this atmosphere of doubt and conflict that writers have now to create," and the lyric "is no more fitted to" it "than a rose leaf to envelop the rugged immensity of a rock" (*GR* 12). New forms will appear, among them a novel "we shall scarcely know how to christen," in prose displaying "something of the exaltation of poetry, but much of the ordinariness of prose," "dramatic, and yet not a play," giving "the outline rather than the detail" and the mind's relation "to general ideas and its soliloquy in solitude"; its writer will "have need of all his courage" (18–19, 23).

44. Elaine Showalter famously deplores *Room*'s "flight" from femaleness in "Virginia Woolf and the Flight into Androgyny," *A Literature of Their Own: British Women Novelists from Bronte to Lessing* (Princeton, N. J.: Princeton UP, 1977), 263–97. But far from denying continuing obstructions to women writers, Woolf's concept of androgyny urges women to claim freedom despite masculine culture's bogeys and to flee not "femaleness" but credulousness and impotent anger. In dismissing Woolf's androgyny as lifelessly "utopian," Showalter ignores the dialectic between realism and utopianism in Woolf's work—characteristic of feminist theory and practice—which challenges social

"reality" to incorporate possibilities that must otherwise remain literally utopian. On androgyny as an alternative to gender, see Carolyn G. Heilbrun, *Toward a Recognition of Androgyny* (New York: Harper and Row, 1973); and essays by Heilbrun and others in *Women's Studies* 2, no. 2 (1974). For Jacobus, Woolf's androgyny is "a harmonizing gesture, a simultaneous enactment of desire and repression by which the split is closed with an essentially Utopian vision of undivided consciousness" (*Reading Woman* 39). I argue that this state of mind requires less the repression of gender than a conscious, hard-won disbelief in it, which *The Waves* exemplifies.

45. *D* 3:295, 1 March 1930; the commission was for a biography of Boswell. See n. 39 above.

46. *RO* 84. Similarly, when Woolf urges Mary Carmichael to record the lives of ordinary women talking with "the swing of Shakespeare's words," she evokes her own project, "the Lives of the Obscure," conceived "to tell the whole history of England in one obscure life after another" (*RO* 89, *D* 3:37, 20 July 1925).

47. *RO* 90; *D* 3:229, 28 May 1929. The moth recurs from *The Voyage Out* on as a naturalized Psyche, a bodiless self or soul evoking what *Room* calls "reality," beyond "the world of men and women." See my chapters 2 and 3; Harvena Richter, "Hunting the Moth: Virginia Woolf and the Creative Imagination," in *Virginia Woolf: Revaluation and Continuity*, ed. Ralph Freedman (Berkeley: U of California P, 1980), 13–28; and my "Out of the Chrysalis: Female Initiation and Female Authority in Virginia Woolf's *The Voyage Out*," *Tulsa Studies in Women's Literature* 5 (spring 1986): 63–90.

48. Wittig, "The Mark of Gender"; see also her novel *Les Guérillères*, trans. David Le Vay (Boston: Beacon, 1971, 1985).

49. *Wh* I:9, cf. 6, my emphases. In citing the holograph drafts I silently omit deleted and extraneous words and make minor editorial corrections.

50. "Odd, that they (the Times) shd. praise my characters when I meant to have none," Woolf wrote when reviews appeared (*D* 4:47, 8 October 1931).

51. As several critics point out, *The Waves* preserves gender stereotypes— and privileges male culture-makers—in its six characters: the coquette Jinny, the earth mother Susan, the mystic Rhoda, versus the writers Bernard, Neville, and Louis; e. g., Eileen B. Sypher, "*The Waves*: A Utopia of Androgyny," in *Virginia Woolf: Centennial Essays* (Troy, N.Y.: Whitson, 1983), sees Bernard as "a male center [chosen] to repress [Woolf's] own voice" and concludes, "However much she valued it, Woolf could not in *The Waves* fully confront female authoring, female creativity" (210). Locating the narrative voice in the voice of the interludes that frames the children's voices, I argue that Woolf abstracts a reality all six voices share, to which gender is accidental, irrelevant. The novel privileges voice over writing; further, no hierarchy of gender exists among the six voices: each shares in the narration until the autobiographical Bernard takes over—not to privilege a male voice (his gender is immaterial) but to dramatize the immateriality of the (historically female) thinker's sex to the "one" who is

the novel's ultimate speaker. My reading thus aligns *The Waves* with something like Maurice Blanchot's concept of "the Neutral"; see *The Infinite Conversation* (*L'Entretien infini*, 1969), trans. Susan Hanson (Minneapolis: U of Minnesota P, 1993) and n. 63 below.

52. W 35. Doris Eder, "Louis Unmasked: T. S. Eliot in *The Waves*," *Virginia Woolf Quarterly* 2 (1975): 13–27.

53. Stephen J. Miko, "Reflections on *The Waves*: Virginia Woolf at the Limits of Her Art," *Criticism* 30 (winter 1988): 66.

54. For a lucid treatment of quantum physics and the descriptions of the cosmos generated by it, see Paul Davies, *Other Worlds: A Portrait of Nature in Rebellion: Space, Superspace, and the Quantum Universe* (New York: Simon and Schuster, 1980); on affinities between quantum physics and eastern mysticism, see Gary Zukav, *The Dancing Wu Li Masters: An Overview of the New Physics* (New York: William Morrow, 1979). On intersections among quantum physics, twentieth-century abstract art, and postmodern philosophy, see my "Quantum Physics/Postmodern Metaphysics: The Nature of Jacques Derrida," *Western Humanities Review* 39 (winter 1985): 287–313. Judith Ann Killen, "Virginia Woolf in the Light of Modern Physics" (Ph.D. Diss., U of Louisville, 1984), reconstructs Woolf's reading on science during the thirties, relates it to *The Waves*, and analyzes Woolf's adaptation of scientific theory to new aesthetic techniques. See also Gillian Beer, *Virginia Woolf: The Common Ground*, chap. 6; and Holly Henry, *Virginia Woolf and the Discourse of Science: The Aesthetics of Astronomy* (Cambridge: Cambridge UP, 2003). Marcus, 242 n. 6, and McGee, 643–44, touch on this connection.

55. Quantum theory demonstrates that the language of classical logic cannot comprehend events at the subatomic level and therefore cannot be considered a system the truths of which would hold in face of any contingency, as philosophers since David Hume have asserted; see R. I. G. Hughes, "Quantum Logic," *Scientific American* 245 (October 1981): 199–213.

56. Henry Stapp, "S-Matrix Interpretation of Quantum Theory," *Physical Review*, D3, 1971, 1303, quoted in Zukav, 93, 96.

57. Davies, *Other Worlds*, 103–4. One month and sixty-six pages into the draft, Woolf wrote, "There is *something* there (as I felt about Mrs. Dalloway) but I can't get at it squarely. . . . I am in an odd state; feel a cleavage; here's my interesting thing; & there's no quite solid table on which to put it. It might come in a flash . . . some solvent. I am convinced that I am right to seek for a station whence I can set my people against time and the sea—but Lord, the difficulty of digging oneself in there, with conviction" (*D* 3:264, 5 November 1929).

58. Davies, *Other Worlds*, 138.

59. W 64. Woolf returns to this autobiographical experience in "A Sketch of the Past": "the moment of the puddle in the path; when for no reason I could discover, everything suddenly became unreal; I was suspended; I could not step across the puddle; I tried to touch something . . . the whole world became unreal" (*MB* 78; ellipsis Woolf's).

60. *D* 3:260, 11 October 1929. Woolf's inspiration for Percival was Thoby Stephen, who died of typhoid in 1906. Woolf thought of dedicating *The Waves* to him; after reading it, Vanessa Bell wrote, "I think you have made one's human feelings into something less personal . . . you have found 'the lullaby capable of singing him to rest' [*Hamlet*]" (*D* 4:10, 7 February 1931; *L* 4:390–91 n. 1, October 1931).

61. *W* 277, 269–70. In writing of Roger Fry's funeral Woolf evoked bleak recognition of death's finality against the renewed will to fight and live: "how we all fought with our brains loves & so on; & *must* be vanquished. Then the vanquisher, this outer force became so clear; the indifferent. & we so small fine delicate. . . . I felt the vainness of this perpetual fight, with our brains & loving each other against the other thing: if Roger could die. / But then . . . the other thing begins to work—the exalted sense of being above time & death which comes from being again in a writing mood. And this is not an illusion, so far as I can tell. Certainly I have a strong sense that Roger would be all on one's side in this excitement, & that whatever the invisible force does, we thus get outside it" (*D* 4:245, 19–20 September 1934).

62. E. g., Patrick McGee reads the "fin" as the *fin*/end of writing, a "third voice" beyond "the symbolic order": "the symbolic Other . . . the symbolic not insofar as it has been inscribed with meanings by a given culture but as the material trace, the historical condition of the possibility of meaning" ("Woolf's Other: The University in Her Eye," *Novel* 23 [1990]: 229–46; 244); Charles Bernheimer, as "division, difference and death" ("A Shattered Globe: Narcissism and Masochism in Virginia Woolf's Life-Writing," in *Psychoanalysis and . . .*, ed. Richard Feldstein and Henry Sussman [New York: Routledge, 1990], 205).

63. *W* 163. Again, *The Waves* resonates with Maurice Blanchot's theoretical naming of literary space as "the neutral," "the outside," *desoeuvement*, "essential solitude," "the other night," and the ambivalence of "being *as* dissimulation: dissimulation itself" (see *The Space of Literature* [*L'Espace litteraire*, 1955], trans. Ann Smock [Lincoln: U of Nebraska P, 1982]).

64. Bernard d'Espagnat, "The Quantum Theory and Reality," *Scientific American* 241 (November 1979): 181.

65. Critics tend to emphasize one or the other. DiBattista, e. g., describes *The Waves* as "a displaced creation myth rendered in distinctly feminine terms and expressing peculiarly feminine ambitions. It describes the formation of a subjectivity which, although common to all minds, finds its representative voice in a female 'She' who reflexively comes to know and identify herself" (*Virginia Woolf's Major Novels*, 162). While diBattista registers *The Waves'* aspirations to "one" ("common to all minds"), her insistence on "a female 'She,' " and on "distinctly," "peculiarly feminine" "terms" and "ambitions," reinscribes the "interest" that, I argue, Woolf labored to surmount. Toril Moi begs the question of "sex . . . unconscious of itself" in identifying Woolf's androgyny with Kristeva's "third position," beyond women's "demand for equal access to the symbolic order" and its rejection in the name of difference: women's rejection

of "the dichotomy between masculine and feminine as metaphysical" (*Sexual/ Textual Politics: Feminist Literary Theory* [New York: Methuen, 1985], 12). Invoking Kristeva's maternally identified semiotic, Minow-Pinkney links *The Waves'* rhythmic, choric prose to the "she" who writes it (*Virginia Woolf and the Problem of the Subject*, chap. 6). Reversing this promotion of "she" over "one," Garrett Stewart rejects the essentialist equation of the semiotic with the maternal and argues that *The Waves* "transmits textual energy along the momentarily ungendered and non-signifying *person* of a vocal agent without identity, whose bodily cooperation alone spans the recesses within that combined cerebration and subjectivity known as reading" (Garrett Stewart, "Catching the Stylistic D/Rift: Sound Defects in *The Waves*," *ELH* 54 [Summer 1987]: 458).

66. Woolf memorializes the organic, bodily locus of *The Waves'* textual production (complete with bloody birth imagery) in a letter to Ethel Smyth: "I wrote this morning; and then took one of Leonards large white pocket handkerchiefs and climbed Asheham hill and lost a green glove and found 10 mushrooms, which I shall eat in bed tomorrow, with bacon, toast, and hot coffee. I shall get a letter from Ethel. I shall moon slowly dressing; shall loiter talking, shall hear about the funeral of our epileptic Tom Fears, who dropped dead after dinner on Thursday; shall smell a red rose; shall gently surge across the lawn (I move as if I carried a basket of eggs on my head) light a cigarette, take my writing board on my knee; and let myself down, like a diver, very cautiously into the last sentence I wrote yesterday. Then perhaps after 20 minutes, or it may be more, I shall see a light in the depths of the sea, and stealthily approach—for one's sentences are only an approximation, a net one flings over some sea pearl which may vanish; and if one brings it up it wont be anything like what it was when I saw it, under the sea. Now these are the great excitements of life. Once I would have written all this [the letter] twice over; but now I can't; it has to go, with its blood on its head" (*L* 4:223, 28 September 1930).

67. In "A Sketch of the Past" Woolf describes the violent perceptual "shocks" that lead to writing: "I feel that I have had a blow; but it is not, as I thought as a child, simply a blow from an enemy hidden behind the cotton wool of daily life; it is or will become a revelation of some order; . . . a token of some real thing behind appearances; and I make it real by putting it into words. It is only by putting it into words that I make it whole; this wholeness means that it has lost its power to hurt me; it gives me, perhaps because by doing so I take away the pain, a great delight to put the severed parts together" (*MB* 72). The "shock" felt as "token of some real thing behind appearances," which the artist strives to "make . . . real"—to endow with material form in the realm of appearances—evokes Kant's proposition that art throws a bridge between the noumenal and phenomenal realms, while Woolf's description of the "great delight," "the strongest pleasure known to me," "the rapture I get when . . . I seem to be discovering what belongs to what" (akin to Lily Briscoe's experience

of "the joy of freedom") bodies forth his view of the artist as "nature's favorite" (*MB* 72).

68. *D* 3:260, 11 October 1929. Following *The Waves*' both/and logic, I would augment Stewart's identityless "vocal agent" (n. 65 above), which relies on the literary text's material silence, with this visual and aural *image* of a woman singing, her (imaginary) sex and voice aspects of organic nature. While the human voice is usually inflected by physiological sex, it is no reliable index to the sex of the body from which it issues; even professional singers cannot always distinguish, say, a countertenor from a soprano and might, for example, mistake Marilyn Horne in Vivaldi's *Orlando* for a tenor.

7. The Sexual Life of Women: Experimental Genres, Experimental Publics from *The Pargiters* to *The Years*

1. The Speech's posthumously published four versions include: 1) Manuscript Notes dated 21 January 1931 (*P/MN* 163–67); 2) Speech typescript (*P/S* xxvii–xliv); 3) *The Pargiters*' First Essay, dated 11 October 1932 (*P/E1* 5–10); 4) the essay "Professions for Women," derived from the Speech (*DM/PW* 235–42). In citing *The Pargiters*, I silently omit words deleted by Woolf and make minor editorial changes for clarity.

2. *D* 5:65, 7 March 1937. See Grace Radin, " 'I Am Not a Hero': Virginia Woolf and the First Version of *The Years*," *Massachusetts Review* (1975): 195–208, and *Virginia Woolf's* The Years: *The Evolution of a Novel* (Knoxville: U of Tennessee P, 1981), 35 and passim; Mitchell A. Leaska, "Virginia Woolf, the Pargeter: A Reading of *The Years*," *Bulletin of the New York Public Library* 80:2 (winter 1977): 172–210; Jane Marcus, "*The Years* as Götterdämmerung, Greek Play, and Domestic Novel" and "Pargetting *The Pargiters*," *Virginia Woolf and the Languages of Patriarchy* (Bloomington: Indiana UP, 1987), chaps. 2–3, first published in *Bulletin of the New York Public Library* 80:2–3 (winter, spring 1977). Cf. Elizabeth Abel, *Virginia Woolf and the Fictions of Psychoanalysis* (Chicago: U of Chicago P, 1989), on *Three Guineas* (106). On her half brothers' sexual abuse see *MB*, esp. 58, 67–68, 169, 177. Biographical treatments include QB 1.44; HL chap. 8; Roger Poole, *The Unknown Virginia Woolf* (Atlantic Highlands, N.J.: Humanities P, 1978), Stephen Trombley, " '*All that Summer She Was Mad*': Virginia Woolf and Her Doctors* (London: Junction, 1981), and Louise DeSalvo, *Virginia Woolf: The Impact of Childhood Sexual Abuse on Her Life and Work* (Boston: Beacon, 1989). Anna Snaith argues that "Woolf abandoned the essay-novel idea not because fact and fiction were in conflict, but precisely the opposite, because she did not need the genre divide, she had already found a balance between fiction and the 'truth of fact' which supported it" ("Negotiating Genre: Re-visioning History in *The Pargiters*," in *Virginia Woolf: Public and Private Negotiations* [New York: St. Martin's P, 2000], 110).

3. M. M. Bakhtin, "The Problem of Speech Genres," in *Speech Genres and Other Late Essays*, trans. Vern W. McGee, ed. Caryl Emerson and Michael

Holquist (Austin: U of Texas P, 1986), 98, 95–96. Recall Woolf's appeal to her audience to help the "good cause" of bringing forth "one of the great ages of English literature" in "Mr. Bennett and Mrs. Brown" (*CDB* 119).

4. *D* 4:338, 5 September 1935. Sidonie Smith writes that in "A Sketch of the Past" "Part of the 'truth' that Woolf tells 'about my own experiences as a body' is the unspeakable truth of repression"; her metaphor of disembodiment "sustains . . . the troubled relationship between the autobiographical subject and the female body" ("The Autobiographical Eye/I in Virginia Woolf's 'Sketch,' " in *Subjectivity, Identity, and the Body: Women's Autobiographical Practices in the Twentieth Century* [Bloomington: Indiana UP, 1993], 102).

5. *D* 4:6, 20 January 1931. Days later Woolf could hardly stop "making up The Open Door or whatever it is to be called" to finish *The Waves* (*D* 4.6, 23 January).

6. *D* 4.7, 23 January 1931; Woolf continues, "Ethel in her blue kimono & wig. I by her side. Her speech rollicking & direct: mine too compressed & allusive. Never mind. Four people wish the speeches printed . . . And now Open Door is sucking at my brain." See Vera Brittain on the program "provided for a large audience by Dame Ethel Smyth and Mrs. Virginia Woolf" (*P/S* xxxv n); and HL 590.

7. See n. 1 above.

8. Woolf's writing was by now a primary source of income. By 1928 her books' popular success had produced a "sudden, large jump" in income (*D* 3:43, 22 September)—a "revolutionary increase" that Leonard attributed "first to the sudden success of Virginia's books and secondarily to the Hogarth Press." While they already had the life they wanted on £1000 a year, he wrote, "life is easier on £3000 a year"; e. g., he could resign as the *Nation*'s literary editor. Owing to *Orlando* and *The Years*, 1929 and 1938, the years of Woolf's major feminist essays, were the two highest-earning years of her career. Leonard tracks the Press's lists and profits during this period and the increased income Vita Sackville-West's books brought it (*Downhill All the Way: An Autobiography of the Years 1919–1939* (New York: Harcourt, Brace, Jovanovich, 1967), 142–43f, 157, 145); see also HL, chap. 31.

9. *P/MN* 164–65. As a professional writer in the line of Aphra Behn (who "makes it not quite fantastic for me to say to you tonight: Earn five hundred a year by your wits" [*RO* 66]) and a breadwinner whose future earnings depended largely upon her continued productivity and sales, Woolf differed markedly from Joyce (who enjoyed Harriet Shaw Weaver's bounteous patronage) and Proust (whose inherited wealth endowed his writing). Leonard, always Woolf's first reader as well as manager of the Press, may have been a factor too.

10. *P/S* xxxiii. See John Maynard Keynes, review of *Clare College, 1326–1926*, ed. Mansfield D. Forbes, 2 vols. (Cambridge: Cambridge UP, 1928, 1930), *The Nation and Athenaeum* 48: 17 January 1932: 512–13; *P/S* xxxiii–xxxv, notes. The sexcentenary history, its editor wrote, sought to give

the men of Clare "some glimpse of the greatness of the rock from which they are hewn" (14).

11. Since 1920, when she began publicly criticizing the sex/gender system that her friends took more or less for granted, Woolf had been conscious of "taking my own line apart from" Bloomsbury's: "One of these days I shan't know Clive if I meet him. I want to know all sorts of other people—retaining only Nessa & Duncan, I think" (D 2:81, 19 December 1920).

12. RO 49–50. This internalized prohibition against writing about sexuality had not thus far prevented Woolf from writing of prostitutes in The Voyage Out, Jacob's Room, and Orlando; menstruation and menopause in "Mrs. Dalloway in Bond Street" and Mrs. Dalloway; illegitimate pregnancy in Jacob's Room and Mrs. Dalloway; same-sex love in Jacob's Room, Mrs. Dalloway, Room, Orlando, and The Waves; and sexual transgressions in The Voyage Out and Mrs. Dalloway.

13. P/S xl. Cf. Nancy Fraser's discussion of contestatory "alternative publics" and "subaltern counterpublics"—"parallel discursive arenas where members of subordinated groups invent and circulate counterdiscourses, which in turn permit them to formulate oppositional identifications of their identities, interests, and needs"—in "Rethinking the Public Sphere: A Contribution to the Critique of Actually Existing Democracy," Social Text 25/26 (1990): 67 and passim.

14. Cf. the endings of The Years, Three Guineas, and Between the Acts; see Radin, Virginia Woolf's The Years, 9.

15. This is the novel-essay portion, dated 11 October–19 December 1932; on 31 January 1933 Woolf began recasting the chapters as the novel that became The Years (P 159n).

16. D 4:6–7, 28, 42 n. 8, P iv. The editors of the diary and The Pargiters assign these titles to Three Guineas (D 4:6 n. 8), though they led first to the essay-novel; as Radin notes, the first page of the first extant notebook is dated 20 July 1931, and headed "Notes for The Knock on the Door?"; the next several pages have been cut out and the next extant page, dated 11 October 1932, begins The Pargiters (reproduced, P 4) (P xv and n. 4; Virginia Woolf's The Years, 9 n).

17. Ottoline Morrell, unpublished diary, 9 November 1932 (HL 155). In Mrs. Dalloway "a tap at the door" just precedes Septimus's suicide (MD 144). Rather than speculate on the events that engendered this psychic trauma, I take Woolf's declaration that "the damage done to the mind is worse than that done to the body" as read.

18. Breuer's patient Bertha Pappenheim/"Anna O." coined the phrase talking cure in 1881 on their discovery that her hysterical symptoms could be "talked away" through systematic description of each occurrence from the latest "back to the event which had led to its first appearance": "[W]e found . . . that each individual hysterical symptom immediately and permanently disappeared when we had succeeded in bringing clearly to light the memory of the

event by which it was provoked and in arousing its accompanying affect, and when the patient had described that event in the greatest possible detail and had put the affect into words" (Sigmund Freud and Josef Breuer, *Studies on Hysteria* [London: Penguin, 1974], 85, 91, 89, 57). First published in 1895, *Studies on Hysteria* was partially translated and published in New York in 1909; the first Hogarth Press edition appeared only in 1955. Woolf appears not to have read it; Abel, *Virginia Woolf*, does not mention it.

19. Woolf added that writing the novel dispelled her mother's almost hallucinatory daily presence (*MB* 81). In 1931, as she makes the unconscious the wellspring of the fisherwoman's creativity, Woolf also complains that Walpole's sealing it over reduces *Judith Paris* to "words without roots," "a trivial litter of bright objects to be swept up"; by contrast, Scott's *Ivanhoe* has "some roots," words "ruffled (but oh how seldom) by some raid from the sub-conscious" (*D* 4:41, 1 September).

Jane Vanderbosch suggests that Woolf may have considered psychoanalysis while at work on *The Years*. In December 1935, at Aldous Huxley's suggestion, Woolf had her hand read by the German-Jewish refugee, psychologist, and palmist Charlotte Wolff, remarking that though it was "sheer and mere drivel," "she's driven out of Germany—a Jewess" (*L* 6:5). Woolf had Wolff to tea, and Wolff wrote that Woolf "wanted to know how I would treat people with nervous disorders and anxiety. [Wolff:] ' . . . No therapeutic shortcuts exist for anxiety states, and nervous tension has many causes. . . . You mean Freudian analysis?' [Woolf:] 'Yes.' [Wolff:] 'I cannot judge it as I had Jungian analysis. . . . In certain cases it is contraindicated.' [Woolf] jumped in. 'You mean, in my case?' 'Yes, I would think so' " (Charlotte Wolff, *Hindsight: An Autobiography* [London: Quartet, 1980], 46, cited in Vanderbosch, "Virginia Woolf and Psychoanalysis," *VWM* 19 [fall 1982]: 4). In Vanderbosch's view, Wolff's memoir dispels the myth that Woolf "never considered the application of Freudian theory to her situation" or "consulted a practicing therapist about her 'case.' " But would Woolf, so well connected to the British psychoanalytic community, have seriously consulted a German Jungian and palmist on this matter? Wolff's "hindsight" report was possibly written years later, and the Woolfs' diaries and letters do not corroborate it.

20. Freud and Breuer, *Studies on Hysteria*, 63.

21. Winifred Holtby's *Virginia Woolf: A Critical Memoir* appeared in October 1932. Woolf disparaged it to various correspondents while it lay about unread and finally wrote Holtby on 15 January 1933 that she had "finished" and "enjoyed it very much," adding that she suspected that "a good many things happened to" its subject "by way of life, that she concealed successfully, but it seems to me, speaking as an outsider, that you have made an extremely interesting story out of her books" ("Nineteen Letters to Eleven Recipients," ed. Joanne Trautmann Banks, *Modern Fiction Studies* 30 [1984]: 183). Presumably Woolf concealed a good deal from a biographer she elsewhere denigrates as "feather pated" and a "farmer's daughter"; "I couldn't help laughing to

think what a story she could have told had she known the true Virginia," she wrote Violet Dickinson (her early confidante about her half brothers' sexual abuse), adding a description of Gerald, whom she had just visited; to Margaret Llewellyn Davies she wrote, "I'm told her book is bad—, vain though I am, I cannot read about myself, and my parents and my education—all lies too" (*L* 6:28, 21 April 1936; 5:125, 10 November 1932).

22. *Three Guineas* cites biographies, memoirs, published letters, and diaries in many contexts, for example, to ventriloquize social critique (Mary Kingsley on the poverty of daughters' formal education) or as "oracles" that women can consult "as our fathers and grandfathers did before us" for prophetic utterances on women's fate and future in civilization: "The question we put to you, lives of the dead, is how can we enter the professions and yet remain civilized human beings who wish to prevent war?" (*TG* 114). Cited texts include works by or about Anne Clough, Mary Kingsley, Elizabeth Haldane, Horace Vachell, Mary, Countess of Lovelace, the Duke of Portland, Anthony, Viscount Knebworth, Henry Chaplin, Josephine Butler, Wilfred Scawen Blunt, Edward Gibbon, Herbert Warren of Magdalen, Mary Butts, Mary Astell, Sir J. J. Thomson, Lord and Lady Amberley, the Baroness St. Helier, Sir Anthony Hope, Gino Watkins, G. L. Dickinson, John Bowdler, C. E. M. Joad, H. G. Wells, Helena Mary Lucy Swanwick, Sophia Jex-Blake, John Collings Squire, Charles Gore, Sir Ernest Wild, Sir William Broadbent, Sidney Low, Winston Churchill, Charles Tomlinson, Ellen Weeton Stock, Octavia Hill, Lady Salmond, Gertrude Bell, Saint Paul, Charles Kingsley, Upton Sinclair, John Nichols, Margaret Oliphant, Sir Edmund Gosse, Douglas Jerrold, Tennyson, Joseph Wright, William Gerhardi, Charlotte Brontë, A. R. Orage, Emily Davies, Margaret Collyer, Laura Knight, Amelia Earhart, Prince Hubertus Loewenstein, and Georges Sand, among others.

23. *D* 4:170. This memoir has not been found.

24. *L* 5:299, 3 May 1934. Hermione Lee finds "no evidence" of the content of Vanessa's memoir, but it is clear from this letter, Fredegond Shove's 1918 letter, and other documents that George's abuses were an open subject between the sisters and with some of their friends (HL 777 n. 68; 156). Lee, in an odd opposition, judges George's abuses "more emotional than penetrative" and finds a "gap between the available evidence and the story [Woolf] drew from it," though she acknowledges that "Woolf herself thought that what had been done to her was very damaging" (156). By focusing on "penetrative" events, Lee slights Woolf's own emphasis on "the damage done to the mind," not least the force of repression in limiting what Lee does construe as evidence. DeSalvo, though her treatment of textual evidence is at times wildly inaccurate, takes psychic consequences more seriously.

25. *L* 6:28–29, 21 April; notably, Thoby, Adrian, Stella, Vanessa, and her mother do not figure in this solicitation. Cf. "the flood" here to the difficulty of finding "a sentence that could hold its own against the male flood"; and to the memoir of George that "flooded" Woolf with horror (*P/MN* 163–64, *L* 3/4 May 1934).

26. "Shy and silent as I am, I remain devoted, grateful, humble and Eternally yr Sp[arroy]" (*L* 6:42–43, 3 June). "£100 in gold" recalls the Hirsts' parlormaid who gave the cook twenty pounds in gold before committing suicide in *The Voyage Out*.

27. Thomas C. Caramagno, *The Flight of the Mind: Virginia Woolf's Art and Manic-Depressive Illness* (Berkeley: U of California P, 1992), 146, cf. 144; see also Jean O. Love, *Virginia Woolf: Sources of Madness and Art* (Berkeley: U of California P, 1977), 208; DeSalvo, 108–11, 119; HL 123–25.

28. *L* 1:472, 25? July 1911. On the Victorian ethos of female "passionlessness," see Nancy F. Cott, "Passionlessness: An Interpretation of Victorian Sexual Ideology, 1790–1850," *Signs* 4 (winter 1978): 219–36. On 3 September 1931 Woolf was reading Montaigne "about the passions of women—their voracity—which I at once opposed to Squire's remarks & so made up a whole chapter of my Tap at the Door or whatever it is" (*D* 4:42). J. C. Squire, editor of the *London Mercury*, broadcast "Idle Thoughts" on August 13.

29. "Lets leave the letters till we're both dead," Woolf replied when Ethel proposed that they publish their correspondence (*L* 6:272, 17 September 1938).

30. I have not been able to document the date of "Professions for Women," nor at the time of my last inquiry had Andrew McNeillie, the editor of the *Essays* (e-mail correspondence). Jane Marcus judges Leonard's decision to print this essay and not the 1931 Speech an "editorial suppression of his wife's anger" in "the interest . . . of protecting her reputation" (*Art and Anger* [Columbus: Ohio State UP, 1988], 137).

31. Woolf's preoccupation with her public in *The Pargiters/The Years* and her eventual judgment of *The Years* as a deliberate failure accord with the reception of incest reports in the early twentieth century and public discourse on sexual abuse more generally. Judith Lewis Herman with Lisa Hirschman, *Father-Daughter Incest* (Cambridge: Harvard UP, 1981), observe that the surprisingly high incidence of incest was discovered and suppressed twice, by Breuer and Freud in *Studies on Hysteria* and by the American sociologist Kinsey in the nineteen-fifties. Only when the American women's movement rediscovered it twenty years later was it brought to public attention (7). Although the Kinsey researchers documented "the largest number of incest cases ever collected from the population at large," this "wealth of information . . . remained buried in the files of the Institute for Sex Research" because the "public, in the judgment of these men, was not ready to hear about incest" (17–18). The Kinsey reports "dared to describe a vast range of sexual behaviors in exhaustive detail," but about "incest, apparently, they felt the less said the better"; Kinsey wished to defend "the unfortunate male" against "the persecution of malicious females" (17), and "even the most courageous explorers of sexual mores simply refused to deal with the fact that many men, including fathers, feel entitled to use children for their sexual enjoyment" (21). "Without a feminist analysis," Herman notes, "one is at a loss to explain why the reality of incest was for so long suppressed by supposedly responsible profes-

sional investigators, why public discussion of the subject awaited the women's liberation movement, or why the recent apologists for incest have been popular men's magazines and the closely allied, all-male Institute for Sex Research" (3). In the United States, virulent public controversies over incest accounts and the problem of testimony raged on in the 1980s and 1990s; various modes of and questions about documentation, vociferous attacks on the credibility of witnesses and defendants, and important exposés of false accusations and convictions have all complicated the issue in the public consciousness without entirely suppressing it.

32. Woolf retrospectively described her intention to Stephen Spender: "a picture of society as a whole," the characters turned toward "society, not public life," and shown "from every side" to reveal "the effect of ceremonies; Keep one toe on the ground by means of dates, facts: envelop the whole in a changing temporal atmosphere; Compose into one vast manysided group at the end; and then shift the stress from present to future; and show the old fabric insensibly changing without death or violence into the future—suggesting that there is no break, but a continuous development, possibly a recurrence of some pattern; of which of course we actors are ignorant. And the future was gradually to dawn" (L 6:116, 7 April 1937).

33. Rose's name associates her with sexuality, in contrast to artist-heroines defined against conventional heterosexuality (Lily Everit, Lily Briscoe, Lilian La Trobe); named after her "invalid" mother, she is also a realist alter ego of Rhoda (Greek: rose) in The Waves. Oscar Wilde's fairy tale "The Nightingale and the Rose" tells of a nightingale leaning on a thorn "until, by her death agony, a rose is born" (Richard Ellmann, Oscar Wilde [New York: Vintage, 1984], 285).

34. On gender as "role call" see Laura Ring, "Sexual Harassment and the Production of Gender," Differences 6:1 (1994): 129–66.

35. See Louise J. Kaplan, Female Perversions: The Temptations of Emma Bovary (New York: Doubleday, 1991), 13. The passage figures gender as a loss of language for men no less than women: if to be human is to have language, the exhibitionist's gibbering marks him as subhuman at the very moment he displays an exaggerated phallic masculinity.

36. See Leaska's close analysis of Rose's sexual molestation as an autobiographical allegory, "Virginia Woolf, the Pargeter," 181f.

37. Radin, Virginia Woolf's The Years, 33.

38. Breuer proposes that hypnoid states—"a kind of vacancy of consciousness in which an emerging idea meets with no resistance from any other"—form "the basis and sine qua non of hysteria" (Studies on Hysteria, part 3, chap. 4).

39. Cf. other out-of-body moments in The Years (25, 74, 267), once titled The Caravan—an image that recurs in The Years and Between the Acts; cf. the "procession" in Three Guineas.

40. Y 358, 381, 367, 336. Leaska terms this father/daughter relationship "emotional incest," 187f.

41. See galley 188, reproduced in Radin, *Virginia Woolf's* The Years, Appendix.

42. Radin, *Virginia Woolf's* The Years, 39–40, 44 and n. 9; *D* 4:149, 6 April 1933; see *PA* 164–67. The name *Elvira*, with its echo of Elijah, means "elf counsel."

43. "I hardly know which I am, or where: Virginia or Elvira; in the Pargiters or outside," she wrote on March 25, but when she arrived at "the scene I've had in my mind ever so many months" on April 6, she felt "so tired! . . . I can't write it now. Its the turn of the book. It needs a great shove to swing it round on its hinges"; a week later: "What fun that book is to me!" (*D* 4:148–150). On April 25 she urged herself to "be bold & adventurous," to make it "a terrific affair" with "immense breadth & immense intensity" (*D* 4:151–52). Touring France and Italy from May 5 to 27, she longed for home, "for I cant stop making up the P.s: cant live without that intoxicant" (*D* 4:159, 21 May). On coming home she felt "damned . . . aimlessness . . . depression . . . my brain is extinct" and could not "look at Ps," "an empty snail shell" (*D* 4:160–61, 30 May). The next day she urged herself "to be venturous, bold, to take every possible fence" (*D* 4:161, 31 May).

44. *D* 5:24–25, 11, 21 June 1936. Radin sees Elvira as "shrill and angry," drawn from "the less stable elements in Woolf's own personality," which Woolf perhaps tried to keep "under control by limiting Elvira's role" (*Virginia Woolf's* The Years, 153). Octavia Wilberforce, a doctor and distant cousin whom Woolf met in 1937 and who brought cream to the Woolfs during the war, noted that Woolf asked her during one visit about "'drink in women—Was it curable?' She had a friend—gifted poetically . . . I thought I knew whom she meant. You can guess, I'm sure. Very distressed about this" (letter to Elizabeth Robins, 14 March 1941, in Herbert Marder, *The Measure of Life: Virginia Woolf's Last Years* [Ithaca: Cornell UP, 2000], 356). In his 1956 memoir Clive Bell finds "the notion of Virginia as a dipsomaniac . . . beyond the limit of absurdity" (*Virginia Woolf: Interviews and Recollections*, ed. J. H. Stape [Iowa City: U of Iowa P, 1995], 106).

45. Cf. Freud's view that mourning's work is never done (chap. 5, n. 56 above).

46. The editor, Mitchell Leaska, notes that Woolf pasted on the label "Diary/Hyde Park Gate/1903?" "presumably at a later date," since she was not certain of the year, perhaps on rereading it for *The Pargiters* (*PA* 163).

47. *PA* 165–66. This is perhaps the earliest of Woolf's many signature trees: Clarissa's Sylvia, the tree in Lily Briscoe's painting, the woman poet of "the trees, the sky, the thing itself" in *Room*, Orlando's oak tree and "The Oak Tree," the singer split like a tree to the core in *The Waves*, the tree pelted with starlings that shelters La Trobe.

48. *PA* 171–72. Following Radin, Leaska observes that, despite the Stephen sisters' hopelessness at society balls ("We aint popular—we sit in corners & look like mutes who are longing for a funeral") and their painful family life

during their father's illness, "with pen and ink at hand, Virginia discovered herself mistress over a world of her own making" (*PA* 163). See also "Thoughts on Social Success," 15 July 1903 (*PA* 167–69).

49. Holograph M42, Berg Collection of English and American Literature, New York Public Library; transcribed from *Virginia Woolf: Major Authors on CD-ROM*, ed. Mark Hussey (Woodbridge, Conn.: Primary Source Media, 1997), 345–46, my ellipsis and emphases; hereafter cited as Holograph M42. Curved brackets enclose a passage canceled by a wavy vertical line.

50. See n. 43 above, April 6 entry, which continues, "As usual, doubts rush in. Isnt it all too quick, too thin, too surface bright? Well, I'm too jaded to crunch it up, if thats so; & shall bury it for a month—till we're back from Italy perhaps . . . Then seize on it fresh" (*D* 4:149).

51. In the 1891 chapter, Abel Pargiter wonders that Digby and Eugénie have "money to spare, with three boys to educate" (*Y* 118); at the Present Day party, Maggie draws a caricature of a big white-waistcoated guest she identifies as "my brother" who "used to take us for rides on an elephant"—not to be confused with another "big man" whose white waistcoat encloses a "magnificent . . . sphere"—"Chipperfield, the great railway man . . . Son of a railway porter" (*Y* 382, 412).

52. Holograph M42, 351. This draft was presumably composed before Woolf left for France on May 5 (since the Third Holograph is dated June 1 and she returned on May 27), perhaps around April 13 ("What fun that book is to me") or April 25 ("a terrific affair").

53. Holograph M42, 347–48; my ellipses and emphases.

54. Holograph M 42, 351. Raped by her brother-in-law Tereus who also cuts out her tongue, Philomela weaves her story in a tapestry of images for her sister, Procne; the sisters plot to kill, cook, and serve to Tereus his and Procne's son Itys. Vengeance done, the sisters are transformed into a nightingale and a swallow, which Woolf rewrites as two nightingales. See Ovid, *Metamorphoses*, book 6, lines 412f: "As they fly from him you would think that the bodies of the two Athenians were poised on wings; they were poised on wings! One flies to the woods, the other rises to the roof. And even now their breasts have not lost the marks of their murderous deed, their feathers are stained with blood" (Loeb, Ovid 3, *Metamorphoses* 1, 335); and cf. Wilde's figure of the nightingale leaning on a thorn to create a rose (n. 33 above).

55. Holograph M42, 350–51. In this version the "irascib[le]" Elvira makes "a sharp jerk of her arm—flinging the hand out, with annoyance: so knocked over the milk" (ibid.).

56. Holograph M42, 353–91. The page before, dated June 1, begins with Elvira as the Pargiter family historian.

57. "Nothing lived there but the two nightingales, who sang to each other calling, answering, nearer, further, night after night. There were pauses: & then replies. But at what intervals?" (Holograph M42, 355).

58. Cf. Radin's transcription, *Virginia Woolf's The Years*, 48.

59. Suffering over this scene, Woolf records what seem to be her own hysterical symptoms: "Absolutely floored. Sally in bed. . . . I think, psychologically, this is the oddest of my adventures. . . . Oh if only anyone knew anything about the brain. And, even today, when I'm desperate, almost in tears looking at the chapter, unable to add to it, I feel I've only got to fumble and find the end of the ball of string—some start off place, someone to look at Sara perhaps—no, I dont know—& my head would fill & the tiredness go"; "Isn't it odd that this was the scene I had almost a fit to prevent myself writing? This will be the most exciting thing I ever wrote, I kept saying. And now its the stumbling block. I wonder why? too personal, is that it? Out of key? But I wont think" (D 4:338–39, 5 and 6 September 1935). Later, headaches ("sharp pain behind the eyes") gave her "mornings of torture" as she revised *The Years* (D 4 and 5 passim, esp. 5:24–25, 11 June and 21 June 1936). The mysterious impediments to Woolf's progress on *The Years* suggest that the "pattern of repetitions" she created as she revised (Radin, *Virginia Woolf's* The Years, xxii) may have been produced unconsciously; see Allen McLaurin's argument that repetition enabled Woolf to "free the phrases and allow them to become pure pattern. If exact words and phrases to some extent falsify, then the truth might be contained in the modified repetition, the rhythm of language" (*Virginia Woolf: The Echoes Enslaved* [Cambridge: Cambridge UP, 1973], 109, cited by Radin, xxii, 45 n.10).

60. In "Sketch" Woolf recalls still feeling the "thrill" of the parties the next morning as she read Sophocles with Janet Case, who began tutoring her in early 1902 (*MB* 155–56, cf. 177, 182). Case's 1911 visit to Virginia at Firle occasioned "a revelation of all Georges malefactions. To my surprise she has always had an intense dislike of him and used to say 'Whew—you nasty creature,' when he came in and began fondling me over my Greek. When I got to the bedroom scenes, she dropped her lace, and gasped like a benevolent gudgeon. By bedtime she said she was feeling quite sick" (L 1:472, 25? July 1911). See also DeSalvo, *Virginia Woolf: The Impact of Childhood Sexual Abuse*, chap. 4, and Leaska.

61. Hermione Lee, Introduction, *The Years*, ed. Lee (Oxford: Oxford UP, 1992), xxvi; cf. Victoria Middleton, "*The Years*: 'A Deliberate Failure,' " *Bulletin of the New York Public Library* 80:2 (1977): 158–71.

62. *MB* 127. *The Pargiters* describes Bond Street as, for daughters, "as impassable, save with their mother, as any swamp alive with crocodiles" (P 37); by 1935 the "interminable" *Years* had "the vitality of a snake"—"some snake thats been half run over but always pops its head up" (L 5:334, 448, 24 September 1934, 1 December 1935). George had died in April 1934; Gerald lived on, old and "melancholy" (L 6:23). Tea at Gerald's was "like visiting an alligator in a tank, an obese & obsolete alligator" (D 5:21, 1 April 1936). If Gerald was "a lethargic alligator," George, "my incestuous brother," survived his own death to judge by a news item Virginia apparently sent Vanessa featuring "an alligator called George at the London zoo which 'resumed his old aggressive attitudes towards his companions,' and was removed to a solitary pool where

he remained motionless for days, 'as though sulking' ": "Look at this from the Sunday Times," she wrote; "I think they might have mentioned us as they put in George" (*L* 6:28, 56, 71 and n; 21 April, 14 July, 6 September 1936).

63. *VO* 22; see n. 60 above.

64. Radin, *Virginia Woolf's* The Years, 54, citing *The Pargiters* 4:51; she attributes Woolf's revisions to a "Victorian upbringing" that "inhibited her own 'powers of expression,' made certain subjects difficult if not impossible to deal with, especially in . . . print" (cf. "I am Not" 206); "even in the draft manuscript she never really tackled" women's sexuality "directly"; "Woolf, whose 'powers of expression' on almost any subject were prolific, found herself nearly as tongue-tied as Rose when she tried to deal with sexual behavior," though the conversations in *The Pargiters* are "a first tentative step toward overcoming this inhibition" (55).

65. Radin, *Virginia Woolf's* The Years, 92, citing *The Pargiters* 6:101. Leaska argues that Woolf wove George Duckworth's name into Rose's toy duck-buying episode as well as into Kitty's first sexual experience ("Virginia Woolf the Pargeter," 181f).

66. Victoria Middleton, "*The Years*: 'A Deliberate Failure,' " reads the last scene as a parody of "those great moments of fulfillment at the end of *Mrs. Dalloway* and *To the Lighthouse*" (170).

67. The ambivalent love between Peggy and North in the Roman camp incident resonates with Octavia Wilberforce's seemingly blinkered report of a conversation with Woolf, who was studying Octavia for a verbal "sketch": "I got a pretty shrewd picture of her en passant. . . . Her step brother George she evidently adored. Did you know him? Oh! and I told her at the start, that the basis of medicine, science, is to try to be truthful—whereas for her I inferred that it wasn't so important. But my immediate difficulty was to be sure of what *was* the truth. I might have added that I spent my time living ahead and not in the past. Again the reverse of that backward-looking spirit" (Wilberforce, letter to Robins, 14 March 1941, in Marder, 356).

68. Cf. Wilberforce, in Marder, 356: "And her father rather went to pieces after her mother's death and 'threw himself too much upon us. Was too emotional and took too much out of us, made too great emotional claims upon us and that, I think, has accounted for many of the wrong things in my life. I never remember any enjoyment of my body.' "

69. *Y* 422. Marcus reads *The Years* as "an opera for the oppressed" in *Virginia Woolf and the Languages of Patriarchy*, 57; "one long series of interrupted discourses, the interruptions themselves marking the daughters' emergence from the tyranny of the father's voice" ("Pargetting," 74).

70. *D* 5:35, 44, 38; 24, 30 November, 30 December 1936. See Radin, *Virginia Woolf's* The Years, 114ff. After surviving an "extraordinary summer" of "almost catastrophic illness" that she had no "wish to analyse," Woolf reread the novel and found it "happily so bad that there can be no question about it. I must carry the proofs, like a dead cat, to L. & tell him to burn them unread"

(D 5:26, 24, 28; 30 October, 11 June, 3 November 1936). Leonard had read it in April and offered tepid approval, well aware that it had pushed her near to madness and that "unless I could give a completely favourable verdict she would be in despair and would have a very serious breakdown"; before, he had always "given an absolutely honest opinion"; now he "praised the book more than I should have done if she had been well," judging it "remarkable" though "a good deal too long" (*Downhill* 155, cited by Radin 115). Woolf could not "bring myself to believe that he is right" (D 5:30, 4 November 1936). At last the "miracle" was "accomplished. L. put down the last sheet about 12 last night; & could not speak. He was in tears. . . . I, as a witness, not only to his emotion, but to his absorption . . . can't doubt his opinion: what about my own? Anyhow the moment of relief was divine" (D 5:30, 5 November 1936). "Vigorous & cheerful" though she felt after Leonard's "wonderful revelation," she continued to feel "despair. It seems so bad," and to fear public ridicule (D 5:31, 9, 10 November 1936).

71. D 5:66, 10 March 1937. *The Years* sold 30,904 copies in the USA and 13,005 copies in its first six months in England (Leonard Woolf, *Downhill*, 144–45).

72. D 5:67–68, 14 March 1937. See the section on *The Years* in VW:CH, 367–99. Selincourt reads *The Years* as a "parable" of "the skein of misgivings, mistakings, misconceptions, misapprehensions, out of which we somehow manage to knit together these half-intelligible lives of ours"; he finds its "deeper intention" to reveal "separation and solitude as mere appearances" (375). When John Brophy judged it "a tired anaemic middle class book," Woolf countered, "no one has yet seen the point—*my* point" (D 5:69, 17 March 1937). Ethel Smyth called it "superb," and Woolf-the-publisher noted "selling power" on hearing that Ethel's friend Alice Hudson had "spontaneously enjoy[ed]" it (D 5:74, 30 March 1937). She felt "found out" when Edwin Muir in *The Listener* and Scott James in the *London Mercury* called it "dead and disappointing" and "suffered acutely" to find that "that odious rice pudding of a book is what I thought it—a dank failure" with "No life in it"; then a brief anonymous notice called it "The best of my books," and she rallied, feeling "the delight of being exploded": "One feels braced . . . amused; roused; combative; more than by praise"; "immune, set on my feet, a fighter" ready to "make a fresh start" (D 5:75, 2 April 1937). She was "floored" to hear that twelve thousand advance copies had been sold in America: "Honestly I do not know what to think . . . is it good or bad?" (D 5:79, 14 April 1937). Keynes, Spender, and Kingsley Martin all thought it "the best of my books," along with Vanessa, John Hayward, and S. Koteliansky; "Vita; Elizabeth Williamson; Hugh Walpole" were against (D 5:79–80, 15 April 1937). Later, she noted that the dean of Durham "sneers at me on the BBC—too clever 'for myself who am only a simple person'—& wrist watches were not invented in 1880" (D 5:84, 30 April 1937); "Scrutiny . . . calls me a cheat";

and William Faulkner had praised her "most intelligently (& highly)" (*D* 5:91, 1 June 1937).

8. St. Virginia's Epistle to an English Gentleman: Sex, Violence, and the Public Sphere in *Three Guineas*

1. *D* 5:57, 19 February 1937, *TG* 3, 49. Among the funding appeals in Woolf's three scrapbooks of 1932–37, held at the University of Sussex Library, are a leaflet from the "International Peace Campaign," signed "Cecil/The Viscount Cecil" (Monk's House Papers B16f[3]); a letter of 19 February 1936 from J. P. Strachey asking Woolf to become a "Patron" of Newnham College to help launch a funding campaign (B16f[2]); and a flyer dated February 1936 from the National Council for Equal Citizenship ("a direct descendant of the National Union of Women's Suffrage Societies"), Dame M. Fawcett, President (B16f[3]).

2. Brenda R. Silver, *Virginia Woolf's Reading Notebooks* (Princeton: Princeton UP, 1983), 22; see n. 1 above. By 1937 Woolf complained of receiving "six letters to sign daily—or nearly so" and many requests for topical essays (*L* 6:112, 7 March).

3. *D* 4:6 n. 8, 361; 20 January 1931, 30 December 1935.

4. On Woolf's figure of the veil to represent Western women's subordination in the modern public sphere, see chap. 1, n. 90 above. On *Three Guineas*' reception see Silver, "*Three Guineas* Before and After: Further Answers to Correspondents," in *Virginia Woolf: A Feminist Slant*, ed. Jane Marcus (Lincoln: U of Nebraska P, 1983), and "The Authority of Anger: *Three Guineas* as Case Study," *Signs* 16 (Winter 1991): 340–70; QB, chaps. 8–9, and Quentin Bell, "Bloomsbury and the Vulgar Passions," *Critical Inquiry* 6 (Winter 1979): 239–56; and Jane Marcus, "Storming the Toolshed," *Signs* 7 (1982): 622–40. Usually hypersensitive to reviews, Woolf was to her own bemusement impervious to "praise and wigging" of *Three Guineas*. Queenie Leavis's nasty *Scrutiny* review gets only brief mention in her diary (5:165–66, 1 September 1938) and letters: "Oh I've had such a drubbing and a scourging from the Cambridge ladies—the professors of Eng. lit: at Cambridge for 3gs. I'm a disgrace to my sex: and a caterpillar on the community. I thought I should raise their hackles—poor old strumpets" (6:271, 11 September 1938). As Silver notes, academic accounts of the British cultural scene of the thirties are almost entirely silent on *Three Guineas* ("Authority," 353 n. 35).

5. *TG* 260 n. 41; 7, 23, 32, 34, 39, 60, 99, 113; 192, 160, 28.

6. James George Frazer, *The Golden Bough: A Study in Magic and Religion*, one-volume abridged ed. (New York: Macmillan, 1922), 624; see especially chaps. 55–59 for possible influences on Woolf's argument. Leonard was reading the 1929 abridged edition during this period (see *D* 4:159 and n. 6, 21 May 1933). Woolf cites *The Golden Bough* in *RO* 30 n. 2. Elizabeth Abel, *Virginia Woolf and the Fictions of Psychoanalysis* (Chicago: U of Chicago P, 1989) dis-

cusses anthropological and psychoanalytic discourses without reference to scapegoat theory.

7. Woolf, owning a press, felt herself "the only woman in England free to write what I like" (*D* 3:43, 22 September 1925; cf. *L* 4:348, 27 June 1931). Mary M. Childers notes that "the Act did not live up to its promise" ("Virginia Woolf on the Outside Looking Down: Reflections on the Class of Women," *MFS* 38:1 (spring 1992): 65f.

8. *D* 4:77, 16 February 1932; *VW: CH* 402. The scrapbooks contain two programs for the Palm Sunday service at St. Paul's on 21 March 1937, with Woolf's notes and comments on the sermon and 1 Cor. 11 (Monk's House Papers B16f[2] and [3]).

9. *TG* 23, 32, 172. Eleanor Pargiter, described as "a fine old prophetess," reflects on Christianity as a religion of love and life (*Y* 154, 328).

10. *L* 1:272, 25 December 1906; 3:457, 11 February 1928; 5:282, 8 March 1934. On Leslie Stephen's agnosticism and *An Agnostic's Apology*, see Noel Annan, *Leslie Stephen: The Godless Victorian* (New York: Random House, 1984), 234–66 and passim; on Julia Stephen's agnosticism, 105.

11. Catherine F. Smith, "*Three Guineas*: Virginia Woolf's Prophecy," in *Virginia Woolf and Bloomsbury: A Centenary Celebration*, ed. Jane Marcus (Bloomington: Indiana UP, 1987), 225.

12. In this matter 1 Corinthians differs from 1 Timothy, which (taking the line followed by the Church for two millenia) prohibits women from preaching (1 Tim. 2:12). Historians question Paul's authorship of the Pastoral Epistles, particularly 1 Timothy, thought to have been composed some sixty years after Paul's death.

13. *TG* 188. See Elaine Pagels's argument that the censored women's voices in the first- and second-century Gnostic Gospels, buried for sixteen centuries in an earthenware jar dug up at Nag Hammadi in 1945, brought to light the diversity of early Christianity and show that the establishment of the "one, holy, catholic, and apostolic Church" required the suppression not just of dissenting voices but of an open concept of spiritual authority (xxii). While the Church Fathers interpreted the Resurrection as a literal event witnessed by the eleven remaining disciples—an ingenious political move that enabled them to restrict spiritual authority to this small band and their chosen successors through the apostolic succession—the gnostics resisted the establishment of an "orthodox" Church that would claim a monopoly on the mediation of spiritual authority. Holding that those who had received *gnosis* or spiritual self-knowledge had gone beyond the Church's teaching and transcended the authority of its hierarchy, the gnostic Christians argued for experience over "all secondhand testimony and all tradition" as "the ultimate criterion of truth" and "celebrated every form of creative invention as evidence that a person has become spiritually alive"; for them, authority could "never be fixed into an institutional framework" but remained "spontaneous, charismatic, and open" (*The Gnostic Gospels* [New York: Random House, 1979], 25).

14. Rachel Bowlby, *Virginia Woolf: Feminist Destinations* (New York: Basil Blackwell, 1988), 15.

15. "Violence and the sacred are inseparable"; "I might as well have said 'violence *or* the sacred.' For the operations of violence and the sacred are ultimately the same process" (René Girard, *Violence and the Sacred*, trans. Patrick Gregory [Baltimore: Johns Hopkins, 1977], 19, 258; hereafter cited as *VS*).

16. Cf. James George Frazer, *Encyclopaedia Brittanica*, 9th ed. (1878), s.v. "taboo."

17. René Girard, *The Scapegoat*, trans. Yvonne Freccero (Baltimore: Johns Hopkins, 1986), esp. chaps. 13–15; hereafter cited as *S*. Girard argues that the scapegoat mechanism functions in "all mythological and religious beginnings," shaping "dynamics that other religions succeed in concealing from themselves and from us by suppressing or disguising collective murders and minimizing or eliminating the stereotypes of persecution. . . . The Gospels . . . expose these same dynamics with an unequalled severity and strength" (*S* 165). While Girard treats "the Christian Bible, the combination of the Old and New Testaments," as the proverbial key to all mythologies to unlock readings of the scapegoat mechanism in many historical and mythological texts, he views the Gospels as a heterogeneous text whose narrators do not always grasp the import of the stories they tell, and he takes a gnostic stance toward the Church's claims to authority: "Christians have failed to understand the true originality of the Gospels. . . . Unwittingly, they play the game of their adversaries and of all mythology. They once more make sacred the violence that has been divested of its sacred character by the Gospel text," whereas the gospel revelation "concerns not only the early Christians persecuted by the Jews or by the Romans but also the Jews who were later persecuted by the Christians and all victims persecuted by executioners" (*S* 100–02, 126, 212). Girard exemplifies the interdependence of the Hebrew and Christian Bibles by Christ's allusion to Psalms 35:19 ("let not those wink the eye / who hate me without cause") in speaking of his own condemnation: "It is to fulfil the word that is written in their law, 'They hated me without a cause'" (John 15:25); and notes that "Jesus is constantly compared with and compares himself with all the scapegoats of the Old Testament, all the prophets that were assassinated or persecuted by their communities: Abel, Joseph, Moses, the Servant of Yahweh, and so on" (*S* 117).

18. Girard argues that the Gospels not only precede but make possible the modern Western scientific spirit: "The invention of science is not the reason that there are no longer witch-hunts, but the fact that there are no longer witch-hunts is the reason that science has been invented" (*S* 204).

19. Girard derives his account of the potential violence between men that the scapegoating of women defuses from Freud's observation that "Sexual desires do not unite men but divide them" (*VS* 211f); cf. my chapter 9.

20. *Public* and *pubic* derive from Latin *pubes*, which means both "adult" and "the adult male population." The root *pubes* thus founds the idea of the

public on the site not only of biological maturity but of sexual difference; and the shift from the gender-neutral literal meaning to a male body politic parallels the cultural transformation of biological signs into gender hierarchy. That the public is etymologically the privates highlights this arbitrary construction of the public sphere as an arena of male *pubes* that subordinates (or veils) female *pubes*. Cf. Nancy Fraser, "Rethinking the Public Sphere: A Contribution to the Critique of Actually Existing Democracy," *Social Text* 25/26 (1990): 60.

21. Writing before Kristallnacht, the concentration camps, and the then unimaginable Nazi genocide of the Jews, Woolf could make this case in a way those events now make more difficult to understand. The Woolfs had witnessed the Nazis' persecution of the Jews firsthand as they motored through Germany in 1935, carrying a diplomatic letter "to protect [Leonard] from the Nazis' anti-Semitism" (Leonard Woolf, *Downhill All the Way: An Autobiography of the Years 1919 to 1939* [New York: Harcourt Brace Jovanovich, 1967], 185–86). Virginia describes with irony their obsequiousness toward the customs guards coupled with their mounting anger as they passed through streets hung with anti-Semitic slogans (D 4:311, 9 May 1935). In July 1937 Woolf's nephew Julian Bell was killed in the Spanish Civil War, evoked in the photograph of "dead bodies" and "ruined houses" she calls to readers' minds (*TG* 15). Quentin Bell considered *Three Guineas* to some extent an "argument . . . with what she supposed to be Julian's point of view" (QB 2:203). After England declared war on Germany, the Woolfs made provision for suicide in case the Nazis should invade, aware that "the least that [Leonard] could look forward to as a Jew . . . would be to be 'beaten up' " (Leonard Woolf, *The Journey Not the Arrival Matters: An Autobiography of the Years 1939–1969* [New York: Harcourt Brace Jovanovich, 1969], 46). Unbeknownst to them, they were listed on the 2,300-name Gestapo Arrest List prepared in 1940 in anticipation of Hitler's invasion of England (*Die Sonderfahndungsliste G. B.*, 222, Hoover Institution on War, Revolution and Peace Archives, Stanford University); see my chapter 9.

22. While other biological and quasi-biological signs of difference—most obviously, race and ethnicity—are subject to cultural coding and hierarchizing, only sexual difference cuts through and across races, ethnicities, classes, nations, and religions. The coincidence of femaleness with other signs of difference puts women who bear them in double jeopardy. Thus, as Nancy Fraser points out, Anita Hill, not Clarence Thomas, became the scapegoat on whom many Americans displaced "a range of class, ethnic, and racial resentments"; Hill's detractors described her not as a self-made black woman who, like Thomas, came from impoverished origins but as a tool of elite white feminists; and "large numbers of people who believed Hill nonetheless supported Thomas's confirmation" ("Sex, Lies, and the Public Sphere: Some Reflections of the Confirmation of Clarence Thomas," *Critical Inquiry* 18 [Spring 1992]: 608, 611).

23. Woolf notes the Church's historical opposition to what it characterized as women's "obstinate and perhaps irreligious" desire for learning, citing

Bishop Burnet's obstruction of Mary Astell's plan to found a women's college in 1694 by dissuading a certain "prominent lady" (Princess Anne or Lady Elizabeth Hastings) from donating £10,000 on the grounds that the college would resemble a nunnery and so "encourage the wrong branch . . . of the Christian faith" (*TG* 37, 233 n. 21).

24. *TG* 99. See Marcus's discussion of "The Sheep Motif" in "Pargetting *The Pargiters*," *Virginia Woolf and the Languages of Patriarchy* (Bloomington: Indiana UP, 1987), 62–65.

25. *TG* 36, 232 n. 20. Woolf wonders whether "a biography from the pen of an educated man's daughter of the Deity in whose Name such atrocities have been committed would resolve itself into a Dictionary of Clerical Biography" (ibid.).

26. On the scapegoat's ambivalent status as *pharmakon* (remedy/poison), see Jacques Derrida, "Plato's Pharmacy," *Dissemination*, trans. Barbara Johnson (1971; Chicago: U of Chicago P, 1981), 61–171, and Girard, *VS* 296–97.

27. *TG* 101. The guinea originated in the British slave trade with the African West Coast, first named Guinea (*Guiné*, from Berber *gyana*, "black man") by the Portuguese. The English coin was made of Guinea gold "in the name and for the use of the Company of Royal Adventurers of England trading with Africa"; it was "first struck in 1663 with the nominal value of 20s., but from 1717 . . . circulat[ed] as legal tender at the rate of 21s." A "Guinea merchant" or "Guinea trader" was a slave-dealer; a "Guinea ship" or "Guinea-man," a slave-ship. The guinea was no longer struck after 1813 and had long been out of ordinary circulation by 1938, although it remained the unit of value for such luxuries as professional fees, works of art, racehorses, landed property, and subscriptions to such societies as Woolf's three correspondents represent (*OED*). Marcus notes that Woolf's title plays on Brecht's *Threepenny Opera* while defining "the class of her audience" (*Virginia Woolf and the Languages of Patriarchy* 79). It also marks Woolf's class position as an "educated man's daughter" who has achieved a measure of economic parity with her brothers through her profession and can now use her economic power toward social change. (Woolf's income for 1937, chiefly from the bestselling *The Years*, was £2,466 [Leonard Woolf, *Downhill*, 142]; "for the first time she found herself really wealthy" [QB 2:203]). Woolf's antiracist conditions on her contribution for professional women subvert the guinea's history in the act of spending it.

28. *TG* 152. Mary P. Ryan, *Women in Public: Between Banners and Ballots 1825–1880* (Baltimore: Johns Hopkins UP, 1990), documents unofficial participation in public life by nineteenth-century American women of various classes and ethnicities, some (e. g., philanthropic and moral-reform societies) adapting values linked to domesticity and motherhood. Julia Stephen's nursing of the poor exemplifies women's work at the border of private and public spheres.

29. *TG* 119, 122. Woolf's diary records one occasion for "derision" when E. M. Forster reported that the London Library Committee had considered (and rejected) her membership, citing Leslie Stephen's view that women were impossible; she experiments with converting anger into *Three Guineas*' more

measured language: "The veil of the Temple—which, whether university or cathedral, was academic or ecclesiastical I forget—was to be raised, & as an exception [I] was to be allowed to enter in. But what about my civilisation? For 2,000 years we have been doing things without being paid. . . . You cant bribe me now" (4:298, 9 April 1935).

30. Sandor Goodhart, " 'I am Joseph': René Girard and the Prophetic Law," in *To Honor René Girard, Presented on the Occasion of His Sixtieth Birthday by Colleagues, Students, Friends* (Saratoga, Cal.: ANMA Libri for the Department of French and Italian, Stanford U, 1986), 89.

31. On *Three Guineas'* treatment of women's complicity with war, see Sandra M. Gilbert, "Soldier's Heart: Literary Men, Literary Women, and the Great War," *Signs* 8 (Spring 1983): 422–50. One letter Woolf received from a reader of *Three Guineas* taxed her with failure to address women's responsibility in perpetuating the infantile fixation in their sons (Silver, "*Three Guineas* Before and After," 265; see Anna Snaith's edition of the eighty-two letters from readers, "Wide Circles: The *Three Guineas* Letters," *Woolf Studies Annual* 6 [2000]: 1–168).

32. *TG* 217–18. For an eloquent exposition of this passage see Patricia Klindienst Joplin, "The Authority of Illusion: Feminism and Fascism in Virginia Woolf's *Between the Acts*," *South Central Review* 6 (1989): 89–104.

33. *TG* 156. Walter Benjamin, "Theses on the Philosophy of History," in *Illuminations*, ed. Hannah Arendt, trans. Harry Zohn (New York: Schocken, 1969), 256.

34. Silver, "*Three Guineas* Before and After," 263–64.

35. Silver, "*Three Guineas* Before and After," 268, 275 n. 29. Smith's letter of 7 November 1938 (98–103) and another of 28 November (105–6) are transcribed in Snaith, "Wide Circles"; Woolf's letters to Smith are lost.

36. This logic may explain Woolf's eccentric-seeming historical examples: the mayor of an armaments-manufacturing town who announces that she would not darn a sock to help in a war, the organizers of women's sports leagues who rule out prizes and awards, women students who are absenting themselves from church services in record numbers.

37. The Commission's recommendation that women's ministry be confined to the lower orders of deaconesses, lay workers, and theology teachers in women's colleges contradicts Grensted's argument that the idea that "man has a natural precedence of woman . . . cannot be supported" and "must not be confused with . . . any type of precedence which could have a bearing on the admissibility of one sex rather than the other to Holy Orders" (*TG* 191).

38. Grace Radin, " 'I Am Not a Hero': Virginia Woolf and the First Version of *The Years*," *Massachusetts Review* 16:1 (winter 1975), 207. Like Mrs. McNab in *To the Lighthouse*, Crosby suffers and survives familial loss and disintegration.

39. *Y* 281, *TG* 210. Elvira/Sara reads *Antigone* in *The Years*; see my chapter 7.

40. Abel argues that Woolf's vignettes of tyrannical Victorian fathers and their miserable captive daughters (Charlotte Brontë, Elizabeth Barrett, Sophia Jex-Blake) depict a quasi-incestuous society that normatively sacrifices daughters' desire to fathers' and substitutes the seduction theory for the Oedipal complex as the root of men's irrational opposition to women's public authority (*Virginia Woolf* 105–6).

41. 1 Cor. 11:8–16; *TG* 253 n. 38. Betraying infantile anxiety about maternal power, Paul invokes Adam's rib/womb fantasy, with its inversion of the son's birth from the mother into the mother's cultural birth from the male. His resort to hairstyles to fashion a social sign of sexual difference pantomimes male lack (shorn hair) compensated by social privilege (unveiled head) and female fecundity (unshorn hair) mitigated by social subordination (veiled head).

42. *TG* 253 n. 38. In Abel's view, Woolf "cannot sustain ironic mastery of" what Abel interprets as a psychoanalytic rather than Pauline veil: "*Three Guineas*'s adaptation of the psychoanalytic veil unexpectedly complies with the presumption of female lack"; "The mother's body in *Three Guineas* is the site of both a horrifying excess and a lack; whether disgustingly prolific or castrated . . . it consistently fails to possess positive attributes" (106–7). Yet Woolf explicitly attributes lack to Paul not the maternal body (*TG* 253 n. 38); far from questioning the maternal body's positive attributes, she debunks essentializing representations of it that purport to authorize women's subordination.

43. *Three Guineas* anticipates Nancy Fraser's arguments that Habermas's "uncoupling of system and lifeworld institutions tends to legitimate the modern institutional separation of family and official economy, childrearing and paid work," amounting "to a defense of an institutional arrangement that is widely held to be one, if not the, linchpin of modern women's subordination" ("What's Critical about Critical Theory? The Case of Habermas and Gender," in *Unruly Practices: Power, Discourse, and Gender in Contemporary Social Theory* [Minneapolis: U of Minnesota P, 1989], 113–43, 121–22); and that "It is not now and never was the case that women are simply excluded from public life; nor that men are public and women are private; nor that the private sphere is women's and the public sphere is men's. Rather, feminist analysis shows the political, ideological nature of these categories" ("Sex" 609).

44. Cf. contemporary psychoanalytic arguments that the infant's early perception of maternal plenitude and power underlies unconscious anxiety about female authority; that the "powerful, unconscious" hostility to women's full participation in the public sphere arises from atavistic dread of a perceived advantage bestowed upon women by nature, for which their cultural subordination compensates; that this anxiety helps engender a war-making public culture; and that this psychology would perhaps change if women and men shared equally in childcare and the public world; e. g., Dorothy Dinnerstein, *The Mermaid and the Minotaur: Sexual Arrangements and Human Malaise* (New York: Harper, 1976); Bruno Bettelheim, *Symbolic Wounds: Puberty Rites and the Envious Male* (Glencoe, Ill.: Free Press, 1954); Robert J. Stoller, *Sex and Gen-*

der: *On the Development of Masculinity and Femininity* (New York: Science
House, 1968); Nancy Chodorow, *The Reproduction of Mothering: Psychoanalysis and the Sociology of Gender* (Berkeley: U of California P, 1978); and
Helen Cooper, Adrienne Munich, and Susan Squier, "Arms and the Woman:
The Con[tra]ception of the War Text" in *Arms and the Woman: War, Gender,
and Literary Representation*, ed. Cooper, Munich, and Squier (Chapel Hill: U
of North Carolina P, 1989), 9–23.

45. *TG* 224 n. 10, 82. Cf. "A Society" (1920): "While we have borne the
children, they . . . have borne the books and the pictures. . . . We have populated the world. They have civilized it. . . . Before we bring another child into
the world, we must swear that we will find out what the world is like" (*CSF*
119); and "Thoughts on Peace in an Air Raid" (1941): "if it were necessary, for
the sake of humanity, for the peace of the world, that child-bearing should be
restricted, the maternal instinct subdued, women would attempt it" (*DM* 247).

46. *TG* 211. Sallie Sears, "Notes on Sexuality: *The Years* and *Three
Guineas*," *Bulletin of the New York Public Library* 80 (Winter 1977): 211–20,
argues that the female characters in *The Years* tend to "eroticize liberty; the
males, tyranny" (220).

47. At its 1992 General Synod, the Church of England—following "a bitter
and exhausting debate," and by a margin of only two votes—finally voted to
ordain women as priests (*New York Times*, 12 November 1992, A1, A6). At
the 1992 National Conference of Catholic Bishops, women's ordination was
hotly debated despite the Vatican's insistence that the issue is closed, one bishop
opining that a "woman priest is as impossible as for me to have a baby" (*New
York Times*, 18 November 1992, A13).

48. Mathews continues, "the Church is a living organism, . . . continuous
with its past but not bound by it, and . . . the Ministry . . . is so high and arduous a vocation that the full resources of humanity ought to be available for its
fulfilment" (*Report of the Archbishops' Commission* 74, 76, 78).

49. *TG* 157; cf. n. 18 above.

50. Woolf's compound audience of two professional women and one "civilized" man overleaps Fraser's "alternative publics" and "subaltern counterpublics"—"parallel discursive arenas where members of subordinated groups
invent and circulate counterdiscourses, which in turn permit them to formulate
oppositional identifications of their identities, interests, and needs"—by
addressing a representative of the mainstream public on the Enlightenment
premise of open debate ("Rethinking" 67 and passim).

9. The Play in the Sky of the Mind: *Between the Acts* of Civilization's Masterplot

1. *D* 5:284, 292; 14 May, 9 June 1940. A copy of the "automatic arrest list
of more than 2,300 persons," "originally compiled after the fall of France" and
"found by Allied investigators in the Berlin headquarters of security police" as
described in an attached news item, its cover stamped "*Geheim*!", is held in the

Hoover Institute on War, Revolution and Peace, Stanford, California. The list reads: "115. Woolf, Leonhard, 1880 geb., Schriftsteller, RSHA VI G1. / 116. Woolf, Virginia, Schriftstellerin, RSHA VI G." Others include Winston Churchill and his cabinet members, Stefan Zweig, Jan Paderewski, Sigmund Freud, and other prominent political exiles and Jewish refugees. Besides petrol, the Woolfs possessed fatal doses of morphia supplied by Adrian Stephen in June 1940.

2. For recent critical views see Clive Ponting, *1940: Myth and Reality* (London: H. Hamilton, 1990), Richard Overy, *The Battle of Britain: The Myth and the Reality* (New York: Norton, 2001), Clement Liebovitz and Alvin Finkel, *In Our Time: The Chamberlain-Hitler Collusion* (New York: Monthly Review P, 1998).

3. *D* 5:318, 169, 290, 326; 11 September 1940, 13 September 1938, 30 May, 2 October 1940.

4. *D* 5:293, 354, 355; 9 June, 26 January, 7 February 1940–41.

5. Mitchell Leaska calls *Pointz Hall* "the longest suicide note in the English language" ("Afterword," *PH* 451); Daniel Ferrer writes that for Woolf "the result of the book was not life, but madness and death" and that it "cannot be read without being linked to this biographical extension which puts it in its true perspective" (*Virginia Woolf and the Madness of Language*, trans. Geoffrey Bennington and Rachel Bowlby [New York: Routledge, 1990], 115). In fact critics respond to the novel as variously as the spectators to La Trobe's pageant. Leaska, Renée Watkins ("Survival in Discontinuity—Virginia Woolf's *Between the Acts*," *Massachusetts Review* 10 [1969]), Elizabeth Abel (*Virginia Woolf and the Fictions of Psychoanalysis* [Chicago: U of Chicago P, 1989], chap. 6), Gill Plain ("Violation of a Fiction: *Between the Acts* and the Myth of 'Our Island History'," *Women's Fiction of the Second World War: Gender, Power, and Resistance* [Edinburgh: Edinburgh UP, 1996]), and others see a parched and barren wartime world, a mid-century waste land from which hope of regeneration has largely receded; for Alex Zwerdling (*Virginia Woolf and the Real World* [Berkeley: U of California P, 1986], chaps. 10–11), pessimism about civilization's future dominates. Judy Little ("Festive Comedy in Woolf's *Between the Acts*," *Women and Literature* 5 [1977]: 26–37), Brenda R. Silver ("Virginia Woolf and the Concept of Community: The Elizabethan Playhouse," *Women's Studies* 4 [1977]: 291–98), Maria diBattista (*Virginia Woolf's Major Novels* [New Haven: Yale UP, 1980]), Makiko Minow-Pinkney (*Virginia Woolf and the Problem of the Subject* [New Brunswick: RutgersUP, 1987], 189–95), Melba Cuddy-Keane ("The Politics of Comic Modes in Virginia Woolf's *Between the Acts*," *PMLA* 105 [March 1990]: 273–85), Mark Hussey, " 'I' Rejected; 'We' Substituted': Self and Society in *Between the Acts*," *Reading and Writing Women's Lives: A Study of the Novel of Manners*, ed. Bege K. Bowers and Barbara Brothers [Ann Arbor: UMI Research P, 1990]), and others see a comic revival of the green world and communal spirit: "art as gift, mere gift, free gift . . . gratuitous, fragile, and free" (diBattista 234); a "testament of hope" (Hussey 152).

6. *TG* 166. On the novel's Englishness, see Gillian Beer, *Virginia Woolf: The Common Ground* (Edinburgh: Edinburgh UP, 1996), chap. 7; and Joshua D. Esty, for whom the novel "proceeds under the sign of the nation because it seemed both possible and necessary to resignify 'England' as a meaningful (but geopolitically 'minor') social collective" ("Amnesia in the Fields: Late Modernism, Late Imperialism, and the English Pageant-Play," *ELH* 69 (2002): 269.

7. *Y* 212, citing Dante, *Purgatorio* 15:56–57. Woolf judged "1911" "about the best, in that line, I ever wrote" (*D* 5:18, 18 March 1936).

8. On "the cult of the 'pageant' " inaugurated by Louis Napoleon Parker and "in spirit . . . closely akin to . . . 'folk art'," see Allardyce Nicoll, *English Drama 1900–1930: The Beginnings of the Modern Period* (Cambridge: Cambridge UP, 1973), 92–93, 130–31; L. N. Parker, *Several of My Lives* (London: Chapman and Hall, 1928); and Robert Withington, *English Pageantry: A Historical Outline*, 2 vols. (Cambridge: Harvard UP, 1918–1920). Ayako Yoshino-Miyaura, "Redefining Englishness: *Between the Acts* and the History of the Modern English Pageant" (MLA paper, Chicago, 1999), discusses the "modern" or "Parkerian" pageant ("actually inspired by German village plays" [1]) and La Trobe's departures from it. Parker's first pageant, in Sherborne, Dorset, in 1905, had nine hundred participants and fifty thousand spectators; over the next two decades seventy-three towns invited him to be their pageant master, and he undertook five more. His 1909 York pageant—in his words, "all English history," "Drama lifting our souls to God, and our hearts to the King—is not that National Drama?"—had thirteen thousand participants and half a million spectators over its twelve-week run (Yoshino-Miyaura, 1–2). Parker's grandson carried on his "method of producing History without Tears"; see Anthony Parker, *Pageants* (London: Bodley Head, 1954), 12.

9. *BA* 212, cf. 23, 213; "An Essay in Criticism" (1927 review of Hemingway's short stories *Men Without Women*), *E* 4:454. See also Woolf's review of the Arts Theatre's "The Cherry Orchard" (14 July 1920), *E* 3:246–49; and my "The Play in the Sky of the Mind: Dialogue, 'the Tchekhov method,' and *Between the Acts*" in *Woolf Across Cultures*, ed. Natalya Reinhold (New York: Pace UP, 2004), 279–91. John Maynard Keynes (married to the Russian ballerina Lydia Lopokova) thought *The Years* Woolf's "best book," "very moving[;] more tender than any of my books," and that "one scene, E[leanor]. & Crosby, beats Tchekov's Cherry Orchard" (*D* 5: 77–78, 4 April 1937). The Woolfs had seen recent productions of *Uncle Vanya* and *The Three Sisters* and dined with the director, Michel Saint-Denis, at Vanessa's (*D* 5:57 and n. 7, 128, 129 n. 1; 18 February 1937, 10 March 1938).

10. With its Chekhov affinity, La Trobe's pageant springs at once from English soil and from what Woolf calls in "The Leaning Tower" the "common ground" of the world's literature: "Literature is no one's private ground; literature is common ground. It is not cut up into nations; there are no wars there. Let us trespass freely and fearlessly and find our own way for outselves. It is thus that literature will survive this war and cross the gulf—if commoners and outsiders like our-

selves make that country our own country, if we teach ourselves how to read and
to write, how to preserve and how to create" (*The Moment and Other Essays*
[New York: Harcourt Brace Jovanovich, 1948], 154).

11. *D* 5:285, 237, 302; 15 May 1940, 23 September 1939, 12 July 1940.

12. Erich Auerbach, *Mimesis: The Representation of Reality in Western Literature*, trans. Willard R. Trask (1946; Princeton: Princeton UP, 1953), 552–53.
Auerbach wrote *Mimesis* in Istanbul between May 1942 and April 1945; his
example is *To the Lighthouse*, but *Between the Acts* would serve as well.

13. Henceforth I shall use quotation marks to distinguish what is "real" in
the fictional characters' lives (as opposed to the pageant's illusion) from the real
(historical) world outside the novel.

14. Clarke, "The Horse with a Green Tail," *VWM* 34 (1990): 3–4, reconstructs these events from the London *Times* of 28, 29, 30 June and 26, 30 July
1938. The Early Typescript reads:

> "A girl who lives down our way," she read, "used to go out with the Guards. One of
> them asked her to come and see the horse with the green tail." [If you crossed the
> Horse Guards' parade, you saw the sentry from behind. He sat in his box with his
> cloak stretched out to meet the horse's tail.] In imagination she ran her eye to the
> horse's tail where the trooper's cloak met it. It was set like a black wedge in the horse's
> rump. But it was black; not green. "She found it was just an ordinary horse; and they
> dragged her up to the barrack room and she was thrown down on a bed, the troop-
> ers having removed part of her clothing. And then she screamed and hit him about
> the face"—the girl who lived down our way, the girl with red lips and white cheeks
> who had gone skylarking. The horse had a green tail; and the grass outside the win-
> dow was green. A flower bent. A certain pleasure mingled with her disgust; [with her
> sense of Stuart Princesses;] the window in Whitehall from which Charles stepped to
> his execution; Nell Gwyn and orange sellers. "She screamed and hit him about the
> face," the girl down our way [who had gone to the troopers' bedroom.] She looked
> at old Oliver wrinkling his nose over the paper; reading so pompously about politics.
> The trembling veil of summer air quivered; it was down our way it was an alley in
> which the girl lived. . . . The door opened (*PH* 54–55, Early Typescript).

If Leaska's tentative dating of this passage (20 May–15 June 1938) is correct,
Woolf must have read earlier news accounts than those of the trials Clarke
cites. The casual opening, "A girl who lives down our way" suggests a journal-
istic genre different from the *Times*'s trial reports, or perhaps a fictionalized
report. The Woolfs were traveling in Northern England and Scotland from 16
June to 2 July 1938.

Awaiting *Three Guineas*' June 2 publication, Woolf considered founding
"an illustrated sheet to be called 'The Outsider' "; "Oh my Outsider papers: the
TLS is now a paper like any other, not my paper"; and: "Ann Watkins says the
Atlantic readers haven't read enough of Walpole to understand my article.
Refused. That's another reason then for my Outsider to be born" (*D* 5: 128
and n. 8, 132, 160; 7 February, 26 March, 7 August 1938). On Woolf's analysis of censorship, see my chapter 7.

15. *Civilization and Its Discontents*, trans. and ed. James Strachey (1930;
New York: Doubleday, 1964), 61, hereafter *CD*. Woolf read *Civilization and*

Its Discontents, Group Psychology and the Analysis of the Ego, and *Moses and Monotheism*, among other works (*D* 5:250 and n. 5; and 5:252 and n.12; 9 & 17 December 1939). See Abel, *Virginia Woolf*, esp. chap. 6, and Cuddy-Keane, "Politics."

16. *Totem and Taboo* (1913), *SE*, v. 13, 144; *Group Psychology and the Analysis of the Ego*, trans. and ed. James Strachey (1921; New York: Norton, 1959), 67f. On the anthropological critique of Freud, see W. Arens, *The Original Sin: Incest and Its Meaning* (New York: Oxford, 1986).

17. René Girard, *Violence and the Sacred*, trans. Patrick Gregory (Baltimore: Johns Hopkins, 1977), 211, 219, commenting on *Totem and Taboo*'s fuller version of the masterplot summarized in the epilogue of *Group Psychology and the Analysis of the Ego*. Girard continues, "Strictly speaking, between members of the same community, legitimate sexuality exists no more than legitimate violence"—as Lily Briscoe seems to intuit in picturing Mrs. Ramsay leading "her victims . . . to the altar" (*TL* 153).

18. *CD* 51; cf. "Women represent the interests of the family and of sexual life. The work of civilization . . . confronts [men] with ever more difficult tasks and compels them to carry out instinctual sublimations of which women are little capable" (50). Cf. Freud, *The Future of an Illusion*, trans. W. D. Robson-Scott, rev. and ed. James Strachey (New York: Doubleday, 1964): if "a culture has not got beyond a point at which the satisfaction of one portion of its participants depends upon the suppression of another, and perhaps larger, portion— and this is the case in all present-day cultures—it is understandable that the suppressed people should develop an intense hostility towards a culture whose existence they make possible by their work, but in whose wealth they have too small a share" (15). For fuller discussion see my chapter 4.

19. Joseph Conrad, *Heart of Darkness*, ed. Robert Kimbrough, 3d ed. (1899; Norton, 1988), 49 and n; see my chapter 2.

20. As Claude Lévi-Strauss puts it, "Woman could never become just a sign and nothing more, since even in a man's world she is still a person, and since [although] she is defined as a sign she must be recognized as a generator of signs"; "woman has remained at once a sign and a value. This explains why the relations between the sexes have preserved that affective richness, ardour, and mystery which doubtless originally permeated the entire universe of human communication" (*The Elementary Structures of Kinship*, 496, cited by Gayle Rubin, who highlights this leap from sacrifice to romance, in "The Traffic in Women: Notes on the 'Political Economy' of Sex," *Toward a New Anthropology of Women*, ed. Rayna R. Reiter [New York: Monthly Review P, 1975], 201).

21. The gang rape resonates with Girard's claim that there is "Strictly speaking" no such thing as legitimate sexuality between members of the same community (n. 17 above) by dramatizing the violence of (male) insiders upon (female) outsiders within the community. Dorothy Dinnerstein, *The Mermaid and the Minotaur: Sexual Arrangements and Human Malaise* (New York:

Harper and Row, 1976) analyzes gang rape as an extreme act in the continuum of practices that constitute the sacrificial traffic in women, one that forces a woman into the role of surrogate victim, "communally possessed in a spirit of ritual counterassertion against the sexual rivalries that weaken male solidarity" (58). On the sacrificial dynamics of marriage and rape in Greek and Latin texts, see Patricia Klindienst Joplin, "The Voice of the Shuttle Is Ours," *Stanford Literary Review* 1 (1984): 25–53, rpt. in *Rape and Representation*, ed. Lynn A. Higgins and Brenda R. Silver (New York: Columbia UP, 1991), 35–64.

22. "The girl said that she was crying and shouting, and he said that if she shouted it would be the worse for her. She screamed and tried to push him away and punched him, and he said he would hit her back and hurt her, as he had been a champion boxer"; "Since Pullin was tried separately from Thomas and Reeves, the girl had to give her evidence twice" (Clarke 3, citing the London *Times*).

23. Although the novel does not mention the trials, its setting on a June day (albeit in 1939 not 1938) ties it to the news of the late-June rape trials; the abortion trial took place in July. Although we might suppose that the novel's first English readers would have recalled this shocking case, it goes unmentioned in the early reviews; the American Malcolm Cowley takes the rape as fictional ("twice the heroine finds herself thinking—she doesn't know why—about a newspaper story she had just read of a girl raped by soldiers," *VW: CH*, 449). Would it have registered as real had Woolf been living at the novel's publication?

24. E.g., Ellen Bayuk Rosenman, *The Invisible Presence: Virginia Woolf and the Mother-Daughter Relationship* (Baton Rouge: Louisiana State UP, 1986), relates "the mother-figure, the lady in yellow" in the dining room portrait, to "her unlikely daughter artist, Miss La Trobe" by a "line of descent" that traces not "personal" but "cultural history" (114); in her view, "what optimism resides in the ending is seriously qualified by the failure" of pageant and narrative "to carry forward the communal art of the mother" (133). Jane Marcus argues that the novel depicts the mother-figure as victim and collaborator to show that "the militaristic patriarchal state needs . . . women to make war" and "casts her in two crucial and needed roles of mother and nurse" ("The Asylums of Antaeus: Women, War, and Madness—Is There a Feminist Fetishism?," in *The New Historicism*, ed. Aram Veeser [New York: Routledge, 1989], 134). For Abel, a "conceptual as well as actual void haunts *Between the Acts*, a new inability to think or write the mother, who is always already absent or subsumed . . . to patriarchy. . . . There is no maternal realm of nature exterior to culture in this text, whose bleakness derives in part from the collapse of this distinction, central to *Mrs. Dalloway* and to *To The Lighthouse*"; absent "the possibility of some position 'before' or 'outside' culture," an "originary source" of "creativity," the novel's world becomes a "parched" metaphysical landscape (*Virginia Woolf*, 118, 120–21, 114).

25. Cf. my chapters 5–6.

26. *D* 5:35, 24 November 1936, *BA* 210–11. Marcus offers a darker reading of the Antaeus allusion in *Virginia Woolf and the Languages of Patriarchy* (Bloomington: Indiana UP, 1987), 93–95.

27. *PH* 78, my emphasis; cf. *BA* 58. Cf. "Florinda's story": "her name had been bestowed upon her by a painter who had wished it to signify that the flower of her maidenhead was still unplucked. . . . she was without a surname, and for parents had only the photograph of a tombstone beneath which, *she said*, her father lay buried" (*JR* 77, my emphasis).

28. *BA* 211. Implicitly challenging the legitimacy of what Freud calls civilization and Woolf "half-civilised barbarity," La Trobe recalls Woolf's Antigone's wish "not to break the laws, but to find the law" (*TG* 210, cf. 124, 215–16; *Y* 414).

29. Abel observes that Woolf noted, "End w/ the deification of the primal father of the horde" on the "Postscript" of *Group Psychology and the Analysis of the Ego*, in Woolf's Holograph Reading Notes, vol. 21, Berg Collection, New York Public Library (*Virginia Woolf* 27). Patricia Klindienst Joplin, in "The Authority of Illusion: Feminism and Fascism in Virginia Woolf's *Between the Acts*," *South Central Review* 6 (1989): 89–104, finds La Trobe "a comically mixed" leader who inspires "not fear but laughter" and raises "the question of whether it is possible to constitute an identity, whether as individual or group, except at the expense of an other who is at once model, rival, authoritarian persecutor, and ultimately, victim to the self" (101, 95, 97–8). For Cuddy-Keane, the outsider La Trobe, herself incorporated in the community, "redefines inclusiveness" in a way that counters Freud's analysis of the group leader as a father-hero-poet who constellates the group through mutual identification ("Politics," 279).

30. Leaska dates the ur-biography between 29 August and 1 September 1938 (*PH* 26, 78).

31. *D* 5:171, 189, 16 September, 22 November 1938. On the other hand Woolf noted lunch party gossip about "2 cabinet ministers in favor of giving me the O[rder of] M[erit]," which did not materialize (*D* 5:192, 19 December 1938).

32. Rose Macauley's book, with its salute to Forster, left Woolf unimpressed, "jealous as I am, rather mean always about contemporaries" (*D* 5:130, 12 March 1938). Later she urged the need to "fight Hitler in England" against such externally directed protest demonstrations as that of the Association of Writers for Intellectual Liberty against Franco, to which Forster was invited and the Woolfs were not; when Forster agreed ("Thats what I'm always saying. But how?"), Woolf referred to her connections "with Pippa [Philippa Strachey] & Newnham" (*D* 5:142, 24 May 1938).

33. Forster consulted Woolf on a literary reference in his pageant for the Abinger Church Preservation Fund, performed near Dorking one "Wet black cold" weekend of July 1938, but she did not witness what Esty calls its "historical insipidness" firsthand ("Amnesia in the Fields," 258). She did attend (possibly with Eliot) Stephen Spender's *Trial of a Judge*: "A moving play: genuine;

simple; sincere; the mother like Nessa. Too much poetic eloquence. But I was given the release of poetry: the end, where they murmur Peace freedom an artist's, not an egoist's end" (D 5:131, 22 March 1938). In 1939 Hogarth published Leonard's play *The Hotel*, which Spender thought "a roaring comedy & very original"; it had a private reading at the Keyneses' but was not performed (D 5:183, 30 October 1938).

34. Eliot began work on "Little Gidding" (1944) early in 1941; five years earlier he had made a pilgrimage to that site of a seventeenth-century Anglican religious community, of which he may have told the Woolfs (Peter Ackroyd, *T. S. Eliot: A Life* [New York: Simon and Schuster, 1984], 263). After seeing *Murder in the Cathedral* Woolf wrote her nephew Julian, "Oh Lord—how I hate these parsons! We went to Toms play . . . and I almost had to carry Leonard out, shrieking. . . . the tightness, chillness, deadness and general worship of the decay and skeleton made one near sickness. The truth is that when he has live bodies on the stage the words thin out, and no rhetoric will save them. Then we met Stephen Spender, who was also green at the gills with dislike"; after seeing *Romeo and Juliet*, she wrote "how it curled up Toms Cathedral and dropped it down the W. C.!" (L 5:448–49, 1 December 1935). In the Early Typescript La Trobe chides herself for her nasty competitive feelings toward William Dodge; see *PH* 139.

35. *D* 5:135, 26 April 1938; *L* 6:230–31, 26 May 1938.

36. *D* 5:210, 22 March 1939. Woolf missed seeing Eliot's religious pageant, *The Rock*, at Sadler's Wells (28 May–9 June 1934) because of flu, but she read it and—acknowledging her "anti-religious bias"—was "disappointed" by its "cheap farce and Cockney dialogue and dogmatism" (L 5:315, 10 July 1934).

37. La Trobe's and the narrator's dialogic poetics diverge from Bakhtin's Dickensian paradigm of a ruling narrator imposing interpretive judgment on other voices within the text.

38. *BA* 217-19. Cf. George Macauley Trevelyan, *History of England* (1926; London: Longmans, Green & Co., 1937): "For many centuries after Britain became an island the untamed forest was king. Its moist and mossy floor was hidden from heaven's eye by a close-drawn curtain woven of innumerable tree-tops, which shivered in the breezes of summer dawn and broke into wild music of millions upon millions of waking birds; the concert was prolonged from bough to bough with scarcely a break for hundreds of miles over hill and plain and mountain"; "Much of modern London was once a swamp or lake" (3, 17 n. 2). Brenda R. Silver notes that Woolf cites the former passage in "Anon" and "The Reader," begun in late November 1940 (" 'Anon' and 'The Reader,' " ed. Silver, *Twentieth Century Literature* 25 [1979]: 356-441; see also 401-2; and *PH* 245-46).

39. *BA* 74. I am indebted here and in this chapter's last section to Hannah Arendt's *Lectures on Kant's Political Philosophy*, ed. with an interpretive essay by Ronald Beiner (Chicago: U of Chicago P, 1982), 26, cf. 12-27, 115; hereafter cited as *LK*. Arendt notes that "Kant understands history also as part of

nature—it is the history of the human species insofar as it belongs to the animal species on earth" (14); her reading of Kant's *Critique of Judgment* links the freedom at play in aesthetic pleasure—" 'a predicate of the power of imagination and not of the will' "—with " 'political thinking par excellence,' because it enables us to 'put ourselves in the minds of other[s]' " (*LK* 102). See also my chapter 1.

40. Woolf writes in "The Leaning Tower": "We have got to teach ourselves to understand literature. Money is no longer going to do our thinking for us. Wealth will no longer decide who shall be taught. . . . [W]e must become critics because in future we are not going to leave writing to be done for us by a small class of well-to-do young men. . . . We are going to add our own experience, to make our own contribution. That is even more difficult. For that too we need to be critics" (*Moment*, 152). Cf. Roland Barthes's metaphorical "death" of the author, simultaneous with the birth of the active, critical, meaning-making reader.

La Trobe's avant-garde stagecraft has been likened to Brecht's epic theater (Herbert Marder, "Alienation Effects: Dramatic Satire in *Between the Acts*," *Papers on Language and Literature* 24 [Fall 1988]: 423–35, and Joplin, "Authority"), Artaud's theatre of cruelty (Ferrer, *Virginia Woolf*, chap. 5), Bakhtin's dialogic poetics (David McWhirter, "The Novel, the Play, and the Book: *Between the Acts* and the Tragicomedy of History," *ELH* 60 [1993]: 787–812), Parker's modern pageants (Yoshino-Miyaura, "Redefining Englishness"; Esty, "Amnesia"), John Cage's "living" theatricality (Cuddy-Keane, "Politics"), and feminist performance theory (Penny Farfan, "Writing/Performing; Virginia Woolf Between the Acts," *Text and Performance Quarterly* 16 [1996]: 205–15).

41. *BA* 157, 179. *PH* 401: "Mrs. Mayhew had sketched her own version of what was to be the conclusion. . . . she would have a splendid finale. The Army; the Navy; the King and Queen. Very likely that was what Miss La Trobe had planned"; cf. pageant master Anthony Parker: "on to the Finale. The Arena is a blaze of light as the Choir sings the Triumph Song in praise of the Pageant town and all its people. Group by group, the entire casts of all the Episodes enter, forming a great semi-circle of colour right across the Arena, with all their horsemen and all their flags and banners. Then there appear one or more symbolic figures, perhaps representing the Spirit of the Pageant Town, or perhaps the central figures of the Pageant itself. They speak some short verses in praise of the Past and looking with hope towards the Future, and leading up to the National Anthem, which is sung by all the players and the audience. Then, to the stirring music of the March Past, the whole of the performers pass in review before the stands, and our Pageant is over" (*Pageant* 44–45).

42. *BA* 58–9, 63, 180. In the "Essay in Criticism" Woolf aligns "the Tchekov method" with the "moderns" who "make us aware of what we feel subconsciously" and "even anticipate it," "giv[ing] us a particular excitement"; by contrast, Hemingway's characters seem like "people one may have seen

showing off at some cafe" who are "terribly afraid of being themselves, or they would say things simply in their natural voices" (*E* 4:451, 453).

Apart from her brief fantasy of "*the* play" without an audience, La Trobe is the antithesis of the "authoritative director" promoted by Gordon Craig in *The Art of the Theatre* (1905) as "in effect . . . the only artist in the playhouse," possessing "paramount supremacy," "independence," and "untrammeled authority," and ideally also the play's author. Craig eschewed scripts by living playwrights, since "his genius was so much mightier than their poor talents"; living actors were an imposition too, which he addressed in an essay on the advantages of marionettes (Nicoll, *English Drama*, 106–8). Woolf would have known of Craig's ideas, whose influence derived less from memorable productions than from his notoriety as their executor; her essay on Ellen Terry mentions Craig, Terry's son (*Moment* 205). Woolf also knew Gordon's sister, Terry's lesbian daughter Edith (Edy), an actress, theatrical director, designer, and producer to whom Woolf's idea of La Trobe seems more than a little indebted. After attending a rehearsal Woolf described "Miss Craig" as "a rosy, ruddy 'personage' in white waistcoat, with black bow tie & gold chain loosely knotted," and sketched her directorial manner: "Beautiful lady, you go up to the balcony. Can you step to the left? No: I won't take risks. Young man, Dunlop, you walk straight—straight, I say—straight—Can't you move that table? No? Well then to the right. Miss Potter (this with some acerbity) *you* needn't dance" (*D* 2:174, 30 March 1922).

43. *BA* 113. A version of Isa's knife scene exists in a typescript titled "Possible poems for P. H." (*PH* 559).

44. *BA* 156. Woolf worked this prose poem into the Later Typescript in autumn 1940, when both 52 Tavistock Square and 37 Mecklenburgh Square were bombed to ruins (see *PH* 28, 373–77). At Tavistock she "cd just see a piece of my studio wall standing: otherwise rubble. . . . So to Meck. All again litter, glass, black soft dust, plaster powder. . . . A wind blowing through. I began to hunt out diaries. What cd we salvage in this little car? Darwin, & the Silver, & some glass & china. . . . Exhilaration at losing possessions—save at times I want my books & chairs & carpets & beds—How I worked to buy them—one by one—And the pictures. . . . But its odd—the relief at losing possessions. I shd like to start life, in peace, almost bare—free to go anywhere" (*D* 5:331–32, 20 October 1940). Struggling with salvage and storage she added: "oh that Hitler had obliterated all our books tables carpets & pictures—oh that we were empty & bare & unpossessed" (*D* 5:343, 16 Dec 1940).

45. In the "poems for P. H.," Isa's wish "that the waters should cover me" follows lines linking a news story of a man who stripped and killed "the girl who came up from the country" with images of blighted or perverted desire ("a worm in the rose," "a knife in the red hot poker") and with a dream of love between "brother and sister" (*BA* 103, *PH* 559). The "withered tree" recalls the leafless tree in *The Years* and "A Sketch of the Past" (cf. my chapter 7). Louise A. DeSalvo, *Virginia Woolf: The Impact of Childhood Sexual Abuse on Her Life and Work* (Boston: Beacon, 1989), relates these poems to Isa's memo-

ries of childhood visits to a versifying clergyman-uncle and finds a suppressed incest narrative in her "Songs my uncle taught me," as Dodge calls them (201f).

46. *BA* 120. Anthony Parker (n. 8 above) continues, "our Pageant . . . should span the centuries up to, say, Victorian times. I am against the introduction of modern events, as I consider the Present is not a suitable subject for a Historical Pageant"; "current affairs, manners, customs and clothes are and have always been divorced from glamour in the contemporary eye. Censorship and the laws of Libel forbid the portrayal of the Great Ones of today. Let us rather confine ourselves, in part of our great Finale, to verbal eulogy of current wonders and our Destiny" (*Pageants* 40, 14).

47. *BA* 180. Cf. "Not a sound this evening to bring in the human tears. I remember the sudden profuse shower one night just before war wh. made me think of all men & women weeping" (*D* 5:274, 24 March 1940).

48. Isa echoes Milton's "On the Morning of Christ's Nativity" ("Time is our tedious song should here have ending"); Woolf noted in her contribution to F. W. Maitland's biography of Leslie Stephen that Milton was the "old" writer her father "knew best; he specially loved the 'Ode on the Nativity,' which he said to us regularly on Christmas night. This was indeed the last poem he tried to say on the Christmas night before he died; he remembered the words, but was then too weak to speak them" (cited by Leaska, *PH* 239).

49. *BA* 182. As Zwerdling (292–93) and Abel (116) note, Bloomsbury intellectuals were instrumental in founding the League of Nations through their pacifist work in World War I but lost faith in it by 1935; Leonard was "personally . . . convinced that Baldwin and the French statesmen . . . had finally destroyed the League as an instrument for controlling aggression and preventing war" (*Downhill*, 243). The scene recalls Woolf's summary of a conversation with the "genial" Lord Robert Cecil, President of the League of Nations Union from 1923–45, who was "In good spirits, in spite of the world. But he said, I think there is more vitality both in men & in institutions, than one expects. We have failed (the L. of N.) no matter we must try again" (*D* 5:33, 17 November 1936).

50. *LK* 113, 141.

51. Speech to the House of Commons on 4 June 1940, after the massive evacuation of Allied troops from Dunkirk.

52. Entry to "sum up the whole of life" at the end of a year (*D* 4:135, 31 December 1932; cf. *D* 5:352, 9 January 1941, cited above in the text).

53. *BA* 209; cf. Lily Briscoe's tree/self, *Orlando*'s oak tree, *Room*'s feasting "plant" and Woolf's exhortation to women writers to see the "trees, sky, or whatever it may be in themselves," *The Waves*' sea-green woman split to the core, the withered tree outside Virginia/Elvira/Sara's window, Maggie's laughter like a tossing tree hung with bells in *The Years*, and the Outsider who pelts the tree with laughter in *Three Guineas*.

54. *Y* 382. In the Early Typescript Lucy tiptoes upstairs "telling herself the story of the world" (*PH* 188).

55. The Conrad allusion appears in neither the Early nor the Later Type-

script (*PH* 188–89, 554–55); see my chapter 2, and cf. Mary Beton's remark that men's long opposition to women's emancipation is "more interesting perhaps than the story of that emancipation itself" (*RO* 55).

56. *CD* 92. *Between the Acts*' end resonates with Freud's closing evocation of his audience: "I have not the courage to rise up before my fellow-men as a prophet, and I . . . offer . . . no consolation," though everyone from "the wildest revolutionaries" to "the most virtuous believers" longs for it; instead he poses the "fateful question" of whether the human race will master the aggression that, with modern war technology, can "exterminate" it "to the last man" and calls his readers to fight on the side of Eros for the uncertain future—"But who can foresee with what success and with what result?" (*CD* 92). Freud added the last sentence in 1931, as Hitler was on the rise. Freud's and Woolf's refusals to prophesy recall Dante's prophets, plunged deep in *Inferno*, their heads twisted backward in the *contrapasso* to punish their presumption against free will.

57. *LK* 43, 55. In making the faculty of judgment the basis of a political philosophy, Arendt retains the negative, abstract power of moral reason to free human beings from prejudice and violence while emphasizing that reason is made for community, not isolation and "truth is what I can communicate" (*LK* 40). Cf. Tobin Siebers, "Kant and the Politics of Beauty," *Philosophy and Literature* 22:1 (1998): 31–50.

58. *LK* 40, 141; cf. Arendt, *On Revolution* (New York: Viking, 1965).

59. As we saw (chapter 1, n. 48), Kant distinguishes the "*common sense*" based in feeling, which underwrites the "subjective universal validity" of aesthetic judgments, from "common understanding, which people sometimes call common sense (*sensus communis*)" (*CJ* §20 75, *CPJ* 122). Arendt, finding in the *Critique of Judgment* "not yet . . . political philosophy, but . . . certainly . . . its condition *sine qua non*," makes a kind of bridge between these meanings (*LK* 141). As we saw in chapter 6, Kant distinguishes between the determinative judgments of science and ethics—bound, respectively, by natural law and moral law (to which all rational beings subject themselves in their freedom)—and the reflective judgments of aesthetics, which partake of the imagination's freedom; Arendt extrapolates reflective judgment to the realm of politics and sociability: the beautiful calls out the reflective judgment of "actual inhabitants of the earth" who are made by nature for sociability, for thinking together in public toward a *sensus communis* (*LK* 26).

60. *LK* 73, *BA* 192. Cf. Kant's 1759 essay on optimism, cited by Arendt: "I call out to each creature . . . : Hail us, we are!" "The whole is the best, and everything is good for the sake of the whole" (*LK* 30).

61. See n. 1 above. The Woolfs had sold Virginia's share in the Hogarth Press to John Lehmann in March 1938, a development intended to free her for writing. While the sale relieved her to some extent, she remained heavily involved in the Press and the care of the staff, inventory, and hand-press, an especially heavy burden after Mecklenburgh Square was bombed. Although

there was never any question that Hogarth would publish whatever Woolf wrote, still, no longer was she "the only woman in England free to write what I like" in quite the same sense. The risks she was used to taking in her writing (think of *Three Guineas*, of her "growing detachment from the patriarchy") would no longer be borne by her and Leonard alone (*D* 5:347, 29 December 1940). Lehmann praised *Between the Acts*, but a day or two before her death Woolf, worried that its publication would mean "a financial loss," wrote asking him to withdraw it from the spring list; she planned to revise it for the autumn (*L* 6:486, 27? March 1941).

62. Arendt comments, "What Kant said is . . . that a bad man can be a good citizen in a good state. . . . I can will a particular lie, but I 'can by no means will that lying should be the universal law.' . . . The bad man is, for Kant, the one who makes an exception for himself; he is *not* the man who wills evil, for this, according to Kant, is impossible" (*LK* 17).

63. By 1997 *Between the Acts* had been translated into some eighteen languages (B. J. Kirkpatrick and Stuart N. Clarke, *A Bibliography of Virginia Woolf*, 4th ed. [Oxford: Clarendon P, 1997]).

64. Leonard Woolf, *Barbarians Within and Without* (New York: Harcourt, Brace and Co., 1939), 176–77; Hitler, he wrote, posed only "a temporary danger," since "he and his political system carry within them the seeds of their own disintegration."

65. *D* 5:268, 16 February 1940; see n. 44 above.

66. *D* 5:304, 24 July 1940. "Question of suicide seriously debated among the 4 of us," Woolf recorded after Kingsley Martin and Rose Macauley visited; "French are to be beaten; invasion here; 5th Coln active; a German pro-Consul; Engsh Govt in Canada; we in concentration camps, or taking sleeping draughts" (*D* 5:292, 7 June 1940). See also her last letters to Leonard and Vanessa (*L* 6:485–87, 23?–28 March 1941).

GENDER AND CULTURE

A series of Columbia University Press

Edited by Carolyn G. Heilbrun and Nancy K. Miller